ENGINEERING ANTHROPOMETRY METHODS

WILEY SERIES IN HUMAN FACTORS

Edited by David Meister

Human Factors in Quality Assurance

Douglas H. Harris and Frederick B. Chaney

Man-Machine Simulation Models

Arthur I. Siegel and J. Jay Wolf

Human Factors Applications in Teleoperator Design and Operation

Edwin G. Johnsen and William R. Corliss

Human Factors: Theory and Practice

David Meister

Human Factors in Highway Traffic Safety Research

T. W. Forbes, Editor

Applied Maintainability Engineering

Clair E. Cunningham and W. Cox

Prediction and Development of Industrial Work Performance

Gavriel Salvendy and W. Douglas Seymour

Perception and Performance Under Water

John Adolfson and Thomas Berghage

Engineering Anthropometry Methods

J. A. Roebuck, Jr., K. H. E. Kroemer, and W. G. Thomson

ENGINEERING ANTHROPOMETRY METHODS

J. A. ROEBUCK, JR., M. S.

Space Division
Rockwell International Corporation
Downey, California

K. H. E. KROEMER, DR. ING.

Federal Institute for Occupational
Safety and Accident Research
Dortmund, Federal Republic of Germany

W. G. THOMSON, M. S.

Naval Undersea Center
San Diego, California

A WILEY-INTERSCIENCE PUBLICATION

JOHN WILEY & SONS New York • London • Sydney • Toronto

Library of Congress Cataloging in Publication Data:

Roebuck, John Arthur, 1929–
Engineering anthropometry methods.

(Wiley series in human factors)
Bibliography: p.
Includes index.
1. Human engineering. 2. Anthropometry.
I. Kroemer, K. H. E., 1933– joint author.
II. Thomson, Walter Gary, 1939– joint author.
III. Title.

TA166.R63 620.8′2 74-34272
ISBN 0-471-72975-2

Printed in the United States of America

10 9 8 7 6 5 4 3 2 1

SERIES PREFACE

Technology is effective to the extent that men can operate and maintain the machines they design. Equipment design which consciously takes advantage of human capabilities and constrains itself within human limitations amplifies and increases system output. If it does not, system performance is reduced and the purpose for which the equipment was designed is endangered. This consideration is even more significant today than in the past because the highly complex systems that we develop are pushing human functions more and more to their limits of efficient performance.

How can one ensure that machine and machine operations are actually designed for human use? Behavioral data, principles, and recommendations—in short, the Human Factors discipline—must be translated into meaningful design practices. Concepts like ease of operation or error-free performance must be interpretable in hardware and system terms.

Human Factors is one of the newer engineering disciplines. Perhaps because of this, engineering and human-factors specialists lack a common orientation with which their respective disciplines can communicate. The goal of the Wiley Human Factors Series is to help in the communication process by describing what behavioral principles mean for system design and by suggesting the behavioral research that must be performed to solve design problems. The premise on which the series is based and on which each book is written is that Human Factors has utility only to the degree that it supports engineering development; hence the Series emphasizes the *practical application* to design of human-factors concepts.

Because of the many talents on which Human Factors depends for its implementation (design and systems engineering, industrial and experimental psychology, anthropology, physiology, and operations research, to name only a few), the Series is directed to as wide an audience as possible. Each book is intended to illustrate the usefulness of Human Factors to some significant aspect of system development, such as human factors in design or testing or simulation. Although cookbook answers are not provided, it is hoped that this pragmatic approach will enable the many specialists concerned with problems of equipment design to solve these problems more efficiently.

David Meister
Series Editor

PREFACE

A large, although still incomplete, body of published data exists in reports, articles, handbooks, and various textbooks which can be identified as "the literature of engineering anthropometry." However, no textbook sets forth the full content of approaches and techniques for both the generation and the application of anthropometric data in a cohesive, integrated manner suitable for use in industry or in teaching. Many colleges and universities have regular courses in human factors or ergonomics, in which the teaching of physical anthropometry and its applications are included. A few publications provide some text material. However, there is still a need for a compilation of information on techniques and tools for measurements and for extensive practical guidance dealing with the "real world" of unknown dimensions and incomplete reporting. Additional needs include "tricks of the trade," generalized procedures, and emphasis on application of fundamental engineering principles, supported with recent and wide-ranging examples of applications.

To meet such needs, a general plan for this manual was conceived by John A. Roebuck, Jr., as a further development of the themes in his 1957 article, "Anthropometry in Aircraft Engineering Design."* In 1968, the plan was crystallized in an outline, which was accepted for the Wiley Series on Human Factors by Dr. David Meister, the series editor. Three years later, K. H. E. Kroemer and W. Gary Thomson joined forces with Roebuck to enhance and complete the manuscript, which was at that time already far advanced. Material was included that Kroemer had planned for a similar text, and independently proposed to the publisher in 1969.

The focus on *technique* in measurement and application, which is unique to this methods manual, makes it complementary to compilations of *data* found in many other handbooks. The content includes historical material, descriptions of measurement techniques, and explanations of methodology, abstracted and developed from a wide variety of reports on special anthropometric studies and applications carried out in research institutions and engineering departments in the United States and many other countries. Such studies by manufacturers

* References are listed alphabetically by author and date in the Bibliography.

of airframes, spacecraft, automobiles, and industrial equipment and furniture have contributed significantly to the development of needed data and application techniques.

The presentation of material is designed to aid two types of users. First, the text may be used by the relatively knowledgeable human factors specialist as a reference manual for a variety of specific problems. The book is divided into ten chapters, each having utility in design, with increased emphasis on applications as one proceeds from the early chapters to the later ones. The other usage is an educational one. If one reads the entire book, he will gain a deeper understanding of the underlying unity and generality of the presented approach and procedures and will gain from cross-fertilization of ideas expressed in a rich diversity of application areas.

The historical background material, presented mainly in the first chapter, provides understanding of how the present technological level was achieved. It gives insights for future research in related parent and parallel disciplines, which can carry the reader beyond the handbook stage of understanding. Trends in the field are pointed out to suggest future needs for research and methodology development.

Chapter II provides detailed information on instruments and techniques for human body dimension measurement, primarily dealing with static body positions and classical anthropometric approaches. Subjects included are personnel training and facilities planning for surveys, and concepts of measurement standardization.

Chapters III and IV cover the measurement of more dynamic body movements, of inertial properties and of statically exerted muscular forces. The measurement of movement and description of envelopes of limits of movement are considered together with new concepts in terminology for describing angular positions of limbs in space. Many of these measurements are also appropriate for fields of study called biodynamics or biomechanics.

In Chapter V, there is a brief review of statistical data reduction concepts and of analytical procedures as they particularly relate to engineering anthropometry. Statistical aspects of planning for anthropometric surveys are included. Methods are presented for using available data to produce estimates of dimensions that are not available in the literature.

Chapter VI discusses biometric relationships in terms of factors that relate or differentiate groups of persons in ways specific to engineering anthropometry. General "rules of thumb" concerning body proportional relationships and population characteristics are discussed. This chapter provides a broad overview of the dimensional and strength exertion capability aspects of humans, as applicable to engineering design.

Applications of engineering anthropometry are presented in Chapters VII through X. Selected basic tools and techniques for applications are discussed in

Chapter VII. In Chapter VIII, the focus is on design of the shape of space surrounding men and women at work or rest in the context of a basic procedure for design applications. Chapter IX refers to the design of clothing and personal protective equipment. Chapter X concentrates on detail items such as control knobs, tool handles, pedals, and small appliances.

An extensive bibliography provides starting points for further research and data access. Appendices provide supporting detail to text topics, including a glossary and tables of correlation coefficients. An index is provided to aid access to selected topics.

In writing this textbook, we were confronted with much more material than could possibly be included. Hence, it was necessary to omit many interesting references and examples. Undoubtedly, the reader will find occasional misinterpretations, misspellings, or other errors. We invite and sincerely appreciate our readers' corrections, suggestions, and comments. We hope that the text defines and explains the field of engineering anthropometry in an operationally useful manner, through presenting fundamental principles and sufficient examples to show how the principles are applied. Work in this area has been "tough, but interesting." Many frontiers await exploration and standardization. To those who elect to apply themselves to solution of such problems, we give our good wishes and hearty encouragement.

John A. Roebuck, Jr.
K. H. E. Kroemer
W. Gary Thomson

September 1974

ACKNOWLEDGMENTS

The authors acknowledge their indebtedness to the encouragement, good graces, and direct aid provided by many teachers, friends, colleagues, and technical and editorial assistants. Credit is due Mr. D. T. Hanifan for his persistent encouragement of J. A. Roebuck early in the planning stages of the writing, and to Mr. S. Lippert, who introduced the subject and supervised the work of Mr. Roebuck at the Douglas Aircraft Company Human Factors Group in Santa Monica. Thanks are due Dr. John Lyman and Dr. Gershon Weltman, whose classes at UCLA provided incentive and opportunity to research and develop several of the subjects in the book as term papers and master's theses. Credit is given to the several supervisory personnel at Space Division of North American Rockwell, who permitted, encouraged, and aided the preparation, especially Dr. J. G. Wells, D. B. Morris, and E. W. Johnston.

We thank K. H. E. Kroemer's colleagues and friends, M. Alexander, C. E. Clauser, H. T. E. Hertzberg, and K. W. Kennedy for their advice and help with data. To Mr. Jack Mallonee, for his important assistance in preparing bibliographic material and reviewing the early text, and to Mr. Roebuck's parents, who aided in the bibliographic collation, we are indebted for an extensive set of references. We gratefully acknowledge the assistance of the many, many secretaries who have typed the manuscript, especially Mary Wright, Patricia Hahn, Yvonne Kupsh, Carol Baxter, Carol Thomas, Patricia Hall, Mrs. Jack Mallonee, Maxine Harrison, Cathy Holmquist, and Ruth Pantzalas.

We are especially appreciative of the editorial assistance and helpful suggestions given by Dr. David Meister, the series editor. Credits to the many publishers, from whose publications we have quoted or reproduced art work, are noted in the text, or by inclusion with the detail listing in the bibliography. All the above work would have led to naught without the patient acceptance and sacrifice of our wives and children, for which we owe humble thanks.

J. A. R., Jr.
K. H. E. K.
W. G. T.

CONTENTS

ENGINEERING ANTHROPOMETRY METHODS

I
HISTORICAL DEVELOPMENT OF ENGINEERING ANTHROPOMETRY*

1.1 INTRODUCTION—OVERVIEW

The contribution of the science of measurement to the history of civilizations has been told many times. However, seldom has the contribution to technology of the measurement of the physical dimensions of man been presented, especially with the point of view expressed here. This section traces the history of human body measurement methods from the development of selected activities derived from a series of diverse parent disciplines to their present maturity as elements of a new, cohesive discipline known as engineering anthropometry.

The idea that the physical size of a person is somehow related to his ability to function in the world is so old that it is surprising how often the concept is neglected in everyday thought. Even in biblical times there was recognition of differences in size and build, with much talk of "giants" and even comparison of body types, such as the brothers, Jacob and Esau. The artists of Greece and Rome studied body dimensions to develop standards of body proportions.

Closely related to the artist's canons are *folk norms* for proportioning hand tools, furniture, and various items of architecture. The names for many units in use today derive from names of segments of the body. Drillis (1963) points out that *le pied* and *le pouce* in French, *il piede* and *il pollice* in Italian, and *peda* and *pirksts* in Latvian had the same meaning as units of measure as foot and thumb had in English. He also notes that, "during the Middle ages, the 'thumb-ell', a distance measured across the hand to the tip of the outstretched thumb (14–18 cm), was used for the handles of swords, files, scutches and jugs. Farmers and dealers in horses still measure the height of horses or the length of scythe blades in 'hands'."

The development of arms and armor based upon military engineering prin-

* The term "anthropometry" is derived from two Greek root words: *anthropo(s)*—human, and *metrikos*—of, pertaining to, measuring. (A glossary of terms is provided in Appendix A.)

ciples has a traceable and useful history that continues into the present. The production of clothing and development of housing and transportation are other important hereditary lines combining engineering principles and concern with human dimensions. These, of course, were developed through mathematics and its derivative, statistics, suppported by the Age of Reason and the scientific method. The Industrial Revolution focused these activities on mass markets and mass health measures because of the need to apply man's measurements to the design of articles for mass production. The notion of "normality" in proportion and size was gradually replaced with statistical tables and charts.

From 1940 to 1970, there has been a significantly increasing need for human body dimension data in many industrial fields. The trend has been particularly strong in engineering design in the aircraft industry, where weight and size become so critical in the performance and economics of aircraft. As man has entered the space age, these factors have become even more critical as the cost per pound of payload has increased exponentially. For example, the introduction of the pressure garment as a means of exploring space further created unique problems in design and evaluation of habitable volumes.

1.2 PHYSICAL ANTHROPOLOGY

The origins of physical anthropology as a recording and comparing science may be traced to the travels of Marco Polo (1273–1295), which revealed a great number of human races differing in body size and build. Linné (1707–1778), Buffon (1707–1788), and White (1728–1813) inaugurated the science that was later called comparative racial anthropometry, in showing that there were differences in the bodily proportions of the various human races. These researchers formalized the classification of man into the zoological system.

Blumenbach (1752–1840) reported, for the first time, the complete anthropometric data available in his treatise, *On the Natural Differences in Mankind.* The statistician Quetelet (1796–1874) is credited with founding the science and with devising the term "anthropometry." He conducted the first large-scale somatometric survey.

Humphrey, in 1838, made careful measurements of humerus, radius, femur, and tibia in 25 skeletons each of white and Negro men. He calculated indices of each individual length divided by the subject height in order to have numbers that were directly comparable. The next advance was the realization that many of the bone lengths could be measured on the living subject, obtaining their termini by palpation. Other "landmarks" (nipples, umbilicus) were also found to be of value in the study of proportions. Broca (1824–1880), founder of the École d'Anthropologie in Paris, influenced the upsurge of anthropology significantly through his theoretical research as well as by devising many measurement techniques and devices. In 1914, Martin published the first edition of his famous *Lehrbuch der Anthropologie,* which remained the standard textbook for several decades.

The late nineteenth and early twentieth centuries saw the development of a widespread interest in the detailed study of the living human and of the skeletal remains of early man, in which physical anthropometry played an important part. Martin (1914) and Hrdlička (1939) describe the development and the main contributors in some detail. In the United States, the activities in anthropometry were triggered by comparing the many relics of ancient man with modern body dimensions and by the anthropometric differences observed among the U.S. citizens stemming from such a multitude of racial, ethnic, and national origins.

Recruiting statistics provided military surgeons with data for research during the nineteenth and twentieth centuries. Among their interests was the relation of body dimensions to occupation (occupational anthropology). Especially notable are the monumental anthropological studies in the United States during the Civil War and World Wars I and II (Gould, 1869; Baxter, 1875; Davenport and Love, 1921; U.S. Selective Service, 1943; Hooton et al., 1948; Hooton, 1949; Randall, 1947–1949; and Randall and Baer, 1951). Bertillon, in 1882, devised a system of 11 easily taken body measurements for establishing the individual identity of criminals. This was the beginning of forensic anthropometry.

By the beginning of the twentieth century, anthropometry had become an important branch of anthropology, expressed in an extensive and rapidly increasing literature. However, individual investigators used different methods and measurements. As a result, comparisons between results were difficult. Standardization of skull measurements was first attempted as a result of the International Congress of Anthropologists, meeting in Monaco during April, 1906. The 38 skull dimensions and 19 living head and face measurements have become the standards followed by anthropologists everywhere. A second standardization of measurements on the living body (excluding the head), applying mainly to the skeleton, resulted from the International Congress of 1912 in Geneva. Martin's *Lehrbuch* in effect unified the measurement techniques to a large degree. However, with the development of more practical needs and rigorous screening techniques, the necessity for more clearly defined and standardized (comparable) data become apparent again in recent years (Hertzberg, 1968; Garrett and Kennedy, 1971).

The aims and attitudes of the earlier investigators were somewhat different from those of the present-day engineering anthropometrist; consequently, their methods were different. However, many of their results are useful in design, and their methods can be adapted to the present problems. Some of their findings are still the only data available, so a knowledge of their methods is vital to understand what the data really mean and to evaluate the degree of applicability to an engineering problem.

1.3 ENGINEERING ANTHROPOMETRY

During approximately the same period that the study of static, structural body dimensions was developing for racial comparisons, an interest in the study of movement was also developing (Giedion, 1948). The important concept of graphical representation of movement had been discussed by Nicolas Oresme as early as the fourteenth century. At the beginning of the 1880s, Marey in Paris and Muybridge in California began to use photographic methods for the study of movement. They recorded human walking movements in a series of photographs. Around 1881, time study was introduced by F. W. Taylor, and aspects of work were quantified (Giedion, 1948). Exhaustive studies of human muscular action and body motion were made by several German investigators in the late 1880s and early 1900s (Braune and Fischer, 1889; Hultkrantz, 1897; Fischer, 1906 and 1907; Strasser and Gassmann 1893; Strasser, 1917; Fick, 1904–1911).

In 1912, the Gilbreths began their important contributions to the scientific study of movement as a management technique to improve industrial work efficiency (Barnes, 1949). Recognition of the value of placing the work within easy reach of the operator led to the study of maximum and normal work space dimensions. The body dimensions of the worker were studied by investigators such as Legros and Weston (1926) in order to properly place the seat and bench for alternate sitting and standing postures. Detailed studies of seating comfort and comfort angles were made by Lay and Fisher (1940) and Hooton (1945) for vehicle seat design criteria.

In the above studies the emphasis was on the use of human body kinematics and dimensions to improve work output. Such an interest, based on the application of physical sciences rather than biological sciences, could readily be classed in that group of activities called engineering. Taylor, the Gilbreths, and the latter investigators, being product oriented, were concerned with applications, rather than just the study of man for the sake of scientific curiosity.

Many systematic studies of human body dimensions were carried out during the late 1800s and early 1900s for various purposes related to commercial products, medical records, or military selection (Baxter, 1875; Gould, 1869; Davenport and Love, 1921). However, it is doubtful that the investigators considered themselves part of a new discipline. Much military anthropological research has been devoted to establishing effects of body dimensions and build on design and use of military equipment (Randall, 1948). These studies eventually helped in the converging of disciplines such as psychology, anthropology, physiology, and medicine with engineering, a synthesis that later came to be called human engineering in the United States, and ergonomics in most other countries. The branch of this work involving body dimensions was called applied physical anthropology (Randall, 1948). The need for an integration of life science disciplines for engineering applications was brought into focus by World War II, which created a whole new series of man-machine-environment problems. In addition to such problems as defining clothing dimensions for Army troops, great numbers of accidents in training and operational aircraft pointed to the need for study of basic causes. Psychologists, who were asked to study the actions of men under stress of flying, found that the complexity of modern military equipment was outstripping the abilities of men to operate them (Damon and Randall, 1944). Although extensive training could be used to get the most out of the man, this approach was costly and time consuming. Even at best, some equipment could not be operated at maximum efficiency because of a poor matching of human control and sensing abilities to the demands of the machinery as it was designed.

Among other problems, it was found that cockpits were often actually too small for many pilots, thus hampering or even preventing certain pilot movements. The study of body dimensions took on a renewed interest when it was found that very few reliable data on sizes of military pilots existed to help solve these problems. Physical anthropologists were called into service to measure pilots and flight crewmen, to define design criteria for future aircraft and selection criteria for current machines. A major milestone in this work was the report by Randall, Damon, Benton, and Patt (1946), *Human Body Size in Military Aircraft and Personal Equipment.*

After World War II, the emphasis on fitting the machine to the man became more fully developed as both commercial and military agencies continued the study of body dimensions and work space requirements along with the physiological and psychological factors involved. For example, Hooton surveyed 3867 adult men and women in Boston and Chicago railroad stations to obtain dimensions for railroad seating (Hooton, 1945). Other similar and related studies were continued at the Harvard School of Public Health, during the late 1940s, to improve safety in the use of all types of equipment. Evaluations were made of representative trucks, busses, and automobiles from the point of view of human engineering, anthropometry in particular. Over 300 bus and truck drivers were surveyed in conjunction with these studies to develop relationships between measurements such as Sitting Height, Eye Height, Arm Reach, and Leg Length and the interior dimensions of vehicles (Damon and McFarland, 1953; Damon, Stoudt, and McFarland, 1966).

Since the early 1940s, a stream of anthropometric data has come out of the U.S. Air Force laboratories at Wright-Patterson Air Force Base, near Dayton, Ohio, and the use of these data has increased throughout the airframe and transportation industry. Notable in the early portions of this work were Randall, Damon, and Benton. Later, H. T. E. Hertzberg directed these studies. A highly significant large-scale study of 132 dimensions of Air Force flying personnel was conducted during 1950 (Hertzberg, Daniels and Churchill, 1954). In other military-related anthropometry, R. W. Newman and R. M. White have contributed greatly to clothing design by anthropometric studies at the U.S. Army Quartermaster Research and Development Command in Natick, Massachusetts. Across the Atlantic, in England, Morant has published several valuable studies of RAF personnel. Data from the foregoing studies were applied to many fields other than those originally intended, by various applications engineers (e.g., Carlyle, 1960; Lippert, 1949–1965; Roebuck, 1952, 1957, 1968; Kroemer, 1966a, 1967a) and industrial designers (Dreyfuss, 1955, 1960, 1966; Sahley, 1957).

Although much of the engineering application work uses techniques from the early physical anthropologists, there have been many changes in approach, types of data gathered, and special instruments for measurement which arose from practical needs. In particular, a distinctive necessity to establish spatial relationships in three-dimensional coordinates was developed as characteristic of engineering applications of anthropometry. That is, engineers must know not only the length of body parts but also where they are located during human activity. In addition, many of the users of anthropometric data were not trained in anthropology originally but in fields such as physics, engineering, or design. It seems fitting, then, to classify their work into another specialized field of applied anthropometry which is herein called *engineering anthropometry,* formally defined as follows:

> *Engineering anthropometry is the application of scientific physical measurement methods to human subjects for the development of engineering design standards and specific requirements and for evaluation of engineering drawings, mock-ups, and manufactured products for the purpose of assuring suitability of these products for the intended user population.*

To set this definition in perspective to the parent discipline, it is appropriate to examine the purposes of anthropological anthropometry as stated by Hrdlička (1939) to see if they are appropriate here.

"The objects of anthropological anthropometry are:

1. To secure data on body measurements which reliably describe the characteristics of the group, race or stock being studied, and
2. To publish the data in a form which may be readily and safely used for anthropological comparisons and deductions."

By the substitution of "engineering" for "anthropological" and the interpretation of "characteristics" to include reach capabilities, work areas of normal and maximum usage, comfort angles, weight distributions, volumes, and so on, one has a good beginning to a description of the aims of engineering anthropometry. A further qualification should be added by substituting for "publish" the more inclusive term "communicate."

An outline of the scope of engineering anthropometry, relating actual and potential applications in terms of types of activities, typical products affected, data obtained or used, and the purposes of the activities is presented with examples in Table 1-1. Each of the terms used has specific meaning to the field of engineering anthropometry as explained in the remainder of the text. For now, it suffices to point out the utilitarian flavor and ultimate monetary considerations involved in the purpose for the listed activities. As fascinating as the measurements and analyses may be from a scientific viewpoint, the reasons for engineers to be engaged in these activities relate to the reasons manufacturers should invest in them: more profits from a better product. Actually, this is easier to say than to prove, since it is difficult to find objective methods for accurately evaluating a product's value solely in relation to one attribute, such as anthropometric adequacy. Past experience has shown such obvious evidence of serious problems resulting from flagrant violations of the practices espoused in this book that a detailed, accurate accounting of cost benefits should not be needed.

Traceable mainly from works of Braune and Fischer before the turn of the century, a special science of body structures, of the kinetics and the kinematics of the human body has developed. This field of scientific endeavor, now commonly called *biomechanics* (or biodynamics), can be defined as follows:

Biomechanics is the interdisciplinary science (comprising mainly anthropometry, mechanics, physiology, and engineering) of the mechanical structure and behavior of biological materials. It concerns primarily the dimensions, composition, and mass properties of body segments; the joints linking the body segments together; the mobility in the joints; the mechanical reactions of the body to force fields, vibrations, and impacts; the voluntary actions of the body in bringing about controlled movements, in applying forces, torques, energy, and power to external objects like controls, tools, and other equipment.

The relationships between classic anthropometry, biomechanics, and engineering anthropometry are so close and interwoven that it is very difficult (and rather useless) to draw demarcation lines between them. Physical anthropology is obviously the basic input to each of them, and designing man's environment to fit his dimensions and meet his capabilities is the practical output. In this sense, biomechanics is part of engineering anthropometry. Hence, this book does not treat biomechanics separately.

Interest in biomechanics, coupled with the need of clear terminology and

Table 1-1. Outline of Applications of Engineering Anthropometry

General Uses and Examples	Anthropometric Data Required	Purpose for Activity
Design criteria development and selection		
Determine general and specific population characteristics of users. *Measurement of sample subjects, statistical description of sizes, design population selection.*	Major body dimensions (Height, Weight), age, sex, job, color, nation/extraction, geographic areas.	Realistic design and evaluation of dimensional specifications. Customer acceptance, maximize sales, minimize legal liabilities.
Design requirements		
Workspace design and development—aircraft cockpits, automobile interiors, seats, consoles, tables, cabinets, maintenance access space, hatches and doors, tunnels, ladders. Includes any gross volume designed for human occupancy, for work, pleasure, hygiene, rest, treatment, or education.	Reach limits, body clearances, and clothing allowances, forces, torques, centers of mass, moments of inertia, mobility, volume, eye locations.	Assure operator/occupant has adequate volume, proper location of controls, displays, devices, tools. Maximize work efficiency, sales and profits, safety.
Clothing and personal equipment design and development—pressure suits, cooling and heating garments, fuel handler's suits and armor. Harness, life support, and temperature control packs. Emphasis on "engineered" clothing, not on home or business dress.	Circumferences, surface lengths along body, contours, areas, volumes, diameters, limb movements and restrictions.	Proper fit to the wearer, minimize restriction of movement, define range of sizes and number of each required to prevent overstock. Assure proper workspace interface.
Components and devices—electrical switches: knobs, levers, buttons, etc., handholds, latches, wheels, cranks, stick controls, small appliances, instruments.	Emphasis on the details of body parts in contact with product—fingertips, face contours, foot and shoe shape.	Assure proper interface with hand, foot, head, etc. to enhance operability, safety, convenience, comfort. Maximize sales, reduce rework costs.

Table 1-1. (Continued)

General Uses and Examples	Anthropometric Data Required	Purpose for Activity
Evaluation criteria and testing		
Specify bases for determining if design drawing or product/work space is adequate for design population or other intended users. Perform comparative measurements and test operability.	As required by above	According to above goals
Measurement of sample subjects—select persons representative of design limits.	Per critical design limits	Evaluation to determine if design meets goals, or to develop limits for rework of design if required.
Population description—prepare drawings, tables or graphs.		
Evaluation device design—prepare reach envelopes, contour templates, articulated drafting manikins, anthropomorphic dummies.		
Testing—perform measurements on product, workspace, clothing, and subject.		
Operator selection		
Specify operator dimensions—prepare list of measurements to be taken and limits for acceptance for critical spaces or clothing, etc.	As required by specific cases. Usually Height, Weight, Sitting Height, Breadths, Strength tests.	Assure personnel are of proper size range for equipment design limits (size or stress). Assure correct methods and accuracy.
Personnel measurement—train and initiate program of selection.	As above.	

coherent data, has led to some changes in anthropometric content and philosophy. For example, one of the authors and his colleagues have devised a new system of angular movement notation and terminology, and new tools and techniques for measurement of human body limb movements (Roebuck, 1968). There have been studies of dynamic body movement envelopes, or volumes, required to perform various work functions and of envelopes of capability to perform various tasks (Dempster, 1955a, Kennedy, 1964; Garrett, Alexander, and Matthews, 1970). Photography and electronic technology have improved measurement techniques (Tanner and Weiner, 1948; Gavan, Washburn, and Lewis, 1952; Seaford, 1959; Hertzberg, Dupertuis, and Emanuel, 1957; and Chaffee, 1961a,b).

During the last 20 years the development of computers permitting the rapid analysis of voluminous statistical data has greatly enforced the demand for and improved the quantity and quality of numerical data reported from large anthropometric surveys. Even more important was the innovation of computerized methods for handling mathematical models of biomechanical processes. The concepts and breadth of data available today have put a wide variety of mathematical models of man within the range of feasibility, and investigators have begun to develop such models. These attempts have identified specific areas of knowledge that are weak or deficient in data directly useful for developing such conceptual models. There is an increasing interest and new emphasis on three-dimensional descriptions of the body and *functional body link* measurements. For example, instead of measuring bone lengths, we attempt to measure distances between effective joint centers (Dempster, 1955; Snyder, Chaffin and Schutz, 1972). Visco-elastic properties* under various load conditions and other vital keys in these theoretical systems of analysis are also under study. Other examples are the mathematical model approach used by Hanavan (1964) in a study of moments of inertia. In the automotive field, McHenry and Naab (1966) have published results of a detailed computer simulation of the automobile crash victim in a frontal collision. An ambitious program to develop a series of mathematical models for computer analysis of cockpit geometry has been initiated by Hickey, Springer, and Cundari (1968). Several similar efforts are being pursued at government agencies here and abroad.

1.4 THE FUTURE OF ENGINEERING ANTHROPOMETRY

A "historical section" is supposed to deal with past events. However, it seems appropriate here to continue the discussion of broad perspectives of the field with a bit of speculation about its future. Certainly, some form of anthropometric activity will continue to take place for years to come. For example,

* See Appendix A.

one would expect to see the application of anthropometric techniques to populations of "emerging nations." New mores, population stereotypes, and comfort conditions will be studied in depth.

In the advanced technological areas, increased precision and automation of measurement technique and data reduction will free the technician to more fully define human body size and functional mechanics for work space, clothing, and other equipment designs. As more leisure is created and wealth distributed, a wider range of adjustments and personal convenience will be demanded. People will become increasingly discontented with being in the "left out" larger or smaller 5 or 10% of a population (see Chapter VIII).

"Instant anthropometry" will be needed and developed for custom-fitted clothing, chairs, and electromechanical extensions of man's senses and capabilities for work. Detailed descriptions of fine details of body surface features such as fingertips, eyelids, nostrils, lips, ears, and so forth, will be needed. A variety of new phenomena will be investigated to peer into the depths of human bodies, and possibly alien life forms, to locate bones, vital organs, and other internal structures. Among these may be electronic, sonic wave, and thermal (IR) effects.

Engineered clothing will further compensate for wide extremes of environment, on the city street, in ocean depths, and in extraterrestrial planetary atmospheres. Medical and engineering sciences will further overlap and merge in many areas to provide substitute organs and prosthetic body structures and to rebuild body organs from cellular tissue. Remote control of many exploratory devices will be commonplace. In all these activities the basic problems will involve some aspect of numerical definition of human shapes and physical characteristics which are closely related to those activities herein called engineering anthropometry.

II
METHODS FOR STATIC ANTHROPOMETRIC MEASUREMENTS

2.1 INTRODUCTION

Different approaches to body measurement reflect diverse interests of the investigators. For example, the anthropologist wants to describe the structure of the body as a means of studying development differences. The engineer, however, is interested in describing the body as a functional system component or as valuable but sensitive cargo. Thus the anthropologist seeks standard positions, which eliminate such variables of posture as muscle tone, motivation, comfort level and clothing.* The engineer, while recognizing the value of these standards, also tries to measure and apply the *effects* of these variables to optimize the design of machinery. In the following discussion, the criterion of selection is usefulness to the practical problems of engineering anthropometry. Techniques and the appropriate associated instruments are classified roughly according to the kind of physical body measurement for which they are particularly suited. However, many instruments have multiple use.

This discussion first considers general aspects of anthropometric surveys, and then the various methods and tools for measuring the relatively static aspects of the body, such as simple lengths and circumferences, contours, areas, and volumes.

2.2 ANTHROPOMETRIC SURVEYS

General requirements of the anthropometric survey include: the standard terminology and techniques that must be adhered to, the organization and training of the survey team, the precautions necessary to ensure accuracy of the results, and the presentation of the survey results.

* See, for example, Davenport (1927a,b), Hrdlička (1939), and Montagu (1960).

2.2.1 Standardization of Anthropometric Terminology and Techniques

Prior to beginning training for or performing a survey, the actual methods for performing measurements must be clearly defined. Special anatomical terms, which unambiguously specify the measurements to be performed, may be required. Furthermore, *standardization* of terminology and technique specific to each type of measurement will be needed.

The discovery of historical growth trends and the accurate extrapolation of dimensions for similar populations are two examples wherein anthropometric studies may benefit from consistency in method. Academic anthropologists recognized this need for standardization early in the twentieth century and held international conferences in 1906 and 1912 to resolve such questions. Another significant conference of anthropologists, primarily concerned with health and engineering applications, was held in 1967 because of the considerable differences in approach, technique, and terminology that seemed to be developing (Hertzberg, 1968).

Standardization of the Measurement Technique

An example of how a single body dimension can be measured in many different ways with correspondingly different results is contained in the following discussion of the apparently simple question of measuring stature. The 1967 conference (Hertzberg, 1968) considered stature in terms of its appropriate measurement techniques, descriptive terms, and the information content of its definition. Because the considerations for the measurement of stature also apply in some degree to other measurements, this first important dimension was used as a model for discussion. Hertzberg's report on the conference included the following key points and recommendations.

Four frequently used ways to measure stature were named and described: (1) "Stature"*—standing naturally erect, not stretched; (2) "Stature Against Wall"—back flattened and stretched to maximum height; (3) "Maximum-Stretch Stature"—free of the wall with back stretched to maximum height; and (4) "Recumbent Length"—lying supine. Tests have shown dimensional differences averaging .4 in. (1 cm) between techniques 1 and 2. All stretch techniques (e.g., 2 and 3) depend on motivation. Method 1 is recommended, as it requires minimal motivation, minimal language difficulty, and provides maximal access around the subject. A recent study report by Garrett and Kennedy (1971) provides an excellent source for comparing techniques used by previous investigators for a large number of common dimensions.

The engineering anthropometrist is concerned with anthropological stan-

* Titles of measurements formally defined in the literature are normally capitalized in this text.

dards for comparison to other studies and because they often represent a possible, though often temporary, working position. For example, the rigid, upright posture for the standard Sitting Height dimension (distance from plane of buttocks to top of head) may be representative of a "stretch position" for a seated operator, although he would normally assume a "slumped," relaxed posture, leaning forward or back into his seat. The latter type of body position also requires an engineering type of standard for comparing work space design dimensions, such as eye position and reach. These are discussed in Chapters VII to X.

Definition of Measurements

Actual practice in selecting nomenclature tends to polarize about one or the other of two types. There may be a description of the two points between which the distance is to be measured ("descriptive" type), for example, elbow-to-elbow, buttock-to-knee. The merits of this type are that it is simpler to prepare and results in a shorter report. The other, called the "instructive" type, involves a more extensive statement that indicates the subject's body position, names the anthropometric instrument, and describes the technique to be used by the measurer. Its value is that it presents more relevant information, informing the beginners and skilled anthropometrists alike. The description thus aids both standardization and instruction needs. The 1967 conference adopted the instructive type as preferable for standard practice.

Criteria for Terminology Selection. Dimension titles and descriptions should strive for clear, precise, and complete specifications of body posture, instrument used, technique, and body zone measured in a brief, simple but unambiguous manner within the constraints of grammatical correctness and compatibility with as many languages as practical. A consistent order of key words arranged in logical structure aids both writer and reader.

Four words found in previous widely used references, "diameter," "distance," "arc," and "projection" were replaced by other terms as active descriptors. The term "diameter" was dropped because it does not connote direction; and "distance" because it is generic—all dimensions are distances. Reasons for rejection of the other two terms are given later. The new verbal structure as recommended by the group is presented below.

Recommended Terminology. A glossary of terms is contained in Appendix A. Measuring instruments are described in Section 2.3.1 of this chapter.

Heights are vertical distances, usually measured with an anthropometer from the floor as the subject stands (or sits), or from a horizontal surface on which he sits: for example, Knee Height, Sitting or Sitting Height. (The terms "floor" and "standing surface" are largely synonymous, the latter including a solid box or table on which the subject stands for the convenience of the measurer.)

Breadths are horizontal lateral diameters, measured with the top anthropometer segment or suitable caliper: for example, Hip Breadth.

Depths are horizontal anteroposterior diameters, measured with the same instruments: for example, Chest Depth.

Lengths are dimensions usually measured with the anthropometer or sliding caliper along the long axis of a body segment, usually implying no direction: for example, Hand Length. Thus, they are "floating" dimensions, often being parts of a larger distance.

Reaches are distances along the long axis of the arm, often measured with a segment of the anthropometer, although wall-to-measuring-block techniques are permissible also: for example, Thumb-Tip Reach. Reaches can be considered a special variety of length.

Circumferences are distances in a single plane around a body segment or area, measured with a flexible steel tape. The plane of the tape may be horizontal (Waist Circumference) or vertical (Vertical Trunk Circumference), or at any convenient angle in between (Lower Arm Circumference, Extended).

Curvatures are the surface distances between two points on the surface of the body, measured with a flexible steel tape. This term replaces the former term, "arcs," which carried geometrical implications not necessarily present in anthropometry.

Prominences are distances by which one point on the body protrudes from another, as "Ear Prominence" or "Nose Prominence." This word replaces the former term, "protrusion," which cannot be easily translated into some languages.

In general, three types of descriptive terms are needed, which may be called the "locator," the "orientator," and the "positioner"; for example, Eye Height, Sitting. The locator identifies the point or landmark on the body (as Eye, Cervicale, Trochanterion, etc.) whose distance from some other plane or point is being measured; the orientator (as Height, Depth, etc.) identifies the direction of the dimension; and the positioner designates the body position required (—, Sitting;—, Flexed). When dealing with Heights, for example, the subject is usually assumed to be standing unless the positioner "Sitting" is added.

Normally, the locator term should appear at the beginning of the title and the orientator at the end, as in Eye Height. The positioner term is needed when the body changes position. The positioner term should follow the others, as in Eye Height, Sitting. This order retains emphasis on what is measured.

Many dimensions are measured from flesh surface to flesh surface, with only light pressure exerted. Others are measured by applying pressure to compress tissue overlying bones. When such pressure needs to be stated in the description of the measurement, the word "bone" (as in Elbow Breadth-Bone) may be added. However, a more precise terminology to assure better repeatability would include a specification of applied force, for example, "4.0 N force compression," since the actual bone surfaces are not normally accessible in the living subject. The addition of a word can serve to distinguish between slight variations in location, as in Waist Height-Omphalion versus Waist Height-Iliocristele.

Selecting the Measurements

Engineering anthropometrists often desire, and hence would try to measure, a great many more dimensions than might satisfy anthropologists as a reasonable minimum. To adequately describe key body landmarks in three-dimensional space could easily require 300 dimensions or more. Such a large number is not practical for manual measurements. Investigators planning large-scale surveys usually settle for approximately half that number or less. Therefore, the listed measurements must be carefully selected. Often those selected will fall within one of the broad categories whose characteristics are later described in the applications chapters: work space design and evaluation (Chapter VIII), clothing design and evaluation (Chapter IX), and design and evaluation of smaller devices and components (Chapter X). The handbooks listed in Chapter VII and comprehensive reports such as those of Hertzberg, Daniels, and Churchill (1954) or Clauser, Tucker, McConville, Churchill et al. (1972) provide further suggestions.

2.2.2 Organization for Surveys

For any reasonably large survey, considerable thought should be given to organization of the work and indoctrination of measurement personnel. The required data should be carefully defined and explained to the participating investigators. The measurements selected should be tried on a small pilot group of persons with a wide range of body types representative of the group to be measured.

Reliable measurements of Waist Breadth, for example, may be more difficult on persons with extensive abdominal fat as compared to slim or very muscular body types. Determination of landmarks about the shoulders may be confused by fatty deposits. Measurements of Chest Depth for adult females poses different problems than for men; is the body cage depth or the flesh depth at the nipples desired for the study objectives? Facial features pose a wide variety of differences which may make difficult certain nasal or chin measurements.

These pilot measurements should be designed to check consistency between trials for a given measurer, between different measurers, and between any different techniques that might be employed. For an example of the latter, Kemsley (1957) found that there was no practical difference between body measurements made when the female subject wore a slip or was nude.

The layout of the measuring room and scheduling of subjects are other items that can be investigated in the experimental period. A separate room for disrobing is an important point in the physical arrangements, and adequate storage facilities for the subject's clothing are necessary to obtain good cooperation. Flow diagrams and motion studies may be justified if the sample taken is to be large or must be measured in a very limited time.

A receptionist to obtain preliminary personal data will save the time of the measurers for their specialized task. A minimum team size would consist of a measurer and a recorder. When a considerable number of landmarks is to be applied, it may be economical to have a very experienced measurer (preferably an anatomist or physical anthropologist) to mark each subject. For large surveys, it is advantageous to divide the measurement task into segments, or "stations," for example, so that all measurements on a sitting subject are taken by one measurer, and all of a standing subject by another measurer, or that all the measurements to be taken with one instrument are performed by one person. When all team members are trained to work interchangeably, fatigue and monotony are reduced.

The training of completely naive persons to serve as members of the measuring team may take considerable time. This should be anticipated in developing the plans for the survey. This training should include at least a brief introduction to the skeletal structures of the body involved in areas to be measured, a description of the anticipated uses of the data and the importance of precision in measurement. If guidelines (e.g., charts, graphs, tables) for checking readings are to be used, the derivation and meaning of these should be explained. Statistical variations between persons should be discussed as they relate to the planned measurements. Of course, actual practice under the observation of an experienced person is essential to achieve smooth operation. The length of training will vary with type and size of the survey.

For example, Hertzberg, Daniels, and Churchill (1954) reported that their preparations required one week of intensive training. Twelve untrained subjects from a local college were each measured by the two supervisors; then each student in turn had to demonstrate his ability to match these measurements on each of his fellows. Practice sessions were eight hours each day, with the men subdividing into six pairs, each to specialize in a specific series of measurements. On the road, the survey team was composed of a supervisor, a photographer, and six pairs of measurers. Each pair had a portion of a data blank to fill in; each planned to require about equal time. The pairs alternated between measuring and recording at about two-hour intervals to minimize fatigue. The subject carried his own data sheet along through a series of measuring stations manned by a pair of men, and then handed the form to the photographer, who took four photographs of him to complete the record. Over 4060 subjects were measured for 132 different dimensions in this study. (In addition, personal background data were gathered, establishing place of birth, age, Air Force rating and location, parental birthplace, education, race, marital status, and religion.) The average schedules ran to about 100 to 120 subjects per day. Top speed was found to be 170 men processed in a seven-hour day, averaging one man per 2.5 minutes.

In setting up teams, allowances should be made for illness and other absenteeism. Planning should also take into account the considerable cultural idiosyncrosies of various nationalities and religious groups. For example, removing any part of the clothing may be forbidden, or the concept of a scientific test incomprehensible. Ingenuity and knowledge of native customs will be essential in obtaining data in many "emerging nations," where cultural values are different from those of western civilization.

Data recording and data analysis methods can have great effects on the planning and conduct of the survey. Manual recording requires very different techniques and procedures from automatic recording. If, as in Hertzberg's classic surveys, the data are to be transferred to punched cards for analysis, the form of recording the measurements may be quite unique. Grouping of the measurements that are best taken with the same instrument (so that they are sequential and in close proximity on the data sheet) will save time, and arranging the technique so that all measurements to be taken in any special positions are taken in the same sequence is also helpful. When data are to be added or subtracted to obtain the measurement of interest, a place to perform the work on the form may be of value unless the computations are to be performed by machine.

2.2.3 Accuracy and Precision

Two important factors that should be considered when conducting an anthropometric survey are accuracy and precision, according to the following definitions.

Accuracy refers to the closeness of the measurements to some reference or standard value accepted as the "truth"—whereas *precision* refers merely to their closeness together, or grouping. Thus, *accuracy* expresses a relation to a value external to the measurement process; *precision* to a value internal to the process.

In practice, the true value is generally best approximated by use of precisely calibrated, rigid instruments carefully positioned by trained investigators under controlled environmental conditions. Even then, some small deviations may be observed between successive readings. Therefore the average, or arithmetic mean, of several such readings is usually used to improve the accuracy of the results. The standard deviation of these instruments about their average is a measure of the *precision* of the method.

Several precautions against mistakes are advisable. First is the practice of a double reading, then recording and checking again. Another precaution is to take the same measurement by two independent methods, such as measuring Head Height directly and also finding it from the difference between Stature and height of the tragion from the floor. If time and funds permit, two independent teams may take the same measurements on each person. Tables of normal ranges of body dimensions expected for given heights and weights may be used for comparison to call attention to grossly impossible values.

The instruments used must, of course, he accurate, and the survey team should be familiar with their care and operation in order to get the best out of them. Instruments should be periodically checked against reliable standards to maintain their accuracy. The description and application of special instruments for use by anthropologists will be discussed later in Section 2.3.1.

2.2.4 Survey Data Reporting Formats

Reported anthropometric data serve a dual role—that of a record of what was done (and thus how to do it again—the educational role) and that of a source of information. The latter is considered in Chapter VII in a discussion on source documents and preparation of handbooks. The former is discussed here. Examples of the instructive type of titles and definitions are presented. Figure 2-1 provides an example of a data reporting format developed by Hertzberg, Daniels, and Churchill (1954). It attempts to achieve a harmonious blending, visually as well as technically, of the following elements of anthropometric data presentation:

1. The title.
2. An outline sketch of the body or body part, with a bold but accurate dimensional arrow indicating at a glance the distance to be measured.
3. A clear photograph or perspective drawing showing the subject being measured with the proper instrument according to the correct technique.
4. A verbal definition of the procedure carefully worded for clarity and completeness of information.
5. The relevant data,* including at least the mean, standard deviation, coefficient of variation, number of subjects, and selected percentiles from the first through the ninety-ninth and other material as necessary.†

To accomplish this presentation requires the services of a competent artist, a photographer and, of course, a typist. These services must be included in the preparations for anthropometric surveys and scheduled as a portion of the total budget of time and money.

* Note that the common units in anthropometry are metric. However, conversion of results to English units may still be required in some engineering contexts.

† See chapter V for definitions of statistical terms.

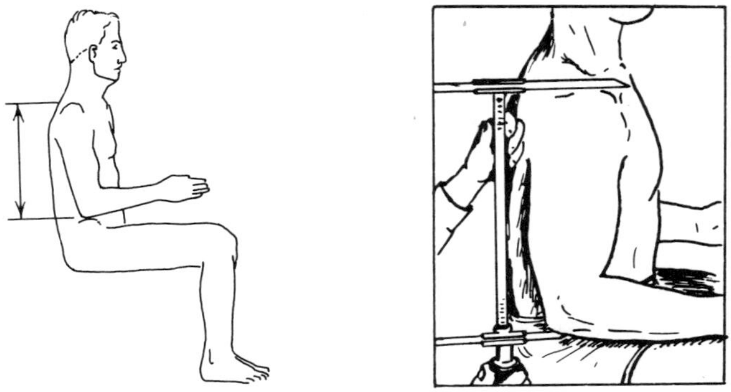

Shoulder-Elbow Length

Subject sits erect, his right upper arm hanging at his side and his forearm extended horizontally. Using the anthropometer, measure the vertical distance from right acromion as marked to the bottom of the elbow.

Mean: 36.37(.03) cm; 14.32(.01) in.
Standard deviation: 1.75(.02) cm; .69(.01) in.
Range: 29–46 cm; 11.42–18.11 in.
$V = 4.81(.05)\%$ $N = 4059$

Percentile Values

%	cm	in.	%	cm	in.	%	cm	in.
1	32.4	12.8	35	35.7	14.1	80	37.9	14.9
2	32.9	13.0	40	36.0	14.2	85	38.3	15.1
3	33.2	13.1	45	36.2	14.3	90	38.7	15.2
5	33.6	13.2	50	36.4	14.3	95	39.2	15.4
10	34.1	13.4	55	36.6	14.4	97	39.6	15.6
15	34.5	13.6	60	36.9	14.5	98	39.8	15.7
20	35.0	13.8	65	37.1	14.6	99	40.3	15.9
25	35.2	13.9	70	37.4	14.7			
30	35.5	14.0	75	37.6	14.8			

Figure 2-1. Example of data reporting format (Hertzberg, Daniels and Churchill, 1954).

2.3 MEASUREMENTS OF BODY FORM

Methods of measurement that involve direct contact of instruments with the surface of the subject (contact methods) or on-site readings of optical devices (optical methods) are classified as *direct* methods. These are distinguished from *photographic* methods that produce a long lasting detailed record that is later measured or interpreted.

2.3.1 Direct Methods

The discussion of methods for direct measurement of body form will begin with the simple linear and curvilinear dimensions, and finally go to the more complex two- and three-dimensional contour recordings. Angular measurement methods are discussed in Chapter III.

Linear Dimensions

The term "linear dimensions" refers to measurements of the shortest distance between two points on the body. In general, this includes the lengths of the long bones, breadths and depths of the body, and the so-called projected dimensions, such as the heights of the various body landmarks as measured from the floor for a standing subject. Other examples include the distance from the eye to the tip of the finger or other dimensions not directly involving a limb or segment of the body.

Except for very rough checks with a yardstick and tape, quite good accuracy for engineering purposes can be achieved with very simple equipment. For measurement of overall body lengths such as Stature, Sitting Height, Knee Height, and so forth, a wall and a scale or grid taped to it at convenient heights can be sufficient. It is helpful to use a triangular block of wood with one right angle, or some similar device, to bridge the gap between the body and the wall and ensure that the desired height is being properly indicated on the wall grid. Hrdlička (1939) provides other historical refinements.

Morant (1945) used two sheets of plywood, marked with a grid of squares, hinged together so they could be opened at right angles. A low bench was placed in the corner. With various adjuncts such as blocks of wood for raising the seat and squares for application to the body point being measured, he obtained a portable, simple setup for measuring seating dimensions with sufficient accuracy and low cost (see Figure 2-2).

Certain body points are not conveniently reached by the blocks or squares mentioned above. For these dimensions, several instruments have been developed by anthropologists (Figure 2-3). One of these is the anthropometer, a term encompassing a number of related instruments which consist of a graduated rod, frequently sectionable for ease of transport and storage, equipped with one fixed and one sliding and extendable perpendicular branch, Figure 2-3*a*. The sharply pointed end of the sliding branches can reach reentrant corners and folds of the body not accessible to the squares used with the reference planes. The investigator must either hold the rod upright carefully (Figure 2-4), or provide a sturdy base to assure verticality when accurate measurement of vertical dimensions is desired. With the sliding and fixed extendable branches used together the anthropometer can be used as a sliding compass (Figure 2-1).

The regular sliding compass (*compas glissier*), Figure 2-3*d*, is more convenient for some smaller measurements. Figure 2-5 shows a typical use of the sliding compass for measuring breadth of hand. A larger version of the sliding compass is sometimes used for measurements such as Chest Depth (Hrdlička, 1939).

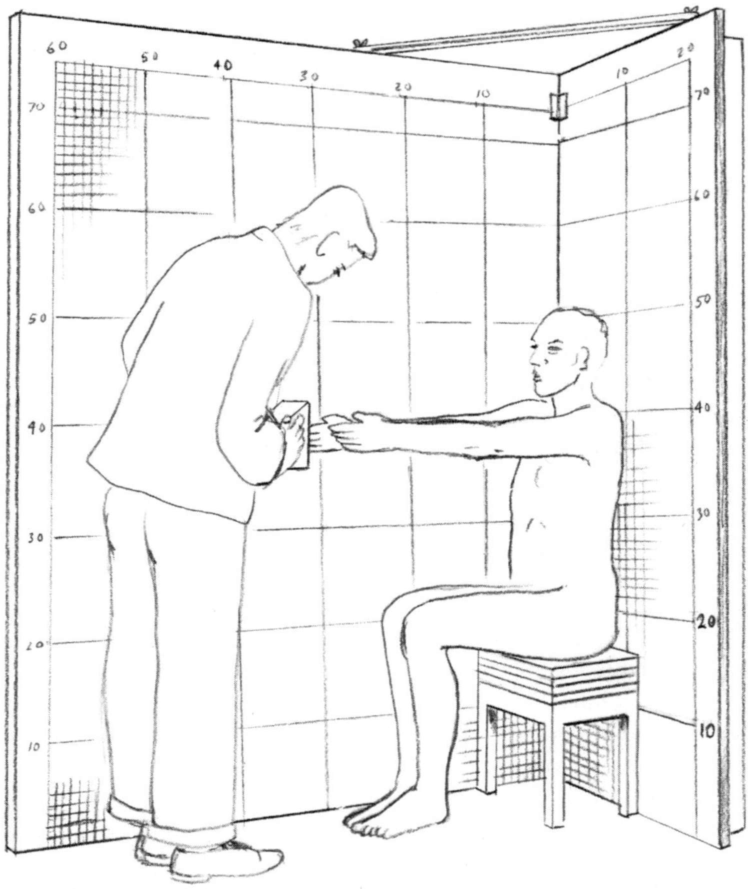

Figure 2-2. A simple, portable linear measurement device.

Another instrument is useful for measuring diameters of the head and other irregular parts of the body. This is the spreading calipers (*compas d'epaiseur*), Figure 2-3*c*, which is made in several varieties.

1. Small compass of Broca: primarily used for skull measurements.
2. Standard larger compass of Paris Ecole d'Anthropologie: used for ordinary work on the living subject.
3. Hrdlička compass: this is similar to the smaller compasses, but has slightly larger branches, with terminal parts horizontal at the spread

of 10 cm and with a guard on the lower portion of each branch 8 mm from the point to regulate the distance of introduction into the meatus of the ear.

4. Bertillon compass: has greater rigidity and bluntness of branches.

The above devices (described in more detail by Hrdlička, 1939) generally have an accuracy greater than the consistency of size of the man being measured. That is, breathing, tremor, muscle tone, changes due to fatigue, and so forth, may alter the dimensions of the subject between one measurement and the next more than the inherent misreading of the measurement device. Considerable skill developed from practice is required for consistent results with about .1 cm on either side of the mean. For some measurements, (e.g., skin folds) consistency requirements make a scale necessary for controlling the force of application of the points of the instrument. For most engineering purposes, accuracy to the nearest ½ cm is sufficient on larger dimensions and to the nearest millimeter is adequate for smaller ones, such as Hand Breadth.

Another source of inconsistency (nonrepeatability) of measurements may be

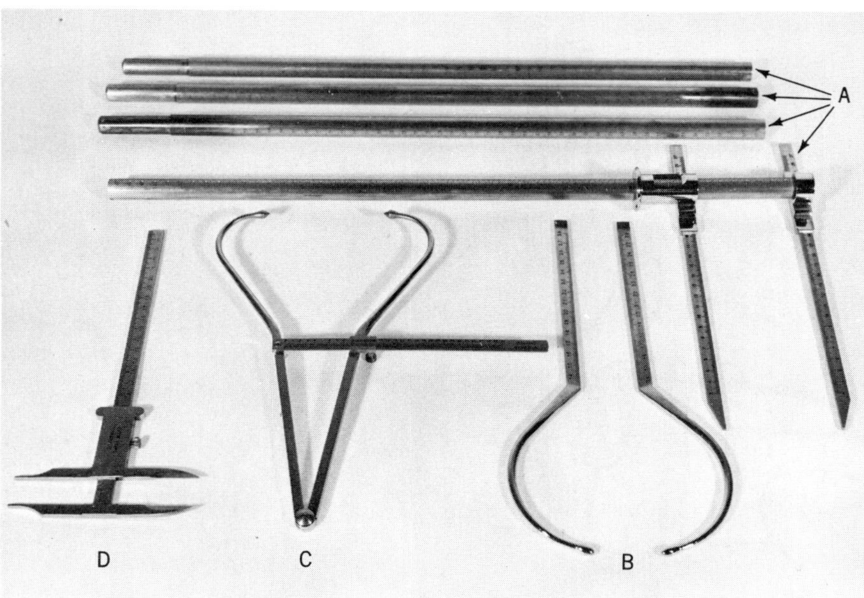

Figure 2-3. A common set of anthropometric instruments. (*a*) Anthropometer, with straight branches, divides into sections for storage, travel. (*b*) Curved branches for anthropometer, useful for measuring large diameters between reentrant surfaces. (*c*) Spreading calipers. (*d*) Sliding compass. (Anthropometric tape, not shown, would usually be included in basic set of instruments.) (Purchased from catalog of Siber Hegner and Co., Inc., 1956.) Photo by James Abbott.

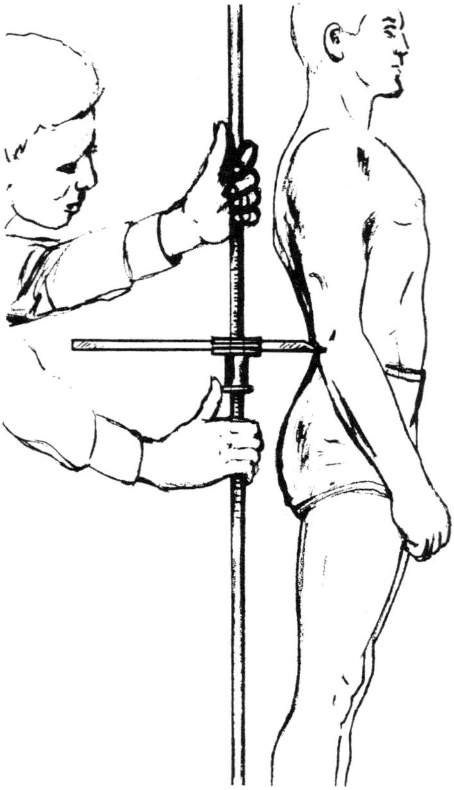

Figure 2-4. Anthropometer in use.

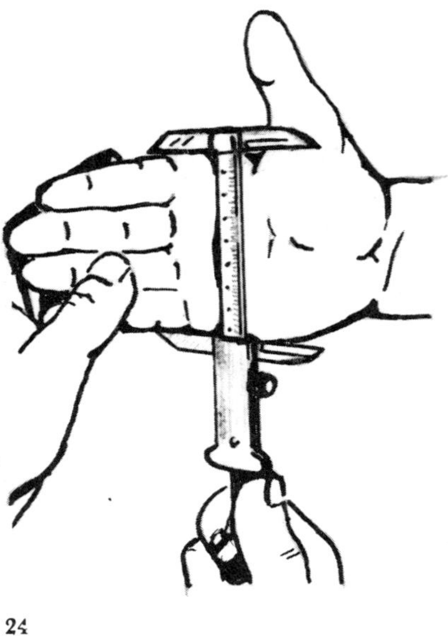

Figure 2-5. Use of the sliding compass for measuring Hand Breadth. (After Hertzberg, Daniels and Churchill, 1954). Many additional examples are illustrated for the use of this and other anthropometric instruments in the same source report.

time of day. The height, for instance, may vary up to one cm or more between morning and evening. Dietetic intake may increase the stomach girth during the day. The length of time required for maintaining a given posture may affect the blood volume in a limb to give different dimensions.

Unless these variables are of interest, the recommended practice is to reduce such variations to a minimum by the selection of uniform conditions for all measurements. Heights and weights should be taken at a selected time of the day. Another alternative is to record several measurements and prepare graphs of measurement magnitude as a function of time. Weights of food and water intake may be recorded for all meals and snacks if Weight is the critical parameter in a study. In large surveys, randomization of measurements in effect eliminates sequential factors.

For special measuring tasks one may develop a large variety of devices. Figure 2-6 shows a measuring box that was used to obtain Foot Length, breadth and Instep Length. A small block (also shown) with millimeter scale along one edge was used in the same survey to obtain Ankle Height. Figure 2-7 shows two devices for measuring diameters,* one for the finger and the other for the grip. Hooton (1945) described a complete chair for body measurements pertinent to railroad travelers seating accommodations.

Circumferential Dimensions

The term "circumferential dimensions" includes those measurements along the surfaces of the body between two points or returning to the same point to obtain a perimeter. Such measurements are of some use in physical fitness and occasionally in special equipment design, but are primarily useful in the design of protective clothing, such as described in Chapter IX.

The use of a flexible tape is the obvious solution for obtaining circumferential data. Although steel tapes are acceptable, specially treated cloth tapes are generally not as cold, do not rust, and are more flexible, but may be sub-

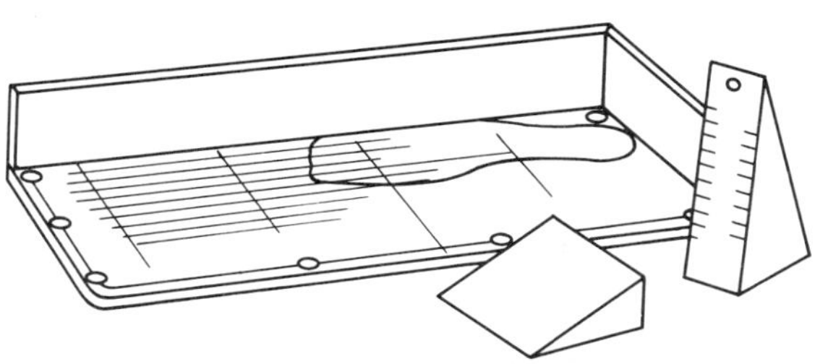

Figure 2-6. Foot measuring box and blocks. (After Hertzberg, Daniels, and Churchill, 1954.) For use in measuring Foot Breadth, Foot Length, and Instep Length. Ankle heights are taken by means of the block on the right with a millimeter scale mounted along the vertical edge.

* Special cases where "diameter" is appropriate terminology, contrary to recommendations on page 14.

ject to stretching. Since so many of the important dimensions include soft fleshy areas that tend to be compressed by a tape, it is advantageous to have a device for providing constant tension on the tape to obtain good reproducibility.

Specifying the way that tape is to be released from the reel for a given measurement does not provide sufficient reproducibility of pull force between different tapes and for different degrees of extension. Kemsley (1957) showed that mean differences of about 1% in waist and 4% in bust circumference can result from different tape tensions by different measurers.

Morant (1945) employed a tailoring tape having thin wires running through it to prevent stretching, and two spring gages attached to ensure that a constant force is exerted when measurements are taken. As shown in Figure 2-8, one of the gages is attached to the end of the tape and the other is attached to a buckle that can be fixed at any convenient distance along the scale. Morant claimed the system gave more assurance of accuracy, was faster to use, and did not require the measurer to touch the subject with his fingers.

It is clear that tissue compression (and, hence, the measurement obtained) depend on interactions among tissue plasticity, friction between tape and skin,

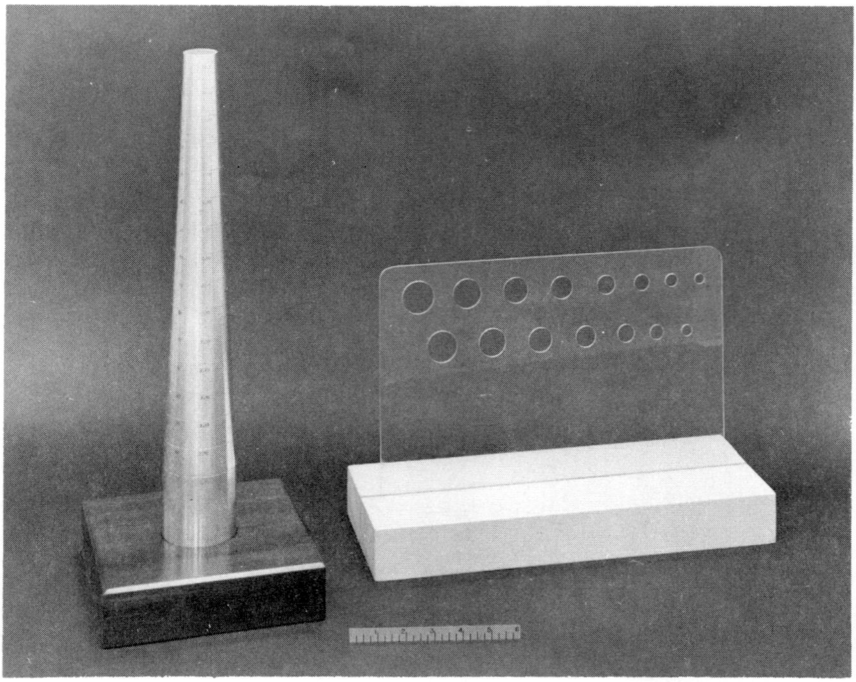

Figure 2-7. Special devices for measuring finger and grip diameters. (Courtesy of Space Division, Rockwell International Corporation.)

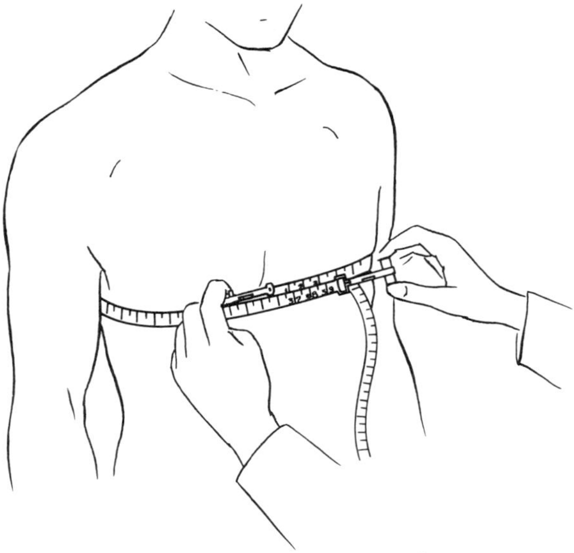

Figure 2-8. Use of the pressure tape (Sketch based on illustration from Morant and Gilson, 1945).

curvature of the tape, and pull force as measured at the free end(s) of the tape. Hence, controlling the pull force is only one step toward standardization of measurement.

The chest girth changes with the breathing cycle. Therefore, care should be taken to define just what is desired. For a rigid armor design, one would like to have the full expanded chest measurement. The *common* anthropometric dimension is the arithmetic mean between the expired condition and the inspired condition. Similarly, other dimensions may change with body posture (e.g., Waist Circumference), or with muscle tension (e.g., Biceps Circumference).

The exact definition of the dimension desired is especially important in taking arcs* and circumferences of the body. Not only can body posture or muscle contractions change the contour but also there are folds and reentrant corners of the body that can be spanned over by a tightly pulled tape. In some cases, the complete surface is of interest, and the tape may have to be held in several places to conform to the body contour. In other cases, the minimum tape length is appropriate.

Position in Space and Body Contours

All dimensions discussed previously were obtained by measurements taken relatively independently of each other. In general, they could not be used to

* Also called "curvatures". See Section 2.2.1.

numerically describe the body posture and contours in a set of Cartesian coordinates, with each body dimension exactly related to each other. It is often said that these are "floating" dimensions.

For many engineering design solutions, however, detailed information on position is necessary. In fact, it is desirable to define the spatial location of *any* point on the surface of the body, or the centers of joint movement, or the centers of mass of body segments, or the static body surface contours. Similarly, the loci of points reachable by a man with his fingertip, elbow, or heel may be considered to define an envelope of static reach or dynamic movements in space. This chapter considers mainly static body form description; dynamic measurements of envelopes of movement and paths of movement are discussed in Chapter III. Since many tools and techniques for both static and dynamic measurements have similarities, such that they can be used interchangeably or with some adaptation, techniques discussed here may be useful for dynamic problems and vice versa.

Direct Measurement, Tracing, and Shadow Methods. Using the Morant grid boards, one can reference points on the surface of the body to a fixed point by reading both height and distance from the corner. Continued application of the technique outlines the body contours on each of the two grid boards. Using a graduated scale on the indicator block allows measurement of body surface points at their location out from the plane of measurements, but this location of points in three dimensions is awkward.

A marking device, such as a grease pencil, can be perpendicularly mounted to a movable base and used to trace body outlines on a flat background grid. This technique, of course, cannot be used to locate eyes or other sensitive areas accurately.

The technique of shadow graphs, projecting one's shadow on a background grid, also falls in this category. Although it is useful for a limited number of anthropometric situations, it suffers from problems of parallax distortion which will be discussed further in relation to photographic methods.

Template Methods. For a small area of the body, it is appropriate to cut plates of cardboard or plywood and fit them to the contours of the body. The accuracy of these methods can be tempered to the time, skill, and patience of the experimenter.

Also feasible is the use of malleable materials that can be fitted to the body by pressure or formed by hand and fitted by successive trials. Applicable materials are strips of lead or soft aluminum wire. Problems relating to these devices include preserving the shape while handling and recording it, and defining the relation of the shape to some reference axes or planes in space.

Multiple Probe Method. Direct mechanical measurement of contours of the body may be obtained by a framework that holds a large number of sliding probes. Typically, this may consist of a box with holes, in opposite faces, aligned so that metal or wood rods, when inserted in the holes, are parallel to each other. Each rod is pushed until it touches the skin, and its protrusion recorded. Such devices have been used to measure face contours, total body shape, and reach envelopes.

The multiple probe principle was used by Roebuck in measuring space suit and body contours (Figure 2-9). The device was primarily intended for recording surface contours of the posterior, from the buttocks upward to the helmet neck ring, but can be used for other contours as illustrated. Special support rods were provided near the shoulder scye areas, to prevent body rotation about the trunk length axis. A back and side "box" at 90° to each other were provided to assure accuracy in the side contours. Removable extension pieces were used for the tops of the shoulders and the crotch area.

Casting Methods. Instead of attempting to describe contours by numerical

Figure 2-9. Multiple probe contour measuring device. Device may be adjusted vertically and leveled by support post fittings. Straps retain subject in position during measurement. The shoulder contour measuring board is in place. The investigator shows the measuring technique for side probes. All rods are the same length. (Courtesy of Space Division, Rockwell International Corporation.)

offsets or contour maps, a direct three-dimensional recording by casting or molding may be desirable. The method is probably the most accurate means of direct measurement for the complicated shapes such as the head, hands, and feet. The use of plaster of paris is a classic method. The skin must be prepared so that the mold will easily part from the skin when desired. This may include shaving the skin. The plaster heats up as it sets, so that discomfort may be felt if the mass of plaster is large and the area covered is extensive. Fortunately, the material sets quite quickly if mixed to the right consistency, which mitigates the problems. An excellent example of plaster of paris applications for developing body molds of children is presented by Boyd (1935). Newer materials have partially replaced plaster of paris.

The use of casting methods for recording of contours has been continued in modern times for many fields. A significant engineering anthropometric example was the development of the astronaut couch for Project Mercury. In that design, only the dorsal surfaces of the crewman's body were of concern. The major forces acting on the spacecraft were such as to cause very high pressures on the back of the body so that a form-fitting couch was necessary. In developing the casting for the couch, the eye location of the astronaut, which was of critical concern in the cockpit, was precisely placed with the aid of a locating device in the casting fixture. Representative clothing was also worn during the casting process to account for this extra thickness during operational conditions.

The manned space program has used casting techniques for other applications as well. The Apollo pressure garment gloves began with a casting of the hands of the intended wearer. A fabric reinforcement was formed around this casting before being dipped into a special rubber compound. Casting techniques were used in development of urine transfer and storage devices worn under the space suits.

Casting is primarily used when:

1. A detailed description of an intricately contoured body surface is desired.
2. The product can be developed directly from the cast form without the intermediate step of numerical description (coordinates, contour maps).
3. The product must fit closely.
4. Intermediate or subsequent steps require pressure of instruments or apparatus that would deform or damage the surface contours.

For many projects, the advantages outweigh the disadvantages of the mess, the preparation and cleanup time, requirements for materials, protection for the subject, and curing time for the cast part. The time requirements are seemingly high as compared to a few measurements with the anthropometer

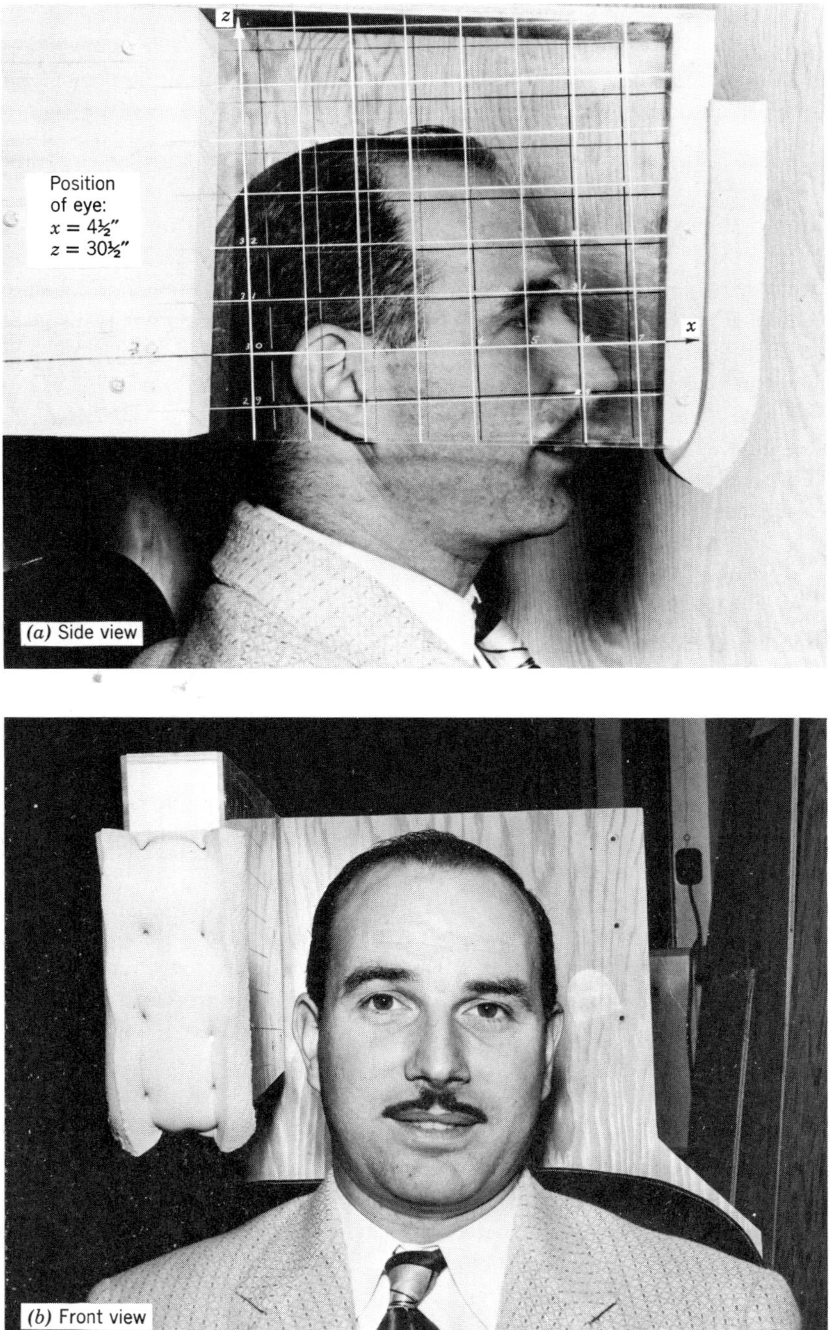

Figure 2-10. Parallel transparent grid measurement device. (Courtesy of McDonnell Douglas Co.)

and calipers, but the extent of information obtained in terms of number of data points per unit time is much higher.

Optical Methods. Certain parts of the body which are of great importance in engineering design are too sensitive to touch by direct techniques. For example, the eyes are so easily hurt by undue pressure that indirect methods, such as optical sighting are desirable. Setting up a surveyor's transit is often too cumbersome and time consuming. A compromise method developed by Roebuck is indicated in Figure 2-10. A device containing two transparent parallel planes, scribed with grid like coordinate lines, is shown. In use, one aligns the grid lines in the two planes and records the location of the eye on these grids, estimating the distance between the lines on one plane by balancing the offset of the more distant lines between the nearer set of lines.

This concept of parallel transparent grid planes can be used for whole body measurements as well by enlarging the enclosing box. The subject and his adjacent seat, control panel, and the like, can be measured in the grid enclosure.

2.3.2 Photographic Methods

To obtain complete outlines of the body by the foregoing manual techniques is time consuming and awkward. Subject fatigue introduces errors of movement during the process. In general, photographic processes are to be preferred if the time required for data reduction is available and if special precautions against parallax can be taken.

The use of photography in anthropometry has gradually evolved from qualitative recordings to precise measurement methods. Significant published descriptions of photogrammetric techniques for measuring contours and landmarks in space are presented in Tables 2-1 and 2-2. Several of these are discussed in detail in the following paragraphs, beginning with simple, single viewpoint methods and ending with complex stereo photogrammetric techniques. Reduction of parallax errors is a key issue in anthropometric applications of photography.

Background or Superimposed Grid Techniques

One of the most commonly used methods for making photographic measurements is to place the subject of interest in front of a background grid. Unfortunately this technique greatly magnifies the parallax problem. To illustrate this point, Figure 2-11 shows a subject wearing a pressure suit with a known diameter neck ring. When a photograph is taken of this subject, the camera does not "see" the true neck ring diameter, x, but a slightly smaller one x' due to the curvature of the neck ring. This illustrates the normal parallax problem. If the distance from object to camera is large compared to the object ($\gtrsim$20X), the error is almost negligible. However, if measurements of this

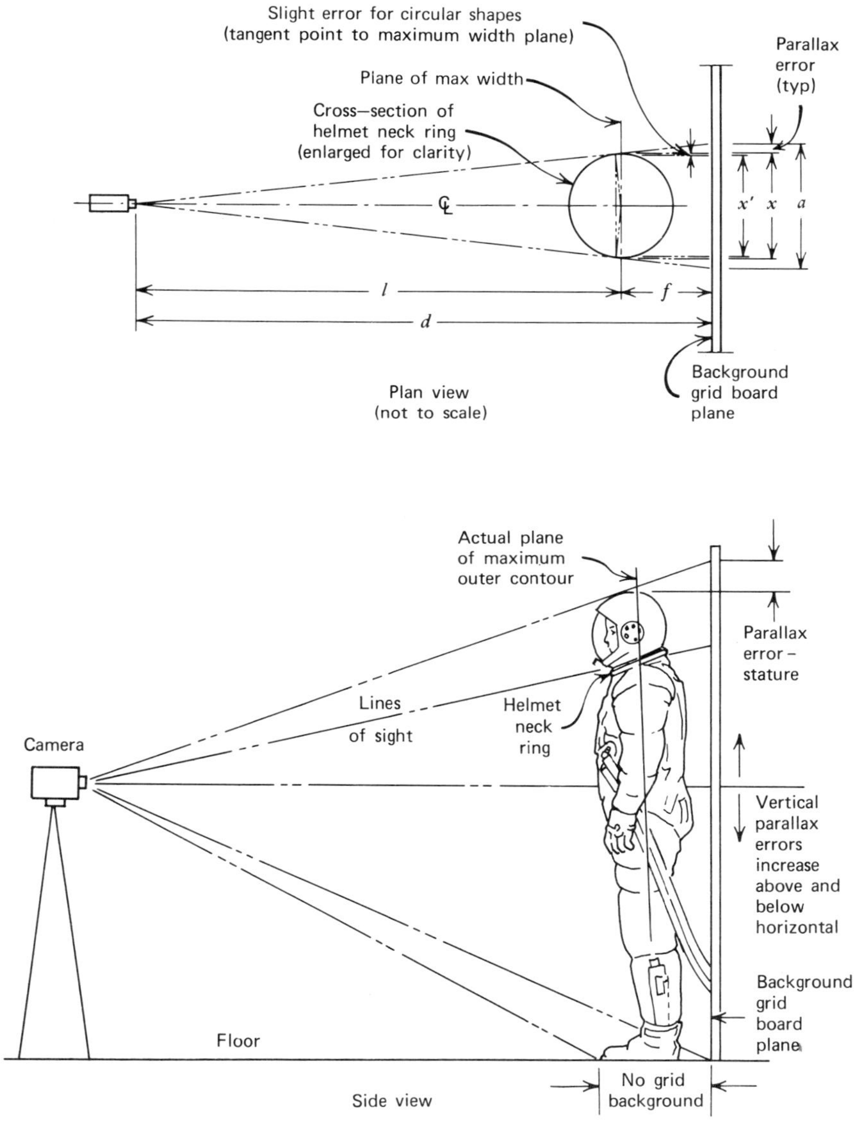

Figure 2-11. Geometry for calculation of scale factor.

Table 2-1. Photogrammetric Methods for Static Anthropometry (Nonstereophoto)

Investigators Reference/Year	Equipment	Subject Matter	Remarks
Hrdlička (1925)	Camera	Subjects measured	Qualitative record
Simon (1926)		Facial features	Advocated
Broadbent (1931)	Radiographs	Skull	Standardized lateral and posteroanterior
Hofrath (1931)	Radiographs	Skull	Standardized lateral and posteroanterior
Sheldon et al. (1940)	Camera	Somatotyping, two views, special pose	Quantitative measurements from negatives
Tanner and Weiner (1948)	Photogrammetric camera	Anthropometric dimensions—head and face	"Accuracy equal to anthropometric methods"
Dupertuis and Tanner (1950)	Photogrammetric camera	Anthropometric data/somatotypes	Discussed importance of posing subject, accurately
Axelsson (Deschin, 1950)	Narrow light beam camera rotating subject	Face and head	Used for sculpture

Lippert (unpublished)	String shadows cast on subject camera at 90°	Face and head	
Gavan, Washburn, and Lewis (1952) Hunt and Giles (1956)	Photometric camera system, nine mirrors	Whole body standing	Bulky complex system but useful for front and side elevations
Seaford (1959)	Photometric camera system modified	Whole body sitting	Equipment modified for mobility, sitting posture
Herren (1961)	Radiograph	Bones of face 3-D analysis	Proposed new technique
Chaffee (1961)	Three cameras at 90°	3-D measurements of body landmarks in space—whole body	Used for escape capsule design
Tanner (1962)	Photogrammetric camera	Body growth measurements	Used many years for head
Roebuck (unpublished) 1965–1970	Camera with inplane grid frame, alignment mirror	Helmet and whole body—space-suited subjects	Convenient for equipment drawings, workplace dimensions

Table 2-2. Stereo Photogrammetric Methods for Static Anthropometry

Investigators Reference/Year	Equipment	Subject Matter	Remarks
Zeller (1939)	40 cm base Wild stereo-camera, A4; Wild auto-graph plotting machine	Man's face contour map 10 mm separation between lines	
Zeller (1952)	Stereo photogrammetric camera and plotters	General use	English text translation
Thalman-Degen (1944)	40 cm base Wild stereo-camera A5 Wild plotting machine	Orthodontic diagnosis, 10 mm steep slope, 5 mm gentle slope, spot height—mm	Posing of head, measurement relative to wall
Lacmann (1950)	40 cm base Wild stereo-camera, A5 and A6 Wild plotting machine, auto-matic planimeter attached	Post operative swellings on face, volume measurements	
Bjorn, Lundquist, and Hjelmstrom (1954)			
Berner (1954)	K17 aerial cameras to give stereo pair, "Kelsh" plotter	Whole body	90° rotation
Miskin (1956)			
Hertzberg, Dupertuis, and Emanuel (1957)			
Miskin (1960)	Stereo photogrammetric camera	Hand-volume	
Savara (1965)	Custom built "Kelsh" camera	Facial contours	Accuracy: .2 mm
Beard and Burke (1967)	Stereophotogrammetric camera method	Facial morphology	New technique development
Burke and Beard (1967)	Special stereophoto setup	Face	Simplified method, less expensive
Herron (1972)	Many	Whole body and segment	Review of methods

diameter are to be made from a background grid, the apparent neck ring diameter, a, is considerably larger than the true diameter due to parallax. Thus, the basic problem when using grid techniques is to effectively place the measuring scale or grid in the same plane as the subject matter to be photographed. This may be done analytically, optically, or physically.

Analytical Corrections for Parallax. A simple first approach is to determine if any specific diameters of personal equipment items on the body are of known dimensions. In the pressure suit example, the helmet neck ring and wrist attachment rings are often very well defined, machined parts that can be used as a check or a standard for deriving length scales. Other such distances may be landmarks of known separation on the body. The Interpupillary Distance is a very useful scale check for full face photographs. This distance in American males is 2.5 ± .125 inches for the fifth to ninety-fifth percentile range. Thus, helmet dimensions and other features can be approximately estimated (to ± 5%), when the eyes are clearly visible.

Given a known length or diameter on the body and known distance between lines on a background grid board, the scale factor can be estimated by the simple ratio:

$$\frac{\text{known distance}}{\text{its apparent length on grid}} \doteq \text{Constant} \qquad \text{(Eq. 2.1)}$$

or in terms of distance labeled in Figure 2-12.

$$\frac{x}{a} = \frac{l}{d} = k \qquad \text{(Eq. 2.2)}$$

then

$$x = ka \qquad \text{(Eq. 2.3)}$$

If there is not a known distance on the subject's body for a scale check, knowledge of the approximate distance of the subject from the grid (f in Figure 2-11) and of the distance of the camera lens from the grid (d in Figure 2-11) can be used for the estimation.

$$x = \frac{a(d - f)}{d} \qquad \text{(Eq. 2.4)}$$

Roebuck has used a set of background grids at right angles to each other similar to that shown in Figure 2-2. The side grid is seen in foreshortened view, with horizontal lines apparently converging to a virtual horizon. This set of lines forms a convenient variable scale relating the distance of the plane of interest from the background grid. Figure 2-12 is an illustration of this technique.

38

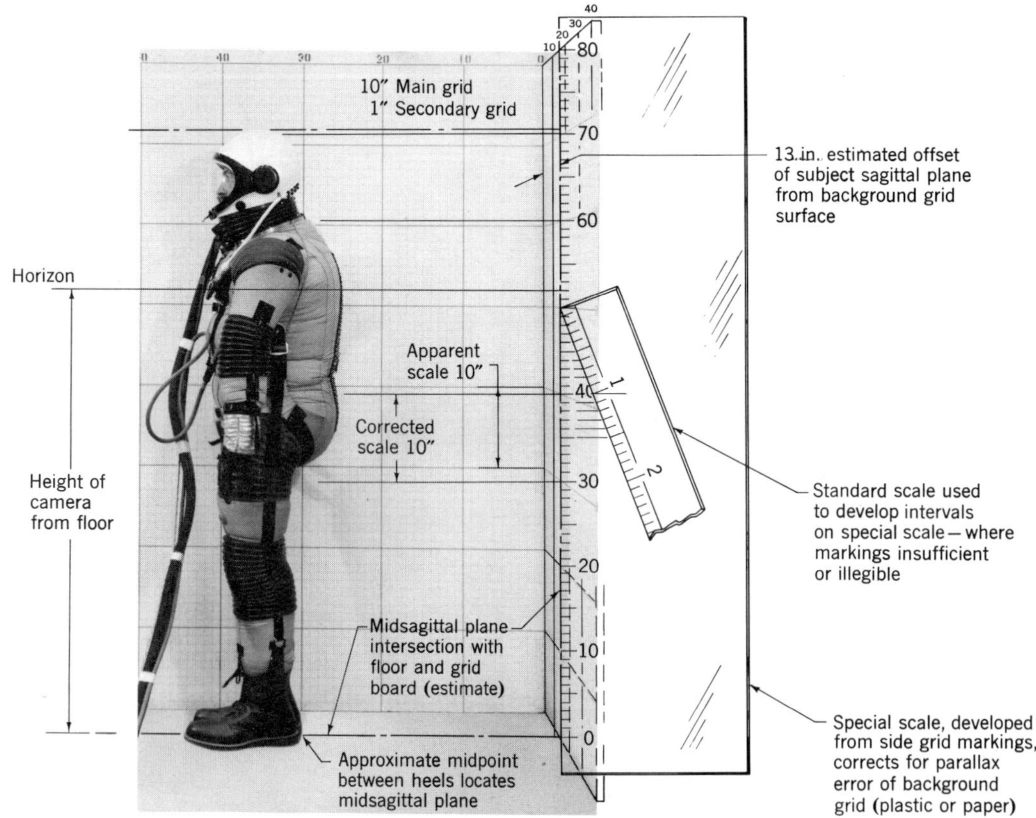

Figure 2-12. Illustration of the use of right angle grids to form a variable scale.

Optical Methods for Parallax Correction. Another solution to the parallax problem involves placing an apparent image of a desired grid plane in coincidence with the plane of the features being measured photographically. This may be done optically by projection of a grid from another source onto the film plane so as to make it a known scale factor with relation to that of the subject's plane of measurement. One simple method is to provide a partial mirror in front of the lens at 45° to the axis of the camera, then, at 90° to the axis, a grid board is set up at the same distance from the mirror as the subject plane of interest. Figure 2-13 illustrates this arrangement schematically. Such a system requires careful placement of the subject and grid and a laboratory room of both sufficient width and length. Since one usually tries to get the camera a long distance from the subject to reduce distortions of scale and body curvature, the distance to the grid must also be large.

Physical Methods for Parallax Correction. A more fundamental approach, which approximates the same result as the foregoing optical grid projection method, is to construct a grid board frame, with appropriate cutouts or shape to fit around the subject. Two successfully used examples are shown in Figure 2-14.

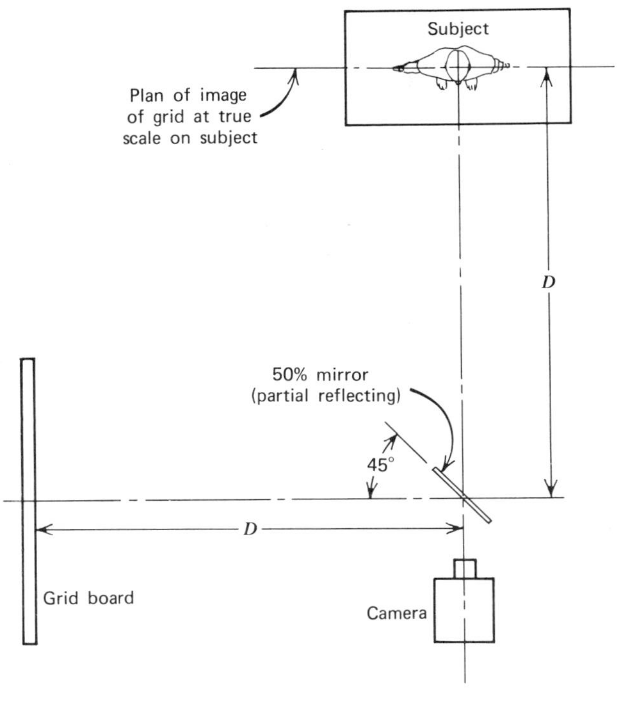

Figure 2-13. The partial mirror method for parallax correction.

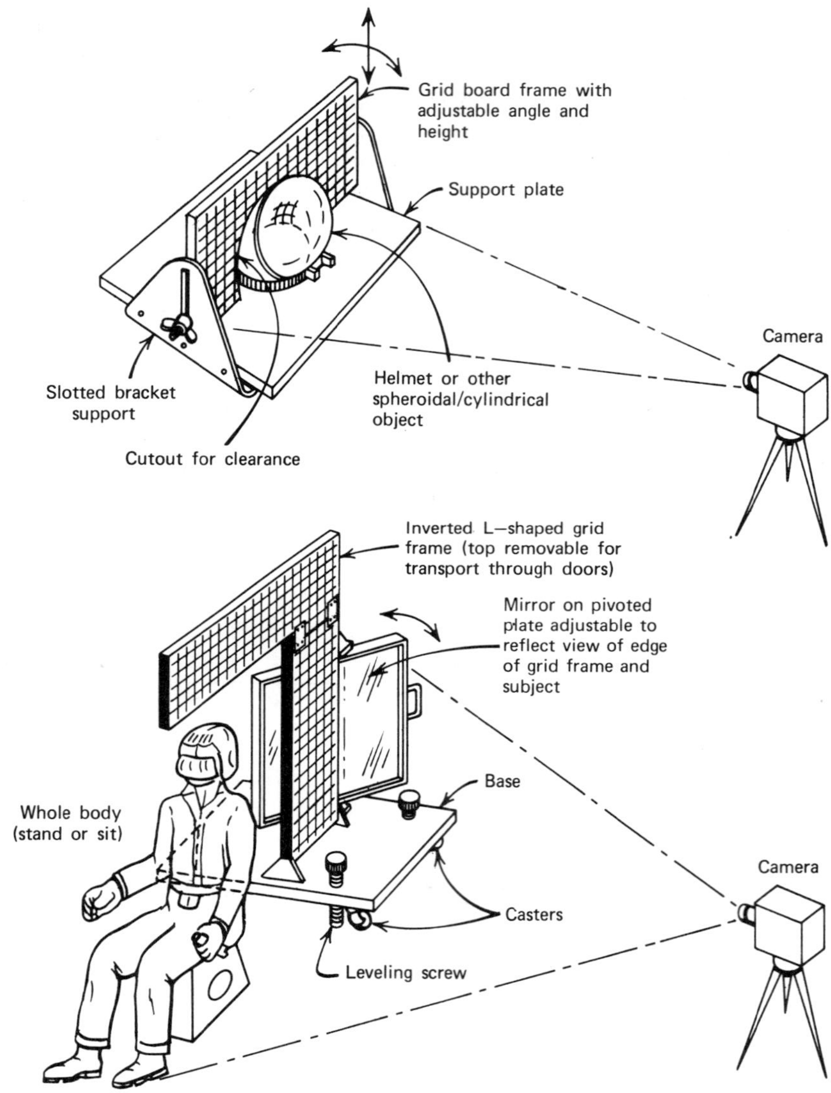

Figure 2-14. Grid board frames for photographic recording of contours.

The "Photo-Metric" Camera System

More sophisticated, although more expensive, single camera techniques have been developed. An example of one of these techniques is the "Photo-Metric" camera system. This system is a combination of fixed mirrors, synchronized electronic flash units, and camera that provides a relatively long effective distance from camera to subject within a small space (Figure 2-15). According to Hunt and Giles (1956), "the mirrors are arranged so that four complete views of a standing human subject are concurrently visible as mirror images at the site of the camera: front, left side, rear, and overhead." All views are exposed at once. Figure 2-16 shows the format of the exposures. Manually taken measurements with graduated scales are said to be within $\frac{1}{16}$ in. per 72 in., or approximately 0.1%.

The system has the disadvantage of being bulky and difficult to set up. This

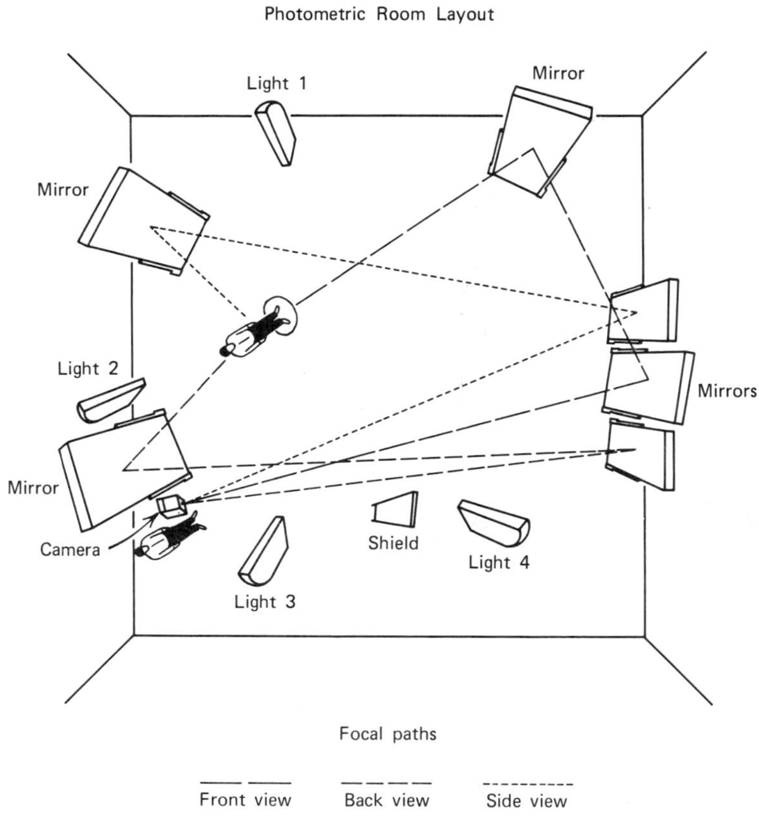

Figure 2-15. PhotoMetric room layout (partial) (Hunt and Giles, 1956).

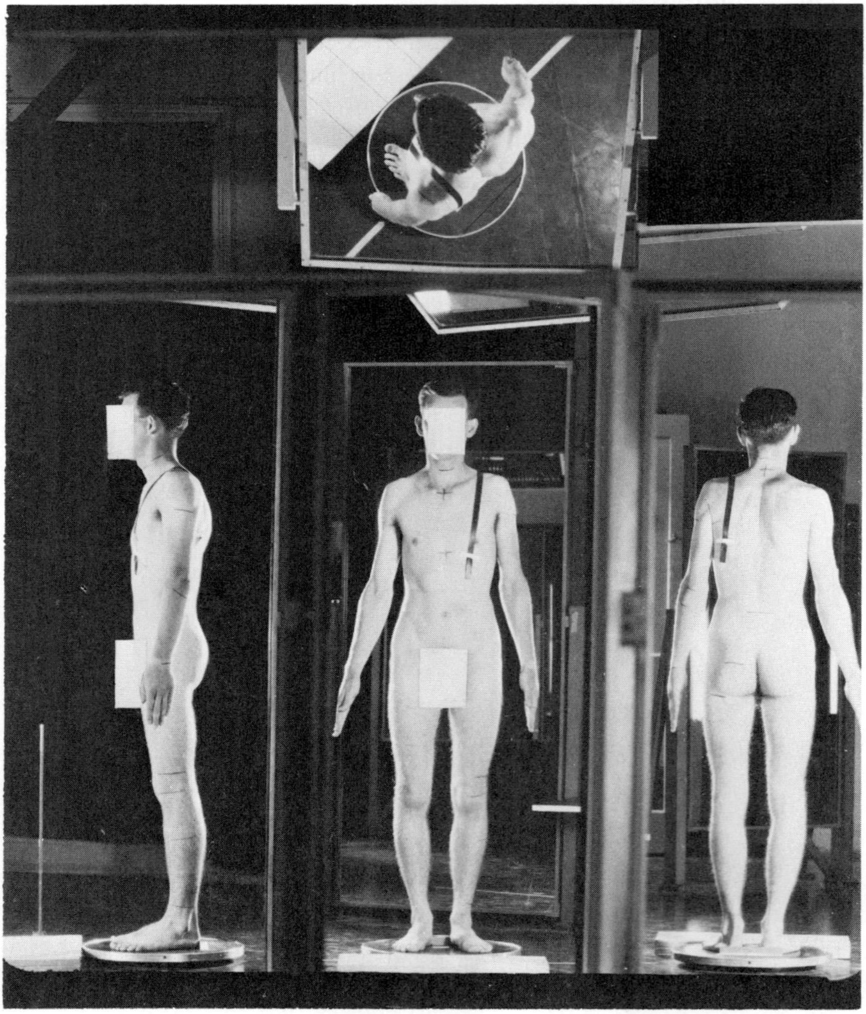

Figure 2-16. Format of exposures (PhotoMetric camera system). (Courtesy Mr. Charles Clauser.)

immobility is a considerable detriment for some types of surveys. However, a significant advantage is that the subject is close to the operator, which permits convenient repositioning, as necessary.

The system has been used for scientific purposes at Yale University (Blesh, Meyers, and Kiphuth, 1954) as well as by clothiers. Seaford (1959) used it in a study of more than 2000 men in the United States Air Force.

Andrometric Camera System

Another photographic measurement technique has been devised and reported by Chaffee (1961a,b). It was developed to meet the need of measuring military pilot body positions in ejection seats. However, it can readily be applied to other situations.

Essentially, the technique consists of obtaining simultaneous photographs from two or three cameras located on mutually orthogonal axes at precisely determined distances from a given axis origin. Measurements of specific marked points on the body are obtained from the photographic negatives and converted to true scale values by a series of trigonometric transformation equations. The arrangement of subject and cameras for this technique is shown in Figure 2-17. The data are obtained by direct measurements of the negatives with either a finely calibrated scale or, preferably, a film reader or oscillograph reader.

Expressions of precision for this technique were given as follows: the standard deviation of the photogrammetrically estimated coordinates was found to vary from a high of 0.9 mm (0.36 in.) to a low of 0.6 mm (0.023 in.). Using a

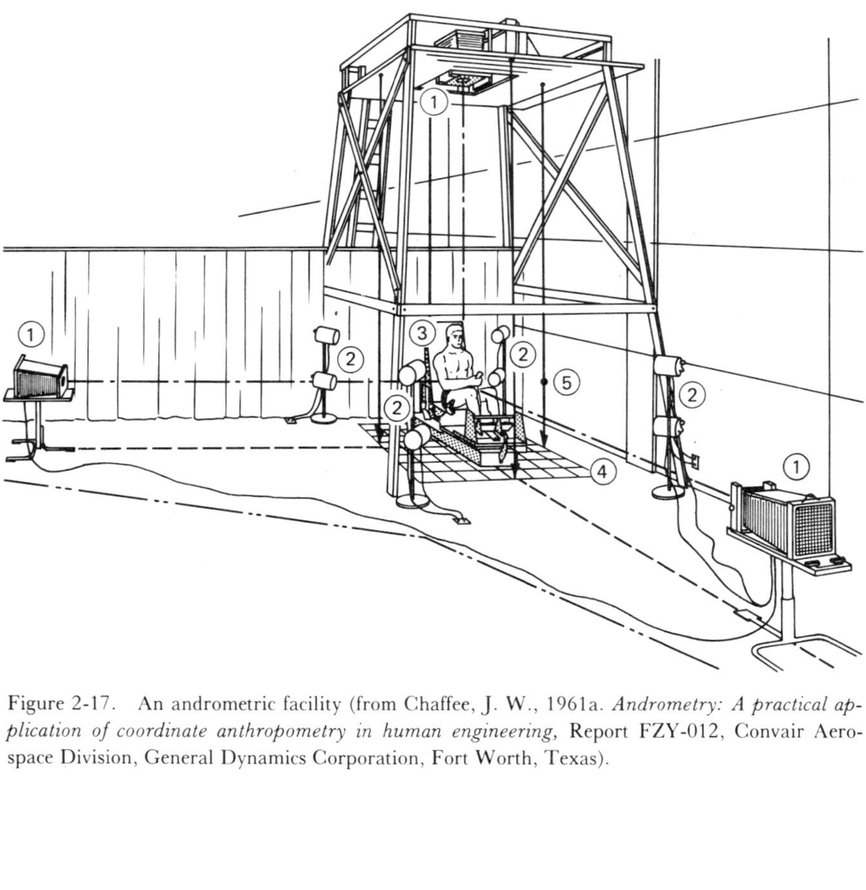

Figure 2-17. An andrometric facility (from Chaffee, J. W., 1961a. *Andrometry: A practical application of coordinate anthropometry in human engineering,* Report FZY-012, Convair Aerospace Division, General Dynamics Corporation, Fort Worth, Texas).

3σ criterion for maximum expected error gives a range of 1.0 mm to 2.7 mm. (See Chapter V for statistical discussion.)

Stereophotogrammetric Methods

Another photographic technique of great value, but considerable expense, utilizes methods developed in aerial contour mapping. The principle of stereoscopic vision is applied to determine the depth of body parts as well as length and breadth. As reported in Hertzberg, Dupertuis, and Emanuel (1957), this technique of stereophotogrammetry had use in the early 1920s in the medical and dental fields and was later shown by Zeller (1939), Thalmann-Degan (1944), and Lacmann (1950) to be useful in obtaining extensive contour maps of human heads, determination of body surface areas (Berner, 1954; Miskin, 1956), and in shaping sculpture (Saralegui, 1954; Englemann, 1956). Herron (1972) gives a detailed overview of the literature.

Hertzberg, Dupertuis, and Emanuel Technique. The apparatus used by Hertzberg et al. (1957) consisted of two K-17 aerial cameras mounted 3.5 ft above the floor, 5 ft apart and 12 ft from the datum plane, their optical axes

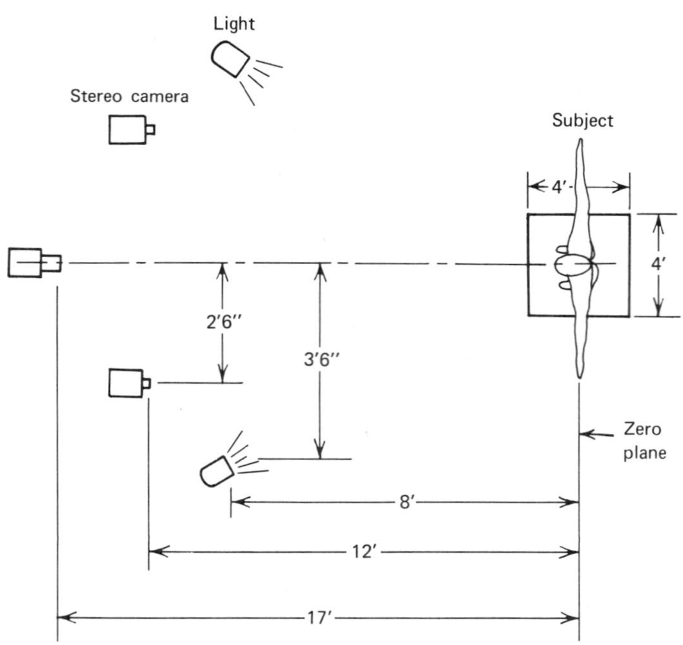

Figure 2-18. Apparatus arrangement for stereophotogrammetry. (After Hertzberg, Dupertuis and Emanuel, 1957.)

Table 2-3. Comparison of Manual and Photographic Methods[a]

Measurement	Manual (in.)	Photographic (in.)
Upper chest arc	9.65	9.58
Intra nipple arc	8.30	8.24
Lower abdomen arc	12.50	12.40
Upper shoulder arc	10.50	10.35
Trunk shoulder arc	39.50	39.51
Circumference—nipples	37.7	37.3
Waist	37.7	37.2
Suprasternale height	57.1	57.0

[a] After Hertzberg, Dopertuis, and Emanuel (1957).

parallel. The cameras were modified for synchronization with electronic flashlamps and their lenses focused on the datum plane. A 4 × 5 view camera was also mounted 17 ft from the zero plane between the two K-17's. The arrangement is illustrated in Figure 2-18.

The subject was marked in two ways:

1. Marks for body measurement to permit comparison of direct anthropometric data with data derived from photographs.
2. Stippling marks to provide contrast from one area to another.

The posed subject was photographed by the three cameras, rotated 90°, and shot again. This process was continued each 90°. The negatives were then developed and diapositives prepared for the Kelsh plotter. With the Kelsh plotter, contour maps were drawn of front, back, and side elevations to a scale of 1:4 and contours were laid out at intervals of ½ in. From the profiles so plotted, surface arcs or circumferences at any elevation as desired may be obtained.

The authors claim that the method is more accurate than the shape of the man. In other words, changes in contour due to breathing, movements, and so forth., are larger than the errors of measurement of the photographs. Table 2-3 presents some comparative values found by measuring the man by manual and photographic contour methods.

Burke and Beard Technique. Burke and Beard (1967) have developed a relatively inexpensive setup for recording facial contours which uses the same basic instrument as camera and plotting machine. They used two "multiplex" projectors, adapted from an aerial survey plotting instrument. Such projectors normally project a series of overlapping transparencies of aerial photographs onto a flat surface using alternate red and blue light sources. Viewing the images with spectacles having one red and one blue lens, the trained operator mentally fuses these images for a three-dimensional impression.

Using a point source of light that appears to float above or below the surface, the correct height is registered in a vernier gage when the "floating spot" just rests on the surface of the three-dimensional image. In this way an experienced operator can build up, from carefully prepared photographs, a map of the face consisting of a number of contour lines related to the datum plane, as shown in Figure 2-19. This is a time-consuming process; "spot heights" of identifiable landmarks can be recorded rapidly. (Modern computer-aided techniques can greatly facilitate and speed up the data reduction.)

The accuracy of the method was investigated using a plaster model of the face. Measurements were made of various spot heights on the plaster model. Upon comparing these measurements with micrometer measurements of the same points, differences of less than 1 mm were found.

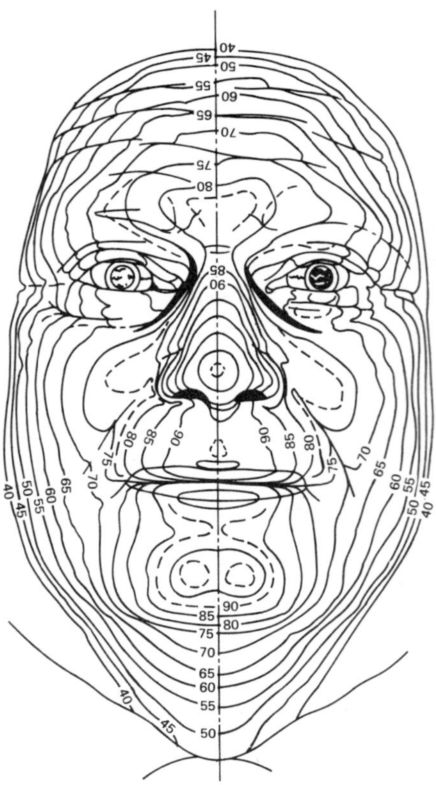

Figure 2-19. Facial plot with contour interval of 5 mm and landmarks for clarity. (From Burke, P. H. and Beard, L. F. H.: Stereophotogrammetry of the face. A preliminary investigation into the accuracy of a simplified system evolved for contour mapping by photography, *Am. J. Orthod.* 53: 769–792, 1967.)

2.4 AREA MEASUREMENT

Several types of body area measurements are of interest to the engineer designing machinery for human operation. There is the total "wetted" area of the human body, the portion that is covered by skin. There is the emitting thermal radiation area of the human body, the area available for the body to use as a surface from which to transfer heat, and the absorbing radiation area, the projected area seen by a radiation source, thermal or ionizing, outside the body. For calculations of windblast effects and decelerations in ejection, the aerodynamic area of the body is of interest. For special situations such as seating, crash protection, vibration, and the like, there is concern with partial areas of the body in contact with other surfaces. This is a broad subject, but limitations of this book permit only a brief discussion of total body area.

2.4.1 Direct Body Surface Area Measurement

Major interest in total body area has arisen from the theory that heat production in the body was proportional to surface area of the body (Rubner, 1883).* Although later theories suggested that Weight is more nearly proportional to heat production, lack of data on surface area made either theory hard to prove. Hence, there has been a continued interest in accurate methods of measurement of total body area. According to Boyd (1935), the methods of measuring surface area fall into three categories: coating, surface integration, and triangulation.

Coating Methods

The coating methods consist of covering the whole body or marked-off regions with a substance of known or measurable area. In some instances, these areas have been measured by fitting together the pieces of the coating on cross-section paper. In some, the areas have been measured with a planimeter. In others, the areas of the pieces of the coating were calculated from their weights or from the weight of their duplicates cut from a substance of more uniform thickness. The major technical problem is to find a nonelastic, pliable substance, preferably of uniform thickness, that can be readily applied and removed without injury or discomfort to the subject. Table 2-4 provides introductory literature references about the technology.

Other Direct Methods

Integration of surface by planimeters has been described by Roussy (1899c)* and Bordier (1901).* These devices consisted of two wheels at a selected spacing apart, connected to revolution counters. The area to be measured was

* Cited by Boyd (1935).

Table 2-4. Linear Geometric Methods for Estimating Body Surface Area (Abstracted from Boyd, 1935)

Investigator(s) and Reference	Assumed Geometric Model	Technique
Abernethey (1793)	Cylinders[a]	The circumference of each body component was measured at several places and the mean circumference was the assumed circumference of that component "cylinder."
Sappey (1852)	Cylinders	Same as above but also included models of the hands and feet.
Letulle and Pompillian (1906)	Trapezoids	Considered body surfaces as a series of trapezoids.
Worner (1923)	Truncated cones	Measured the maximum and minimum circumference and slant height for each body "cone." Head and neck surface = 4 × (average diameter of head)^2.
Roussy (1911, 1924a, c, 1925a, b)	Truncated cones combined to form a large cylinder or rectangle.	Assumed that all the "truncated cones" of the body could be combined in a large cylinder, and later a large rectangle, by his formula or "law of rectangulation."
Du Bois and Du Bois (1915)	Proportionality model	Proposed that the surface areas of the parts of the body are proportional instead of equal to the surface areas of the geometric solids they resemble.

[a] Excluded the head, hands, and feet and measured separately.

either premarked or marked by ink applied by the wheels as they were rolled over the body.

The method of triangulation consisted of marking off regular geometric figures, chiefly triangles, on the body and calculating the area of these figures from their linear dimensions. Fubini and Ronchi (1881), Bouchard (1900), and Lassabliere (1910) are typical investigators cited by Boyd (1935).

2.4.2 Indirect Body Surface Area Estimation

Formulas and techniques have been developed to estimate body surface area without having to actually measure the area with one of the methods discussed above. These techniques require only a few easily obtainable measurements of the body from which the area is then calculated. There are two general classifications for these estimating techniques: linear methods and photographic methods.

Linear (Geometric) Methods of Estimation

These techniques approximate the surface area of the body by assuming the body is composed of regular geometric solids. Thus, one or two measurements for each geometric component is all that is needed for calculation of body surface area using standard geometric formulas. Examples of this technique are listed in Table 2-4. See Chapter VI for a commonly used formula.

Photographic Methods of Estimation

Roussy (1907)* developed a photographic method of estimating the surface of the living body. He considered the surface area of the body to be equal to the sum of the photographic silhouettes of the anterior, posterior, and two lateral views of the whole body, and two special profiles of the arms and soles of the feet, corrected for photographic reduction. The areas of the silhouettes were measured with either cross-section paper or with a planimeter. The surface area estimated by this method for a manikin was within $\frac{1}{100}$ to $\frac{1}{180}$ of the area obtained by his coating method.

Benedict (1916) obtained sharply outlined silhouettes by photographing subjects standing between a window and a sheet, which were then photographed with a scale against the sheet for data processing with a planimeter, yielding an average experimental error of 1.6% and a range of −2% to +5%.

2.4.3 Radiation Area

Measurement of radiation area is occasionally requested of engineering anthropometrists to support studies of environmental conditions. For detailed discussion of techniques, the reader is referred to articles by Guibert and Taylor (1952) and by Bohnenkamp and Ernst (1931).

* See Boyd, 1935.

2.5 VOLUME MEASUREMENT

Data on body volume are often needed in engineering anthropometry in such uses as the calculation of limb and body inertial properties, suit design, and environmental control system design. Several different techniques for obtaining the various volumes of interest are described here.

2.5.1 Immersion Methods

The simplest, in terms of a direct answer with a minimum of calculation, is the Archimedes method. The subject is immersed in a container filled with water and the overflow water is either weighed or its volume measured in a graduated container. The result is influenced by the point of inspiration at which the immersion took place, because of the lung volume. The method can be used to obtain volumes of each limb or parts thereof, also (see Dempster, 1955a).

2.5.2 Cross-Sectional Analysis Technique

Indirect methods of obtaining volume are useful when a record of body contours has been obtained but not for the purpose of volume measurement specifically, and the subject is no longer available. These methods depend on obtaining measurements of cross-sectional areas sufficiently close together that the cross sections between can be assumed to vary linearly with distance. The cross-sectional areas can then be plotted as a function of height from the heel. The area under a smooth curve drawn through the points then represents an approximation to the volume in question. An alternative is to use a mathematical formula that multiplies the distance between cross-section cuts times the average cross-sectional area.

$$\bar{A}_i = \frac{\Sigma A_{i-1} + A_i}{2} \qquad \text{(Eq. 2.5)}$$

$$V = \Sigma \bar{A}_i \Delta h_i \qquad \text{(Eq. 2.6)}$$

where

Δh = distance between cross-section cuts
A_i = ith cross-sectional area
A_{i-1} = preceding or other area
$\bar{A}_i$ = average area
V = volume

Dempster (1955) used two methods of obtaining the requisite data on cross-sectional areas of the body. The first involved obtaining sections of frozen cadavers. The second method, using living subjects, involved tracing sections by means of a pantograph.

"The error of the pantograph-planimeter system, when applied to rigid blocks and cylinders, where volume could be computed from dimensional data and where the pantograph tracing arm could ride on a rigid surface, was nearly 2%." (Dempster, 1955a) Body sway and irregularities in tracings due to the body's soft skin contour contribute to the error.

Other approximations (Weinbach, 1938) use the assumption that body sections are nearly elliptical in shape, so that with only a breadth and depth of a given dimension, the area can be calculated as follows:

$$A_i = \pi \, a_i \, b_i \qquad \text{(Eq. 2.7)}$$

where a is the semimajor axis and b is the semiminor axis. The volume can then be calculated as above.

Burke and Beard used their stereophotogrammetric method discussed above (see p. 00) to estimate facial volume. As opposed to the cylindrical sections assumed above, they treated the contour area measurements as frusta of cones between the levels of the contour measuring planes. Assuming an equal height (H) between contours and using (h) as the height of the summit cone, the total volume (V) can be expressed as:

$$V = \frac{H}{3}\left\{2\sum_{i=1}^{n} A_i + \sum_{i=1}^{n-1} A_i^{1/2} \cdot A_{i+1}^{1/2} - (A_i + A_n)\right\} + \frac{h}{3} \cdot A_n \qquad \text{(Eq. 2.8)}$$

Where the slope of the contours is not very steep, the difference between A_i and A_{i+1} may be negligible, and a simple height times area estimate may be used as above.

2.6 SOMATOTYPING

Selective uses of the foregoing measurement techniques are employed in developing data for a type of application and analysis of body build classification called somatotyping. Because such body build classifications are seldom directly useful in engineering applications, detail descriptions of somatotyping procedures and classification schemes are not included in this text. However, body build descriptions do have indirect, predictive value in certain relationships to human dimensions, mobility, force exertion, and mass properties. Such relationships are introduced in Section 3 and following.

For information on somatotyping, readers are referred to works of Sheldon, Stevens, and Baker (1940), Sheldon, Dupertuis, and McDermott (1954), Dupertuis and Tanner (1950), Dupertuis (1950), Heath and Carter (1967). Croney (1971) also has given an interesting summary of body configuration characteristics, especially as they relate to changes during growth. Selected key somatotyping terms are contained in the Glossary, Appendix A.

III
MEASUREMENT OF DYNAMIC CHARACTERISTICS AND MOVEMENT

3.1 INTRODUCTION

The foregoing measurement techniques dealt primarily with static aspects of the human body. This section discusses dynamic aspects, particularly movement measurements, and related topics. The discussion will first consider the inertial properties of the body, such as weight or mass, mass distribution, moments of inertia, and the related subjects of density and density distribution.

The description of measurement of human mobility, agility, or flexibility as it is variously referred to, follows the discussion of inertial properties. There are two different approaches to the problem of movement description and effects. One is concerned with the "final effect" or description of end points (e.g., reach envelopes) or results of motion which is the subject of Section 3.3. The other considers the fundamental capabilities of each joint and the synthesis of these individual joint motions into the final resulting movement. Techniques for this approach are described in Section 3.4. Each approach has advantages, and often the two must be combined for a satisfactory and economical engineering solution. Some of these combination techniques are described in Section 3.5. In particular, dynamic movement measurement techniques involving photography are described which provide both gross data on envelopes and detailed data on individual joint movement range, velocity, and accelerations.

3.2 MEASUREMENT OF INERTIAL PROPERTIES

Inertial properties of the human body of interest in engineering anthropometry include total weight, or mass, whole body center of mass,* and the distribution

* The expression "center of mass" is used throughout this text (except in quotations), where other authors or previous common usage may have used "center of gravity."

of mass throughout the body, especially for the limb segments. Also useful are the whole body moments of inertia about various axes and the moments of inertia of limb segments and segment combinations, especially about the joint centers of rotation. In order to estimate some of the above quantities, and also for buoyancy considerations, densities of body tissues are also desired. Less closely related are studies of body composition in terms of percentages of fat, water, muscle, and so forth. To obtain these data, considerable variety of methods are available. They are listed in Table 3-1 (density), Table 3-2 (body composition), Table 3-3 (centers of mass), and Table 3-4 (centers of mass and moments of inertia).

3.2.1 Weight

Weight is the simplest inertial property, measured with balance and spring scales. Since the human body is nearly always weighed in air, there is a slight error due to buoyancy effects.

3.2.2 Density and Body Composition

The determination of density is considerably more complicated than that of total weight W_b or mass M_b. Using volume data, one can divide total body weight by body volume, V_b and by the gravitational acceleration g to get average density, D_M (mass per unit volume). The average specific gravity D_s can then be found by dividing by the density of water, D_w.

$$D_M = \frac{M_b}{V_b} = \frac{W_b}{g \cdot V_b} \qquad \text{(Eq. 3.1)}$$

$$D_s = \frac{D_M}{D_w} \qquad \text{(Eq. 3.2)}$$

Weighing the body in water at the same time its volume is determined yields estimates of the variations in density for limb and trunk segments.

Density measurements have been obtained from weight and volume measurements of *cadaver* body segments by several investigators (Dempster, 1955a; Blanton and Biggs, 1968; Clauser, McConville, and Young 1969). Both composite tissue density and density of various specialized types of tissue have been measured in a small number of studies (Clauser, McConville, and Young, 1969). The difficulties associated with weight estimates of cadaver material are numerous. Loss of fluids may be quite significant. Special precautions such as cool moist air and covering with damp cloths reduce drying. Preserving introduces errors when body fluids are replaced by or immersed in preservative solutions. Chemical changes in tissues may also affect results. The best criterion for evaluating the relative fidelity of such preserved body seg-

Table 3-1. Measurements of Density of Body Tissues

Investigators/ Authors and Dates	Preserved	Non-preserved	Living	Type[a]	Remarks on Methods
Davy[a] (1840)		×		1, 2, 3, 4	
Harless (1860)				5	Immersion
Kapff and Vierordt (1906)		×		3	
Krause and Vierordt (1906)		×		2	
Behnke, Feen, and Welham (1942)			×		Gaseous desorption or adsorption
Leider and Buncke (1954)		×		1	
Behnke (1954)			×	5	(Whole body immersion)
Dempster (1955)	×				Segmented by dissection
Cleveland (1955)			×	5	Weighing in water hammock suspended on spring scale (total body and segments)
Drillis and Contini (1966)			×	5	Immersion and segment zones
Blanton and Biggs (1968)	×			4	(Canellous and compact bone measured)
Clauser, McConville, and Young (1969)	×			1, 2, 3, 4 5	Immersion

[a] Type of tissues studied: 1 = skin; 2 = muscle; 3 = fat; 4 = bone; 5 = whole body or combined tissue.

ments seems to be that they "look natural" (are not obviously puffy or dessicated).

The above measurements yield an average density measurement for all types of tissues contained in segments or the whole body (composite tissue). In contrast, another potentially useful concept of lean body mass (LBM) or weight (LBW) involves the idea that there is a basic structural body component of bone, muscle, skin, and the like that is relatively constant in percentage composition from individual to individual. To this basic component is added a component of fat that varies in percentage of total weight according

Table 3-2. Measurements of Body Composition (in vivo)

Authors	Methods	Components Measured
Stuart, Hill, and Shaw (1940)	X-ray photos of soft tissue	Fatty tissue thickness
Behnke, Feen, and Welham (1942)	Densimetric-gaseous desorption or adsorption	Lean body weight
Soberman, Brodie, Levy, Axelrod, and Steele (1949)	Chemical dilution with antipyrine to determine total body water content	Total body water
Brozek and Keys (1951) Newman (1952)	Skinfold calipers measurements of various sites	Fatty tissue thickness
Best and Kuhl (1953)	X-ray photos	Bone, muscle, fat, and skin (humeral arm segment)
Garn (1954)	X-ray photos	Bone, muscle, fat, and skin
Pascale, Grossman, and Sloane (1955)	Skinfold calipers measurements	Fatty tissue thickness
Walmsley and Roberts (1963)	Chemical dilution with deuterium oxide to determine total body water content	Total body water

to the individual (Behnke, 1953). Thus, total weight is expressed as

$$W = (\text{LBW}) + (\text{fat weight}) \qquad \text{(Eq. 3.3)}$$

The lean body weight (LBW) may be functionally related to basal metabolism or other standardized metabolic measurements (Behnke, 1953).

One approach to determine body fat uses skinfold measurements. Selected areas of the loose body skin are grasped and folded and their thickness is measured with a special caliper. Such measurements must be correlated with other more fundamental measurement studies to determine estimates of body fat (Best and Kuhl, 1953; Newman, 1952).

Table 3-3. Inertial Properties Measurement Methods Limited to Centers of Mass and Weight Distribution

Method	Investigators/Authors and Date	Results of Methods Center of Mass: Whole Body	Segments CM	Segments Wt	Continuous Distribution
Balanced platform					
Single platform	Weber and Weber (1836)	L			
	Harless (1860)	C	C	C	C
	Mosso (1884)				
"Balance plate"	Dempster (1955a)		DC	DC	
	Clauser et al. (1969)		DC	DC	
Multiple platforms (5)	Swearingen (1953)	L			
	Clauser et al. (1969)	L			
Platform on fulcrum and weight scale	DuBois-Raymond (1900)	L			
	Basler (1931)	L			
	Bernstein (1931, '67)	L	L		
	Reynolds and Lovett (1909)	X	(1)	(1)	
	Duggar (1962)	X	(1)	(1)	
	Drillis and Contini (1966)	X	(1)	(1)	
	Swearingen, Badgley, Braden, and Wallace (1969)	L			
Platform on two weight scales	Basic engineering texts	X	X	X	
Differential tilting	Cotton (1932)	X			
Statography	Åkerblom (1948)	L			
Suspension	Braune and Fischer (1889)	C			
	Hertzberg and Daniels (1950a)	L			
	Chaffee (1961c)	L			

Abbreviations: L = living body; C = cadavers; D = dissection; X = unknown (living or deceased); CM = Center of Mass; (1) = either weight or CM if other is known.

[illegible] Inertial Properties Measurement Methods for Centers of Mass and Moments of Inertia

Method	Investigators/Authors and Dates	Results of Method						
		Center of Mass				Moments of Inertia		
		Whole Body	Segments CM	Segments Wt	Contin. Distrib.	Whole Body	Segments	Continuous Distribution
Immersion								
By segments (volume and density)[a]	Meeh (1895)			L				
	Cleveland (1955)		L	L				
	Dempster (1955a)	L, DC	L, DC	L, DC				
	Drillis and Contini (1966)							
	Clauser et al. (1969)	DC	DC	DC				
By graduated sections[a]	Dempster (1955a)	L, DC	L, DC	L, DC	L, DC	L, DC	L, DC	L, DC
	Drillis and Contini (1966)							
Torque and angular acceleration	Drillis and Contini (1966)						L	
Pendulum, gravity	Dempster (1955a)						DC	
Compound gravity pendulum	Santschi, DuBois and Omoto (1963)	L				L		
Torsional pendulum	Drillis and Contini (1966)					L		
Cross-sectional[a] graphic analysis—pantograph (for volume)	Dempster (1955a)	L	L	L	L	L	L	L
Photographic[a] contour, elliptical approximation (vol.)	Weinbach (1938)	L	L	L	L	L	L	L

[a] Indirect methods. Abbreviations: L = living body; C = cadavers; D = dissection; CM = Center of Mass; Wt. = Weight.

3.2.3 Center of Mass—Whole Body

Measurements of whole body human body centers of mass (CM) are subject to several problems:

1. *Breathing.* Respiration causes small shifts of mass in the torso and imparts slight force changes to supporting surfaces.
2. *Fluid shifts.* As the body is moved from one position to another, gravity acts to move blood and other fluids to different concentrations, thus shifting the total center of mass. Automatic physiological reactions may aggravate these conditions as a result of position, temperature, or excitement.
3. *Muscular contractions or relaxations.* These also can significantly change distribution of mass, especially in the torso, but also in limbs. The standing subject shows a small but incessant oscillation as his balance is maintained by internal control systems.
4. *Intake of fluids and solids.* A diurnal variation takes place as food and liquids are consumed and excreted. Over a longer period, loss or gain of fluids and fats causes a change.
5. *Exercise and rest.* Exercise causes migration of blood to limbs and rest causes return to head.

Hence, care must be exercised in selection of the conditions and technique of measurement and in the interpretation of the results. One should select instrumentation with consideration of the possible orders of magnitude of errors involved. "A one-percent error in a simple balance will be in the same order of magnitude as error caused by such natural phenomena as breathing" (Duggar, 1962). Dynamic movements and vibrations in working situations induce larger motions than suggested above (Weis and Primiano, 1966).

Balanced Platform Methods

A direct method suggested by the definition of CM is balancing the body on a previously balanced board or other support. However, the practical problems of shifting the body on an unstable platform make this system nearly useless for extensive surveys. Mosso (1884) partially overcame this difficulty by attaching a 25 kg mass to a vertical rod attached to the platform bottom, such that the mass was 80 cm below. Rather than move the subject, he placed containers of liquid at the head or feet of the supine subject.

Swearingen (1953) approached the problem by using a series of adjustable platforms. The Swearingen equipment consists of five platforms (Figure 3-1) mounted one above the other. The top platform, which supports the subject, consists of an adjustable seat with arm and foot rests. This chair can be rotated about a horizontal axis. The second and third platforms slide horizontally at

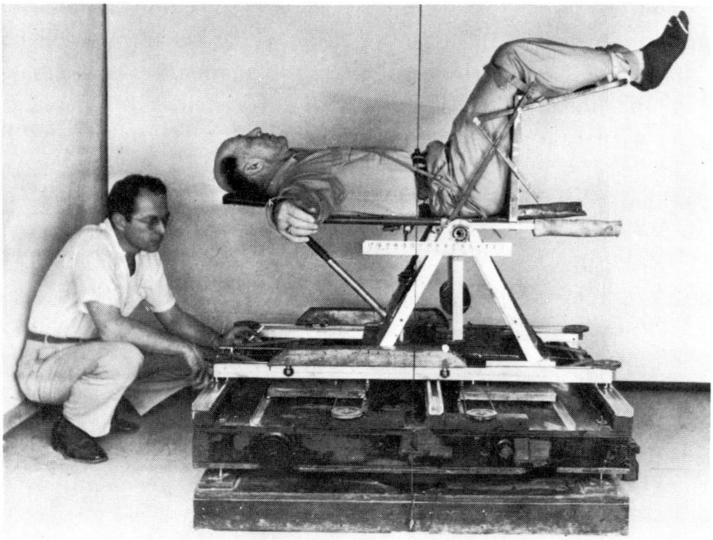

Figure 3-1. Multiple balanced platform device for determining center of mass of body (Swearingen, 1953, courtesy of Federal Aviation Administration).

right angles to one another. Each of these platforms has its own counter-balance system, keeping the equipment as a whole in perfect balance regardless of position with reference to the bottom platform. The fourth platform is separated from the bottom plalform by means of a ball and socket joint in the center and four electrical contact points, one at each corner of this 4-ft-square platform. Each of these contact points lights a lamp in its corner if the platform is tilted in that direction. The subject was placed in the supporting structure with the seat back in the horizontal position, the equipment balanced, and a reading taken on a horizontal scale, from the vertical cable aligned with the balance point to the ischium (seat), representing the distance of the CM of the subject from the ischium point. A point was marked at the intersection of cable and seat back. The seat was then tilted and rebalanced. A second measurement was taken on a scale aligned perpendicularly from the seat back at the marked point of intersection of the cable up to an intersection with the vertical cable. This point of intersection approximates the subject's CM location, in the attitudes measured. The aforementioned fluid shifts and pressure redistributions will, of course, affect the result.

Suspension Methods

To overcome the problems of apparatus instability, one may resort to suspension methods. According to theory, the CM of any irregular rigid body may be found by suspending it from two different positions by a string, since the CM always lies along the extension of the string line through the body. Although the human body is not rigid, an approximation has been attempted by supporting the limbs, head, and trunk in a framework or seat and firmly strapping it in place, then suspending the whole mass (Hertzberg and Daniels, 1950a; Chaffee, 1961c).

The technique of Chaffee (1961c) supposedly permitted determination, in two dimensions, of locations for the center of mass for a group of men at various angles of the back with respect to the gravitational field. A schematic of Chaffee's technique is shown in Figure 3-2. The lines passing through the CM were located by a plumb line attached to the center of the pivot point. To obtain the center of mass location, the occupied seat back was first suspended in a position a few degrees (5° or 10°) forward of the desired angle. The plumb line was then marked on the card, which was also marked with the seat reference point of the seat. Then the angle was changed to the desired angle to be measured and another reading taken. Finally, another additional reading was taken after the seat was moved an additional few degrees (5° or 10°). The three plumb lines then form a triangle within which Chaffee thought the center of mass was closely approximated for the individual at the midpoint of the 10° or 20° range of angular adjustments.

Unfortunately, the very movement of the CM under such conditions creates an error of measurement that is greater as the movement of the CM increases and as the movement direction becomes perpendicular to the plumb line. Chaffee thus incorrectly concluded that the CM moves anteriorly as it moves headward, when the body reclines from upright to supine angles. Other data support the theory that the CM moves posteriorly as it moves headward under such conditions.

Accurate measurement of the CM along two coordinates in a given body orientation requires *two fundamentally different methods* in combination, one for each axis. One of these may be chosen from the foregoing or the nonbalanced platform methods described next. The other could be a pendulum method, such as described in Section 3.2.4.

Nonbalanced Platform Methods

Another platform support method that eliminates the problems of instability and of finding the balance point by iterated trials involves using two scales and precisely located support points (Figure 3-3). The horizontal location of the center of mass can then be calculated by the moment equation as follows:

$$W_1 l - W_m \bar{y}_2 - W_b d = 0 \qquad \text{(moments about } W_2\text{)} \qquad \text{(Eq. 3.4)}$$

and

$$\bar{y} = \bar{y}_2 + a \qquad \text{(Eq. 3.5)}$$

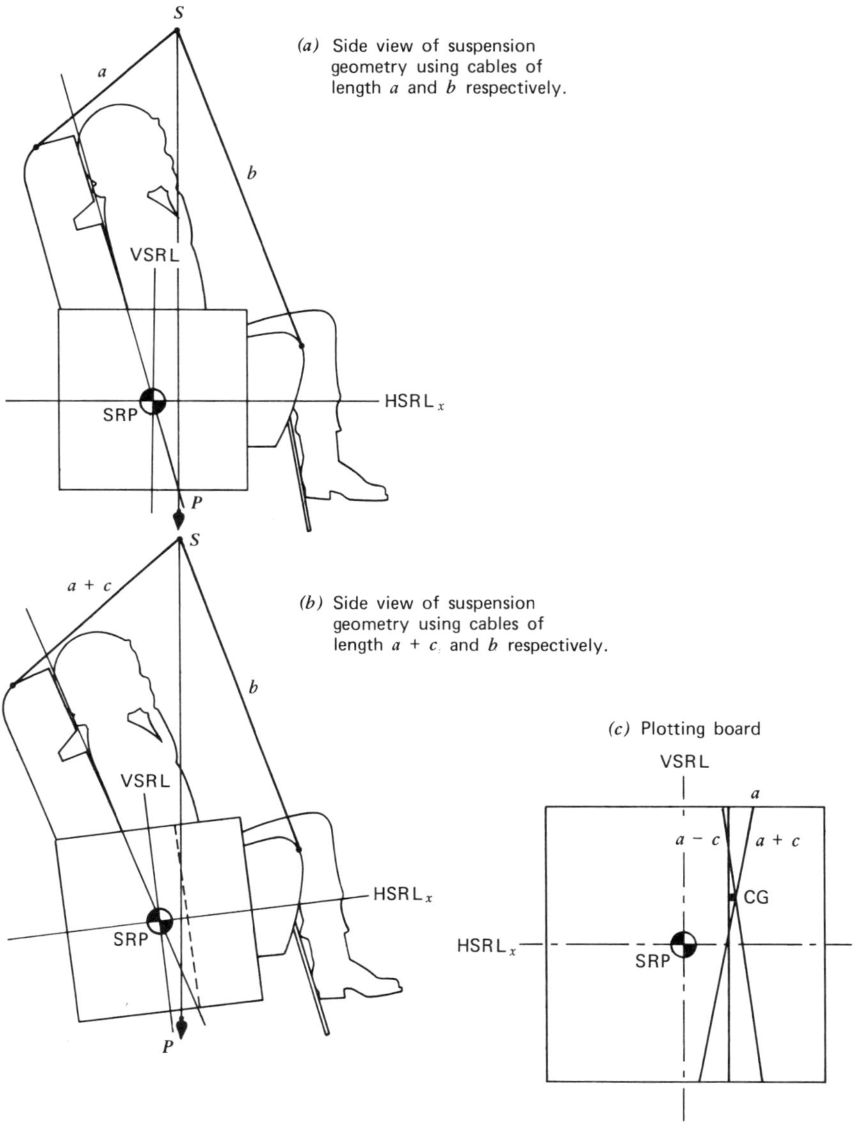

Figure 3-2. Suspension method of locating seat-man center of mass (from Chaffee, J. W., 1961c. *The effect of acceleration of human centers of gravity.* Report FZY-013, Convair Aerospace Division, General Dynamics Corporation, Fort Worth, Texas).

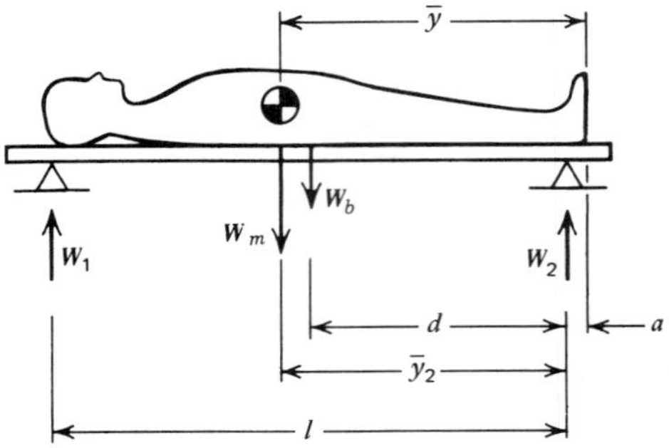

Figure 3-3. Two-scale method for finding center of mass of body.

Since W_1, W_b, W_2, l, d, and a are known and $W_m = W_1 + W_2 - W_b$, then (Eq. 3.6)

$$\bar{y}_2 = \frac{W_1 l - W_b d}{W_1 + W_2 - W_b} \quad \text{(Eq. 3.7)}$$

and

$$\bar{y} = \frac{W_1 l - W_b d}{W_1 + W_2 - W_b} + a \quad \text{(Eq. 3.8)}$$

where

W_1 = weight registered on scale 1 (left)
W_2 = weight registered on scale 2 (right)
W_m = weight of subject acting at his CM
W_b = weight of board acting at its CM = sum of weights registered without subject on board.

(Note that W_m, the weight of the subject, does not need to be determined separately.)

Although a reclining figure is shown, the method is general (applicable for any body position) and the CM can be located relative to any reference point on the body or supporting structure (which is included in W_b).

A variation of the two-scale method involves replacing one scale by a simple fulcrum. The method, described by Reynolds and Lovett (1909), consists of simply equating the moments about the fulcrum and solving for the unknown distance x. For this solution, the weight of the subject must be known.

3.2.4 Center of Mass and Moment of Inertia—Whole Body

To measure rotational moments of inertia (MI) requires application of rotational accelerations. The most practical means to do this is to introduce oscillatory motion to prevent excessive forces and angular velocities. Gravitational pendulum and torsional pendulum methods have been successfully applied.

Gravitational Compound Pendulum Method

A method of obtaining data on both whole body center of mass and moment of inertia is the generalized compound pendulum method in which mean body density, utilized in computing a small second order buoyancy correction factor, is assumed. This method was used by Santschi, DuBois, and Omoto (1963):

"The compound or physical pendulum is an elementary dynamic system consisting of an extended mass oscillating about a fixed horizontal axis under the force of gravity. If two parallel axes of oscillation are provided, it is not difficult to show that the simultaneous solution of the torque equations for the two axes yields expressions for the moment of inertia and center of gravity of the pendulum in terms of its weight, periods, axis separation and acceleration due to gravity. Since the sums of the moments of inertia of two or more masses with respect to the same axis equals the moment of inertia of the combined masses with respect to that axis, the moment of inertia and center of mass of a human subject distinct from the double axis pendulum can be found."

Figure 3-4 shows a simplified schematic drawing of the essential elements and dimensions of the physical pendulum system. The center of mass is located by its distance from the short suspension axis (B in Figure 3-4) by calculating the distance L_s using the following formula.

$$\frac{4\pi^2\Delta L\left[\left(\frac{W'}{g}+\rho V'\right)(2L_s'+\Delta L) + \Delta L\left(\frac{W}{g}+\rho V\right) - \frac{T_{pl}^2}{4\pi^2}(W+W')\right] - W'L_s'(T_{pl}^2 - T_{ps}^2)}{W(T_{pl}^2 - T_{ps}^2) - 8\pi^2\left(\frac{W'}{g}+\rho V\right)\Delta L} = L_s \qquad \text{(Eq. 3.9)}$$

The moment of inertia of the subject about an axis parallel to the fulcrum axis and passing through his center of gravity is given by

$$I_0 = \frac{T_{ps}^2}{4\pi^2}(W'L_s' + WL_s) - I_s' - \left(\frac{W}{g}+\rho V\right)L_s^2 \qquad \text{(Eq. 3.10)}$$

In the above equations, the notation used is defined as follows:

T_{ps} is the period of the pendulum about the short suspension axis
T_{pl} is the period of the pendulum about the long suspension axis

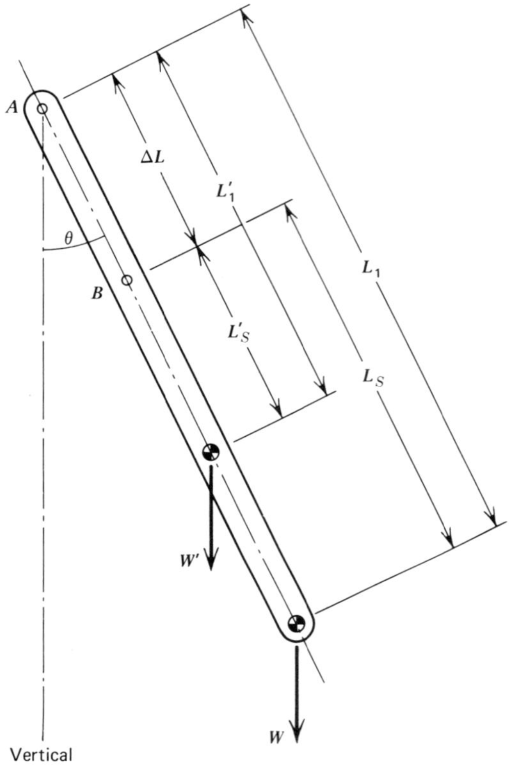

A Long suspension axis,
B Short suspension axis,
θ Angular displacement of pendulum,
W' Weight of pendulum without subject,
W Weight of subject,
ΔL Distance between support axes,
L_s' Distance from short suspension axis to CM of pendulum,
L_1' Distance from long suspension axis to CM of pendulum,
L_s Distance from short suspension axis to CM of subject,
L_1 Distance from long suspension axis to CM of subject.

Figure 3-4. Schematic of compound pendulum (Santschi, DuBois and Omoto, 1963).

I_s' is the moment of inertia of the pendulum (without subject) about the short axes
g is the acceleration due to gravity
V is the subject volume based upon body weight and an assumed mean body density of 65.246 lb/ft^3

V' is the pendulum volume
ρ is the ambient air density

The remaining symbols are as given previously.

A determination of center of mass and moment of inertia involves only five measurements: air temperature, subject weight, the two pendulum periods about the short and long suspension axes, and a reference distance from the subject to the short suspension fulcrum. All other constants in the equations are determined, once, prior to the actual subject measurements.

It is also noteworthy that the center of mass measurement is made in proper relationship with the gravity vector as contrasted with other methods (Hertzberg and Daniels, 1950; Swearingen, 1953) in which the displacement of subcutaneous fat and viscera is orthogonal to the direction of measurement.

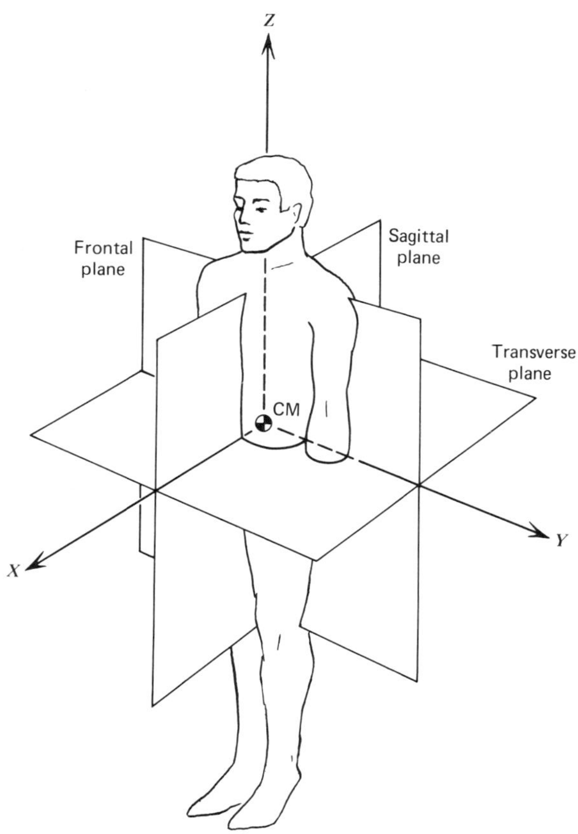

Figure 3-5. Body coordinate system (figure from Santschi, DuBois, and Omoto, 1963).

Provided the crucial experimental variables are carefully controlled, accuracies of $\pm 2\%$ for maximum I_0 values and $\pm 8\%$ for minimum I_0 values can be obtained. The distance to the center of mass can be measured to within $\pm 0.5\%$ or better along the X and Z axes.

Previous discussion of lengths and contours has laid little stress on coordinate systems for describing the body, although a need for some reference axes and datum planes was implied. A considerable variety of systems of coordinates have been used for different purposes. However, many of them are minor variations on the scheme depicted in Figure 3-5. The three-dimensional Cartesian orthogonal axis system is defined by the intersection of three planes passing through the center of mass of the body. The names of the *principal planes* are in common use in the literature, except that the frontal plane shown in Figure 3-5 is often called the *coronal* plane. The Z-axis is formed by the intersection of the sagittal plane and the frontal plane; the Y-axis by the intersection of the frontal and transverse planes; and, the X-axis by the intersection of the sagittal and transverse planes.

The theoretical concept shown is useful for many purposes, but has practical drawbacks. For one, the center of mass moves continuously as the body moves and reorients its limbs. Furthermore, one cannot establish a plane on the body and make measurements from it by use of simple anthropometric tools until

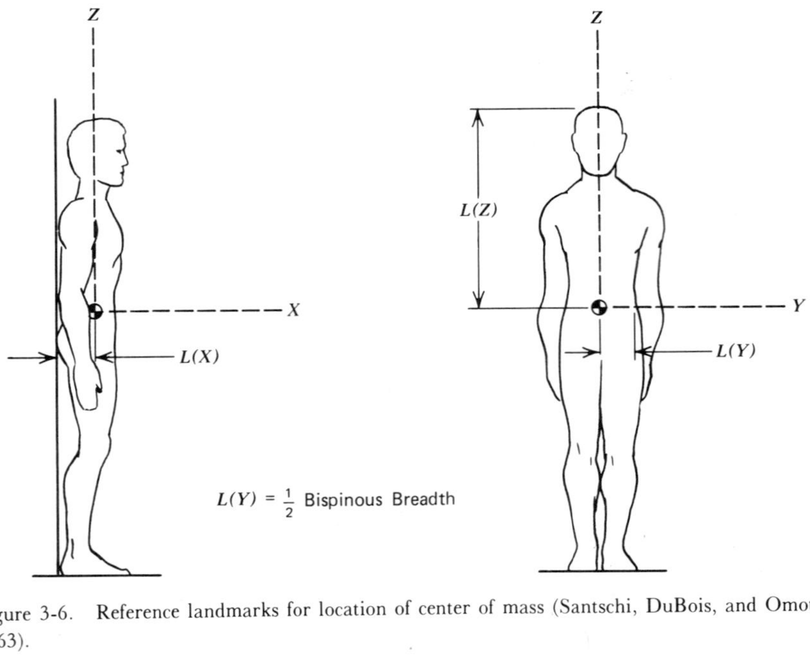

Figure 3-6. Reference landmarks for location of center of mass (Santschi, DuBois, and Omoto, 1963).

Figure 3-7. The compound pendulum framework for measurement of I_{ox}/I_{oy}. (Courtesy of Rockwell International Corporation.)

the CM is defined with respect to the body. Therefore, it is common to select some physically accessible body landmarks as a basis for actual measurements. For example, Santschi, DuBois, and Omoto (1963) referenced the orthogonal axis system to the body back surface and top of head as shown in Figure 3-6.

A brief description of the apparatus used by Santschi et al. provides an understanding of the complexity and cost factors involved in the technique: two compound pendulum structures were designed to accommodate the subjects in eight selected positions. One pendulum was used to determine the moment of inertia about the X and Y axes (I_{0x}/I_{0y}), the other for measurement about the Z-axis (I_{0z}). The pendulums, weighing in the range of 40 to 60 lb, were constructed mainly of welded 1-in. aluminum tubing. The cone fulcrums were fabricated of steel and tipped with a hard-facing alloy. These cones rested on hardened steel pads, secured to a heavy steel support that was anchored solidly to concrete. A hoist mechanism was devised to transfer the pendulums from the short to the long suspension axis and to rotate the I_{0x}/I_{0y} pendulum. The I_{0x}/I_{0y} pendulum is shown in Figure 3-7. The subjects were restrained in their proper positions in the lower portion of the structure by use of pressure-sensitive tape and Velcro tape to ensure rigidity in the pendulum.

An electronic timer system was designed to provide the accurate measurement of pendulum period needed for this method. Based on interruption of a light source, the system provided accuracy to within ± 0.0001 sec.

Torsional Pendulum Method

Another type of pendulum measurement device depends on a torsional spring bar to produce the restoring forces in place of the gravitational attraction in the above described technique. Gravitational effects are eliminated by supporting the subject horizontally on a table. The combined bar and table physical constants are first determined. The inertia of the body, when added to the system, changes the period of oscillation, permitting calculation of the mass moment of inertia (*Product Engineering,* 1967; Drillis and Contini, 1966).

3.2.5 Center of Mass—Body Parts

The amount of data on centers of mass of body components is necessarily small, since accurate measurements on the living body are very difficult, and methods using cadavers depend on the very limited sample as well as time-consuming and difficult methods. Classic historical examples are described by Harless (1860), Meeh (1895), and Dempster (1955). More recent data are given by Clauser, McConville, and Young (1969), who describe the earlier work and their own methods.

3.2.6 Moment of Inertia—Body Parts

Dempster (1955a) and others have determined the moments of inertia for body parts of cadavers by measuring the period of oscillation about a selected suspension point. Freezing the parts enabled treatment as a rigid body.

The estimation of moments of inertia of limb segments of the living subject can be performed by model analog measurements. For example, Pearson, McGinley, and Butzel (1963) made models of cork and linoleum disks, which they selected to closely approximate the actual density and mass distribution of the arm. They were swung as pendulums in the same manner as Dempster used for cadaver limb dissections.

Another method is based upon the fact that rotational acceleration of a body about a fixed point in space is directly related to its moment of inertia and rotational torque. Therefore, it is necessary to find a means to measure the exerted torque about a joint and to prevent translation of the joint in order to measure I_j, the moment of inertia, on any combination of limb segments distal from the selected joint. The distal segments must, of course, be rigidly held relative to each other. The elbow and knee joints are relatively simple joints that lend themselves to such treatment in that they do not engage in significant translation if the proximal limb segment (upper arm or thigh, respectively) is held fixed. An effective system for determining a self-induced torque by the subject and the resulting rotational acceleration of the fore-arm-hand has been devised by Drillis (1959). The apparatus is shown in Figure 3-8.

A string is attached to a band on the wrist of the arm and to a force

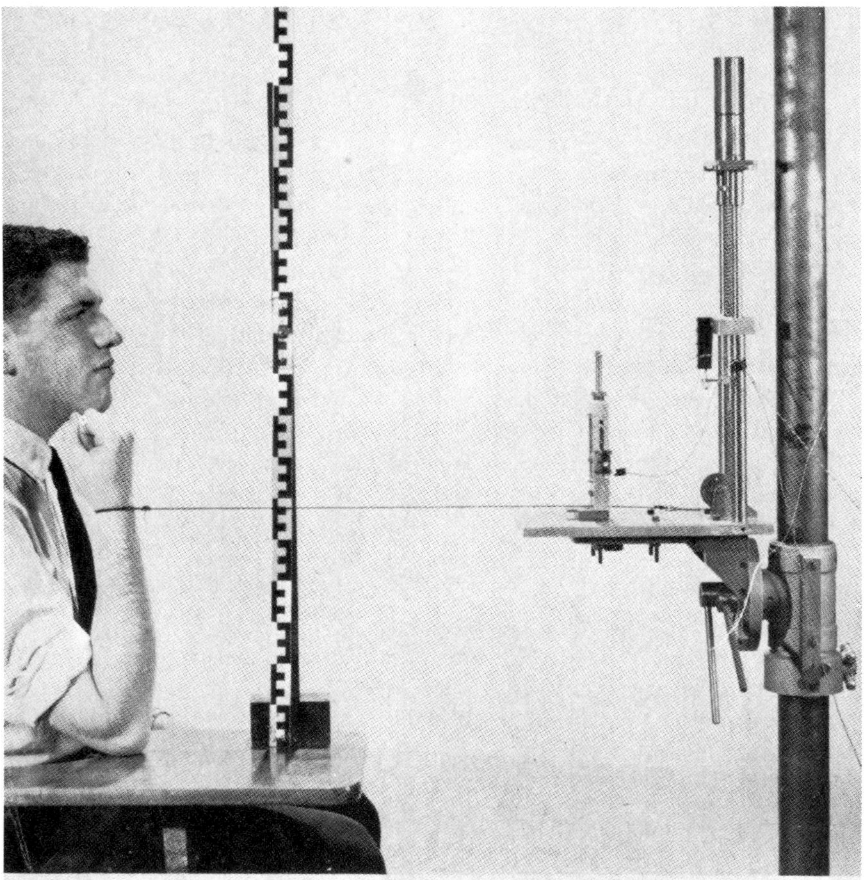

Figure 3-8. Subject in position to measure forearm hand acceleration and force. (Courtesy *Product Engineering*. Copyright, Morgan-Grampian, Inc., 1967)

measuring device located on a line perpendicular to the arm axis. The string is then pulled taut by the subject until the force is strong enough to break the string. The resulting rotational movement is recorded photographically by multiple exposure photography or a gliding cyclograph technique (described later, Section 3.5.3). Analysis of the record yields the angular acceleration (α) due to the torque about the elbow exerted by the subject at the time of release.

The force measured at the instant the cord breaks defines a torque Fd by introducing the distance from the string to the elbow center of rotation. The mass moment of inertia I about the elbow is determined from the equation

$$I = \frac{Fd}{\alpha} \qquad \text{(Eq. 3.11)}$$

The moment of inertia about the center of mass can then be estimated by the formula $I_0 = I - Mb^2$ where b is the estimated distance from elbow to center of mass.

3.2.7 Analytical Methods

The previously discussed measurements of body cross sections and the volumes and density between successive cross sections provide data from which approximations of both whole body and limb or trunk segment centers of mass and moments of inertia can be calculated. Multiplying average density by the estimated or measured volume within closely spaced cross-sectional body elements provides mass estimations for the segments. Since the center of mass locations of each of these elements can be closely estimated (assuming uniform density), the elemental masses can be combined to estimate segment center of mass and, thence, whole body center of mass. Similarly the moments of inertia of the elements can be estimated individually and then combined to form estimates of limb segment moment of inertia and/or whole body moment of inertia.

Weinbach (1938) used an approximate method of estimating the cross-sectional shapes by assuming they were ellipses having major and minor axes equal to observed measurements obtained by photography. The general expression for moment of inertia of such a regular shape is defined in engineering and mathematical tables.

The Dempster (1955a) planimetric measurements of cross-sectional areas should yield more accurate (but less regular) shapes. The center of mass and moments of inertia of these irregular shapes must be individually determined by numerical integration or by measuring models cut from materials of uniform density. This is a very tedious process unless aided by computer techniques.

Approximation methods using larger segments are generally more satisfactory. The allowable error is usually quite large in view of the known changes in center of mass and moment of inertia due to the fluid shifts, and so forth, previously described. Knowing the mass and center of mass location of a limb segment, one can select a representative geometric shape such as the frustum of a cone which has the same relative center of mass location and volume as the limb. If the weight is known, by similarity or by estimation from density calculations, moments of inertia can be estimated with reasonable accuracy.

3.3 STATIC REACH ENVELOPE MEASUREMENTS

Practical engineering considerations often lead to the realization that the simplest, most direct approach to measurement of movement capabilities is that of defining "final effects." In many engineering design and evaluation problems, the desired answer can be presented in a simple "yes" or "no" to a question such as "Can the operator reach and operate this control if it is located here?"

Without prior knowledge, the most obvious method of solution is to make a representative mockup of the situation and test a sample of subjects who represent design limit conditions to see if they succeed in performance of the task.

Of course, after the answer is obtained, one has knowledge of only a single specific situation that may never be repeated. To deal with a larger number of similar problems, one may seek a more general solution in terms of defining a reachable spatial volume by its boundary surfaces, or its *envelope*. Within such a volume, a certain class of control operations can be performed by a specified group of human operators. General purpose definitions of mobility by such means may become a very time-consuming task because of the infinite and subtle variety of control types, clothing restrictions, and subject percentile variations involved in the reach components. Therefore, anything that can be gleaned from former attempts to accomplish such measurements may save large amounts of effort and expense in measurement apparatus, testing time, and validity assessment.

The following descriptions of example studies suggest approaches that the anthropometrist may adapt for future studies. In both envelope and angular movement studies, two basically different approaches are employed. The first is essentially a series of static measurements of a number of possible positions of the body or points on its surface. The second approach involves recording of the body positions and envelopes of movement while in motion, a considerably more difficult problem discussed mainly in Section 3.5.

Early studies of reach envelopes of 139 Naval pilots were reported by King, Morrow, and Vollmer (1947) and King (1948). The testing apparatus for the reach measurements consisted of a pilot seat mounted on a platform and equipped with suitable horizontal and vertical measuring rods. The horizontal arm was pivoted at a point directly above the reference point of the seat. This reference point was taken as the upper level of the seat cushion at its line of intersection with the small lower cushions of the back pad.

The subject reached for and touched successive points on the vertical measuring rod as it was brought toward him by moving it along its horizontal support. Horizontal distances from a vertical line from the seat reference point to the vertical measuring rod at the extreme fingertip reach were measured for 99 points on each subject.

Another device for work space analysis was described by Swearingen (1949). It was "an adjustable cockpit mockup" consisting of 15 vertical frames, mounted at 15° intervals to 105° right and left of the median plane. On each frame were 15 horizontal measuring members, and in the ceiling were mounted 21 vertical measuring rods. The device could locate in space a total of 246 points to simulate shapes of work spaces. Although capable of reach envelope measurements, the device seems to have been used primarily as a mock-up device to evaluate existing work spaces.

Another work space measuring device was developed by Dempsey (1953) for determination of optimum, maximum, and minimum space requirements of Air Force pilots. The device consisted of ten horizontal arms and five vertical arms each equipped with individual friction locking catches (Figure 3-9). The horizontal and vertical arms were spaced 6 in. on center.

"When the subject adjusts any sliding arm the actual vertical and horizontal distance from that point can be read directly from the scale on the side of the

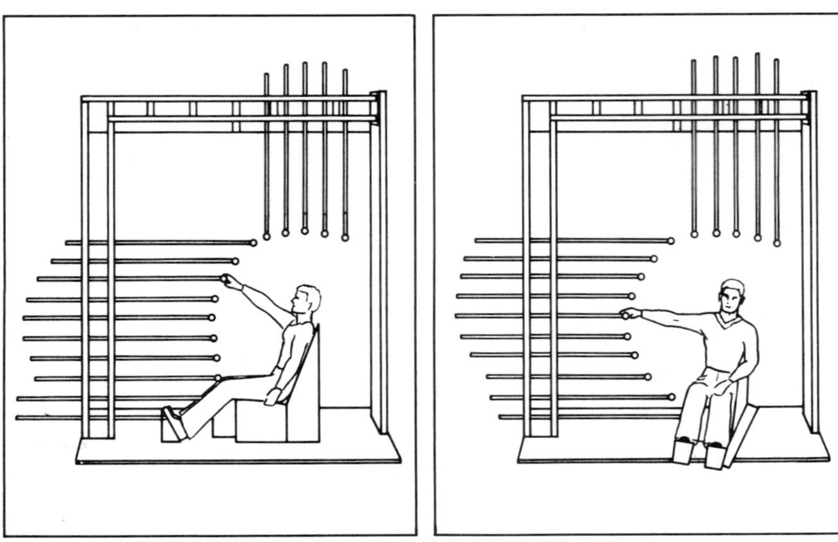

Figure 3-9. Arm reach measurement device. (After Dempsey, 1953.)

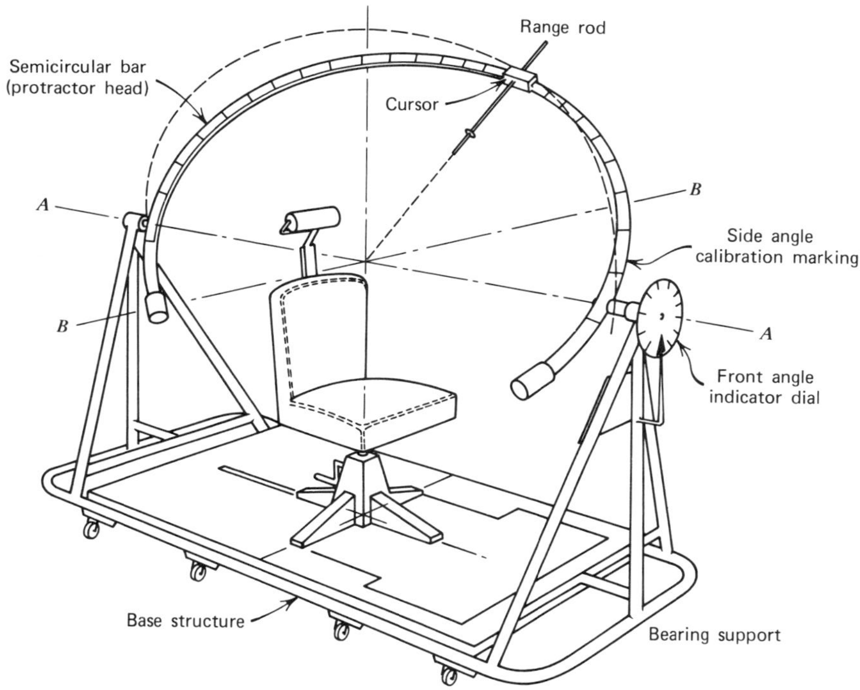

Figure 3-10. The Frankenstein anthropometric measuring apparatus (Courtesy of Wright, 1963 and the *Journal of the British Interplanetary Society*).

arm. The inner end of each arm is equipped with a 2 inch square cap which can be pivoted 45° above or below the arm centerline. Movement of this cap through the 90° arc by the subject provides data on the optimum angle for the end point of each vertical and horizontal arm with reference to the shoulder. . . . A rotating knob which can be operated through a 360° range is mounted on the face of each pivoting cap.

"The seat and rudder pedals are attached to a platform which rotates around the Seat Reference Point in a horizontal plane and is calibrated in 15° increments up to 135° on each side of center."

Kennedy (1964) described a device developed by P. Frankenstein and Sons which pivots about a fore-aft axis through the chest/neck area, as shown in Figure 3-10. In place of a multitude of bars, a single range rod is mounted to a cursor which moves on a semicircular bar. The bar can be pivoted about the seated subject to the desired increments of angular position. The data are reported in terms of the "front angle" (inclination of the semicircular bar), the "side angle" (location of the cursor), and the radial distance read off of the

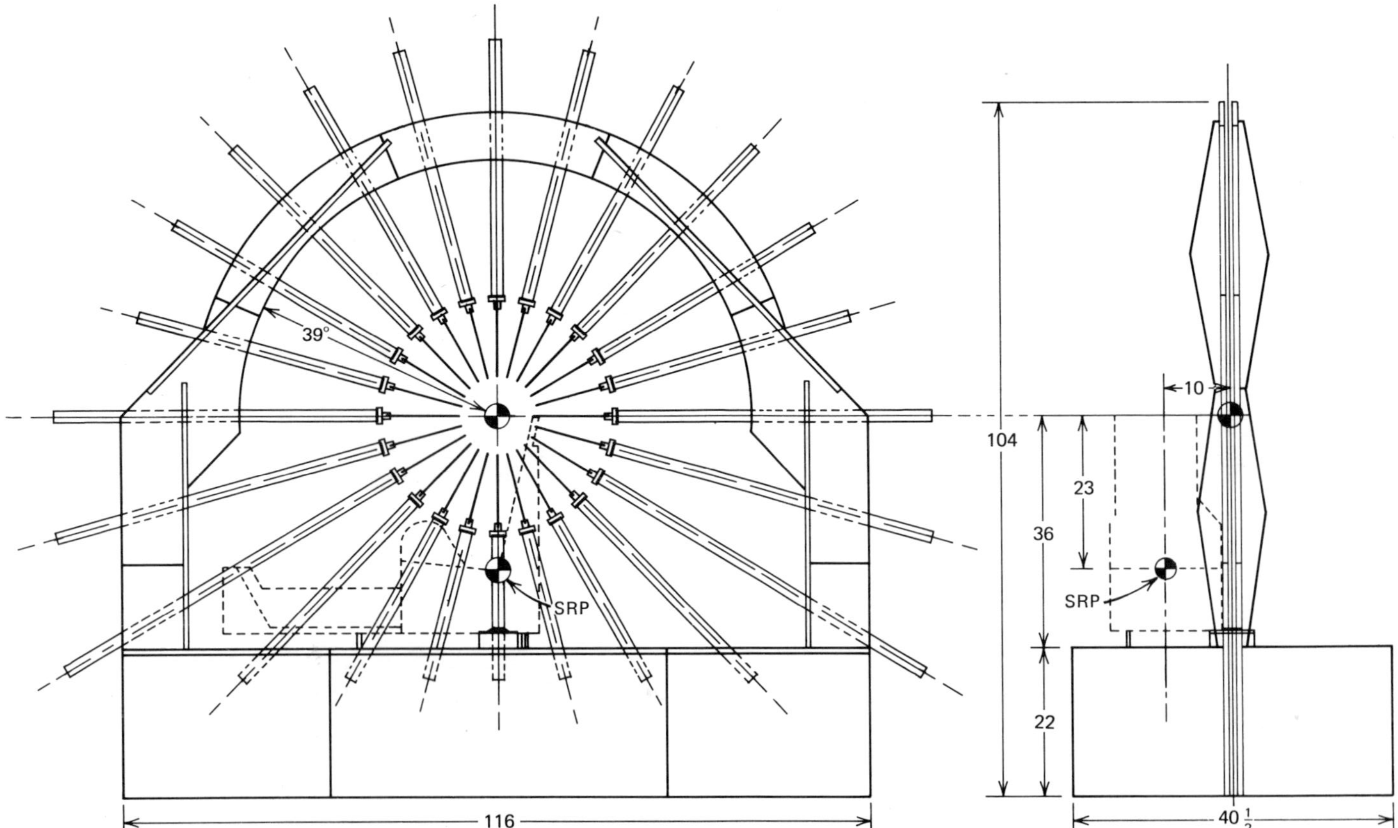

Figure 3-11. Grasping-reach measuring device platform. The axis of seat rotation is within the plane of the arch and its measuring slats (Kennedy, 1964).

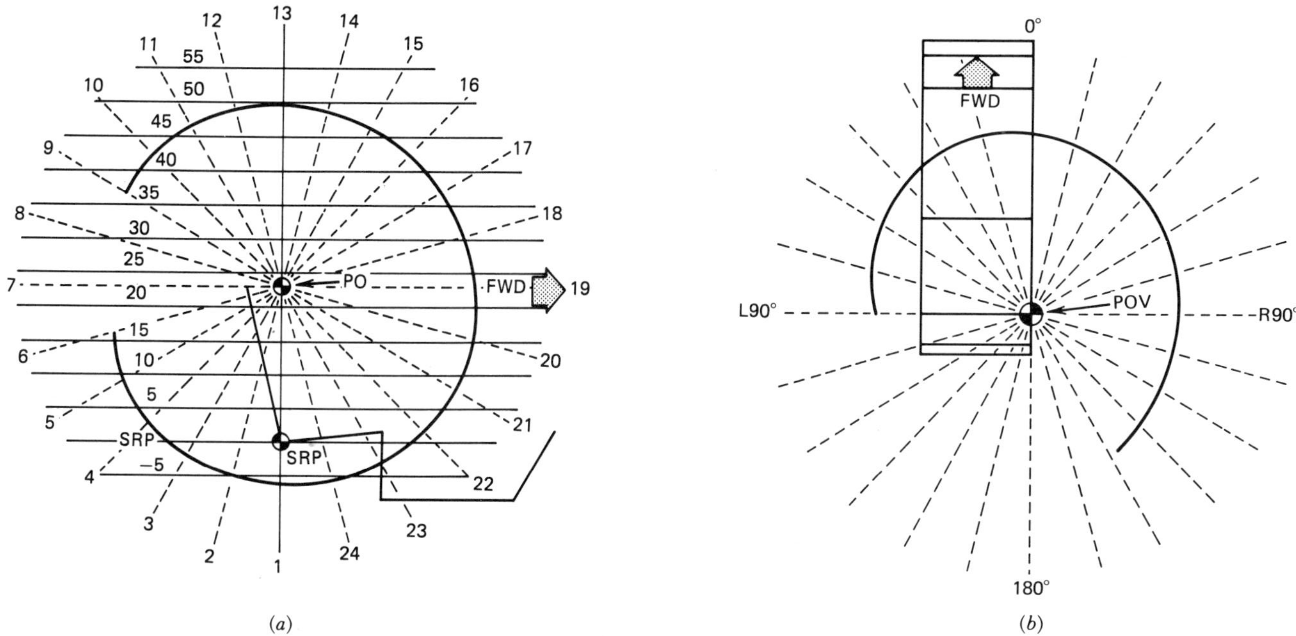

Figure 3-12. Data reduction method for reach envelope contours (from Kennedy, 1964). (*a*) Side view of the vertical section at 0°–180° (through PO) through the grasping-reach envelope of one subject. Horizontal lines are at 5-inch intervals from SRP level. (*b*) Top view of the horizontal section through the grasping-reach envelope of one subject at the 25-inch level, referenced to POV.

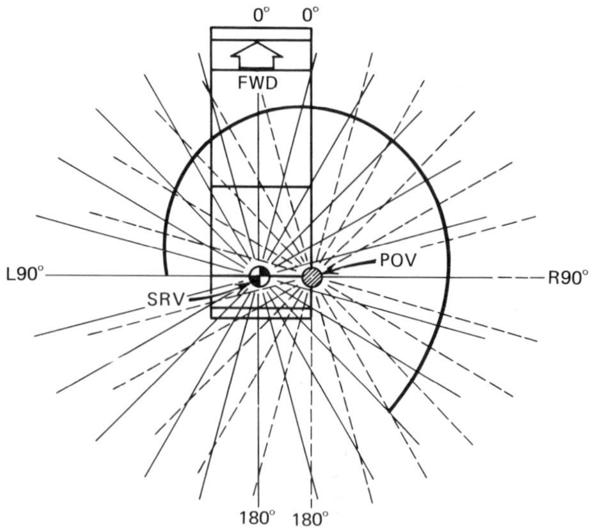

(*c*)

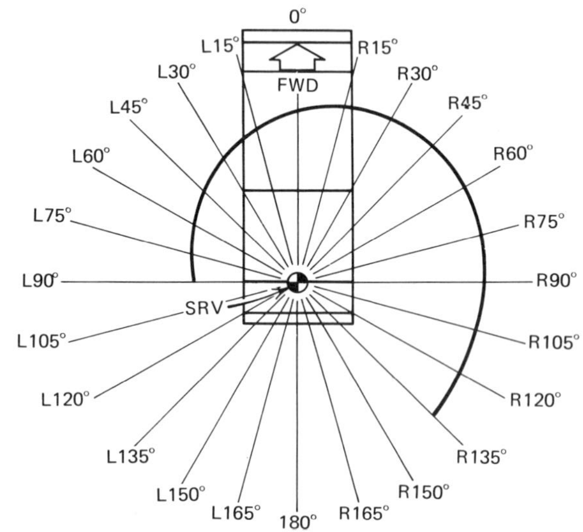

(*d*)

Figure 3-12. (Continued). (*c*) Diagram showing method used to transfer reference from POV to SRV. Indentical system of radiating lines is superimposed so that its center is over SRP. Distances from SRV along line to envelope boundary are measured. (*d*) Top view of the horizontal contour through grasping-reach envelope at the 25-inch level, referenced to SRV (vertical axis through SRP).

range rod. The device can be used as a mobility measuring device for clothing and to describe the complete reach envelope.

A larger and more stable device was described by Kennedy (1964), which measures distances in a vertical plane, radially from an approximate shoulder center (Point of Origin, PO) located to the side of a rotating mockup chair (Figure 3-11). The arch and platform contain friction-held measuring slats, radiating at 15° intervals.

Data reduction involved a conversion from measurements about the PO to distances related to the Seat Reference Point (SRP). Also, the data were expressed as horizontal cross sections of the envelope rather than vertical cuts through the SRP. Figure 3-12 presents a sample of the results.

3.4 MEASUREMENT OF BODY SEGMENT ANGULAR POSITIONS

Another method for determining or defining reach capabilities and other aspects of body mobility involves an elemental approach. Each piece of the body linkage is first defined as accurately as is feasible in terms of joint centers and connecting axes. Then, their angular positions in space and their relationship to each other are measured or specified. For example, in work space analysis, one can derive an estimate of reach areas on panels by knowing the arm length, shoulder axes location, and range of shoulder joint movements. When the work environment requires bulky or restrictive clothing, such as a space suit, one must take into account these different angular motion and bulk restrictions. If these are unknown, ways to measure them must be devised. This section is primarily concerned with such methods of measurement of elementary human joint motion capabilities and the notation systems that may be used to describe and organize the records of such measurements for engineering applications.

3.4.1 Mobility Terminology and Standardization

Mobility and, in kinesiology and physical education, *flexibility* are used as synonyms. However, Holland (1968) quotes other equivalent terms, including "mobilization," "freedom to move," and "the measurement of range of motion in the joints." The term flexibility implies just flexion and therefore should be considered a misnomer and replaced with a more appropriate designation, such as mobility.

Classical Anatomical Terminology

For many years movement terminology has depended on a set of anatomically related terms in use by the medical profession. Although there are several semantic problems associated with these terms, students and engineers dealing with the literature will need to understand their basis. Therefore, a brief description of these "standard" or classical anatomical terms is first presented, together with some of the inherent problems. Later, a new terminology that is more suited to engineering use is offered.

Movements in the classical terminology systems are considered to begin from the so-called anatomical position. This is defined as that of a man standing upright, head facing forward, arms hanging down with palms facing forward. Three mutually perpendicular principal planes are defined for reference in description of motion: the frontal (or coronal) plane, the sagittal plane, and the transverse plane. The orientations of planes were illustrated in Figure 3-5 with their common intersection at the center of mass of the human body. (A point of common intersection for the three planes is apparently not actually defined in most anatomical texts. However, engineering usage requires some sort of precise definition to form a basis for measurements.)

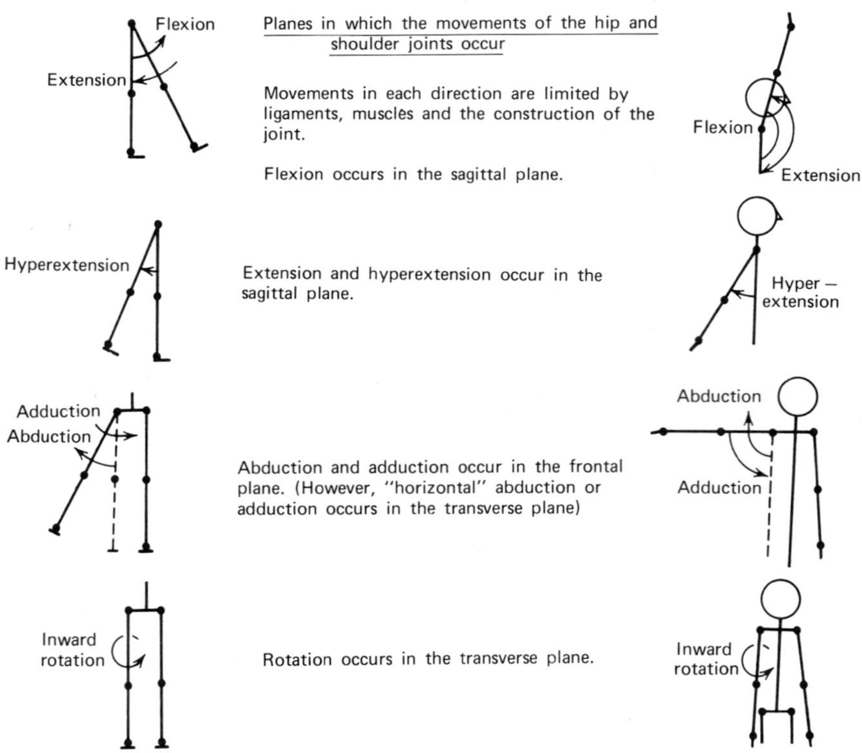

Figure 3-13. Classical terminology for major movements (redrawn from Bilger, A. J. and Greene, E. H., 1973, "*Winters*" *Protective Body Mechanics. A Manual for Nurses,* Copyright, 1973, Springer Publishing Company, Inc., 200 Park Avenue South, New York, N. Y. 10003, pp. 38, 39).

Winters prepared a well-illustrated description of classical movement terminology (Bilger and Greene, 1973), and many other authors of anatomical and kinesiological texts have included such descriptions in various forms. The most general components of classical movement terminology are summarized in Figure 3-13. The terms are said by Winters to apply to hip and shoulder joint movements, but they are also applicable to movements of other joints.

Although the classical movement descriptions found in anatomical texts appears well organized, many terms are actually misleading and inappropriate. Furthermore, it is notable that writers in this field are equivocal and inconsistent about using some of the terms, and often redefine or use different combinations. Some confusion in the classical terminology is possible because the same terms are applied interchangeably to movement of joints and to movements of limb segments.

Certain motions, said to occur in a given plane (Figure 3-13), may also occur in others. For example, note that rotation of the arm can occur in the sagittal, frontal, or transverse planes or almost any other orientation. From an engineering standpoint the movement of the *joint centers* in space, with respect to some defined reference planes, could also be of interest. However, the terminology here does not apply to that concept.

The most controversial set of terms involves shoulder joint motion, where the anatomical terminology seems particularly inadequate. For example, "abduction" is defined to mean motion away from the body (trunk) centerline. However, once the upper arm is "abducted" to 90° sidewards, every element of the straight arm actually begins to move *toward* the body centerline as *any* further motion is imparted in any permissible direction. Codman (1934) gives one of the best and most amusing discussions of shoulder joint motion and difficulties with the standard anatomical movement terminology.

Another more paradoxical example involves the problem of describing inward and outward rotation of the humerus/forearm group. Consider horizontal angular movement of the forearm with the elbow bent to 90° and the humerus hanging vertically: "inward" and "outward" are consistent with direction of movement from the trunk centerline. However, keeping the elbow at right angles and elevating the humerus to a vertical upward position, and placing the forearm over the head (as it must be, due to joint construction), rotation in either direction now seems to move it *away* from the body centerline. Furthermore, there is a semantic paradox created by return movement of the upper arm *forward* and downward as compared to *sideward* and downward (in both cases keeping the elbow bent at 90°). In the former case, the end result is a position of "inward rotation" but in the latter the final result is a position of "outward rotation." Yet, there is no sensible rotation of the humerus about its longitudinal axis in either motion. Here, the physical fact and body sensations are not in agreement. Thus the terminology becomes confusing. This is sometimes referred to as the Codman paradox.

Additional general terms describing surfaces of the body, planes through the body, relative positions of one structure to another, and so forth, are presented in Appendix A, part 2.

A basic problem with some of the standard anatomical terms (such as adduction, abduction, extension), is that they are based on the wrong model of movement (Roebuck, 1968). They seem to assume that body segments move about upon a rectangular lattice work, by *translation* rather than by the actual rotation, necessitated by swinging about joint centers. In fact, the structure in the body permits pure translation only in distal members, which have several degrees of freedom with respect to the trunk. Engineering analysis of each joint will reveal that the major mode of movement is *rotation* about instantaneous centers, which shift about slightly as the movement progresses (Dempster, 1955a). Recognition of this basic problem in semantics of the standard anatomical terminology has led to a new notation system based upon *rotational* movements (Roebuck, 1968). The development of this system is discussed in the following paragraphs.

Before proceeding into that development, it is appropriate to discuss two additional special problems of body movement terminology. The first has to do with limb segment shape and the meaning of certain types of body limb movements. In engineering dynamics, any motion of a body about any defined axis is called *rotation* about that axis. In discussing limb segments, it appears useful to classify rotations into two types (MacConaill, 1966; Codman 1934). One type is rotation about a joint center in which the longer axes change their relative angulation to each other. Thus, a pendulous or swinging motion occurs, in which the distal end moves in space with respect to the proximal end (or vice versa). The second type involves rotation about the length axis. There is negligible relative movement of the distal end in relation to the proximal end; they rotate together at the same time and do not change spatial relationships of the principal axes. The latter type of motion is generally called *rotation* in standard anatomical terminology (except in the case of supination-pronation and certain compound movements). It is the terminology of the former type of movement that leads to confusion. Admittedly, some body segments do not have an obvious longer axis; they are about the same length in several directions. In such cases, an arbitrary decision is needed. It should be such as to assist in memory or to fit with a basic scheme of terminology.

Another problem of notation in medical anatomical usage is the lack of precise definitions of relative orientation of body parts. "The anatomical position," for example, contains no precisely located landmark distances from specified planes or specific angular orientation of the body structure in space. This is only a qualitative definition, using a pictorial presentation without specified axes or angles. Following such lack of coordinates, some investigators report angular movement ranges, but do not tell where the movement started.

Therefore, an engineering draftsman cannot use such data to lay out ranges of movement in a work space with respect to the floor, seat, or other reference planes.

A New System of Notation for Mobility Evaluation

In response to problems of designing for space-suited crewmen in Project Apollo, development was initiated on a new notation system and measurement methodology that would insure precise, unequivocal description of coordinates and movements. Goals selected for the system included the following: the system of description of movement and position should be capable of handling gross and fine movements and should be compatible with common methods of engineering analysis, such as drafting layouts, trigonometrics and machine computation, using concise shorthand notation. Yet, it should be related readily to common experience and stereotypes of description where feasible. The descriptions of measurement techniques for joint and limb positions should be clear, simple, and effective in yielding reproducible results, calling for a minimum of costly, special equipment.

The resulting notation system provides several improvements over the classical approach. First, the major axes of the coordinate systems are related to the human body pelvic area, regardless of the positions of the other segment orientations, or the orientation of the body with respect to other objects or force fields. The primary coordinate systems are shown in Figure 3-14. When the subject is standing erect, the angular zero position is footward for both the frontal and sagittal planes as suggested by Eshkol and Wachman (1958). The transverse plane zero position is directly forward, perpendicular to the frontal plane.

The three planes facilitate use of standard three-view orthographic drawing presentation. Angular measurements avoid many problems related to differing body dimensions among subjects. Use of a full 360° circle scale provides for nonambiguous notation for limb orientation. Cartesian coordinate system axes compatible with acceleration terminology, center of mass description, and vehicle control locations are also defined in Figure 3-14. A global angular coordinate system, more appropriate to certain types of analysis, is shown in Figure 3-15.

For brevity in data recording, specification, and convenience in machine computation, limb and suit segments are assigned specific numbers according to examples in Figure 3-16. Two digits designate major body segments; up to four digits may be used for smaller segments if required (Figure 3-17). In general, the first digit of right limbs is even and the first digit for left limbs is odd. Segment numbers generally increase from head to toe and from proximal to distal segments.

For uniqueness in specifying direction, each body segment (link) is assigned

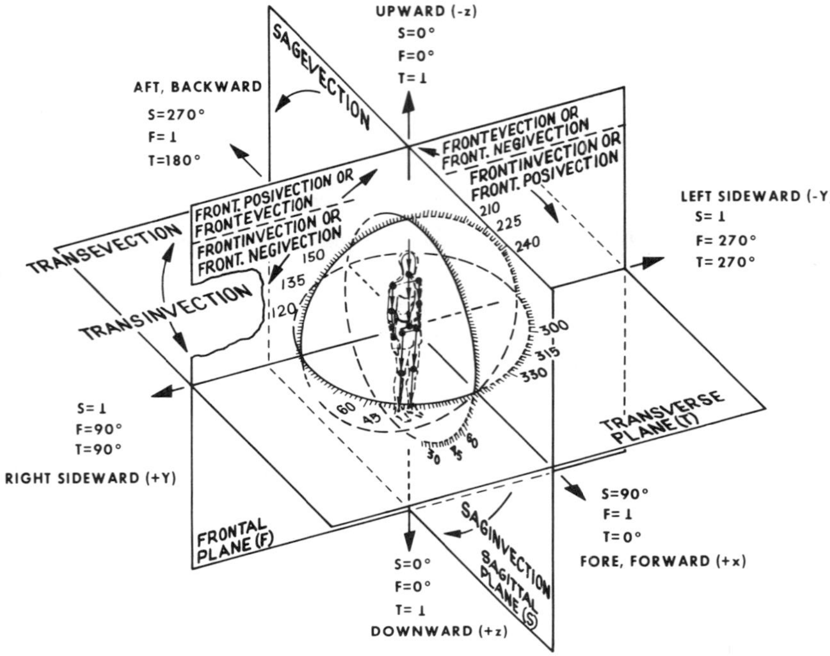

Figure 3-14. Mobility terminology: triplanar angular coordinate system (Roebuck, 1968).

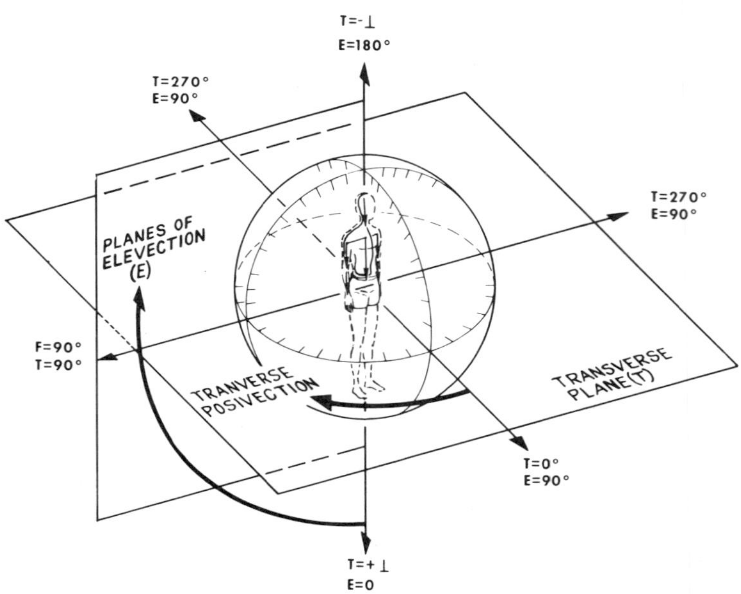

Figure 3-15. Global coordinate system (tentative) (Roebuck, 1968).

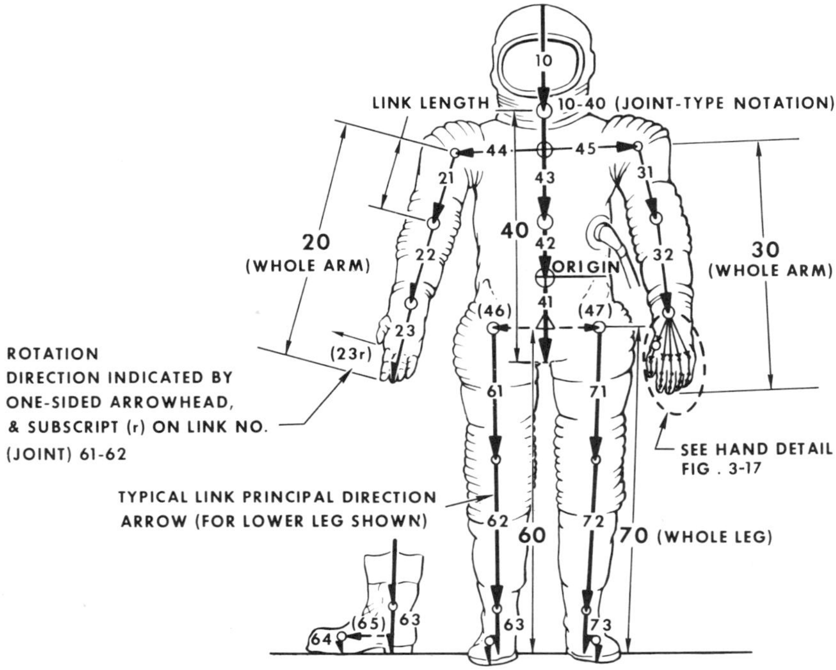

Figure 3-16. Link diagram and numerical notation system (Roebuck, 1968).

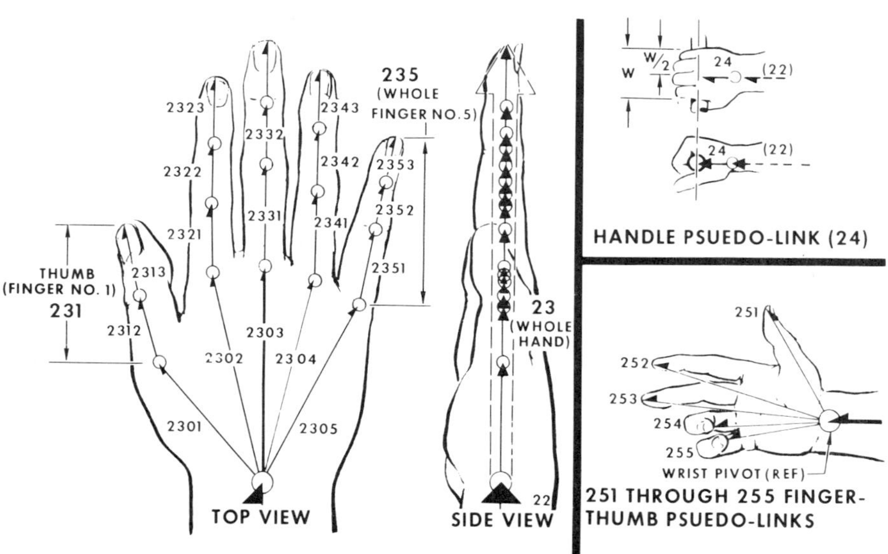

Figure 3-17. Basic hand link and pseudolink details (Roebuck, 1968).

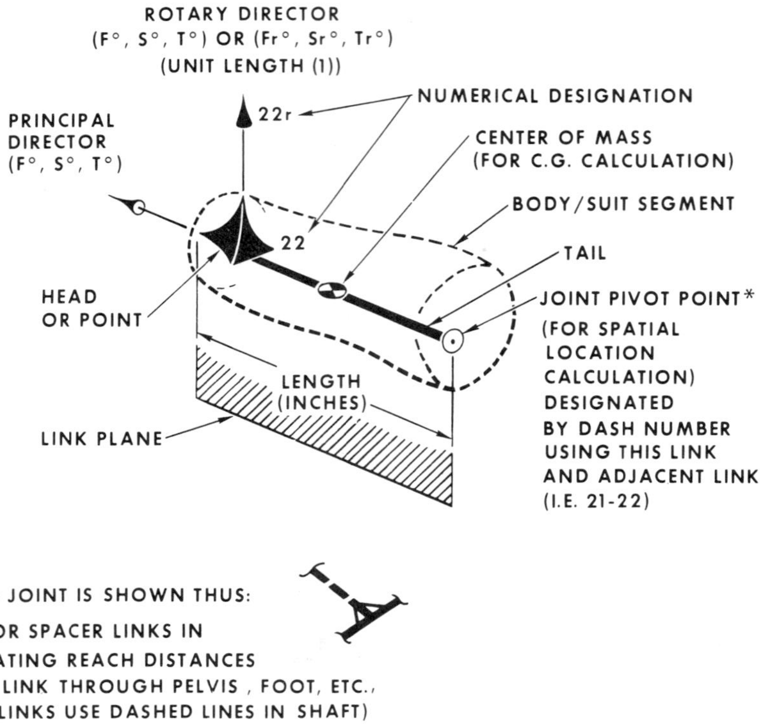

Figure 3-18. Link properties and picturizations (Roebuck, 1968).

a principal direction vector (called the Principal Director) as shown in Figure 3-18, along with other nomenclature associated with these vectors. The Principal Director for the pelvic region (No. 41) determines the direction in space of the zero axis for the angular coordinates and of the Z-axis for Cartesian coordinates. For most pressurized space suits, the trunk is quite rigid, and may be considered as a single link instead of several. The direction of this overall link (No. 40) is determined by the line connecting two points. The first point is at the top of the iliac crest, midway front to back on the sagittal plane, and the second is at the nipple level, midway front to back on the sagittal plane (Figure 3-19).

One method of describing direction is to write the angular position of the projection of each vector on the three principal planes. Theoretically, only two planes need be specified, but it is often more accurate and useful to specify all three angles. The shorthand notation utilizes the capitalized first letter of each principal plane, then a colon preceding the angle in degrees. This arrangement helps avoid confusion with the commonly used notation for temperature. Examples are shown in Figure 3-20.

1. Subject stands erect (barefoot) and looks directly forward (head oriented in Frankfort plane).

2. a. Measure and record distance from floor to center of right nipple.

2. b. Measure and record distance from floor to right side midway in body depth at level of iliac crest.

2. c. Measure and record height.

3. Measure height with suit, but without helmet, while subject is standing erect. The difference between this height and that in 2c gives shoe height. This is added to height readings in 2a and 2b.

4. While subject stands erect and normal in pressurized suit with helmet, mark adjusted nipple and iliac heights on suit at midpoints in pressurized suit depth.

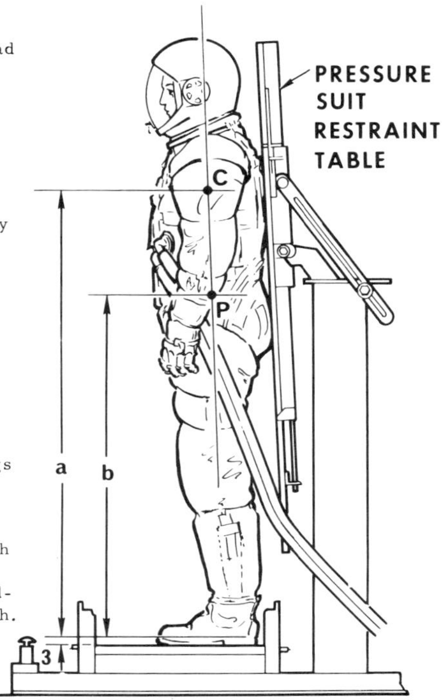

Figure 3-19. Method of obtaining midbody points. (Roebuck, 1968.)

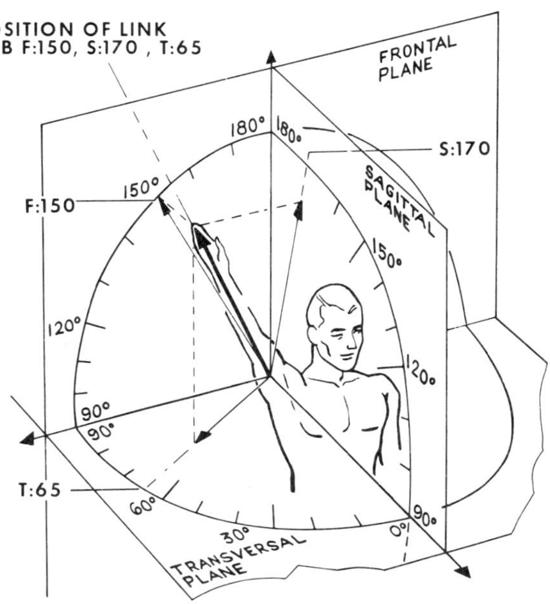

Figure 3-20. Example of shorthand notation (Roebuck, 1968).

Space-suit joints (or other clothing) may accomplish motion in quite a different manner than the human body, and thus require some means to distinguish them from the human body parts. A suffix (s) is used for this. For example, in supination and pronation of the hand and forearm within a suit, the forearm section of the suit (22s or 32s) may be fixed while the glove section (23s or 33s) and the hand (23 or 33) revolve. However, in the human, the forearm section takes an appearance of torsion due to the radius and ulna crossing over one another. For most purposes, this latter condition will be sufficiently described as a simple rotation of the forearm (22 or 32) in which the Rotary Director for the human forearm will take a new set of angular readings.

Dempster (1955a) has suggested two alternative approaches to the problem of joint centers. The first is to apply techniques which he describes to actually follow the instantaneous centers. For most engineering purposes, however, this is unnecessary, and one may use the second approximate approach wherein a single pivot-point for each joint is selected and angles are measured from these points.

Angular Motion Terminology for Limb Motions. Basically, the idea for new terminology is to provide a consistent means to describe movements of the links (rather than the joints) with respect to the spatial coordinate reference system previously described. Each movement term always refers to motion in the same direction of rotation with respect to the spatial coordinates, although sometimes they may not be the same direction in a muscular or anatomical sense. In comparing motion descriptions of two men, one starting from the anatomical position and one from the newer standard position, one will at first be hard put to find significant differences. As the extent and complexity of motion is increased, however, the "engineering" terminology proves to be more precise, consistent, manageable, and easily learned.

The medical terminology is largely based upon the Latin terms *ducere, ductum,* "to lead." This gives the root word "duction." For example, "adduction" means "to lead toward" the sagittal or reference plane. These definitions are not satisfying since one is not really told how to express the motion once one *passes* the reference plane. To solve this semantic difficulty in the medical terminology, some authors use the prefix "hyper" as in hyperextension. The engineering terminology avoids the problem, since it is based upon definition of rotary directions of movement as *clockwise or counterclockwise when looking in a certain direction.* Therefore, no matter what position of the circle in which one starts, the word describing the direction of rotary motion in space is the same. In order to make a unique distinction from the medical root words, a new root word has been selected, "vection," based on the Latin verb *vehere, vectum,* "to carry," which implies no end point of movement. It is, of course, related to the common engineering term "vector," and one is then speaking of changing the direction of vectors in using the root, "vection." The next step was to select a series of unique prefixes that convey a sense of movement in the three principal planes. The scheme of word formation selected is shown in Table 3-5.

Because of the basic difference in philosophy of the system, new prefixes were selected. Abbreviations of the names of the planes in which the action was to take place and the direction of movement was incorporated. Thus, terms like "sagevection," contain the components "sag-" for sagittal plane, and "-e" indicating movement initially outward from the rest position, but specifically defined as a positive, increasing-angle sense of angular movement for the right limb.

Admittedly, this system resulted in some long words, but they are words perhaps less difficult to pronounce, and all carry the same rhythm. Furthermore, there is a savings in learning time since the terms all start with one of three prefixes based on the names of the Principal Planes, which must be learned anyway. The list is essentially complete with the use of three movement terms: the new one, "vection" and two old ones, "rotation" and "torsion." The latter two words were selected for the case of movements such as pronation and supination, which appear to be a twisting of the forearm as a whole when viewed as a complete unit. In summary, the use of eight building-

Table 3-5. New Movement Terms, Triplanar System (Plane + Direction + Type = Motion)

Plane	Direction	Type	Motion
Front(al)	-e-	Vection	Frontevection
Sag(ittal)	-in-	Rotation	Frontinvection
Trans(versal)	posi-	Torsion	Sagevection
	negi-		Saginvection
			Transevection
			Transinvection
			Fronterotation
			Frontinrotation
			Sagerotation
			Saginrotation
			—
			—
			—
			etc.

block letter combinations permits the formation of a logical, consistent set of just 18 words for major dual body-segment movements.

Next, because not all body segments are dual links, it was considered useful to have terms for movement of the singular links, such as the head and the thorax, in the Principal Planes. This led to the adoption of the terms "posivection" and "negivection," denoting increasing and decreasing angular readings as the movements progressed. A more complete glossary of these terms is presented in Appendix A, part 3, which lists all the combinations from Table 3-5.

In describing movement, one must also have terms for *joint* action, independently of spatial orientation. For these considerations, it appears that the classical medical terminology still serves quite admirably in many instances, especially for flexion-extension of the knee and elbow and for some of the more complicated specific applications such as supination-pronation, and inversion-eversion. However, when used in this context, the terminology should be rigorously limited to description of movement with respect to the next proximal local joint, not with respect to the anatomical position or the spatial coordinate system described above. Local anatomical landmarks should be incorporated in the terminology to describe direction of flexion. For example, describe the wrist as moved in "radial flexion" instead of in "abduction." Such detailed description of hand and finger motions requires further development.

In the case of rotation and torsion, there would be many more occasions to reference the action to the axis of a control, such as a rotary selector or dial knob. In such cases, the usual engineering terminology for positive and negative rotation (also called right and left) would be directly applicable.

A proposed standard graphic presentation system for body segment orientation description has been devised for communication of the new concept. A sample presentation is shown in Figure 3-21*a*. The graphic scheme emphasizes description of *rotational* (rather than translational) movement with respect to a segment of a protractor scale. The scale starts from the 0° reference direction and extends in the increasing (positive) sense of the angular scale, to the end point of the movement, whether or not the actual movement is positive. The actual direction of movement is shown with an arrow symbol placed peripherally parallel to the scale of degrees.

Starting positions and ending positions are indicated by outlined figures, the latter by a shaded outline of the limb segment. Orientation of the segment at the limit of movement is depicted by an arrow, representing the principal director links, using the conventions in Figure 3-18. An open circle is placed over the scale of degrees at the point of intersection of the scale and an extension of the link arrow. Within this circle may be placed a code number for the measurement, which relates to a tabulated set of results or a specification

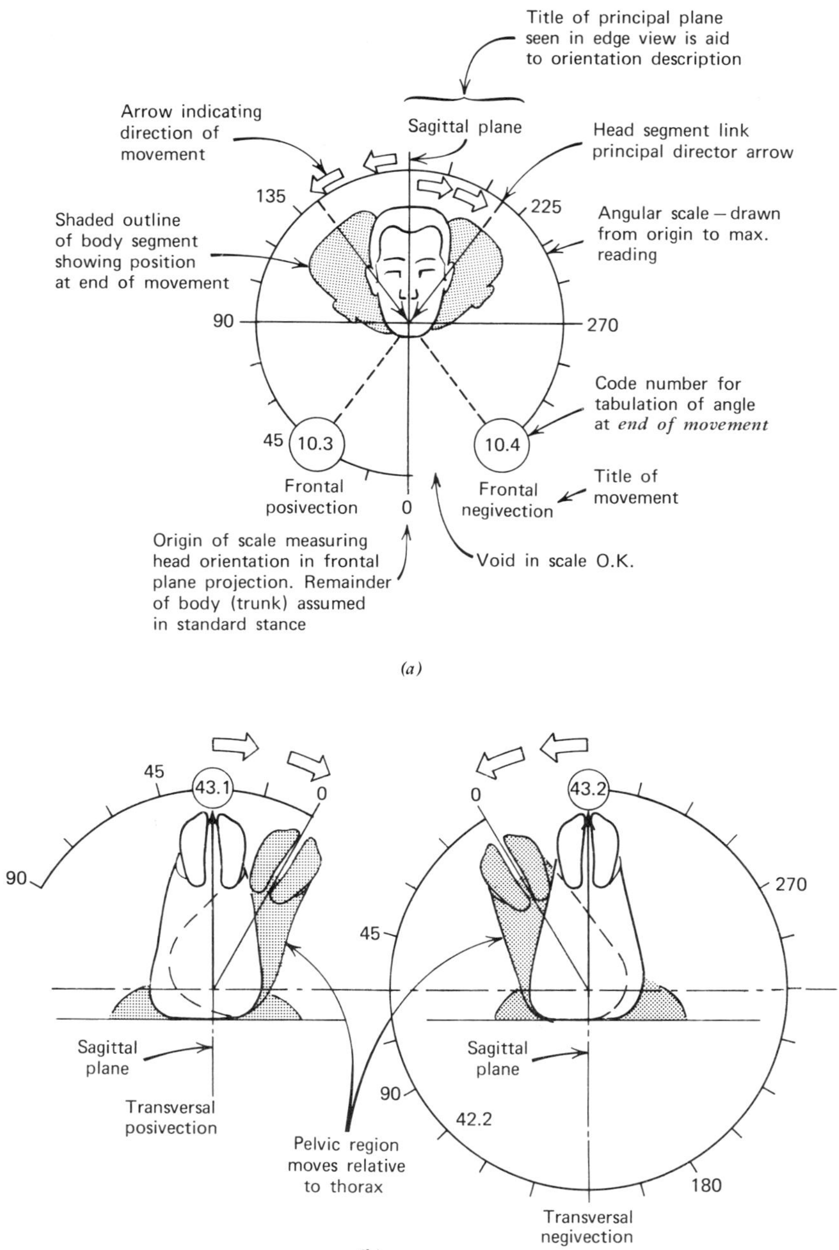

Figure 3-21. Proposed standard graphic description technique for movements. (*a*) Head mobility. (*b*) Trunk-torso mobility.

Table 3-6. Standard Movements for Space Suit Mobility Measurement[a]

Number	Type of Motion (engineering anthropometry and classic terminology)[f]	Instruments[b] and Fixtures
1.	Head saginvection—sagevection (Neck flexion—extension)	Flexometer[c] Table vertical[d]
2.	Head frontal posivection—negivection (Neck lateral flexion left—right)	Flexometer Table vertical
3.	Hand frontinvection—frontevection (Forearm supination—pronation)	Flexometer Table vertical Upper arm support
4.	Hand frontinvection—frontevection (Wrist palmar flexion—dorsiflexion)	Flexometer Table vertical Forearm support
5.	Leg frontevection—frontinvection (Hip abduction—adduction)	Flexometer (2 Required) Table vertical
6.	Upper leg (thigh) sagevection—saginvection (knee may be bent) (Hip flexion—extension)	Flexometer Table vertical
7.	Arm sagevection—saginvection (Shoulder flexion—extension)	Bubble level goniometer[e] Table vertical
8.	Arm frontevection—frontinvection (Shoulder abduction—adduction)	Flexometer Table vertical
9.	Head transversal positrotation—negrotation (Neck rotation right—left)	Flexometer Table horizontal
10.	Forearm saginvection—sagevection or humeral (upper arm saginrotation—sagerotation) (Shoulder rotation inward—outward)	Flexometer Table horizontal Upper arm support
11.	Forearm transinvection—transevection (projected—movement in F:45°) Right arm plane of elbow flexion—extension (terminology equivalent in both systems)	Flexometer Table horizontal Upper arm support
12.	Wrist radial flexion—ulnar flexion (terminology equivalent in both systems. Same plane of movement of hand as in 11, above)	Flexometer Table horizontal Forearm support
13.	Foot transerotation—transinrotation (leg in anatomical position) (Hip rotation outward—inward)	Flexometer Table horizontal Lower leg support
14.	Foot sagevection—saginvection (Ankle flexion—extension)	Flexometer Table horizontal Lower leg support

Table 3–6. (Continued)

Number	Type of Motion (engineering anthropometry and classic terminology)[f]	Instruments[b] and Fixtures
15.	Thorax (chest) transerotation—transinrotation (Trunk rotation—right, left)	Flexometer Table horizontal
16.	Upper arm transinvection—transevection (Shoulder horizontal adduction—abduction)	Flexometer Table horizontal
17.	Lower leg saginvection—sagevection (Knee flexion—extension and hyperextension)	Flexometer Table horizontal Upper leg support
18.	Toe sagevection Toe dorsiflexion	Flexometer Table foot stand and use as balance support
19.	Chest (thorax) sagevection—saginvection (Trunk flexion—extension)	Flexometer (2 required)
20.	Chest frontal negivection—posivection (Trunk lateral flexion—left, right)	Flexometer (2 required)

[a] Based on use of gravitational direction-indicating instruments. Details under development, based on work of Mobility Notation Standardization Committee composed of personnel from companies under contract to National Aeronautics and Space Administration. (see Roebuck, 1968). Adapted from Grumman Aerospace Corporation report by Schwartz and Visconti (1965).

[b] Proposed for gravitational direction-indicating instrument methods by Mobility Notation Development Committee (see Roebuck, 1968) and following sections of this text.

[c] Trademark. See Leighton (1955).

[d] Mobility Measuring Table—original designed by Hamilton Standard Div. of United Aircraft (see Section 3.4.5).

[e] Required by concurrent rotation of upper arm as it is raised above 90°. Flexometer would no longer be parallel to sagittal plane.

[f] See Appendix A, parts 2 and 3, for terminology definitions.

requirement; or, an actual magnitude (in degrees) may be appropriate. It must be remembered that this presentation, by definition, is *schematic,* not an actual depiction of motion in all cases, because other link motions may well be involved, causing *translation* in addition to the simple rotation intended to be pictured in this graphical presentation. One may select a "fixed-scale" or "fixed-body" system of reference. The illustration shown in Figure 3-21*a* could be either, since movement is referred to the trunk/pelvis region. However, in some measurements it is easier to fix a portion of the body, such as the thorax, and move the pelvic region, to which the reference axes are considered as fixed. To indicate this, as a measurement technique, one may depict a fixed trunk and a scale reorientation following the pelvic movement in space, as in Figure 3-21*b*.

Consistent use of such scales, reference axes, planes, and vectorial representation of links will reduce uncertainty and encourage consistency and rigor in description of human body movements, thus leading to more accurate design data and clear specifications for mobility requirements.

Elementary Movement Standardization

Elementary movements of the nude subject have been described by a variety of investigators. Among the more significant are Sinelnikoff and Grigorowitsch (1931), Glanville and Kreezer (1937), Gilliland (1921), Leighton, (1955, 1956, 1957, 1960, 1964) and Dempster (1955a).

Following these leads, a series of 20 standard movements appropriate for work space design and space-suit mobility were described by Schwartz and Visconti (1965). They are listed in Table 3-6.

3.4.2 Angular Mobility Measurement Techniques (Goniometry)

Angular movement measurement involves characteristics analogous to the measurement of linear dimensions. Contact methods and indirect methods are both used, and photographic methods provide a versatility for deriving a variety of types of information, including centers of rotation, and range of movement envelopes. As before, contact methods will be first discussed.

Instruments for measuring joint angular movement or positions are called *goniometers*. Although subject to inherent errors due to the complexity of human body joint mechanisms, joint goniometry provides a potentially versatile and powerful tool for analysis for many engineering problems.

An extensive early literature on joint goniometry has included Clark (1920), Rosen (1922), Wiechec and Krusen (1939), Moore (1949a), Hellebrandt, Duvall and Moore (1949), Glanville and Kreezer (1937), Sinelnikoff and Grigorowitsch (1931), and Gilliland (1921). More recently Leighton (1942, 1955, 1957, 1960, 1964), Karpovich and Wilklow (1959), Karpovich, Herden, and Asa (1960), Karpovich (1960), and Tipton and Karpovich (1964) have contributed through development of new goniometry and procedures.

Leighton Flexometer. For measuring angles of movement without regard to shifting to joint centers, Leighton's flexometer (1955) has been found quite useful for the elementary movements. With this device, all angles are measured with reference to the direction of gravitational attraction. Once the standard reference position is identified, the instrument is attached parallel to the plane in which the angle of movement is to be measured. The scale is then zeroed and locked. The movement from zero is then measured by unlocking the dial (Figure 3-22). Since the scale and dial are independently controlled, either can be used as a reference to the limb or to gravity.

Leighton's instrument was originally developed for measuring agility of athletes. However, it has proved extremely useful in measuring mobility of men clothed in pressurized and unpressurized space suits (Roebuck 1968). The attachment strap can be wrapped around a suit arm, leg, helmet, or trunk section as well as on the nude body. Also, it is adaptable to attachment to rods on handles with a sturdy gummed tape or clamp system. A significant drawback in usage is the lack of damping in the dial and scale motion. One must wait several seconds for oscillating movement to subside, or take the mean of the extremes of movement as the reading.

Bubble Level Goniometer. Leighton's flexometer will not work where the measurement must be made in a horizontal plane. Also, in some areas there is not enough room to fasten the flexometer. As a means of overcoming some of these problems, the simple goniometer shown in Figure 3-23 has been developed. This device is used by visually aligning the two arms with appro-

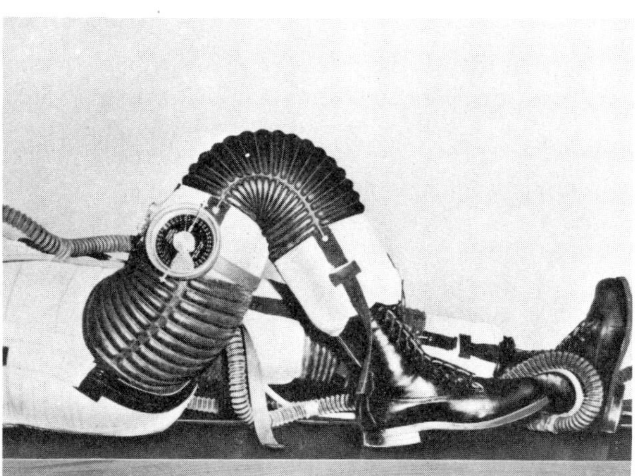

Figure 3-22. Flexometer for elementary movement measurements. (Roebuck, 1968. Photo courtesy Space Division, Rockwell International Corporation.)

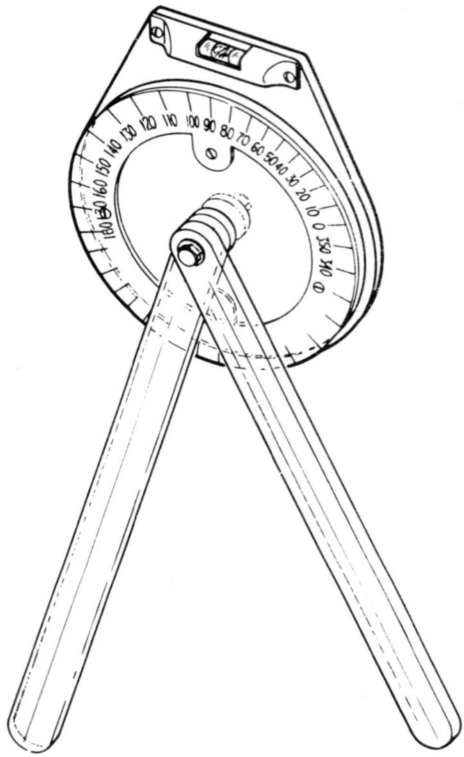

Figure 3-23. Bubble level goniometer for space suit mobility measurements (Roebuck, 1968).

priate reference lines on the structure or man or suit. It also contains a bubble level that can be set to any desired reference angle (Roebuck, 1968).

Electrogoniometer. In the category of electromechanical devices, a contact method of measuring angular movement which offers the advantage of continuous, direct, permanent recording of angles as a function of time was pioneered by Karpovich and Wilklow (1959). Several units are required to sense, amplify, and calibrate the signal. These include the electrogoniometer instrument itself (abbreviated elgon), calibration board, meter unit or control panel, and a recorder.

An elgon is very similar to the simple goniometer described previously, except that a linear, variable resistor potentiometer replaces the protractor. In use, the elgon is attached to the body or suit segments on each side of a joint by means of tapes and straps (Figure 3-24). The potentiometer is normally connected by wires with the meter unit, which includes a microammeter panel meter, batteries, balancing and gain controls and reversing switch. Current is sent through the potentiometer. The current is changed proportionately to the change in angle of the elgon arms as the joint moves. The affected current provides the input to the paper tape recorder which, when suitably calibrated, provides a record of movement in degrees. The record thus provides data from which one can calculate range, amplitude, angular velocity and angular acceleration, and can determine sequence of movement.

The elgon is limited to measurement of joint action in one plane and thus cannot provide direct measurement of apparent or projected movement on other planes. [Detailed instructions, materials list, and costs for an instruction model electrogoniometer are described by Adrian (1968).]

Figure 3-24. Elbow, wrist elgons on right arm, and index finger and forearm elgons on left. (Courtesy of M. J. Adrian and *Kinesiology Review, 1968.*)

In using the elgon, care must be exercised to locate the center of rotation as close as possible to the average center of rotation of the joint. Since instantaneous joint centers shift about during joint movement, the elgon cannot measure exact angle of position at all points along the motion.

Gyrocompass. Another approach to angular movement measurement which is independent of the instantaneous center of rotation and of gravity involves use of a gyrocompass. Theoretically, a magnetic compass device could also be used, especially for horizontal motion. However, most laboratory situations involve masses of metal, wiring, and so forth, in the vicinity, which may produce uneven magnetic fields.

The commonly available gyrocompass is an aircraft instrument, with a dial meter and a vacuum line hose attach point. A source of vacuum (low pressure tank or suction pump) is required. The size and mass of the gyrocompass may be an obstacle to some types of body movement measurements. It is best suited for larger limb segment motions, where it is strapped onto the limb in much the same way as the Leighton flexometer.

3.4.3 Determination of Joint Centers of Rotation

Estimates of joint centers of rotation can be obtained by detailed anatomical analysis of cadaver joints, x-radiography, or indirect photographic measurements of instantaneous centers during motion studies. The latter two techniques also generally provide data on the angular position in space and range of joint motion.

Articular Surface Measurements. Dempster (1955a) performed a series of measurements of the radius of curvature of joints using cadaver material. Although the techniques used are interesting from a mechanical engineering viewpoint, they yield little of direct use on the living human being, except to establish that instantaneous centers move about considerably as the joint is flexed and extended.

Estimation by Apparent Movement of Markers. More successful methods employed by Dempster (1955a) involved photography and x-rays for recording movement of the limbs on living subjects to whom various markers had been applied. The photographic technique involved fixing one limb and moving the other side of the joint to its limits, with an open lens and a speed lamp flash at each limiting condition providing the controlled exposure. The process requires a darkened room, black background, and sometimes auxiliary contrasting point or line markings. Frames of the strip of negatives were projected as enlarged images and the best estimates of the link lines connecting joint centers were ruled on paper. Angles were then simply measured to the nearest degree. Similar methods have been reported by Moore (1949a,b) and

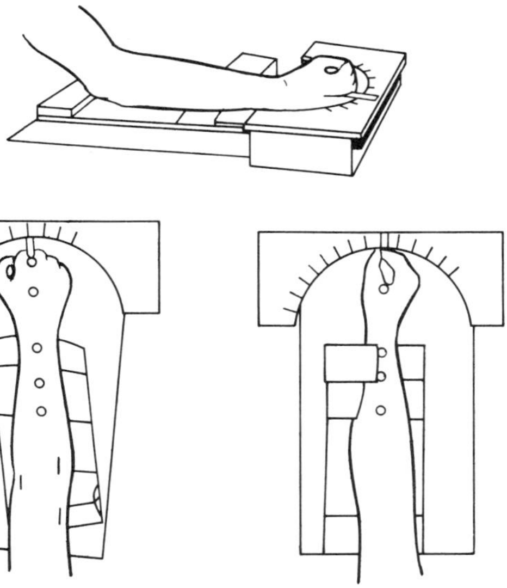

Figure 3-25. Special method for determining wrist centers (after Dempster, 1955a).

by Hellebrandt, Duvall, and Moore (1949). Advanced methods of film data reduction are available today that would facilitate the process.

The wrist movement measurements employed x-ray exposures by an angiocardiograph machine, lead shot taped to the skin, and a support jig of wood, shown in Figure 3-25. Records of successive positions were superimposed and arcs of movement derived, from which instantaneous centers of joint motion were determined.

3.4.4 Reference Plane Definition—Pelvis and Thorax

In order to measure the changing position of the pelvis and thorax due to different postural changes, Dempster (1955a) contrived two guides, or harnesses, to place on the subject when the photographs were to be taken.

The pelvic guide (Figure 3-26) consisted of a narrow metal plate with a plane of plastic set perpendicular at its middle. At the free end of the plastic plane, a rod covered with light-reflecting tape was set in place to provide a line of reference in the photographs. Three pillars, which could be adjusted in height, provided supports for the metal plate and its reference gear. One pillar (*C*) in the middle of the plate fit over the pubic bones at the symphysis, and the others (*A* and *B*) fit over the anterior-superior spines of the right and left ilia. The positions of each pillar could be moved sidewise and set anew to allow for any pelvic size.

To keep the pelvic guide in contact with the three pelvic landmarks, a belt

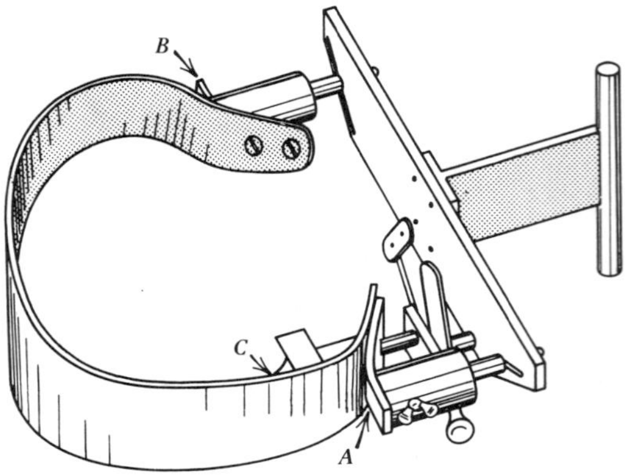

Figure 3-26. Pelvic guide (after Dempster, 1955a).

was cut from $\frac{3}{16}$-in. sheet lead. Each man was provided with an individual form-fitting belt, and the foot pillars of the guide were screwed into lugs placed on the belt at points corresponding with the locations of the anterior-superior spines of the ilia. The belt was fashioned after a paper pattern had been molded to the subject's form. Strips of heavy, gummed, manila paper (such as one uses for sealing packages for mailing) were pasted on the subject's skin to a thickness of three or four layers, so that the papers overlaid and girdled the upper pelvic bony landmarks. On drying and hardening, the paper was trimmed so that it in no way interfered with trunk or lower limb movements. Then it was removed to provide a pattern for the cutting of the sheet lead.

The lead belts fit snugly over the upper pelvis with the guide against the three landmarks; there appeared to be virtually no shifting of the belt with changes in posture. After the belt and guide were fitted to a subject, the guide

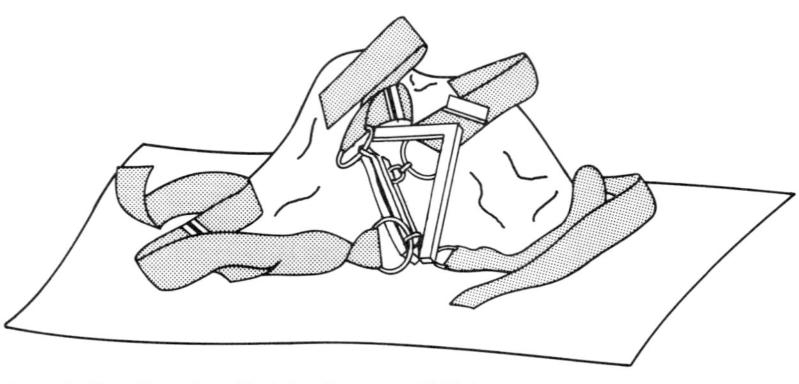

Figure 3-27. Thoracic guide (after Dempster, 1955a).

plate was tilted as needed by means of the adjustments until the light-reflecting reference line lay vertical when the subject stood squarely on both feet. Any tilting of the pelvis associated with the seated posture was thus indicated by an angulation of the reference line.

Thoracic tilting was measured by another type of guide (Figure 3-27). This consisted of a metal plate shaped to fit against the sternal manubrium. The metal had a perpendicular, sagittally directed, 30° triangle of clear plastic attached. To serve as reference lines, the free borders of the plastic plane were marked with light-reflecting tape. The manubrial guide was strapped to the subject with elastic rubber strips passing behind the neck and around the chest, so that it fit firmly on the manubrial plane uninfluenced by any shoulder girdle and trunk movements. The guide was not adjustable, so that its initial angulation was determined for the standing posture, then deviations from this position determined in other postures.

Figure 3-28. Hamilton standard measuring table. (Roebuck, 1968.)

The pelvic and manubrial angles were determined for each posture from photographic negatives. The images were enlarged and guide angulations were measured by protractor relative to a true vertical within the field of view.

3.4.5 Mobility Measurement Table

A significant concern of these mobility measurement techniques is the prediction of reach from specified supporting surfaces. To this end, considerable effort is justified to define the reference supporting surface carefully and to assure wherever possible that one is actually measuring a specific limb angle from a specific joint and not some other combination of joints and limbs. A special measuring table shown in Figure 3-28 has been designed by the Hamilton Standard Division of United Aircraft to provide a standard means for supporting the body, when applying the space suit mobility measurement techniques developed by the NASA-Apollo aerospace engineering committee described above (Roebuck, 1968). This table can be tilted from a vertical position to a horizontal position and several parts can be removed to permit specific limb movements.

There is a height adjustment on the platform used for standing measurements, so that the subject can be properly centered on the central panel which provides shoulder strap, crotch strap, and cross-abdomen straps for stabilizing the trunk. The base framework provides casters for in-plant relocation with minimum difficulty.

3.5 DYNAMIC MEASUREMENT OF POSITION IN SPACE

Drillis (1959) and Ayoub (1972) have well summarized the problems and practices of the dynamic recording and measurement of human movement.*

The requirements for an exact and objective method of recording movements are as follows:

1. Proper precision and constant relationship to the particular dimension chosen.
2. Noninterference with performance of subject.
3. Sensitivity and range sufficient to pick up and record the changes of position of the joints and limbs under study.
4. Ease of interpretation.

Five recording systems are possible: mechanical (transmission by rods, levers, or pulleys), pneumatic (transmission by a change in air pressure), optical (transmission by light rays or x-rays), electrical (transmission by change in voltage or current), and sonic (transmission by sound waves). All are useful in certain applications.

* Giedion (1948) also gives an interesting historical background on this subject.

3.5.1 Mechanical Recording of Range of Movement

Dempster (1955a) used a mechanical technique for determination of the space ahead of the seat into which the foot could be positioned. The basic procedure was simply that the foot was moved at floor level to its limits in all directions. A tracing of the maximum circuit was recorded. Then the foot was similarly moved at different horizontal levels, 3 in., 6 in., and so forth above the floor and movement was recorded for each level. When summated, the pattern of movement could be visualized in the three dimensions of space. A wooden replica of a standard aircraft seat (pilot cockpit) provided a fixed reference for foot movements. The seat could be raised or lowered to different heights relative to a low reference platform.

The platform on which the foot rested consisted of a plate that slid over the floor on four ball-type casters. The base plate was rigged to two link systems. Both linkages were pivoted on a fixed point. One link mechanism consisted of a drafting machine-type of linkage that kept the foot continuously oriented straight forward in a sagittal plane. The other linkage was a 1:5 pantograph that traced a reduced outline of the foot excursion.

3.5.2 Electromechanical Recording of Movement

Swearingen et al. (1962) used a method of recording the motion of a point on the top of a head which involved a mechanical framework and grid for an electrical pickup. His electromechanical apparatus consisted of a lightweight vertical rectangular carriage mounted on rollers and tracks, free to move fore and aft along a platform. This vertical rectangle lay in the frontal plane of the subject, and its two uprights served as tracks for a horizontal bar that was restricted to move vertically only. A flying helmet was secured to the center of this bar in such a manner as to locate the pivot point less than ¼ in. from the apex of the head. Each component (horizontal and vertical) of this equipment carried a wire spring switch to make contact with wires spaced at 1-in. intervals and activate a writing needle on a moving tape. Thus, the abscissas and ordinates of the curve of forward motion of the head were directly recorded.

3.5.3 Photographic Recording of Movements

Four basic methods are used:

1. Still photographs—long exposure.
2. Interrupted light photography (chronophotography).
3. Gliding cyclograms.
4. Motion pictures.

Variations of these methods are also used in x-ray recording of internal movements (Weis, et al., 1967; Weis and Mohr, 1967).

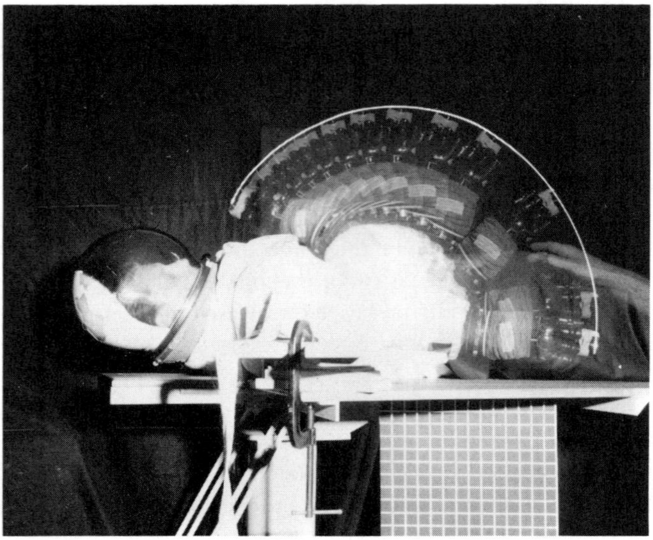

Figure 3-29. Continuous point light source combined with multiple exposure photography. (Courtesy of Space Division, Rockwell International Corporation.)

Still Photography

Still photography, using a long exposure, is primarily useful for obtaining envelopes of movement or tracing pathways of a point on the body. To avoid washing out the image, a black room and darkly clothed subject are used. A point source of light or a very thin line of light (such as a neon tube) is attached to the subject to trace the image of the movement in space. In Figure 3-29 the fingertip motion envelope was recorded by this technique. Accelerations and velocities can be determined by controlled blinking off and on of the moving point light source. A brief flash of light at the beginning and end of the exposure of the movement helps in orienting the subject movements to his background and in interpreting the record. Small battery-powered lamps are most readily adapted to the continuous use of the interrupted point light source on the subject. A grid of known scale, oriented in the plane of motion provides for later graphical analysis.

Interrupted Light Photography

For nonrepetitive activity such as a throw or single forearm contraction, or for activity such as walking, which is progressing along a linear axis, a constant illumination source that is interrupted by a slotted rotating disk can be used. The advantage of this technique is that a complex record can be obtained on one film frame. Reduction of data is greatly simplified, since the measures of vertical and horizontal displacement are all taken directly from a single set of reference axes. The time intervals may be well controlled, by taking advantage of the mass of the rotating disk, which helps to reduce small variations in speed, and a synchronous motor drive, which has inherent speed stability.

This technique is very useful for measuring work area envelopes, limb position and joint angle changes, velocities, and accelerations. In addition to the continuous point light source for fingertip reach envelope recording, Figure 3-29 provides an example of electronic frequency-controlled stroboscopic light exposures to show arm positions for a pressure-suited subject. Figure 3-30 is an example of a longer term multiple exposure study of gross motion of seated subjects. In each case, the usual problems of scale markings, parallax, and magnification errors inherent in photography must be controlled.

Pearson, McGinley, and Butzel (1963) describe a typical example of kinematic measurments of the upper extremity in sagittal planar motion, using photographs of a sequence of exposures taken at constant time intervals. The resulting multiple exposure picture recorded the upper arm and forearm in several positions, defined by reflective tape. To minimize recording of skin movement relative to the arm axes, the tape was attached to the posterior surface of the arm. To locate the arm axis for subsequent analyses, a template was made showing the posterior surface and axial relation. The analysis was performed by projecting the film onto a screen. This technique yielded stick diagrams similar to those shown in Figure 3-31.

Figure 3-30. Two subjects performing comparable desk activities. Example of multiple-exposure photographic record of motion to develop envelopes (Dempster, 1955b).

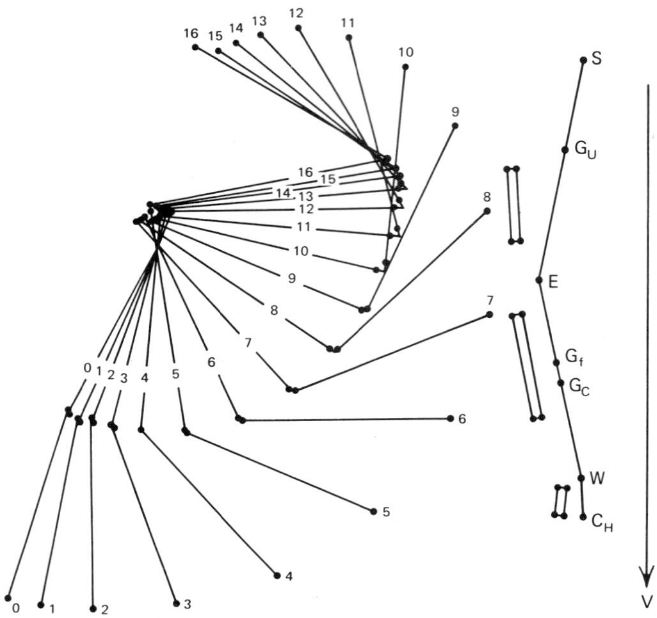

Figure 3-31. Stick diagram of arm motion (Pearson, McGinley, and Butzel, 1963).

Gliding Cyclograms

When the motion to be recorded is repetitive, or overlapping in a limited space, the interrupted light method cannot be readily applied, for the pattern of points cannot be distinguished as to occurrence in time. To overcome this difficulty, Bernstein* and slightly later Drillis* independently developed the gliding cyclogram method which is now seldom used. It is similar to the interrupted light method, except that here the film is transported across the field at a constant rate. If, in a repetitive motion, a point on the moving body is returned to its initial position, the image on the cyclogram in the initial and succeeding instances will be displaced on the film by the distance the film has been transported in the elapsed time interval. The distance the film is transported in an interval of time must always be subtracted from the measured horizontal displacement of a point. The advantage is that it greatly increases the sensitivity and range of motion studies, and it is especially useful in recording the motion of arm activities, many of which are repetitive and overlapping.

* Cited by Drillis (1959).

Several methods of recording three-dimensional aspects of movements can be used:

1. Three synchronized motion picture cameras, one for each of the reference planes of motion (University of California, Berkeley; Eberhart and Inman, 1947).
2. Two still cameras or synchronized motion picture cameras with parallel optical axes (similar to the stereophotogrammetry technique of Hertzberg Dupertuis, and Emanuel, 1957; and of Bullock and Harley, 1972).
3. Two cameras or gliding cyclographs with a 90° angle between the crossing optical axes as used by Drillis (1930b) or one camera and a 45° mirror.
4. One camera with suitably arranged mirrors.

The special problem at hand, and the equipment available, determine which of these (or other) methods will be used.

Motion Picture Photography

Motion pictures are not very suitable for some types of simple measurements because, in the data reduction process, each frame must be oriented in relationship to two of the three major coordinate axes, which introduce possible sources of error. Also, the film transport mechanism does not always respond at the same rate, so that the time intervals between consecutive frames vary significantly and contribute to errors of measurement. The use of an electrical clock in the field of view for the determination of consecutive time intervals increases accuracy but also increases the data reduction time.

However, motion pictures have been successfully applied in a wide variety of types of motion analysis (Eberhart and Inman, 1947; Barnes, 1949). For example, Taylor and Blaschke (1951) devised a unique method for kinematic analysis of the motions of the shoulder, arm, and hand complex using motion picture recordings. They listed six steps:

1. Measurement of the experimental subject.
2. Fitting of the subject with visual landmarks.
3. Cinematography of the subject performing the activities under study.
4. Obtaining the Cartesian earth coordinates of the visual landmarks from selected frames of the developed film, and correcting these coordinates for parallax.
5. Analysis of the coordinate data to yield the axes and angles of the idealized kinematic system.
6. From serial frames, obtaining angular velocities and accelerations of the members of the kinematic system.

The article is a useful basic presentation of technique and contains helpful graphics of the subject markings and the results which are meaningful to engineering analysis.

3.5.4 Sonic Technique

Displacements, velocities, and accelerations in three dimensions are measurable by a system developed by Goldman and Nadler (1956). The system is called Unopar (Universal Operator Performance Analyzer). It consists of a small cylindrical emitter that is strapped to the test subject (e.g., his wrist), an oscillator, three microphones, and various recording instruments. Ultrasonic waves generated by the oscillator and broadcast by the emitter are picked up by the microphones. At each microphone, the frequency received

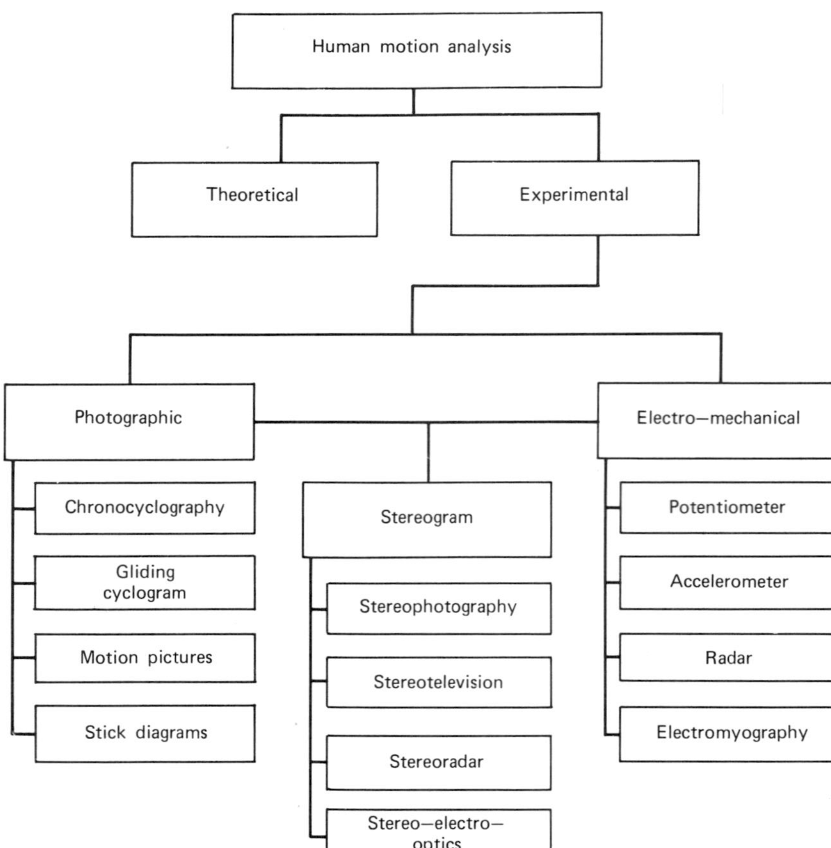

Figure 3-32. Techniques of motion analysis (Ayoub, 1972).

will vary from the emitted frequency according to the Doppler effect. Hence, change in location of the emitter (and the body member to which it is attached) can be calculated from the changes in the received frequency. Although some practical difficulties had to be overcome, this technique was found to be useful in recording body movements in such noisy environments as factories.

3.5.5 The Most Promising Techniques Currently Available

Ayoub (1972) discussed most of the methods to record and analyze human motion in three-dimensional space, as known from the literature. Figure 3-32 depicts his breakdown of applicable techniques. He tried, in his laboratory, the accelerometer system, the potentiometric technique, and stereophotogrammetry. His conclusion is that, although each method has its own advantages, stereophotogrammetry has the greatest potential. This assessment is supported by Bullock and Harley (1972) who were able to develop a stereophoto system that fulfills the requirements of accuracy, noninterference with the task, simple data recording, and quick data reduction. However, special requirements or circumstances may well lead to the selection of another system for a given experiment.

IV
MEASUREMENT OF MUSCULAR STRENGTH CAPABILITIES

4.1 INTRODUCTION

Engineering anthropometry has a unique interest in muscular force measurements as compared to other fields. In classical anthropological studies, force measurements were used in an attempt to characterize and compare populations. The measurements selected have been relatively few and as simple as possible. Grip strength is a typical example. Medical anthropometry has somewhat broader interests that include detection of disease and measurement of rates of improvement of specific muscular capabilities. Engineering applications, however, deal with the capability to operate specific controls, to lift equipment, to perform useful work, and to stress structures. The range of applications is broad and so is the need for data to support these applications. Structural "strength" of muscles (or of other components of the human body) are not discussed in this text, although it is a valid engineering concern in some applications. This section first presents definitions needed to understand the concepts and techniques. A list of variables to be considered and descriptions of typical apparatus needed for measurements are then presented.

As compared to the anthropometric dimensions, biomechanical strength data typically have a much greater variability or spread between individuals. Strength is significantly affected by many more conditions of both the mental and physiological state of the subject, which must be taken into account in planning surveys of human force exertion capability. This section discusses several of these factors, presents recommended procedures to deal with them, and provides supporting examples.

4.2 DEFINITION AND EXERTION OF STRENGTH

Many published studies on human muscular strength capabilities suffer from one or several of the following shortcomings:

- Failure to define terms, or the inappropriate or imprecise use of terminology.

- Insufficient consideration of physiological, biomechanical, and psychological aspects involved.
- Use of inadequate instrumentation.
- Failure to report clearly experimental procedures and statistical analyses.

Surprisingly enough, "strength" or the capability to exert force on an outside object has, until a short time ago, not been defined in a generally accepted form. Kroemer (1970b) proposed a definition that will be used throughout the following text: *static strength is the maximal force muscles can exert isometrically in a single voluntary effort.* Strength has vector quality and must therefore be described in direction, magnitude, and location relative to the body of the operator. Strength is measured as the external static effect of internal isometric muscle efforts, modified by the mechanical advantages of the body members involved. Dimensions of strength are *force* or *torque* × *time*, that is, impulse over a given time, or *force* or *torque* alone if the effort is exerted instantaneously or during a very short period of time, such as a few seconds.

As defined, strength is exerted "isometrically," or "statically," indicating that during the contraction period the length of the muscles involved is kept constant and, therefore, attached body segments remain motionless. Without motion, all acting forces must be in balance. Neither the terms "isometric" nor "static" gives information about the magnitude or steadiness of muscle tension.

"Isotonic" may be the most misused term in strength testing. It means "constant (muscle) tension." Although theoretically not limited to this combination, an isotonic effort is normally found combined with an isometric force exertion, as in holding a weight motionless. Muscles are *not* strained isotonically when moving a body segment against a constant resistance; during the motion, the tension of the involved muscles changes with their changing lengths and with the changing mechanical advantages. "Dynamic" is really the appropriate term.

Exertion of muscular strength requires that the actively involved muscles be tensed (contracted). For this purpose, chemical energy must be converted into mechanical energy at the muscles. During this process, oxygen is consumed and heat, carbon dioxide, as well as other metabolites (such as lactic acid) are produced. Sufficient blood flow through the muscles (to supply them with oxygen and to remove heat and metabolites) is necessary to maintain the process of energy conversion. Such blood flow can be facilitated by the pumping action of dynamic work (as in turning a crank) but can be largely or completely cut off in strong and longer-lasting static efforts (as in holding a load) during which the capillaries (connecting the arteries with the veins) can be compressed and occluded.

These few remarks (for further information see typical references such as

Lehmann, 1961, 1962; de Vries, 1966; Hoyle, 1970; Astrand and Rodahl, 1970) should indicate that there is a significant physiological difference between static and dynamic exertion of muscular force; and that static (isometric) efforts can be extremely fatiguing.

The term "endurance" signifies man's ability to continue to work or, in the static case, to exert force. It is common experience that small forces can be exerted over long periods of time while maximal efforts have to be terminated soon because of fatigue or exhaustion. Monod (1956), Rohmert (1960), Molbech (1963), and Caldwell (1961, 1963) showed that a nonlinear relationship exists between the fraction of strength required and length of time during which it can be maintained. Figure 4-1 schematically shows this relation. If less than about 15% of total strength is required, such a force can be maintained over periods of time "indefinitely" longer than ten minutes. With increasing force requirements, the endurance time decreases quickly; "maximal strength" can be maintained for only a few seconds.

Generally, a muscle connects two body segments rotatable about a common joint. If the muscle is under tension, it applies torque to each segment. The magnitude of torque depends on the amount of internal muscle force, on the distance between the joint and the location of the muscle or tendon attachment to the bone, that is, the lever arm, and on the pull angle between the vector of muscle force and the limb. Usually, neither pull angle nor lever arm are known, and for practical purposes, the muscle is inaccessible. Therefore, the magnitude of internally developed muscle force cannot easily be measured directly.

However, for engineering purposes the force applied to an outside object is

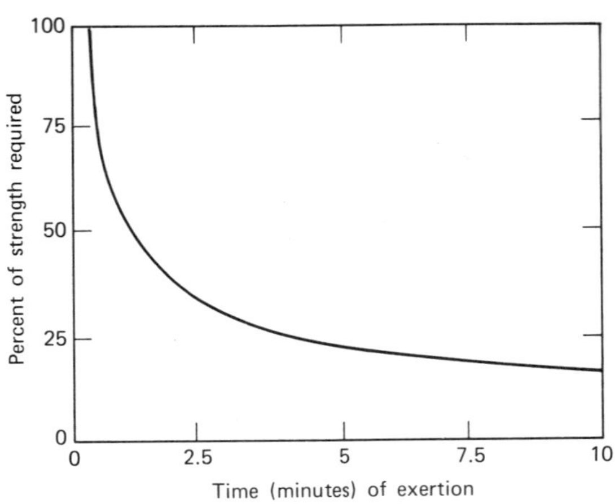

Figure 4-1. Endurance time as a function of strength requirement (Kroemer, 1970b).

of primary interest. Since this force depends on the inherent strength of the muscles as well as on the prevailing mechanical advantages, the location of the force-measuring device must be specified with respect to the body, usually to the next joint, to make the measurement meaningful.

Human muscular strength is, for engineering purposes, expressed as the linear, or translational, force exerted at the interface with the measuring device in terms of a vector (magnitude and direction). Torque measurements (force multiplied by the prevailing lever arm) or pressure measurements (force evenly distributed over a known surface area) can be conceived as modified assessments of linear force.

By definition, strength data refer to maximal static efforts only. The relevance of such maximal data to submaximal, optimal, reasonable conditions is discussed in Chapter VI Section 6.12.

Of major importance for the experimental determination as well as for the engineering application of strength data is the fact that strength scores, even when exerted by the same subjects, are only weakly correlated with each other. Thordsen et al. (1972) and Laubach et al. (1972) report on strength data measured on 51 male subjects who were asked to exert their maximal strengths in 44 different exertions. Of the 768 intercorrelations among the 44 exertions, only 13 had coefficients of .71 or higher (i.e., at least 50% of variance of the predicted value would be accounted for by the primary variable). The authors conclude that, if data are desired on strength scores other than previously measured, such information usually has to be gathered experimentally rather than computed, for example, by regression analysis.

4.3 PROBLEMS OF DATA PRESENTATION AND TYPES OF MEASUREMENTS

One of the more difficult problems in the assessment and application of human strength data is the presentation of data. This point is emphasized here because of its impact on planning for types of measurement to be taken. Forces important to design engineering may be exerted by an operator in any direction at any point in space reachable by him. Furthermore, for any given population, each of these force vectors has a statistical variability in magnitude and direction. More complex is the problem of describing the force/torque data over a specified pathway for a control lever actuation or over a complete specified surface of a control-display panel. In addition, force exertion depends on a variety of other variables, such as body position, clothing, environmental conditions, and motivation. For strength experiments, a large number of the variables must be kept under control (i.e., often constant) and their status must be clearly specified in the protocol or final report. The failure to specify the experimental conditions has caused the results of many studies to be of questionable validity and generality.

4.3.1 Checklist for Strength Measurement

The following checklist (Table 4-1), adapted from Kroemer and Howard (1970a), summarizes the variables to be used in planning research and serves to insure that the most important factors in strength testing are considered and reported adequately: how force is measured; where force is applied; what body parts are mainly involved and what posture is employed; how the subject is instructed to exert force; what role motivational factors play; and what index is selected to rate the subject's performance. There are interactions among apparatus/subject/experimenter/environment, causing some redundancies in the list. For example, the subject's body posture as well as the magnitude of exertible force are affected by the support (reaction force) available to him. Such cross references are useful since they point out the multiple effects of a single factor.

The following discussion presents examples of previously used techniques that may aid in the planning and data collection procedures. The discussion will first consider instrumentation, then procedures, test scheduling, and finally selection of subjects.

4.4 MEASUREMENT OF FORCES

In each individual laboratory situation, resources may dictate selection of one of the several primary modes of transducing muscular capacity into a measurable quantity. The following section is therefore divided into descriptions of four types of measuring devices: mechanical, hydraulic, pneumatic, and electrical.

The electrical instruments generally are basically mechanical, hydraulic, or pneumatic devices, the output of which is converted into an electric signal proportional to the strain induced to the device by force application.

Reports by Hunsicker (1955) and Hunsicker and Donnelly (1955) give an excellent overview of strength measurement device development up to the early 1950s and are recommended to the reader interested in historical background.

4.4.1 Mechanical Devices

The Frenchman Regnier is generally credited with developing the first practical spring dynamometer* in or about 1803, although similar devices must have been in use before that date (Hunsicker and Donnelly, 1955; Pangle

* Though the term "dynamometer" should be used only in connection with dynamic measurements, it is used in this text also for static assessment, in accordance with the common usage in the literature.

Table 4-1. Variables Affecting Muscular Strength Measurements

---

The following list has been compiled for force measurements. It can easily be adapted to tests of torque, work, and the like.

A. Measuring Device

1. General identification:
   a. function
   b. model, manufacturer
   c. last calibration
2. Attachment of measuring device to the subject
3. Output-Readout
   a. digital/analog
   b. units read
4. Other (specify)

B. Description of the Force Vector

1. Coordinates of the point of force application in space and relative to subject
2. Direction of force application
3. Other (specify)

C. Subject(s)

1. Drawn from what population
2. Anthropometric data (including inertial properties)
3. Sex
4. Number required (consider statistical distribution of scores, accuracy required)—See Section 5.2
5. Occupation, or specific training
6. Sports activities (especially weight lifting, swimming, football, and other strenuous sports)
7. General state of health
8. Dominant hand
9. Age or age range of group
10. Other (specify)

D. Posture of the Subject

1. Coupling of the subject to the measuring device (see A2, H2, H4)
2. Body parts and muscles chiefly used
3. Body posture during force exertion
4. Body support/reaction force available
5. Other (specify)

Table 4-1. Variables Affecting Muscular Strength Measurements (continued)

E. Method of Force Exertion

Exact wording of the instructions given to the subject; or, especially if no specific instructions given, how was force actually exerted. In particular:

1. Requested magnitude of force (maximum effort, or submaximal)
2. Requested manner of force exertion:

    a. how to build up force
    b. what to do after requested magnitude has been reached
    c. how long to exert force
    d. is muscle length kept constant during exertion (isometric)
    e. is muscle tension kept constant during exertion (isotonic)

3. Time interval between subsequent tests
4. How many repetitions
5. Practice/training
6. Other (specify)

F. Motivational Factors

1. Selection of subjects
2. Voluntary/required participation
3. Mode of payment
4. Knowledge of the purpose of the experiment
5. Knowledge of the experimental procedure
6. Feedback of performance
7. Supervision during the experiment
8. Stimulating factors such as encouragements, rewards, competition, spectators
9. Restraining factors such as danger, fear of injuries, adverse environmental conditions, fatigue, lack of interest, spectators
10. Other (specify)

G. Environmental Factors

1. Accelogravitational environment (including shock and vibration)
2. Atmospheric pressure
3. Liquid pressure (underwater)
4. Liquid density of environment
5. Viscosity of environment
6. Temperature, heat flux
7. Humidity

Table 4-1. Variables Affecting Muscular Strength Measurements (continued)

H. Clothing and Protective Equipment
  1. Potential movement or position limits
  2. Forces induced by clothing—especially pressure suits (at pressures used in test)
  3. Weight of clothing and equipment
  4. Protection against pain, chafing injury (see D1 F9)

I. Selection of Performance Score
  1. Amplitude-dependent value (maximum, minimum, or . . .)
  2. Time-dependent value (at or over a specified time)
  3. Other (specify)

Kroemer (1970b) proposed:

"Use the peak (i.e., the largest instantaneous amplitude) occurring any time during the exertion period if force is exerted for less than 3 seconds.

"Use the average of the middle second if force is exerted for 3 or more seconds. However, use the peak (see above) if this score exceeds 110% of the average at any time."

The recommendation of the Ad Hoc Committee . . . for Strength Testing (1973) is to use the mean score of three consecutive seconds instead of one second. Otherwise, the recommendations are in essence the same as listed above.

---

and Garrett, 1966). This instrument, like most dynamometers of today, is essentially a spring whose deformations are proportional to the forces that produce them.

Smedley (1900) and Hertzberg (1955) pointed out the importance of the size of hand strength testing instruments. Hertzberg found that a separation of 2.5 in. between grip elements was best of four separations studied. However, the differences in recorded grip strength are relatively small unless gross misadjustments occur (Montoye and Faulkner, 1964).

A multitude of specialized force measurement devices are available today. However, for preliminary tests, an inexpensive "fish scale" device can be used to get some information on the overall magnitude and range of force capabilities. Force ranges of 0 to 10 lb, 0 to 50 lb, 0 to 100, or 0 to 250 lb are convenient for many "quick and dirty" tests.

Humans can exert force on objects by hanging from them, standing, sitting, leaning, or lying upon them when in an accelerational or gravitational field. To measure such mass-induced forces, many types of balance scales or spring scales (bathroom scales) are available.

One should not overlook that most fundamental mechanical device, the calibrated, configured weight. However, while the ability to hold a weight and, maybe, to move it very slowly, are measures of static force capability (i.e., strength), any rapid accelerating or moving of masses (such as weightlifting) are dynamic efforts that test the subject's capacity to perform work, but do not measure his isometric strength.

4.4.2 Hydraulic Devices

Kellogg (1893) developed a hydraulic dynamometer that enabled him to test the major portion of the voluntary muscles of the body. About 60 years later, Hunsicker (1955) used one of the original dynamometers which he found still to be in excellent working order.

In 1949 Newman introduced a hydraulic "myometer" consisting of a cylindrical housing 2 in. in diameter and about 3 in. long. At one end is the pressure transmitting button. At the other end, a dial gage. The gage has a pointer that remains at the maximum reading until it is manually reset (Hunsicker, 1955).

Within the range of possibilities, framed by Kellogg's instruments, exists a variety of other hydraulic pressure measurement devices available for specific purposes. Among the newest is a hydraulic grip dynamometer with electrical output developed by Van Patten and Rubinstein (1970).

4.4.3 Pneumatic Devices

Hamilton (1875) and Geckeler (1939) developed hand grip dynamometers with a bulb that is squeezed to compress air and a device to measure the resulting pressure change. However, such compressible bulbs do not yield information on the direction(s) of exerted force(s) and hence do not meet the requirement of a vector—they do not measure force. Nevertheless, the pneumatic principle can be used like hydraulic devices for strength measurements, if appropriately applied.

4.4.4 Electrical Devices

The principle of locating strain gages on structural parts that will be (ever so slightly) deformed by the force applied, is used in the majority of electric force measuring devices. A typical example is the apparatus used by Hunsicker (1955) in tests of arm strength. The dynamometer apparatus was built in the form of a hand grip pivoted on a steel beam that extended into the hollow shell of the grip. The other end of the beam was mounted on an adjustable supporting framework. On the beam, strain gages were located that transduced the structural strain (due to applied force) to a pointer instrument. Not only can the principle be utilized with beams but it can also be used almost as easily on any other structural parts of a device. Rather well known is the ring equipped with strain gages. Here, force and reaction force act on opposite sides (say, 0° and 180°), flattening the ring into a slightly elliptical shape. Strain gages are glued to the intermediate parts of the ring (at 90° and 270°) which are mostly bent (at the outside) and compressed (inside) by the pair of forces. Using four strain gages ("Full Bridge") instead of the usual two gages ("Half Bridge") switched in the usual Wheatstone scheme, high sensitivity can be achieved. Kroemer (1969b) and Kroemer and Robinson (1971) have used this design successfully in a number of experiments to assess muscular force capabilities. Because strain gages often can be attached to suitable parts of stressed equipment without structural changes, and since only simple rules need to be followed to obtain sensitive and reliable instruments, the strain gage technique has been widely accepted and is described in many engineering texts and industrial pamphlets (see the subject index of an engineering library for current information).

Kroemer and Gienapp (1970) described their patented design and use of a strain-gaged, hand-held device to measure finger (thumb) strength as follows: "The device is held in the hand. Force exerted by the thumb (or another selected digit) deforms an instrumental beam. This deformation is sensed by strain gages and transmitted electrically to a recorder."

The device was designed to have the following features: (1) to measure the thumb force vector exerted isometrically in defined location and direction; (2) to assure a direct flow of force vectors between the thumb and the hand without interfering force inputs from arm or shoulder muscles; (3) to describe the position of the thumb with respect to the hand by readings taken from scales on the device itself; (4) to yield, in combination with a recorder, a histogram of the force exertion; (5) to be calibrated easily; (6) to be small and light in weight; and (7) to adapt to a large range of hand sizes. The principle employed is adaptable to measurements of thumb and finger forces in other locations and directions.

4.5 MEASUREMENT OF TORQUES

Instrumentation developed to measure maximal torque capability follows the same pattern as the linear strength test devices. Since applications of pneumatic or hydraulic devices for torque assessment are infrequent, only two types of devices will be discussed here: mechanical and electrical.

4.5.1 Mechanical Apparatus

The apparatus of Hedberg and Lobron (1954) consisted of a rod, with one end machined in knob form, a lever arm, and a spring scale that was attached to one end of the lever arm and secured to the main structure of the apparatus. The other end of the lever was used to attach counterbalance weights.

The mechanism was mounted in a box such that only the knob projected out from a surface facing the subject. There were no special data reduction devices. The maximum spring deflection was the value read by the observer.

Another approach to torque measurement is to place a carefully machined and tempered spring steel bar in torsion and read the resulting deflection of one end. This deflection is directly proportional to the torsional stress as long as the elastic limit of the metal is not exceeded. Figure 4-2 illustrates two such devices designed to measure different ranges of torque. A deflection of 55° accompanies full-scale readings on these instruments, so they do *not* qualify as essentially isometric devices.

A convenient method for many engineering anthropometry applications is the use of a torque wrench of suitable size (Roebuck, 1965; Garrett, 1968). These wrenches are designed to provide a dial reading of torque when applied to a nut or bolt during critical assembly operations. They are generally available in many large manufacturing company tool cribs or may be readily purchased. By providing suitable shaft connectors, such as a hexagonal bar or Allen head screw, and a mounting jig (such as shown in Figure 4-3), torque exertion on tools, knobs, or handles may be measured. The torque wrench of Figure 4-3 is a dial reading type. There are also types that have a deflection type measuring scale.

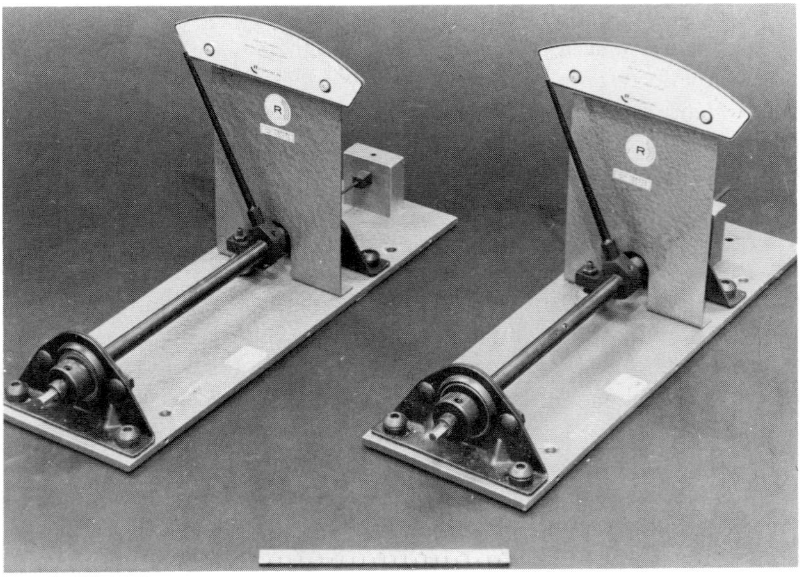

Figure 4-2. Mechanical torque measurement devices (Roebuck, 1965).

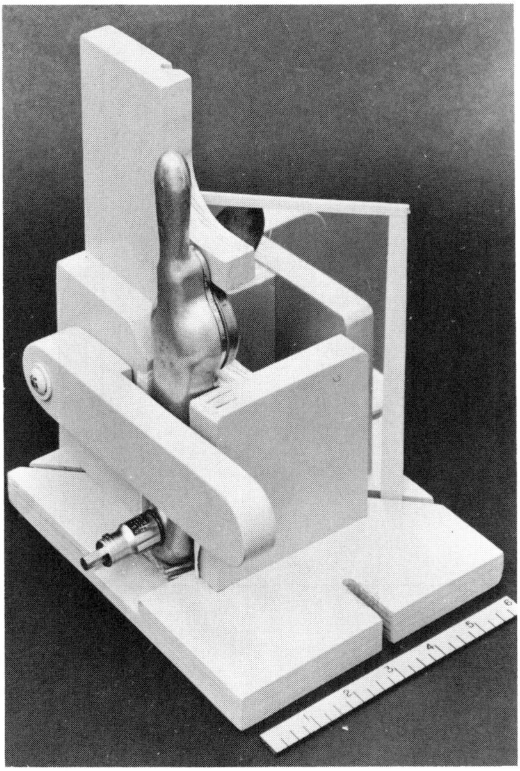

Figure 4-3. Torque wrench mounting fixture. The mirror in the rear is used to read the dial of the torque wrench from the side of a low-pressure test chamber (Roebuck, 1965).

4.5.2 Electrical Apparatus

The strain gage dynamometer of Darcus (1951) was one of the early electrical devices specifically designed to measure human arm torque strength (see Figure 4-4). It consisted of a wooden handle connected by a metal stirrup to a tubular metal spindle, which passed through a ball bearing in the center of a rigid metal plate. A tempered steel bar traversed the spindle immediately in front of the plate. Both ends of the bar could be firmly fixed to the plate by metal pegs in angular positions at 30° intervals. The hand grip spindle was provided with a pointer which indicated, on a scale attached to the metal plate, the angular position of the handle. The whole apparatus was mounted so that it could be tilted in all directions and was clamped to a vertical support such that it could be adjusted in height.

The rigidity of the tempered steel bar was sufficient to allow only one degree angular rotation of the handle with a torque of 10 Nm (86.5 in.-lb). The

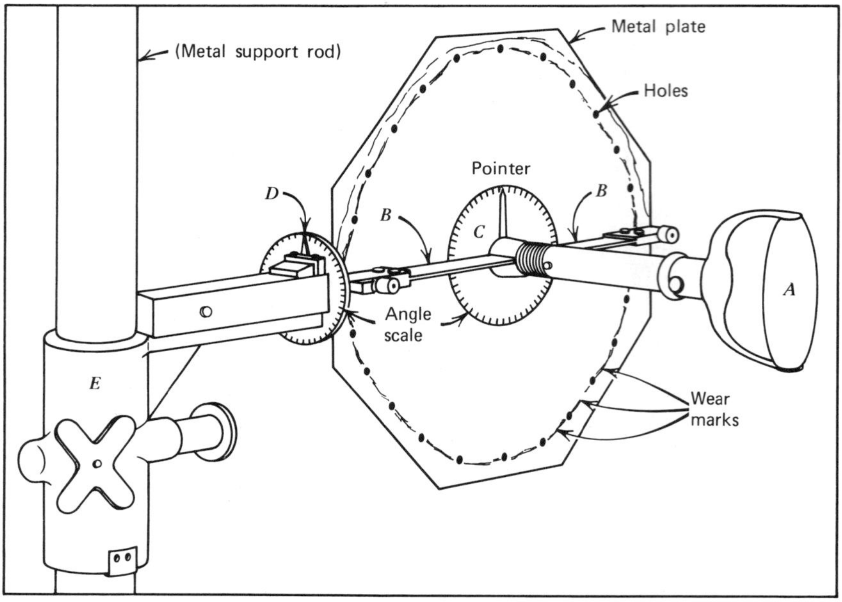

Figure 4-4. Darcus strain gage dynamometer. (*a*) Hand-grip connected to metal spindle; (*b*) tempered steel bar to which electrical strain gages are fixed; (*c*) scale indicating position of hand-grip; (*d*) scale indicating tilt of dynamometer; (*e*) adjustable support (sketched from Darcus, 1951).

degree of deformation as a function of load was measured by two strain gages fixed to the upper surface of the tempered steel bar on opposite sides of the hand grip spindle. The gages formed two arms of a Wheatstone bridge, the output of which was read on a galvanometer.

The apparatus used by Dzendolet and Rievley (1959) involved a novel approach to torque measurement since they attempted to simulate the weightless conditions of space flight.

Two types of measurements were made. The first involved a man standing on a platform that was supported on a thin cushion of air to make it practically frictionless. A (dynamic) torque was exerted about the vertical axis of the body by reaching overhead to grasp a fixed hand hold. Time to complete a revolution after exerting torque for one second was the quantity measured. This was then related to an estimated moment of inertia to calculate the force exerted.

The second measurement technique, also at least partly dynamic, involved a subject seated on a similar "frictionless" platform consisting of three "pads" providing an air cushion. Torque was exerted about a hand hold mounted parallel to the coronal plane in front of the seated subject at approximately shoulder height. The attempt was to rotate the body in a horizontal plane about the hand hold as a center. To measure the torque, a strain gage device was arranged at a radius of 2 ft from the hand hold to measure push or pull forces normal to a radial line connecting the hand hold and force pickup. This, then, measured the amount of axial force exertable on a screw driver or other tool located 2 ft away from a hand hold when the operator is in weightless conditions. The torque exerted was about an axis perpendicular to the forearm rather than parallel to the forearm as for turning a knob.

The record obtained was a continuous tracing of force versus time from the output of the bridge amplifier used with the strain gage. Since the torque applied by the subject varied considerably with time, an average force was reported. This was calculated by reading the force at 1-sec time intervals for a total of 4 sec after the torque was first applied by the subject. The mean of these four readings was called the "long term" force for that trial.

4.6 MEASURING DEVICES: SUMMARY AND RECOMMENDATIONS

Dynamometers operated on a principle of metal deformation have been used for more testing than any other kind. All types, with the exception of the electrical strain gage, were developed with the idea of indicating the largest amplitude ("peak") achieved. The electrical strain gage device has the unique advantage of recording the total time history of the strength effort. This allows the experimenter to examine, at any time he chooses, the record of the effort. He can reject results that are the outcome of apparently irregular or unwanted methods of force exertions (e.g., jerking instead of steady exertions). From the record, he can select the strength score that appropriately describes the subject's achievement (Kroemer and Howard, 1970a,b; Ad-Hoc Committee, 1973). The record of the time history is especially valuable if the raw test results are directly (on-line or on-time) fed into a computer for automatic data processing.

It is useful at this point to distinguish clearly between the two functional parts of any measuring device: the strained part, which is deformed by the acting force or torque (the beam bent, the spring compressed), and the transducing part, which senses the stress/deformation and indicates (the mechanical pointer on a dial) or records (the electrically operated pen on a chart recorder) amount and direction of the stress or deformation. Calibration of the measuring device is, of course, a prerequisite—but often neglected.

The purely mechanical device (like the common grip strength measuring device) is usually the cheapest, simplest, and most rugged. However, its output is generally via a pointer moving over a scale in proportion to the stress actually applied. This induces the experimenter to read, often hastily, the largest pointer excursion occurring during the subject's effort. This "peak" is always used with "maximum indicator" devices on which a secondary pointer is pushed to the maximal excursion by the primary pointer and left there until reset.

In order to evaluate the subject's effort thoroughly and adequately, a time record of the performance is often necessary. This cannot be achieved with simple mechanical, pneumatical, or hydraulic devices alone; an electric recording device has to be added to the strained unit. This leaves the "indicating" devices for preliminary and pilot studies, while the "recording" instruments will usually be required for proper experimentation. With adequate planning, the higher cost of recording instruments can be distributed over many experiments and long periods of time, since the same amplifiers and recorders can be used with a large number of different sensors.

4.7 PROCEDURES FOR TESTING

4.7.1 Subjects

Selection of subjects for strength testing involves much more than selection for anthropometric dimensions surveys. Some of the key factors that affect selection, and therefore should be recorded to describe the sample of subjects, were previously listed in Table 4-1, item C. Ideally, the sample should be drawn from personnel who will use the device being designed. More commonly, persons who seem to match the user population closely are selected. Although strength has relatively low correlation with dimensional factors, a few key dimensions are significant.

Among the anthropometric measurements to be taken, Stature and Weight are basic. Additional measurements should be selected to establish the body segment link lengths which determine the angles of the joints when force is applied, mass properties, body muscle and relative fat contents, and possibly the body somatotype. Dimensions taken should be relevant to the joints and limbs most directly involved in the force exertion. Suggested dimensions meeting the above criteria in a general way are listed in Table 4-2. Dimensions specific to link and joint geometry were described in greater detail in Chapter III.

It is important to estimate the potential range of strength of the sample population; otherwise the measuring device may be too weak. Weak exertions also have to be taken into account, since their adequate recording may require special measures to achieve the necessary sensitivity amplification.

4.7.2 Strength Test Situation Variables

The specification of body positioning in strength measurements is also crucial. Textures greatly influence frictional forces. Surface shapes may greatly affect

Table 4-2. Recommended Anthropometric Dimensions and Description of Subjects for Strength Tests

General	*Hand-Arm Strength*
Stature	Upper arm length and circumference
Weight	Forearm length and circumference
Eye height (s&s)[a]	Wrist circumference
Acromion height (s&s)	Hand width and length
Shoulder breadth	Finger length and width
Thumb-tip reach	
Skinfold thickness (triceps, juxtanipple, subscapular)	*Foot-Leg Strength*
Grip strength	Trochanterion height (may be substituded by buttock-knee length)
Somatotype	Thigh circumference
Measures of mobility	Knee height
	Calf circumference
	Ankle height
	Foot dimensions (shoe size)

[a] s&s: sitting and standing.

pressure on the body, often causing a tolerance limit of pain from local high pressures. Supports and constraints, restraint harnesses, hand or foot grips, tools, clothing conditions, humidity, and temperature may also affect results. Timing and frequency of testing are much more critical in strength measurements than in body dimensions measurements, and will be discussed separately.

Body Positioning

The angular relationships of body parts during strength exertion can have substantial, even surprising, effects on the force or torque exerted to an outside measuring device. (Chaffin, 1969; Linford and Rarick, 1968; Williams and Stutzman, 1959; Clarke and Baley, 1950) The elbow angle, for instance, determines to a great extent the amount of force that can be exerted in push or pull with the hand, perpendicular to the axis of the forearm. Similarly, the force or torque exerted with the foot depends on thigh and knee angles and/or on the angle between the lower leg and the foot (Kroemer, 1969b; 1972d; Kroemer and Robinson, 1971). This dependency between strength and joint angle derives from two main factors: The tension of the muscle depends on its amount of stretch (its length) at the moment of exertion, and on the mechanical advantages prevailing at this instant, that is, on the pull angles between the muscles and the body members at each side of the joint. This relationship is further complicated if a muscle connects body members that are separated by two intermediate joints, or if an external support offers an additional fulcrum (as in applying a lift force with the hand to an object, but with the elbow supported by an armrest).

Related phenomena are often encountered in the various testing methods employed in physical education. Disregarding the too often dubious "fitness" tests (Ricci, 1970), even simple strength tests suffer frequently from a lack of "experimental cleanliness." Care must be taken to control, and to report, in which direction strength is exerted, and at what point it is exerted. One simply cannot report "peak" efforts if "smooth" or "steady" efforts are required. Some tests in physical education, for example "back lift," require that the subject lift parts of his body (here, the upper trunk) slightly off the supporting surface. Lifting a body part means that the area of support, and the location of this surface supplying reaction force, are changing in an uncontrollable manner; this, in turn, means changing and unknown lever arms, and the like. "Measurements" like these are almost useless for engineering purposes.

These few remarks will suffice to demonstrate the importance of controlling and reporting the positions of body parts with respect to each other, and in relation to the supporting surfaces as well as to the force and torque vectors exerted.

Acceleration

The influence of variable accelogravitational force fields was listed as related to human force exertion in Table 4-1. How can these conditions be altered for strength tests? In a broad sense, one must consider systems and devices that affect the subject's force field environment within the category of instrumentation and test apparatus. Among these apparatuses are large centrifuges, rocket- and steam-powered sleds and water or mechanical braking systems, drop towers, catapults, and aircraft.

Lombard and Drury (1947) studied the influence of positive (head to foot) radial acceleration on the ability of a subject to manipulate a control stick using a centrifuge at the University of Southern California. Other similar studies on pilot capabilities were performed on this centrifuge by Lombard et al. (1951), Basler and Morehouse (1948), and Morehouse and Wells (1948). Cochran (1953) of the U.S. Navy School of Aviation Medicine, Pensacola, Florida, reported tests to determine the ease with which pilots can grasp and pull on ejection seat face curtain handles, using a centrifuge. Kroemer (1972a, 1973) studied the effects of G_z accelerations on strength available for the operation of aircraft controls in the human centrifuge at the USAF Aerospace Medical Research Laboratory in Dayton, Ohio. These data show specific acceleration effects on available muscle strength when compared to the results of preceding studies in the laboratory (Thordsen et al., 1972; Laubach et al., 1972).

Rocket sled tests have been primarily used for studies of human capability to tolerate high accelerational loads, under emergency conditions. The time available for activity under such conditions is very short and the system is not usually practical for generating long-term accelerational fields for strength testing.

Aircraft have a capability to simulate a wide range of accelerational fields within the cabin, including the sensation of weightlesness or "zero-g" experienced by astronauts in orbit. Although limited by structural strength and altitude considerations, test periods up to 30 seconds or more of near weightlessness can be obtained by a parabolic flight path. During pullout maneuvers and turns, fields of two to three times the force of gravity can be obtained by some large aircraft, and even higher loads, to five or seven "g," by aerobatic or military combat aircraft.

Finally, complex suspension systems for the human operator are conceivable (and have been tried) which allow an approximation of weightlessness in the regular laboratory. However, even with large expenditures in effort, machinery, and cost, such simulators have shown only limited validity and success.

Motivation

Subject motivation is very important in strength testing, although often disregarded and only superficially treated in the human engineering literature. The experimenter should try to interest the subjects in the experiments to be performed by a brief but careful explanation of purpose and procedure, by assuring that no injuries would occur, and by avoiding any forms of contest or competition among the subjects. Crucial information and instructions should be carefully worded, fixed in writing, and related to each subject in the same manner.

How to Exert and Score Strength

Instructions given to subjects can definitely affect the outcome of strength tests as Kroemer and Howard (1970a,b,) showed. They told their subjects to exert their maximal push forces in three different ways as specified in the following instructions read to them:

"*Hold*-Exert and hold your maximal force for five seconds—then release."

The subject had to exert maximal force without changing the length of the involved muscles (isometric) and to maintain the reached force level (isotonic). A period of five seconds was chosen as sufficient time to build up and maintain a "constant" force and yet short enough to be endured without perceptible muscle fatigue.

"*Increase*-Apply gradually increasing force until you reach your maximum—then release."

The subject had to apply an increasing force until he felt that he had reached his largest possible force, and then release. Self-paced, the subject attained a peak force in a predominatly isometric way.

"*Jerk*-Apply your maximal force suddenly, twice."

The subject had to apply peak forces in sudden sharp thrusts of the body. During such "jerks," kinetic energy of moving body parts is released by sudden deceleration at the measuring device (actually a dynamic exertion). Figure 4-5 shows schematically the results of the different techniques of force exertions.

It is remarkable that two isometric techniques of force exertion, almost undistinguishable when merely observing the subjects and not checking the recorded strength curves, could bring about distinctly different peak forces. This is in contrast to the convenient assumption that "a maximum is a maximum." Since the magnitude of exerted peak forces depended so distinctly on the actual manner of force exertion (i.e., on the instruction given to the subjects on how to exert force), it is not sufficient to instruct the subjects to apply their "maximal" or "strongest" or "hardest" force. The actual technique of force generation must be described.

Using "peak" scores to indicate the subjects' performance is an adequate procedure if instantaneous maximal amplitudes of force are actually requested, as in the "increase" experiments. It is hard to justify the use of the peak score if exertion of a "constant" force is really required, as in the first experiment. In this case, a scoring system should be used that takes into account the

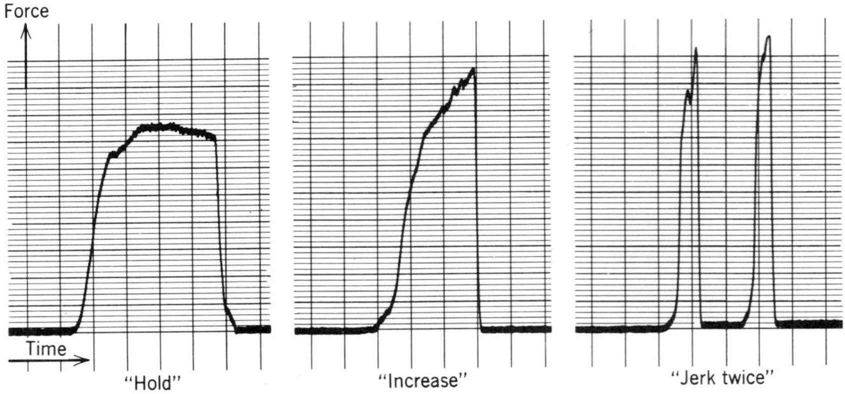

Figure 4-5. Force curves resulting from different techniques of force generation.

requested evenness of the exertion curve. Hence, an integrated or averaged score is appropriate which results, of course, in an index lower than the peak.

Duration and Scheduling of Tests

Of concern in scheduling experimental trials are sequential artifacts, fatigue effects, motivation, cost, availability of subjects, date when results are needed, time to adjust apparatus, and data-recording techniques.

Some of those factors can be fairly accurately determined according to the purpose of the tests, but others are selected according to experience, judgment, and available materials. As a consequence, most authors state the selected schedule without much justification or comment, and often ascribe the selection to the "results of pilot tests" without further explanation. In spite of this paucity of information, a few guideposts may be discerned.

Human performance shows a diurnal variation usually with a maximum in the morning and another in the afternoon, but the exact time varies with different observers. It is widely accepted that persons may be classified along a continuum of early-rising types and late-rising types, who reach their peak of motivation and energy at different times of day. It is not known whether these effects significantly affect static muscle strength.

Müller (1970) has shown that static strength of muscles can increase as a result of training in a predictable manner. This is important to investigators interested in obtaining the "normal" or "usual" static strength level of a working population group. Müller's data indicate the following.

1. To avoid introducing any training effect in testing of static strength, one may make several trials during one day, but the next set of trials using the same muscles should occur either two weeks later or the next day (see 4).
2. To have a training effect, a muscular contraction must be at least 50% of the existing strength and last one second or longer. As a rule of thumb, an exertion of two-thirds of actual strength usually brings about a further strength increase.
3. The length of muscle contraction time beyond several seconds has little effect on strength training. Fatigue and exhaustion does not influence the training effects.
4. Strength tends to fall off in time at about the same rate at which it was built up. "Only if again and again muscles are forced to strong contractions for months does the body allow a lasting increase of muscle substance" (Müller, 1957). The effect of a single muscular contraction is to increase strength for approximately seven days, after which it decreases for the next seven days.
5. No substantial cross-training of opposite limb occurs due to static

strength training. This implies that opposite limbs may be tested in turn, with the probability that the nontested limb can be considered at rest, recovering for the next test. This permits a saving in testing time when both limbs are to be tested.

The effects of muscular fatigue and their relation to maximum strength are less clearly defined. Problems of motivation introduce a host of difficulties in any discussion of "fatigue." Volume 14, number 1, 1971, of the journal *Ergonomics* is completely devoted to a discussion of the numerous aspects of "fatigue."

An intermission of three to five minutes or more between short-time (five seconds or less) maximal exertions of the same muscles should be sufficient to avoid fatigue effects. In the meantime, other muscles can be tested.

The question arises whether the same test should be repeated or not. Statistically it appears that a single effort is as reliable as the best of several (Henry, 1967; Alderman and Banfield, 1969). In the sense that there is no assurance that a higher value will appear in retesting, just one trial is sufficient. For a large number of subjects, the random chances tend to even out and a single trial may be quite acceptable.

V
STATISTICAL METHODS

5.1 INTRODUCTION

This section deals with the problems of selecting subjects and of summarizing anthropometric data into meaningful statistics that serve the dual role of describing the measured sample group and of providing a basis for inference about some larger group or population. Emphasis is on the statistics and methods that are especially useful for planning engineering anthropometry surveys, for performing data analysis, and for development of anthropometric requirements for engineering design. Also covered are related considerations such as (1) the number of sample measurements required in order to achieve a selected level of accuracy and confidence; (2) estimates of body dimension variability; and (3) combinations of statistical data to approximate unknown body dimensions, composite populations, and so forth.

Further discussions of the meaning of such data in terms of biometric relationships and of the implications for engineering design are presented in Chapter VI. However, selected data from Chapter VI are used in examples here to avoid duplication. Design applications examples are illustrated in greater detail and variety in Chapters VII through X.

5.2 BASIC STATISTICAL DEFINITIONS AND CONCEPTS FOR ANTHROPOMETRY

5.2.1 Population

A major anthropometric concern in design and evaluation of engineering products is the statistical description of all those persons who may, throughout the life of the product's usefulness, be involved in its operation, consumption, maintenance, or other anthropometric relationship with the product. This group of persons may be defined as the *total user population*. For specific design criteria, smaller populations may be usefully defined, such as the assembly personnel population, maintenance personnel population and the operator population. Any of these can vary from an explicitly described group of individuals to a group so ill-described as to allow only gross approximations to their anthropometric measurements.

In the case of the NASA Mercury Program to put a man into space, the operator population was a very well-described group of seven pilots. Further, only one of the seven was to operate each vehicle. Each pilot was thoroughly measured and his dimensions recorded. Statistical calculations were hardly needed.

Near the other extreme, the design of the passenger seating space for a jet transport, intended for international service, involves a wide variety of persons—any sex, age, occupation, race, or nationality. The anthropometric description of such a population is much more complex. Typically, a set of *summary statistics* is used. These give some expressions of the upper and lower limits of each dimension, the central tendency or midpoint of the set of data and the relationships between the various dimensions.

5.2.2 Samples

It is usually impossible or economically undesirable to measure every individual in a population. Instead, a smaller group, called a *sample*, of individuals thought to be like the population is measured. The larger the sample selected, the more likely it is to be representative of the total population. That is, the central tendency (such as the average) of the various different sizes (distribution) for the sample is very nearly the same as the central tendency for the distribution of the population. Also, the measures of how widely different are the sizes (dispersion, or *spread* of the sample distribution of measurements) are approximately the same as that of the population. Other implied characteristics of the population are also probably common within the sample.

5.2.3 Random Selection and Bias

It is necessary to take a random sample from a population for the sample to be representative (unbiased). For example, suppose one has a list of 1000 persons in a population, and the listing has been arranged in order of increasing stature. An incorrect procedure might be taking the first 10 (or 100 or 500) persons from this list, resulting in a smaller average height estimate for the population height than if the sample had been selected from the other (taller) end of the list. Instead, one might take a series of 1000 cards that contain the names of all persons in the population, mix the cards thoroughly, and have a blindfolded person pick a sample. This would approach the major requirements for random selection:

1. Each individual in the defined population should have an equal chance to be included in the sample.
2. The selection of one individual shall in no way affect the selection of another.

Inadvertantly biasing, or selecting a sample such that there is an unlikely concentration of one characteristic, must be of constant concern to engineering anthropometrists in planning surveys and analyzing data. Consider the experimenter who included in his first sample all subjects whose last name started with the letters A through M, and assigned the remainder to the second sample. The resultant data was biased, as this technique introduced a division between two basically different nationality groups!

Recommended tools for insuring random sample selection are random number tables frequently published in statistical texts. For example, the 1000 cards in the above example could be numbered from 0 to 999. Entry could be made into the tables at some random point, and the next 10 (or 100 or 500) three-digit consecutive numbers would represent the item numbers of subjects to be measured.

5.2.4 Stratified Sampling

Another method by which the selection of a sample group can be made to correspond more closely to known population characteristics is by stratified sampling. Where a sample contains distinctly different groups, such as men and women, the percentage can be made the same as for the main population, for example, 50% each. Within each group the selection may again be random. On further stratification, age groups known to be in the main population can be selected in corresponding percentage mixes. Where available subjects of one type are preponderant in the sample, but not in the population, a technique of weighting may be necessary to assure that no one type of subject gets too much emphasis in the averaging of the data.

5.2.5 Selection Standards and Design Limits

In engineering anthropometry, a major use of statistical calculations is to develop design criteria specifying the range of each body dimension for which a product must be designed. These criteria also provide the basis for selection standards to be used in screening potential candidates for the user population. Examples of occupationally related dimensional characteristics are discussed in Chapter VI, Biometric Relationships.

Principles for setting such anthropometric limits are essentially the same as for selecting tolerances and fits for design of machined parts, familiar to many engineers. However, the variabilities of human beings are vastly different than those of machinery, so that many engineers have difficulty grasping the similarities and significance. In both cases, too tight a "tolerance" excludes use of many manufactured parts (persons in the user population) and raises costs (selection and recruitment of personnel, scrap waste in parts). On the other hand, a design that accommodates the full range of observed variations in population dimensions requires added complexity of adjustments and thus raises costs to an uneconomical stage.

5.2.6 Percentiles

It has become common practice to specify anthropometric design limits and selection standards in terms of statistical numbers called *percentiles,* which simply indicate the percentage of persons within the population who have a body dimension of a certain size (or smaller). The concept is more easily explained than the concept of variance or standard deviation to persons who have no statistical background, and most persons are familiar with it. Also, there is no need to discuss characteristics of the population dimensional distribution such as normality, skewness, or kurtosis in such introductory discussions, since the concept applies to any distribution.

To find out what percentile rank applies to a particular person in a population or a sample, one may perform the following steps.

1. Arrange data of given dimension in ascending order of size.
2. Group data into convenient class intervals and record frequency of occurrence in each class.
3. Count number of individuals below upper limit of each class and divide by the total number of individuals. Multiply by 100 to determine percentile rank.
4. Tabulate and/or graph percentile versus size. Graphs may be shown with simple linear scales on the ordinate and abscissa or with cumulative normal probability scales for the percentiles. The development of normal probability scales is explained later.

If the data are from a sample of the population, the resulting percentiles are statistics that are descriptive of the sample. They also constitute a prediction of the population statistics, a prediction that is subject to certain statistical measures of confidence of prediction and possibility of error in prediction, which will be further discussed after the basic formulas concerning central tendency and dispersion are presented.

The resulting percentile tables and graphs also can be useful for the reverse process: finding the permissible limits for dimensions of individuals, given a specification of design limits in terms of percentiles. Work space or clothing sizes may also be evaluated or ranked in terms of population percentiles accommodated or fitted by determining the largest body size (hypothetical or actual) for a specified dimension that can work efficiently within a work space or effectively operate a device or comfortably fit within a garment, and expressing these body dimensions as percentiles. The expression of body dimensions in terms of percentiles is one of the first goals in reducing measured body size data for engineering anthropometry.

It has been the experience of the authors that percentiles, although useful, can also cause misleading results when improperly applied. Although closely related to biometric relationships described in Chapter VI, the following four characteristics of percentile values are emphasized here to alert the reader to the more frequently occurring errors committed when using percentiles.

1. *A percentile is a point on a cumulative percentage scale for a specified population.* A man of 95th percentile Height would be taller than 95% of the *particular group* (population or sample) upon which this percentile is based. For example, percentile ratings used in the Apollo project were based on data describing Air Force Flying personnel in 1950 (Hertzberg et al., 1954), since this was a population most similar in nature to the still incompletely selected astronaut corp. Misleading results would be expected if percentile values were selected from a less representative population such as a survey of midwestern college students or of U.S. Army truck drivers.
2. *A percentile scale is an ordinal scale.* It shows the order of a rating on the scale, but in itself gives no information about the intervals between ratings. Thus, with respect to some arbitrary body dimension, the interval between the 70th and 75th percentiles may be only 0.2 in., while that between the 95th and 99th may be 2 in. In practice, linear interpolation between five percentiles or less is subject to relatively small error; but linear extrapolation is seldom valid.
3. *Anthropometric percentiles on actual individuals refer to one, and only one body dimension,* such as Height, Weight, Arm Length, or Head Circumference. When the occasion warrants, it is permissible to refer to more than one dimension with the same percentile rating, that is, 90th percentile Height and Weight. In all cases, however, it must be indicated to which dimensions the rating refers. A statement, unqualified by reference to a specific dimension, such as, "the 90th percentile man," can only apply to a theoretical statistical concept, like a collection of dimensions each of which is 90th percentile in magnitude (see Section 6.3.3).
4. *The magnitude of percentile ratings should not be used to infer exact percentile ratings of other dimensions.* Only invalid and misleading information will result from attempting to add the percentile ratings of body parts to infer the rating of a greater part, that is, 90th percentile Knee Height plus 90th percentile Knee to Crotch Length does *not* equal 90th percentile Inseam. This will be discussed further in Sections 5.5 and 6.3.

5.2.7 Statistical Distributions

To be able to predict population percentiles from other statistical information or from sample data requires additional statistical concepts and mathematical tools. Specifically, one needs information about the *distribution* of the accumulated data, expressed in terms of frequency of occurrence versus magnitude. These data are the basis of most predictions of design criteria for engineering applications. To learn more about the distribution of data, it is useful to group the data into equal intervals, or classes, such as 10 to 11 in., 11 to 12 in., and so forth, then determine how many persons fall into each class (i.e., the class frequency). An an example, the measurements of Standing Height for a sample from the Army aviator population might be grouped in intervals as shown in Table 5-1. This simple frequency table provides the first indication of the distribution of the data. Plotting the data in a histogram, or frequency polygon, Figure 5-1 reveals more clearly the nature of the distribution. The more data one has, the smaller one can make the class intervals and the more nearly the distribution plot will approach a smooth curve.

The distribution most commonly approximated in anthropometric data is

Table 5-1. Example of a Frequency Table

Standing Height of Army aviators in inches. The data in the frequency column are the number of measurements occurring within each interval (data after White, 1961).

Interval	Midpoint	Frequency
62.5–63.2	62.85	1
63.3–64.0	63.65	3
64.1–64.8	64.45	3
64.9–65.6	65.25	16
65.7–66.4	66.05	20
66.5–67.2	66.85	47
67.3–68.0	67.65	48
68.1–68.8	68.45	64
68.9–69.6	69.25	73
69.7–70.4	70.05	63
70.5–71.2	70.85	48
71.3–72.0	71.65	43
72.1–72.8	72.45	37
72.9–73.6	73.25	14
73.7–74.4	74.05	10
74.5–75.2	74.85	9
75.3–76.0	75.65	1

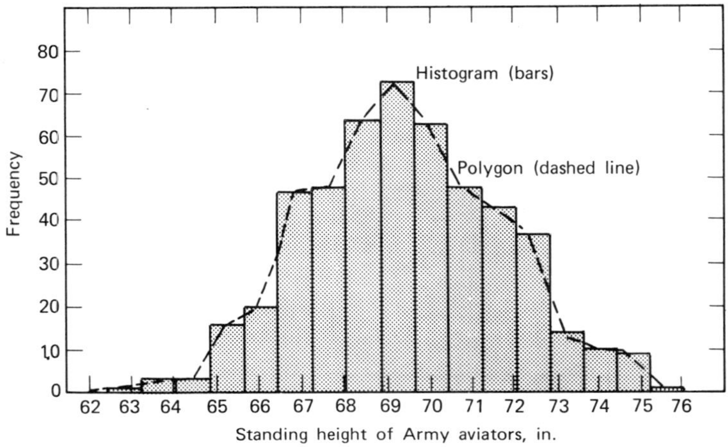

Figure 5-1. Example of a frequency histogram and frequency polygon.

the *normal* or Gaussian distribution, a bell-shaped, symmetrical curve resulting from a plot of frequency of occurrence versus size, as illustrated in Figure 5-2. Such a curve has been "fitted" to the sample data using the functional relationship shown. The theoretical normal distribution curve becomes asymptotic to the abscissa, but never touches it. Many anthropometric population and sample data, when properly grouped into a set of class intervals of appropriate size will closely approximate the theoretical formulation as

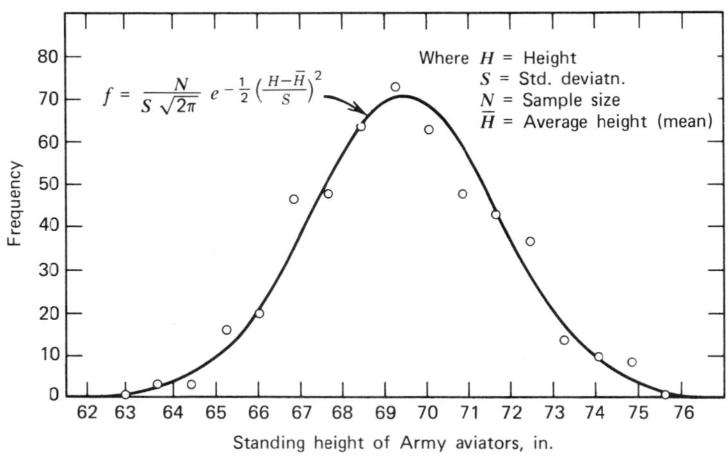

Figure 5-2. A normal distribution curve fitted to sample data.

illustrated by Figure 5-2. (Exceptions are described in Section 6.3.2.) Therefore, this theoretical curve is the mathematical model for most of the applicable statistical theory discussed in the following sections. The degree to which the data match this model determines the validity of many of the following procedures.

5.2.8 Cumulative Distribution Graphs

The cumulative frequency distribution graph is a convenient tool for locating percentile values for a given set of data. This graph is prepared by expanding the frequency table (Table 5-1), by calculating cumulative frequencies and the cumulative percentage for each interval as illustrated in Table 5-2. The cumulative frequency for an interval is obtained by adding all the frequencies below it (smaller measurements) to the frequency for the interval of interest. The cumulative percentage is then calculated by dividing this sum by the total number of measurements. These cumulative percentages are then plotted on the vertical axis against the scale of dimensions on the abscissa to obtain the cumulative frequency distribution graph, Figure 5-3. For example, the cu-

Table 5-2. Cumulative Frequency Table

Standing Height of Army aviators (data after White, 1961)

Interval	Midpoint	Frequency	Cumulative Frequency	Cumulative Percentage
62.5–63.2	62.85	1	1	0.2
63.3–64.0	63.65	3	4	0.8
64.1–64.8	64.45	3	7	1.4
64.9–65.6	65.25	16	23	4.6
65.7–66.4	66.05	20	43	8.6
66.5–67.2	66.85	47	90	18.0
67.3–68.0	67.65	48	138	27.6
68.1–68.8	68.45	64	202	40.4
68.9–69.6	69.25	73	275	55.0
69.7–70.4	70.05	63	338	67.6
70.5–71.2	70.85	48	386	77.2
71.3–72.0	71.65	43	429	85.8
72.1–72.8	72.45	37	466	93.2
72.9–73.6	73.25	14	480	96.0
73.7–74.4	74.05	10	490	98.0
74.5–75.2	74.85	9	499	99.8
75.3–76.0	75.65	1	500	100.0

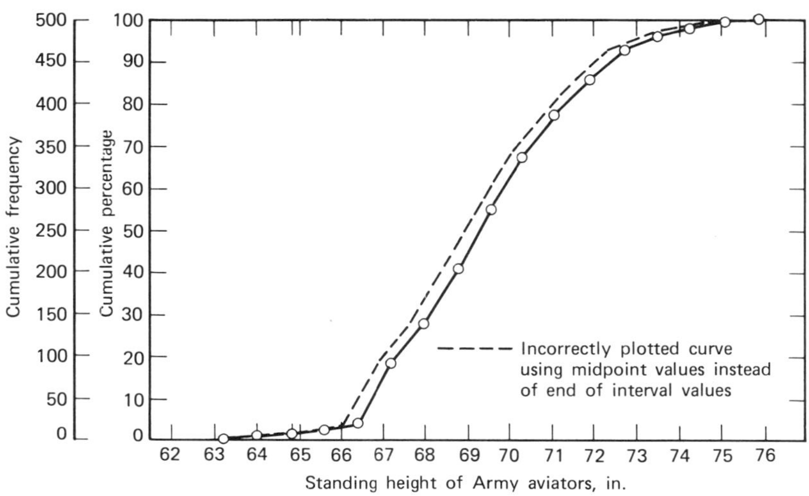

Figure 5-3. Cumulative frequency distribution graph.

mulative frequency for the interval 65.7 to 66.4 is obtained by adding 20, 16, 3, 3, and 1. This value is then divided by 500, the total number of measurements, to obtain the cumulative percentage or percentile value for that interval.

Note that in preparing a simple frequency polygon one uses the *midpoint* of the class interval to express the size of the class. However, in plotting a cumulative frequency distribution graph, it is more correct to use the upper limit of the class interval, since each point on the curve is to represent *all* the sizes up to that selected size. When plotting data on both types of curves, this correction factor should be considered. Otherwise, the values obtained from the cumulative frequency graph for a given percentile will be too small, as illustrated in Figure 5-3. If it is desired to plot the midpoints of the class intervals, one should adjust the percentiles downward to account for only one-half of the number of observations in the class being plotted.

With the above graph, it is a simple matter to find the corresponding value for a given percentile. For example, the value of the 50th percentile can be determined by finding the 50th percentile value on the vertical axis, extending a horizontal line from it to the intersection with the curve and then a vertical line downward to the scale of dimensions on the lower axis. Alternately, one can determine the percentile rank of a given dimension on the abscissa (e.g., 71 in.) by extending a line upward to the curve and horizontally to the vertical scale where the corresponding percentile rank may be read (75th percentile).

5.2.9 Normal Probability Graphs

Another very useful method of representing a cumulative frequency curve is shown in Figure 5-4. Here the scale of percentages has been distorted so that a straight line relationship will result between the percentage scale and the linear dimensional scale if the data are from a normal (Gaussian) distribution. In order to do this, the scale must be continually expanded as it moves away from the 50 percentile area of the scale. It may be seen that the 100 percentile mark and the 0 percentile mark cannot be depicted, since they are theoretically at infinity. However, for engineering problems, approaching the upper and lower extremes to a tenth or hundredth of a percent is sufficient. This so-called *normal probability graph paper* can be purchased from graph paper suppliers and is of considerable time-saving advantage in making predictions and estimates of distributions based upon very few distribution descriptions.

1. Drafting time is saved in collection, reduction, and communication of data by the use of straight lines where possible.
2. Only a normal distribution will appear as a straight line, so that non-normal curves may be easily detected.
3. The standard deviation for a normal distribution can be determined graphically, thus eliminating a lengthy calculation.
4. A complete normal population distribution may be reconstructed from only two given percentiles, or more commonly, from the mean plotted at the 50th percentile and the mean plus the standard deviation plotted at the 84.13th percentile.
5. New population distributions can be constructed conveniently by combining given proportions of known populations.
6. Considerable information may be condensed into a small area for ease of reference and rapid visual estimation of body dimension distributions.

5.2.10 Measures of Central Tendency, Dispersion, Symmetry and Peakedness

The following tables and figures summarize factors that characterize frequency distributions and provide formulas that allow one to precisely define them. Table 5-3 is a key table, which refers to following tables and figures for examples. Further details are in standard statistical texts.

5.2.11 Measures of Correlation

The discussion so far has dealt only with individual dimensional distributions. However, there are many very important engineering anthropometry problems that require information about the relationship of one dimension to one or more other dimensions. The simplest and most common case is the bivariate

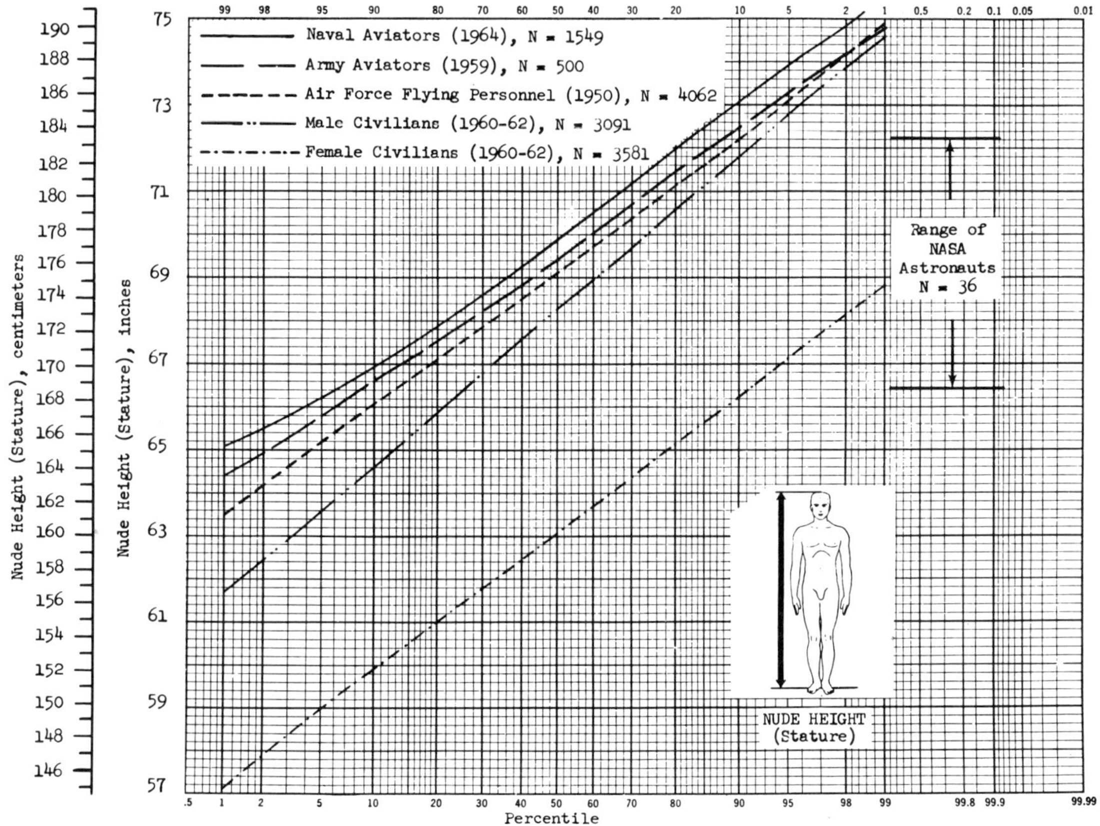

Figure 5-4. Normal probability graph. (Thomson, 1969. Data from Gifford et al., 1965; White, 1961; Hertzberg et al., 1954; Stoudt et al., 1965. Standing body illustration from Hertzberg et al., 1963. Courtesy of General Dynamics Corporation.)

Table 5-3. Measures of Central Tendency, Dispersion, Symmetry, and Peakedness

Statistic Definition	Remarks
A. Measures of central tendency	
Mean: $\overline{X} = \dfrac{\sum_{i=1}^{N} X_i}{N}$ (Eq. 5.1) or for data grouped in m classes: $\overline{X} = \dfrac{\sum_{j=1}^{m} f_j X_j}{\sum_{j=1}^{m} f_j}$ (Eq. 5.2)	Generally the most useful, unbiased, stable central value. X_i = magnitude of a given dimension for any individual. N = number of individuals in the sample or population. f_j = frequency of the class (number of individuals)
Median: That value in a series of measurements above and below which are the same number of measurements (average of two middle measurements if N is even)	Easy to compile. Often considered a better measure of central tendency than mean for skewed distributions.
Mode: The measurement of maximum frequency	Valuable for small sample statistics with variables having large or discrete changes. Highly dependent on size of class intervals.
B. Measures of dispersion *Standard deviation*: $S = \sqrt{\dfrac{\sum_{i=1}^{N} (X_i - \overline{X})^2}{N - 1}}$ (Eq. 5.3) alternate, more efficient calculation:	Significant points on the normal distribution curve are described in terms of S. Examples: 68.26% of the area under the curve lies between $\pm 1S$ form the mean. See Figure 5-5 and Table 5-4. Commonly used design percentiles can be expressed in terms of the mean and a ratio of S units from the mean (Table 5-5).

Table 5-3. Measures of Central Tendency, Dispersion, Symmetry, and Peakedness—(continued)

$S = \sqrt{\dfrac{\sum_{i-1}^{N} X_i^2 - \dfrac{\left(\sum_{i-1}^{N} X_i\right)^2}{N}}{N - 1}}$ (Eq. 5.4)	
Range: Difference between largest and smallest measurement	Unstable from sample to sample, but sometimes useful for small sample descriptions.
Percentiles: See text, Section 5.2.6	Most descriptive for normal distributions and large N. More stable as selected closer to the mean. Relatively easy to compile, but may be calculated for normal distributions (see Table 5-5).
C. Measure of skewness (symmetry)	
Moment coefficient: $a_3 = \dfrac{m_3}{S^3}$ (Eq. 5.5) where $m_3 = \dfrac{\sum_{j=1}^{N} (X_j - \overline{X})^3}{N}$ (Eq. 5.6) and S = standard deviation	When a_3 is positive, distribution is skewed to the left. When a_3 is 0, distribution is symmetrical. When a_3 is negative, distribution is skewed to the right. See Figure 5-6. To make skewed distributions approximately fit the normal model, use transformations such as the logarithmic, $Y = \log X$ (particularly useful for skinfold data) or $Y = \log (X + A)$ or the square root transformation $Y = \sqrt{X + B}$.
D. Measure of kurtosis (peakedness)	
Moment coefficient: $a_4 = \dfrac{m_4}{S^4}$ (Eq. 5.7)	For a normal distribution, $a_4 = 3$. Therefore $(a_4 - 3)$ is frequently used as the measure of kurtosis.

Table 5-3. Measures of Central Tendency, Dispersion, Symmetry, and Peakedness—(continued)

Statistic Definition	Remarks
where $m_4 = \dfrac{\sum_{j=1}^{N} (X_j - \overline{X})^4}{N}$ (Eq. 5.8) and S = standard deviation	When $(a_4–3)$ is positive, the distribution is leptokurtic (peaked). When $(a_4–3)$ is zero, the distribution is normal. When $(a_4–3)$ is negative, the distribution is platykurtic (flat). See Figure 5-6.

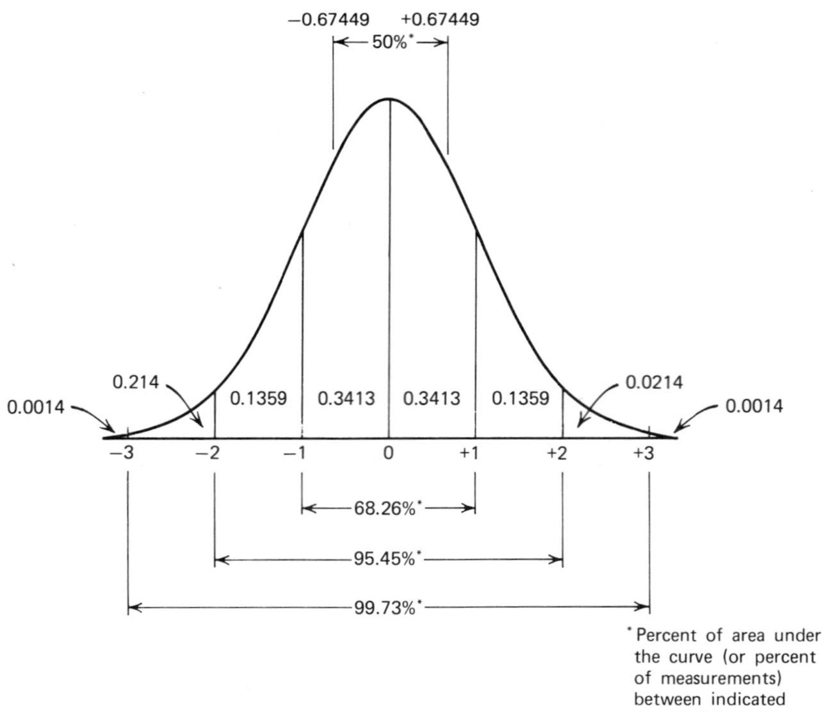

Figure 5-5. Areas under the normal curve between specified standard deviations (after McNemar, 1962).

Table 5-4. Probability of Occurrence of Statistical Deviations of Different Magnitudes (After Arkin and Colton, 1939)

Number of Standard Deviations	Probability of Occurrence of Deviation as Great as or Greater than Designated Number of Standard Deviations	Odds Against the Occurrence of a Deviation as Great as or Greater than the Designated Number of Standard Deviations
0.67449	50.00%	1.00 to 1
0.7	48.39	1.07 to 1
0.8	42.37	1.36 to 1
0.9	36.81	1.72 to 1
1.0	31.73	2.15 to 1
1.1	27.13	2.69 to 1
1.2	23.01	3.35 to 1
1.3	19.36	4.17 to 1
1.4	16.15	5.19 to 1
1.5	13.36	6.48 to 1
1.6	10.96	8.12 to 1
1.7	8.91	10.22 to 1
1.8	7.19	12.92 to 1
1.9	5.74	16.41 to 1
2.0	4.55	20.98 to 1
2.1	3.57	26.99 to 1
2.2	2.78	34.96 to 1
2.3	2.14	45.62 to 1
2.4	1.64	60.00 to 1
2.5	1.24	79.52 to 1
2.6	.932	106.3 to 1
2.7	.693	143.2 to 1
2.8	.511	194.7 to 1
2.9	.373	267.0 to 1
3.0	.270	369.4 to 1

distribution, for two dimensions. Such relationships can be expressed graphically, by various forms of scatter diagram and regression graphs, and by mathematical expressions such as the coefficient of correlation and the so-called regression equations.

A rough order of magnitude of the dependency relationship between two dimensional variables, such as Height and Weight, can be seen by a plot of points on a graph with a scale for one dimension along the abscissa and a scale for

Table 5-5. Factors for Computing Percentiles from Standard Deviations (Roebuck, 1957)

Percentile		K_1	Central Percent Covered	$K_2 = 2K_1$
30	70	0.524	40	1.045
25	75	.674	50	1.349
20	80	.842	60	1.683
15	85	1.036	70	2.073
10	90	1.282	80	2.563
5	95	1.645	90	3.290
2.5	97.5	1.960	95	3.920
1.0	99.0	2.326	98	4.653
0.5	99.5	2.576	99	5.152

Examples:

1. To find the 95th percentile, use $K_1 = 1.645$. When $\overline{X} = 35.1$ in. and $S = 1.5$ in.;
   $1.5 \times 1.645 = 2.5$ in.
   $35.1 + 2.5 = 37.6$ in., the 95th percentile.
2. To find the adjustment needed for the middle 90% of the same group:
   $1.5 \times 3.29 = 4.9$ in., the range of adjustment.

the other dimension along the ordinate. Examples of several forms of scatter diagrams are shown in Figure 5-7. Other more detailed forms specify the frequency of data points (Table 5-6) or the percentage of the data for each block defined by designated intervals on each axis.

In reporting anthropometric data, the preparation of scatter diagrams is highly desirable for two reasons. First, such presentations enable the user to observe quickly whether the bivariate distribution gives promise of some possible adjustment mode that can fit more persons for minimum expense or space requirement. Such a case would be like that of Figure 5-7*b*, which exhibits a definite change in the average ordinate magnitude with a reasonably small variation or spread in the ordinate at each point on the abscissa. On the other hand, when the distribution is so unsystematic as in Figure 5-7*a*, one can observe no significant trend or correlation between the observations. Adjustments to accommodate either variable must be independent of one another.

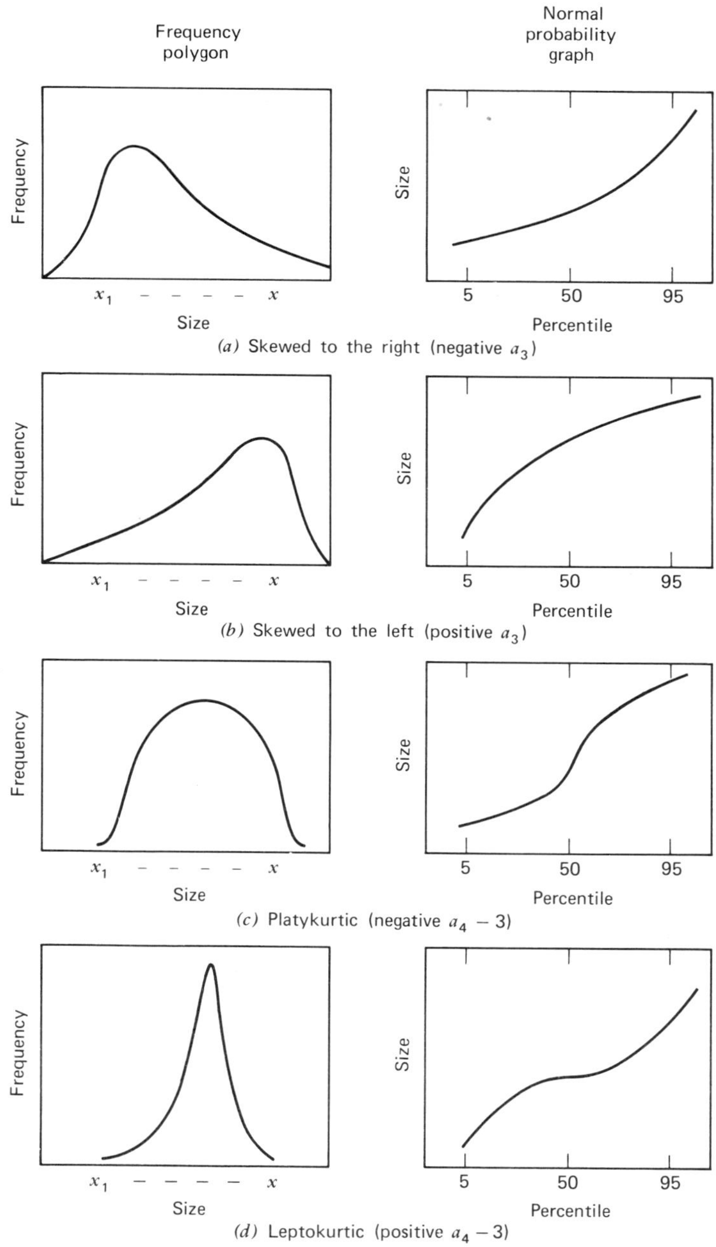

Figure 5-6. Examples of skewness and kurtosis.

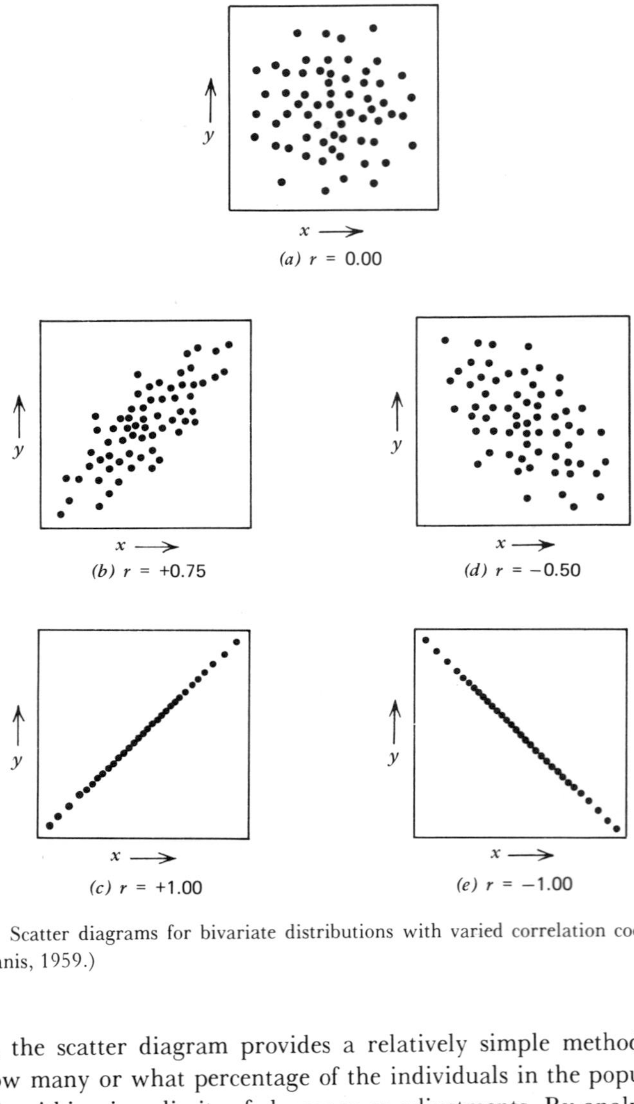

Figure 5-7. Scatter diagrams for bivariate distributions with varied correlation coefficients (r). (After Chapanis, 1959.)

Second, the scatter diagram provides a relatively simple method of determining how many or what percentage of the individuals in the population are likely to fit within given limits of clearance or adjustments. By analyzing samples of subjects with various combinations of sizes, one may define regions on the chart into those in which the subjects are or are not accommodated. By merely counting the number of subjects in these areas and dividing by the total number of persons on the chart, one can approximate the percentage accommodated. Example applications of this technique are given in Chapters VIII and IX.

The scatter diagram, while of great usefulness, is expensive and tedious to

Table 5-6. Bivariate Frequency Distribution Table[a]

Y variable (weight, lb)	X variable (height, in.)							
	60	62	64	66	68	70	72	74
230					1		1	3
220						4	4	3
210					5	1	2	1
200		2	1	3	9	1	7	1
190		1	3	8	16	3	5	
180		1	5	8	15	12	1	
170		2	8	18	26	8	1	
160			19	40	20	4		
150		5	15	26	9	2		
140	1	4	6	5	1			
130	2	3	1	1				
120	1	1						

[a] From *Introduction to Statistical Analysis*, 3rd ed. by W. J. Dixon and F. J. Massey, Copyright 1969, McGraw-Hill Book Co. Used with permission of McGraw-Hill Book Company.

prepare and file, and to transmit or communicate to others in reporting results. A more concise expression is often desirable. Furthermore, a numerical expression summarizing the degree of the relationship or correlation between two dimensions is desirable for direct comparison and for several mathematical manipulations of data for design. The commonly used summary statistic that expresses this relationship is the Pearson coefficient of correlation, which is calculated as follows:

$$r = b\, S_x/S_y \qquad \text{(Eq. 5.9)}$$

or

$$r = \sqrt{bb'} \qquad \text{(Eq. 5.10)}$$

where

$$b = \frac{\Sigma X_i Y_i - (\Sigma X_i \Sigma Y_i/N)}{\Sigma X_i^2 - [(\Sigma X_i)^2/N]} \qquad \text{(Eq. 5.11)}$$

$$b' = \frac{\Sigma Y_i X_i - (\Sigma Y_i \Sigma X_i/N)}{\Sigma Y_i^2 - [(\Sigma Y_i)^2/N]} \qquad \text{(Eq. 5.12)}$$

S_x = the standard deviation of variable X.
S_y = the standard deviation of variable Y.

The correlation coefficient is a measure of closeness of the relationship between two body dimensions. When one dimension is essentially independent of the other, the correlation is zero, Figure 5-7*a*. When large values of one variable tend to accompany large values of the other variable, the coefficient is positive, Figure 5-7*b*. When they are perfectly dependent, as in a straight line or linear relationship, the correlation coefficient is 1.0, Figure 5-7*c*. When the reverse is true, large values of one variable accompany small values of the other, the coefficient is negative, Figure 5-7*d*. The sign of the coefficient only indicates the direction of the relationship and not the degree. For anthropometric data the coefficients are usually positive. Additional anthropometric data correlation relationships are discussed in Section 6.4.3. A typical tabulation of coefficients of correlation is presented in Appendix B.

Churchill (1966) used the following example to provide some basis for judging whether two variables are meaningfully correlated (i.e., the coefficient r is large enough to be meaningful): if 100 individuals are above average in one dimension such as Height, the following table gives the number (p) of individuals that will be above average on a second dimension as well. This approximation will be reasonably good for data that fit the normal distribution curve.

The correlation coefficient is like a concise code signal for transmitting information about relationships. It must usually be decoded, or reconstituted into a set of numbers or graphs to apply the information to a design. One simple method depends on having a series of prepared theoretical bivariate distribution tables for various values of r. The scales of length would be in terms of nondimensional distribution expressions with a mean of zero and intervals expressed in terms of fractions of the standard deviation. One selects the table having the closest approximation to the given correlation coefficient and calculates the actual scale factors in appropriate units from knowledge of the individual statistical distributions, producing a table similar to Table 5-6.

Another approach, yielding a different form of information, is to calculate the so-called *regression* relationships, which express the average of one di-

Table 5-7.[a] **Number of Individuals above Average on Second of Two Dimensions, Given 100 are Above Average on First**

Coefficient of correlation, r	.1	.2	.3	.4	.5	.6	.7	.8	.9
Persons above average on second dimension, p	55	60	65	70	75	80	85	90	95

[a] Adapted from Churchill (1966).

mension as a function of the other. The regression relationships are given below:
For predicting Y from X:

$$Y = r\frac{S_y}{S_x}(X - \bar{X}) + \bar{Y} \qquad \text{(Eq. 5.13)}$$

For predicting X from Y:

$$X = r\frac{S_x}{S_y}(Y - \bar{Y}) + \bar{X} \qquad \text{(Eq. 5.14)}$$

These equations may be plotted on the bivariate scatter diagram as shown in Figure 5-8. A typical sample problem might involve estimating the range of Sitting Height for stewardesses. Selection standards would generally limit the range of Height for such a group. Thus, from regression relationships of Height as a function of Sitting Height for American women, one can estimate the stewardess average Sitting Height, as well as the average for the shortest and the tallest stewardesses. Estimation of the standard deviation of Sitting Height can be made by a variety of methods discussed in following paragraphs and in Section 6.3.

The accuracy of the regression equation estimates is measured by a statistic similar to the standard deviation, called the *standard error of estimate.* It is based on the differences between the estimated values and the actual values rather than the differences between the data points and the mean. Its formula when calculating Y is:

$$\text{Standard error of estimate, SE} = S_y\sqrt{1 - r^2} \qquad \text{(Eq. 5.15)}$$

For perfect correlations, the standard error of estimate is zero and the regression equations exactly predict the value of the desired dimension. When the correlation is zero, the standard error of estimate equals S. Thus the regression equations could predict no better than within the standard deviation. The predictive value of the regression equations can be illustrated in terms of the correlation coefficient and the standard deviation as shown in Table 5-8.

Just as two-thirds of the data lie within $\pm$ 1 standard deviation from the mean, two-thirds of the estimated values will be within $\pm$ 1 standard error estimate from the actual values, about 95% will lie within $\pm$ 2 SE, and so forth. Therefore, in the above example, if the correlation coefficient is 0.8 between the Height of stewardesses and their Sitting Height, the range of Sitting Height can be predicted with 95% confidence to be within $\pm 2 \times 0.6\ S$ or ± 1.2 standard deviations instead of ± 2 standard deviations if the correlation coefficient and regression equations had not been used.

This procedure can be extended by the use of the multiple correlation coefficient and multiple regression equations. The multiple regression equation is similar in form to the simple regression equation but involves two or more predictor dimensions. Theoretically there is no limit to the number of predictor dimensions that could be used. The multiple regression equations are calculated directly from the simple correlation coefficients plus the appropriate means and standard deviations.

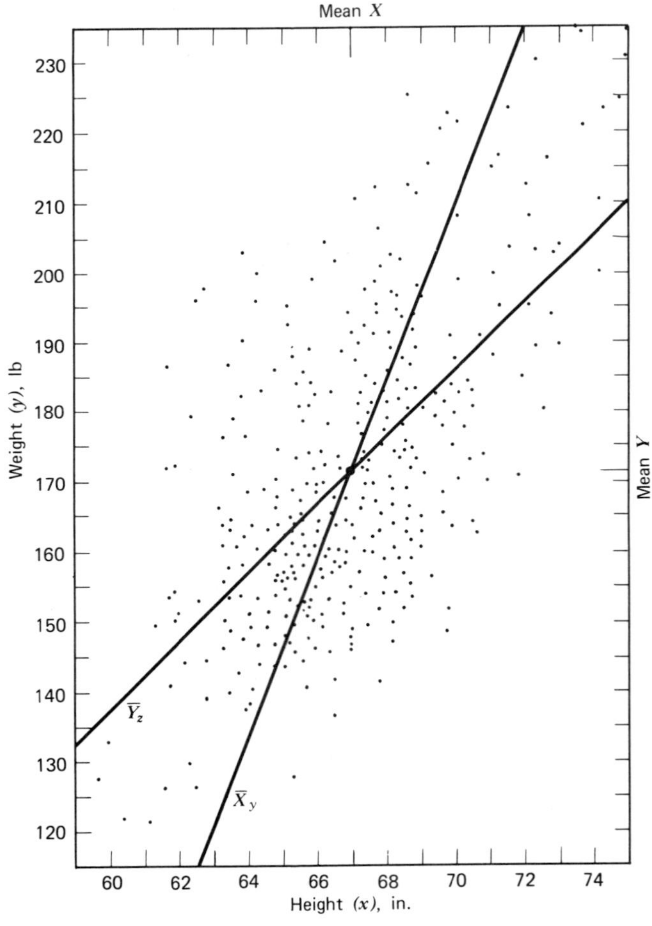

Figure 5-8. Typical scatter diagram and regression lines for a height-weight bivariate distribution (from *Introduction to Statistical Analysis,* 3rd Ed., by W. J. Dixon and F. J. Massey, Copyright 1969, McGraw-Hill Book Co. Used with permission of McGraw-Hill Book Company).

Table 5-8. The Predictive Value of Regression Equations as Shown by the Relationship Between the Correlation Coefficient and the Standard Error of Estimate (Churchill, 1966)

Correlation Coefficient γ	Standard Error of Estimate, SE
0.0	100% S
0.1	99.5 S
0.2	98.0 S
0.3	95.4 S
0.4	91.7 S
0.5	86.6 S
0.6	80.0 S
0.7	71.4 S
0.8	60.0 S
0.9	43.6 S

5.2.12 Standard Errors

The statistics calculated from samples, while correctly descriptive of the samples, are each merely an estimate of population parameters, since not all of the possible measurements are represented. The potential unknown deviation of the sample statistic from the comparable true population parameter is called the sampling error. This unknown error is presumed to be a single estimate of the population of sampling errors that would exist if many samples were obtained, and the statistics calculated for each sample. The single value obtained from the first sampling is thus subject to an uncertainty, which can be concisely expressed as a probability estimate, assuming the population of errors is normally distributed. Any of the usual statistics describing dispersion may be used for the frequency distribution of errors (e.g., standard deviation, quartile, or percentile). However, it is common practice to utilize the estimated standard deviation of this distribution of errors, which is abbreviated, for convenience, to the name *standard error*. The standard error can be calculated for the more common statistics by the formulas listed in Table 5-9.

The standard error of the sampling distribution can be used in a manner similar to the use of the standard deviation of the distribution of measurements. That is, if a large number of samples were taken, 68% of the sample

Table 5-9. Standard Error Formulas for Common Statistics (After Churchill, 1966)

1. Standard error of the mean: $S/\sqrt{N}$
2. Standard error of the standard deviation:

$$\frac{S}{\sqrt{2N}} = 0.71 \times \text{SE Mean}$$

3. Standard error of a correlation coefficient:

$$\frac{1 - r^2}{\sqrt{N - 3}}$$

4. Standard error of the percentiles:

$$\frac{k\,(100 - k)\,S}{100 f_k\, N}$$

where f_k is the ordinate of the normal curve at the kth percentile. Or

30th through 70th	$1.3 \times S/\sqrt{N}$
20th, 25th, 75th, 80th	$1.4 \times S/\sqrt{N}$
15th and 85th	$1.5 \times S/\sqrt{N}$
10th and 90th	$1.7 \times S/\sqrt{N}$
5th and 95th	$2.1 \times S/\sqrt{N}$
3rd and 97th	$2.5 \times S/\sqrt{N}$
2nd and 98th	$2.9 \times S/\sqrt{N}$
1st and 99th	$3.7 \times S/\sqrt{N}$

5. Standard errors of proportions and percentages:

(a) a proportion p: $\sqrt{\dfrac{p(1 - p)}{N}}$

(b) a percentage $P\%$: $\sqrt{\dfrac{P(100 - P)}{N}}$

6. Standard error of the coefficient of variation:

$$\frac{V}{\sqrt{2N}}$$

7. Standard error of the difference between the values of the same statistic computed on two independent samples:

(a) two mean values: $\sqrt{\dfrac{S_1^2}{N_1} + \dfrac{S_2^2}{N_2}}$

(b) two standard deviations: $\sqrt{\dfrac{S_1^2}{2N_1} + \dfrac{S_2^2}{2N_2}}$

(c) generally: $\sqrt{\text{SE}_1^2 + \text{SE}_2^2}$

means would lie within plus or minus one standard error of the population mean, 95% within two standard deviations, and so on.

The application of the standard error is illustrated in the following example. Assume that the Weight of passengers debarking from limousine busses into airline passenger terminals was estimated to be 169 lb by measuring samples of these passengers. Also assume that the standard error was 6 lb. Suppose the resulting data were then transmitted to a bus design company and an airplane design company. In determining acceleration performance of the bus, the designer may use the mean Weight data at its face value or, at best, add 6 lb to the mean to help assure himself that his mean estimate is not too low. The aircraft designer, on the other hand, may be concerned that failure to meet critical performance guarantees for a fully loaded airplane might cost his company loss of several millions in contracts. He would want to have a high probability of being right, say 95%. He, therefore, would multiply the standard error by 1.645 to obtain a 95th percentile estimate (9.870 lb), which he would add to the sample mean to obtain:

$$169 + 9.870 = 178.87 \text{ lb}$$

as his estimate of the population mean to be used as a basis for performance calculations.

The technique for ensuring a high probability of inferring correctly from a sample as illustrated by the previous example is known as establishing *confidence limits*. The most common confidence limit used in anthropometry is the 95% confidence limit. It is obtained by multiplying the standard error of a statistic by 1.96 for a "two-sided" confidence limit and 1.645 for a "one-sided" confidence limit, as in the example. That is, one can be sure that the true value of a population parameter will lie within $\pm$ 1.96 standard errors of the sample statistic, or below a value obtained by adding the sample statistic and 1.645 standard errors, or above the value of sample statistic less 1.645 standard errors, 95 out of every 100 times a sample is taken.

5.3 SAMPLE SIZE DETERMINATION

As discussed earlier, it is often difficult and normally impractical and/or impossible to take measurements on all of the individuals constituting a specified population. If one were able to include the entire population in his "sample," however, he would be assured that the percentiles, for example, which he calculates for establishing design limits, would only be limited in accuracy by the precision of his measuring instruments and the validity of his measuring technique. But a practical sample includes only a fraction of the population of interest, due to the expense and time-consuming nature of data collection procedures. This sample must be selected large enough to assure the accuracy and representiveness of the results while being small enough for the survey to stay within budget and schedule constraints.

The data needed, then, to calculate an appropriate sample size are: (1) the required level of accuracy of the final results and (2) an estimate of the dispersion or variability of the dimension that is to be measured. The latter estimate will be discussed in detail in the following section. The required level of accuracy depends on the specific situation, but most anthropometric measurements are reported to the nearest tenth of an inch or centimeter.

Since the distribution of most anthropometric measurements is approximately normal, the required sample size can be approximated from the following formula:

$$N = \left(\frac{K_1 S}{d}\right)^2 \qquad \text{(Eq. 5.16)}$$

where N = sample size required;
S = estimated standard deviation of the data;
d = the desired accuracy of the measurement ($\pm d$ units);
K_1 = a value taken from Table 5-10 for the statistic of interest.

For example, if it is desired to measure the mean value of Chest Depth with an accuracy of $\pm$ 0.1 in., with the standard deviation of this measurement being 0.75 in., the necessary sample size would be calculated as follows:

$$N = \left[\frac{(1.96)\,(0.75)}{0.1}\right]^2 = [14.7]^2 = 216$$

Note that the K values vary with the statistic being calculated. Also note that the value for the 50th percentile (median) is larger than the value for the mean. This is due to the more frequent fluctuations in the median from sample to sample than the mean; the mean is a more stable measure of central value.

The accuracy of this formula decreases as N drops below 100. If the initial sample size calculated (N_1) is less than 100, a more accurate estimation can be made by recalculating N using K_2 instead of K_1.

For counted data such as obtained in a public opinion poll, the following formulas can be used to calculate the approximate size of a random sample for estimating the proportion of a population with a certain opinion.

$$N = \left[\frac{0.98}{d}\right]^2 \qquad \text{(Eq. 5.17)}$$

where N = sample size required and d = desired accuracy in percent.

For example, a pilot population might be surveyed to determine if they felt a new type of restraint system was comfortable, and accuracy was desired to the

Table 5-10. *K* Values for Sample Size Determination

K_1	Statistic of Interest
1.96	Mean
1.39	Standard deviation
2.46	50th percentile
2.46	45th and 55th percentile
2.49	40th and 60th percentile
2.52	35th and 65th percentile
2.58	30th and 70th percentile
2.67	25th and 75th percentile
2.80	20th and 80th percentile
3.00	15th and 85th percentile
3.35	10th and 90th percentile
4.14	5th and 95th percentile
4.46	4th and 96th percentile
4.92	3rd and 97th percentile
5.67	2nd and 98th percentile
7.33	1st and 99th percentile

If the initial sample size calculated (N_i) is less than 100, a more accurate estimate of N for the mean can be made by recalculation, using in place of K_1 the K_2 value for the appropriate N_i, where $K_2 = 2.00$ ($100 > N_i > 40$); 2.05 ($40 > N_i > 20$); 2.16 ($20 > N_i > 10$); and 2.78 ($10 > N_i$).

nearest 1%.

$$N = \left[\frac{0.98}{.01}\right]^2 = [98]^2 = 9604$$

The above calculations assume that the population is about evenly divided on the question. If the true proportion can be estimated in advance, a smaller sample can be used. If it was known that about 80% thought the system comfortable, the following formula can be used:

$$N = \left[\frac{1.96\sqrt{p(1-p)}}{d}\right]^2 \qquad \text{(Eq. 5.18)}$$

then

$$N = \left[\frac{1.96\sqrt{0.8\,(1 - 0.8)}}{0.01}\right]^2 = [78.4]^2 = 6147$$

Note that in all of the above calculations, the sample size required was related to the square of the required accuracy. To double the accuracy of the results (reducing the allowable error by one half), one must quadruple the sample size. Clearly, there is a very real limit to the accuracy that can be achieved simply by increasing the sample size. Another approach would be to reduce the variability of the measurements.

5.4 POPULATION DIMENSION VARIABILITY ESTIMATION

One of the basic requirements for sample size determination specified above was an estimate of the variability of the dimension to be measured. Estimation of dimension variability is equally important in the process of adding and subtracting body dimensions, which is discussed in Section 5.5. It is possible to make a reasonable estimate of this variability in several ways, some almost purely statistical in nature, others more empirical and based on biometric patterns of human shape and growth.

1. The variability of the same dimension on other populations may be used to calculate the estimate. This assumes that a dimension has approximately equal relative spread on similar populations. A correction factor can be used to account for population differences. For example, the correction factor could consist of the ratio of the standard deviations for some common dimension such as Standing Height, which is known for both populations.
2. A small pilot study could be conducted measuring a few randomly selected individuals from the population of interest. An estimated standard deviation can be calculated from the results.
3. Another approach to estimating dimension variability involves a measure of relative dispersion, called the coefficient of variation (V),* which can easily be calculated by the following formula:

$$V\,(\text{in }\%) = \frac{S}{\bar{X}} \times 100 \qquad \text{(Eq. 5.19)}$$

The V can be used in a fashion similar to the standard deviation, but as a percentage. That is, two-thirds of a population lies between (100

* V is the symbol used by Hertzberg, Daniels, and Churchill (1954) and by Spiegel (1961). It is used here for convenience and learning ease, although the possibility of confusion with volume or velocity symbols could exist in other contexts of engineering.

+ V) % and (100 – V) % of the mean; 95% lie between (100 + 2 V) and (100 – 2 V) % of the mean; and 99% lie between (100 + 3 V) and (100 – 3 V) % of the mean.

The usefulness of this statistical concept is based on empirical biometric data: the V's of standard anthropometric dimensions generally have values that lie within a relatively narrow range from about 3 to 10%. (Tabulated data on such coefficients of variation are presented as part of the biometric relationships data summarized in Section 6.3, Table 6-3) Furthermore, body dimensions of similar type and magnitude, for example, "long body lengths," "large circumferences," and the like, have approximately equal V's. Thus, to complete this procedure requires than one find data from which to select the appropriate V, then estimate the standard deviation by multiplying the V times an estimate of the mean. (The estimate of the mean also can be obtained by a variety of approaches, some involving the biometric relations described in Chapter VI, others involving simple geometric relationships.)

4. If one cannot determine whether the dimension falls into one of the classifications listed in Table 6-3, one may estimate (with less accuracy) the standard deviation as a function of the mean, using plots of these relationships as described in Section 6.3.
5. Another method, almost purely statistical in nature, applies in the special case where the dimension whose variability is to be estimated is the sum or difference of two dimensions with known variability. Then, given the coefficient of correlation (r) between the known dimensions (x and y), the following formulas may be used for normal distributions:

   (a) When addition of two dimensions is involved:

$$S^2_{(x+y)} = S^2_x + S^2_y + 2rS_xS_y \qquad \text{(Eq. 5.20)}$$

   (b) When subtraction of two dimensions is involved:

$$S^2_{(x-y)} = S^2_x + S^2_y - 2rS_xS_y \qquad \text{(Eq. 5.21)}$$

   In practice, suitable correlation coefficient data are often difficult to find. Yet, it is likely there exists a significant degree of correlation between many dimensions. A partial help for this problem is found in Appendix B, containing tables of correlation coefficients for U.S. Air Force males.

The foregoing discussion brings out the often observed close relationship between estimation of variability and estimation of the average in anthropometric applications. It is difficult to discuss the one without considering the other.

5.5 COMBINATIONS OF STATISTICAL DISTRIBUTIONS

It is often necessary to combine statistical data for practical applications in engineering anthropometry. The more commonly occurring requirements are: (1) to develop statistical distributions for dimensions of a composite population from distributions of several known component populations; (2) to estimate an unknown dimension distribution by addition or subtraction of two known dimension distributions; and (3) to estimate the group mean and standard deviation of the distribution of the sum of individual dimensions of three or more persons.

5.5.1 Developing Composite Populations

When anthropometric surveys have been conducted on several specific populations, and it is necessary to know the distribution of these body measurements as a group rather than as separate populations, a composite population must be synthesized. The combination of populations is here illustrated by a hypothetical problem in which it is given that a certain troop transport schedule is to carry 30% pilots (cadets), 45% air crew gunners, and 25% nurses, whose respective heights are given in Figure 5-9. The computation is shown in Table 5-11 and the dot-dash line on Figure 5-9 shows the resulting distribution.

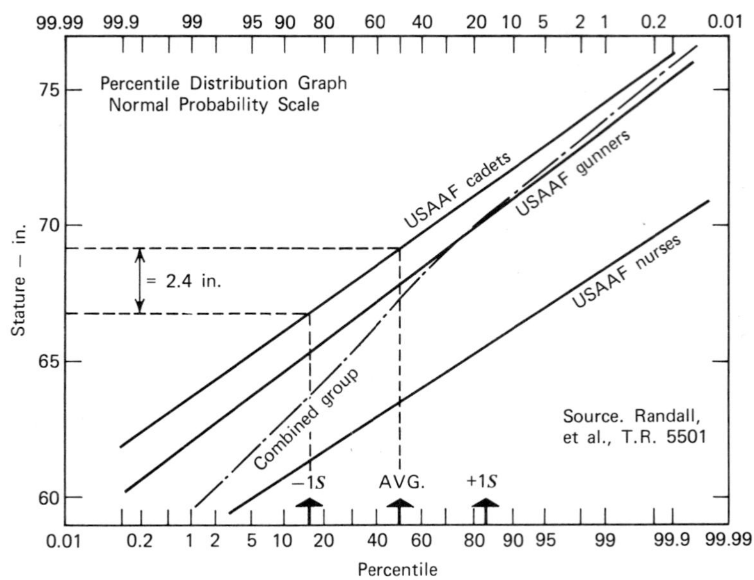

Figure 5-9. Illustration of the use of normal probability paper for developing composite populations (Roebuck, 1957).

Table 5-11. A Method of Forming a Composite Population Dimension Distribution from Three Populations with Different Means and Standard Deviations (Roebuck, 1957)[a]

		Cadets		Gunners		Nurses		Combined
	Stature, In.	Percentile	Percent in New Population	Percentile	Percent in New Population	Percentile	Percent in New Population	Population Percentile
Column no.	(1)	(2)	(3)	(4)	(5)	(6)	(7)	(8)
Operation			Col. (2) × .30		Col. (4) × .45		Col. (6) × .25	(3) + (5) + (7)
	61	.03	0.009	.3	.135	12.5	3.13	3.27
	64	1.4	0.42	6.0	2.7	59.0	14.75	17.87
	67	18.0	5.4	36.0	16.2	94.6	23.7	45.3
	70	64.0	19.2	80.0	36.0	99.9	24.98	80.18
	73	94.6	28.4	98.0	44.1	100	25	97.5

[a] Percentiles determined from Figure 5-9: m = 67.4 in.; 95% = 72.2 in.; 5% = 60.4 in.

5.5.2 Adding or Subtracting Body Dimensions

Unknown dimensions distributions may sometimes be derived by adding or subtracting known component dimensions. The proper procedure is first to add or subtract the means of the known distributions, then estimate the spread (e.g., standard deviation) of the resulting distribution, and finally, calculate the desired percentiles. It is a common mistake to add or subtract two 95th percentile dimensions to obtain the 95th percentile for a new dimension. Only in the case of the 50th percentile may the dimensions be directly added or subtracted. The erroneous results of adding or subtracting the 95th percentiles are shown in the following example.

Suppose it is desired to know the Shoulder-to-Elbow Length for Air force flying personnel, and only the Shoulder Height and Elbow Rest Height dimension distributions are known. (Actually, all three distributions are known and will be used here for comparison with estimated values.) The calculation in Table 5-12 shows the effect of subtracting like percentiles. In this example the estimated mean is in error by 0.18 in., but the estimated 95th percentile is in error by 1.1 in.

This considerable error may be reduced by following one of the variability estimation procedures outlined previously in Section 5.4. For example, one may estimate the standard deviation by referring to Figure 6-3. The dashed lines indicate a value for S between 0.5 and 1.3 in. for the estimated mean. From these values, one can determine the possible range of values of the desired percentile using normal probability paper or factors from Table 5-5. For the latter, the 95th percentile may be found as follows:

S		*Factor*		*Difference between mean and 95th percentile*
0.5	×	1.645	=	0.822 in.
1.3	×	1.645	=	2.14 in.

then,

$$.822 + 14.14 = 14.962, \text{ an estimated minimum 95th percentile}$$
$$2.14 + 14.14 = 16.280, \text{ an estimated maximum 95th percentile}$$

The midrange value for the 95th percentile would be ½ (14.962 + 16.28) = 15.6 in., which gives a true error of 15.6 – 15.4 = .2 in.

Adding and subtracting known dimensions is but one of many procedures using combinations of statistical and biometric relationship data to estimate unknown dimensions for design or evaluation. Others, derived from Chapters V and VI are summarized in Sections 7.3.1 and 7.3.2.

Table 5-12. Error Due to Incorrect Estimation Procedure for 95th Percentile (Roebuck, 1957)

	Mean (In.)	Standard Deviation (In.)	95th Percentile (In.)
Shoulder height (sitting):	23.26	1.14	25.1
Elbow rest height:	9.12	1.04	10.8
Difference: (estimated shoulder-elbow length):	14.14		14.3 estimated by subtraction
True distances (measured distribution)	14.32	0.67	15.4
Error:	0.18		1.1

5.5.3 Estimating Group Mean and Standard Deviations

An example of this type of statistical data combination is the determination of average and standard deviation of seat width for side-by-side arrangement in a passenger aircraft. Assume the sum of N seated passenger shoulder widths sets the total seat width. If random seating is assumed, then the mean and standard deviation of the combined widths may be found from the following formulas:

$$M_N = NM \qquad \text{(Eq. 5.22)}$$

$$S_N = S\sqrt{N} \qquad \text{(Eq. 5.23)}$$

where

N = number of persons sitting together;
M = mean of distribution of shoulder widths for the population;
M_N = mean of distribution of sum of shoulder widths of N persons sitting together in the same row;
S = standard deviation of shoulder widths for the population;
S_N = standard deviation of the sum of shoulder widths for N persons sitting together.

5.6 USE OF COMPUTERS FOR STATISTICAL ANALYSIS

Handling the great mass of data typical of statistical analysis often involves tedious and time-consuming manual calculations, which can be reduced by machine computation. To minimize hand labor, the sample data should be fed to a computer as early as possible in the process. If possible the data should be keypunched or otherwise recorded in machine-readable form at the field site as data are taken, and relayed to a central computing facility. As a minimum, the format for data collection should be designed for ready use as a guide for keypunching of input cards in addition to complying with criteria discussed in Chapter II. Several detailed procedures described by Hertzberg et al. (1954) and Clauser et al. (1972) can save labor and reduce card storage space in preparing anthropometric data for statistical analysis by machine.

VI
BIOMETRIC RELATIONSHIPS

6.1 INTRODUCTION

This chapter provides guidance in evaluating the meaning and significance to engineering design of selected relationships among anthropometric data. Understanding of such relationships aids the investigator, the analyst, and the designer in establishing priorities and scope of planned efforts to achieve cost effectiveness. Most anthropological survey reports and handbooks of data for human engineering contain inadequate discussion of these important concerns. Helpful exceptions are books by Damon, Stoudt, and McFarland (1966) and Van Cott and Kinkade (1972), which are strongly recommended to the reader. The discussions herein provide additional information and emphasize topics found important in the authors' experience and expected to have future significance in this field.

6.2 POPULATION CHARACTERISTICS

Information on population differences of a biological and socioeconomic nature has potential significance to engineering anthropometry. Specific uses for such data include making decisions about whether data from several populations can be combined, when a new synthesis of known data is appropriate, or when a survey of a sample of the population is required.

A checklist of significant general population characteristics appears in Table 6-1. Elements of human choice implied in Group I suggest that people can change jobs, move to different countries, change attitudes and beliefs, and improve income by study and work. Group II characteristics are those of inheritance, or results of irreversible disfiguration, over which humans generally have little control. Further details and examples are presented in following paragraphs.

6.2.1 Occupational Considerations

The majority of engineering anthropometry design problems are associated with occupational groups. "Occupation" is here defined as activity or occu-

Table 6-1. Checklist of Population Characteristics Descriptors for Engineering Anthropometry

Group I: Characteristics Related to Personal Choice
- Occupation—vocation, activity, hobby, sport, study________
- Socioeconomic Class—Income range________Education________
- National Group—Country of origin________Mixture________
- Ethnic Group—Culture, language, religion________

Group II: Biologically Determined, Accidental
- Race—Relatively homogeneous________Mixture________
- Sex—Males________Females________Mixture________
- Historical Period—From________to________
- Personal Age Range—From________to________
- Malformation—Injury________Birth defect________Disease________
- Body build (somatotype)________

pancy, independent of income considerations, and includes sports, hobbies, studies, and so forth. The descriptions of such populations for design or for evaluation can be aided by results from the field of *occupational anthropology* (Damon and McFarland, 1955). Table 6-2 is a list of several examples of job-related characteristics. The selection process in hiring may be explicitly stated and objectively related to valid criteria, or merely the result of prejudice. In either case, the prime goal for engineering design consideration is to describe the physical situation in order to develop design criteria.

6.2.2 National Extraction, Geographical Location and Ethnic Groups

User populations may be characterized by any or all of the groupings in the above title. These classifications may infer differences in proportions, in preferred bodily work or rest positions, or in clothing, all of which are of concern to engineering anthropometry. Further examples and discussion are provided in Van Cott and Kinkade (1972) and Damon, Stoudt, and McFarland (1966).

6.2.3 Historical Variability and Age Variability

Quantification of the well-known increase in growth of individuals from infancy to adulthood is needed for such diverse engineering design projects as school equipment and furniture (Oxford, 1969), automotive safety equipment (Rogers and Silver, 1968), and survival equipment (McFadden and Young, 1971). Data on growth are available from a variety of sources (Martin, 1953, 1954; Stuart, 1961; Snyder, Spencer, Owings, and Van Eck, 1972; Malina et al., 1973). "Shrinkage" related to aging of adults has also been noted (Stoudt, Damon, McFarland, and Roberts, 1965). However, some of this apparent

Table 6-2. Possible Population Selection Factors in Various Occupations and Activities

Occupation/Activity	Selection Factors Stated or Presumed
"Blue-collar workers" (factory, construction, and farming)	1. Special skills, strength, health, endurance, generally lower socioeconomic groups.
Astronaut	1. Minimum weight and length—desirable to reduce volume, weight, and drag of capsule. 2. Age—generally below 40. 3. Excellent health—lean body type, meso- or ectomorphic.
Nurse	1. Females traditionally selected are usually smaller than males.
Stewardess	1. Females—"desirable for U.S. customer image," according to airline officials. Also lighter, requiring smaller reduction of payloads. In current aircraft, probably primarily a cultural requirement.
Military	1. Definite Height, Weight, and other health standards specified for each service. Based upon presumed requirements for stamina, possibly on vehicular or equipment limits in some cases.
Basketball player	1. Taller players can more easily reach closer to basket, guard smaller men, pass ball over heads of smaller men.
Stevedore	1. Strength to handle large crates is desirable, probable mesomorphic type.
College students	1. Higher socioeconomic status than general population—probably better health care; taller than average of population. 2. Younger average age than general population of adults.

change may be related to historical trends discussed below. Figure 6-1 provides an example of a cross section of the U.S. population circa 1960–1962.

Another relationship of body dimensions to time which is of emerging importance is the relatively slow *historical* change of means and standard deviations of adult populations (and children of a given age range) over decades (Trotter and Gleser, 1951a,b; Newman, 1963). Figure 6-2 is an example of such trends in a military population, which are of concern to design of such long-range projects as the NASA Space Shuttle Orbiter and military vehicle weapons systems. Many other examples are given by Van Cott and Kinkade (1972) and by Damon, Stoudt, and McFarland (1966), and by authors of shorter articles describing civilian populations (*Product Engineering,* 1968; Lieber, 1960).

Such considerations force the analyst and designer into the uncomfortable role of predicting the future, as well as analyzing the past, to account for probable trends and their causes. A simple linear extrapolation such as in Figure 6-2 suggests a change in Stature, presumably of biological origin, amounting to 1.25 in. between 1950 and 1980. This implies a rate of 0.0418 in. per year. However, a recent unpublished study by the Aerospace Medical Research Laboratory at Wright-Patterson Air Force Base indicates the growth rate for Air Force males has been closer to 0.032 in. per year during the last two decades. Further analyses of the data suggest caution, for there may be selective attrition of shorter men as a function of duration of service in each year's incoming group. Such a trend would be an example of a nonbiological historical change. The consideration of various competing effects is a part of the methods to improve predictions and thus improve the general state of the art in engineering anthropometry.

6.3 VARIABILITY PATTERNS OF POPULATIONS

Knowledge of variability patterns characteristic of human populations is an important aid to accuracy of estimation of statistical means and standard deviations. Estimations are often required by the press of time and lack of data on specific critical dimensions or other anthropometric quantities.

6.3.1 Variability Versus Average

Roebuck (1957) has described a useful pattern of correlation of variability (standard deviation) with the mean of the distribution of body dimensions, which is revealed in Figure 6-3. Compilations of similar data for previously classified populations can be helpful in estimation of dimensions variability.

For such purposes, it is best to select a frequently reported, well-described datum point, such as stature, then express the scale of ordinate (S) and abscissa ($\overline{X}$) in terms of percentages of that datum. This is simply done by di-

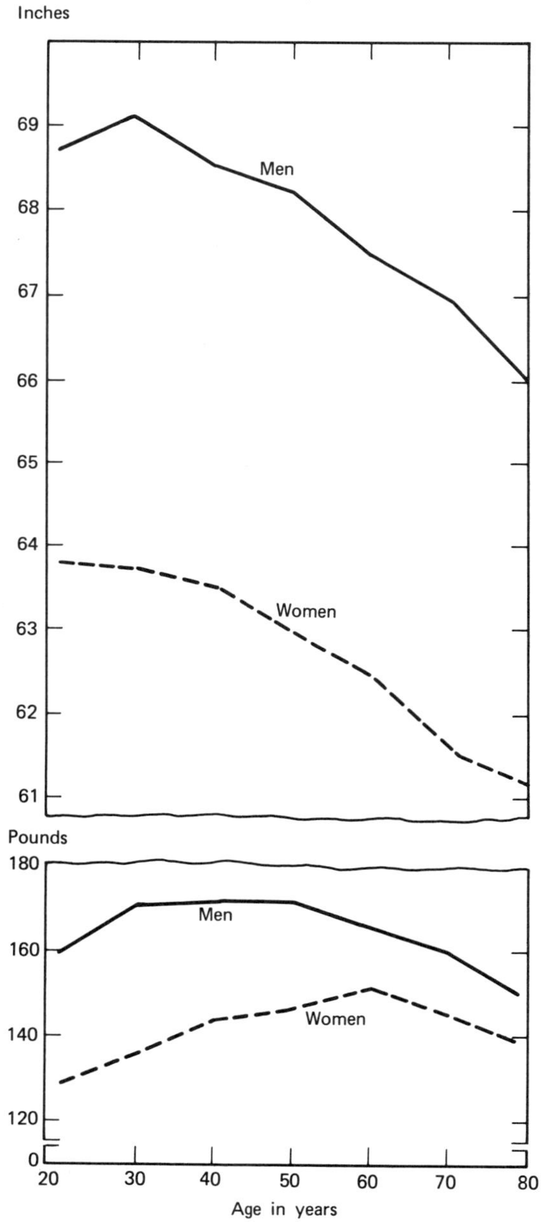

Figure 6-1. Average Height and Weight as a function of age for U.S. adults 18–19 years, circa 1960–1962 (from Stoudt, Damon, McFarland, and Roberts, 1965).

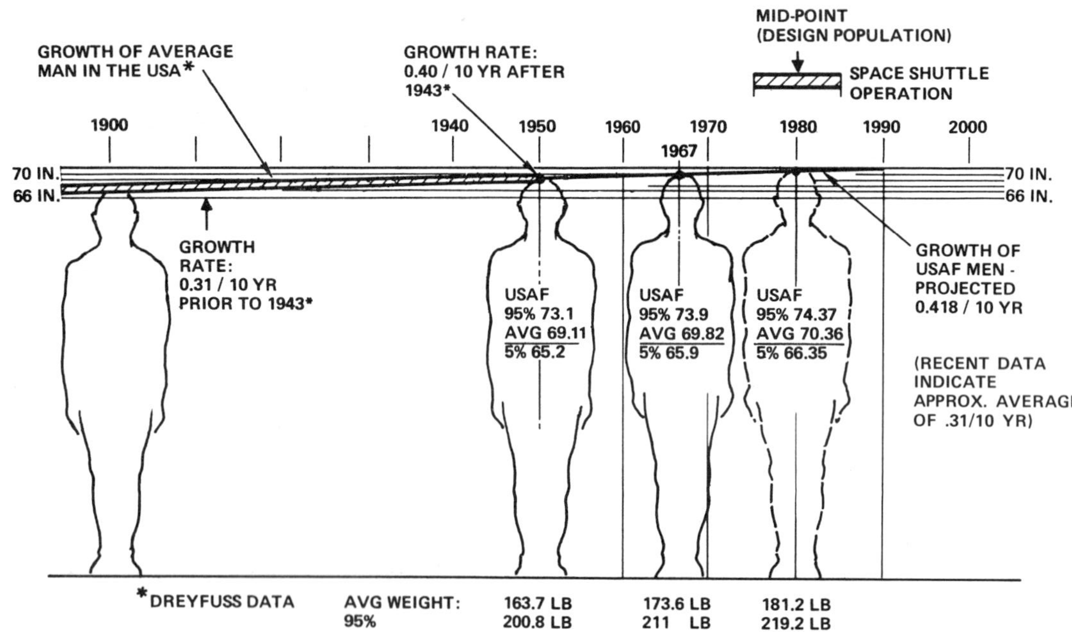

Figure 6-2. Anthropometric projection for U.S. Air Force flying personnel to 1980 Heights and Weights. (Roebuck, Kroemer, and Thomson, 1973.)

viding the magnitudes of all other data points by that of the selected datum and multiplying by 100. The outer scales in Figure 6-3 provide an example.

The predictive value of such similarities depends on selection factors for the population and on the various inherent population differences mentioned in the preceding discussion (occupation, sex, age, nation, race, etc.). This pattern of similarity can be used to obtain a first approximation of standard deviations for populations assumed to have some similar characteristics. For example, the patterns in Figure 6-3 apply best to males in the U.S. Air Force, less to American males in general and probably not so closely to, say, female Japanese.

To express the relationships of means and standard deviations of individual dimensions on a more standardized basis, the coefficient of variation is used:

$$V = \frac{S}{\bar{X}} \times 100 = \text{coefficient of variation (in percent)} \qquad \text{(Eq. 6.1)}$$

This ratio becomes a useful tool for classifying various types of dimensions of the human body according to their variabilities (see Table 6-3).

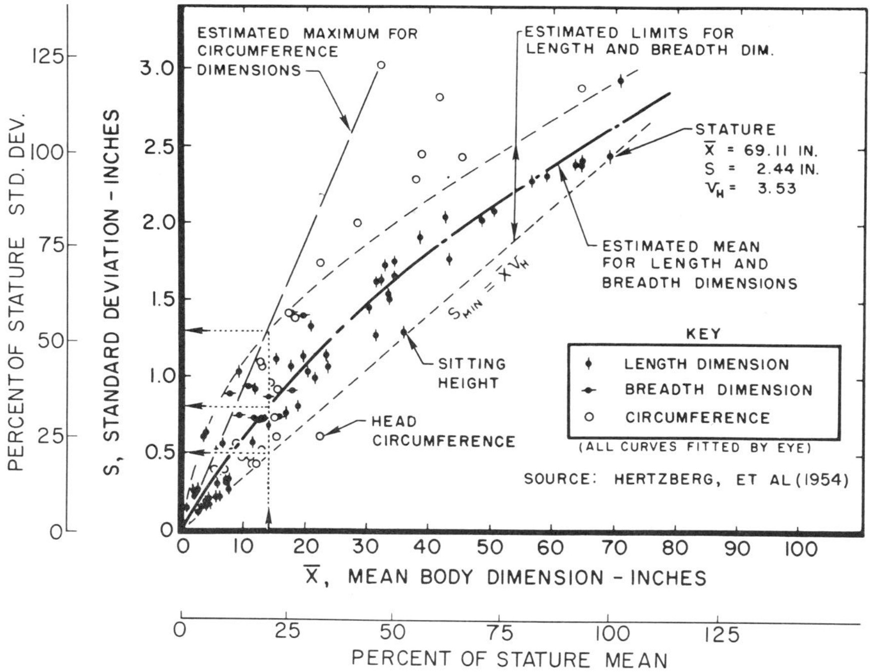

Figure 6-3. Standard deviation as a function of distribution mean for U.S. Air Force flying personnel—1950. (Adapted from Roebuck, 1957).

Table 6-3. Coefficient of Variation for Selected Body Dimensions and Dimension Classes

Body Dimension	Average V^a per Class	Average V^a per Dimension	Range of V from Ten Anthropometric Surveys[a]
Long body lengths	3.69		
Stature		3.48	2.74–3.79
Sitting Height		3.57	3.09–4.04
Eye Height, Sitting		4.01	3.73–4.53
Short body lengths	4.58		
Shoulder-Elbow Length		4.92	4.41–5.99
Forearm-Hand Length		4.46	3.92–4.81
Buttock-knee Length		4.42	4.04–4.80
Knee Height, Sitting		4.66	4.16–5.05
Foot Length		4.45	3.90–4.87
Hand Length		4.59	4.16–5.06
Major breadths	5.92		
Hip Breadth, Sitting		5.94	4.96–6.97
Shoulder Breadth		5.15	4.13–6.23
Elbow-Elbow Breadth		7.16	6.05–8.73
Major depths	8.79		
Chest Depth		7.65	6.19–8.61
Waist Depth		10.80	8.43–14.39
Buttock Depth		8.33	7.27–9.34
Major circumferences	6.83		
Chest Circumference		6.18	5.51–7.14
Waist Circumference		8.81	7.69–10.20
Buttock Circumference		5.77	4.90–6.82
Calf Circumference		6.56	5.88–7.47
Major head measurements	3.53		
Head Length		3.54	3.26–3.77
Head Breadth		3.85	3.33–4.93
Head Circumference		2.67	2.44–2.86

[a] Values (in percent) calculated from data of ten surveys reported by Garrett and Kennedy (1971).

6.3.2 Dimensional Distribution Configurations

Two major groupings of statistical distributions are often found in large, relatively homogeneous populations that have not been severely truncated at upper and lower ends of the distribution. The first, called "bony dimensions" consists of body dimensions that are measured between prominences which have relatively little covering flesh. Examples are Stature, Sitting Height, Biacromial Breadth, Shoulder-Elbow Height, and Knee Height, Sitting. These have cumulative distributions very closely represented by a straight line on normal probability graph paper, that is, they are Gaussian distributions or nearly so.

The second, called "fleshy dimensions" are those covering, starting, or ending at soft tissues. Examples are Abdominal Depth, Waist Girth, Thigh Girth, Neck Circumference, and Buttock Circumference. They are likely to have a cumulative distribution whose shape on normal probability graph paper is concave upward. A few persons have abnormally large amounts of fatty deposits, shifting the distribution unsymmetrically to the high side.

6.3.3 Individual Percentile Analysis: Useful Mythical Men

The following discussion is presented to emphasize that *individuals* are not populations, to illustrate by examples that great deviations of percentiles among an individual's body dimensions and proportions are commonplace, natural, and must be accounted for in design.

The concept of a *profile chart* is a simple, but useful method for visualizing such comparison. A selected group of dimensions of an individual is plotted in terms of percentiles on a scale from 0 to 100. If all of the body dimensions of the individual are equivalent to, say, an 80th percentile of the population, his profile is revealed as a straight line across the chart at the 80th percentile level. Deviations show as an upward or downward displacement of the line. Figure 6-4 presents actual data of three individuals. It will be clearly seen that such profiles have a "sawtooth" character, often with wide swings between peaks and valleys. Selection of the range of percentiles for an operator design standard must be done with care and understanding of consequences. The following discussion concerns some simple approaches to design limit specifications, and points out various associated problems and pitfalls.

One may define an "average man" as the assemblage, or tabulation, of all 50th percentile measurements, or mean measurements. Such a collection of numbers is not a "man," but only a myth, a concept, or model in the mind. Drawings or manikins and dummies that represent such mental images are merely convenient collections of midpoint conditions, from which variations (describing design limits) can be measured. While most designs should be able to accommodate these midpoint conditions, they usually should accommodate much, much more.

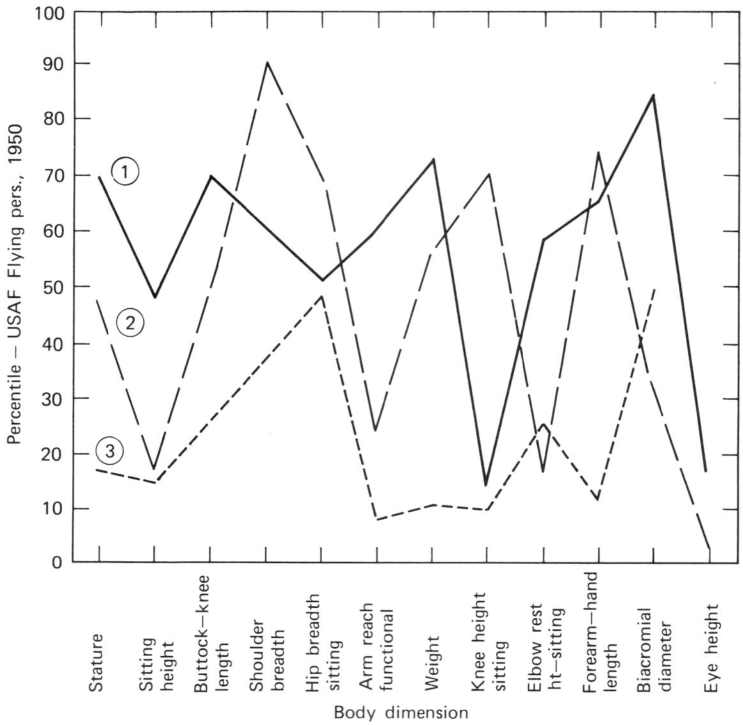

Figure 6-4. Examples of profile chart analysis of individual subject percentiles. The graph lines connect points that indicate the magnitude, on the vertical scale, of percentiles for the various body dimensions of 3 actual individuals listed along the horizontal scale.

A serious problem arises when these representations are thought to represent *all* people in a population. In fact, they represent *exactly no one.* Even taking a broader, more liberal interpretation of "average" to include the 15% above and below the midpoint magnitudes of each dimension will not produce a range of dimensions in which even one single individual's complete set of dimensions can be included. This has been documented by Daniels (1952) in an analysis of only ten measurements of over 4000 flying personnel. This analysis documents the unrealness of the "average man." May its nonreal corporality rest in peace, to plague human factors engineers no more.

A "common percentile man" or "constant percentile man" is a generalization that includes the foregoing "average man." This mythical individual is conceived as the collection of all dimensions of a population that represent one common, specific percentile level of each of the individual dimensions. Rather than the 50th percentile, a more extreme level is usually selected, such as the 5th or the 95th percentile. As living individuals, each is as unlikely and unreal as the "average man." However, manikins and drawings of *both small* and *large percentile figures* are more useful than a single representation of the middle percentiles, since together they represent design criteria range dimensions. Properly used, *in pairs,* these mythical bodies can help prevent many gross errors in work space design or personal equipment and accommodations design.

A further sophistication of the mythical man concept involves selection of varied levels of percentiles, based upon their criticality in the intended design. Thus, one may set a small number of critical design dimension limits at a fairly extreme range, such as the 10th or 90th percentile. The remainder may be allowed to range even wider, such as to the 2nd and 98th percentiles. This "hybrid percentile man," while more complicated to specify, and involving additional complexity in developing design standards, assures a reasonable measure of control with less likelihood of fit problems for the selected population. Proper selection of the cut-off percentiles will also help assure a minimum system penalty at the detail design level, as well as for operator selection.

Figure 6-5 shows comparisons of a two-level design criteria concept to an actual group of astronauts. Fifth and 95th percentiles are represented by shaded areas suitable for each dimension. Since the dimensions are in inches (and centimeters) rather than in percentile scale numerics, the 5th and 95th percentile limits are not representable by straight lines across the graph.

The foregoing percentile selection concepts are implicitly based on a simplistic assumption of a relatively uniform and significantly high coefficient of correlation between all pairs of dimensions. Actually, correlations may vary greatly between given pairs of dimensions, a biometric fact that can greatly influence the overall effectiveness of design criteria selection. This correlation aspect of variability structures of populations is of such importance that it is discussed later in considerable depth, together with the concept of proportional relationships.

6.4 PROPORTIONAL RELATIONSHIPS OF BODY DIMENSIONS

Discussion of population differences has indicated that average body proportions expressed as percentiles may be significantly varied between individuals within a population. There is another aspect of body proportions equally important to engineering design: the differing *ratios* of actual dimensions of body segment lengths between individuals within a given population and between different populations on the average. Some typical situations concerning both aspects will be presented herein for actual populations, primarily because of the engineering value of such data, for predicting unknown body dimensions, in order to design furnishings and personal equipment.

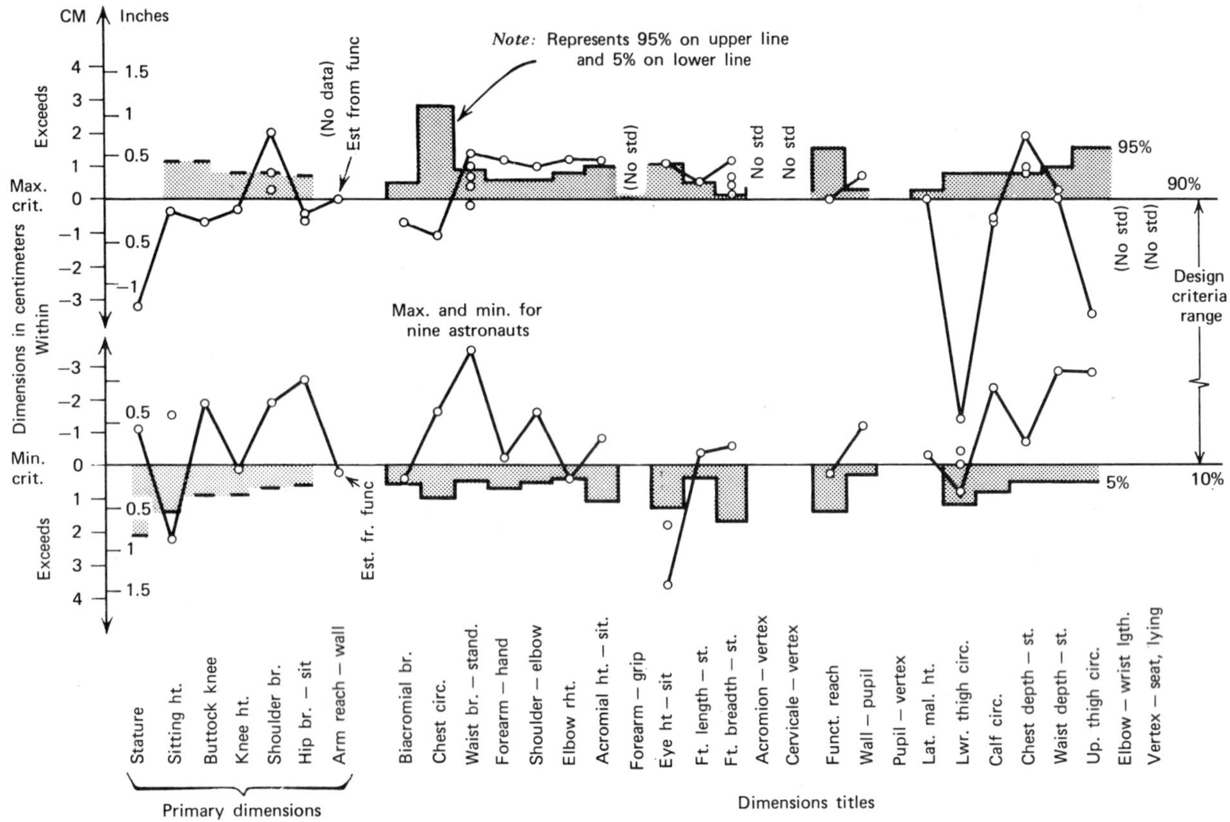

Figure 6-5. Comparison of actual selected population of operating personnel to hybrid percentile design limits.

6.4.1 Anthropometric Ratios

The physical anthropologist who is concerned with characterizing the shape of human beings, often resorts to ratios of dimensions to do so. The engineering anthropometrist can use such data as an aid in estimating unknown lengths from given body dimensions. For example, the anthropologist may be interested in determining whether men or women have longer leg length in proportion to their height. This can be expressed as a ratio of average Leg Length to Stature, which may be written as a dimensionless fraction

$$\frac{\text{Average Leg Length}}{\text{Average Stature}} = K_1 \qquad \text{(Eq. 6.2)}$$

Reported data on the fraction K_1 for a variety of populations can be used to estimate Leg Length if Stature is known, as is often the case. This type of ratio gives no information on individual differences within a population. However, one may obtain such other information by other statistics: the average and the standard deviation of the ratios for the individuals in the sample or population. To obtain such statistics requires that each individual's measurements be known. For example, individual ratios of Height to Sitting Height are summed and divided by the total number of individuals, to obtain the average of the ratio:

$$\text{Average}\,\frac{\text{Height}}{\text{Sitting Ht}} = \frac{\dfrac{\text{Height}_1}{\text{Sitting Ht}_1} + \dfrac{\text{Height}_2}{\text{Sitting Ht}_2} + \dfrac{\text{Height}_n}{\text{Sitting Ht}_n}}{n} = K$$

(Eq. 6.3)

These ratios must be used with a great deal of care and understanding. In particular, stating a relationship in terms of a ratio may seem to imply that the body dimensions are simply related in a proportional, straight line manner, from the smallest to the largest man. Such is rarely (practically speaking, never) the case.

A much more accurate statement of relationship over a range of sizes is the regression formula or the graphical expression of the regression relationship, which were described in Chapter V.

6.4.2 Body Link Proportions

A unique characteristic of many engineering anthropometry applications is the necessity for data on average locations of joint centers and the distances between them, called "link lengths." Several references were introduced in Chapter III which have useful data for further study: Dempster (1955) summarized much research, including his own, and provided estimates of segment length and relations of joint centers to certain anthropometric landmarks. More recently, Drillis and Contini (1966) have provided an "average" set of ratios of segment length to height, shown in Figure 6-6, as a two-dimensional figure. These may be used with great caution as a rough approximation in the absence of better data. Clauser et al. (1969) have provided additional useful data. Snyder, Chaffin, and Schutz (1972) have developed information to link Dempster's extremity (arm and leg) models; hence, they put special emphasis on spinal and shoulder links and their movements. However, there is still a need for comprehensive studies of the whole body, describing the entire set of body links in three dimensional coordinate systems with consistency and statistical validity. Various simplified link systems descriptions have been synthesized for development of mathematical models, using available data and

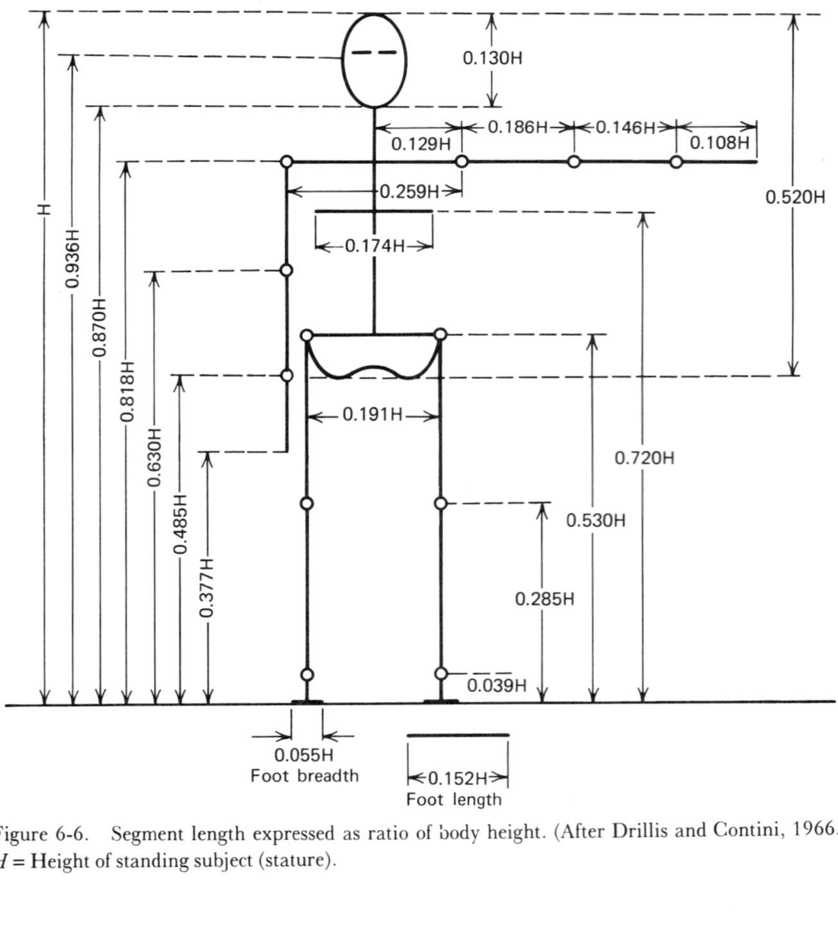

Figure 6-6. Segment length expressed as ratio of body height. (After Drillis and Contini, 1966.) H = Height of standing subject (stature).

engineering approximation methods, which will be discussed later in the applications sections.

6.4.3 Dimensional Correlations

Although body dimensions for given individuals are not simply related by common percentiles nor by simple ratios, populations as a whole do show observable tendencies for proportional relationships between some dimensions. For example, tall individuals as a group tend to have relatively long legs and long arms, while shorter individuals as a group tend to have relatively short arms and legs. As explained in Chapter V, the degree to which such tendencies hold true is often expressed by correlation coefficients, by regression equations, and by scatter diagrams. Major correlation relationships, which are compact and useful statistics, vital to many engineering anthropometry estimates, are briefly described in Table 6-4. Unfortunately, data are few and not widely published concerning such correlation coefficients. Appendix B contains an unusually complete tabulation of correlation coefficients for 96 dimensions of U.S. Air Force flying personnel in 1950 (Courtesy USAF Anthropology Branch, AMRL). These data may be used to verify statements in Table 6-7 and as highly useful engineering approximations, representative of correlations for many American and European military and civilian male populations. The tables are also valuable for sample problems in college level courses. For more precise information on how body dimensions are interrelated, correlation scatter diagram presentations are needed for the population (or a representative sample of it). Moroney, Smith, and co-workers, have pointed out these needs and have prepared several articles and reports concerning use of such data and tables of data from analysis of anthropometric surveys of Naval aircrewmen. (Moroney, 1971, 1972; Moroney and Smith, 1972a, b; Smith, 1972)

6.5 AREA CORRELATIONS

Formulas for estimating total body surface area using simple anthropometric data provide convenient expressions of these relationships. The formula developed by DuBois and DuBois (1915, 1916) is still sometimes used:

$$A = 71.84\, W^{0.425}\, H^{0.725} \qquad \text{(Eq. 6.4)}$$

where A is the total body surface in square centimeters; W is the Weight (mass) in kilograms, and H is the Height (stature) in centimeters. With an error of less than 1%, this formula can be approximated by

$$A = 50w + 80H - 3300 \qquad \text{(Eq. 6.5)}$$

where w = (Weight) in lb, H = (Height) in cm.

Table 6-4. Summary of Major Types of Linear Dimension Correlation Coefficients with Commentary

Types of Dimension Correlations	Commentary on Significance of Relationships
Long bone and major axial dimensions correlations	Relationships highly important to work space design, also useful in clothing design. Tend to be closely correlated with Stature because long bones, such as femur and tibia, are components of Stature. Buttock-Knee Length and Knee Height have higher ρ^a than Sitting Height. Arm dimensions also have fair correlation to Stature, but less. Foot Length, Hand Length, and Arm Reach are lowest. Note Sitting Height vs Anterior Arm Reach: low ρ, which is significant to aircraft and auto design, indicates little change in forward reach as function of seat height. Summary: many such correlations are positive and significant, but many (in the .4 to .6 range) are not much help to design of simple adjustments.
Breadth and depth dimensions correlations with Height and each other	Also important to work space design, especially breadths. Usually low (but positive) correlations with Height. Foot Breadth, and Head Length, of negligible value in work space layout—essentially independent. Many are higher, but few approach Waist Depth vs. Buttock Depth (ρ approx. .8).
Circumference and curvatures dimensions correlations with Breadths, Height, and Weight	Primarily useful for clothing design. Often relatively high correlations to Weight, showing sensitivity to fatty tissue in mass, less in head and foot. Also, usually there are *low* correlations of horizontal section circumferences to Stature and Sitting Height. However, Vertical Trunk Circumference and Sleeve Length have significant ρ's. Most circumferences correlate better with *breadths* of the *trunk* than the limbs, although circumferences of head and foot have quite low correlations.
Circumference dimensions correlations with each other	Circumferential intercorrelations are relatively good, except for those with head.

[a] ρ = coefficient of correlation in this table.

DuBois and DuBois' formula was derived from measurements of only 9 subjects. Furthermore, Stevenson (1928) showed that it may not be sufficiently accurate for different subjects, for example, Chinese as compared to Caucasians. A much larger sample (more than 250 subjects) was used by Sendroy and Cecchini (1954) to develop charts from which, using Height and Weight, one can directly read the surface area. The latest chart published by Sendroy and Collison (1960) is in wide use.

6.6 RELATIONS OF MASS AND INERTIAL PROPERTIES WITH STANDARD ANTHROPOMETRIC DATA

Engineering kinematics analysis of the human body requires data on the relationships between standard anthropometric descriptors (such as body lengths) and body mass distribution, moments of inertia, and radii of gyration. Simple correlations of total body mass (Weight) with a large number of body dimensions are included in Appendix B.

6.6.1 Whole Body Density

Density of the body varies with age, increasing from birth up to the age of 20 to 27 years (for the average of a population), probably due to growth of muscular tissues. It then decreases again as age increases, probably due to accumulation of body fat.

Bashkirew (1954) developed the following formula for whole body density of Russian subjects based on constituent material percentages:

$$d = 1.07554 - 0.00191\,D_1 + 0.00055\,M_1 - 0.0019\,B_1 \qquad \text{(Eq. 6.6)}$$

where d represents body density, D_1 is the relative mass of fat tissue (ratio to the whole body mass), M_1 is the relative mass of muscular tissue, and B_1 is the relative mass of bones. Such ratios may be obtained from the various chemical, radiological, and skinfold methods described in Chapter III. A formula for American males was developed by Dupertuis (1950) to express body density in terms of the somatotype component called endomorphy:

$$d = 1.094 - 0.0119\,X \qquad \text{(Eq. 6.7)}$$

where X is the rating of the first component (endomorphy) in the somatotyping scheme of Sheldon (1940). The formula is based on a negative correlation ($-.853 \pm 0.030$) between specific density and the endomorphic component. Another equation for American men was developed by Drillis and Contini (1966), using data from Behnke et al. (1942):

$$d = 0.6905 + 0.297\,C \qquad \text{(Eq. 6.8)}$$

where C is the ponderal index $= hw^{1/3}$, w is the body Weight (lb), and h is the body Height (in.). Since Height and Weight are readily measured, this index can be more easily obtained than the preceding formulas.

6.6.2 Body Segment Density

Conclusions of several investigators (Harless, 1860; Dempster, 1955; Drillis and Contini, 1966; Clauser, McConville, and Young, 1969) can be summarized as follows:

1. Densities of body components (such as skin, muscle, fat, bone, etc.) vary significantly.
2. The density of segments increases from proximal to distal parts.
3. Segment density increases linearly with the whole body density.

Table 6-5, adapted from Clauser, McConville, and Young (1969) lists densities of body components (skin, muscle, fat, and bone) found in six studies. Averages of the data from three studies of body segment density have been determined by Drillis and Contini (1966) and are presented in Table 6-6. From the same study, data have been combined into Figure 6-7 to show how segment density varies with overall body density.

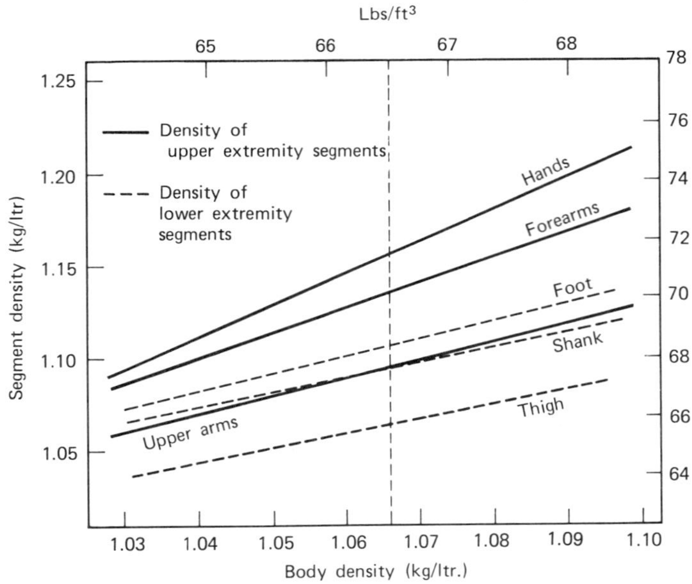

Figure 6-7. Density of extremity segments as a function of overall body density. (After Drillis and Contini, 1966.)

Table 6-5. Densities of Body Components[a] (Adapted from Clauser, McConville, and Young, 1969)

Source (nonpreserved)[d]	Skin	Muscle	Fat	Bone	
Davy[b] (1840)	1.100 to 1.108	1.056 to 1.058	0.942	1.383 to 1.944	
Kapff and Vierordt (1906)			0.971		
Krause and Vierordt (1906)		1.0382 to 1.0591			
Leider and Buncke (1954)	1.102 (S = .010)[c]				
Blanton and Biggs (1968)				Cancellous	Compact
Preserved				1.09	1.85
Fresh				1.08	1.85
Clauser, McConville, and Young (1969), Preserved	1.102 (S = 0.070)	1.087 (S = 0.025)	0.961 (S = 0.036)	1.105 (S = 0.047)	1.800 (S = 0.105)

[a] Densities in kg/liter.
[b] Specific gravity (?).
[c] S = Standard deviation.
[d] Except where noted as preserved.

Table 6-6. Average Body Segment Density (in kg/liter) (From Drillis and Contini, 1966)

Upper arm	1.081
Forearm	1.122
Hand	1.144
Thigh	1.069
Shank	1.095
Foot	1.100
Head and neck	1.111
Trunk	1.030

6.6.3 Center of Mass of Whole Body

Location of the mass center of the whole body is dependent on limb positions. Reports of studies by King, Patch, and Shinkham (1960), Santschi, DuBois, and Omoto (1963), and Swearingen (1953) give examples of the expected range of data. It is frequently useful to know the distance of the body center of mass from the feet for the standing subject. Drillis and Contini (1966) found a range from 55.35% to 60.40%, with a mean of 56.68% and standard deviation of 1.39%. Clauser et al. (1969) report a range of 56.9 to 60.1%, a mean value of 58.81% and a standard deviation of 1.14%.

6.6.4 Body Segment Mass and Center of Mass

Values for the ratio of segmental mass to total body mass have been reported in five different cadaver studies and are compiled in Table 6-7. The location of the center of mass of a given segment is usually described as on the centerline of the segment, at a given distance from the proximal end of this segment. This distance is commonly expressed relative to the total segment length. Table 6-8 lists such ratios as reported in five cadaver studies. It shows that the center of mass of each segment is, in most cases, not exactly in the middle of the centerline of the segment, but located more proximally.

Drillis and Contini (1966) noted significant differences in segment mass distributions between Russian and American subjects. Clauser et al. (1969) discuss such differences between American and Japanese populations. Their report contains step-wise regression equations to predict mass properties of the body segments from one, two, or three anthropometric dimensions easily taken on the respective segment. This method supersedes the more simplistic prediction procedures hitherto used, and allows rather exact mass calculations for individuals instead of populations.

Table 6-7. Segmental Mass/Body Mass Ratios from Several Cadaver Studies (Adapted from Clauser, McConville and Young, 1969)

Source Sample Size	Harless (1860) 2	Braune and Fischer (1889) 3	Fischer (1906) 1	Dempster[a] (1955) 8	Clauser, McConville and Young (1969) 13	Average 5
Head	7.6%	7.0%	8.8%	8.1%	7.3	7.8
Trunk	44.2	46.1	45.2	49.7	50.7	47.2
Total arm	5.7	6.2	5.4	5.0	4.9	5.4
Upper arm	3.2	3.3	2.8	2.8	2.6	2.9
Forearm and hand	2.6	2.9	2.6	2.2	2.3	2.5
Forearm	1.7	2.1	—	1.6	1.6	1.8
Hand	0.9	0.8	—	0.6	0.7	0.8
Total leg	18.4	17.2	17.6	16.1	16.1	17.1
Thigh	11.9	10.7	11.0	9.9	10.3	10.8
Calf and foot	6.6	6.5	6.6	6.1	5.8	6.3
Calf	4.6	4.8	4.5	4.6	4.3	4.6
Foot	2.0	1.7	2.1	1.4	1.5	1.7
Sum[b]	100.0	100.0	100.0	100.0	100.0	100.0

[a] Dempster's values adjusted by Clauser, McConville, and Young (1969).
[b] The sum is calculated as head + trunk + 2 (total arm + total leg).

Table 6-8. Locations of the Centers of Mass of Body Segments, Measured from the Proximal Ends (Adapted from Clauser, McConville, and Young, 1969)

Source	Harless (1860)	Braune and Fischer (1889)	Fischer (1906)	Dempster (1955)	Clauser, McConville and Young (1969)
Total body	41.4%	—	—	—	41.2%
Head	36.2	—	—	43.3%	46.6
Trunk	44.8	—	—	—	38.0[a]
Total arm	—	—	44.6%	—	41.3
Upper arm	—	47.0%	45.0	43.6	51.3
Forearm and hand	—	47.2	46.2	67.7[a]	62.6[a]
Forearm	42.0	42.1	—	43.0	39.0[a]
Hand	39.7	—	—	49.4	18.0[a]
Total leg	—	—	41.2	43.3	38.2[a]
Thigh	48.9	44.0	43.6	43.3	37.2[a]
Calf and foot	—	52.4	53.7	43.7	47.5
Calf	43.3	42.0	43.3	43.3	37.1
Foot	44.4	44.4	—	42.9	44.9

[a] These values are not directly comparable due to variations in the definition of segment length used by the different investigators.

6.6.5 Moment of Inertia and Radius of Gyration—Whole Body

Other expressions of mass distribution are embodied in the moment of inertia and the radius of gyration. Some data on moments of inertia can be obtained from sources referenced in Chapter III. However, complete data have not yet been published.

Whole body moments of inertia are related in a complex manner to limb positions. Simple correlations with a small number of key dimensions are not possible for this great freedom of motion capability, nor are three-dimensional envelopes useful as in locating ranges of center of gravity movement. The most useful approach today is the mathematical model, using computer computation based on limb position inputs (Chapter VII).

6.6.6 Body Segment Moment of Inertia and Radius of Gyration

A less commonly used parameter, of interest for some engineering calculations, is the radius of gyration (ρ). It is related to the segment length, mass, center of mass location, and moment of inertia. Braune and Fischer (1889) found that the radius of gyration for rotation about the axis through the mass center and perpendicular to the longitudinal axis of the segment can be approximated by a coefficient (C_3) multiplied by the segment length (L):

$$\rho = C_3 L \qquad \text{(Eq. 6.9)}$$

The moment of inertia can then be expressed by the formula

$$I_m = M\rho^2 = MC_3{}^2L^2 \qquad \text{(Eq. 6.10)}$$

Braune and Fischer assigned the magnitude 0.3 to C_3, therefore,

$$I_m \approx 0.09\, ML^2 \text{ approximates the mass moment of inertia about the center of mass.} \qquad \text{(Eq. 6.11)}$$

Location of joint center of motion, and determination of segment length were discussed in Chapter III and Section 6.4.2.

Braune and Fischer also developed a similar formula for rotation about the longitudinal axis, using another coefficient C_4, related to the diameter (d) of the segment. Using a magnitude 0.35 for C_4, the radius of gyration becomes

$$\rho = 0.35d \qquad \text{(Eq. 6.12)}$$

Drillis and Contini have accumulated the data in Table 6-9, relating radius of gyration to segment length by the ratio (C_3).

6.7 VOLUME CORRELATIONS

Dempster (1955), Drillis and Contini (1966), and Clauser, McConville, and Young (1969) made volume measurements as described in Chapter III.

Table 6-9. Ratio (C_3) of Radius of Gyration (ρ) to Segment Length (L) (from Drillis and Contini, 1966)

Segment	Braune and Fischer 1 Cadaver Test I		Braune and Fischer 1 Cadaver Test II		N.Y.U. 8 Live Subjects	Weighted Average
			Rt.	Lt.		
Entire upper extremity	—		0.30	0.31	0.24	0.252
	Rt.	Lt.				
Upper arm	0.27	0.27	0.29	0.31	0.26	0.268
Forearm and hand	0.26	0.28	0.29	0.32	0.25	0.263
Entire lower extremity	—		0.32	0.32	0.24	0.256
Thigh	0.26	0.27	0.31	0.31	0.23	0.250
Shank and foot	0.32	0.32	0.33	0.35	0.29	0.303
Shank	0.25	0.26	0.24	0.26	0.27	0.264
Average	0.27	0.28	0.30	0.31	0.25	0.265

However, if the weight (W) is known, the Volume (V) for the total body or for body segments can often be calculated with sufficient accuracy using the formula

$$V = \frac{W}{g \times D} \qquad \text{(Eq. 6.13)}$$

where g is the gravitational constant and D is the density. Data for the density D are contained in Tables 6-7 and 6-8.

In general, volume of the distal parts of extremities (hands and feet) amounts to about 10% of the total extremity volume (arms and legs). The middle parts are about 30% and thus the proximal parts are about 60% (Drillis and Contini, 1966; Clauser, McConville, and Young, 1969).

6.8 ENVIRONMENTAL EFFECTS

An increasing number of human engineering problems concern designs involving wide variations from normal conditions. Undersea exploration, high altitude flight and space exploration produce major differences in atmospheric pressure. Space flight, such as the recent human landings on the moon, potential flights to Mars, and planned space stations, involve partial or multiple gravitational fields, as well as complete weightlessness as working environments. These environmental effects present possibilities of changing anthropometric dimensions from those measured under normal environmental conditions.

6.8.1 Accelogravitational Effects

According to Newton's and Einstein's theories, it is not possible to distinguish between the effects of acceleration and gravitation as regards field forces on the mass of physical bodies. The term "accelogravitational effects" has been coined to describe effects on anthropometric dimensions resulting from changes in either *direction* of application or *magnitude* of acceleration and/or gravitational fields, however produced, or combined.

For example, most standard anthropometric dimensions are measured with the body upright, either sitting or standing, such that the force of the earth's gravitational field on the body is downward, parallel to the spine. However, for the design of spacecraft accommodations, one may wish to know the effect of reducing the forces along the spine to zero, in order to design a couch for the launch phase. Such effects can be simulated by simply reclining the body to a horizontal position, but pressures will now be exerted along the back of the torso, arms, and legs, perpendicular to the spine. Frictional forces developed by such forces will prevent complete freedom, even axially. However, one may expect that the following changes in specific body dimensions will occur, creating a need for new design standards.

1. The pressure on the buttocks of a seated subject will be eliminated or greatly reduced causing return to a more convex, rounded shape and increasing the distance from surface of buttocks to eye, crown, shoulder, sternum, and so forth.
2. The pull of gravity on the arms (parallel to the spine) will be eliminated. This will permit the shoulders to move upward toward the head and the elbows to move headward and akimbo to achieve equilibrium of pressures and tensions of muscles and flesh.
3. Another effect will be to straighten the spine and relieve intervertebral pressures, thus permitting an apparent increase of the trunk length as measured between buttocks and crown, and of other distances from buttocks to eye, sternum, cervicale, and so forth. The relief of pressures on the body in the spinal direction for an extended period (such as sleeping overnight) will cause further "stretch," or "growth," which may be observed by comparing Height measurements made in the early morning with those made in the late afternoon or evening.
4. As a result of the above body dimensional changes and fluids redis-

tributions, the center of mass of the whole body will move headward (Chaffee, 1961c).

Figure 6-8 summarizes some expected changes in several dimensions of major concern to work space design as the seat back is reclined from upright to a reclining position.

This figure does not indicate all the subtle changes in head and eye position as the seat back is reclined. The shaded areas in the figure indicate changes in length as if there is constant orientation of the torso parallel to a straight-backed seat, such as one might use in standard anthropometric postures. In practice, the upper torso and head tend to remain vertically oriented when a relaxed working position is permitted in an aft-reclined seat. This results in a "slump" effect as the seat tilts until the back angle is so extreme that an upright head posture cannot be maintained, or is not desired for other reasons, at which point the subject lies back into the head rest.

Somewhat different, usually smaller magnitude changes result when the subject is tightly restrained by lap belt, shoulder harness, and special clothing before rotating backward in the seat. However, further discussion of these effects is beyond the scope of this text.

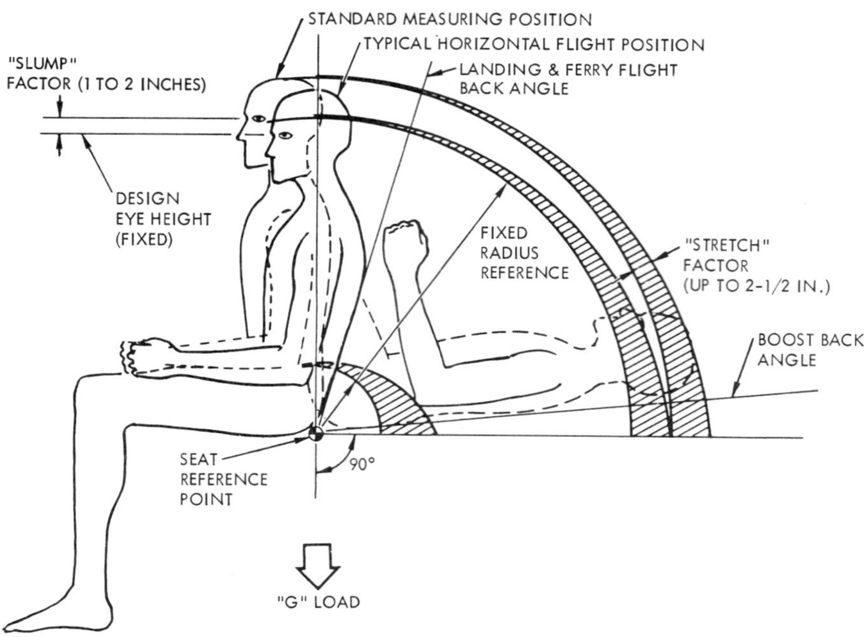

Figure 6-8. Anthropometric dimension changes as a function of back angle in earth gravity. (Roebuck, Kroemer, and Thomson, 1973.)

Upward ejection seat loads and downward impacts can cause significant temporary compression of the spinal column (and presumably, buttocks) resulting in head movement toward the seat pan. Also, impact loading resulting in the "eyeballs-up" acceleration has been observed to cause "stretching" of the head away from the seat pan with subsequent return movement resulting up to 3 in. total amplitude at 10 g.

Even more critical and less apparent is the effect on measurement of the center of mass, which often depends on two different body positions for its location in space. Since the body dimensions change, the center of mass will inevitably move also as the attitude is varied. Therefore, to accurately locate the center of mass one must resort to two different types of determination without changing the body orientation with respect to gravitational (or accelogravitational) forces (see Chapter III).

6.8.2 Atmospheric Pressure Effects

The major concern of engineering anthropometry related to changes in atmospheric pressure (other than those involving pressure suits and equipment) involves swelling of tissue at very low pressures such as may be encountered at high altitudes or in a vacuum (space). Wilson (1961) and Billings (in Parker and West, 1973) have summarized historical research on this subject, and reported results of research that showed that exposure of the hand to very low pressures, of the order of 5 mm Hg, for several minutes caused swelling. The swelling was generally painless, but greatly reduced mobility as it increased the hand volume.

6.9 MOBILITY CORRELATIONS

The terms *mobility* and *flexibility* are used interchangeably in the following discussion. The former is more common for engineering usage while the latter appears to be preferred by physical educators and kinesiologists. Both refer here to the capability of the various human body segments to assume different relative orientations in space. Of special interest is the orientation of the limbs with respect to the torso.

Current indications are that basic human mobility is related to age, sex, somatotype, training or practice, and general condition, such as warmup, fatigue, excitement, or fear and tolerance to pain. Clothing restrictions may form a very significant additional consideration, especially in the case of pressure suits and armor, but will not be considered in this section.

6.9.1 Age and Sex

A great many mobility studies have been performed on children and youth in school and up through college age, while only a few concerned older adults.

Holland (1968) has summarized several studies of children up to 18 years of age. Among these are studies by Leighton (1956, 1964) of male youths, ages 6 to 18 years, indicating that boys 6 to 10 years old showed little change, but from 10 to 18 years there was a steady decrease in the range of motion of 15 out of 18 measurements reported.

Toe touch tests indicated significantly more girls than boys at all ages (between 6 and 15 years) could pass the test. It was also found that the percentage of boys and girls able to pass the test gradually decreased from ages 6 to 12, then slightly increased into the middle teens. (Buxton, 1957; Kendall and Kendall, 1949; Kirchner and Glines, 1957; Phillips, 1955 and Schaffer, 1959). Roebuck and Levedahl (1961) reported a noticeable difference in time of passage through emergency exits for groups in the 20 to 40 age brackets as compared to 40 to 50 and 50 to 60. The time of passage increased with age, indicating possible reduced flexibility or increased caution, related to lower agility and/or fear of injury.

6.9.2 Somatotype

A relationship between body type and mobility has been indicated in results of studies by several investigators, although others have found no significant correlation. Dempster (1955) reported data on a small sample of men which seemed to indicate ectomorphic (thin) types have greater range of motion in many joints. Perbix (1954) studied physical education major and nonmajor women in college, relating somatotypes (ratings by Sheldon) and flexibility. She reported no statistically significant relationship in either group.

Laubach and McConville (1966) have summarized several studies of body type and mobility, and have presented data from their own study of 63 male students. They found low and/or insignificant correlations between flexibility, anthropometric data, and somatotypes, but high negative correlations with body fat. Laubach (1969) confirmed these findings.

6.9.3 Anthropometric Dimensions

Taken without regard to somatotype, basic anthropometric dimensions seem to bear inconclusive relationships to mobility, as defined in terms of angular movement at the joints. However, measurements of mobility that depend on absolute length or changes in linear distances between points on body extremities (such as sit and reach tests) may show significant effects for extreme body proportional variations. For example, Broer and Galles (1958) showed that women with extremely long trunks and arms performed significantly better in the floor touch test. Similar findings for college men were reported by Wear (1963), for the sit and touch test. On the other hand, Mathews and his co-workers (Mathews and Kruse, 1957; Mathews et al., 1957; Mathews, 1959) found no significant correlation in sit and reach tests or the Kraus-Weber floor touch tests.

6.9.4 Variability Patterns in Flexibility

Flexibility does not appear to be a general factor that is applicable to all joint motions of an individual. Wrist motion comparisons for individuals have shown wide variations, as much as 200% in some cases (Hewitt, 1928, Cobe, 1928). Similarly, comparisons between wrist flexion and extension to plantar- and dorsi-flexion by Dickinson (1963) did not show significant correlation. Hupprich and Sigerseth (1950) and Leighton (1960) also agree that flexibility is a specific factor varying considerably with each joint. Further, there appears to be a difference between extent flexibility (so far discussed) and dynamic flexibility, which involves the speed with which maximum range movements can be executed. A discussion of these aspects is outside the limited scope of this text.

6.9.5 Summary: Presentations of Joint Motion Range

Engineering descriptions of human joint motion capabilities are needed for work space design and for evaluating clothing designs. The description of the complete range of motion in a three-dimensional sense requires more refined analytic and pictorial tools than simple planar angle measurements. As a means of pictorially visualizing and describing such complete ranges of motion, the "globographic" technique is useful. The globograph is a three-dimensional sphere with appropriate angular longitudinal and latitudinal scales, whose center is conceptually at the average, or instantaneous, center of rotation of a body joint. An outlined area on the surface represents the total range of angular movement (vection) of the trace of the limb axis with respect to the adjacent limb (or, as required, some other fixed part or plane). An example is shown in a detail inset of Figure 6-9, which also provides a summary illustration of several key limb joint motion capabilities.

6.10 MUSCULAR STRENGTH CORRELATIONS

In order to develop the rationale for strength testing procedures, a great deal of material that could logically be contained in this chapter was presented in Chapter IV. To minimize overlapping and duplication, such items will receive only brief summary herein.

6.10.1 Age and Sex Differences in Strength and Work Capacity

Studies of male and female subjects by Asmussen and Heeboll-Nielsen (1962), Cathcart et al. (1927, 1935), Galton (1881, 1883), Isakawa (1932), Schochrin (1935), and Ufland (1953) are typical of the large-scale static strength tests that have been performed. In general, these and other studies agree that muscular strength increases until approximately 30 years of age and thereafter tapers off (Hunsicker, 1955). With both sexes being about equally strong at

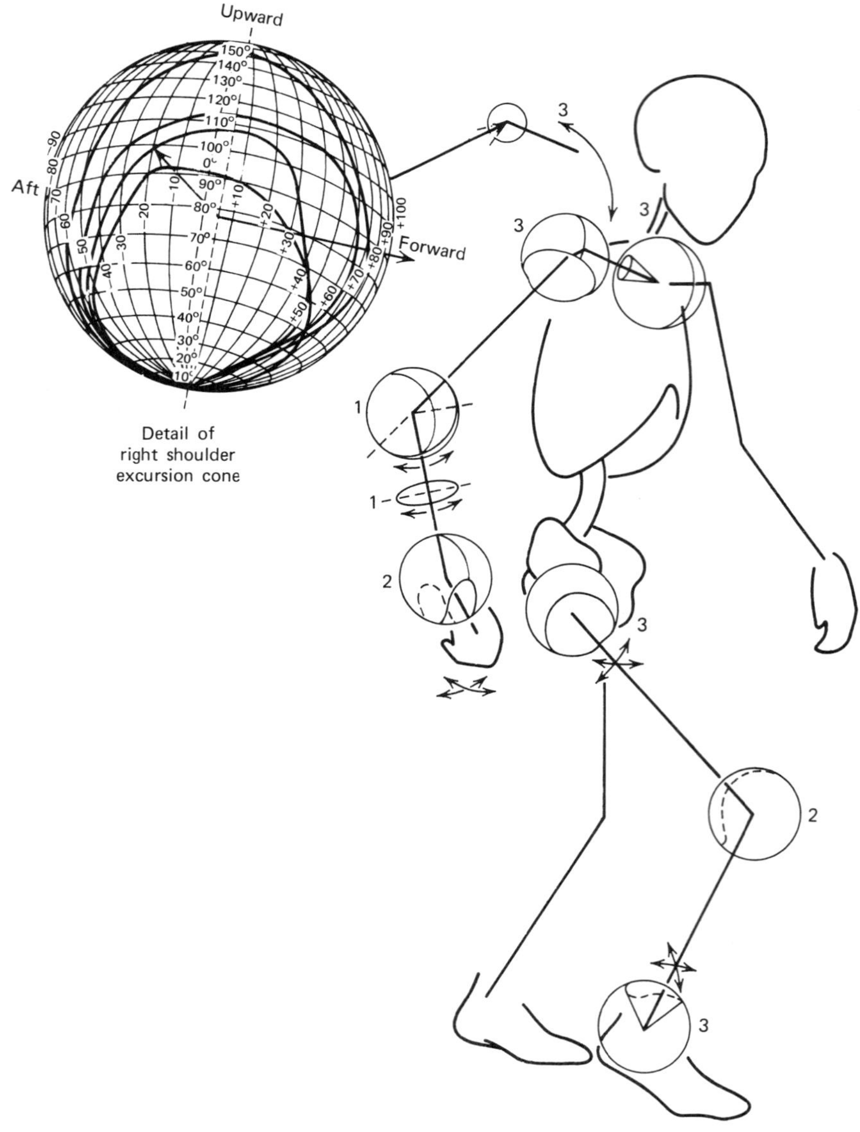

Figure 6-9. Link figure with globographic representations of the joint ranges of the extremity links (after Dempster 1955a,b).

the age of ten, the strength of males increases more rapidly and to a higher amount in the years of 12 to 19, at a rate similar to Weight (Galton, 1881, 1883). In men, strength reaches the maximum in the middle or late twenties. It remains on this level for five or ten years and then drops slowly but increasingly. Only about 80% of the maximum strength of the twenties is still available at age 60. However, not all muscle groups vary in strength in this way. For example, the strength of hand and arm shows a relatively strong ascent after the age of twenty (Ufland, 1953), and later declines less steeply with increasing age.

Strength of women has been measured variously at 0 to 60% weaker than that of men of the same age. A generally accepted overall estimate for the strength of women at age 30 is two-thirds of the men's strength at the same age. Following about ten years of rather constant strength, the strength of women decreases somewhat faster than that of men; at about 50 years, women are only about half as strong as their male contemporaries.

6.10.2 Handedness

Handedness has only relatively small effects on strength and working capacity (Heeboll-Nielsen, 1964). In right-handed persons (approximately 90% of all), the right arm is slightly stronger than the left, though usually less than 10% (Damon et al., 1966; Hunsicker, 1955). Strength differences between the two legs are even less obvious (Elbel, 1949; Hugh-Jones, 1947). For most practical purposes, the slight differences in strength of the two sides of the body can be neglected (Hunsicker and Greey, 1957).

6.10.3 Fatigue

Physiological fatigue greatly reduces strength and working capacity. There is a nonlinear, inverse relationship between the fraction of strength that must be exerted and the time during which it can be maintained. Maximal force (100% of strength) can be exerted for only a few seconds, and only a fraction (less than about 15%) of maximal strength can be exerted for more than 10 minutes (see Chapter IV for more details).

6.10.4 Anthropometric Dimension Correlations with Strength

Anthropometric measurements in themselves give relatively little help as predictors of strength because of the multiplicity of other variables that have such a strong influence (Laubach, Kroemer and Thordsen, 1972). For groups of similar age and build or somatotype, Weight and Height appear to be the best, but still only fair indicators of relative strength. When Weight and Height are held constant, the correlation with mesomorphy becomes 0.61 (Jones, 1947). Weight alone is, for engineering purposes, insufficient for strength prediction (Kroemer and Robinson, 1971). Clarke (1954) found fairly good correlations, around .72, between arm girth and certain arm strength measurements for a selected sample of predominantly mesomorphic subjects, with some meso-ectomorphy tendencies. Jones (1947) concluded that 25% of the variance in strength is relatable to Weight, but when Weight, Height, and components of body build are taken into account, about 75% of the variance is controlled.

Body build is related to strength and working capacity. Significant but often low correlations have been found between strength and body weight, circumferences, and lengths. Among schemes of body-build classifications (somatotypes), only mesomorphy (athletic build) showed significant positive correlations with strength. For endurance and sustained dynamic work, however, normal or even slender build seems to be advantageous (Damon et al., 1966; Caldwell, 1963; Laubach, and McConville, 1966; Tornvall, 1963). For most practical purposes, however, Laubach's and McConville's (1969) statement holds true that measurements of body size, typology, and composition are *not* effective predictors of strength.

6.10.5 Occupational and Training Differences in Strength

Strength differences are often pronounced between so-called laboring groups and more sedentary groups, although sports or health enthusiasts among the latter may create individual discrepancies. This relation was noted early by Quetelet (1835) who found that masons and carpenters had stronger grips than domestic servants. A hundred years later Cathcart et al. (1935) found that the "black-coated" group (called "white-collar" workers more recently) were inferior in strength to manual workers, but superior in Height. Similar findings have been confirmed by the authors. Again, the fact that certain occupations tend to impose selective limitations on groups of people as to age, sex, ethnic, or national background makes more likely the introduction of differences in strength between occupational groups.

The concepts of training and conditioning programs are also considered together in this discussion. An occupation may be considered a "steady state" program which maintains a certain level of physical strength. One must also consider short-term, transient effects of changes in training (see Chapter IV) both for the purposes of building or evaluating specific strength or endurance characteristics and for the purpose of evaluating deconditioning effects such as confinement, bedrest, weightless flight in orbit, and so on.

6.10.6 Body Position Effects

The proper or improper use of the earth's gravitational pull (or lack thereof) can have a surprising effect on exerted force. In fact, the concept of describing force exertable by humans cannot be meaningfully divorced from the specification of body orientation, leverage, friction and accelogravitational field effects. Even very slight, almost imperceptible changes in limb angles can have very different results in exerted force, especially as the limb approaches a straight line wherein the toggle, or "overcenter" effect can operate in push forces of the leg or arm (see, e.g., Kroemer, 1969b; Linford and Rarick, 1968; Rohmert and Jenik, 1971; Williams and Stutzman, 1959). Newton's equation, ACTION = REACTION, has been overlooked surprisingly often in studies of strength: nobody can apply more force than the force that is resisting his efforts. This point is illustrated by a study published by Kroemer and Robinson (1971). Static forces were measured which can be exerted while standing on surfaces of various tractions. The results show small forces, with little scatter of the data, exerted while standing on very slippery surfaces, and large forces, with large variability, under the non-slip conditions.

6.10.7 Grip Strength Correlations to Other Measures of Strength

Measurements of grip strength are commonly taken in anthropometric surveys. They are easy to administer—but unfortunately it is rather dubious whether they yield any data that are of interest to the engineer. Very few controls or tools are grasped and squeezed in the manner of exerting force on the hand dynamometer. Furthermore, a great number of studies showed very little overall correlation between grip strength and other measures of bodily strength (Laubach, Kroemer, and Thordsen, 1972). Thus, it appears at this time that grip strength has developed into an anthropometric criterion of its own standing and value, but that grip strength is of little value for engineering applications, practically only for grasping-squeezing actions as in operating plier-type tools.

6.11 VARIABILITY PATTERNS IN POPULATION STRENGTH

To aircraft engineers, used to working with safety factors of 1.5 in highly refined and chemically controlled metals, the wide range of variability in human strength can hardly be overemphasized (Kroemer, 1972d). Factors of 10 to 1 between personnel are not unexpected to the experienced strength tester, with ratios of 3 to 1 or 4 to 1 being common among different persons. Standard deviations of the order of 30 to 40% of the mean are commonplace among relatively homogeneous groups of subjects. Thus, a 5th to 95th percentile range can easily range from half to one and one-half times the average strength of a group on a given test. These coefficients of variation are thus 5 to 10 times those of human body dimensions.

Strength data frequency distributions are typically skewed to the large values instead of normally distributed as are many dimensional distributions. Thus, prediction of various strength percentiles from means and standard deviations using normal probability statistics are more likely to be in error than for dimensional percentiles.

6.12 STATIC STRENGTH AND THE "REAL WORLD"

Strength has been defined in this text as the muscular ability for maximal isometric contractions (essentially no motion involved). It is recognized that many questions will arise in every day activities involving usage of controls, equipment, and tools in which some motion is certain to result. Related questions of lifting and performing work also constantly arise. Some information on ability to perform dynamic work of a competitive, continuous nature is contained in books on work physiology (Astrand and Rodahl, 1970; Lehmann, 1961; Scherrer, 1967), in articles by Wilkie (1966) and by Snook, Irvine, and Bass (1970) as examples.

It will also be shown in later examples that maximum strength is not the real deciding criteria for design of operating forces (those normally applied, frequently and over long periods of time) which are often related to questions of accuracy and fatigue of "work." However, maximum strength data do set limits within which such operating forces may be investigated, and do set limits for breaking strength of such items for safety criteria.

VII
APPLICATIONS METHODOLOGY

7.1 INTRODUCTION

This chapter is the first of four emphasizing the use of anthropometric data in engineering projects. Selected general methodology, documents and tools for applying anthropometric data are outlined and some are discussed in detail, along with the special requirements and idiosyncrasies of the industrial environments in which the anthropometric engineer generally works. Further details are given in Chapter VIII through X, in conjunction with step-by-step procedures for application.

Differences in design goals among the various industrial organizations alter the requirements and priorities for applications. In Table 7-1, the design "drivers"* affecting these priorities are identified by major type of industry.

The application of engineering anthropometric data normally requires the three common functions of data collection, processing, and communications. These will be discussed in the following sections.

7.2 DATA COLLECTION

Collection of data, in the applications sense, means the gathering and filing of source documents containing anthropometric data in various stages, from raw data to sophisticated condensations. The bibliography provided in this text attests to the multiplicity of sources, basic types of which are discussed below.

7.2.1 Survey Reports

Engineering anthropometric applications are primarily based upon a variety of reports that have originated from surveys using the techniques described in the previous chapters. The majority of such survey reports are prepared by government agencies, such as the U. S. Air Force Laboratories at Wright-Patterson Air Force Base, Ohio, the U. S. Army Quartermaster Corps at Natick, Massachusetts, or the U. S. Department of Health, Education, and Welfare. Various manufacturing companies, industrial design firms and universities also have prepared such anthropometric survey reports.

* See Glossary, Appendix A.

Table 7-1. Design Drivers Affecting the Application of Engineering Anthropometry in Selected Research and Industrial Categories

Industry	Design Drivers
Aerospace	Minimum weight and aerodynamic drag critical to vehicle performance—function of volume and cross-sectional area of crew and passenger compartments. High cost per pound of airframe justifies accurate knowledge of necessary crew space to operate safely and efficiently. Low safety factors (commonly 1.5) require accurate knowledge of human strength, weight, and moments of inertia. Engineering cost is high percentage of product price; efficiency in design process is significant competitive advantage. Safety critical. Emphasis on (1) military populations, (2) general public.
Automotive	Weight and drag less critical than for aircraft or spacecraft, significant to racing cars. High quantities make engineering cost smaller percentage of vehicle cost, but small savings in production cost and material highly significant in very cost-competitive market. Aesthetics, styling very significant. Recent government rulings increase importance of safety features, including reach and vision, forces exerted on controls, restraints. Military vehicles must be rugged, but operable—styling negligible. Emphasis on driver population (15–75 years old).
Maritime	Weight and aerodynamic drag small considerations, but viscous drag critical to high speed vessels. Wide variety of vehicles with varying degrees of criticality as to effects of human space requirements. Probably most critical in submersibles, military craft. Ranges up to architectural approaches in concepts. Strongly oriented to naval populations.
Industrial production machinery and Assembly	Weight negligible, operator efficiency, speed, and fatigue minimization are prime goals for these stationary installations. Volume related to overhead costs. Primarily adult worker population 16–65 years, male and female.
Clothing	Engineered clothing of concern are space suits, high altitude suits, armor, antismoke, antifire, fuel handlers, special cold weather gear, diver clothing. Requires special attention to body size to determine design of patterns, sizing, number in stock required per size, interfaces with work space and machinery. Strongly oriented in a military male population 18–50 years of age.

Table 7-1 (*continued*)

Industry	Design Drivers
Electronics	Applications range from consoles to control and display detail design, communications gear. Forces and torques critical to controls. Maintainability access significant consideration. Wide range of populations.
Furniture	Office, theater, and school furniture benefits from anthropometric data applications. Styling may be more important than comfort in much commercial furniture sold to homes, hotel, etc. Weight usually not critical. Handling forces and torques may be significant. Wide range in populations from babies to senior citizens.
Prosthetics	Extremely critical as regards fitting to subject on individual basis. All ages, both sexes in population, but heavy influence in military population due to war injuries. Most research work in university-sponsored groups.
Industrial design (serves all groups)	Styling and functional value applied to a wide variety of components and devices for the above vehicles and consumer products require anthropometric data for effective product. Emphasis on consumer population.

When such survey reports do not provide sufficient data, one may be forced to resort to in-house testing of a small sample of volunteer test subjects ("subject pool"). The resulting data file can be of great value for specialized dimensions and combinations of data not commonly reported. Subject selection often is directed toward finding individuals representative of design percentiles, such as 5th and 95th for key body dimensions, or key customers (chief pilots, presidents, etc.) in order to anticipate potential product acceptance problems.

7.2.2 Test Reports

Other sources of anthropometric data are engineering reports of work space analyses, equipment and vehicle mockup evaluation, clothing fit tests, and personal equipment evaluations. Basic body dimensions are often measured and reported as control data in order to establish a relationship to a general population for which the devices are being developed. The dimensions of subjects in the nonstandard body positions required for operation of the equipment under study will often be the main purpose of the report. Such data, while specific to a given vehicle or problem, may be of use to designers of other similar work space conditions or equipment.

7.2.3 Analysis Reports

The engineering anthropometry literature also includes articles and reports presenting descriptions of graphical and mathematical combinations and extrapolations of anthropometric data based on previously reported surveys rather than presentations of original data. However, such reports may include data from survey reports normally not available to persons interested in a specific area of engineering applications. In addition, the derived results may be useful when actual survey data are lacking or unobtainable.

7.2.4 Data Handbooks

Handbooks containing anthropometric data are often a useful source of information. Table 7-2 lists representative examples of such publications that contain useful and significant portions of anthropometric data. Because of their eclectic nature, considerable diversity in types of data and methods of presentation are usually carried over from the original sources. Very often such data require additional processing to prepare them for specific problems.

7.3 DATA PROCESSING

Processing includes those procedures necessary to prepare source data for incorporation into a selected format for direct use or for communicating the data to the user. It includes such functions as analyses of subject measurements, conversions of units from source documents, extrapolation of data into expected future time frames, determination of trends, synthesizing of populations, and calculating unknown dimensions. The statistical bases for some of these were presented in Chapter V. Other items, such as the development of nomographs are covered in a following section emphasizing data presentation techniques. The important aspect of synthesizing populations and estimating unknown dimensions will be featured here.

7.3.1 Synthesizing Populations

In spite of the considerable number of published reports containing anthropometric data, it often occurs in industrial applications that one does not have a ready-made set of anthropometric data adequately describing a user population for a specific product. Lack of time or funds may prevent conducting an appropriate survey. Even with adequate funds, a lengthy design and development period (10 to 20 years) may require an extrapolation into the future operational use period.

Under such conditions, the engineering anthropometrist can perform the unique function of synthesizing dimensional distributions estimates for the planned user population. Such applications represent a significant culmination of the statistical estimation techniques and biometric relationships analyses previously described in Chapters V and VI.

A comprehensive outline of the process is shown by an operations flow chart in Figure 7-1. A description of the steps in the process follows.

1. *Engineering Task Description.* This statement of the problem to be solved should reflect consideration of the category of applications (e.g., work space design, clothing design, or design of small devices and components) and what level of detail is required (gross or fine).
2. *Checklist of Anthropometric Data Requirements.* This list helps to scope the size of the task and the structure of the report of results. It is derived from the above category of application and personal experience.
3. *Preliminary Population Description.* A written word description helps clarify the data needs. Some numerical data may be available to begin with, such as Height and Weight. However, this description should identify factors listed in Chapter VI, such as age, sex, ethnic groups, race, training, socioeconomic status, diet, nation of origin, and so forth. Percentage mixtures of various subgroups should be tabulated if known.
4. *Review and Analysis of Data.* Comparison of data and needed information in three basic steps determines needed calculations:
   (a) Equivalency (similarity): population characteristics other than historical should be first considered as to degree or number of like characteristics.
   (b) Sufficiency: determine what additional data must be estimated to satisfy the list in step 2.
   (c) Currency: apply historical trend factors. Determine if survey data are so nearly current that no further adjustments need be made.
5. *Output.* Two types of output product are suggested: a tabulated list of dimensions (means and standard deviations, or percentiles) and a drawing illustrating these dimensions of the body. Many further elaborations of bivariate distributions and the like can be added if required.

7.3.2 Estimating Unknown Dimension Distributions

Recurrent in many engineering anthropometry applications (including the synthesis procedures previously discussed) is the problem of estimating means and standard deviations for dimension distributions that are not found among the available data for the design population. Several formulas and techniques for handling such problems, abstracted from Chapters V and VI, are summarized in Table 7-3, with an emphasis on the typical application aspects. That is, the left column of the table has groups of data such as the analyst is often given or able to collect. The appropriate formulas and procedures for

Table 7-2. Selected Human Engineering Handbooks and Design Guides Containing Anthropometric Data

Title and Contents	Author, Date, and Publisher
1. *Human Engineering Guide for Equipment Designers* General guide to human engineering, contains limited tables of anthropometric data, body motion limits, strength. Very well illustrated.	Woodson, W. E. (1954) University of California Press Berkeley, California *Also:* Woodson, W. E. and Conover, D. W. (1964) 2nd ed., University of California Press Berkeley, California
2. *Annotated Bibliography of Applied Physical Anthropology in Human Engineering* Abstracts, tabulated data, figures, and charts from 121 references. 149 total references.	Hansen, R., Cornog, D. Y. and Hertzberg, H. T. E. (1958); WADC Technical Report 56-30 (ASTIA Document AD 155622) Aero Medical Lab Wright Air Development Center Air Res. and Dev. Command USAF, Wright-Patterson Air Force Base, Ohio
3. *The Measure of Man* A collection of charts and organized, stylized design dimensions for work-space layout by industrial designers.	Dreyfuss, H. (1960), 2nd ed. (1967) Whitney Library of Design 18 East 50th Street New York, New York
4. *NASA Life Sciences Data Book* Size and motion—condensed percentile graphs, males and females, skeletal weights, work space dimensions, pressure suits dimension, sitting area, surface area, radiation area, CM, moments of inertia, limits of motion, handgrip strength, arm strength, leg strength, G-effects.	Editor: Webb Associates, Yellow Springs, Ohio First edition (June 1962) Director of Aerospace Medicine Office of Manned Space Flight Headquarters National Aeronautics and Space Administration Washington, D.C. 20025

5. *Human Engineering Guide to Equipment Design* Anthropometric criteria by dimension for a variety of populations. Work space and maintenance design criteria. A very extensive collection of anthropometric information for military and civilian human engineering design.	Morgan, C. T., Cook, J. S., Chapanis, A., and Lund, M. W. (eds.), 1st ed. (1963) McGraw-Hill Book Co., New York Van Cott, H. P. and Kinkade, R. G., (eds.), 2nd ed. (1972) U.S. Government Printing Office Superintendent of Documents, Washington, D.C.
6. *Human Engineering Design Criteria Standard MSFC-STD-267A* Anthropometric data for work space and maintenance design criteria.	George C. Marshall Space Flight Center National Aeronautics and Space Administration (1964)
7. *The Human Body in Equipment Design* A very large collection of anthropometric data for engineering design, which forms the major part of the text. Also contains variety of other human engineering data and design recommendations.	Damon, A., Stoudt, H. W., and McFarland, R. A. (1966) Harvard University Press, Cambridge, Mass.
8. *Anthropometrics for Designers* A limited collection of data, some with special interest to clothing designers, such as section on growth rates and on body typing. Contains some work space layout data and design approaches, also some control design recommendations	Croney, J. (1971) B. T. Batsford, Ltd., London Van Nostrand Reinhold Co., New York
9. *AFSC DH 1-3. Design Handbook, Series 1-0. Personal Subsystems, Chapter 2, Human Engineering* A comprehensive application-oriented compilation of human engineering data and rules. Continually updated.	U.S. Air Force, Headquarters Air Force Systems Command, 2nd ed. (1972) Wright Patterson Air Force Base, Ohio

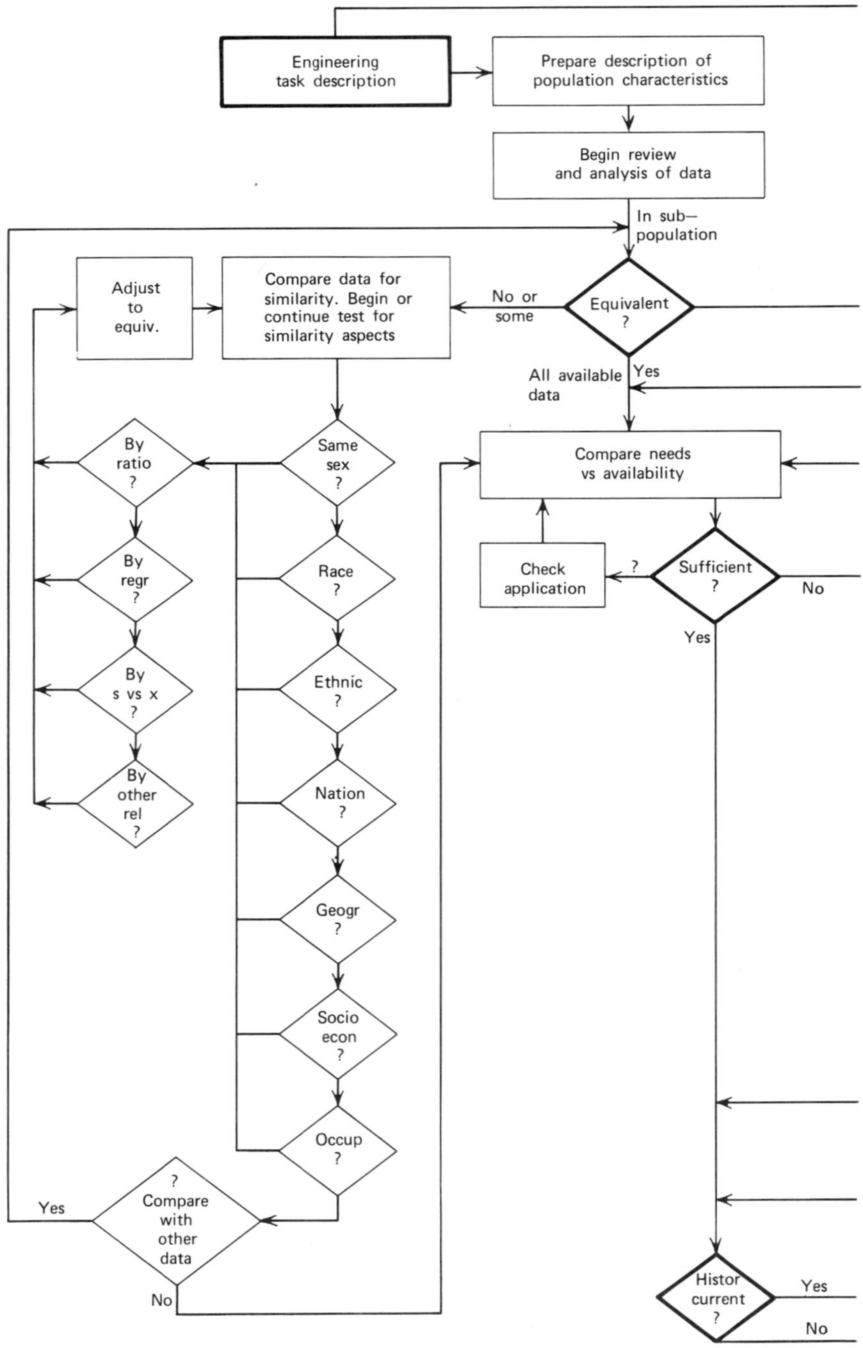

Figure 7-1. Operations flow diagram for synthesizing anthropometric descriptions of user populations.

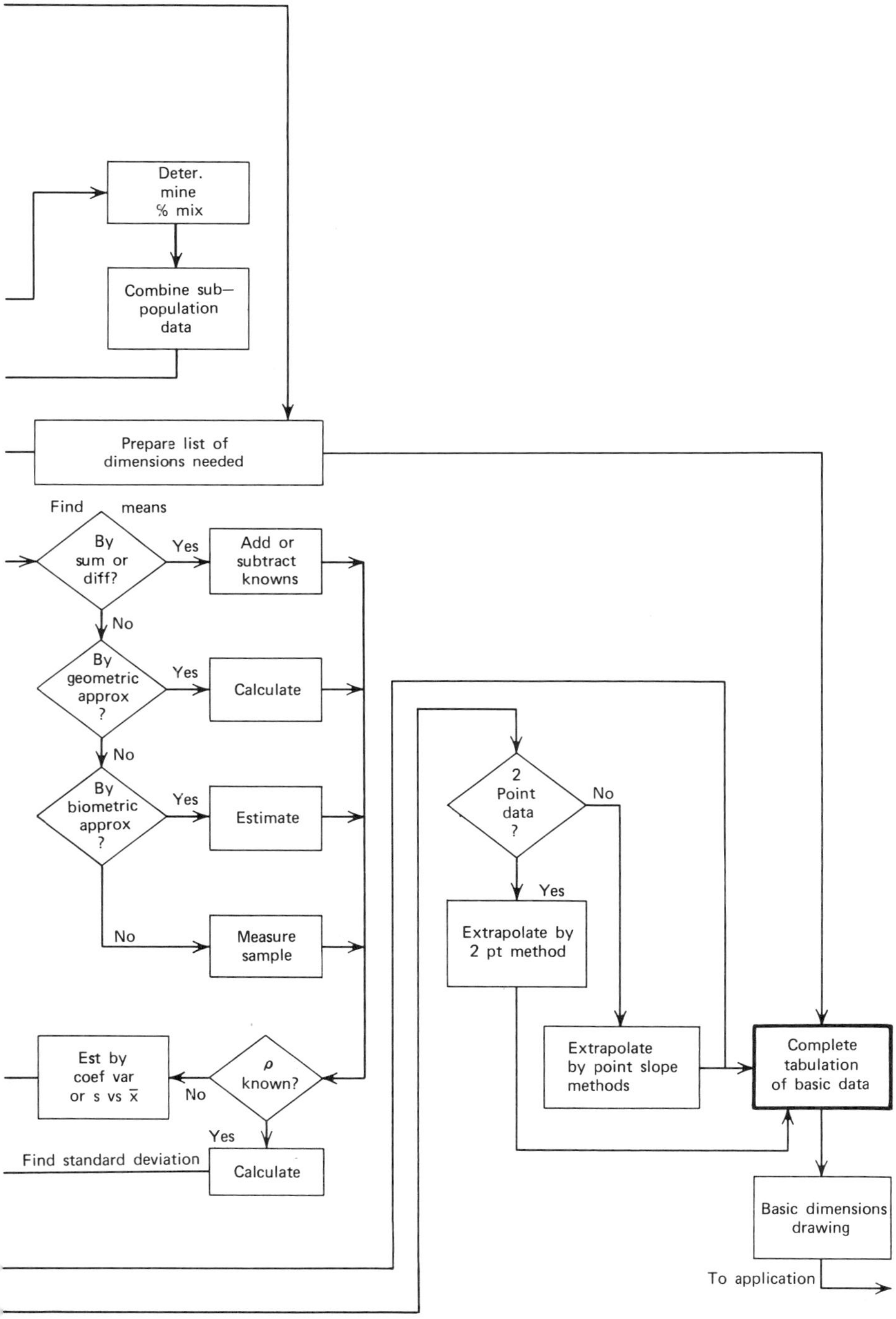

Figure 7-1. (continued)

Table 7-3. Methods for Estimation of Unknown Dimensions, Means, and Standard Deviations

Given Data	Description of Method and Section Ref.
A. Means, standard deviations (or variances), and correlation coefficients for two dimensions which add up to the desired dimension. *Note.* A correlation coefficient estimate from a different survey on a similar population may be used if available.	A1. Add means to estimate the mean (M) for the unknown distribution (Section 5.5.2): $M_x + M_y = M_{(x+y)}$ (Eq. 7.1) A2. Estimate standard deviation by formula (Section 5.4, No. 5): $S_{(x+y)}{}^2 = S_x{}^2 + S_y{}^2 + 2rS_xS_y$ (Eq. 7.2)
B. Means, standard deviations (or variances), and correlation coefficients for two population dimensions such that the smaller is part of the larger and the difference is the desired dimension. See note above.	B1. Subtract means to estimate mean for the unknown distribution (Section 5.5.2): $M_{(x-y)} = M_x - M_y$ (Eq. 7.3) B2. Estimate standard deviation by formula (Section 5.4, No. 5): $S_{(x-y)}{}^2 = S_x{}^2 + S_y{}^2 - 2rS_xS_y$ (Eq. 7.4)
C. Means for two dimensions (from which a new mean for the unknown dimension can be derived by addition or subtractions, A1 or B1 above). Also, a graph of s versus $\bar{x}$ (or data on s versus $\bar{x}$ for the population or a population with similar characteristics; construct graph as in Figure 6-4).	C1. Add or subtract means of unknown dimensions to estimate unknown dimension mean (Section 5.5.2). C2. Select appropriate class data (length, breadth, circumference). (See Table 6-3, Section 6.3.) C3. Read estimate of s corresponding to above estimate of $\bar{x}$ (or M) for selected parameter curve (Section 5.5.2 and Figure 6-3).
D. Means and standard deviation of desired dimension for "similar" population with known differing major body dimensions means	D1. Select appropriate comparable major body dimensions and determine ratio of means and of standard deviations (Section 5.4,

Table 7-3. ***(continued)***

Given Data	Description of Method and Section Ref.
and standard deviations (such as Height, Sitting Height, Buttock-knee Length, Arm Reach).	No. 1; Section 6.4): $$K_m = \frac{M_{p_1A}}{M_{p_2A}} \cong \frac{(M_{p_1B})}{M_{p_2B}} \quad \text{(Eq. 7.5)}$$ $$K_s = \frac{S_{p_1A}}{S_{p_2A}} \cong \frac{(S_{p_1B})}{S_{p_2B}} \quad \text{(Eq. 7.6)}$$ where "A" designates available dimension distribution for both population 1 and 2, and "B" designates dimension data available only for population 2. Unknown in ( ). D2. Estimate unknown body dimension for population (p_1), based upon ratio to known differing population (p_2): $$M_{p_1B} = K_m M_{p_2B} \quad \text{(Eq. 7.7)}$$ $$S_{p_1B} = K_s S_{p_2B} \quad \text{(Eq. 7.8)}$$
E. Verbal description of body dimension and plot of s versus $\bar{x}(\bar{x} \equiv M)$ for "similar" population, expressed in percent of stature. (Example shown in Figure 6-3 as part of discussion on biometric relationships.)	E1. Estimate unknown mean in percentage of body stature based on approximate biometric proportions (e.g., 10%, 50%, 75%) or by analogy to available data on similar population (Section 5.4). E2. From graph of s versus $\bar{x}$, estimate s for appropriate class of dimensions (length, breadth, depth) (Section 5.4, No. 4).
F. Verbal description of body dimension and data on coefficients of variation (V) for dimension classes (per Table 6-3).	F1. Estimate unknown mean (M) same as above. F2. Calculate standard deviation (Section 5.4, No. 3): $$S = VM \quad \text{(Eq. 7.9)}$$

estimating the needed dimension distribution are found in the opposite space in the right column. Note that Table 7-3 is organized to group those data and methods related to a complete distribution description, omitting neither average nor dispersion estimates. This is in contrast to the separate considerations which may be found in Chapters V and VI by use of the accompanying section references in parentheses.

7.4 DATA COMMUNICATION

Many of the significant concepts of this section relate strongly to the proper selection of communications media. Effective data presentations formats for engineering handbooks and requirements documents are described herein, which are generally applicable to example developments in Chapters VIII, IX, and X.

7.4.1 Presentation of Percentile Values of Body Dimensions

Effective communication of data and criteria to the design engineer generally requires presentation of the information in the specific *language of the engineer* which, excluding engineering drawings, is basically in terms of numbers, graphs, and formulas.

Tabular Formats

The simplest means of presenting discrete numerical data is a *table* of numbers from which one can read specific values of interest directly. When listing the full range of percentiles is impractical, the recommended magnitudes are 1st, 2nd, 5th, and 10th at the low end, the 50th, and the 90th, 95th, 98th, and 99th at the high end. If only one low- and high-range value is used, the 5th and 95th are recommended for convenient comparison with other data (unless specific design policy dictates otherwise). Figure 7-2 is an example of such a presentation, containing data from a 1967 survey of the U.S. Air Force personnel. An illustration of the dimension and the method of measurement should be included and verbally described along with the set of tables.

Graphical Formats

It is possible to summarize a great deal of information, while still giving percentiles directly, by the use of graphical form as shown previously in Figure 5-4. The development of the normal probability graph presentation and its several advantages were discussed in Chapter V, as one of the recommended statistical tools for analysis and applications. As noted therein, the "stacking" of many graphical presentations of percentile distributions, permits a compact presentation of a large amount of data for ready reference in design work. Compactness of the presentation is possible because of "nesting" and infrequent crossovers or overlapping of individual graphs of percentiles versus body dimension on the normal probability scale. The separation of lengths, breadths (and depths), and circumferences, also helps achieve line separation and ease of reading the graph. Although preparation of these graphs requires considerable time, they are very useful for direct design use, for incorporation in handbook presentations of anthropometric data, and for data interpretation as regards information on skewness, kurtosis, and other conditions of non-normal statistical distributions.

Statistical Quantities and Formulas

The most compact method for accurately describing perfectly normal (Gaussian) frequency distributions, is to list only means and standard deviations. Such presentations are primarily for limited distribution, to statistically knowledgeable personnel. Although engineers normally are not familiar with statistical techniques, the simple algebraic formulas for calculating percentiles from mean and standard deviation may be readily understood by persons with engineering training. Inclusion of the tables of factors and formulas for their use with the tables of basic statistical data extends their potential usefulness for engineering application.

7.4.2 Nomographs

The nomograph is a powerful technique for presenting human body dimensional data for certain situations. A nomograph, such as the example in Figure 7-3, is a special kind of graphical presentation that enables one, by the aid of a straightedge, to read off the value of a dependent variable when the value of two or more independent variables are given. It is primarily useful as a time-saver for highly repetitive evaluations or when data are required on several body dimensions under conditions where two body dimensions are independently determined. Examples are the determination of clothing sizes, given Height and Weight, or the design of work places, given normal reach and Sitting Height.

Major steps involved in the procedure are outlined by Munro (Hansen and Cornog, 1958) as follows:

1. Select two body dimensions as independent variables that have reasonably good correlations with useful dependent variables.
2. Determine interval size for the independent variables to provide reasonable accuracy with a small number of intervals or "boxes" (area of bivariate distribution bounded by interval limits of dependent and independent variables) as shown in Figure 7-4.
3. Begin chart construction with parallel layout of independent variable scales of convenient size for graphic work.

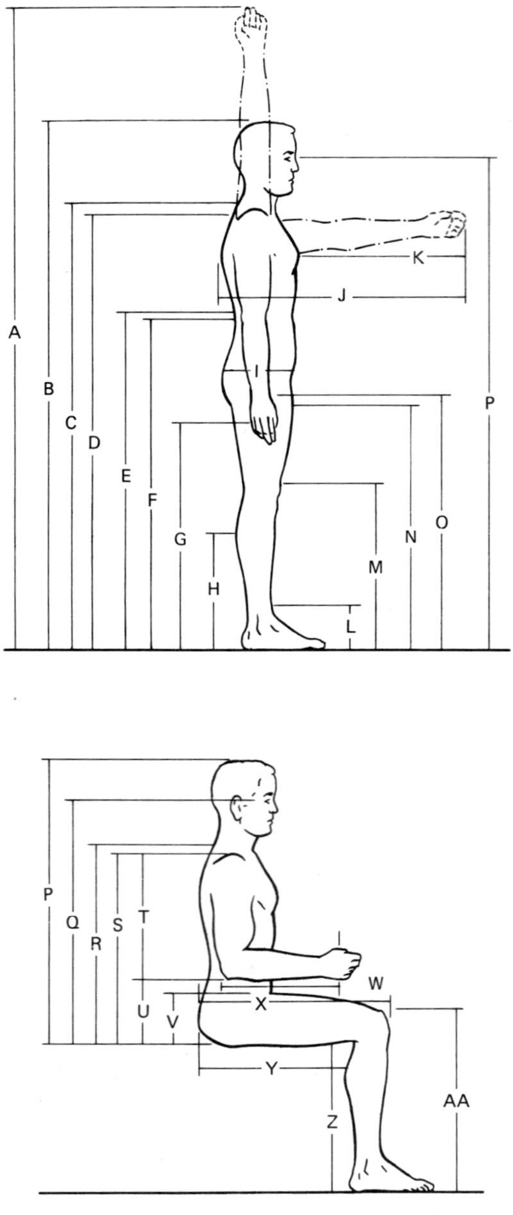

Figure 7-2. Tabular format for presentation of anthropometric percentile data. (U.S. Air Force, 1969, 1972) The 1972 data (shown here) contain two corrections not shown in the 1969 issue.

Key to figure	Dimension	5th* Percentile	95th* Percentile
A	Overhead reach	78.6	87.6
B	Stature	65.9	73.9
C	Cervical height	56.1	63.7
D	Shoulder height	53.4	60.9
E	Elbow height	41.3	47.3
F	Waist height	38.9	45.0
G	Knuckle height	27.7	32.4
H	Calf height	12.6	15.5
I	Depth of reach		
	one arm	20.2	26.8
	both arms	19.2	24.5
J	Functional reach	29.1	34.3
K	Ankle height	4.7	6.2
L	Kneecap height (top)	17.1	22.4
M	Crotch height	30.8	36.2
N	Wrist height	31.6	36.7
O	Eye height	60.8	68.6
P	Sitting height	34.7	38.8
Q	Eye height, sitting	30.0	33.9
R	Mid-shoulder height	23.7	27.3
S	Shoulder height	22.2	25.9
T	Shoulder-elbow length	13.1	15.3
U	Elbow rest height	8.2	11.6
V	Thigh clearance height	5.6	7.4
W	Elbow-grip length	12.8	14.9
X	Buttock-knee length	22.1	25.6
Y	Buttock-popliteal length	18.2	21.5
Z	Popliteal height	15.8	18.7
AA	Knee height	20.4	23.6

* 1967 Air Force officer flying personnel

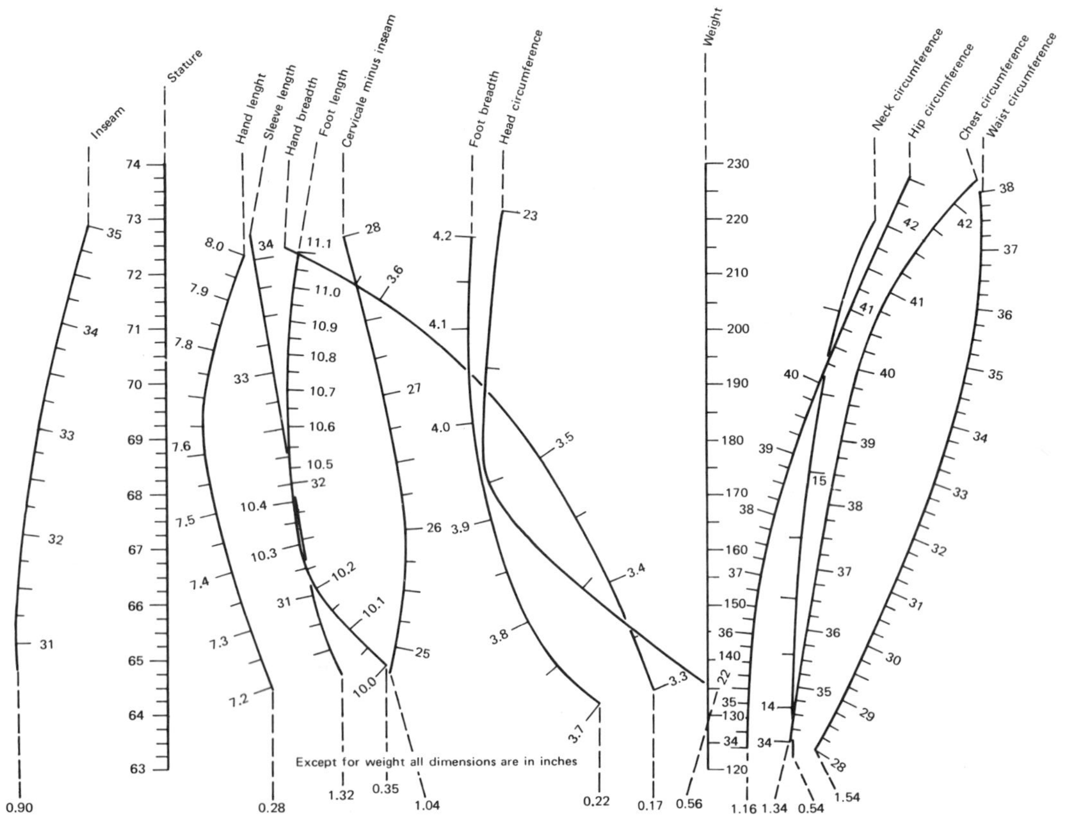

Figure 7-3. Anthropometric nomograph of army men (Munro, in Hansen and Cornog, 1958). A straight line passing through known values of Stature and Weight, will also pass through average values for all other dimensions as shown. Each average value thus indicated is mid-point of a range determined by adding and subtracting the amount shown below each line to the mid-point. This range will include about 67% of men with the original given values of Stature and Weight.

75
74
73
72
71

	Mean	S.D.
Waist Circumference	29.7	1.7
Inseam Length	35.0	1.2
Chest Circumference	35.9	1.5
Cervicale-Inseam	27.0	1.1
Neck Circumference	14.4	0.6
Sleeve Length	33.3	1.4
Seat Circumference	36.5	1.3
Head Circumference	22.4	0.6
Hand Length	7.9	0.3
Hand Breadth	3.5	0.2
Foot Length	10.8	0.4
Foot Breadth	3.9	0.2

9.226%

	Mean	S.D.
Waist Circumference	32.9	2.0
Inseam Length	34.9	1.2
Chest Circumference	38.6	1.6
Cervicale-Inseam	27.5	1.1
Neck Circumference	15.1	0.6
Sleeve Length	33.7	1.4
Seat Circumference	39.1	1.5
Head Circumference	22.8	0.6
Hand Length	8.0	0.3
Hand Breadth	3.6	0.2
Foot Length	11.0	0.4
Foot Breadth	4.1	0.2

6.000%

	Mean	S.D.
Waist Circumference	38.1	2.4
Inseam Length	34.7	1.3
Chest Circumference	42.2	1.9
Cervicale-Inseam	28.0	1.1
Neck Circumference	15.8	0.6
Sleeve Length	34.1	1.3
Seat Circumference	42.4	1.7
Head Circumference	23.0	0.6
Hand Length	8.0	0.3
Hand Breadth	3.6	0.2
Foot Length	11.1	0.3
Foot Breadth	4.2	0.2

0.587%

70
69
68
67

	Mean	S.D.
Waist Circumference	29.1	1.6
Inseam Length	33.1	1.1
Chest Circumference	35.1	1.5
Cervicale-Inseam	25.9	1.1
Neck Circumference	14.1	0.6
Sleeve Length	31.8	1.4
Seat Circumference	35.5	1.3
Head Circumference	22.2	0.6
Hand Length	7.6	0.3
Hand Breadth	3.4	0.2
Foot Length	10.4	0.4
Foot Breadth	3.8	0.2

29.864%

	Mean	S.D.
Waist Circumference	32.1	2.1
Inseam Length	33.0	1.2
Chest Circumference	37.8	1.7
Cervicale-Inseam	26.5	1.1
Neck Circumference	14.8	0.6
Sleeve Length	32.3	1.4
Seat Circumference	38.0	1.5
Head Circumference	22.5	0.6
Hand Length	7.7	0.3
Hand Breadth	3.5	0.2
Foot Length	10.6	0.4
Foot Breadth	3.9	0.2

24.443%

	Mean	S.D.
Waist Circumference	37.1	2.4
Inseam Length	32.7	1.3
Chest Circumference	41.5	1.8
Cervicale-Inseam	27.2	1.2
Neck Circumference	15.7	0.6
Sleeve Length	32.7	1.4
Seat Circumference	41.6	1.6
Head Circumference	22.8	0.6
Hand Length	7.7	0.3
Hand Breadth	3.5	0.2
Foot Length	10.7	0.4
Foot Breadth	4.1	0.2

1.839%

66
65
64
63

	Mean	S.D.
Waist Circumference	28.3	1.6
Inseam Length	31.2	1.1
Chest Circumference	34.1	1.5
Cervicale-Inseam	24.8	1.0
Neck Circumference	13.9	0.6
Sleeve Length	30.3	1.4
Seat Circumference	34.4	1.3
Head Circumference	21.9	0.6
Hand Length	7.3	0.3
Hand Breadth	3.3	0.2
Foot Length	10.0	0.4
Foot Breadth	3.7	0.2

11.848%

	Mean	S.D.
Waist Circumference	31.2	2.1
Inseam Length	31.1	1.2
Chest Circumference	36.7	1.7
Cervicale-Inseam	25.4	1.1
Neck Circumference	14.6	0.6
Sleeve Length	30.8	1.4
Seat Circumference	36.8	1.5
Head Circumference	22.2	0.6
Hand Length	7.4	0.3
Hand Breadth	3.4	0.2
Foot Length	10.1	0.4
Foot Breadth	3.8	0.2

13.178%

	Mean	S.D.
Waist Circumference	36.8	2.2
Inseam Length	30.8	1.2
Chest Circumference	40.7	1.7
Cervicale-Inseam	26.3	1.1
Neck Circumference	15.5	0.7
Sleeve Length	31.4	1.4
Seat Circumference	40.9	1.6
Head Circumference	22.5	0.6
Hand Length	7.4	0.3
Hand Breadth	3.4	0.2
Foot Length	10.3	0.3
Foot Breadth	3.9	0.2

0.746%

100 108 116 124 132 140 148 156 164 172 180 188 196 204 212 220 228 236 244 252

Weight (lb)

Figure 7-4. Dimensional relations to Stature and Weight sorted in "box" format. (Modification of Munro in Hansen and Cornog, 1958.)

4. Perform trial layouts to determine spacing of independent variable scales and evaluate crowding of dependent variable scales between them.
5. Complete layout of selected spacing.
6. Calculate standard error of estimate for each dependent variable.
7. Label scales for variables with names and associated standard errors.

Smoothing of dependent variable scales may be required as a result of experimental errors or random variations in small sample data. The standard error is calculated as follows (Hansen and Cornog, 1958):

$$S_e = \sigma_1 \sqrt{\frac{R}{R_{11}}} \qquad \text{(Eq. 7.10)}$$

where

$$R = \begin{vmatrix} r_{11} & r_{12} & r_{13} \\ r_{21} & r_{22} & r_{23} \\ r_{31} & r_{32} & r_{33} \end{vmatrix} \qquad R_{11} = \begin{vmatrix} 1 & r_{23} \\ r_{23} & 1 \end{vmatrix} \qquad \begin{matrix}\text{(Eq. 7.11)} \\ \text{(Eq. 7.12)}\end{matrix}$$

and σ = standard deviation of the dependent variable.

$$\begin{bmatrix} r_{11} \\ r_{22} \\ r_{33} \end{bmatrix} = 1$$

r_{12} = correlation coefficient of dependent variable with one independent variable
r_{13} = correlation coefficient of dependent variable with other independent variables
r_{23} = correlation coefficient of two independent variables.

(Eq. 7.13)

Munro's report provides further detail and numerical examples of the key steps, and cautions concerning typical problems often encountered.

7.4.3 Presentation of Correlated Data

Simple, readily useful presentation methods for design limit data on correlations between two dimensions are needed for engineering applications. The classic method is to define an elliptical boundary for the bivariate distribution, which encompasses a selected percentage of the total data. More details, dealing with driver's eye location, appear in Chapter VIII. Calculation of such curves is tedious and so is the drafting layout. Furthermore, it does not tie directly to the other usual design limits, expressed as the upper and lower percentiles of the individual variables.

Another, simpler technique, which also overcomes the latter difficulty, is presented here. An example is shown in Figure 7-5. Given the basic regression equations and design percentile limits, a straight line graphic construction is readily developed to any selected scale, depicting a hexagonal boundary for a correlation scatter diagram. In the figure, the key intersection points are labeled with letters as a convenience for discussion and to aid in tabulating coordinates.

A selected range of percentiles for each primary variable defines a rectangle (*AEJP*) of suggested working limit criteria, applicable where correlation is not considered in design. Regression lines for each variable on the other are then drawn. Next, a selected band width (here 5th and 95th percentiles of the standard error of the mean) are shown on either side of the regression lines. Two triangular areas are then defined as outside of design limits, by connecting lines through the intersections of the primary rectangle and the outermost limits of the two regression bands (shaded triangles *DEF* and *NPQ*).

All of the essential data for the coordinates of the lettered points can be tabulated compactly, as illustrated by the table below the figure, which depicts two example combinations of bivariates. The table may be extended vertically as desired for additional bivariate combinations of interest. Including the cor-

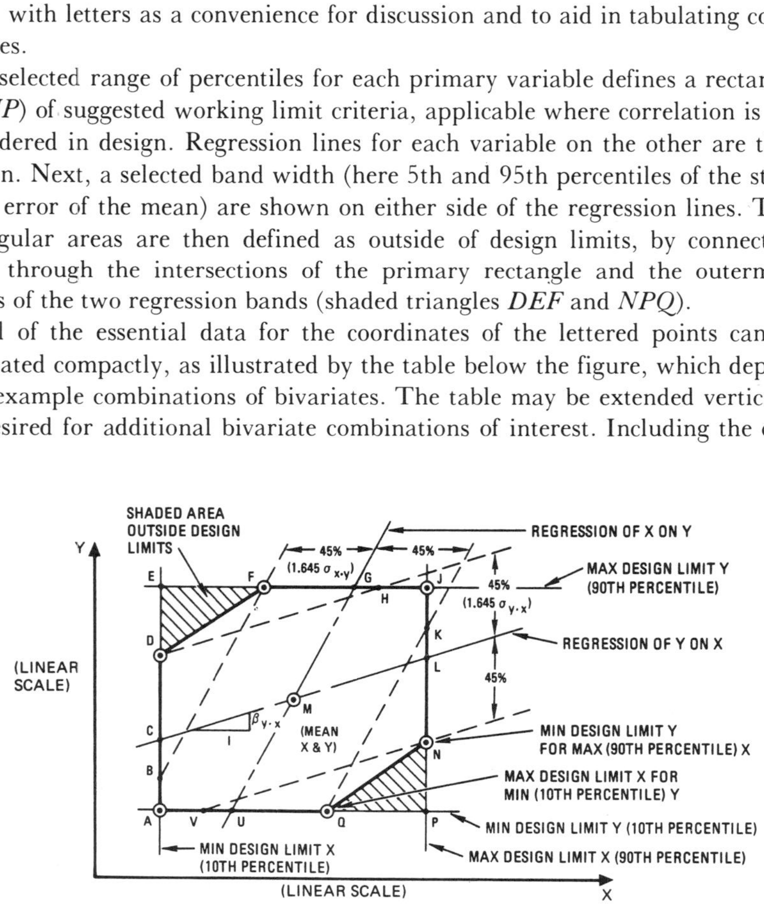

COORDINATES OF KEY POINTS (INCHES) *

VARIATES		A		D		F		J		N		Q		M		P	$\beta_{y \cdot x}$	$\beta_{x \cdot y}$
X	Y	X	Y	X	Y	X	Y	X	Y	X	Y	X	Y	X	Y			
STATURE	SIT. HT	66.0	34.3	66.0	36.4	68.8	37.6	72.2	37.6	72.2	34.5	69.5	34.3	69.1	35.9	0.743	0.305	01.408
KNEE HT., SITTING	BUTTOCK-KNEE L.	22.3	20.4	22.3	21.5	23.8	23.0	25.0	23.0	25.0	21.8	23.5	20.4	23.6	21.7	0.822	0.768	0.880

* BASED ON DATA FROM HERTZBERG, DANIELS AND CHURCHILL (1954)
AND UNPUBLISHED CORRELATION TABLES

Figure 7-5. Roebuck design data correlation diagram. (Roebuck, Kroemer, and Thomson, 1973.)

relation coefficient and slopes of the regression lines in the table aids in extrapolations for different percentile conditions.

7.4.4 Specifications, Standards, and Other Advisory and Regulatory Documents

The primary concern of this text is the *technology* of measurements and applications of anthropometric data which often culminate in specifications, standards, and other regulatory documents. Therefore, a brief discussion of their function is appropriate. Such documents provide direction to designers and testing/evaluation personnel in matters related to the techniques and data in this text (Meister and Farr, 1967). Being expressions of past accumulated knowledge, such documents are most useful and convenient for the more common anthropometric problems. However, when detailed design data for new devices and new environments are needed, these documents often prove inadequate, overly restrictive, or simply not applicable. Familiarity with such specifications and regulations is useful, both for knowing *when* and *when not* to rely on their contents. An extensive listing of such documents has been compiled in a publication by Man Factors, Inc. (W.C.S. Institute, 1969).

7.5 ENGINEERING ANTHROPOMETRY DRAWINGS

Application of the processed data is often performed through the medium of various types of engineering drawings.

The types of engineering drawings of primary concern herein are powerful analysis and synthesis tools for engineering anthropometry, just as they are for surveying, machinery kinematics, airframe structures, and bridge design. In addition, such drawings are also highly effective as a means of communication of man-machine geometric relationships to design engineers.

Descriptions and examples of the different types of drawings are included as integral parts of the procedures and examples in Chapters VIII, IX, and X. However, a general consideration of differences between standard engineering practices and drawings of human beings is appropriate here.

Preparation of engineering anthropometric drawings requires artistic skills not taught in standard engineering curricula. A modest ability to make a reasonably recognizable free hand graphic representation of human beings, both in standardized anthropometric positions and in actual working attitudes is required. A formal course, or considerable informal practice, in drawing the human figure from life is strongly recommended for training of an engineering anthropometrist and his drafting staff. Such training will greatly aid the rapid preparation of drawings of persons from the often very limited anthropometric dimensions available. The other extreme, of course, is the complete contour map of the human body which can be developed from stereophotos, and in which artistic skill is minimally required.

In preparing drawings, articulated two-dimensional templates, or manikins, representing the human body at various scale factors, percentiles, and clothing conditions often are of great benefit, and can substitute for the basic artistic skill requirement to some degree.

Two other important types of engineering drawings closely associated with anthropometry applications are briefly mentioned for completeness of this discussion: (1) design drawings for special anthropometric gages, design aids, and measurement devices, and (2) mockup design drawings of reach and clearance envelopes which are used in mockup evaluations. Such drawings use standard tool design or machine design drawing practice; they are most frequently rough mockup sketches rather than formal drawings. The innovative design content and economic considerations involved in such drawings are significant to success in engineering anthropometry applications.

7.6 ENGINEERING MANIKINS, DUMMIES, AND ROBOTS

Among the very useful engineering aids to work space, clothing, and personal equipment design are accurately scaled engineering models of human beings. These range from simple two-dimensional forms for design layout and analysis to three-dimensional, dynamically similar, instrumented anthropomorphic dummies for escape systems and restraint harness testing. Selected examples of such items are described in detail in the following paragraphs.

7.6.1 Drafting Board Manikins

A useful form of model man for work space layout drawings and two-dimensional mobility studies is the articulated, transparent sheet plastic (or sheet metal) manikin. A set of these manikins is commonly prepared in a range of sizes and scales for use in a design department. They are usually made to represent two-dimensional aspects of a man as seen from the side, but occasionally may represent a fore-aft view or other aspect. Because of the limited quantities required, the cost for each item generally has been very high. They are usually made by skilled model makers, largely by hand and if existing designs such as those illustrated in this section are unsuitable, the analysis and preparation of engineering drawings of such devices involves extensive engineering time.

When considering the acquisition of a set of articulated manikins for an engineering project, factors such as the following should be considered: (1) the number, type, and size of the manikins required to do the job; (2) the degree of manikin fidelity required; and (3) the acceptability of available designs versus the cost of developing new ones. These factors are discussed below.

For maximum flexibility a large number of sizes will be required to represent the desired range of body dimensions and the useful scales for engineering drawings. For example, consider the problem of the design of a set of manikins to represent the 10th, 50th, and 90th percentile sizes, to take into account two clothing conditions: a simple close-fitting undergarment and a fully pressurized space suit, and to be usable in the most frequently drawn scales of engineering drawings, $\frac{1}{10}$, $\frac{1}{4}$, and $\frac{1}{2}$ size. The total number of manikins required will be 18 manikins (3 percentiles × 2 clothing conditions × 3 scale sizes). At a cost of $50 to $100 a piece, the manikin set can become a significant budget item. Yet this set would only satisfy minimum requirements. It would not demonstrate the effects of alternate clothing configurations normally encountered when designing for space suit operations such as the effects of the uninflated suit or the removal of parts of the suit such as the helmet, boots, or gloves.

A second consideration when selecting the number and type of manikins required is the desirability of having some multiple percentile manikins (i.e., a manikin with some dimensions of one percentile, and other dimensions of another percentile). For example, there is an extremely low probability that any one person will have as many as five body dimensions that fall within a range of ± 5 percentiles from some nominal value, such as the tenth percentile. Therefore, it would be desirable to have a manikin representing the most probable worst case combinations of maximum and minimum dimensions of body parts instead of one representing all maximum dimensions and another representing all minimum dimensions. Careful judgment must be exercised in arriving at the optimum selection of sizes, adjustments, and joint designs.

The greater the accuracy desired of the model man, the more elaborate is the manikin. Instead of a simple pin joint, the shoulder action may be represented by a cutout in the body and a slot in the upper arm section as in that by Dempster (1955a). Spinal action may also be simulated by additional segments, springs, or flexible members. Various neck and head motions may be simulated by separate links, but the practical problems of constructing the joints and stops in the shoulder and neck area must be carefully considered in terms of space limits.

When developing manikins to represent the hybrid percentile men described in Chapter VI, special problems arise. For example, a 10th percentile arm reach dimension constrains the location and design of joint pivots at the shoulder in a way that may not be compatible with other shoulder dimensions. In particular, the shoulder pivot may be so close to the acromial point that there in not enough material to form a pivot joint in the manikin.

Elbow Rest Height is another difficult area, since this dimension tends to be near the middle percentile range for all common-percentile combinations. Design limits must be ignored or simulated by use of adjustable upper arm lengths or other approaches.

A brief outline of the design process for manikins is presented below. The first few steps are similar to those for a basic anthropometric drawing. If such a drawing has been prepared, steps 1 through 3 and 6 may be reduced to the physical effort of a new layout at the proper scale factor.

Manikin Development Process

1. Establish the population description and obtain or derive percentile distributions for as many critical body dimensions as feasible. Document data sources.
2. Lay out Height and other major body lengths on a drawing of the standing position at the largest scale desired for the set of manikins (usually ½ scale). Also show the sitting upright position for layout of Buttock-knee Length and Knee Height dimensions, Sitting Height and other sitting upright measurements. Show maximum reach distances forward, upward and downward (and sideways if a frontal plane view is contemplated).
3. Estimate length of body segments and locations of joint centers with respect to the body outline, using data and techniques previously described for basic drawings. Adjust as necessary to account for limitations in work space freedom and clothing requirements. Strive for consistency in major anthropometric dimensions in standing and seated posutres, such as correct Sitting Height, Buttock-knee Length, Knee Height (sitting), Shoulder Height (standing and sitting) and reach forward. Document design decisions and compromises.
4. Determine range of motions for joints suitable for the population, clothing limitations, and expected operating conditions. Document design decisions and compromises.
5. Design tentative joint motion limit systems.
6. Prepare outline of the body shape for standing, sitting, and like positions. Consider clothing thickness and shape additions.
7. Design each body segment outline and clothing or personal equipment item to approximate the desired body outline in conjunction with the selected joint motion limit systems. Modify as necessary. Design attachments for detachable clothing and personal equipment items as required.
8. Calculate locations and layout centers of mass for each segment. A hole large enough for a pencil point or pin should be drilled through the material at each center of mass point. These holes help to make

such points on a drawing for calculation of overall C.M. in different positions. Although more difficult to fabricate, similar holes through the hinge points help to hold certain joints fixed while moving others and to trace arcs and limits of joint motion. A hole at the eye position is also recommended strongly as this is a critical point for window, control, and display visibility assessment.

9. Investigate scale-down problems at critical joints due to minimum sizes for rivets, screws and material thickness. This is especially critical for $\frac{1}{10}$ and $\frac{1}{20}$th scale manikins. Elimination and simplification of some joints may be necessary because of the small size of such manikins. This is generally consistent with the lower level of expected detail for such drawings.
10. Complete engineering drawing callouts and details for joints.
11. Photographically reduce the drawing to the desired scale on dimensionally stable paper or fabric. This step is critical for accuracy of the smaller scale manikins. Shop personnel will need these reduced drawings for template layout guides.
12. Select areas of manikins for placement of labels. Design and order identifying labels. Suggested information: population, percentiles, Height and Weight, data source or descriptive documents, and scale. Special clothing should be noted. Centers of mass and absolute weight or weight percentage or each body segment should be labeled. Specify whether weight is for one (1) or two (2) arm or leg segments. Where applicable, label special reference lines, flesh compression limits and so forth.
13. Obtain bids for fabrication and place order.
14. Inspect tooling and follow up on fabrication process.
15. Inspect final fabricated parts for dimensional accuracy and return for rework if necessary.

Figure 7-6 shows an example of a manikin design for small, one to four-place naval fighters and attack bombers. Some manikins have been designed to appear realistic in any position (standing, stooping, climbing ladders, piloting, etc.). That shown in Figure 7-6 was designed primarily for the seated position in the space limitations which prevent extensive movement. To such a manikin, one may add templates for clothing items such as helmets, boots, parachutes, and so forth.

7.6.2 Anthropomorphic Dummies

Several types of anthropomorphic dummies have been developed for engineering research on aircraft escape systems and other similar rugged service. They are generally designed to have a weight distribution and hinge points based on anthropometric data. They may have, in addition, simulated flesh, bone, and muscular action for specific applications.

Dummies can be obtained for various G levels and a variety of sizes, articulations, and other special features. For example, resistance to accelerative forces at known levels may be incorporated by use of friction joints. Inspection of the dummy following a test, or observing its action by high-speed photography, will indicate whether these loads have been exceeded. Instrumentation can be incorporated into the head, chest, and other body cavities. Telemetering devices can transmit information from parachute drops, ejection seat firings, or car impact tests. Specially selected materials for bones and surfaces can indicate breakage (Cichowski, 1968) and local impact pressures indicating potential injury patterns (Miller and Katz, 1968). Another example of such developments is the "Dynamic Dan" elastic dummy developed for the U.S. Air Force Aerospace Medical Laboratory (Payne and Band, 1971), Figure 7-7. Significant data inputs from engineering anthropologists (Clauser, McConville, and Young, 1969) were incorporated in the development of this dummy.

Statistical considerations of dimensions discussed in the section on design layout manikins also apply to these models of man, but in three dimensions. Similar considerations must be applied to such parameters as bone stress and flexibility, weight distributions, moments of inertia, density, and so forth. Design of these dummies is, in itself, an area of engineering anthropometry application, quite apart from their use as instruments of evaluation. Problems of limb positioning, simulation of slump or extension of the trunk, contours, and the like, are inherent in the design concept. In addition, repair and maintenance are major factors in design of practical, reuseable dummies. The mechanisms must be simple and rugged. A trade-off between cost and fidelity must be considered. Possibilities for adjustments of limb lengths instead of complete replacements for different percentiles should be evaluated.

In the absence of other devices, these rugged, full weight dummies may be used for demonstration of space requirements and clearances of human operators in mockups. However, such use is generally not the optimum approach. It is desirable, for increased convenience and safety, to devise lighter weight, more accurately configured anthropomorphic dummies for such purposes. Examples that point the way are the mechanical models of human joints developed by Dempster (1955a), Rebiffe et al. (1969) and the SAE "H-Point Machine" (SAE, 1970).

Another type of dummy or partial dummy (head, bust, hand, foot) is used for design and fitting of clothing and close-fitting personal equipment. In such dummies the emphasis is upon correct surface contours and circumferences instead of mobility, torques, forces, strength of materials, and inertial considerations. Proper location of hinge points is generally of secondary

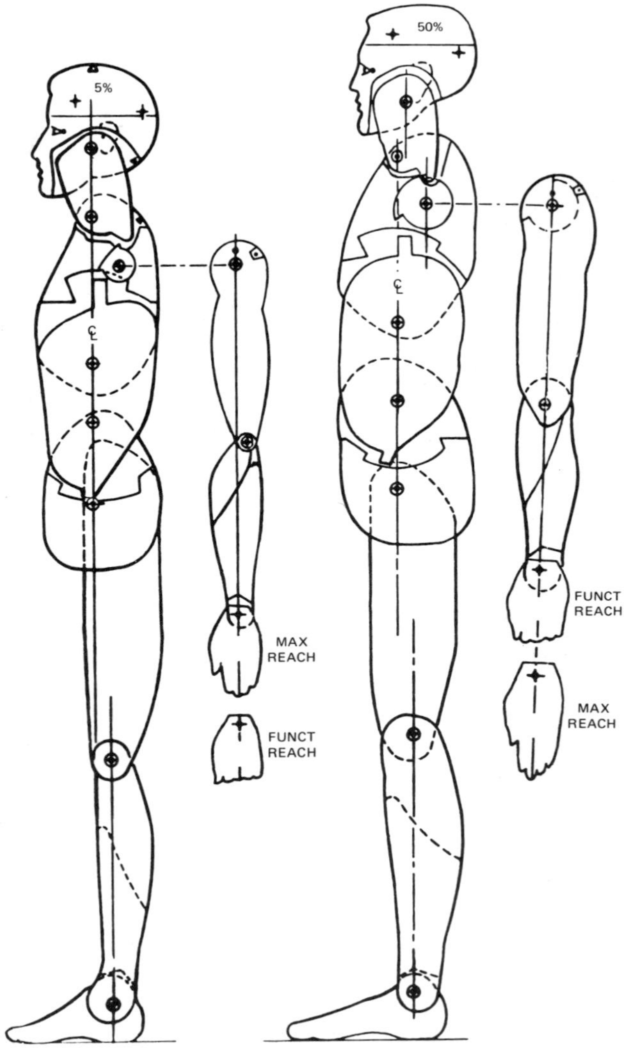

Figure 7-6. Manikin primarily for use in the seated position. Typical construction and configurations for primarily sitting position manikins. Construct as noted: (1) Manikin dimensions per WADC 52-321 (Hertzberg, Daniels and Churchill, 1954). (2) Body and helmet material: 1/16 inch transparent acrylic. (3) Cement double thickness components together. (4) Body articulations marked ⊕ to be joined by flush-mounted rivets. (5) Use same rivets for locator posts in each head and hand. (6) Scribe identification on parts as noted. (After Carlyle, 1960a Courtesy of McDonnell Douglas Corporation.)

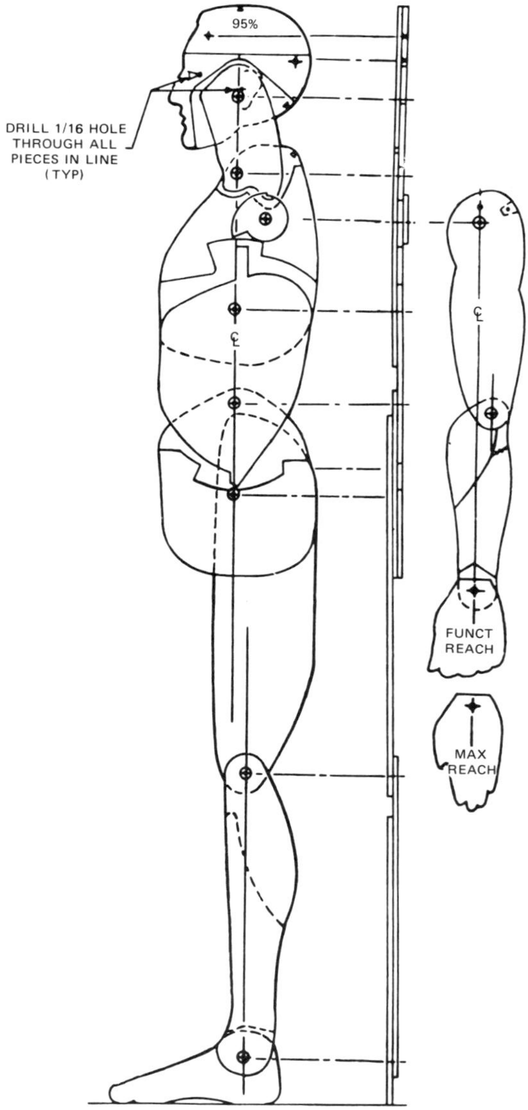

Figure 7-6. (continued.)

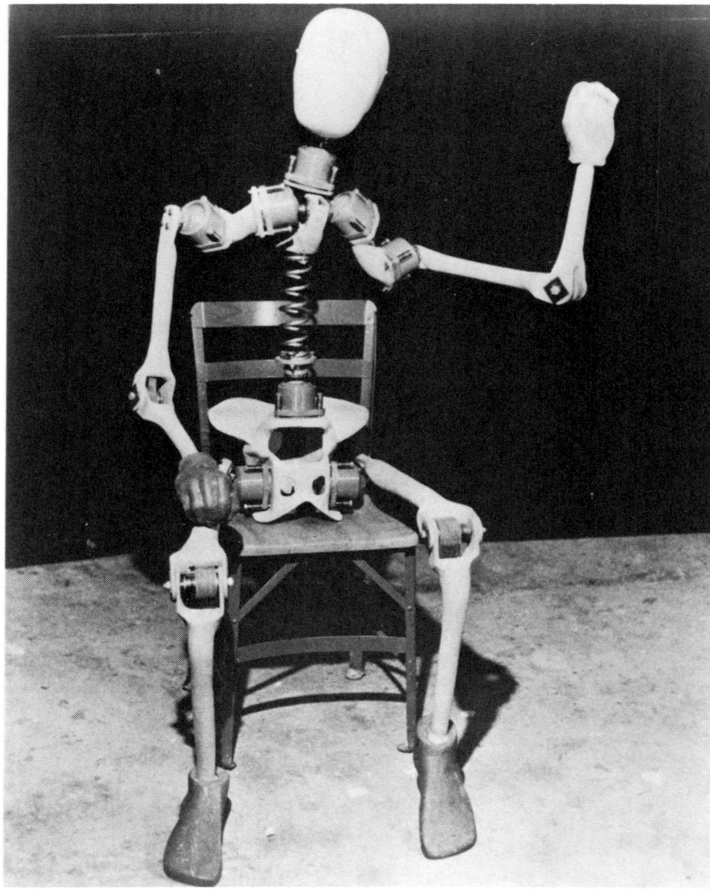

Figure 7-7. "Dynamic Dan" elastic dummy (Payne and Band, 1971.)

concern, except in special cases. Examples of development of such specially prepared clothing dummies (usually called manikins, or forms) are contained in Chapter IX.

7.6.3 Robots

A further extension of the "substitute man" concept is to equip dummies with mechanical activators, servos, force and torque sensors, and the like, to control and measure movements and their results remotely. Such anthropometric robots could determine space suit joint resistance in a wide range of movements and aid in a variety of other investigations. Pertinent publications in this area include Mizen (1965) and Parry et al. (1966). The anthropometric engineering tasks involved in design of such robots are highly challenging applications. However, no practical devices have been produced to date because of the complexity of the device and the relatively high cost for the expected benefits.

7.6.4 Scale Models

Although much less accurate than full-scale representations, small-scale, three-dimensional engineering models may be constructed to demonstrate critical stowage and volume relationships, work space limitations, and analysis techniques. These models should reflect appropriate clothing allowances and provide indications of joint movement limitations. They have several advantages, particularly ease of portability and storage and ability to demonstrate concepts of rearrangement without use of heavy moving equipment and personnel. Although expensive to construct and maintain, such devices can save many dollars and hours in extensive development programs.

7.7 MODELS OF REACH, VISION, AND CLEARANCE ENVELOPES

Between the clearly anthropomorphous two-dimensional and three-dimensional representations of man previously discussed and the mockup representations of machinery to be considered later, lies a special group of three-dimensional representations of man's capabilities and volumetric requirements. This group consists of reach, vision, and/or clearance envelopes to help visualize functional working space requirements, reach or vision capabilities, or other similar concepts. Because of their expense, time requirements for fabrication and the relative lack of reuse flexibility, such devices are not often developed. However, in some cases, these constructions of conceptual space are useful and dramatic demonstrations of significant value to engineering anthropometric practice. Also, lower cost approaches may be expected as technological problems are overcome. An example of such reach envelopes is that developed by Dempster for study of space requirements of seated operators, Figure 7-8.

If a working tool is desired, one that can actually be placed into a workspace to check, measure, and demonstrate functional reach and clearance requirements, the design must be different. Clearance requirements for body parts and movements may be shown with rigid or elastic semirigid materials, but these representations may need to be disassembled for insertion into the cockpit, duty station, and so forth. Reach envelopes are an entirely different problem. It is axiomatic that a proper work space will be designed so that control/display panels, controls, latches, and other manipulative devices are *within* the majority of the nominal reach envelope. Therefore, this conceptual shell must

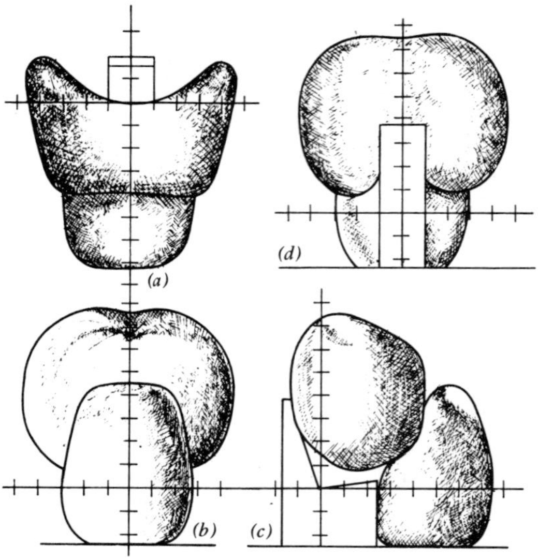

Figure 7-8. Four views of hand and foot reach envelopes. This sketch shows mean limits of hand and foot movement for a group of 22 seated operators. Views shownare top (*a*), front (*b*), side (*c*), and rear (*d*). Coordinates through the seat reference point are scaled off in 6 in. intervals (Dempster, 1955a).

intersect planes and surfaces of the work space and will be mostly out of sight when the envelope device is installed in the actual or simulated working situation. It will be difficult to assess results of changes. Illustrating the volume occupied by use of a *retractible device* with calibrated scales is more appropriate. To date, it appears that successful application of this principle has not been achieved. A series of telescopic rods of selected length, radiating from a central fixture to the limits of the clearance envelope is suggested as a possible means of generating this demonstration. The rods would be retracted during installation in the work space. Later, the rods would be extended to points of contact with panels or structure onto their appropriate length. Where no contact is made, an indication of inability to reach is apparent. Where contact is made, the difference in actual versus potential extension provides a numerical datum. Such a system will not account for reach *around* struts or other obstructions, so it cannot be considered as a final solution. Ingenuity and materials exploitation are needed to provide a satisfactory technology for this general problem.

Another approach is to cut and shape a separate set of simulated parts with printed or three-dimensional controls and displays to fit into and around a rigid, transparent reach envelope representation. This is a less desirable method from a time and cost standpoint, but is possibly more dramatic.

Materials and forming methods can run a wide gamut. Papermaché, plaster, foam, malleable wire mesh, cardboard, glass fiber laminates, heat-softened plastics, and room temperature curing rubbers are some examples.

7.8 MOCK-UP METHODS AND MATERIALS

An extremely important concept and methodology, the "mock-up approach", has been alluded to several times in previous discussions. Its application to engineering anthropometry practice has been urged by several authors (e.g., Morant, 1954), and further definition is appropriate here.

> *Mock-up approach:* a concept of physical simulation and procedures using three-dimensional representations of preliminary designs depicting surfaces and mechanical movements and/or forces characteristic of work spaces and related machinery (mock-ups). Such representations are usually fabricated of low-cost and easily reworked substitute materials and, for engineering anthropometry, are selected items of significance to the human-machine interaction. The measurement procedures involve representative human subjects performing typical task motions and force exertions to evaluate the design concepts and to further develop design requirements. The results are generally stated in terms of how well the machine or work space suits the intended purpose, and how it might be varied to properly accommodate the expected range of users.

The concept can be a powerful integrating factor in many phases of engineering anthropometry. Classic anthropometry measurements and percentile identification (performed outside the mockup) are combined with data on actual working positions, in which emphasis is on locating body surfaces by spatial coordinates, and on defining reachable and visible areas and points of possible contact. These data combinations facilitate estimation of effects due to individual differences between actual subjects and the design population limits.

Looking backward at the engineering graphics discussion, one can see a parallel relationship in the two-dimensional developments of drafting board manikins and their use in design layouts and drawing evaluations. The placing of the manikins in various attitudes on the scaled drawings is verified in three dimensions by use of the human subjects in the mock-up. The results of the mock-up evaluation may be expressed in drawing form, and revised requirements drawn up in this medium. Confidence in their validity is based on both theoretical and practical demonstration.

Because the engineering mock-up is an important "tool of the trade," it is appropriate to consider construction methods and materials for various types of mock-ups.

7.8.1 Work Space Analyzer

In the early stages of work space design, an effective method of mock-up analysis involves use of a sort of full-scale Tinker-Toy* set here called a "work space analyzer." This set consists of a collection of tubes, clamps, and brackets, which may be readily assembled between two parallel panels of pegboard, to simulate essential corners, edges, and planes of a proposed work area or other habitable environment.

The pegboard floor and ceiling panels have holes spaced on a 1-in.-square grid, which accepts a ¼-in. diameter pin at each end of the main vertical tubes. One end of these tubes is adjustable by use of a knurled knob to permit retraction and insertion. Brackets having holes for wood or metal screws to attach wood or sheet metal parts can be clamped to the tubes at the desired angles and positions. Some of the clamps should be designed to clamp to the poles and bars after an initial setup is made. This greatly facilitates minor revisions, additions, and deletions without requiring disassembly of the basic framework.

Within such a basic structure, a variety of readily formed materials may be used to simulate tentative structure and/or equipment. Heavy weight cardboard, paper and foam sandwich materials, corrugated cardboard, transparent sheet plastic, string, wire, plywood panels, foam blocks, and balsa (blocks) are examples of such materials. These may be supplemented later by use of "harder" mock-up components, including metal mechanisms, couches, hatches, or structural frames as appropriate. Much use is made of masking tape for attaching panels, for making edges and points, and for buildup shapes.

By using a highly flexible basic structure such as this, a great many tests and measurements surveys involving only a limited section of a vehicle or other special device can be accomplished without cutting into or delaying further construction on other, more substantial, "mainstream" engineering mock-ups.

Figure 7-9 shows this system as used during a study of spacecraft couch egress with a subject in a fully pressurized suit. Plywood panels form the couch support surfaces, and the main display and control panel. Other support and obstruction structures are simulated by cardboard construction and tape attached to the work space analyzer tubes.

7.8.2 Foam and Paper "Soft" Mock-Ups

Recently, several companies have experimented with a variety of plastic foam and paper sandwich construction techniques for low-cost, rapid mock-up fabrication. Figure 7-10 illustrates a mock-up of the cockpit of a space shuttle orbiter using a foam and paper sandwich material called Fome-Cor.†

* Registered trademark.

† Trade name.

Figure 7-9. Work space analyzer. (Courtesy of Space Division, Rockwell International Corporation.)

Preliminary layout drawings are made on the Fome-Cor which is then cut out for mock-ups. By testing with a selected group of subjects representing design limits of size, the adequacy of the work space can be determined. Refinements can be made on the spot with a stroke of a knife or taped and glued attachments. These changes are then transferred to standard engineering drawings. When such anthropometric feedback is available early in a design cycle, considerable savings can be effected in mock-up and redesign effort and many costly, gross errors can be avoided.

Similar results can be achieved with skillful use of corrugated cardboard at less expense for materials. However, the foam sandwich material is often preferable, because it has no directional characteristic. That is, folds can be made just as easily in any orientation and the edges resulting from cuts are the same in all cases. Also, the strength in bending is the same in all directions.

7.8.3 "Hard" Mock-ups

As engineering details become more certain, more complex and sturdier mock-ups can be constructed for demonstration and testing of critical features or

Figure 7-10. Fome-Cor mock-up of a proposed space shuttle orbiter cockpit. (Courtesy of Space Division, Rockwell International Corporation.)

overall appearance. Plywood, pine, balsa wood, glass fiber resin laminates, sheet metal, and special machined parts are incorporated. Silk screen instrument panels or full-depth representations are installed. More exact anthropometric tests can be performed in these mock-ups such as evaluation of reach, vision, control operability, egress, ingress, and comfort. Figure 7-11 shows a test of reach in the Apollo command module.

It is strongly recommended that removable or transparent sections be incorporated in the design of these mock-ups wherever an enclosed space will inhibit use of anthropometric devices or interfere with photographic recording of activities and critical clearances. Simple creature comforts such as circulating air or air conditioning and adequate lighting should also be incorporated to aid concentration on the main evaluation tasks. Special attention should be paid to devices that help the operator locate his eye at the design eye position. Reference planes, centerline, and index holes should be marked as bases for measurements.

Considerable study and ingenuity are expended in design, selection of materials, and development of philosophy of use of these devices. Several suggestions that reduce preparation time and cost and improve mock-up flexibility have been made by various authors. Deats and Nielsen (1966) have proposed use of vacuum forming techniques for control and display panel mockups. One of the authors has experimented with use of a composition pinboard material and specially prepared pinmounted control and display components. Metal boards and magnetic-backed control display faces are also used. Kubokawa (1968) has described a complete kit of component mock-up parts for ground control and display panels, and has summarized the advantages and disadvantages of different mock-up materials and methods. Hickey, Springer, and Cundari (1968) have studied comparative costs of mock-ups of a simple cockpit made from wood, metal, and Fome-Cor. Their results are shown in Table 7-4.

7.9 COMPUTER AIDS TO CRITERIA DEVELOPMENT

The use of computers for statistical analysis was discussed in Chapter V. Computers are also used for a range of applications leading to development of design criteria. Among these uses are synthesis of new populations and dimen-

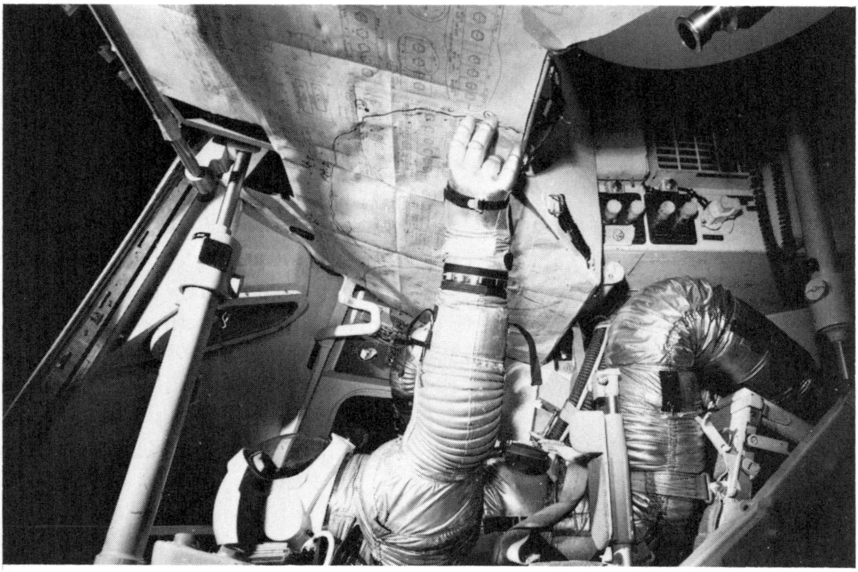

Figure 7-11. Reach limits test in "hard" mock-up of Apollo Command Module. The subject is determining reach limit area on the main control and display panel while he is fully restrained and wearing a fully pressurized pressure garment. The mock-up is fabricated from a combination of metal, wood, plastics, and fabrics to a high degree of dimensional accuracy. A drawing of the main control and display panel is taped over the panel to assist in recording reach limits and rapidly evaluating the results. (Courtesy Space Division, Rockwell International Corporation.)

Table 7-4. Comparative Costs of Three Mock-up Materials (After Hickey, Springer, and Cundari, 1968)

Material	Man-hours	Material dollars
Fome-Cor	300	300
Wood	1500	500
Metal	3400	750

sions, computations of interactions between mathematical models of men and work space, combinations of weights, breadths, and other measurements for specific problems, locations of centers of mass and determination of moments of inertia. Specific examples of these applications are presented in Chapters VIII, IX, and X. Here the emphasis is on the general aspects of the very powerful analysis technique currently being developed for many problems related to engineering anthropometry: the mathematical model approach. Many anthropometric and biomechanical properties of the human body can be expressed by mathematical equations, and hence computerized. This applies to the longitudinal dimensions of the human body, the links connected by joints, as well as the curvilinear and voluminous dimensions, mass properties, elasticity, and structural strength. Biomechanical models of the human body have been categorized either into those representing "external" or "internal" biodynamics, or (in different terminology) into "passive" (reactive) or "active" analogs. Both categorizations distinguish between models that merely react passively to impulses received from the outside, and models that represent the internal muscular activities, and their effects on bodily movements. In each case, the "other side" is assumed to stay constant (passive). Sandover (1971) and Von Gierke (1971) treat, in excellent review papers, the passive (external) model methods, and describe the state-of-the-art. Kroemer (1972b) attempts to describe the state-of-the-art, and a new approach, in active (internal) modeling.

At present, the art of computer modeling is mainly in the phase of describing and assembling selected physical properties of the human body. The simplest efforts in this direction are the various "stickman" models, in which two or three-dimensional joints are connected by straight lines, representing the links or limbs. Hanavan (1964) developed a three-dimensional model of the human body with inertial properties—a large step beyond the stickmen. Since then, the development of man analogs has branched out into a variety of directions.

Most of the models serve to simulate certain parts or characteristics of the human body such as the response of the spinal column to vibrations and impacts as described by Von Gierke (1971). Of more general interest are analogs of the total body and its behavior. Here, the stickman approach is still useful for establishing a "skeletal" system onto which "flesh" is added in terms of geometric volumes, mass properties, and so forth.

7.9.1 Three Phases of Development

At the first level of development, the man-model serves as a reservoir of anthropometric data in one or more of a series of static body configurations. Such a computer model allows more versatile storage, manipulation, and retrieval of anthropometric information than the conventional tables of data.

A second level model is "reactive" (i.e., responds to external forces such as G-fields, vibration, or impact). It requires that mass properties (amount of mass, center of mass, moment of inertia) of the total body and of all major body segments be considered. However, the model becomes "reactive" through incorporation of internal muscular force, torque, work, and power capabilities that are independent of external stressors, and are capable of acting against them.

The third phase of the evolution of a computerized physical man analog places the model at the work station (in the shop, office, or vehicle). Computerization of the work area can be achieved by defining two-dimensional panels or three-dimensional blocks, which can be varied in size and locations to represent an unlimited number of work places or equipment. The work space boundaries can be defined as rigid or deformable, solid or penetrable ("windows"), and the like. The dimensions of specially formed components, such as seats or controls, also can be included in the computer program. Note that one may use nonreactive (Phase 1) models in this work space context. In discussing the merits of certain model approaches, one has to consider the objectives of their design, their specific functions, the experimental data incorporated: the analyst must know the boundary conditions in order to evaluate the validity of a body analog.

Model design depends on the purpose pursued, and the organ, segment, or function of response to be modeled. Specific goals can be to understand pathological processes, physiological or anatomical responses, or to extrapolate from observed conditions to new ones, to validate tests performed with animals or dummies.

Table 7-5 (Kroemer, 1972b) exemplifies the phases of evolution reached or aspired to in seven computerized man analogs. The first one, Dynastick, is, despite its name, a purely static stick-and-joint assembly; however, it does reflect mass properties of the human body according to the data developed by Clauser, McConville, and Young (1969). Both Lift Man and Torque Man are

Table 7-5. Computer Man-Models of Increasing Complexity

Name	Dimensions	Links	Joints	Volume	Mass	Strength	Work	Static[a]	Kinematic[b]	Dynamic[c]	G-fields	Algorithms	Work Place	Remarks
Dynastik	2	13	12	—	X	—	—	X	—	—	—	—	—	Indicates static mass distribution
Lift Man	2	7	6	—	X	X	—	X	—	—	—	—	—	Indicates two dimensional flow of force vectors if external forces and joint angles are known
Torque Man	3	11/18	10/17	—	X	X	—	X	—	—	—	—	—	Indicates three-dimensional flow of force vectors if external forces and joint angles are known
Cinci Kid	3	15	14	X	X	—	—	X	X	(X)	X	—	—	Describes attitude control in g-fields
Sammie	3	18	17	X	—		—	X	—	—	—	—	X	Describes fit of equipment to man
Boeman	3	23	22	X	X	(X)[d]	—	X	(X)	—	(X)	(X)	X	Static work place-geometry model, dynamic capabilities considered
Combiman	3	23	22	X	X	X	X	X	X	X	X	X	X	Dynamic man-work station model

[a] Static: no movement.
[b] Kinematic: considers movement without relation to mass and force.
[c] Dynamic: considers movement with relation to mass and force.
[d] ( ): projected capabilities.

static, but they incorporate data on isometric muscle strength (Chaffin, 1969). Cinci Kid (Passerallo and Huston, 1971) incorporates kinematic and dynamic aspects of the human body and also considers the environmental effects of G-fields. Sammie (Bonney, Evershed, and Roberts, 1969) is basically a static model, but incorporates several possible work place configurations. This model simulates, to some degree, task performance by utilizing elementary motion times. Boeman (Boeing Company, 1970) is a rather advanced model of man sitting in a cockpit, intended to be used in the evaluation of the geometry of aircraft cockpits. Although basically static, a number of dynamic aspects is considered in this model.

Combiman is being developed as a Computerized Biomechanical Man-Model to represent the static and dynamic characteristics of the human operator, to incorporate variable environments and work stations, and to assess the interactions between man, environment, and work place and their combined effects on task performance. (Kroemer, 1972b; Krause and Bogner, 1971). Hence, Combiman is one of the first truly ergonomic computer models. Additional examples are discussed in Chapter VIII (see automotive applications).

7.9.2 Modeling Approaches

In modeling a human's physical actions at the work place, one has to produce a body configuration for the man-model approximating that of a human at specified instants during the execution of tasks.

Three modeling approaches exist: (1) Stored Data Model; (2) Specific Algorithm Model; and (3) General Algorithm Model (Boeing, 1970).

The *Stored Data Model* is the simplest model as it uses virtually no mathematics. It depends on the collection and computer storage of large volumes of human motion data to be recalled where specific man-model tasks are to be performed in a crew station. For a static anthropomorphic body configuration, this can be the appropriate approach. For a dynamic model, this is a clumsy approach which does not efficiently use available information.

The *Specific Algorithm Model* uses explicit mathematical procedures for moving the link system to perform a given task. Many human motion data have to be collected and analyzed to develop valid algorithms to specify man-model motion under all the conditions required. However, this modeling method offers significant computer efficiencies.

The *General Algorithm Model* requires the least amount of data on human movement parameters. This modeling approach uses a general mathematical problem-solving technique, as opposed to specific link-system motion algorithms. Such a model is highly flexible for future improvements. If appropriately formulated, special governing functions can be transferred from a Specific Algorithm Model to the General Model.

7.9.3 Modeling Criteria

Two major criteria are associated with the man-model development: the man-model must be accurate and efficient. Accuracy means that the man-model must be human-like in its performance. Efficiency means that computer storage and processing time for the man-model must be reasonable. Accuracy is the most pressing criterion, because it is technically much more complex than computer efficiency. Therefore, this aspect of the development has received the greatest attention. If an accurate model is realized, efforts to improve computer efficiency will follow.

7.9.4 Future Developments and Limitations

Further developments must be made to improve efficiency of computer techniques and to ensure manlike performance. Two major lines of development are necessary. One is to conduct research on new objective functions and constraint techniques to improve man-model accuracy. The other is to take evolutionary steps toward specific algorithms. This development requires the acquisition of many new dynamic and ergonomic data and their subsequent analyses.

It is recommended that persons who are interested in engineering anthropometry as a career become familiar both with computer programming methods and with the anatomical and mathematical bases for modeling of the human form. Development of newer, more accurate models will be a significant factor in the future of engineering anthropometry, giving impetus and direction to detailed study of the anthropometry of human joints, and of the control functions of the moving muscles.

Because of the necessity of quantifying all the aspects of the human form which are to be studied in computer analyses, the cost of research and development for the mathematical model and the computer program may be too high for some engineering project needs. It may be better to proceed directly to manned testing for the required insight and solution to work space problems. Because the mathematical expressions are always merely simplifications and approximations to reality, some manned testing effort ultimately is required. However, as more experience is gained in developing mathematical models and various computer programs, costs will be reduced and effectiveness increased. Computer analysis can be used profitably to carefully select those areas of critical concern and uncertainty where only a mock-up test with human subjects will provide the desired data. Thus the number of tests and their preparation costs can be reduced.

VIII
WORK SPACE DESIGN APPLICATIONS

8.1 INTRODUCTION

The necessity to provide adequate work space and habitation space arrangements for manned vehicles and to assure efficient operations at stationary work sites has resulted in development of general principles and procedures supported by a special series of anthropometric application techniques and devices for engineering design and analysis. The more that volume and weight affect the performance of a vehicle, the more important applications of these techniques become, and the greater the degree of training and specialization required of the design engineer. Yet, in many areas of preliminary design and analysis, an estimate of feasibility and avoidance of costly major errors can be accomplished by persons with relatively little background, if they understand a few basic fundamentals, which are illustrated by examples in the following pages.

From where does one get information and guidance concerning design of work space? Pertinent information is contained in the handbooks and sources of anthropometric data listed in Chapter VII, and in articles (Morant, 1955b; Mayo, 1953; Teeple et al., 1956). In the handbooks, a set of very simplified, general rules or "laws" are provided, together with parametric human engineering data which may be applied as needed by the designer. There is little information given concerning the derivation of these rules, how to select or modify them for specific situations, or *what to do if the handbook data do not apply*. Procedures primarily oriented toward *psychological* aspects of control and display panel layout are often found in the literature on work space design, (e.g., Meister and Farr 1966a,b and Lear, Inc., 1960). Anthropometric considerations are only briefly discussed in these reports as a means of ensuring adequate reach capability to controls and adequate visibility of displays. Examples in this book are designed to overcome some of the foregoing deficiencies in work space design information.

8.2 GENERAL APPROACH: INSTALLATION ENGINEERING FOR PEOPLE

The fundamental problem of any *equipment* installation engineer is to see that adequate volume, clearance, attachments, supports, and systems connections are provided to permit a selected item of equipment to perform its intended function, and to assure that the surrounding environment is controlled to meet the operational limitations for the equipment.

Designing work space and habitation space for *humans* can also be viewed as an unique "installation engineering" problem, similar to installing machinery. The above viewpoint is a *minimum* basis for assuring that human operators will get *at least* as much consideration as machinery does in systems design! Although the human mechanism is vastly more complex than any man-made machinery, even *basic dimensional* engineering problems of "installing" people have often been given less attention than those of a simple fuel tank or a motor. To help overcome this problem, the engineering anthropometrist and other human factors specialists must act as educators, as well as technical researchers in their speciality.

8.3 AEROSPACECRAFT CONTROL STATION—A MODEL FOR THE WORK SPACE DESIGN PROCESS

As indicated in Table 8-1, many general and special work space design concerns must be considered in aerospacecraft. This specific application area has been selected as the model for introductory discussion of general procedures, philosophy, and considerations applicable to many work space designs. The presentation is organized as a generalized, step-by-step procedure for work space design with supporting descriptions and examples, from concept to deployment. An information flow chart for this procedure is presented in a highly abbreviated form in Figure 8-1. Various portions of this chart will be emphasized, detailed procedures will be developed, and other information flows will be shown as the discussion proceeds.

8.3.1 Step 1. Establishing Requirements

Before beginning a work space layout, considerable study should have been performed, or experience gained from similar situations, to establish the following requirements:

1. Purpose or mission of the system. Example: "land men on the moon before 1970 and return safely to earth."
2. Mission profile, or detailed phases and environments in a typical mission. Example: launch vertically, accelerate to 4.5 g, orbit earth (weightless), accelerate at 1 g to translunar coast flight (weightless

Table 8-1. Spacecraft Design Areas with Unique Anthropometric Considerations

Design Area	Unique Considerations
Crew couch and body supports	Reentry and launch loads, supine position, space-suit mobility and bulk, landing impact, weightlessness, astronaut population dimensions.
Controls, latches, and hand holds	Space-suit glove bulk, mobility limitations. Space-suit reduction of tactile sensation. Suit leak and abrasion sensitivity. Astronaut population strength.
Personal equipment	Space-suit interface shape, connections, mobility limits, visibility limits.
Hatches and tunnels	Space-suit bulk and limited mobility, zero-G locomotion, vacuum environment, metabolic costs, suit safety.
Portable environmental control systems	Zero-G, need for suit support, suit mobility and vision. Metabolic requirements for suits.
Tool design	Space-suit glove: limited mobility and bulk. Weightlessness. Loss of traction, use of tethers for restraints.
Restraints and tethers	Weightlessness requirements.
Personal maneuvering units	Six degrees of freedom—no friction. Weightlessness, space-suit bulk, contour, and mobility limits. Lighting and vision.
Clothing	Space suit, helmet, gloves, boots. Astronaut population.
Emergency ground egress and rescue	Space-suit bulk, weight, and mobility limits. Supine position, pressurized vessel. Oxygen environment fire hazard. Umbilical tower environment. Astronaut training and agility.

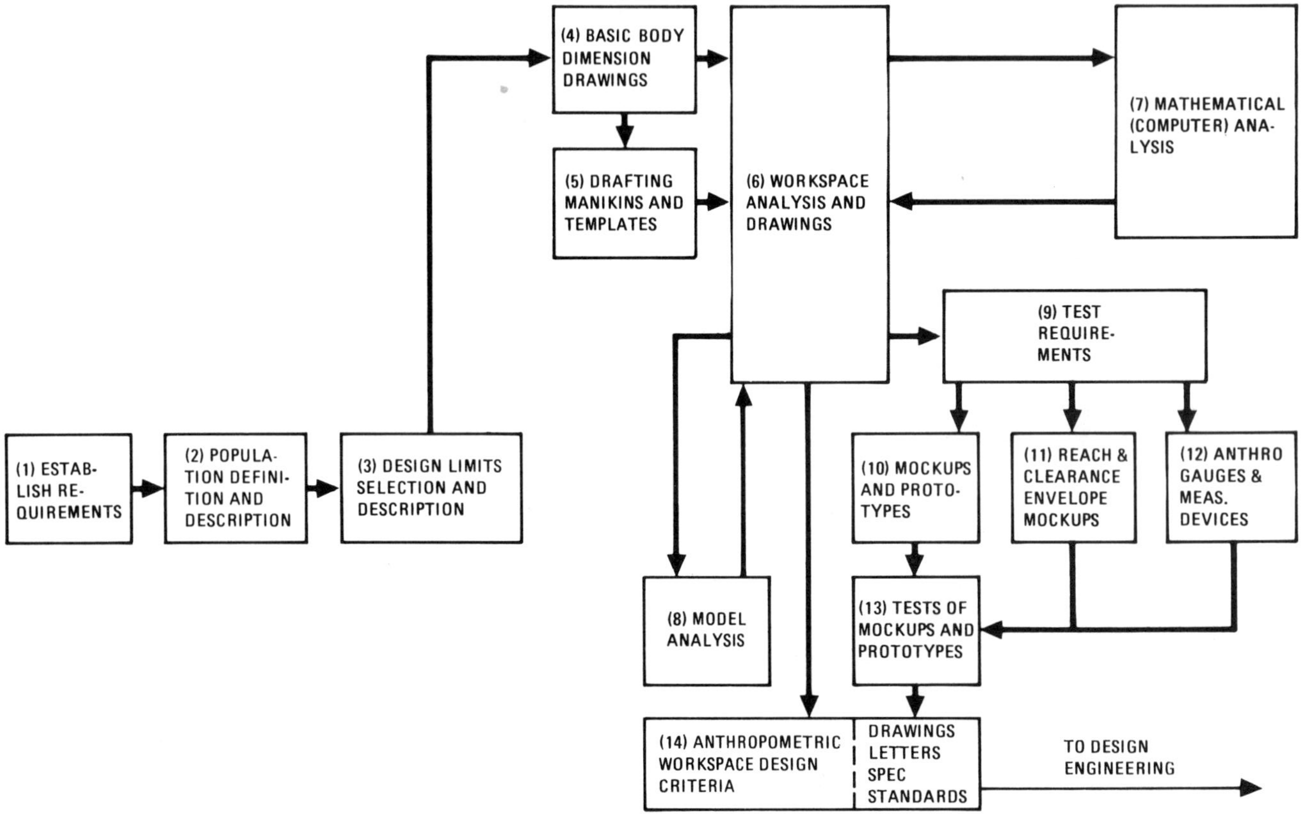

Figure 8-1. Information flow chart for applications of anthropometry to work space design. (Roebuck, Kroemer, and Thomson, 1973.)

again), decelerate to lunar orbit, then to lunar landing. Return to earth by similar sequence.

3. Tolerances allowable in the performance of the system (i.e., limits for accuracy, speed, force, etc.). Examples: launch time, aiming accuracy, reentry velocity, "G" limits, oxygen consumption rates, atmospheric pressures.
4. Effects upon system performance when various tolerances are not met. Examples: miss moon, lose vehicle and crew; miss earth, lose vehicle and crew; high G—blackout, miss landing site.
5. Vehicle definition: geometry and dimensions, location of functional work areas, fundamental structural characteristics.

Major challenges in spacecraft design derive from extremes of accelogravitational forces and thermal environments, for which special protection may be required. Pressure and thermal protection requirements have led to use of the so-called space suit, or pressure garment assembly, creating new interfaces between the man and the work space, and new suit design and fitting applications, as described in Chapter IX.

The extremes of environments have also led to special selection criteria for the crewmen, thus defining new design populations, called "astronauts," in the USA, and "cosmonauts" in the USSR.

Most of the activities in this step are nonanthropometric, yet they will help to define crew and passenger work positions, equipment and clothing constrictions, and later will dictate mock-up test requirements. "Vehicle definition" leads to further engineering definition of structures and subsystems, which will set constraints for models, mock-ups, and work space design layouts. Also, establishing system requirements affects selection of the user population (Step 2).

8.3.2 Step 2. Population Definition and Descriptions

Crew skill and selection requirements derived from mission analysis often are stated in words, such as "the driving public" or "military pilots." The detailed numerical tabulation of the population anthropometric characteristics (strength and dimensional statistical distributions) is usually derived by the anthropometric specialist, based on his knowledge of appropriate surveys.

This activity may consist almost entirely of searching for pertinent literature in files and libraries. However, "Populations Synthesis" (described in Chapter VII) may be needed to process the data and to prepare tables and graphs of new populations.

Test subject selection and measurement is another related process, involving sample subjects selection and obtaining measurements on aspects not included in available data. The subjects selected and measured as part of an in-house "subject pool" (Chapter VII) will be used later in Step 13 for mock-up testing.

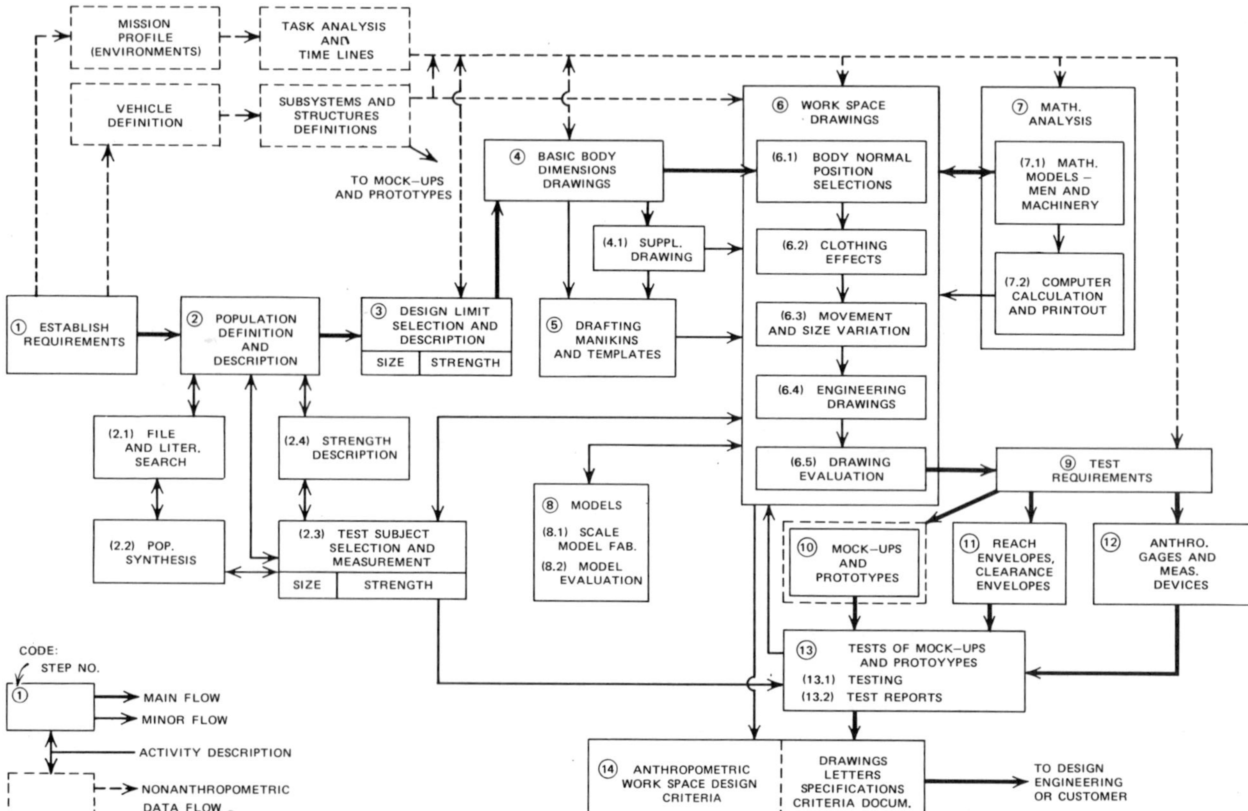

Figure 8-2. Work space design procedure summary flow chart.

Anthropometrists may also participate in the operator selection process by identifying meaningful dimensional and strength criteria and by making screening measurements to determine if the criteria are met.

The above described substeps for Steps 1 and 2 and for remaining portions of the procedure have all been summarized in Figure 8-2, which will be frequently referred to in the following discussions.

The selection of the first seven astronauts provides an appropriate example of crew selection procedures involving many of the above steps (Swenson, Grimwood, and Alexander, 1966). The population was to be selected from graduates of test pilot school, have active service as a military test pilot, a total of 1500 hours flying time, and excellent physical condition. Only males between 25 and 40 years of age, less than 5 feet 11 inches in height, with at least a bachelor's degree were acceptable. Once accepted, a battery of anthropometric measurements was administered to define the group's range of dimensions.

8.3.3 Step 3. Design Limits Selection and Numerical Description

Having made an estimate of the user population from which design criteria are to be selected, the next step is to define how many persons or *what range of percentiles* will be used for design criteria. This decision defines the theoretical design limits for the persons actually to be "installed," in effect, a *design criteria population.*

Study of economic factors in selecting percentiles in an optimum manner has actually received little attention due to the many uncertainties involved, the variety of skills, and the time required to perform it. (Some work along this line is described later in respect to airplane pilot selection.) At present, however, the usual practice is to select some wide percentile range (such as 5th to 95th) for design limits. The wise designer will hold these limits only at most critical dimensions and provide as much additional freedom as possible in all others.

The design criteria population for Project Mercury was the total original seven (already highly selected) astronauts as regards the control display panels, windows, overall capsule shape, and other features common to all spacecraft. However, for the crew couches, which were cast to individual contours, and for many special items in each vehicle, the design criteria population consisted of *one individual.*

For Project Apollo, the anthropometric criteria were somewhat more generous and more typical, being originally given as 10th to 90th percentile for the U.S. Air Force. Further definition was incorporated into the basic design criteria document as follows.

First, a basic population was selected, whose measurements were well documented in terms of statistical distribution. Thus, specifying percentiles automatically provided specific dimensions by reference to the report. Additional studies of correlations, clothing dimensions, and other anthropometric information based upon this population were also available.

Next, a statement was prepared, describing which major work space dimensions would be related to the above design criteria, and what to do about the others (Rockwell International, 1962):

"The flight crew shall consist of three men. The size of each crew member shall be between the 10th and 90th percentile as defined in the following reference:
Hertzberg, H. T. E.; Daniels, G. S. and Churchill, E. "Anthropometry of Flying Personnel," 1950, WADC TR 52-321, 1954.

"The above percentile limits shall apply to the following nude dimensions: standing height, weight, sitting height-erect, buttock-knee length, knee height-sitting, hip breadth-sitting, shoulder breadth-bideltoid, and arm reach from wall. All other body dimensions shall fall within the 5th and 95th percentile. Body dimensions undefined by applicable documents will be estimated by the most appropriate statistical and anthropometric methods."

In order for each man to be able to fit all couches in the Apollo Command Module, each of the three couches were made to adjust for all men meeting the above criteria.

The 10th to 90th percentile criteria, based on a 1950 population, were generous by Project Mercury standards, but more stringent than first appears: the first manned Apollo flight was not launched until October 11, 1968, *18 years after the U.S. Air Force population survey.* Recently published Air Force data for a 1967 survey has indicated that the 90th percentile had risen from 72.2 in. in 1950 to 72.9 in. in 1967. There were, indeed, some suggestions to raise the upper limit to 73 in. However, sufficient volunteer personnel were readily available to accomplish the small number of Apollo flights. Future space flight projects may involve larger numbers of persons, possibly foreign nationals, females, and a wider range of skills and ages, potentially requiring a wider range of percentiles, and a mixture of populations.

8.3.4 Step 4. Preparation of Basic Body Dimension Engineering Drawings

This drawing type shows orthographic views of maximum and minimum dimension limits of the population with the body in standard anthropometric positions. For work space design, there is particular emphasis on human lengths, breadths, and widths, and few circumferences. In order to develop manikins for work space layouts, and mathematical models for analysis, link dimensions, joint locations, and centers of mass of body segments should be included. A separate drawing is suggested to summarize ranges of motion possible and desirable for the major body joint systems. For large populations,

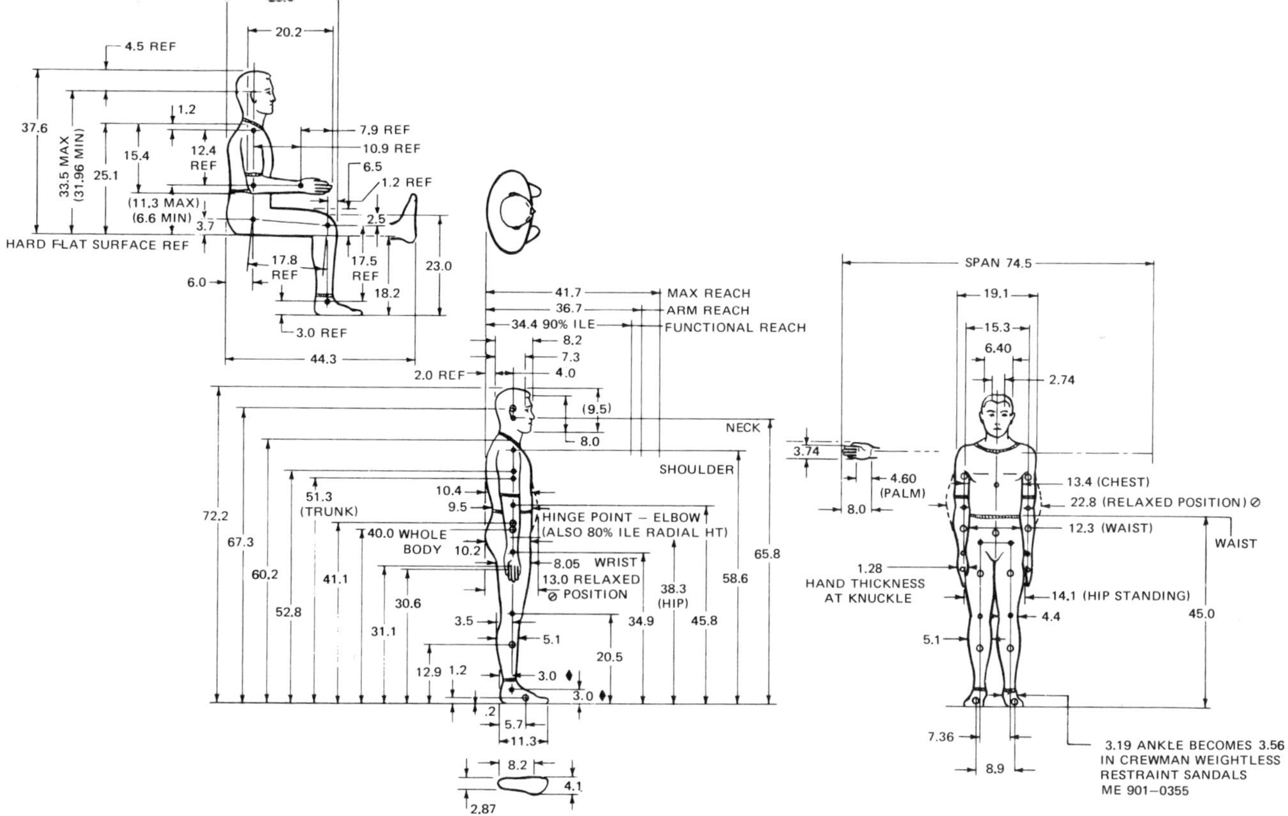

Figure 8-3. Example of basic body dimensions drawing for work space design. (Courtesy of Space Division, Rockwell International Corporation.) An important by-product of such systematic synthesis of data is the identification of "missing" dimensions that must be estimated to provide complete engineering data.

it appears most useful to collect all of the minimum design criteria dimensions together in pictures of a stylized, imaginary small man (such as 5th percentile man) and on the same drawing, with separate figures, show the maximum design criteria dimensions in similar features of a large man (95th percentile man). A caution note should be included, warning of possible dimensional differences in *working positions drawings* (see Step 6, Section 8.3.6). The first basic dimensions drawings (here considered as Step 4.1) may include nude body dimensions only, but the effects of clothing, equipment, and the like should be included whenever possible. A partial example of a basic body dimension drawing is presented in Figure 8-3.

Step 4.2, "Preparation of Supplementary Drawings," is a further extension of the concept of drawings that define components of the "human installation." Drawings of special clothing, personal equipment, and tools that are usually attached or carried by the operator for use in the work space should be separately drawn to a scale compatible with the work space layout drawings (Step 6). These component drawings also may form the basis for specially "clothed" manikins or separate drafting templates.

8.3.5 Preparation of Drafting Aids

A by-product of the basic drawing, that is frequently used as a drafting and design aid to obtain a first approximation of man's size, is an accurately scaled three-view drawing of man at small scale factors, such as in Figure 8-4. These drawings are often reproduced on 8½ × 11 in. transparent sheet plastic for convenience of storage and handling. Three such overlays can illustrate the size of the 5th, 50th, and 95th percentile man at selected scale factors such as 1/10 or 1/4. Other body positions are also frequently used in accordance with the design application area in the early stages of design.

The design and fabrication of articulated two-dimensional manikins, (Chapter VII), will greatly aid in the initial preparation of work space drawings and the subsequent evaluations and revisions usually found necessary. Therefore, it is highly recommended that they be prepared *before* extensive work space layout drawings are begun.

For Project Apollo, four sets of manikins were constructed. Each had 1/10, 1/4, and 1/2 scale, "small" (10th percentile) and "large" (90th percentile) men represented in nude and fully pressurized space suit profiles. Manikins of 1/20 scale are recommended as useful for preliminary design.

8.3.6 Step 6. Preparation of Workspace Layouts

Having defined the basic structural and kinematic design limits of the human beings, clothing, and personal equipment to be installed in the work space, the next major step is to define the design limits for the human being in actual *working attitudes and constraining conditions*. Conceptually, this may be

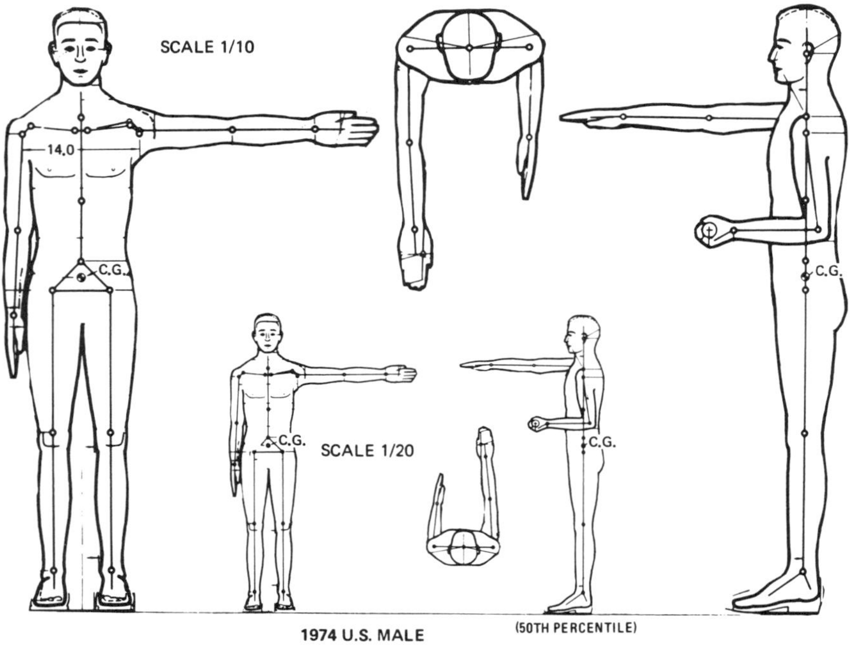

Figure 8-4. Three view overlay of man in two scale factors. (Roebuck, Kroemer and Thomson, 1973).

divided into several parts: (6.1) analysis and definition of static/neutral body positions; (6.2 and 6.3) analysis and description of clothing and movements; (6.4) presenting of these definitions in "engineering language" (layout drawings) as design requirements; and (6.5) evaluation of such work space drawings. Graphical analysis techniques comprise a highly versatile and powerful unifying approach advocated for accomplishing and integrating these steps.

The essential engineering skill for successful work in this area is descriptive geometry. The analyst must be able to project views and cross sections of the work space geometry or other device and the human subject into various auxiliary planes which often are not parallel to the normal planes of the three-view orthographic engineering drawings. Also, for visibility considerations, concepts of perspective must be mastered. Intersections of regular and irregular solids with flat and curved planes must often be determined for reach studies or determination of clearances. The ability to mentally visualize the descriptive geometry problem and to accurately prepare the layout drawing depicting the relationships can save many trials in mock-up studies. Such capability also can be a highly effective aid in selecting test measurements and analyzing and presenting test results.

Step 6.1 Selection of Nominal Work Space Body Position

Determination of human body *orientations* required to perform the defined work is the *essential first step* in engineering anthropometry analysis or synthesis of work space. In many areas of work space design one may rely on a long-developed tradition which also correlates with well-accepted physiological and psychological principles of design. However, in new situations, such as aerospacecraft design, one should review basic physiological and mechanical principles concerning body segments orientation to determine whether new methods of body support (and thus, work space dimensions) are indicated.

The fundamental goal for design of body support crew seat, couch, or other harness is to position and orient the human operator so that he survives and functions optimally (or at least adequately) over the whole range of vehicle operating conditions. To provide equilibrium, he must be "properly supported" by surfaces, straps, pads, and the like, engineered to resist internal (muscular) and external (acceleration) forces. For each angular direction of vehicle acceleration force and/or gravitational force exerted in a specified plane, he experiences pressures and physiological effects to which he has various levels of tolerance and performance. These tolerance levels and operating efficiencies are functions of many variables such as temperature, fatigue, general health, training, stress, and so forth, and are related to rate of onset, duration, and previous exposure to various environments. With sufficient data, one could plot polar graphs of human G tolerance and performance vectors in all directions about the man for a given duration. The ends of these vectors define "surfaces" which are envelopes of capabilities in "conceptual space."

Similarly, a vehicle, such as a spacecraft, has a normal mission and emergency performance profile to which it is designed, which also can be defined in terms of G level vectors at given orientations, thus defining capability envelopes comparable to those of the human operator/occupant.

A major task of any vehicle design group is to so orient and support the crewman with respect to the vehicle that his G-vector tolerance and performance envelopes encompass the greatest possible amount of required vehicle performance G-vector envelope in all mission phases and expected attitudes. Figure 8-5 graphically depicts two situations in cross section at the *X-Z* (sagittal) plane for hypothetical spacecraft design and crew performance/tolerance envelopes. Orienting the crewman to a near-supine position at launch, which is typical of current spacecraft (right side of Figure 8-5), results in human tolerance and vehicle performance envelopes that are compatible.

Tolerance concepts also can be extended if warranted, to include visual acuity, color discrimination, reaction time, tracking accuracy, comfort, control operability, mobility, and the like, for all orientations and over a complete mission profile.

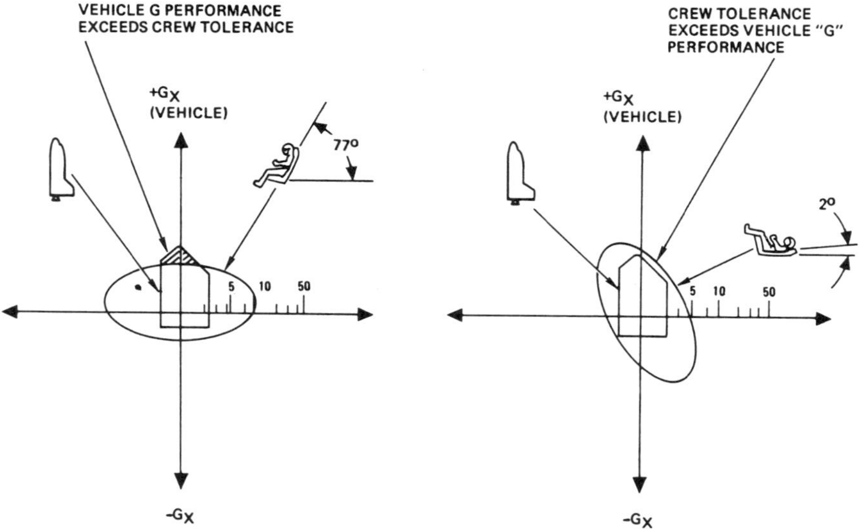

Figure 8-5. Crew body positioning for optimum G tolerance. (Roebuck, Kroemer and Thomson, 1973.)

To minimize costs of experiments and mock-up testing, body positions which are known by experience of many persons to be acceptable should be selected, where possible. As a general rule, the major body positions for control stations design considerations are: (1) sitting, in an upright, comfortable, aft-reclining position (automobile, airplane), (2) sitting, in a leaning-forward, working position (as at a desk), (3) standing, (4) supine, in the sense that one is lying down with legs outstretched, (5) the semisupine couch position for aerospacecraft, in which the knees are raised considerably and lower legs are parallel to the body, and (6) the prone position.

A rule of thumb for comfortable limb angles is to use the *midpoint of the range of joint movement.* This usually puts the least stress on the muscles, as evidence by low electromyographic readings, and therefore, such limb orientations generally can be endured for the longest time. However, the gravitational attraction or accelerational forces may tend to pull the limb into a position that is not the midpoint of its travel, yet one that is considered relatively comfortable, because the limb does not have to resist accelogravitational forces. Special attention to body positions requiring a minimum of volume or minimum length in specific directions is often required in vehicular design. Also, operator positions should be considered as to suitability for exerting force, or for accomplishing a wide range of motion, perhaps with low force.

Two or more major positions in crew/passenger seat angles or adjustments may be required for a given vehicle to provide for different mission phases. Such designs have been used in experimental, vertical take-off aircraft, and are planned for the Space Shuttle Vehicle.

Steps 6.2 and 6.3 Clothing Effects and Deviations from Nominal Body Position

The next steps are key efforts in engineering anthropometry, equivalent to *kinematics analysis of mechanisms,* which is performed to assure *operational clearance* for all moving parts in an installation. All work space criteria dimensions can be conceived as made up of *vectorial components.* These are as follows:

B = the basic, "static," nominal or neutral nude human body dimensions, selected as previously described (Step 6.1).

C = added dimensions or effects due to personal clothing or equipment worn. Both are measured by anthropometric tools in a carefully controlled, generally static, laboratory situation and are determined from the foregoing types of overall tolerance/performance effects analysis (Step 6.2).

N = the vector sum of additions or modifications required for dynamic working situations, such as vibrations, accelerations, gravitational field variation, comfort movements, operational control movements, egress, ingress, breathing, and pressure suit expansion effects, which are further discussed in the following paragraphs. The composite envelope defined by all these **N** dimensions outlines a work space volume "bubble" around the nominal body position (Step 6.3).

The vector sum of the above individual dimensional vector components defines the design dimension vector **D**:

$$\mathbf{D} = \mathbf{B} + \mathbf{C} + \mathbf{N} \qquad \text{(Eq. 8.1)}$$

The composite envelope of design dimensions defines the total work space volume.

It is helpful to consider the term **N** as divided into two categories defined below:

$\mathbf{N}_K$ = known dimensional modifications, those factors over which the designer has some control or about which he has statistically valid test data.

$\mathbf{N}_u$ = unknown, or hypothetical effects, "ignorance factors," that comprise all the remaining effects about which the designer or anthropometric requirements engineer knows little of a quantitative nature. These are often estimated upon the basis of experience. The above two form the vector sum:

$$\mathbf{N} = \mathbf{N}_K + \mathbf{N}_u \qquad \text{(Eq. 8.2)}$$

A long-term goal of anthropometric research is to minimize and ultimately eliminate components in class $\mathbf{N}_u$. Notice that in this discussion, the confidence level of the statistical data is not being considered. There is always an element of risk that design for a given percentile factor will be insufficient to account for some (perhaps too many) of one's customers; however, this is a known, *calculated risk*. The effects relegated to components for class $\mathbf{N}_u$ are those for which measurements are not available or calculable so as to define percentile factors or assignable risk.

There are often many effects in the various categories to be considered:

$$\mathbf{B} = \mathbf{B}_1 + \mathbf{B}_2 + \mathbf{B}_3 + \ldots = \Sigma \mathbf{B}_i \qquad \text{(Eq. 8.3)}$$

where $\mathbf{B}_i$ is any basic individual component. A similar equation applies to clothing and equipment static effects.

$$\mathbf{N} = \mathbf{N}_{k_1} + \mathbf{N}_{k_2} + \mathbf{N}_{k_3} + \ldots = \Sigma \mathbf{N}_{k_i} \qquad \text{(Eq. 8.4)}$$

where $\mathbf{N}_i$ is any individual dynamic component effect, including clothing changes.

Some effects increase dimensions while some decrease. For example, inflating a pressure garment may increase many outside dimensions since gas is being introduced between the suit and the body, but the suit construction may force a "slumped" position when worn in a pressurized mode, thus *reducing overall height.*

In addition to pressure suit changes, other dynamic conditions described in Chapter VI, such as changes in vehicle accelerations, transition from horizontal to ascent or descent attitudes, impact conditions, vibrations, and air pressures or motions, may affect both neutral and dynamic operating body dimensions and positions. Local pressures of cushions or supporting surfaces will affect body contours and may require frequent alternate positions in addition to normal stretching, flexing, or relaxing. Nearly every work space requires access space for ingress and egress. Many operations require head movement to obtain better vision and require gross motions of the limbs to operate certain controls. Movements and body positions are conditioned by certain clothing and personal equipment, such as helmets and visors, boots, gloves, goggles, spectacles, masks, weapons, tool carriers, holsters and bags, life support apparatus and survival gear, parachutes, and restraint harness. Each industry and design area has characteristic items and situations that the practicing anthropometrist and designer must consider. Development of a detailed checklist and applicable data tables are strongly recommended at the outset of a project.

Measuring and applying dynamic, nonstandard dimensions are characteristic of engineering anthropometry. Thus, one may ask the obvious question: "Wouldn't it be better to get a single, overall measurement for a representative group of subjects which combines all of the component effects?"

This type of measurement is indeed desirable, but seldom sufficient. In practice, it is often impractical, for a variety of reasons, to obtain a sample subject group, which is, in fact, truly representative of the design population in all desired dimensional limits and physical aspects. Wherever the subject's dimensions do not quite match those of the design population, the difference is used as a small correction to the dynamic test results. The smaller such corrections, the less likely they are to contribute significantly to errors in the final results. Therefore, attempts to find representative sample subjects and correctly allocate uncertainties are quite worthwhile. Certain dynamic dimensions and force data are derived from high-risk or near fatal case histories (from a small sample of accident victims, for example). Such victims most probably do not exactly match the limits of any design population. Again, a correction must be derived to account for differences between actual subjects and the design population, using extrapolation or interpolation.

Such considerations point to the long-range benefits of collecting basic anthropometric data on test subjects (and accident victims, etc.) and of attempting to separately account for clothing, equipment, and dynamic effects correlated with such basic measurements or core dimensions, wherever possible.

Early development of dimensional *interface drawings* showing both the suit and couch surfaces is strongly recommended ("Step 14" function). Except for helmets and metal fittings around the wrist, neck, and the like, a pressure suit usually will have smaller and more indefinite dimensions when in the "ventilated" condition as compared to when it is in a fully pressurized state. These "instant growth" considerations of pressurization affect design of adjustments for head supports, arm rests, flight controllers, and couch movements for vehicles that must accommodate both conditions. In one Apollo suit prototype model, it was found that the helmet (and the man's head in it) moved 3.5 in. in a headward direction when the suit was pressurized without restriction from couch restraints.

The *reduction of operator mobility* in a pressure suit is of great significance to work space design, and thus requires quantification by development and testing using mobility measurement methods in Chapter III.

Graphical Synthesis Procedures—Spacecraft Couch Design

Clear and precise description of body orientation and movement envelopes requires reference to detail, true-scale sketches, or drawings that include key landmarks, planes, and axes from which angles are measured.

Work space layout drawings generally begin with a series of small-scale (1/20 to 1/4) design concept sketches to work out the key dimensions and angles in a consistent and complete pattern. Where lack of data prevent completion of the layout, a need for further literature search, mock-up measurement or other analysis is indicated. The articulated drafting manikins described in Step 5 are a great help in this work, for they have inherently built into them all the major link lengths and an estimate of body depths and contours for selected percentiles.

Layout Drawing Determines Nominal Body Position and Shape

After determining the gross body orientation, per Step 6.1, the next question is "where to start?" The following example is based on the *fixed seat reference point* approach used in the Apollo spacecraft main duty stations, in which there was relatively little need to accurately control eye position (except during docking and special sightings) and there were no foot controls. The seat reference point (SRP) is at the intersection of the seat back and seat bottom (thigh support surfaces). This "fixed seat" layout concept has general application advantages even for other seat designs, (especially when considered apart from the work area): It will minimize overlapping views as various seat extremity adjustments are developed (e.g., headrest, foot support, arm rest, cushions).

From the selected reference point, angles are defined with respect to a selected set of spacecraft vehicle reference axes to show orientation of the trunk and thighs, the arms, the head, the lower legs, and feet.

Basically, two approaches to graphic layout of these lengths and angles are used:

1. "Outside-in," based on first specifying orientations and contour of supporting surfaces of the seat.
2. "Inside-out," based on first specifying orientations of body segment links, or "centerlines."

Because seat surfaces are relatively accessible and measurable (as compared to human body hinge points), they are preferred as reference lines for many applications, especially when the seat is comprised of simple, hard surfaces without cushions (or with very thin cushions), and is generated by straight, parallel lines (as seen from the side view), or when the seat is a simple set of plane surfaces. Clear definition of the "seat back angle" is relatively simple with such surfaces, no matter how the man inside it slumps. However, when couches are contoured in complex ways, or cushioned deeply, descriptions of both the "body orientation" and the description of the supporting surfaces are more difficult, requiring other methods that are described later (Sections 8.5 and 8.6).

Engineering kinematics analysis, computer mathematical modeling, and mechanical drawing procedures are especially compatible with the "inside-out" approach, using link centerlines and joint centers to define the body orientation in space, then defining the supporting surfaces to achieve such

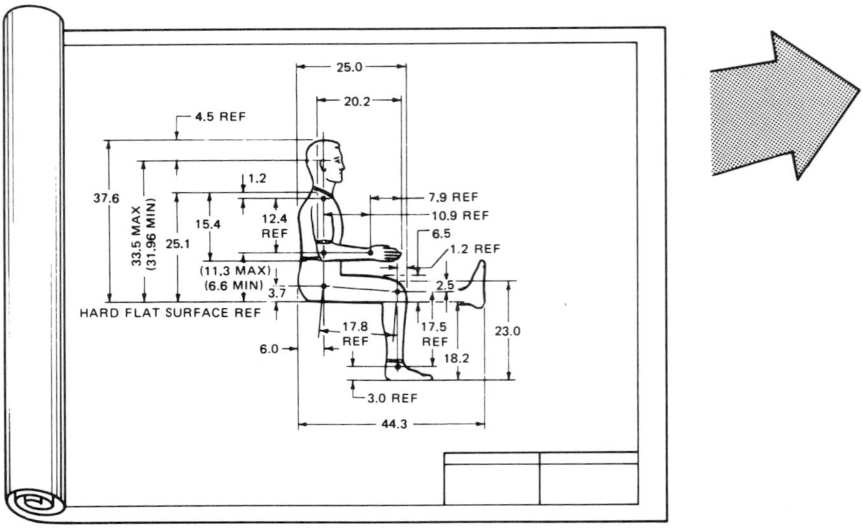

① BASIC ANTHROPOMETRY DRAWING

- SURFACE DIMENSIONS (STD)
- LINK DIMENSIONS (BASIC)
- CENTERS OF MASS LOCATIONS (STD)

Figure 8-6. Example of spacecraft crew couch layout—initial steps.

orientations. However, trunk orientation is quite difficult to describe because of the many "pieces" and inaccessible joint centers. In fact, a combination of both techniques listed above is often employed in specific problems, especially for arms and legs. Link description is the primary system selected for the following discussion, to illustrate the concept.

A side view of the operator or occupant, with the given preferred link angles and dimensions for a large man is first drawn, as shown in Figure 8-6, using the basic body dimensions drawing (Step 4) and modifications due to accelogravitational forces and to clothing (Steps 6.1 and 6.2). The relationships of body surfaces and supporting surfaces to the link centerlines must then be determined and drawn on the layout. In Figure 8-6 the concept of "terminal link" vectors is used to indicate key points on contours of this nature.

The first side view is often an approximation, with body segment lengths all indicated as if they were aligned parallel to the sagittal plane, in true length. The next step is to lay out a frontal view and such auxiliary views as necessary to show probable limb angulation in space. Descriptive geometry is then em-

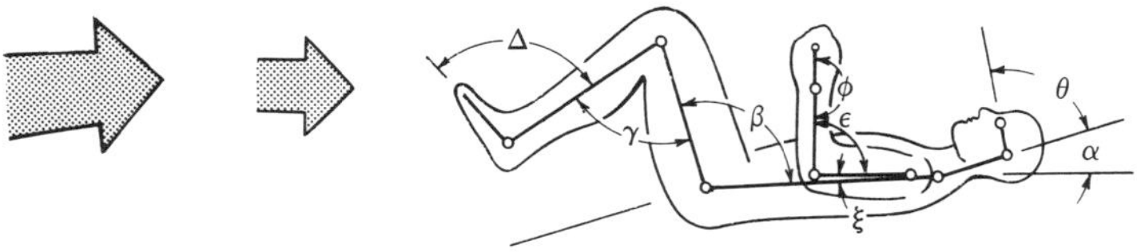

② PREFERRED BODY ANGLES AND ORIENTATION

ANGLE	NUDE	VENTED	PRESSURIZED
α	15°	15°	15°
β	110°	120°	135°
γ	110°	120°	170°

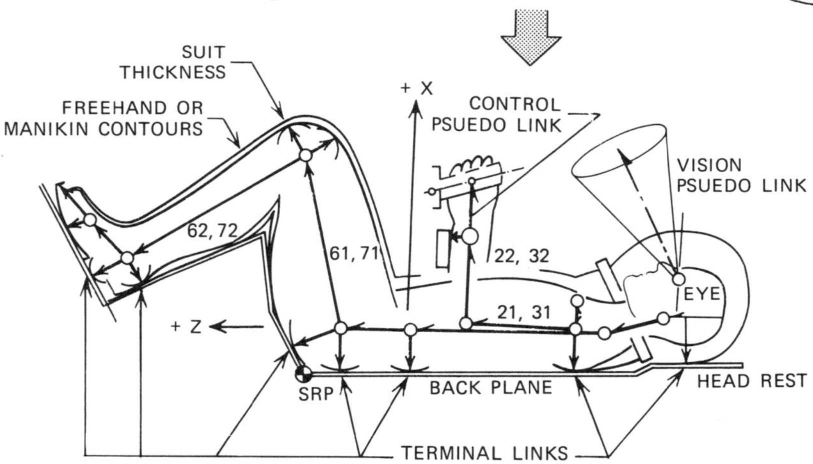

③ BODY SUPPORT PLANES DEFINITION – PRELIMINARY

NAME AND LOCATION OF TERMINAL LINK	LINK NO.	LENGTH – ONE G FIELD (IN.)						REMARKS
		NUDE		VENTED		PRESSURIZED		
		SIT	SUP	SIT	SUP	SITTING	SUPINE	
BACK OF HEAD FROM HEAD LINK (RADIUS)	11	4.5	4.5	6.0 *	5.5 *	6.0 *	5.5 *	*1″ HELMET PAD + SHELL THICKNESS ADDED
TRUNK BACK – FROM STERNOCLAV. JOINT 43–46	51	4.6	4.0	5.2 **	4.3	6.0	5.0	**NO COMPRESSION

Figure 8-6. (continued)

ployed to determine the actual projected lengths of each link on the principal planes of interest (main views). The link length concept facilitates such drawing work. Once the body link orientations are determined to a reasonable degree of accuracy, artistic experience or drafting manikins and other contour data may be applied to supply the surface contour outlines and cross sections.

The terminal link lengths and the body contours are functions of forces due to accelogravitational fields (described in Section 6), restraints, clothing thickness, and suit pressurization conditions, and therefore may require further modifications in a third iteration from fixed manikin shapes. Frequently, these data must be developed by mock-up test measurement (Step 13) when previous experience is not available.

Dimensional Variations and Body Movements Determine Clearances

To deal with the dimensional statistical variation, one may prepare a series of similar drawings that incorporate the various combinations of significant link dimensions for small, medium and large men. The resulting data may then be superimposed, using a common seat reference point, and an envelope drawn around the extremes. The adjustment ranges may be derived for the head rest, arm rest, leg supports, and so on. Often small variations in link angles are used to reduce adjustment ranges of supports, and thereby simplify the design and save weight.

In the Apollo command module, knee clearance to the main display and control panel was very critical in several phases of the mission, even more than is usual for desks, workbenches, and other work stations of more mundane situations. Figure 8-7 illustrates how the potential range of knee positions due to body size variations was determined. Also, the figure provides an example of application of the hexagonal boundary diagram for design limits of bivariate distributions, which was described in Chapter VII. The procedure includes the following steps.

Hip joint centers (H_1, H_2), ankle joint centers (X_1, X_2), and knee joint centers for the maximum and minimum percentiles (*A*, *J*) were first laid out using the estimated link dimension systems previously described. Drafting manikins are convenient for this step. The maximum boundary limits for knee joint centers were next found by intersecting circles with radii equal to maximum and minimum leg links from respective hip centers to form a roughly four-sided figure (*EJPA*). Boundary limits for the low probability area triangular figures (*EDF*) and (*NPQ*) were then determined by the regression methods outlined in Chapter VII, for simplified presentations of bivariate design limits. Outer clearance limits for the knee are formed by adding the terminal link lengths for shin and top of knee to points *F*, *J*, and *N*, then fairing these distances as radii to form the envelope.

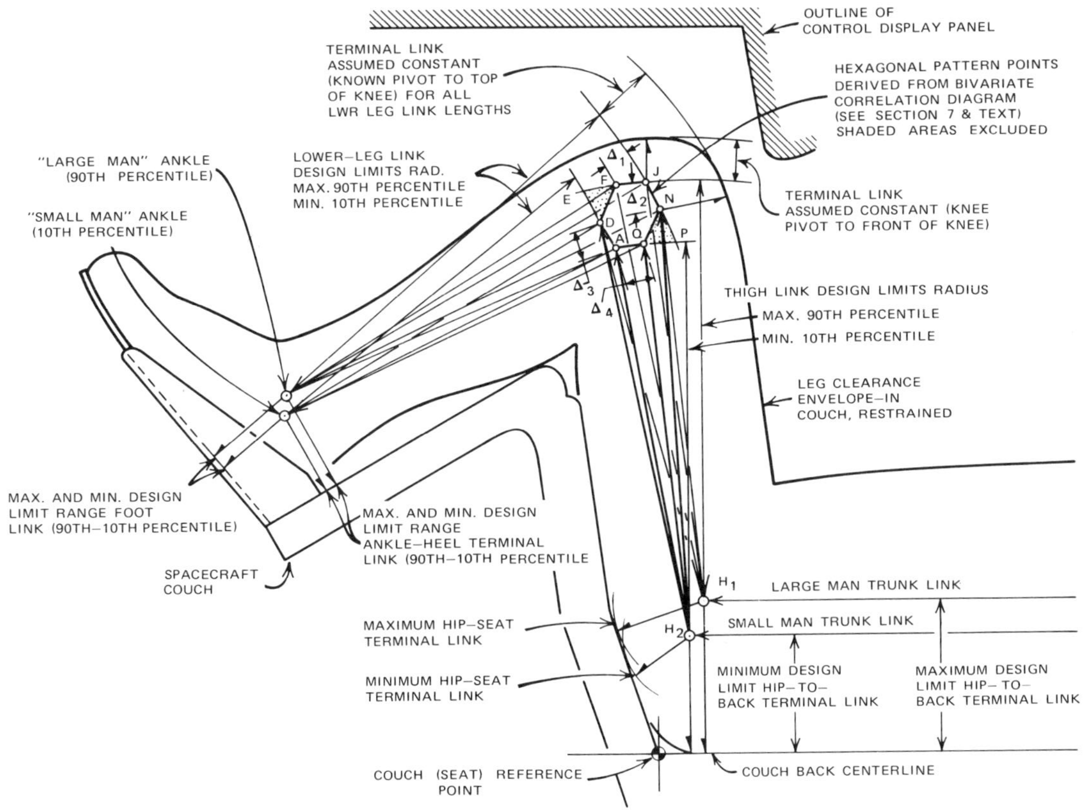

Figure 8-7. Development of design limits for knee location to determine clearance.

Reach Envelope Determines Panel Location, Area and Control Location

Within the reach envelopes (described in Chapter III) of the smallest design criteria dimension combinations, the controls must be located, many of them mounted on control and display panels. In considering the design criteria combinations, long and short trunk lengths must be considered among those persons with short arms. Thus, using only the 5th percentile dimensions may be misleading as regards footward reach, since persons with 5th percentile arm segments, but longer (e.g., 15th to 90th percentile) trunk are also statistically viable combinations. Figure 8-8 describes an example analytical determination of reachable areas on a panel by descriptive geometry, which depicts the intersection of a reach envelope surface and a panel plane.

Reach also may be limited by restraint harness, inflated pressure suit, parachute harness, life vest, and the like. Mock-up testing (Step 13) is mandatory for final data development and verification. For such testing, one should generally select subjects with short arm lengths (i.e., 5th or 10th percentile), but having long and short trunk lengths and wide and narrow shoulders to determine worst case downward/upward and inward/outward limits of reach. Those points, areas, and volumes not reachable by *all* subjects should not be used as control locations.

Since subjects available for such tests often do not represent anthropometric design limit combinations, another approach is sometimes used, particularly for generalized reach envelope description data such as found in handbooks and laboratory studies (Kennedy 1964; Garrett, Alexander, and Matthews, 1970; Dempster, 1955; King, Morrow, and Vollmer, 1947; Rebiffé, Zayana, and Tarrière, 1969): A variety of subject sizes are tested. The reachable limits and arm orientation at selected angular positions are measured. A correction is then added or subtracted to account for the difference from the design limit condition. With sufficient subjects who are representative of the population, at each angular position, the statistical distribution of reach data may be plotted and a percentile curve or statistical estimate prepared. Then, all points corresponding to a given *percentile of the reach condition* are plotted as the resulting envelope. The resulting data points are not necessarily the same as those developed with selected subjects representative of the design criteria arm reach and trunk length percentiles, but the error should be small, in most cases, and probably more representative of actual requirements. In either case, the panel intersection boundaries can be derived by the methods shown in Figure 8-8.

Step 6.4 Engineering Drawing Presentations of Anthropometric Work Space Requirements

As the graphical analyses are completed, results are communicated to designers, either by direct prints or by use of engineering layout sketches and

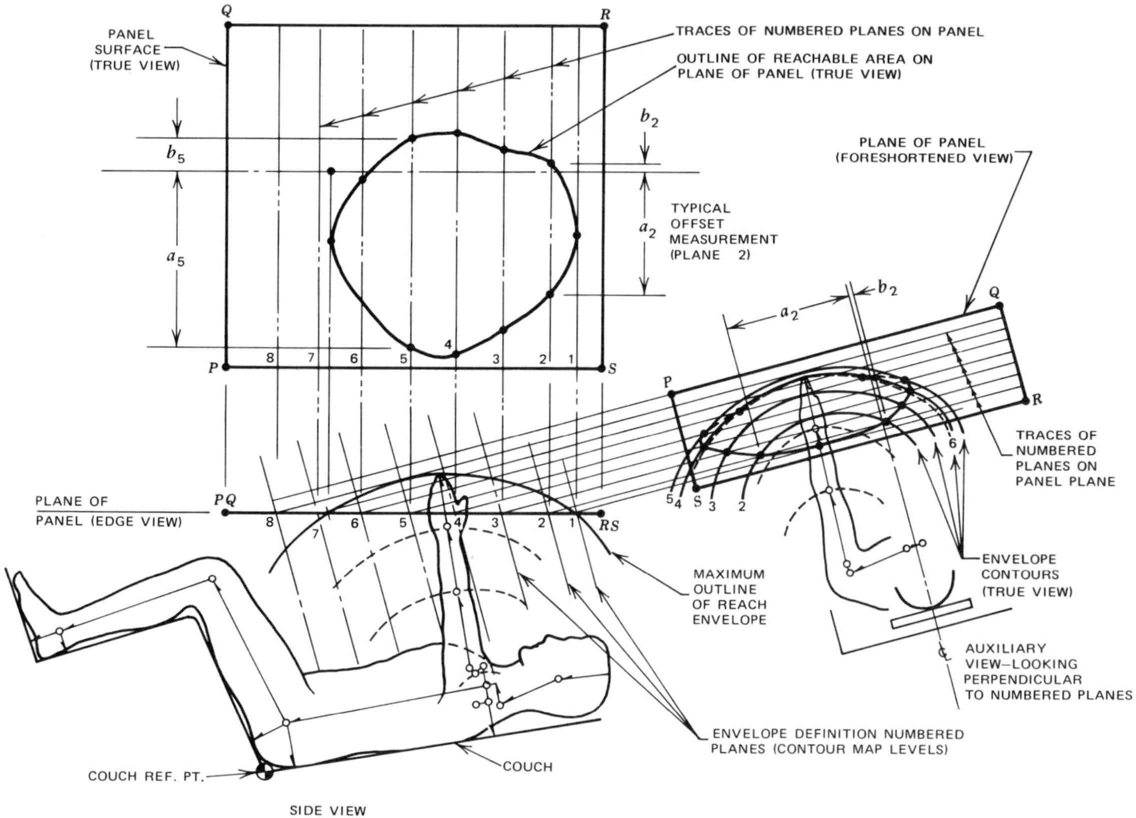

Figure 8-8. Method of developing reachable panel area from each envelope intersection. Several iterations with a variety of seat positions and combination of body dimensions are required to identify reachable area common to all persons within anthropometric design limits.

drawings summarizing work space volume envelopes and depicting typical body positions in seats, couches, at consoles, maintenance task, rest stations, and other critical work areas, and describing ingress or egress requirements. These sketches and drawings are key products for use in work space design. They are, in effect, the *installation drawings* of the human "machinery." They are not released to the shop (since no parts are fabricated from them), but are prepared to define anthropometric man-machine interface requirements to be considered by the crew compartment design engineers.

Such graphic presentations must be accurate, preferably all drawn to a consistent scale (usually 1/10, 1/4, or full scale) and should be well labeled as to station planes, reference points, loft contours, and critical dimensions. Two types of drawings can be prepared: (1) criteria drawings, stating "how it should be," and (2) record drawings, stating "how it is." The latter records and evaluates the actual state of affairs as engineering design layouts are completed or as drawings are released and mock-up tests completed. These show current problem areas (interferences, lack of reach, etc.) implying need and criteria for correction by redesign.

The design group should be provided with the idealized concepts (criteria) early in the development cycle as an aid to preliminary layout work. These should be carried along until mock-up tests or revised mission requirements indicate good reason for a change, and eventually phased out as the designs are finalized. The "how it is" record (analysis and evaluation) should be started as soon as practicable following first preliminary vehicle design layouts, and maintained as long as practical, to record inevitable changes, and to provide a historical record to aid potential later similar projects.

When there are several different phases to a mission, such as launch and boost, orbital flight, docking, reentry and landing, a separate drawing for each phase is recommended.

Step 6.5 Evaluation of Work Space Drawings

As the drawings of work space are being prepared, preliminary evaluation is performed by mental visualization of three-dimensional relationships. Needs for additional data may become apparent. Data not found in the literature must be developed, either by mock-up tests or by iterative statistical/geometric calculations, perhaps using computer calculations. Because many persons find two-dimensional drawings difficult to visualize in three-dimensions, scale models may be developed (Step 8) to "get a new viewpoint." This understanding is then incorporated into the drawing evaluation process. Where it appears that mathematical analysis or model visualization techniques may not be effective, a full-scale mock-up evaluation, including a special test procedure of the actual task, may be initiated by preparation of test requirements (Step 9). Such tests may call for further selection and measurement of test subjects to carry them out (Step 2.3).

8.3.7 Step 7. Mathematical Analysis

A potential powerful adjunct to the engineering work space analysis and layout drawing activity is found in computerized mathematical calculations of geometric interrelationships between man and machinery. Although one could theoretically proceed directly from a basic description of population anthropometrics to mathematical expression of a crew station layout, it is not practical to do so. The capability of most persons to visualize geometrical relationships from mathematical expressions in coordinate systems is very limited. Therefore, it is generally recommended that the basic scheme for preparing the mathematical models should be developed graphically on layout drawings before the mathematical analysis is undertaken. This baseline can then be used as a check on machine output, whether in numbers or automatically produced drawings. The resulting machine computation outputs should usually be expressed in the context of actual work space drawings, with lettered explanations, in order to make a useful engineering analysis report or criteria presentation.

Data from Steps 3, 4, and 5 may be used directly for preparing initial mathematical models of *man,* without resort to work space context, (Step 7.1 in Figure 8-2). However, work space geometry must be input in Step 7.1 and considered in the computation and evaluation of the output data (Step 7.2).

Computer-aided mathematical analysis was applied to the Apollo Command Module in the analysis of crew and couch movement at ground landing impact. The mathematical model used was that of a rigid body, characterized by a set of points and surrounding spheres representing key areas of concern on the couch and crewman. (Examples: toes, head, knees, couch strut attach points.) The computations showed numerical coordinates of paths and end points of travel due to various G versus time imputs to the extendible strut system. By plotting these points on a layout of the crew compartment, an envelope of couch motion was developed. A variety of sled tests and rotating table tests provided data for estimates of additional crew body movement *within* the couch, as a result of the applied G-loads. Combining these movements vectorially, a complete crew-couch clearance envelope drawing for each set of impact conditions was developed.

8.3.8 Step 8. Physical Small-Scale Model Analysis

As the three-dimensional requirements are being defined on the drawing board and through mathematical model analysis, verification will be desired in a physical, three-dimensional form. Small-scale models of the crew work space have been used to accomplish this preliminary visualization economically in both the Apollo and Space Shuttle programs. Three-dimensional models of the operators were also constructed to assist in such evaluation. Simple cardboard, foam, and wood models are often constructed for a first check, then more functional representations of metal, transparent plastics, mechanisms, and the like, may be appropriate to represent more realistically complex parts, clearances, and orientations.

The second part of this effort involves systematic evaluation. Procedures can include physical measurements, placement of body models in various working positions, relocations of equipment, movement of seats, and so on, through their range of travel to check for possible interferences/clearances and visual sighting from various vantage points. Photographic records of these activities are useful for future reference. Results of these evaluations may lead directly to design decisions (Step 14) or to reevaluation by new drawings (Steps 6.4 and 6.5).

8.3.9 Step 9. Preparation of Functional Test Requirements

Functional test or experiment requirements must be formulated, either informally (in the mind of the analyst) or formally, for execution by others. The tests are needed to verify criteria or obtain original data on the desired quantities, and include measurements of accelogravitational effects, clothing effects, force and torque capabilities, visual obstructions, reach and clearance around obstacles. Proposed developmental modifications to a design may be evaluated by "on the spot" changes to the mock-up as part of the testing effort. Accomplishment of such changes requires planning for adjustable features and/or provision of labor, tools, and materials in anticipation of expected needs. Another function of test requirements is to define and control the number of subjects required (for statistical validity), and what types of subject sizes, mock-ups, measuring apparatus, and support equipment are required to accomplish the tests. Examples are: reach and clearance envelopes (Step 11), special gages and measuring devices (Step 12), cutouts and removable panels for photography, air conditioning, plumbing for breathing gas for space suit support, lighting, and other power requirements and safety provisions in mock-ups (Step 10).

8.3.10 Step 10. Preparation of Mock-ups and Prototypes

The activities involved in this step include not only the fabrication of engineering design representations but also the construction or installation of special provisions necessary to perform photography, measurements, and other engineering evaluation activities within the mock-up. For example, one of the earlier mock-ups of the Apollo Command Module was constructed in two halves, which could be separated in order to observe and photographically record motion and crew positions in one of the side couches. Other Apollo mock-ups had removable sections, removable windows, plumbing for space suit air cooling and pressurization, transparent tunnel and panel sections, and cutouts for suspension harness.

8.3.11 Step 11. Preparation of Reach and Clearance Envelopes Mock-up Representations

Concurrently with, or shortly after, preparation of the equipment mock-ups, three-dimensional mock-up representations of the operator's reach envelopes and movement clearance requirements envelopes are recommended for construction as aids to visualizing critical volumetric relationships (as described in Section 7.7). Because such applications techniques are relatively new, examples are not available for actual physical constructions of *reach* envelopes that have been built and evaluated in direct mock-up evaluation of operational spacecraft. However, it is planned to utilize them in the Space Shuttle development program. *Clearance* envelope constructions, on the other hand, have been built and used to verify and demonstrate volume relationships for the Apollo spacecraft, as described in the following examples.

Among the several types of clearance envelopes to be considered is allowance for movement of the nonrigid human body within the restraint harness due to landing impact or abort loads. At the knees, this may amount to 3 in. forward. The head may move 9 to 12 in. forward, or more, depending on the suit and other constraints. If a piece of structure is located in this envelope of movement, an impact injury may occur. On the other hand, a high degree of head restraint against forward or sideward motion is usually to be avoided because of the possibility of shearing or compressing the neck structure, as the torso moves within its harness. The hands and legs are more easily restrained and consequences of a broken or gashed arm or leg are usually less irreversible. Few data are available regarding typical magnitudes of this movement as a function of harness type, g-loads, time of load application and suit design, and those are primarily for the upright seated man (Swearingen and Hasbrook et al., 1962; Young, 1967; USAF, 1968b; Ewing and Thomas, 1972).

Further compounding this problem in the Apollo Command Module is the potential movement of the couch itself. The set of three crew couches is supported as a unit on struts, which may absorb shock by extension or compression deformation during a severe landing impact. The most severe case could occur during an emergency land impact with high horizontal wind components. Actual operations of the very successful Apollo Command Module have been restricted to water landings, as a result of an extensive series of land and water drop tests (using dummies), an analysis of resulting loads, and description of the total possible envelopes of crew bodies and couch movement (relative to the module) during high wind conditions. Because of concern that these movements be clearly understood by customer and company management, a mock-up representation envelope was prepared demonstrating the estimated envelope of total range of crew-couch movement, for conditions caused by winds up to 26 ft/sec in any direction. The device was fabricated of

Figure 8-9. Crew movement clearance envelope mock-up in Apollo Command Module mock-up. Clearance from forward window, side wall longerons and hatch structure is demonstrated by this photograph. Potential spaces for new installations in critical areas are readily apparent and directly measurable. (Courtesy of Space Division, Rockwell International Corporation.)

plywood formers with balsa wood filler blocks (Roebuck, Kroemer, and Thomson, 1973). It was constructed in several parts, each small enough to be inserted through the hatch of the mock-up Command Module, then bolted together. Head motion envelopes of both outer crewmen received the most careful investigation and contouring, since these were considered most critical in terms of impact injury potential and because interior installations were not entirely symmetrical. A series of photographs, such as shown in Figure 8-9, recorded the spatial relationships to specific structural protrusions inside the crew compartment mock-up.

8.3.12 Step 12. Preparation of Special Gages and Measuring Devices

Frequently, new and unusual devices may be needed for a given work space evaluation. For example, a transparent acrylic device was specifically designed to fit the left forward viewing (docking) window on mock-ups of the Apollo Command Module. The device provided the subject with visual cues for locating his eye in the best position for use of a planned optical sighting device for aligning the Command Module and Lunar Module prior to docking (example of fixed eye reference point concept). A double grid, based on a concept similar to one shown in Chapter II also was provided at the side, to assist the anthropometrist in checking and positioning the subject, as shown in Figure 8-10. Head and helmet clearance to various structures, interior stowage items, and components (lamps/electronic control and display units, instruments) were the subject of several clearance tests in Apollo mock-up evaluations and development efforts.

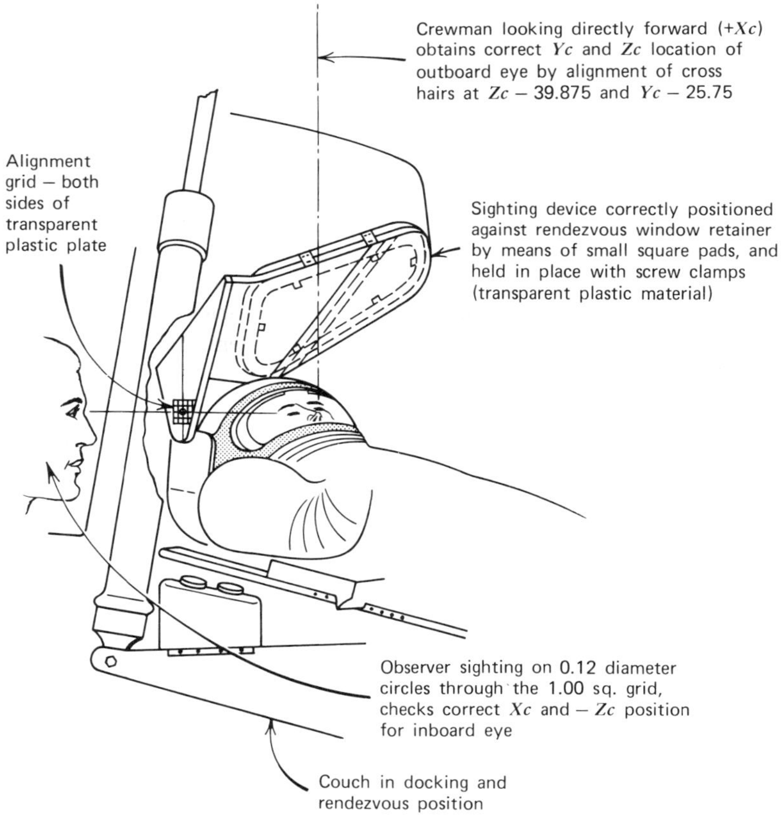

Figure 8-10. Example of special anthropometric measurement and gauging device for use in mock-up. Device is uniquely designed for fitting mock-up Apollo Command Module window and docking eye position. Grid permits measurement (visual estimation) of deviation from ideal conditions. (Courtesy of Space Division, Rockwell International Corporation.)

8.3.13 Step 13. Mock-up and Prototype Testing

Manned testing of mock-ups or prototypes, either to develop new data or to verify design criteria, provides results that may be reflected in revised work space drawings (Step 6) or revised design criteria (Step 14). The effort includes arrangements for test subjects, procurement of test apparatus, scheduling of tests, procurement of recording and photographic services, performance of the test, and recording of data. Data reduction, analysis, and reporting also are included. Chapter VII contains illustrations of activities from several of the numerous tests that were conducted during the spacecraft developments in the 1960s to determine adequacy of reach to each control, of external visibility and of visibility of instruments and markings, of clearance for ingress and egress, of operations of critical equipment and of normal "housekeeping" or "habitability" equipment. These were all performed under a variety of clothing and environmental conditions: ground operations, water recovery operations, and space operations were tested. Mock-ups were placed into large transport type aircraft especially fitted for parabolic flight maneuvers to simulate up to 30 sec of zero-g, or weightlessness. This technique is described by Hammer (1961) and by Pigg and Kama (1961). Operations that could not be performed in one such parabola course were performed in a series of partial operations, with pauses between each portion during the pullout at up to 2½ g between each parabola. Long term zero-g effects were also evaluated using underwater simulations with subjects and various movable objects balanced to neutral buoyancy. Estimates of body movement of crewmen in couch and harness were obtained by rotating subjects in mock-up couches through a complete range of 360° in the sagittal (X-Z) plane, using a pivoted table, and by a variety of sled tests using anthropometric dummies and live subjects while simulating a range of impact vectors.

Documentation of tests involving work space mock-ups and prototypes, either by informal memo or formal reports is *strongly recommended* as a means of recording results and related test conditions for *future use*. Careful planning of test data sheets can materially assist accuracy of report preparation and time for data reduction. For example, when using pressure suits, the manufacturer's specific model, serial number, and general description of the suits, gloves, helmets, boots, and the like should be recorded. Dimensions of the subject with and without the suit, and mobility measurements of the suited and nonsuited subjects should be included where feasible. Records of other personal equipment used should also be included. Mock-up tests involving work space should be reported with a view to answering the question, "What kind of information would I need to prepare a three-view orthographic drawing of the work space and operator, including reach, clearances, and interferences?" Sketches and photographs in the report help to explain precisely the dimensions measured. Accurately prepared graphs, tables, and photographs may require considerable preparation time for typing, processing, printing, and so forth. To satisfy a more immediate need, one should prepare a simple, short letter, recording key data, conclusions, and perhaps recommendations pertinent to a decision on the design being evaluated.

8.3.14 Step 14. Preparation of Work Space Design Criteria Letters, Memoranda, Standards, and Specifications

The major output from the foregoing activity to work space designers is advice, in the form of requirements or commendations that are transmitted both verbally and by written means. These letters and memoranda, together with graphical and tabular enclosures, generally constitute the primary end product of most of the reading and interpreting, statistical analyses and syntheses, work space mock-up testing and evaluation, sketching and drawing. Many of the intermediate products (drawings, test reports, tables, etc.) will be referred to or will accompany the design criteria document to substantiate or further explain the recommendations or requirements.

Not all advice is accepted, even if it has cost a great deal to obtain. To be convincing, it is necessary that those who prepare the letters and other documents of advice clearly explain its meaning and the *expected consequences of proper use, of no use or misuse* of the recommendations presented. While the description of consequences is admittedly difficult, as in any prediction of the future, one must consider that the experience of a person who has worked in the field usually provides a better basis for such prediction than that of one who has not.

Work space design recommendations may be also documented formally as design standards, "Interface Control Documents," and specifications for work space design, using generalized drawings and formulas as discussed in Chapter VII.

8.3.15 Summary of Work Space Design Procedures

The detailed steps and interrelationships discussed in the foregoing presentation are graphically summarized in Figure 8-2. Section 8.3 is a keystone for the entire structure of this text. All previous sections lead up to and support it, all subsequent sections are derived and adapted from it, or otherwise support and contribute to its concepts and the accomplishment of results expected from application of its principles.

8.4 AIRPLANE COCKPITS

Work space for aircraft cockpits (or flight stations or flight decks, as they are sometimes called) can be designed using the same principles and procedures as those previously defined for spacecraft crew stations. Significant differences in detail practice relate to the more normal environments, wider range of populations, striving for minimum drag cross sections and profiles, and need for good external visibility.

For many years, aircraft design has presented highly challenging technological problems in work space design for both crew and passengers. A great many of the concepts and techniques discussed elsewhere in this text are direct applications or outgrowths from aircraft design problem solutions. Examples selected for specific discussion herein are (1) the multiengine civilian passenger/cargo transport, and (2) the single place military fighter.

8.4.1 Population Description and Design Limit Selection

Air crew selection standards and examples of design criteria analysis provide an opportunity to further illustrate and emphasize the statistical concepts previously outlined for Steps 2 and 3 in Figure 8-2. Figure 8-11 illustrates the basic problem of limitation of the operator personnel availability which results from specifying restrictive ranges of percentiles or a large number of body di-

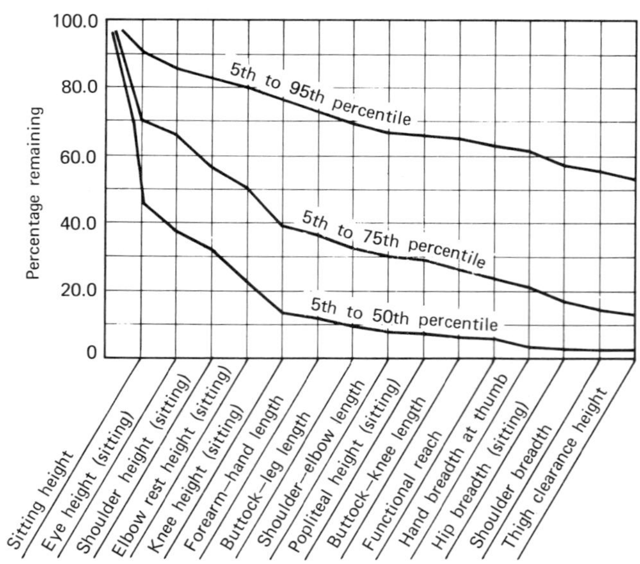

Figure 8-11. Potential reduction in pilot population due to anthropometric selection standards. Three different percentile limit criteria are plotted as a function of selected body dimensions. The more restrictive the range of percentiles and the more the number of dimensions used in selection, the smaller the percentage remaining in the qualifying pilot population. Correlations between dimensions also have a strong effect on these results: the lower the correlation coefficient, the greater the reduction in percentage remaining.

Table 8-2. Entrance Requirements to Military Aviator Programs[a]

Service	Age (yr)	Height (in.)	Weight (lb)	Miscellaneous
U.S. Air Force	$20\frac{1}{2}$–$26\frac{1}{2}$	64–76 (maximum sitting height of 39)	113–230 (depends on age and height)	Vision—20/20 uncorrected College graduate Physically and mentally fit
U.S. Army	18–30	62–75	103–200 (depends on age and height)	Vision—20/50 uncorrected High school graduate Physically and mentally fit
U.S. Navy and Marine Corps	20–28	60–78	120–280 (depends on age and height)	Vision—20/20 uncorrected College graduate Physically and mentally fit.

[a] Adapted from Thomson (1969). Courtesy of General Dynamics Corporation, Convair Division, San Diego, Calif.

mensions. Thus, in selecting persons from the total national population for military pilot training, one must permit a reasonable range of percentiles and limit only a few dimensions to those percentiles, or there will be too few persons left to quality for the service. Among the various services there are significant differences in such selection criteria (see Table 8-2), and air crew stations designed for one service may not accommodate some air crewmen from another. Once percentile standards are applied to define extremes of a design population selection, one may again consider the factors in Figure 8-11 to derive design criteria for such specific populations in designing a particular aircraft fleet.

8.4.2 Design Eye Point—A Starting Point for Cockpit Work Space Layout

In order to minimize windshield and canopy weight and drag, yet maintain sufficient external and internal vision, it is desirable to begin design of an aircraft cockpit from a single design eye point (DEP). This theoretical point is a simplified, "average" eye position representation, often a relaxed, "cruise" position of the pilot's body, but more specifically and frequently a position selected to provide vision adequate for overnose visibility (especially for landing) and for taxi, takeoff, turns, and watching for other aircraft during cruise flight. Once selected, it also helps define the angle, location, and thickness of glare shields in many cockpits. These glare shields usually are parallel to and located just below the line of downward external vision. Thus the upper edge of the visible area of the instrument panel is defined by the eye location and glare shield shape. Any deviation from the selected point must be analyzed as to seriousness of effect on both the internal and external vision requirements. Of course, the pilot does move; he turns to scan, looks up and down, and leans fore and aft from this base point. Also, not all seats and vehicle combinations permit the full range of adjustment needed to assure one exact eye location of all pilots at the theoretical location. Additional defined eye points may be required for specific cockpit tasks. These deviations affect subsequent approaches to window design and to control and display locations, as will be discussed in the following examples.

Window vision requirements based on the single design eye point are the subject of design standards and specifications, in which limits of "external vision" are described geometrically by angles (with respect to a forward sight reference line) plotted on a graph, as shown in Figure 8-12. For military craft, gunsight visual alignment requirements arise which require mock-up study and analysis and which may indicate that further seat adjustments are required. The exact physical relation of the eyes to the design eye point may vary by differing definitions, although in the early phases these details are not important. Some persons define the midpoint between the eye *pupils* as their

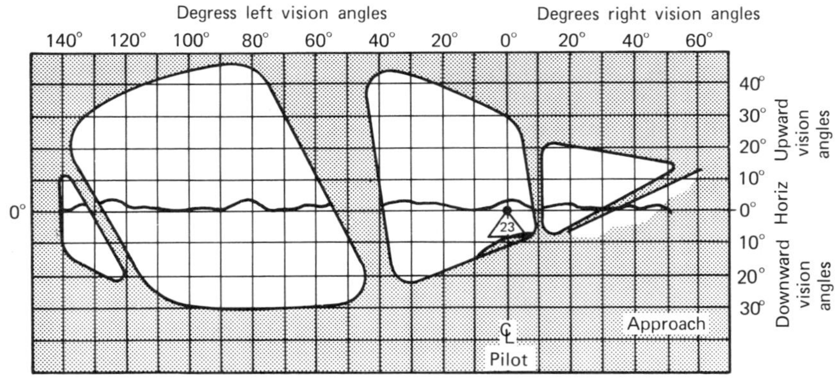

Figure 8-12. External window visibility diagram. Idealized standards for a cockpit window system and actual structural limitations in a given cockpit window system can be compared in a meaningful way on this type of presentation. For simplicity, the angles are measured from a design eye point, but pilots eyes are actually offset on either side of such a point. More accurate presentations would superpose both image plots. (Courtesy Rockwell International Corporation.)

design eye point, while others prefer the midpoint between the approximate centers of rotation of the eyeballs (approximated by the external canthus) approximately ½ in. further toward the back of the head.

Considerations of actual positions of individual eyes are needed to analyze binocular vision around posts and to account for head movements, as detail design layout progresses. Other surfaces or volumes for location of eye points in space are then introduced to more realistically examine visibility. For example, the Federal Aviation Administration (FAA) has developed a special binocular vision camera mount arrangement for measuring cockpit vision. This device is based upon an average distance between eye (pupil) centerlines of 2.5 in. and a fore-aft distance from the pupils to center of neck of $3\frac{5}{16}$ in. In this "second approximation" device, upward and downward head movements are not considered.

Although highly important from a functional, operability viewpoint, the design eye point faces serious practical difficulties as a standard point for design reference. It is difficult to locate and to measure from in mock-ups and actual vehicles, since it is not near any physical object. It is difficult to accurately place a subject's eyes in proper relation to it, since there are many subtle forces and personal differences affecting the eye location in relation to seats, harnesses, nearby structure of window frames, and so forth. Rather than expend the time and money to solve such problems, it has been the practice, particularly in military aircraft, to locate controls and general cockpit features from a point at the intersection of seat back and seat bottom surfaces, when the seat is at the middle of its range of adjustment. This point is called the neutral seat reference point (NSRP). Eye to seat relationships are further discussed in the following paragraphs on seat design.

8.4.3 Seat Design for Airplane Cockpits

The design of a cockpit body support system is a complex compromise between many different factors, including pilot comfort and control efficiency, aircraft weight, overall cost, cockpit volume, aerodynamics, and crew safety. Although the Wright brothers pioneered heavier-than-air craft designs by using a prone pilot body position, the position has had little use and only brief periods of serious study since then (Hertzberg and Colgan, 1948; Brown et al., 1949a, b, c, 1950). The approach to body positions description herein follows the "outside-in" tradition, emphasizing location of key hinge points and links by their distances from given upright seat and floor support surfaces. This is in contrast to the previous approach described for spacecraft design, based on first specifying link orientations, then surfaces. The key relationships of body dimensions to seat design and the inherent impact on, and blending with, relationships to cockpit work space design are developed in the following discussion by means of examples and related explanations. However, the discussion of seat comfort factors that determine how the shapes of body support surfaces are selected is deferred to Sections 8.5, 8.6, and 8.8.

Among the most critical sideview dimensions of interest for crew *positioning* are the seat back surfaces and the seat bottom surfaces. The lengths, curvatures, and angles defining these surfaces determine the body position, hence the vertical distribution of heights of the normal eye position above the seat pan and the fore-aft distribution of eye positions with respect to the seat back surfaces, as well as the operability envelopes for controls (for a given pilot population). The vertical distance from the support surface in contact with the ischial tuberosities is not simply the same distribution as the anthropometric dimension called Eye Height, Sitting. Usually it averages 1 to 2 in. less, an effect called the "slump factor," which is due to (1) the curvature of the spine with the head balanced erect on the shoulders, (2) the angle of the seat back surface, and (3) the pelvic tilt angle.

Similarly, the fore-aft eye position is a complex function of statistical variables related to the above-mentioned factors. Surprisingly few test data are available concerning these fore-aft relationships. Frequently, mock-up tests are required, such as outlined in the following example.

8.4.4 Example: Eye Point Distribution for a Commercial Aircraft Cockpit Seat

Applications of Steps 10 through 13 of Figure 8-2 were implemented to determine the seat adjustment requirements for a fixed pilot's eye location during the development cycle for the DC-8 jet transport (Roebuck, 1954). The study was performed using a custom-made eye location measurement device, employing the parallel grid method. The device was mounted in a simple wooden frame mock-up cockpit, with dimensions as shown in Figure 8-13. In addition to the primary eye location measurements, measurements of control wheel aft position limits and basic anthropometric data were obtained on each subject.

The resulting data on distribution of eye location are outlined on the 1 in. grid pattern in Figure 8-13, and are typical of results from other similar studies as regards magnitude of spread. These data were used in the layout design drawings of crew compartment work space to refine the adjustment range and mean location for the crew seat.

Seat adjustment increments of 0.5 in. are usually satisfactory for the vertical motion, but somewhat larger increments (0.75 to 1.0) are permissible for the horizontal motion.

To locate the eye with respect to the seat (and vice versa) requires an accurate, repeatable measurable engineering definition of a seat reference point.

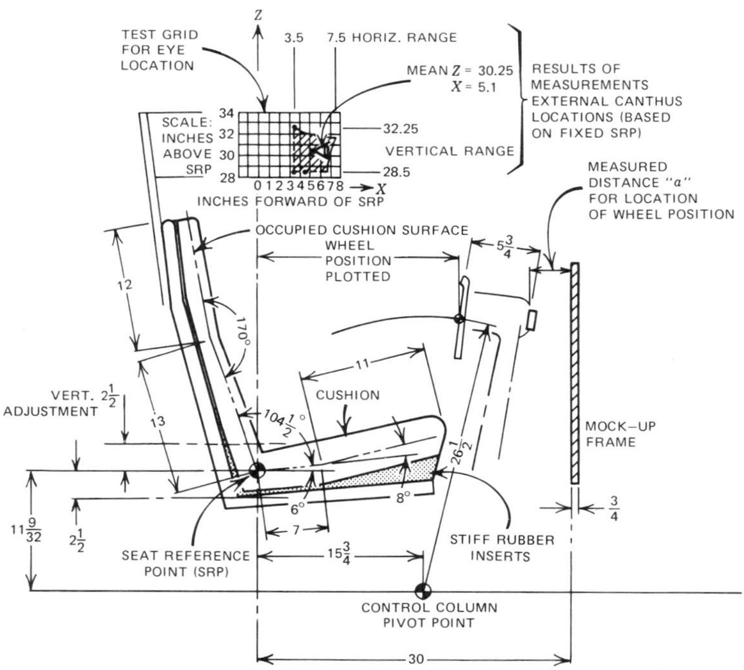

Figure 8-13. Mock-up configuration and results for seated eye position measurements. (Courtesy of McDonnell Douglas Corporation.)

When the back and bottom surfaces are hard, flat planes, one can easily define a so-called Seat Reference Point (SRP) at the intersection of these two planes and the lateral midline of the seat. When cushions are introduced, one should refer to the intersections of the occupied cushion surfaces although the surfaces are likely to be complex and curved, difficult to measure, and subject to variation among pilots. In such cases, rather arbitrary rules, or conventions, define the seat reference point location. A third approach, currently used for automobiles (which is described in Section 8.6), might well be considered for future use in aircraft.

Despite the small uncertainties of definition of the SRP, the SRP has important anthropometric, as well as practical physical advantages as a cockpit design reference point. Anthropometrically, the SRP has the advantage of being at about the middle of the "branched-chain system" of trunk-legs-feet, trunk-arms-hands, and trunk-head. The SRP connects the least mobile body section with the seat. Thus, statistical variations can be more easily described and previous measurements related to the SRP can be readily interpreted and applied with fewer manipulations, and inherent uncertainties, as compared to the use of the DEP.

Considerations of theoretical and practical aspects of design reference points has far-reaching consequences in relation to what measurements are taken in surveys and in mock-up development studies, in relation to the necessary measurement devices and gages for such studies and in relation to the reporting of data. Assuming that windshield and cabin weight and aerodynamics continue to be critical in design, *it is recommended that any future cockpit studies of reach and clearance should include mock-up measurements, locating eye positions (fore-aft and vertical) as well as seat reference points, and describe the cockpit design dimensions with reference to the design eye position.*

8.4.5 Example: Layout and Development of Body Positions and Work Space in Military Aircraft Cockpits

Military aircraft cockpit design will generally begin with one of the military standards documents (Chapter VII), which summarize past experience (including mock-up studies) in terms of key dimensions for seats, controls, and the like, as a function of various cockpit missions requirements. Figure 8-14 shows recommended dimensions for a single seat, fixed wing cockpit configuration, which was derived from a series of anthropometric studies using the foregoing approaches (Sections 8.4.2 and 8.4.3). Note that this specification shows a single design eye position, but only vertical adjustment (except for small coincident fore-aft movement along the 13° line of the seat back). In effect, only a design eye height or eye line is accommodated. The DEP shown is an "average" or nominal fore-aft location, since the seat is constrained to adjust along the ejection rails only.

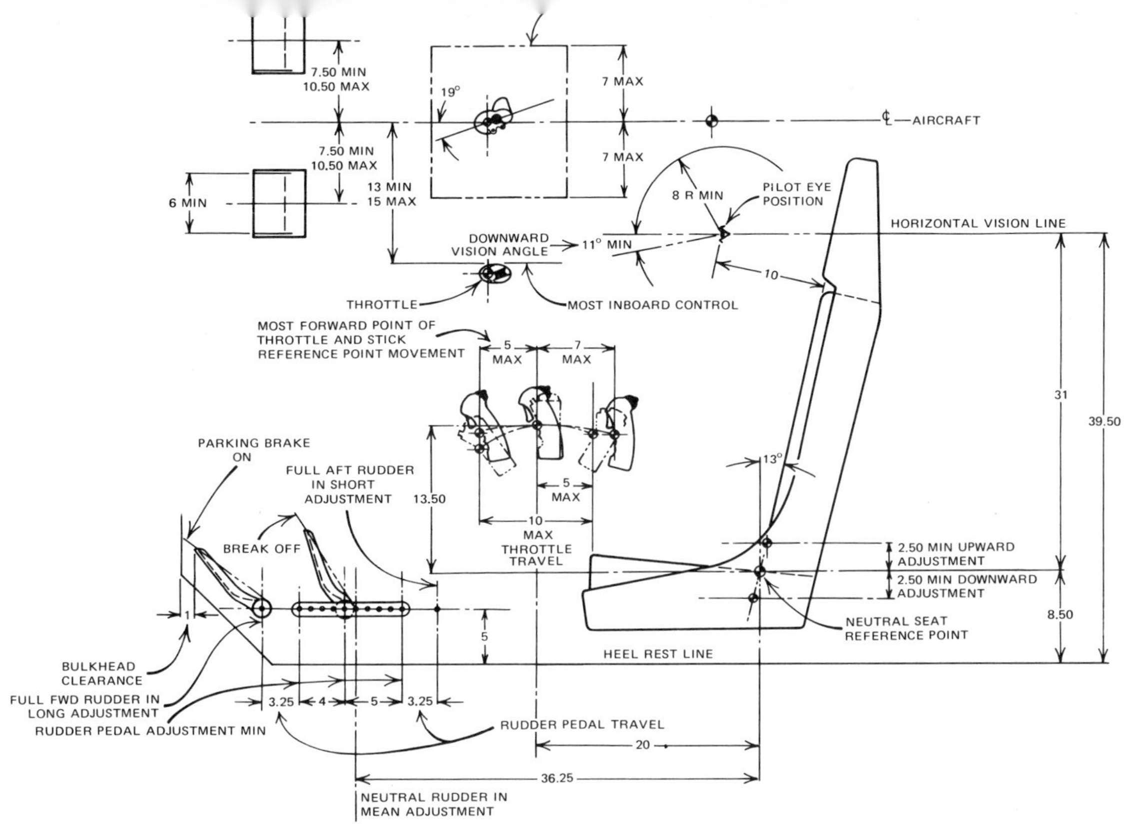

Figure 8-14. Typical standard design guide for dimensions of military cockpit with ejection seat. Such design guides are based upon anthropometric studies of pilot personnel in the USA, circa 1950. These might not be applicable to other populations, such as Japanese military pilots (Dimensions in inches). (Source: US Air Force, 1968a.)

The DEP position shown is probably a "worst case" (furthest from instruments) rather than an average. The US Air Force specification for cargo and bomber cockpits (which often do not have ejection seats) recommends 3 in. of independent fore-aft seat adjustment.

Side view manikins for work space layout should be provided with additional templates for helmets, boots, parachutes, survival gear, and the like, as required. Using these manikins, and other data on reach envelopes (Dempster, 1955a; Kennedy, 1964; Morgan et al., 1963; Garrett, Alexander, and Matthews, 1970), a preliminary crew compartment engineering layout is prepared for the selected range of body positions. This layout will show instrument panel and control panel locations and clearances based on vision limits and analysis of reach envelopes. The men with shortest reach distance determine control locations, as discussed previously in Section 8.3. Elbow restrictions and other mobility limits for the long-armed men determine location of close-in controls. Allowable head and eye movements, knee locations, shoulders, helmet, goggles, and so forth, determine fire control sight locations, instrument locations and orientations to assure adequate visibility. The envelope of crew knee and shin clearance, while operating pedals to appropriate limits of travel and adjustments, determine the lower edge of the instrument panel. Such clearance envelopes are based on all allowable combinations (statistically determined) of Buttock-Knee, Knee Height, and seat adjustments, translated into link diagrams of the legs per Section 8.3.

Laterally, the Bideltoid Shoulder Breadth, Elbow-Elbow Breadth, Chest Breadth, and Hip or Thigh Breadth are critical dimensions for seat design. The Elbow-Elbow breadth in the comfortable or "working" flight position, helps determine overall work space width and arm rest width at the arm rest height, (and often the fuselage width in small aircraft). Flight clothing (especially pressure suits) and other encumbrances, often unknown at the start, tend to force the arms akimbo to achieve a comfortable working position. Ejection seat clearances (dynamic movements) may determine other criteria. Thus, standard anthropometric data may show an Elbow-Elbow Breadth of 19.8 in. for the 95th percentile nude pilot, but the final cockpit clearance requirement for elbows may need to be as much as 30 in. Such dimensions must be determined by measurements, in cockpit mock-ups, of representative subjects in expected flight clothing.

These dimensions may be considered to define a conceptual package or envelope of the seated pilot functional shape, such as that described by Carlyle (1960a), in terms of critical dimensions shown in Figure 8-15. Ingress-egress clearance requirements and ejection envelope requirements further define canopy, instrument panel limits, and upper cockpit open space. The ejection envelope is usually comprised of a 30 in. square "tunnel" oriented parallel to ejection rails and with the aft surface passing through the seat reference point.

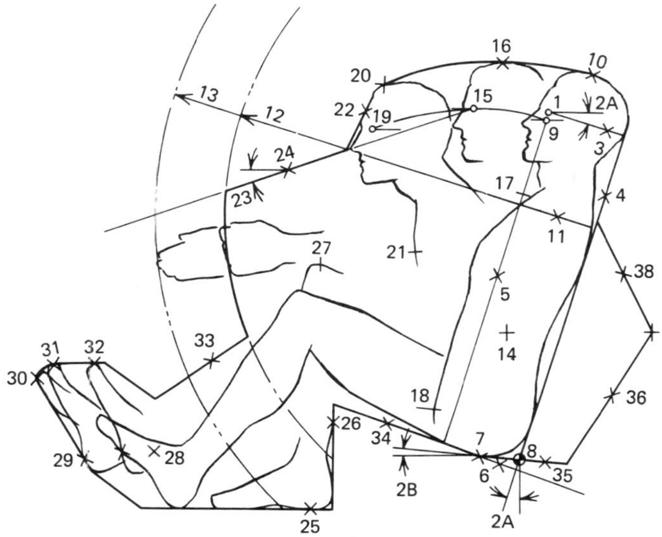

1 Basic eye position
2A Back angle
2B Seat angle
3 Eye-to-back line
4 Back line
5 Eye height
6 Base line
7 Seat depression point
8 Seat reference point
9 Catapult eye position
10 Catapult head top
11 Catapult shoulder top
12 Functional reach
13 Maximum reach
14 Body pivot point
15 Erect eye position
16 Erect head top
17 Erect shoulder top
18 Erect abdomen front
19 Fully flexed eye position
20 Fully flexed head top
21 Fully flexed chest front
22 Forward face limit
23 Down vision angle
24 Down vision line
25 Heel rest line
26 Aft shin limit
27 Maximum knee height
28 Aft rudder pedal position
29 Forward rudder pedal position
30 Forward toe position
31 Maximum toe height
32 Aft toe position
33 Forward shin limit
34 Lower thigh limit
35 Lower hand limit
36 Aft forearm limit
37 Aft elbow position
38 Aft arm limit

Figure 8-15. Basic functional envelope—military aircraft. (After Carlyle, 1960a.) Ejection envelope and crash impact clearance, ingress, and egress requirements are not shown. (Courtesy McDonnell Douglas Corporation.)

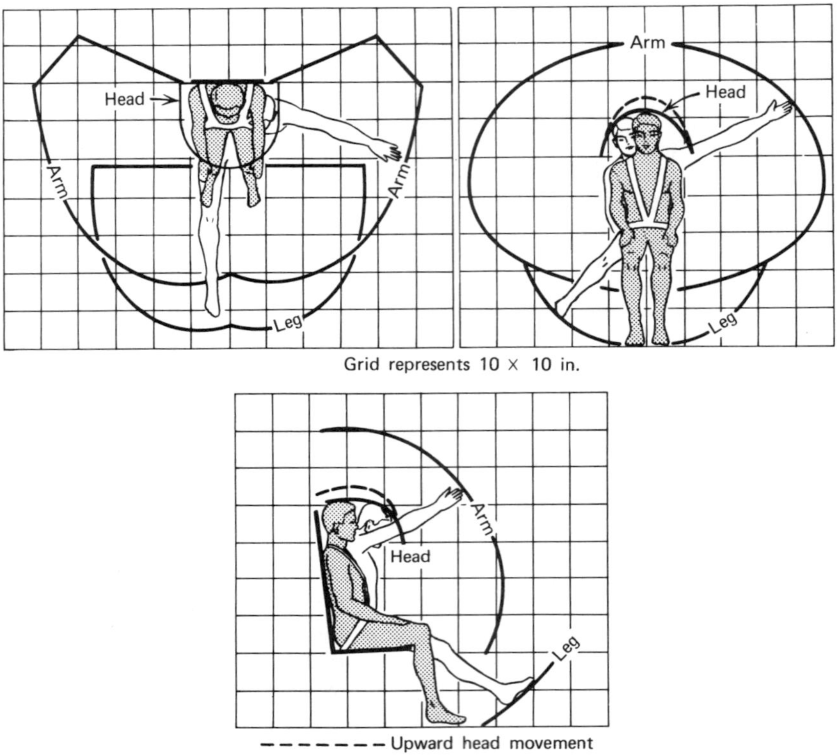

Figure 8-16. Head and arm movement envelopes during crash impact. USAF design data presentation showing frontal, sagittal, and transverse plane clearance envelopes allowing for head movement and arm movement at impact. (Source: US Air Force, 1968b.)

Meeting this requirement generally satisfies the normal ingress-egress space requirements for smaller cockpit designs.

Further mention here is warranted concerning the significant envelope of clearance for potential head and body motion due to crash impact. An example of such data for aircraft design (assuming a rigid seat) is shown in Figure 8-16. Other sources, were mentioned in Section 8.3.11. Such considerations apply to *all* vehicle designs, which can achieve high speeds.

8.4.6 Computer Mathematical Models for Analysis of Cockpit Work Space (Step 7)

Cockpit design analysis has generated much of the interest in computer programs to mathematically generate envelopes of reach and clearance for work space evaluation, and to compare them to surrounding structure. For example,

Hickey, Springer, and Cundari (1968) have outlined the Cockpit Geometry Evaluation Research Program of the Boeing Company (1970) which was an early major effort to establish a mathematical computer modeling analysis of the man-work space geometry. It was conceived as a multimethod approach involving experimental laboratory work, computer modeling, flight simulators, and actual flight test validation effort, divided into six phases, each of 12 months duration. The initial effort was to describe and validate a "stick pilot" concept that had 23 joints, as shown in Figure 8-17, called BOEMAN-1. The

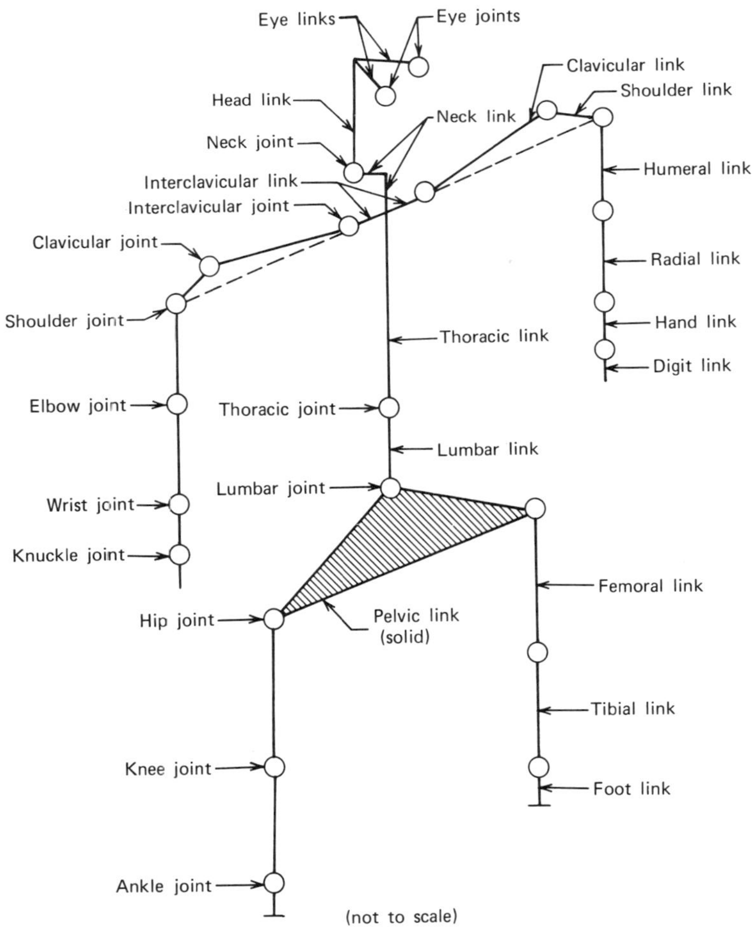

Figure 8-17. Conceptual model for mathematical analysis of cockpit work space: Boeman - 1. (After Hickey, Springer and Cundari, 1968.) The baseline model has 23 joints, which must be described in the orientation description.

next phase involved putting "skin" volumes on the figure to provide three-dimensional definition and improve cockpit control volumes estimates. Additional details and refinements were to be added as the program progressed, until a fully articulated, realistic "pilot" model is validated and programmed into the computer along with cockpit dimensions (including control-display locations) and realistic shapes of all its elements. Such a computer model is a powerful analytical tool, capable of evaluating any cockpit geometry in terms of any human anthropometric combination and any set of flight crew task sequences. The model output may describe display and control accessibility, control actuation, and interferences between flight crew appendages and cockpit structure/equipment. Further developments can provide workload in terms of energy expended, body mass displacements, and distances traveled by the flight crew's eyes and appendages (useful for link analysis and time studies).

However, development of man-work space models requires detailed, consistent syntheses of anthropometric data at a level far beyond that presently available for any population. A report on the link system of the human torso by Snyder, Chaffin, and Schutz (1972) is an example of these new concepts and harbinger of trends in this area of application and supporting measurements.

Other aircraft applications of mathematical biomechanical models have dealt with the inertial properties and stresses of the human body in emergency conditions, such as ejection seat operation or crash impacts. Such considerations have an effect both on design of the space around the pilot and on other mechanical engineering characteristics (sequencing, load vectors, materials) of the affected aircraft structures and escape seat propulsion devices such as rockets, catapults, and the like (Band 1971).

8.4.7 Physical Model and Dummy Applications Examples (Steps 8, 11)

In developing and demonstrating the mathematical model concepts previously described, Boeing engineers utilized models of the cockpit work space and wooden, articulated models of crewmen.

A further extension of the model concept into a blend with the work space measurement device and dummy concepts was used in an anthropometric program of evaluation of U.S. Navy aircraft cockpits (Jones, W. L., and Gifford, 1964). A two-dimensional, adjustable, plastic manikin was developed *to full scale.* This device could be "seated" at the proper position in actual aircraft cockpits. Length adjustments were made until contact was made with structure clearance spacers placed on the critical surface of the manikin. Aircraft were then rated in terms of the Sitting Height and Stature for anthropometric ranges of pilots.

Other frequently used physical models of the human body are the anthropomorphic dummies (Chapter VII), some of which have been called

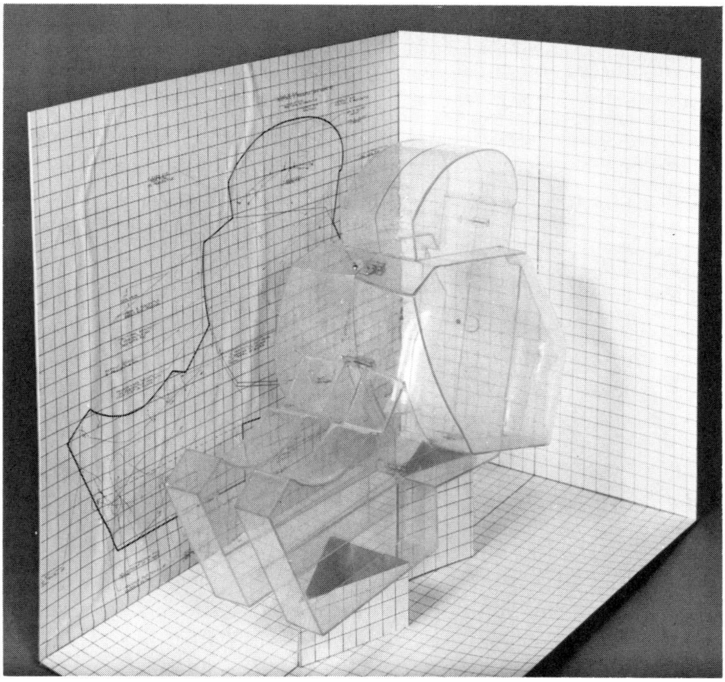

Figure 8-18. Composite functional envelope model—military aircraft. (After Carlyle, 1960a Courtesy McDonnell Douglas Corporation.)

rather inhuman in their design and response characteristics. Hertzberg (1969) discussed a number of anthropometric inputs to dummy design. Dummies have been used for years in the testing of ejection seats for military aircraft, primarily to simulate the aerodynamic and inertial properties of man. Thus the interest in centers of mass, moments of inertia, and distribution of weight to the various segments of the body, described in Chapter VI, stemmed in large degree from ejection seat applications.

In another type of modeling approach, Carlyle (1960a) prepared a plastic model, shown in Figure 8-18, to help designers clearly visualize cockpit work space volume limitations for a naval fighter type of aircraft. The model represents a combination of two types of design requirements: (1) reach envelopes, within which controls must be placed, and (2) clearance envelopes, outside of which cockpit sidewalls, controls, display panels, and other structure must be placed. The representation shown is conceptual only; the construction of the reach envelope portion prevents actual installation in a vehicle mock-up or model cockpit.

8.5 PASSENGER AIRCRAFT CABIN SEATING SPACE

The following discussion of application of anthropometry to the aircraft cabin design concerns passenger seating contours and the seating space requirements. Similar considerations apply to busses, trains, subway cars, and marine taxi vehicles. Some typical anthropometric areas of concern, which are not included in this discussion, relate to configuration of the cabin, stewardess and passenger access to storage, design of minimum size sanitation facilities, design for crash worthiness, (Swearingen et al., 1962) and design of emergency exits (Roebuck and Levedahl, 1961). Discussion of this application area is limited to selected examples from Steps 6 and 7 described in Section 8.3. However a broader introductory overview, including significant points of emphasis such as occupant population description and activities related to the beginning numbered procedural steps previously listed in Figure 8-2, is presented in Table 8-3.

8.5.1 Position in Space for Passenger Seating

One of the first formally stated design procedures for aircraft passenger seating (Lippert, 1949), was developed by combining automotive seating positional and dimensional information (Lay and Fisher, 1940), with rail-traveler dimensional data (Hooton, 1945) and U.S. Army Air Force data (Randall et al., 1946). The resulting simplified diagram, shown in Figure 8-19 "defines the position in which optimum comfort of 90% of the traveling public can be achieved in a fixed seat." While one might quarrel with the semantics and statistical validity of the description, the diagram does provide an example of a practical, convenient basis for seat engineering design that has been derived from valid anthropometric data and principles, and accepted by large numbers of passengers. Furthermore, its simplicity provides ease of reproduction at various scales, since there is no need to lay out elaborate curves by offsets. Lippert's approach is still conceptually valid, but more adjustments in contour are now being considered.

Since compromises between comfort and other requirements must often be made in seat design, Lippert offered the following "practical order of importance" of the dimensions shown in Figure 8-19.

1. Height of seat above floor, *AB* (measured to the projected intersection).
2. Length of seat from front to back ($BC + CD$).
3. Width of seat.
4. Included angle between bottom and back ($\angle CDE$).
5. Break in seat back ($\angle DEF$).
6. Length of seat back (*DEFG*).
7. Foot rest.

Table 8-3. Aircraft Passenger Cabin Work Space Design Applications

Step Numbers (per Fig. 8-2)	Outline of Highlights, References
1	Establishing Mission Requirements: *Primary:* Contain passengers in a reasonably safe and comfortable position during majority of flight. *Secondary:* Food service, sanitation, stowage, recreation (reading, movies, cards, music), study, conversation, etc. Access to/from seats, and vehicle (normal). Exterior vision, lighting (normal and emergency). *Emergency:* Crash impact protection, emergency egress/rescue, oxygen mask and life vest access. Refs.: Roebuck, 1957; Roebuck and Levedahl, 1961; Lippert, 1949, 1950, 1957
2	Population Definition and Descriptions: Synthesized from other available data. In the United States, prior to 1945, primarily those of railroad travelers (Hooton, 1945) and military air crew (Randall et al. 1946). Currently, much like U.S. public (Stoudt et al., 1964, 1965; Damon, Stoudt, and McFarland, 1966). Consider foreign populations and historical growth effects. Special group: Stewardesses—must operate food preparation and service, operate all emergency devices and reach stowage.
3	Design Criteria Population Selection: Fifth to 95th percentile separately applied to male and female passengers for statistical convenience (some other syntheses logically justified but statistical distribution would be platykurtic or bimodal). Provisions for short adult women accommodates many teenagers. Few special provisions for children, except cribs or special restraints in some cases. Use of full range (100%) for stewardess facilities design is recommended.
4, 5	Basic Body Dimensions Drawings and Design Aids: Same considerations as for Section 8.3, however, more varied population groups: stewardesses, male and female adult passengers and children, of various nationality groups may increase number of drawings, manikins, other design aids required.
6	"Work Space" Layout Analysis and Synthesis: Consider normal passenger activities as "work" to be performed (see Requirements). "Normal" is seated position. Consider, also, unusual cases involve lounges, berths, or military air evacuation litters.

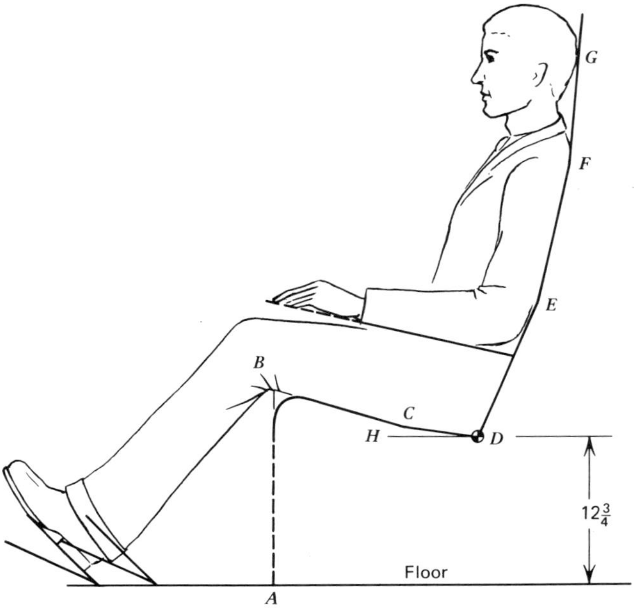

	Length (In.)	Angle	
AB	$16\frac{7}{8}$	BCD	172°
BC	12	CDH	8°
CD	6	DEF	170°
DE	13	EFC	$172\frac{1}{2}$°
EF	11	CDE	105 ± 2°
FG	10		

Arm rest height $7\frac{1}{2}$ in. to 9 in. above a line between B and D.

Arm rest length 13 in. to 18 in.

Seat width—19 in. minimum which will accommodate 95% of shoulder width and hip breadth of 95+% of traveling public.

The foot rest should be adjustable through an angle between 26° and 48° from the horizontal and through a distance, from 28 to 33 in. forward of the projection of point *D* upon the floor.

Figure 8-19. Supporting surface for passenger in fixed seat, according to Lippert (1949). The simplified surfaces shown were developed to accommodate anthropometric dimensions of U.S. traveling public to approximately a 95% level. Slight reductions may be required in dimension ***BD*** for small women and children. The surfaces shown are *occupied* contours for cushioned seats. (Courtesy McDonnell Douglas Corporation.)

8. Clearance between shin and forward seat structure.
9. Inclination of seat.
10. Height of arm rest above seat.

"As an example of the application of the above sequence, ∠*ABC* can be compromised with little effect on comfort, whereas ∠*CDE* is critical . . . A preferred adjustment for a limited range of motion is one where ∠*ABC* alone changes. If this is not possible, a change in ∠*ABC* together with a change in ∠*CDE* is desirable. An adjustment in ∠*CDE* alone is the least desirable but most common type of adjustment" (Lippert, 1949). Some seat studies before and since have recommended an angle greater than 180° in angle *DEF* (Åkerblom 1948, 1954; Cumberland and Bowey, 1945; Dreyfuss 1966; Grandjean 1969b). Lippert admitted that "if it were possible to so position support for the small of the back that a large number of people would be comfortable, it might be worthwhile including in the design." In 1972, some aircraft passenger seats have been equipped with aircushions at the lumbar-sacral region. The passenger can inflate this built-in "Åkerblom-pad" to his liking.

Lippert also stated that the "forward tilt of *EF*, [in Figure 8-19] not only gives more comfort than a straight backed chair, but gives an extra two inches of clearance for passengers in the seat behind." (Especially significant for ingress-egress).

Lippert felt that transverse contouring, which is excellent for the optimum comfort position, might be restrictive when the seat occupant desires to change his position. "It is best, therefore, not to consider lateral contouring of the seat bottom unless the spring and cushion system deflects less than one inch. Gentle lateral contouring of the seat back can improve comfort if it does not restrict broad shouldered occupants".

In designing a seat, according to criteria in Figure 8-19, "the spring rates of the cushion and cushion supports, and the applied pressures at various points on the cushion, must be so regulated that the passenger occupies this position." The normal condition for the statically deformed cushion is usually at about half thickness in a well-designed seat. Further deflection occurs due to the support straps or pan under the cushion.

Design of seat cushions to achieve stated deformations depends on knowledge of body pressure applied on seat bottom and back. Hence, direct pressure level measurement methods and indirect (seat area and weight) measurements are of interest to engineering anthropometry specialists for design of seat contours and seat cushions. Lay and Fisher (1940) during their study of automobile seat cushion attempted direct measurements of pressures. They give 0.4 psi. as the maximum pressure under the buttocks for their average seat occupant. However, calculations on the average pressures under the thigh and buttocks of cadets and gunners in Randall et al. (1946) yielded

0.5 psi, which means that peak pressures are above this value. Crude checks on a few subjects indicate that the peak pressures are approximately three to four times the value given by Lay and Fisher. The low peak pressures found by Lay and Fisher can be ascribed to the area covered by each spring, and the linking of springs by means of canvas strips and the top cover. Later studies by Hertzberg (1955, 1972) indicate much higher pressures on hard surfaces.

8.5.2 Fore-Aft Seat Spacing

There are a large number of structural, anthropometric, psychological, and safety considerations and interactions between dimensions of the seat and the fore-aft spacing of seat rows in passenger aircraft. A method for evaluating aircraft seat spacing and developing design standards, which is also applicable to trains, busses, shuttle boats, and other multiple passenger vehicles is illustrated in Figure 8-20. First, a graded series of leg positions was selected, based on studies of comfortable positions (Swearingen, 1949). Next, the allowable variations of the upper and lower segments of leg length were described for a given restriction, such as corners or surfaces of the seat, in front of the passenger. This was accomplished by making a layout of the combinations of leg length components, expressed as Patella Height and Buttock-Knee Length, showing variations allowed by given restrictions. For each restriction, a "cutoff line" was plotted on a correlation scatter diagram of Buttock-Knee Length versus Knee Height (Step 3). The percentile fit for each seat spacing was determined as the ratio of the number of persons accommodated to the total number in the sample group.

In this application, the correlation scatter diagram permits a simple, direct count of persons accommodated. If only the means, standard deviations, and correlation coefficient were known, more complicated and extensive mathematical analysis would have been required.

The foregoing procedure can be extended to define design criteria envelopes for any percentage fit and set of hypothetical clearance conditions. These "pre-packaged answers" can then be presented in the form of transparent overlays, layout drawings or mock-up forms.

8.5.3 Side-by-Side Seat Spacing

The critical considerations involved in side-by-side spacing may be classified as seat-related (Shoulder or Elbow Breadth, Hip Breadth and arm rest width) and vehicle-related (aisle width, fuselage diameter, and weight/drag considerations).

The Shoulder Breadth is here considered the critical human dimension of interest. This is based upon reference to basic anthropometric data, which show that Shoulder Breadth for American men at any percentile is greater than the corresponding percentile Hip Breadth for men or women. The space

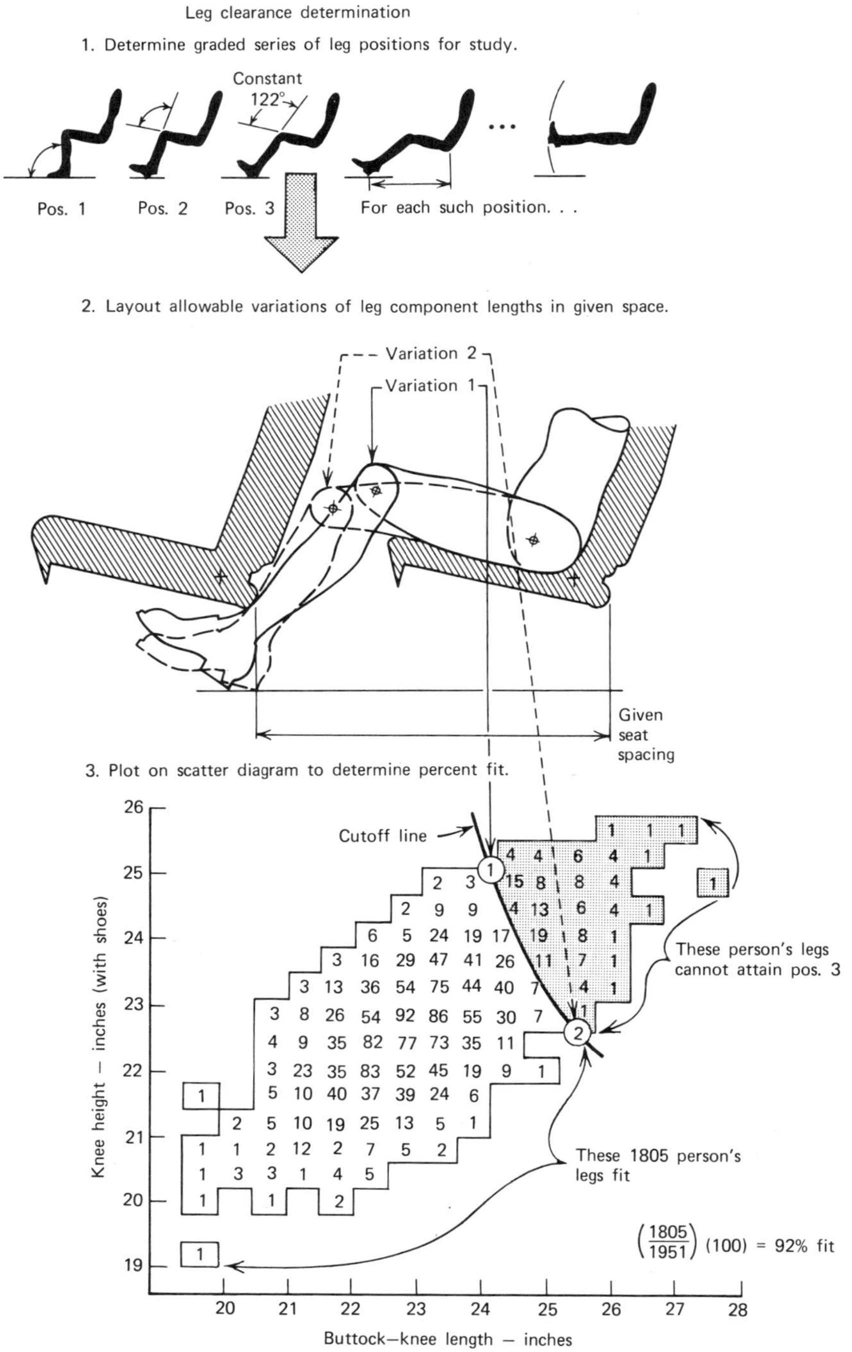

Figure 8-20. Method of estimating leg space requirements for seat spacing study (from Roebuck, 1957).

between hips may then determine the allowance for arm rests. Desirable "elbow room" in addition to that required by shoulder breadth is not considered in this analysis.

The following example shows statistical treatment for seating three persons in a row in two lines of 22 rows each, spaced on both sides of a central aisle.

In each row of three abreast the problems of shoulder interference are potentially eliminated on any aircraft which is less than two-thirds full, since the center seat in each three-seat set could be unoccupied. Therefore, the fit problem is primarily a matter of accommodating the load conditions greater than 66% full, especially the case when all three seats are filled. In many seat rows, one or more persons of below average Shoulder Breadth could be seated with one or more persons of above average breadth. Two criteria were selected for analysis. The first, called the bench criterion, ignores centering effects of armrests and other structure, assuming passengers will slide sideways or lean such as to reduce the problem to calculation of the *distribution of the sum of three Shoulder Breadths* in a set of seats. The second, called the seat criterion, is concerned with probabilities of overlapping shoulders when three passengers are centered in their seats.

In Figure 8-21 only the 100% load factor criteria are considered as a matter of simplifying the presentation of benefits possible with statistical averaging (curves 1 and 2). As a basis for comparison, a third criterion is shown in curve 3. These data, taken directly from Hooton's study (1945), a combined sample

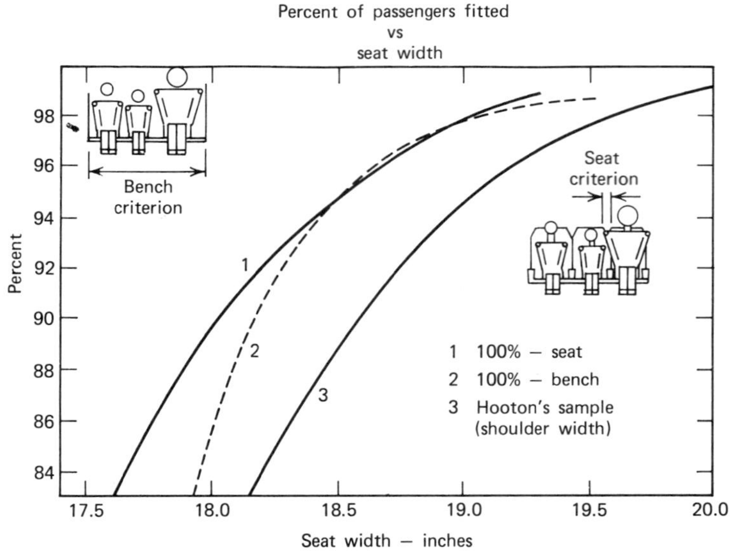

Figure 8-21. Results of analysis of seat width for three abreast combinations (from Lippert, 1958).

of men and women, conservatively imply that each seat is placed between immovable walls fixed at a given distance on the sides (no statistical averaging). From the more optimistic approach of curves 1 and 2, it is seen that seat widths in excess of 19 or 19.5 in. benefit only 1 or 2% *of the population studied.*

8.6 AUTOMOTIVE VEHICLE INTERIORS

Design of personal, commercial, and military automobiles involves many engineering anthropometry considerations in common with design of aircraft cockpit and passenger seating space. However, there are significant and interesting differences as to the type and range of population accommodated, the selected fixed points for geometry reference, and the approaches to protection of the user from both accelogravitational and environmental conditions.

In addition, a significant difference is found in the relatively slow evolution of the automobile work space over many model changes. This has permitted the Society of Automotive Engineers (SAE) in the United States to develop a degree of standardization in approach that contrasts to the more turbulent aerospace industry. Devices that are developed to incorporate and represent accumulated experience of work space designers can be used many times in evaluation of similarly-shaped work spaces. One such device is the SAE standard H-point machine, and the related two-dimensional articulated drafting template manikin. These devices are described early in this discussion, in contrast to previous procedures, in order to assure understanding of subsequent presentations based on the use of the devices.

8.6.1 Seat Reference Point and H Point

The reference point used in automobile seat design and work space layout up to 1961, was the "A" point. This was located 5 in. forward of the undepressed seat back on the surface of the cushion. However, since seat cushions on automobiles provide a wide variety of depression under load, this was not a reliable point for comparing available interior space and reach between cars. To overcome this problem of seat location definition, the Society of Automotive Engineers has developed the concept of the "H" point which is approximately at the mean of the distribution of hip joint centers for seat occupants. By *definition*, it is located in a particular seat by use of a standard three-dimensional partial manikin (called the H-point machine) which is briefly described below. For more detail see SAE Standard J 826a (SAE, 1970).

8.6.2 The H-Point Manikin and Drafting Template

The three-dimensional manikin of SAE J 826a uses the weight and body contour of the mythical 50th percentile male. The main parts of the manikins are one trunk and pelvis section, and two thigh, calf and foot sections. The leg segments are adjustable to different percentile lengths. Simple one-degree-of-freedom hinges allow relative displacements.

For preliminary design, a two-dimensional articulated drafting manikin representation of the H-point machine is used to establish approximate leg clearances using 90th or 95th percentile leg segments. Then, a "seating buck" is often built (Kyropoylos and Roe, 1970). This is a three-dimensional mock-up of the driver and passenger compartment (Step 10, Figure 8-2). Although the mock-up is simply constructed of wood or foam, the seat is fully sprung and trimmed.

The three-dimensional manikin is then placed on the seat using carefully defined procedures. Because of its weight, it sinks into seat pan and back, establishing the H point for further layout analysis. If the designer is satisfied with the appearance of the seating buck, more elaborate mockups are constructed and tested with actual subjects until the final design is tested in an actual vehicle.

In concept ("50th percentile male") and realization, both two- and three-dimensional manikins have limitations as representations of human beings; however, simplicity in design furthers the use of these phantoms for standardization of "H point" and a gross evaluation of the leg clearances of the operator or passenger. Additional mock-up tests can establish envelopes of clearance with respect to the defined "H" point and heel point references, and establish seat adjustment requirements. Attempts to improve the manikins, and the procedures for their use, are continuing through the Design Devices Subcommittee of the SAE Human Factors Engineering Committee, Society of Automotive Engineers.

8.6.3 User Population-Definition and Description

Some significant anthropometric descriptors, based on recent studies of automobile driver and passenger populations in the United States are briefly summarized in Table 8-4, together with some related effects on design of automobile interiors. The cited references should be read for further details on sample descriptions and design-related considerations.

In addition to those listed, an early report by McFarland, Damon, Stoudt, Mosely, Dunlap, and Hall (1953) gives many data on body dimensions and mobility pertinant to vehicular design in general and automobiles in particular.

8.6.4 Step 6.1. Body Position Selection

Although some delivery vehicles and street cars provide for standing attitudes, the majority of automobiles and trucks require only the seated position, and involve normal driving tasks, such as steering wheel rotation, reaching for controls, and looking out of windows and through rear-view mirrors.

Orthopedically handicapped drivers introduce variabilities into the body position and dimensional ranges, in effect constituting a "new population," which, if provided with a rearrangement of controls, power brakes, and power steering, can compete very well with the nondisabled driver in vehicle handling.

As in the case of passenger aircraft seating, comfort is a significant design criterion for automobile passengers and drivers. Not only the previously discussed aspects of sitting in a well-supported attitude (as outlined in Section 8.5) but also the driver's ability to perform the operations of driving the car with ease, and isolation from road impacts, mechanical vibrations, noises, unpleasant temperatures, and so forth, are included in this comfort concept. These considerations are similar to the emphasis on pilot tolerance and operating efficiency in Section 8.3.6. Any body position, or seat profile, even if very comfortable in the beginning, becomes increasingly uncomfortable in long uninterrupted sitting and, finally, is unbearable. In one response to this problem, Hertzberg (1949) tested a pulsating seat cushion, the contours and pressure distribution of which were changed periodically to delay sitting discomfort. However, economic and safety considerations have prevented general usage of such devices.

8.6.5 Heel Location: Package Origin Point

In contrast to the aircraft cockpit "design eye" or "seat reference" points, present automotive work space layout in the United States usually starts from an accelerator pedal heel location reference point. This is possible because of the permissible large expanse of windshield and relative reduced criticality of downward vision over the hood. This automotive work place reference point has been variously called the "heel hard point" or "accelerator heel point" (AHP) and Package Origin Point (PGO). The former AHP is defined by some as the actual point of contact of the heel on the floor. The latter is located at the same forward distance from the seat but is on the centerline (sagittal) plane of the driver seat. The layout drawing (often at full scale) defining the body seat and compartment space is called a "package" drawing or "package" layout. The seat range of adjustment and reference location is then defined (in terms of the "H" point) with respect to this vehicle reference point (AHP or PGO). For example, a medium passenger car body style for the general US public may have fore-aft seat adjustment range of 6 in. along a slanted line dropping 2 in. as it traverses from front to back. Constraints such as this are intended to permit all drivers within the selected percentile range to comfortably reach the accelerator pedal, the steering wheel, and other controls, and to see a sufficient portion of the roadway for safe driving. Note, however, that long legs are not necessarily coupled with long trunks (or longer Eye Height, Sitting). Between Sitting Height and Buttock Leg Length for USAF

Table 8-4. Population Characteristics and Design Considerations for Automotive Drivers and Passengers

Population Name and Selection Characteristics	Other Population Descriptors	Samples Investigated	References and Sampling Area, Dates	Significant Design Considerations
Drivers				
General: age 15–75 years; male and female; average health and whole-bodied	Wide range of income, education, race, age, body build, strength	18–79 years, 6672 persons represent U.S. population.	Stoudt et al. (1965) U.S.A., 1959–62	Wide design range for adjustments of seat, other controls is desirable. Some selection by model size
		524 female, 509 males represent U.S. driver population	Stoudt, Crowley et al. (1970) U.S.A.	
Bus and truck: primarily male; healthy, whole-bodied Long-haul Civilian	Stockier, more mesomorphic, less gynandromorphic than average American male, bigger in weight, breadths, girth, not height.	272 bus and truck drivers. 103 were champions, "roadeo" competitors.	Damon and McFarland (1955) U.S.A.	Design truck cabs for large sizes of men Consider improved controls if smaller, weaker men or females needed as drivers
Champions	Taller, broader shoulders, longer forearms than average			
Military	Smaller, younger than other soldiers.	Military truck drivers	See also Damon, Stoudt, and McFarland (1966) U.S.A.	

Orthopedically handicapped: male and female, limb or limbs missing	See reference	See reference	McFarland et al. (1968) U.S.A.	Design special controls as required for handicap prosthesis form/capability (e.g., power boosting brakes, steering)
Pregnant women, age 15–45 years (Also need special attention as passengers)	Average eight years younger, 13 lb heavier than average females, abdominal depth 2 in. greater than other women measured	203 healthy women (in 3rd to 9th month), Boston, Mass.	Stoudt, Crowley et al. (1970) U.S.A.	Special assistance for ingress/egress, fit behind wheel Special protection against impact injury in crash Adjustability for controls to assist reach.
Passengers				
Infants and children, age 0–15 years, male/female	Body proportions different from adults, relatively high center of mass (top heavy) See Chapter VI	82 child occupants in auto collisions Accident studies	Siegel, Nahum, Appleby (1968) {Burdi et al. (1969) {Snyder (1970a)	Special attention in auxiliary seats and restraints for impact protection, consider relatively higher center of mass, potential injury from more fragile auxiliary seat structure
Elderly persons	See references	65–79 years 133 Spanish-American war veterans	Stoudt et al. (1965) U.S.A. 1959-62 Damon and Stoudt (1963)*	

* "The Functional Anthropometry of Old Men," *Human Factors*, 5:5, 485–491.

males, the coefficient of correlation (as found in Appendix B) is only .451. Therefore, adjustability of the seat pan height should be essentially independent from the fore-aft adjustment, to maintain equivalent vision and head clearance. The commonly used, simple, rearward declined seat adjustment is usable largely because of the wide allowances in eye height permitted by automotive window design and loose standards for required forward visibility. The small range of vertical adjustment offered effectively controls the head clearance from the interior ceiling.

8.6.6 Eye Position Standards

Based upon limits of steering wheel clearance and reach, heel reach, vision requirements, seat adjustments, fore-aft eye position distribution, and sitting eye height distribution in a relaxed, comfortable body attitude, the driver's eyes may be assumed to be located in a roughly elliptical space (in the side view). In a joint effort of the automobile industry (Meldrum, 1966), 2300 people (mostly exhibition visitors) were seated in either a Ford, Plymouth, or Chevrolet 1963 convertible. Two cameras set at 90° took pictures of each subject, from which the eye positions were then calculated. Scatter diagrams resulting from the study were processed by computer to generate elliptical eye range contours. Data were weighted to produce a one-to-one, male-to-female population ratio. The resultant Driver's Eye Range contours are described in SAE recommended practice J941a (SAE, 1967).

The contours (elliptical by definition) of the eye range distribution depict perimeters of envelopes in plan and side view, which encompass selected percentiles (e.g., 95th percentile). Tangent lines drawn to these contours represent lines of sight such that *at least* those selected percentages of eyes (e.g., 95%) are located toward the midpoint side of the line. The tangents provide a conservative estimate because some locations of eyes are outside the ellipses but still not outside the sight lines. Subsequent studies provided methods of (a) accounting for viewing targets located at extreme lateral angles, including limited head and eye movements (Devlin and Roe, 1968) and (b) accounting for changes in the eye ellipses locations brought about by changes in body position at different seat body angles (Roe and Hammond, 1972).

A number of prepared templates can be used to locate the eye ellipses at different seat angles. The H point serves as the reference point in this technique. Such templates are applicable to passenger cars, trucks, and busses with bench or bucket seats. The procedures recommended, and the eye ellipses are described in detail in SAE J941c. These same basic concepts are applicable to any work space design not dictated by a fixed eye reference point. Of course, the contours will be different since they are not based on conditions existing in the exhibition and the three vehicles manufactured in 1963.

8.6.7 Style, Clothing, and Dynamic Considerations

To the static, nude dimensions of the driver and passenger must be added the effects of ingress-egress, vibrations, road-induced jostling, impacts, clothing, and hair styling, which, in almost all cases, require an increase. However, clothing may reduce the reach capability. Also restrictive of reach and affecting other dynamic body movements are restraint harness devices, such as seat belts and shoulder straps, which are now standard equipment on cars in the United States. Restraints for children also are on the market (as optional equipment). These can be attached to the standard interior equipment to offer the child a seat of compatible size as well as provide protection in case of sudden deceleration. However, Snyder (1970b) found that many of the existing child seats offer little or no protection to the occupant or may even be dangerous. In contrast to adults, the child should not be restrained at the shoulder level while the head is free to more: the relatively large mass of the head can "snap" forward on the restrained torso with serious neurological injury possible, since the cervical structure of the child's neck is rather weak. Net or webbing systems, or airbags, that catch the child are advantageous since they distribute the impact force over larger areas of the elastic and fragile body. Snyder proposes a "capsule" protection system (offering protection to side impacts also) for adults and children. Snyder's report on Human Impact Tolerance (1970a) and the one already mentioned (1970b) on restraint systems in land, air, and space vehicles given an excellent overview on the state-of-the-art and on future concepts and design directions. Related articles have frequently appeared in the proceedings of the Stapp Car Crash Conferences (Siegel, Nahum, and Appleby, 1968; Rogers and Silver, 1968; Severy et al., 1968). Injury protection of pregnant occupants is another serious problem (Snyder et al., 1966).

8.6.8 Reach Envelopes

The critical reach dimensions for automotive design purposes involve the forward reach areas around the steering wheel to the dashboard, from the sidewall across to the center of the vehicle. The introduction of shoulder restraint harness has created a significant new need for reach data, and the government safety regulatory activity has enforced this concern. With the heel reference point being at one extreme of the human body, and the fingers at the other extreme of the human link-joint system, the relation of the heel point to the sweep of the fingers (the reach envelope) is difficult to determine by a statistical combination of basic body dimension data. Therefore, it is understandable that for the development of special automotive design standards, current practice relies on Steps 10 through 13 (See Figure 8-2); that is, taking measurements on a sample of drivers seated in car mock-ups, using the Accelerator Heel Point (AHP) for reference. In an article describing such a study, Chaffee (1969) took pains to point out that the envelope of reach must represent a given percentile of *reach capability* of the sample population, not the reach capability of a mythical phantom such as the infamous 50th percentile man or woman, nor even of a "5th percentile man or woman."

To take advantage of normal (Gaussian) distribution concepts and thus simplify the statistical analysis, Chaffee advocated the selection of radial reach directions from a midpoint between the shoulders of the seated drivers, which he called the "ergosphere origin" (EO).

Reach data can be affected by the task to be performed at the reach end points. There is obvious value in setting up the experimental procedure to simulate actual tasks in automobile operation, taking into account different body positions brought about by various seats, their adjustments, and restraint harnesses. Chaffee implemented these concepts in a mock-up arrangement for reach measurement, not previously described in Chapter III. He used a 9 ft-square panel located in front of the subject at various distances and a similar set of positions to the side. The forward reach panels were cut out to clear the subject's legs. The subject's task consisted, using the left hand only, of positioning a 1 in. diameter knob as far out as possible along each of 15 numbered radial lines on the panel. Ergosphere origin points were then determined by a process of analysis of each radial plan trace. This resulted in a different EO for forward reach and sideward reach ergospheres. Figure 8-22 shows a rear view of the reach contours in a plane 22 in. behind the accelerator heel point.

Before and since Chaffee's study, several automobile manufacturers and research agencies have conducted (mostly unpublished) reach surveys using a variety of methods. In trying to evaluate and collate resulting data, one must consider not only the body dimensions (i.e., sample selection), but also seat design, seat positioning, body restraints, garments and equipment worn, and the reaching task itself. In the future, reach data could be computerized to facilitate analysis and applied to development of standard reach envelope gaging devices, similar to the H-point machine, but keyed to the package origin point.

8.6.9 Human and Cabin Dimensions

Selected anthropometric characteristics of the human body that have a crucial, direct bearing on certain dimensions of the interior of the automobile are summarized in Figure 8-23 and Table 8-5 (after McFarland, Damon, and Stoudt, 1955; Kirk, Edwards, and Hindle, 1964; Kroemer, 1966a). Typically, in some cases, large dimensions determine the design, while in other instances, the anthropometry of small persons proves to be crucial. Crossovers and interactions are frequent and confound the problem.

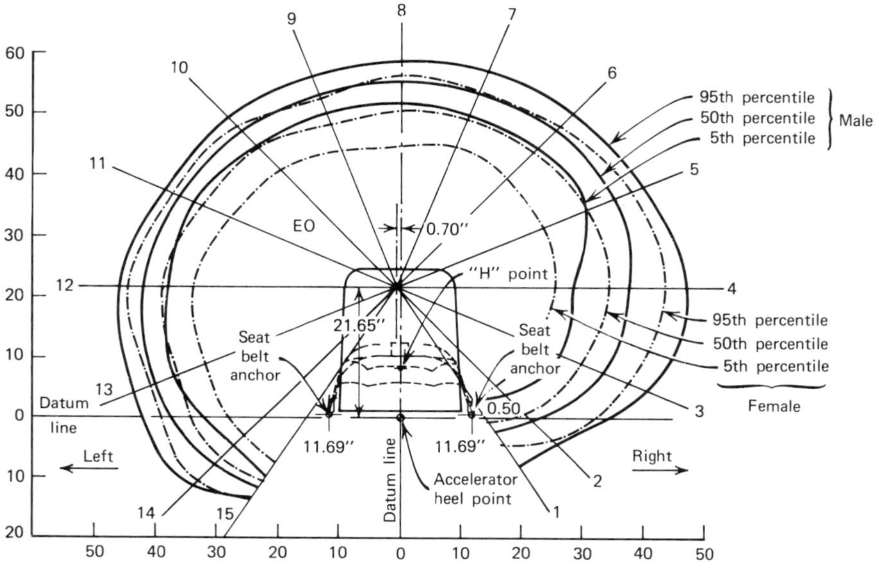

Figure 8-22. Reach contours (rear view) of males and females in a plane located 22 in. behind AHP. (from Chaffee, 1969.)

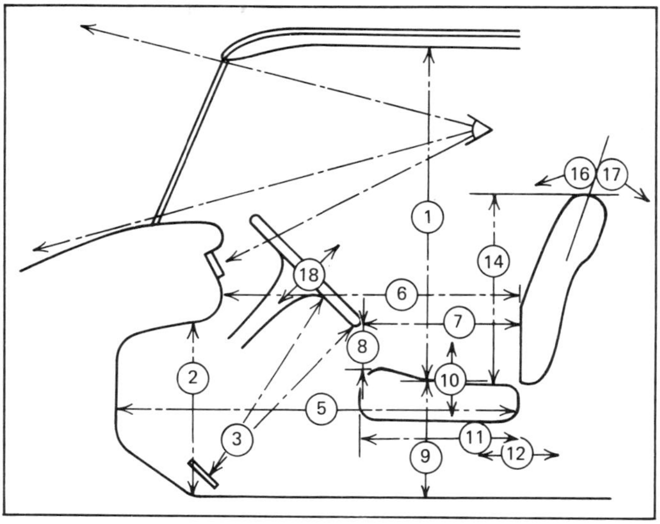

Figure 8-23. Crucial work space dimensions for automobiles (see Table 8-5 for further description) (Kroemer, 1966a). Used with permission of VDI-Verlag GmbH, Düsseldorf, Germany.

Table 8-5. Crucial Dimensions of the Cabin of Automobiles (Kroemer, 1966a)

No.	Design Dimension	Related Anthropometric Dimensions
1	Head clearance: must accommodate tall occupants possibly wearing hats or helmets	Sitting Height
2	Knee clearance: must accommodate long-legged occupants; dimensions also important in accidents	Patella Height, Crotch Height, Trochanterion Height
3	Pedal-steering wheel distance: must allow knee travel connected with rapid foot movements between pedals	
4	Width of space allotted to occupant (not shown): must accommodate big occupant wearing thick garments	Shoulder Breadth, Elbow Breadth, Hip Breadth
5	Depth of leg room: should allow stretching of legs	Buttock-Foot Length, Trochanterion Height
6	Distance to hand-operated controls on the board or near the steering wheel: must be within easy access of small, restrained occupants.	Hand Reach
6a	Distance to pedals (not shown): must accommodate short-legged occupants	Trochanterion Height
7	Clearance, seat back—rim of steering wheel: must accommodate heavy occupants wearing thick garments	Waist Circumference, Weight/Height ratio
8	Clearance seat pan—rim of steering wheel: must accommodate thick-thighed occupant wearing heavy garments (preferably adjustable)	Thigh Circumference, Thigh Height
9 and 10	Seat height: must accommodate *all* drivers, hence must be adjustable independently from seat distance adjustment (12)	Popliteal Height, leg, trunk and arm lengths; Reach; Eye Height
11	Seat depth: Must be "comfortable" for all occupants	Buttock-Knee Length
12	Seat distance adjustment: must accommodate all drivers, hence must be independent from seat height adjustment	Buttock-Foot Length, Patella Height, Trochanterion Height, Reach

Table 8-5 (*continued*)

No.	Design Dimension	Related Anthropometric Dimension
13	Breadth of seat (not shown): must accommodate broad and heavy occupants; must allow changes in sitting posture.	Hip Breadth, Buttock Circumference, Weight/Height ratio
14	Height of backrest above seat pan: determines (in combination with its contour) mobility of shoulders (arms) and head support.	Shoulder Height, Cervicale Height, Sitting Height
15	Breadth of back rest: determines support (see 14) and choice of body postures.	Shoulder Breadth
16 and 17	Seat back angle: must accommodate all occupants, hence adjustability (in small increments or continuously) is desirable	—

The dimensions shown in Figure 8-23 are generic rather than specific to a given work space layout. In an actual engineering work space layout, each type of dimension must be more precisely defined as to its *starting and ending point in space* or its orientation. All such dimensions and points must be related to each other in a consistent coordinate system rather than "floating" semiindependently as shown. Similarly, body dimensions need to be precisely related to either known envelopes of clearance or to joint centers and link dimensions derived from the listed exterior dimensions of the body. This philosophy of coordinated dimensioning, knowing *where*, as well as *how long*, is typical for engineering anthropometry in its concern with work space design, and different from the "anthropological," traditional anthropometry approaches.

8.6.10 Mathematical and Physical Analogs of the Human Body

Models of the human body (both three-dimensional articulated dummies and mathematical analogs) have begun to play an important role for automobile crash research affecting vehicle design, similar to their role in ejection seat evaluation and crash research for aircraft and spacecraft sciences. Such models represent the integument, the soft and hard tissues of the human body, and its biomechanical behavior in various force environments. The following discussion will be largely restricted to passive (external) models, to date of most interest in automobile engineering. One of the most important uses of biodynamic models in automobile engineering is in the design of force environments to obtain maximum protection and/or performance. Typical examples of mathematical models used in automobile crash research are those representing the body kinematics under the deceleration impulses and restraint forces, as acting on an automobile occupant in a collision (McHenry and Naab, 1966; McHenry, 1971). Figure 8-24 depicts such a restrained body mathematical model in a simulated automobile cabin. Such models will allow the evaluation of body movements likely to occur, of the points of impacting structures of the cabin, of the sequence of such impacts. If tolerance limits of the body parts are considered in the model, type and severity of resulting injuries can be assessed (Cichowsky, 1968). Using a mathematical model with varied parameters allows one to establish restraint systems, cabin configurations, and properties of construction materials which, in combination, reduce the seriousness of probability of injuries to the human occupant involved in an accident of the modeled type (Martinez, 1968; Thompson, 1968).

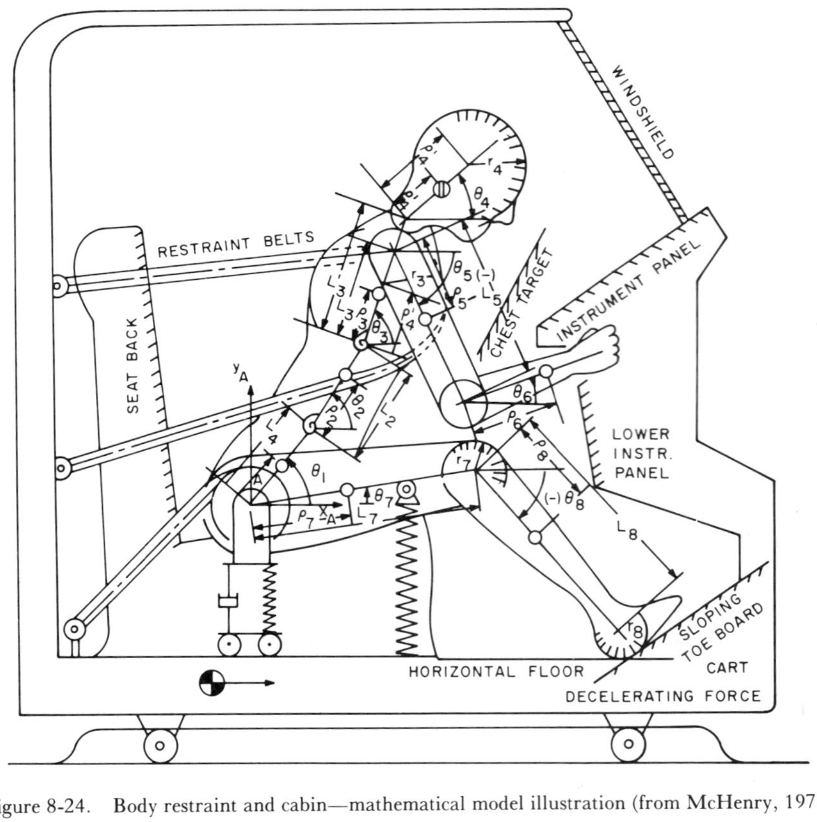

Figure 8-24. Body restraint and cabin—mathematical model illustration (from McHenry, 1971).

Clearly, the best physical analog of the human body is the human body itself. Hence, a number of heroic self-experiments have been conducted; among the best known are the impact experiments of J. G. Stapp at Holloman Air Force Base (NM) in the 1950s. Other experimenters have utilized human cadavers. Lange (1971) was able to show the movement and impact pattern of cadavers, and their injuries sustained, in simulated accidents with and without restraint harnessess, with steering wheels and seat designs of several types and arrangements, in frontal, oblique, and rear collisions. Yet, lack of muscle tonus in cadavers, as well as anthropometric variations, makes use of mechanical dummies necessary and desirable in verification of many designs and various types of mathematical modeling techniques.

Thus the literature on automotive crash injury research contains multiple examples of applications of mathematical models, cadavers, and anthropomorphic dummies. A typical cross section of applications is often contained in the annually published proceedings of the Stapp Car Crash Conferences (Society of Automotive Engineers, 1968, for example).

8.6.11 Steps 12 and 13. Adjustable Mockups

To solve complex reach, adjustment and comfort problems, an interesting combination of the mock-up concept and a remotely controllable and adjustable measuring device concept has been conceived by a major automobile manufacturer (*Machine Design*, 1970). The fixture can accommodate six persons with bench seats or five with front bucket seats and rear bench. The seats adjust horizontally and vertically, and platforms simulating a car's floorpan, toe board, and seat bases can be moved vertically and horizontally by electrically actuated screw jacks. Adjustable roof stringers simulate the roof clearance lines. Brake and accelerator pedals, toe board angle, and steering column are also adjustable. Key reference points are recorded onto a large readout board by means of a laser beam projection system. Additional studies using other ingenious approaches are being carried out in mock-ups to evaluate and to standardize requirements for automotive work space design, both by industry and by government funded contractors.

8.7 MARINE VEHICLE APPLICATIONS

To assure efficient and safe operations, work space design is also important to the design of marine vehicles. Although vehicle volume and weight do not have the same degree of criticality for surface ships as compared to spacecraft, for example, careful work space design for efficient operations is still mandatory in such areas as the command and control centers for large Navy ships, and the like.

Darcus and Weddell (1947) have studied naval weapon operator's seating.

However, descriptions of anthropometric applications specific to surface ship and underwater vessel operator work space design are difficult to find in the scientific/engineering literature. It appears that most of such applications utilize data and approaches previously developed for aircraft, automotive vehicles, or fixed base installations (Panel on Psychology and Physiology, 1949). The remainder is apparently based upon tradition or architectural standards. For this reason, the discussion of marine applications will be quite brief, more a suggestion as to what should be considered than what is done, and with few examples. The following text discusses two example applications.

8.7.1 Example 1—A Shipboard Electronics Station Operator's Chair

Figure 8-25 shows a seat specifically designed to help the operator accommodate to shipboard motion in heavy seas. As noted by the authors of the handbook from which this example was chosen (Woodson & Conover, 1970), the armrests and lower trunk supports resist side loads effectively. The armrests also pivot inward to act as a "thigh clamp," thus providing a seat that holds the operator in. The fully retracting armrest makes it simple for the operator to slide out of the seat. The swivel capability of these seats should have means for stopping and securing at least every 45° (also for resisting wave motion loads). "The fore-aft adjustment of the seat pan should also have fixed stopping positions. All adjustment handles should be placed where the operator can operate them while seated in the optimum position he has selected."

8.7.2 Example 2—Star III Submersible Work Space Design Considerations

It is in the undersea class of marine vehicles that the greatest engineering anthropometry effort is necessary. From the largest nuclear submarine to the smallest research submersible, space is at the premium, and its efficient use is a must.

The work space design of undersea vehicles is remarkably similar to that of aerospacecraft design, discussed in Section 8.3. Selected examples of these procedures are used below to illustrate the application of this process to the design of a current undersea vehicle: the General Dynamics Star III Underwater Research Submersible.

The Star III is a two-man research submersible with both crew stations contained within a 64 in. diameter sphere (Sroka and Hill, 1967). This confining work space requires careful anthropometric analysis in such areas as clearance envelopes for seating arrangements and viewport accessibility, functional reach envelope of the pilot to the necessary controls, and body working

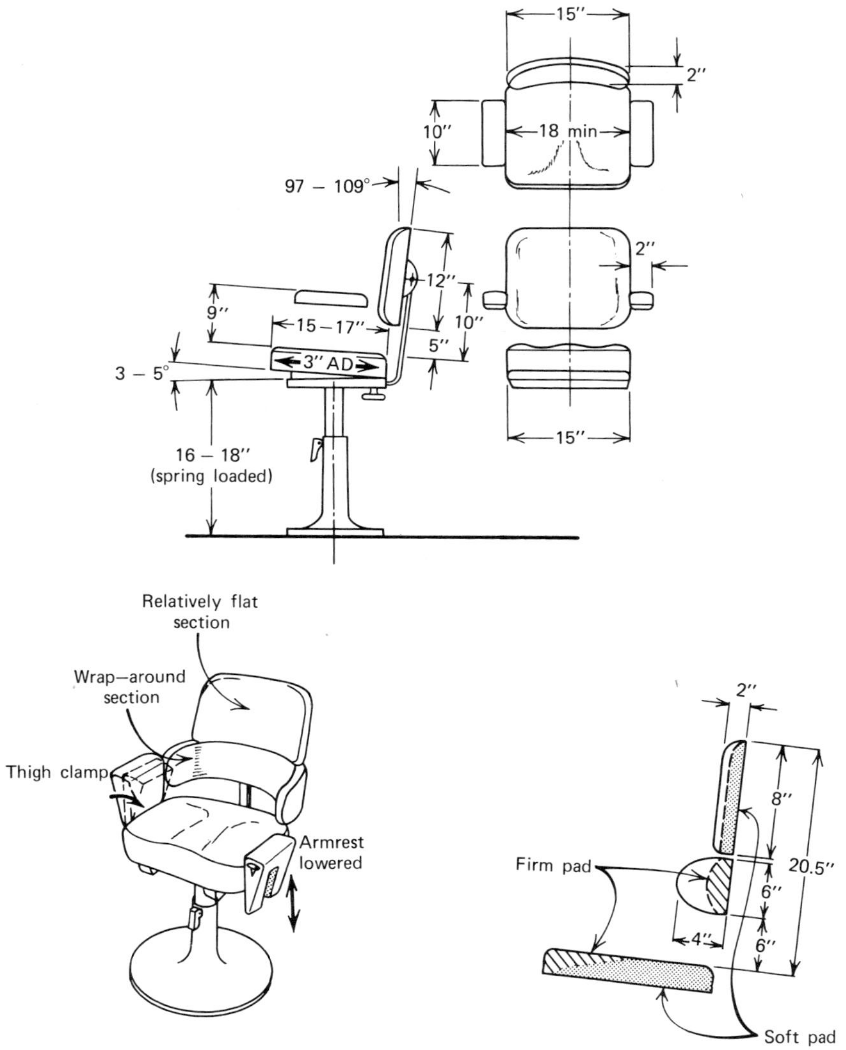

Figure 8-25. Marine vessel operator's chair. (Woodson and Conover, 1970.)

positions to ensure adequate visibility and viewing angles to the appropriate displays.

An example of the mock-up testing procedure with representative subjects, discussed in Section 8.3 (Step 13), is illustrated in Figure 8-26. The pilot can be seen checking his reach to the port control panel and the potential for blockage or interference by the observer.

Figure 8-26. Star III seating arrangement showing both pilot and observer, and pilot's reach. (Stroka and Hill, 1967. Illustration courtesy of General Dynamics Corporation.)

Examples of the anthropometric workspace design criteria (Step 14 in Section 8.3) resulting from this mockup test, are the following:

1. A clearance between the seats was found necessary to facilitate kneeling at the forward viewport for visual observation.
2. A folding observer's seat was desirable to provide more room in the sphere's interior and to increase the size of the above kneeling space.
3. The faces of the instruments in panels not directly in front of the pilot should be canted to minimize parallax.

These results are typical of the anthropometric design criteria that are generated from mock-up testing.

The mock-up testing also verified the results of the work space drawing analysis, Step 6. For example, some of the results were: (1) all display/control components for the trim and ballast system should be grouped in a location of prime viewability and accessibility to the pilot; (2) a wrap-around panel design was the most desirable; and (3) since the pilot is seated to one side of the centerline of the vehicle, the port panel should be canted at a greater angle than the starboard panel for optimum viewability.

8.8 OPERATOR WORK SPACE DESIGNS FOR STATIONARY INSTALLATIONS

In the following paragraphs, examples are given of engineering anthropometry applications to operator/occupant work space designs for nonvehicular work stations, such as offices, launch sites, checkout stands, manufacturing and assembly, and schools. Scientific investigations of such work stations, initiated by persons with engineering background, have led to a body of *industrial engineering* lore and work space design practice (Barnes, 1949) and an extensive literature. The principles previously set forth (Section 8.3 to 8.7) are again applicable with appropriate modifications. Emphasis in the examples is primarily within the context of "Step 6" described in Section 8.3.

As in other human engineering design areas, anthropometric data, although basic and of primary concern, do not suffice for the design of work places in shop or office. Biomechanical, orthopedic, physiological, and other ergonomical aspects must also be considered in a systems approach to arrive at suitable dimensions, as pointed out in the following discussion, abbreviated and adapted from Kroemer (1971a).

8.8.1 Design Philosophy for the Seated Operation Work Space

From foregoing discussions on vehicle work space, it should be obvious that mismatches between the operator and his equipment in an office, command/control station, factory, or home, can be avoided by "building the work place" around the sitting operator. As in vehicles, the task-regulated positions of the hands, arms, shoulders, and eyes determine body posture and specifically affect the usage and adjustment of the seat. Chair and work areas (desk, table, stand, workbench, etc.) must be *selected or designed as a unit,* the dimensions of one dependent on the others, and all dependent upon human variability. However, the static environment permits some freedom in selection of different sizes and designs for different-sized people, as well as providing adjustability for a wide range of requirements to meet the design goals.

Convenience of presentation dictates emphasis on each of the components separately. Following consideration of the seat, the corresponding work table and its reachable working surface area are discussed. Finally, sitting-standing operations are treated.

8.8.2 Body Dimensions, Sitting Posture and "Comfort" (Step 6.1)

Body positioning for factory and office work has received a great deal of attention because of the large percentage of time spent by many persons in such postures (Brookes and Kaplan, 1972). Many apparently subtle effects can be serious when applied continuously for many hours per day to the human body over a period of years. The positions for factory and office work may be significantly different from those used for vehicles. Anatomists, biomechanists, orthopedists, physiologists, artists, and psychologists have tried to evaluate the essentials of "good" posture for sitting. However, as in the story of the blind men feeling the elephant, they do not always concur, and their individual and collective findings often do not seem sufficient for establishing design standards for chairs.

Anthropometric approaches can contribute in two significant ways to the optimum solution of these seating design problems.

1. Prevention of grossly uncomfortable and badly proportioned seat designs that force the body into obviously "bad" postures (as agreed upon by even the above specialists).
2. Assurance that a selected range of reasonable postures can be attained by a large percentage of the users through incorporation of statistically correct adjustment ranges and through knowledge of body linkages and proportions, clothing considerations, and provisions for work movements.

"Comfort" is often one of the stated design goals; however, this may be difficult to define, except as the absence of "discomfort." The latter is operationally definable by a combination of observable effects on operator actions and work output, such as fidgeting, squirming, frequent getting up and walking about, complaints and, in the worst cases, refusal to use the chair, high rates of absenteeism, or actual illness. Ultimately, these are reflected in poor operator performance (errors, low output, etc.) and/or employee grievances that affect operating costs and efficiency of production. By properly fitting the seat to the body of the occupant, the anthropometric engineer can contribute significantly in a concrete manner toward reduction of the symptoms and economic penalties associated with discomfort. Further, he can supplement and assist in improvements by working with specialists from the other disciplines listed previously. Detail considerations of body posture are an integral part of the following discussion of ideal seat shapes and dimensions and the consequences resulting from design deficiencies.

8.8.3 The Seat Dimensions

The prototype of all seats used "on the job" in offices and shops is the secretary or typist chair. It is small to medium in size with an adjustable seat height, with a back rest, without arm rests, and relatively inexpensive. This commonly used chair allows, if properly designed, the nearest approach to the correct seat. Thus, this chair can serve as a model for the following discussion.

Figure 8-27 illustrates the principal parts, dimensions, and adjustments of the standard seat.

At some work places, the standard typist-type chair cannot be used. A large work area may require that the chair can be moved easily and quickly into a variety of locations. Figure 8-28 shows several highly mobile seats, none of which can be pushed over. Many of the design principles developed for standard chairs can be applied to these seats.

In repair shops, at assembly lines, and the like, simple stools, sometimes mounted on casters, are often used. Even boxes of different lengths, depths, and heights (e.g., 20 × 30 × 40 cm; 8 × 12 × 16 in.) may be useful, since they can be rotated to approximate the desired sitting height. Finally, there is a group of so-called props or "stand-seats" that support part of the body weight while the worker leans on them. Figure 8-29 shows two such props.

The Height of the Seat Surface

This is correct for many work stations if the sitting individual has his thighs horizontal when the lower legs are vertical and the feet are flat on the floor (or

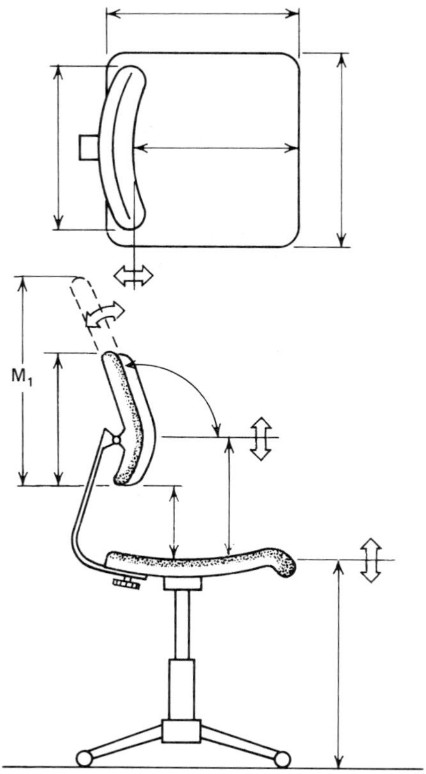

Figure 8-27. Principal parts, dimensions, and adjustments of standard secretary chair and modifications. Dimension M_1 indicates an extension for back support as discussed in the text (Kroemer, 1971a).

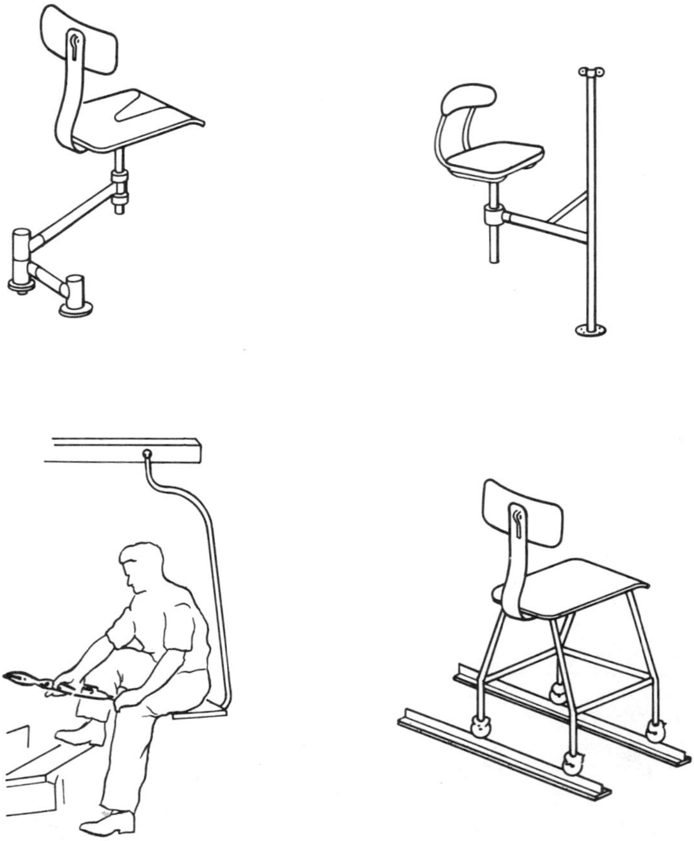

Figure 8-28. Mobile, nontipping seat design concepts (Kroemer, 1971a).

foot rest). Thus the height of the seat is slightly *less* than the distance from the floor to the underside of the thigh near the knee (popliteal area). As this distance (Popliteal Height or Seat Height) varies considerably among individuals, the seat must be adjustable so that each user can choose the proper height. Additions for shoe heel height (or lack) and clothing must be considered in selecting the design range. As in aircraft or automobiles, provisions for extended forward leg positions may require lowering the seat to clear the popliteal area. (See also the discussion on raised foot rests, to follow.) With the correct height, the person can sit fully on the entire seat surface; shifting the buttocks and flexing or extending the legs is facilitated.

Pressure from the front edge of the seat is distinctly uncomfortable because the soft undersides of the thighs are not adapted to sustain compression for any but short periods of time. If the seat is too high, such pressure is always present, even if the front ridge of the seat surface is well rounded or upholstered. To avoid thigh compression, people tend to sit on the front portion of a high seat. Although this leads to a desirable blunt angle between the thighs and the trunk, it also causes an unstable and fatiguing posture, requiring static contraction of muscles to be maintained.

Pressure on the underside of the thighs will certainly be eliminated if a low seat is used. When sitting on a chair that is too low, however, an acute angle between the thighs and the trunk is likely to occur, because many working positions require the operator to tilt his trunk forward over a bench, desk, and the like. This acute angle causes an unfavorable position of pelvis and spinal column, and also brings about pressure on the abdominal organs. Furthermore, tall, heavy, or elderly people often find it difficult to get up from low chairs.

Shape and Dimensions of the Seat Surface

In general, pronounced shaping of the seat surface limits the possible variations of the sitting posture. One of the most important features of a good chair seems to be that it permits changing the posture. When sitting for prolonged periods of time, even the most comfortable position becomes more and more uncomfortable and eventually unbearable. However, the "multiposture-principle" should not be applied uncritically. It can be quite comfortable to be held fairly securely by the chair in a very restricted range of postures.

To cause forward rotation of the pelvis, so as to attain a lordosis of the

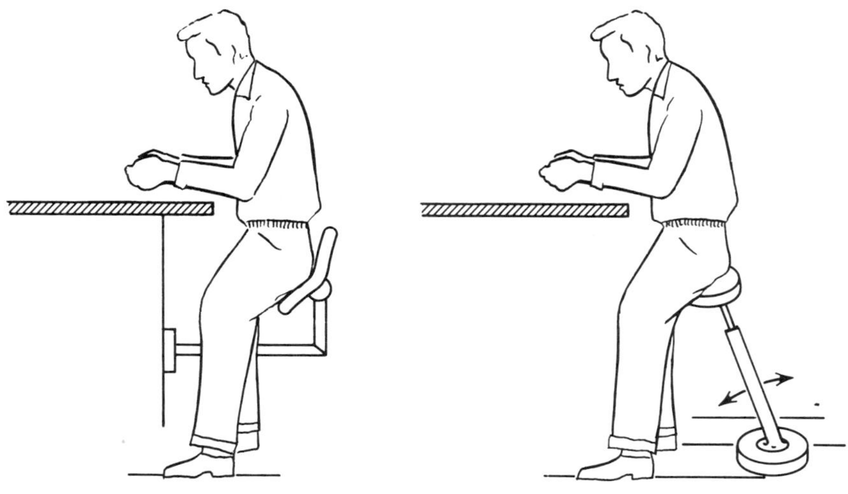

Figure 8-29. Props or "stand-seats" (Kroemer, 1971a).

lumbar spine (Figure 8-30), it has been suggested that the entire seat surface be tilted forward. Such a slope can tilt the pelvis, but can also cause the body to slide forward. Such sliding may be prevented by friction between the seat pan and the clothes of the occupant. However, the ensuing pull on the dress may be uncomfortable. The forward thrust can also be counterbalanced by action of the leg muscles. However, continuous muscle tension may become fatiguing.

Instead of tilting the total surface, it has been proposed to leave the front part of the seat about horizontal, but to elevate by about 30° the rear portion of the seat to tilt the pelvis forward. However, experiments showed that the elevation of the rear portion of the seat does not necessarily cause lordosis of the lumbar spine in healthy subjects. Even on seat pans inclined distinctly forward, no systematic relationships between pelvis position (seat tilt), and curvature of the upper spine were found.

A slight rearward slope of the entire seat surface has also been proposed. This declination is supposed to tilt the trunk toward the back rest and, at the same time, prevent forward slipping of the buttocks. However, if one does not lean against the back rest during work, a distinct rearward slope of the seat tends to rotate the pelvis backwards, causing kyphosis of the lumbar spine.

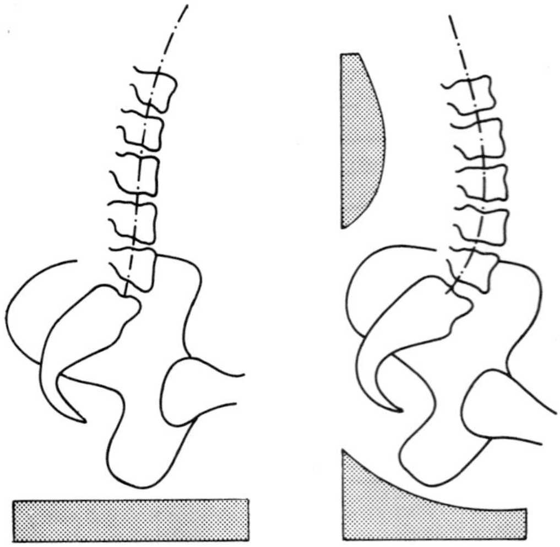

Figure 8-30. Lumbar spine orientations during sitting. The figure on the left indicates usual working posture. The posture on the right is considered more desirable by many ergomists. The curvature being concave toward the back (called "lordosis") is similar to that of the standing individual, and is dependent on the pelvic angle (Kroemer, 1971a).

Adjustability of the slope of the seat pan between 6° above and below horizontal is very desirable. Except for special purposes, any pronounced nonadjustable slopes of the seat surface (to the front or to the rear) are unsatisfactory because they enforce certain postures. If not adjustable, a generally horizontal seat, slightly concave in the center, appears to be most suitable. This concavity facilitates sitting in the center of the seat, prevents the buttocks from slipping off, and still permits various postures.

Upholstery for the seat is generally recommended. On a hard surface, the weight of the trunk is transmitted to the seat through small areas. This causes high local pressure, resulting in diminished blood flow, numbness, and even pain (Hertzberg, 1972). Upholstery enlarges the load-bearing area and consequently reduces pressure. A flat, stiff upholstery that gives way not more than 1 in. is recommended. Using such material, the pressure-loaded area is sufficiently enlarged, yet the posture may be altered easily. Seat cover materials must be carefully selected with respect to their reactions to pressure, temperature, perspiration, and other properties such as slipperiness and flame resistance.

Breadth and depths of the seat surface must be sufficient to accommodate large people and to facilitate changes of posture. This demand sets certain minimum requirements. Seat width is set by reference to the anthropometric dimensions Hip Breadth, Sitting or Thigh Breadth (measured at widest part of thighs while sitting). Provisions for a relaxed, spread position of the thighs adds further to the seat pan width. As a *minimum*, seat width should extend approximately 2 in. on each side beyond the center contact points of the ischial tuberosities for largest operators. As a result of thigh cross-sectional curvature, the seat pan total width may be reasonably 2 in. less than the Hip Breadth, but arm rests or side supports must clear these dimensions.

While the seat may be as wide as reasonable, the depth (front to back) of the seat must not be excessive. If the seat is too deep, an individual tends to sit only on the front part to avoid pressure on his thighs and calves. Consequently, he will not be able to lean against the back rest. This fore-aft seat depth dimension should be sized for the smallest practical individual in a population, such as the 1st or 5th percentile female, if only one chair is to be provided. Where many very large men are also involved, a separate, larger size, adequate for the 50th or 60th percentile and larger may be the answer. Another possibility is a concave shape to the front edge so that spreading the legs allows more support. The corresponding anthropometric measurement, Seat Length, is usually too long for design use, as it is measured along the aft surfaces of the legs. If the chair is hard and thick (vertical dimension of front edge) it contacts the lower leg near the bulge of the calf, thus approximately one inch should be subtracted to account for this contour.

The Back Rest

If at all possible, a chair should have a well-designed back rest even if it is used only occasionally to relax during a break. The back rest should either have an opening or recede just above the seat surface so that the sacrum can be pushed back and lumbar contact made.

If free mobility of the shoulders and arms is necessary, only the lower part of the back below the scapula can contact the back rest. A lumbar back support can be provided by a small back rest (see Figure 8-27). When leaning against such a back rest, support is given at the lumbar spine. Such a forward thrust can also be provided with a full-sized back rest (also indicated in Figure 8-27 as dimension M_1). For support at the lumbar region, the rest may protrude anteriorly at the lumbosacral junction. Such a fullsize back rest gives the desired lumbar support if leaned against only slightly. During breaks, however, one can lean back completely and relax comfortably.

The Arm Rests

If free mobility of the trunk, shoulders, and arms is required, arm rests can be hindering. Arm rests, if feasible, may be used for propping the arms for a while, decreasing the load on the spinal column. For delicate assembly or adjusting tasks, the elbows or lower arms can be supported by individually adjusted arm rests to stabilize the hands. Arm rests are also helpful in changing position or an aid in getting up from the chair. Often, however, and especially in the office, arm rests are primarily a status symbol.

The anthropometric measurement, Arm Rest Height, is independently distributed ($r \approx 0$) as regards Sitting Height or Shoulder Height, Sitting. Adjustment is made either by inward/outward and fore-aft positioning of the upper arm, to shorten the vertical distance between shoulder and elbow, or by elevating the shoulders. Therefore, the arm rest should be set 1 to 2 in. (2.5 to 5 cm) *above* the mean anthropometric measurement for fitting most persons.

The Foot Rest

A foot rest helps to compensate for a seat pan that is too high for the occupant and thus may be considered a part of the seat or "body support system." Foot rests with very small surfaces are undesirable, since relaxing changes in foot and leg position are hindered. Horizontal rods, attached to table or seat, are unsatisfactory, for they generally require continuous muscle tension to keep the foot on the bar.

Ideally, the surface should be as large as the floor area upon which the sitting person could possibly place his feet. The surface of the foot rest may be inclined up to 30° in front of the sitting person, providing support for the feet so

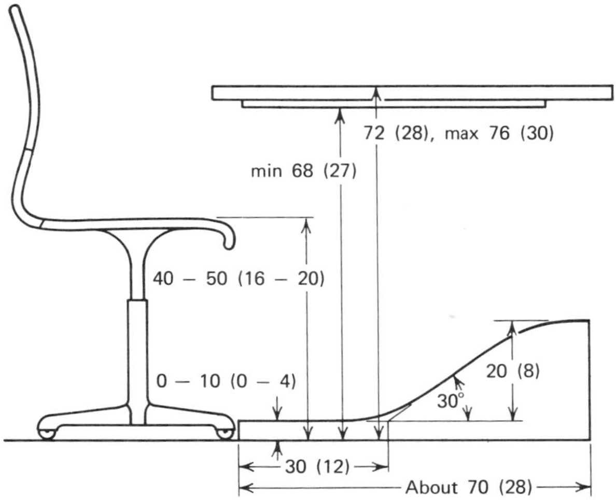

Figure 8-31. Recommended seat, table, and foot rest relationships. Dimensions in parentheses are in inches, others are in centimeters (Kroemer, 1971a).

that even with the "legs stretched out," the front edge of the seat does not cut into the underside of the thighs. The foot rest in Figure 8-31 has a raised platform supporting the heels when the legs are fully extended.

Summary of Seat Design Applications

Surveys of the literature (Grandjean, 1969b; Kroemer, 1971a; Kroemer and Robinette, 1968) showed that most recommendations for the design of the standard seat are in fairly good agreement, since they are generally based on the body dimensions of the user population. The existing differences fall within the range of adjustability. Avoidance of extreme design features (except for special purposes), and provision of adjustability are considered overriding principles. Table 8-6 is an example of recommended dimensions for standard work seats, for adult American and European populations (Step 14). Of course, dimensions will vary for children and youth (Oxford, 1969).

8.8.4 Manual Work Area and Leg Room

Of obvious economic interest is the area where the work gets done: the assembly station, machine stand, console, or desk. Each type of situation has peculiar dimensional requirements for operational efficiency, some of which are discussed in the following paragraphs.

Table 8-6. Recommended Dimensions in Centimeters (and Inches) and Shape of Standard Work Seats

Seat pan	
Height:	Adjustable between 40 and 50 cm (16–20 in.) above floor or foot rest
Width:	Approximately 40 cm (16 in.)
Depth:	Approximately 40 cm (16 in.)
Slope:	Adjustable ±6° about horizontal
Shape:	Essentially plane, only slightly concave [less than 2 cm (0.8 in.) in the center part.] No hard or sharp edges, front edge rounded with a radius of at least 2.5 cm (1 in.). Upholstered stiffly, giving not more than 2.5 cm (1 in.).
Back rest	
Small back rest (lumbar support only)	Approximately 32 × 18 cm (13 × 7 in.), slightly concave toward the sitting person in the top view, slightly convex in the side view. Tiltable ± 15° against vertical about a horizontal axis. Adjustable forth and back between 35 and 42 cm (14–17 in.) from the front edge of the seat pan, and in height so that the lower edge can be between 8 and 15 cm (3–8 in.) above the seat. Attached to seat pan with stiff spring. Edges well rounded. Stiffly upholstered.
Full-size back rest	Up to 12 cm (4 in.) over seat pan open or recessed. At least 38 cm (15 in.) wide, slightly concave towards the sitting person in the top view. In the side view, slightly convex so that the most forward protruding part (the "lumbar pad") is 18 to 20 cm (7–8) above the seat pan. Above the pad, rest may raise up to shoulder height, 50 to 60 cm (20–24 in.) over the seat, 15 to 30° declined behind vertical. Edges well rounded. Stiffly upholstered.

Leg Room

A large amount of volume is devoted to providing clearance for the human legs, again often nonproductive except where foot operated controls are used (such controls should be designed using principles described in Chapter X).

The 95th percentile Hip Breadth, Sitting is a reasonable criterion for *minimum* width of the open leg room, as it permits some natural separation between inner thighs for the larger persons. For the U.S. civilian population 1960–1962 this was 15.9 in. or 40.4 cm (Damon, Stoudt, and McFarland, 1966). A width of 25 in. is recommended (Woodson and Conover, 1970) to accommodate a higher percentile and to permit freedom of lateral movement and rotation of the femur. The minimum depth should accommodate insertion of the knees of a 95th percentile abdomen-knee length (or larger) so that the abdomen may be in contact with the desk/bench front: such a dimension practically never appears in survey data. To estimate this dimension, one may subtract Chest Depth (selected in preference to Standing Abdomen Depth to partially compensate for increase of abdomen depth in sitting position) from Buttock-Knee Length. For the U.S. civilian population, mean Buttock-Knee Length is 23.3 inches (Damon, Stoudt, and McFarland, 1966), but Abdominal Depth is not given. Using the principle of similarity, one may use a large male population such as the U.S. Air Force Flying Personnel in 1950 (Hertzberg, Daniels, and Churchill, 1954) which averages 9.0 in. (22.9 cm). The calculation described in Chapter V and VII is as shown below, using the coefficient of correlation shown in Appendix B ($r = .384$)

$$M_{(1-2)} = 23.3\text{–}9.0 = 14.3 \text{ in. } (36.3 \text{ cm}), \text{ mean difference} \qquad \text{(Eq. 8.5)}$$

$$\begin{aligned} S^2_{(1-2)} &= S_1^2 + S_2^2 - 2rS_1S_2, \text{ variance of difference} \qquad \text{(Eq. 8.6)} \\ &= (1.06)^2 + (.75)^2 - 2(.384)(1.06)(.75)^* \\ &= 1.124 + .563 - .61 \\ &= 1.075 \text{ in.}^2 \\ S_{(1-2)} &= 1.037 \text{ in. } (2.63 \text{ cm}) \text{ standard deviation of difference} \\ \text{95th percentile} &= M_{(1-2)} + 1.645 S_{(1-2)} \qquad \text{(Eq. 8.7)} \\ &= 14.3 + 1.645(1.037) \text{ in.} \\ &= 14.3 + 1.7 = \underline{16.0} \text{ (to nearest tenth inch)} \\ &\qquad\qquad\quad = (40.6 \text{ cm}) \end{aligned}$$

This dimension is measured from the drawer knob or whatever other obstruction or projection may be touched by the abdomen at the front of the desk or bench. In many operations, a clear distance for the abdomen is desired or a leaning forward position pushes the buttocks back, so that a shallower recess is permissible.

A recommended minimum leg room depth of 18 in. is found in some handbooks (Woodson and Conover, 1970). This permits some torso slump, assures clearance space in front of the knee and allows 90° knee angle if there is relief at the bottom of the desk (usually 4 in. high) to permit foot forward extension of 6 to 8 in. A more generous open leg room is certainly desirable, to permit forward movement of the lower legs. Leg/shin clearance envelopes may be developed by methods described in Section 8.5.

The foregoing width and depth dimensions generally can be met easily. It is much more difficult to establish and meet the height requirements for the leg room, which are discussed in following paragraphs.

* Standard deviations obtained from same references as means noted above.

Height Dimensions of Office Equipment

In the office, the work area of the hands is at, or very little above, desk height. Thus the surface of a desk should correspond to the elbow height. In deriving this measure, one has to take into account some slumping of the trunk and shoulders as well as the great variability among body dimensions of men and women. A range of 72 to 76 cm (28 to 30 in.) for the desk surface height should accommodate practically everybody.

Desks as low as 69 cm (27 in.) generally do not pose a problem even for persons with long legs, provided that the thickness of the desk or table top is not excessive. For smaller people, especially for many women, desks and tables with 30 in. tops are rather high. To compensate, shorter persons tend to sit on chairs adjusted too high for their legs. Then the legs dangle, and/or the person cannot lean against the back rest. Appropriate foot rests help to improve this undesirable condition.

Typists, teletypists, or operators of desk calculators, card punches, or computer keysets have to keep their hands at the keyboard to direct their eyes at the text or copy, and often must operate a switch with a foot. The operator's trunk should be effortlessly upright. The upper arms should hang down vertically. The forearms and the palms of the hands should be about horizontal.

Undesirable body postures of keyboard operators are often caused by the location of the text to be copied, and by the large vertical distance between the underside of table, stand, or console and the keyboard surface. With this distance often being 4 in. or more, the operator simply cannot achieve a correct posture. (Anthropometrically, the elbow is only between 1 and 2 in. above the level of the thighs, with the thighs and forearms horizontal, the elbow angle 90°, and the trunk erect). Hence, the elevation of the keyboard over the table top should be reduced and the table top kept as thin as possible. Adjustability of the height of the keyboard between about 64 and 76 cm (25 and 30 in.) above the floor would greatly improve working conditions.

The seated worker's needs for minimum vertical legroom can be estimated from the 95th percentile knee height of a representative U.S. population (23.4 in. plus 1 in. for shoe heel height = 24.4 in.). Thus, the top surface of a desk, table, bench or machine stand cannot be less than approximately 64 cm (25 in.) if it must accomodate a male seated operator with lower leg vertical.

Height Dimensions of Assembly Stations and Machine Stands

Recommended dimensions for the open leg room (height, depth, and width) are illustrated in Figure 8-32 and summarized in Table 8-7 for adult American and European populations. This table also contains minimum dimensions that must at least be met. It should be kept in mind that such minimal leg rooms are quite uncomfortable and should be avoided.

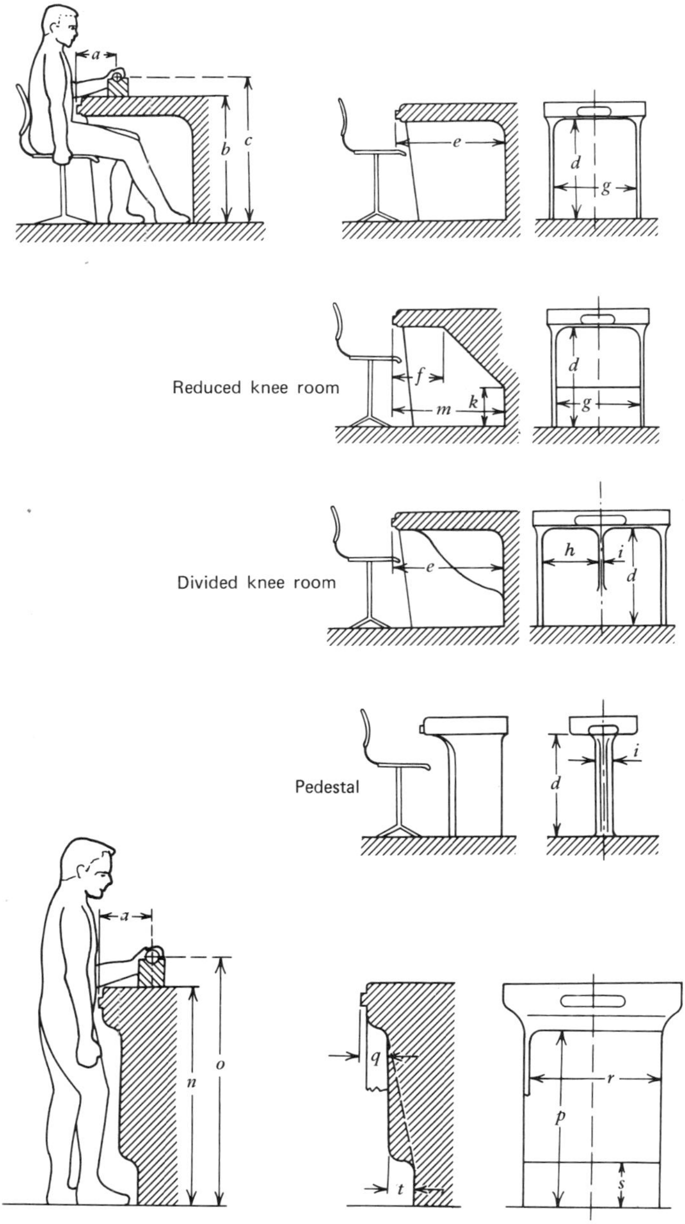

Figure 8-32. Leg room dimension diagram for sitting and standing operator. See Table 8-7 for recommended dimensions for American-European populations (Kroemer, 1971a).

Table 8-7. Dimensions in Centimeters (and Inches) of Industrial Work Places for Sitting or Standing Operators[a]

	Sitting Operator		Standing Operator	
		Outside Dimensions (see Figure 8-32)		
a	15–30 (6–12)	a	15–30 (6–12)	Horizontal distance of work area from front edge
b^b	65^b (25^b)	n	approx 90 (35)	Height of top surface
c	65–100 (25–40)	o	90–140 (35–55)	Height of work area
		Leg Room		
d	75 (30); 60^b (24^b)	p	80 (32)	Height
e	65 (25) if limited	q	10 (4)	Depth
f^b	30^b (12^b) if "e" impossible	—	NA	Minimum depth
g	65 (25); 40^b (15^b) if limited	r	65 (25)	Width
h^c	30 (12); 20^b (8^b) with divider	—	NA	Width with divider
i^c	2.5 (1); at front edge	—	NA	Maximum breadth of divider or pedestal
i^c	7.5 (3); 12.5 (5) from front edge	—	NA	Maximum breadth of divider or pedestal
i^c	15 (6); 25 (10) from front edge	—	NA	Maximum breadth of divider or pedestal
		Foot Room		
k	25 (10)	s	20 (8)	Height
m	65 (25)	t	12.5 (5)	Depth
g	65 (25); 40^b (15^b) if limited	r	65 (25)	Width (same as leg room)
h^c	30 (12); 20^b (8^b) with divider	—	NA	Width with divider (same as leg room)

[a] For alternate sitting and standing, use all appropriate dimensions with the exception of b and c.
[b] Minimum requirement. If it cannot be met, work place must be designed for standing operator.
[c] Avoid divider or pedestal.

Table 8-7 also contains some recommended dimensions for work places at which work must be performed by a standing operator (American–European populations). To facilitate standing close to the front edge of the work surface, the front side of the work stations should be recessed under the work surface to provide some room for his legs and feet. Figure 8-32 also illustrates desirable dimensions of the knee and foot room for the standing operator.

Alternate sitting or standing is required at some work stations. In designing such a work place, the height of the work surface and the knee and foot room appropriate for standing operation should be considered first. Then, the leg room necessary for the sitting operator is superimposed, with the bottom surface of the leg room for the sitting operator about 40 cm (15–16 in.) above the floor on which the operator stands. Accordingly, the height of a seat to be used at such a work station should be adjustable between about 75 and 90 cm (30 and 35 in.).

In some situations one may be given a fixed height countertop or table and need to select a seat adjustment and foot rest adjustment to match. Data on Thigh Clearance Height then are needed to assume clearance. Such data for several populations appear in recent handbooks (Damon, Stoudt, and McFarland, 1966, for example). An adjustment range must be so selected that it accommodates predetermined percentiles of the user population.

Reachable Areas for Factory Assembly Operations Work Space

Manual assembly workbench, tray, and tool arrangements have long been an area of interest to industrial engineering. General procedures previously described for work space design are, of course, readily applicable to these cases, with provision that special attention be paid to specific populations and environments.

For example, the reach envelope concept can be applied to determine the reachable area on horizontal work surfaces and above them for optimum location of trays and bins, tools and gages. Typical reachable areas are commonly presented in human engineering handbooks (Morgan, Cook Chapanis, and Lund 1963; Woodson and Conover, 1964; Damon, Stoudt, and McFarland, 1966). Earlier texts (Barnes, 1949) have indicated the optimum work surface on a table is closely approximated by two overlapping semicircles (one for each arm).

This conclusion was based on a study of 30 subjects (Asa, 1942). Later, Squires (1959) concluded that description of such optimal work area limits should more correctly be described as prolate epicycloids, due to the biomechanical restrictions of the arm. In any special case, mock-up studies are recommended to determine comfortable and maximum reachable areas within actual work space constraints, for the actual population of workers under consideration, and the actual tools, forces, orientations, lighting, and the like to be used.

Dimensions of Consoles

Console operators generally monitor displays on the consoles and/or events happening elsewhere within the viewing range, and operate controls located on the console. Visual observation as well as control activation will be facilitated by proper design of the console. Main design principles for consoles are: locate the displays within the normal viewing range; locate the controls within the natural reach envelope; allow the operator a body posture enabling him to perform his tasks over long periods of time without undue fatigue. Consequently, the location of the operator's eyes determines the position of the displays; the locations of the shoulder, elbow, and hand (and, in some cases, of the foot) determine the positioning of the controls. Thus, anthropometric characteristics of the human body are basic design parameters.

Table 8-8 and Figure 8-33 contain dimensions developed from mock-up studies to define standardized consoles (Kennedy and Bates, 1965). By combining two

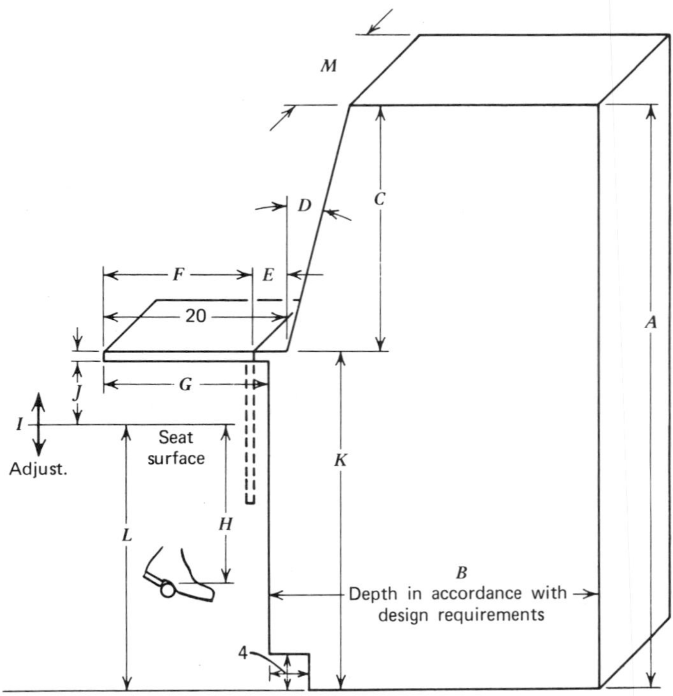

Figure 8-33. Console dimension diagram. See Table 8-8 for recommended dimensions.

Table 8-8. Dimensions (in Inches) for Standard Consoles (After Kennedy and Bates, 1965)

	Maximum Console Height from Standing Surface	Console Depth	Vertical Dimension of Panel Including Sills	Console Panel Angle—from Vertical	Minimum Pencil-Shelf Depth	Minimum Writing Surface Depth—Including Pencil Shelf	Minimum Knee Clearance	Foot Support to Seat	Seat Adjustability	Minimum Thigh Clearance at Midpoint of "I"	Writing Surface Height from Standing Surface	Seat Height at Midpoint of "I"	Maximum Console Panel Breadth
Type of Console	A	B	C	D	E	F	G	H	I	J	K	L	M
1. Sit-stand	62.0	Opt.	26	15[a]	4	16	18	18	4	6.5	36.0	28.5	36
2. Sit (with vision over top)	47.5[a] to 58.0	Opt.	22	15[a]	4	16	18	18	4	6.5	25.5 to 36.0	18.0 to 28.5	36
3. Sit (without vision over top)	51.5[b] to 62.0	Opt.	26	15[a]	4	16	18	18	4	6.5	25.5 to 36.0	18.0 to 28.5	36
4. Stand (with vision over top)	62.0	Opt.	26	15[a]	4	16	—	—	—	—	36.0	—	36
5. Stand (without vision over top)	72.0	Opt.	36	15[a]	4	16	—	—	—	—	36.0	—	36

[a] "A" must never be more than 29.5 in. greater than "L."
[b] "A" must never be more than 33.5 in. greater than "L."

of five standard components, five different consoles can be built that allow:

alternately sitting or standing;
sitting with vision over the top;
sitting without vision over the top;
standing with vision over the top; and
standing without vision over the top.

Each of these consoles accommodates about 95% of the male and about 60% of the female U.S. population with respect to body size as well as to visual and reach capabilities.

8.8.5 Architectural Fixtures

The foregoing office equipment items may be considered special cases of architectural fixtures or features, which have a wide range of involvement with anthropometric aspects. Other examples are: doorways, stairs, windows, counters, sinks, ceilings (height), light switches and fixtures, shelves, cabinets, doors, closets, fireplaces, beds, sofas, and other furniture of a variable degree of portability (Schroeder, 1951). Among those more intimately related to the human anatomy are bathroom fixtures, a subject worthy of a whole book in itself (e.g., Kira, 1966). As with vehicles, there are handbooks and standards for the building industry, applicable in various degrees of criticality to individual population design requirements (Freese, 1934; Ramsey and Sleeper, 1941). The principles contained in this chapter and Chapter X are generally applicable to such situations.

8.9 MAINTENANCE WORK SPACE APPLICATIONS

Engineering anthropometry applications to maintenance work space and equipment design cover a wide range, from thumbscrew torques to volume requirements for unusual working positions. In this text, discussion of considerations involving tool design (for operation, assembly, or maintenance) are presented in Chapter X. Herein, the grosser body positioning, reach, and clearance aspects are considered. The discussion concentrates on work space analysis, clothing effects, and the need for and techniques used in supporting mock-up tests and experiments.

8.9.1 Preparation of Working Position Drawings

In contrast to many of the foregoing work space situations, nearly all maintenance activities require more varied and less carefully controlled body positioning. Thus the processes of determining work space requirements are less straightforward than for cockpits or driving positions in vehicles. Developments of body position descriptions are based on more empirical approaches.

Many standard body positions can be hypothesized, of course, or selected from observation of typical activities. These body positions can then be assumed by a representative group of subjects and anthropometric measurements made to the various extreme limits and landmarks from selected reference planes. Examples of such measurements are shown in Figure 8-34. Similar studies

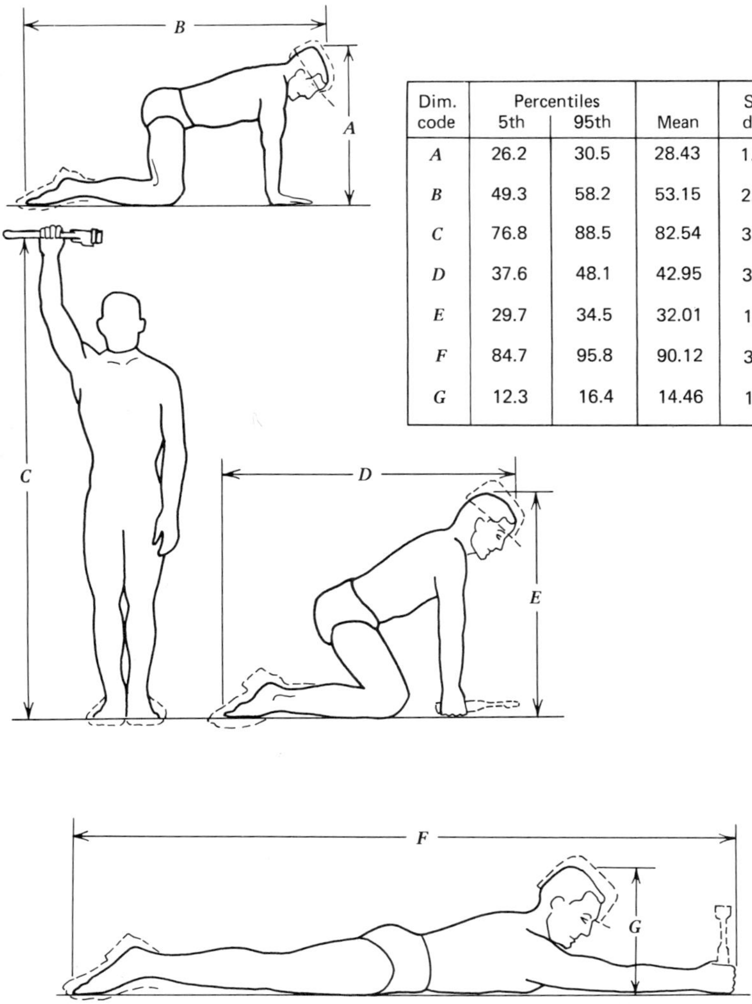

Dim. code	Percentiles 5th	95th	Mean	Std. dev.
A	26.2	30.5	28.43	1.30
B	49.3	58.2	53.15	2.61
C	76.8	88.5	82.54	3.33
D	37.6	48.1	42.95	3.26
E	29.7	34.5	32.01	1.57
F	84.7	95.8	90.12	3.41
G	12.3	16.4	14.46	1.28

Figure 8-34. Dimensions of common maintenance working positions. Key anthropometric dimensions for Air Force personnel are shown for each position. (After Hertzberg, Emanuel, and Alexander, 1956.) Tabulated dimensions in inches.

have been performed by Alexander and Clauser (1965). Forces exertable by persons in various working positions have been reported by Kroemer (1969b) and Kroemer and Robinson (1971). There is no guarantee that the maintenance personnel will actually utilize such positions, but the studies indicate that there is at least one credible position to accomplish the work.

8.9.2 Mock-up Development Procedures

The adequacy of a work space design, or the work space requirements, can be determined by proceeding to Steps 9 through 13: planning, setting up a mock-up of the task area and performing activities like those of the planned task. To obtain a three-dimensional record of the volume required, several of the contour measurement methods described in Chapters II or III may be employed. Examples are the multiple rod method, and the use of multiple planes of cardboard or foam core, cut out to provide sufficient clear space to work.

Direct development of such envelopes can be obtained by an "outside-in" approximation approach. One such approach involves setting up a series of small plates (preferably transparent plastic sheet material) on ball joint fittings at the end of rods, which are adjustable as to length and orientation. The plates are arranged around the work volume with all rods pointing away from it. As the subject simulates maintenance work, the rods are withdrawn as necessary to permit him the needed or desired working space, or pushed in to "fill up" the space not needed. Kama's report (1965) provides an example of an ingenious arrangement of wood plates, adjustable so as to form sides of a box around the work area.

Many removal, replacement, and adjustment activities involve reaching through an opening to a specified distance, using one or two hands. A simple mock-up device with rods or plates horizontally and vertically adjustable to form various sized openings can be used to mock-up the opening size. A tape measure or an extension rod with marked scales can be used to measure reach distance. Kennedy and Filler (1966) used such a device to obtain data on limits for vision to work area and for arm access for subjects in shirtsleeves and in full pressure suits.

Many occasions arise involving manual removal or replacement or tool operation involving one component within a group of components that are relatively closely spaced. This problem has been studied using the photographic record technique previously suggested for use in whole body maintenance space studies (Baker, McKendry, and Grant, 1960a, 1960b; McKendry et al., 1960). Since the studies used only two cameras whose axes were at right angles to each other and to an axis of the part or tool, it is uncertain what the true cross sections of the hand work space would be. However, the data can be expressed as a set of rectangular cross sections in various plane stations at increasing incremental distances from a point on the

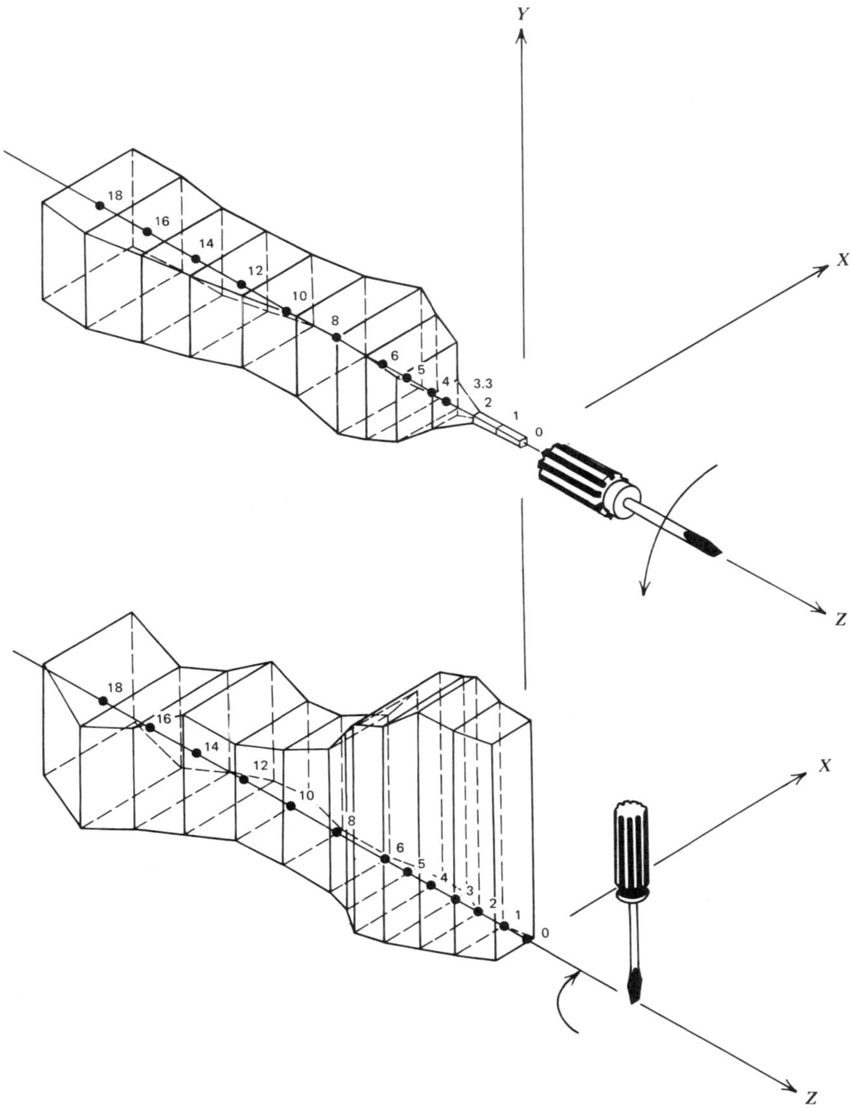

Figure 8-35. Typical results of hand work volume studies. (From Altman, Marchese and Marchiando, 1961.) Upper: Swept volume for screwdriver, used on screw in the vertical plane. Lower: Swept volume for screwdriver, used on screw in the horizontal plane.

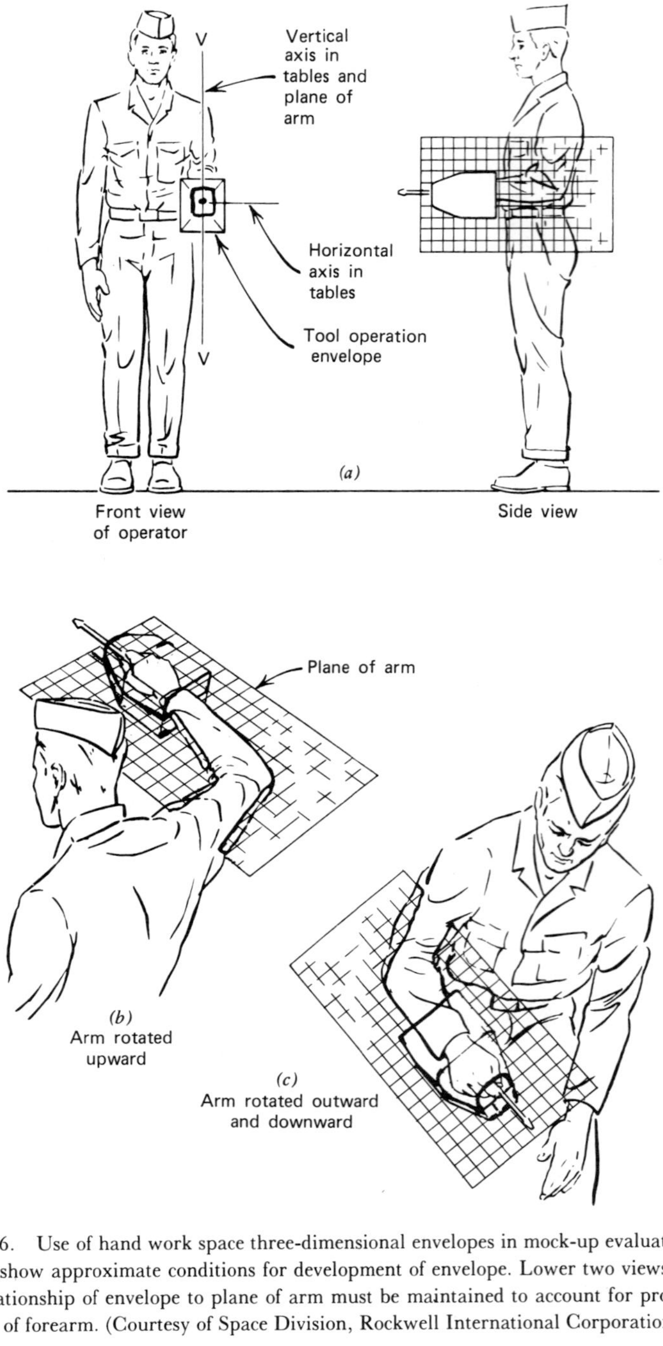

Figure 8-36. Use of hand work space three-dimensional envelopes in mock-up evaluation. Upper two views show approximate conditions for development of envelope. Lower two views show how correct relationship of envelope to plane of arm must be maintained to account for pronation and supination of forearm. (Courtesy of Space Division, Rockwell International Corporation.)

hand such as the extreme tip of a finger. Figure 8-35 illustrates such an envelope. Roebuck has constructed some of these conceptual envelopes as physical, three-dimensional forms using glass fiber, impregnated with a resin plastic (example of Step 11). Figure 8-36 indicates how such envelopes must be properly oriented in space with respect to the operator's arm, during mock-up evaluations.

8.9.3 Clothing Effects

Maintenance may have to be performed under unusual and extreme weather conditions or unusual environments, requiring anthropometric concerns related to the introduction of thick clothing layers of clothing, such as arctic suits or space suits. Altman, Marchese, and Marchiando (1961) provide typical data.

IX
CLOTHING DESIGN APPLICATIONS

9.1 INTRODUCTION

This chapter describes selected engineering anthropometry applications unique to "engineered clothing" and related protective and convenience garments and devices. Typical examples are weather-protective clothing, flame- and heat-protective garments (as for firemen or furnace operators), fuel handler suits, anti-G suits, pressure suits, ear muffs and helmets for noise protection, crash helmets, face masks, boots and gloves, body armor, strength amplifiers, prostheses, and personal communication devices.

Whereas the foregoing chapter on work space design was concerned with the exterior shape of clothing worn by operators and occupants and its effect on shape and size of the work space, this chapter is primarily concerned with internal shape of clothing. Secondary concern is also given to how the work space affects the outer shape and mobility needs of the garment. Following a general discussion of typical concerns, specific examples are presented, in which pressure suits are used as the model to illustrate the anthropometric procedures and techniques used in clothing design, development, and evaluation. Additional examples provide insight to other unique differences.

9.2 CLOTHING DESIGN APPROACH

The critical role of engineering anthropometry in clothing design has been surveyed and the rather limited quantity of pertinent literature has been reviewed by Staples (1966), whose report is highly recommended for additional reading. Garments and equipment that have to serve such special purposes, and often must fit selected population groups closely, are generally developed with careful consideration given to the anthropometry and biomechanics of the user.

Clothing design differs significantly from work space design in a number of ways. One difference is that in many cases the materials used are *flexible or pliable* to a high degree, and thus are less susceptible to standard engineering design drawing practice. They must be developed on body forms, or by experience and fit tests on the wearers. However, in most "engineered" clothing, a significant number of hardware devices and rigid forms are used, for which standard engineering practices are appropriate.

Applications of human strength data, although appropriate in the broad sense to design of certain suit components such as helmet latches, zippers, glove locks, and mobility joint design, are not included in the discussion of chapter IX. Such concepts are covered in Chapter X of this text.

In contrast to the breadths, depths, lengths, and angular movement ranges needed for work space design, clothing design applications typically require a multiplicity of circumferential dimensions. An even more specialized dimensional concept for clothing was investigated in an interesting and unusual study by Iberall (1964): he mapped those lines on the human skin that do not stretch during body motion. These lines of nonextension were used to fit a pressure suit allowing high mobility.

A major difference in approach involves the concept of *sizes*. Instead of one "vehicle" with sufficient adjustments to accommodate a high percentage of the population, it is generally necessary to provide a set of differing sizes, each having a more limited set of adjustments, if required, but each designed to accommodate a much smaller percentage of the basic population. The selection of the number of sizes is a major focus of attention, to balance functional requirements with the economics of development patterns and of stocking in stores and supply depots.

Development of street clothing in ready-to-wear sizes has been fairly successful as a result of trial and error rather than of a logical program of measurement, statistical analysis, and application (Staples, 1966). This has been satisfactory for two reasons. First, such garments fit relatively loosely or are formed of stretch fabric materials, Second, some alteration is usually made that can correct discrepancies in sizes.

However, draft patterns for the general clothing industry were, into the 1960s, apparently based on measurements taken on small samples, often too small to truly represent the general population. The sizing intervals used by the garment trade were, as shown by reliable anthropometric data, not always in accord with the way the human body develops. (For further related data, Croney recently (1972) provided a useful and convenient summary of growth patterns for clothing designers.) Such methods have proven inefficient and expensive (Emanuel et al., 1959). Reliable anthropometric data have mainly been applied to the development and fit of military personal protective clothing, but only in a small scale for civilian populations and purposes (Lonie, 1948).

The U.S. Department of Agriculture actually had measured and analyzed data over 30 years ago, on a series of children (O'Brien, Girshick and Hunt,

1941) and of civilian women (O'Brien and Shelton, 1941). Also, the U.S. Department of Commerce has published standards for civilian women's clothing (U.S.D.C., 1954). However, more typical data reports are those of the Quartermaster Corps of the U.S. Army, which has published a variety of types of information on clothing sizes (Randall, 1948a; Randall and Munro, 1949a,b; Newman and White, 1951; White and Winston, 1951; Munro, 1952; Newman, 1953b). Similarly, the U.S. Air Force, faced with needs for closely fitting, high altitude pressure suits has studied the problem of clothing sizes in great depth with extensive statistical analyses for a variety of clothing components, such as the basic torso suit (Emanuel, Alexander, Churchill, and Truett, 1959), the helmet (Alexander and Hertzberg, 1957; Zeigen, Alexander, Churchill, Emanuel, and Velsey, 1960), face masks (Emanuel, Alexander, and Churchill, 1959), and gloves (Barter and Alexander, 1956).

These analysis reports form a valid basis for anthropometric applications to design of various types of clothing using statistical-anthropometric data. However, to develop a sizing program that will meet stringent requirements (such as a high-altitude partial pressure suit) requires several nearly simultaneous considerations of both a practical and statistical nature. Practically, one must consider the "mission," or function of the clothing, its work space environments and its cost, in order to determine what type of dimensions are critical and which should be used as a basis for statistical sizing systems. On the other hand, one must still consider the natural anthropometric variability which will be found in statistical studies for sizing analysis. Clothing occurs at many of the vital *interfaces between man and machine* as well as atmospheric environment, and thus must be responsive to requirements on *both sides* of the interface.

9.3 DESIGN OF PRESSURE SUITS—MODEL FOR DEVELOPMENT CYCLE

The following presentation parallels, in some degree, that for work space design applications by providing a series of steps to be accomplished in a development cycle. The steps are schematically shown in Figure 9-1.

9.3.1 Step 1. Establishing Requirements for Clothing

The first step in the clothing design process has several counterparts to the work space design process discussed in Section 8.3.1. From the proposed usage ("mission") and environments, one may derive a functional implementation concept for the structure and mechanisms of the suit. Such operations are indicated by dashed line blocks in Figure 9-1 in the upper left corner. Further analysis of the mission leads to description of typical tasks to be performed by the suit wearer, which influence mobility requirements and thus pattern

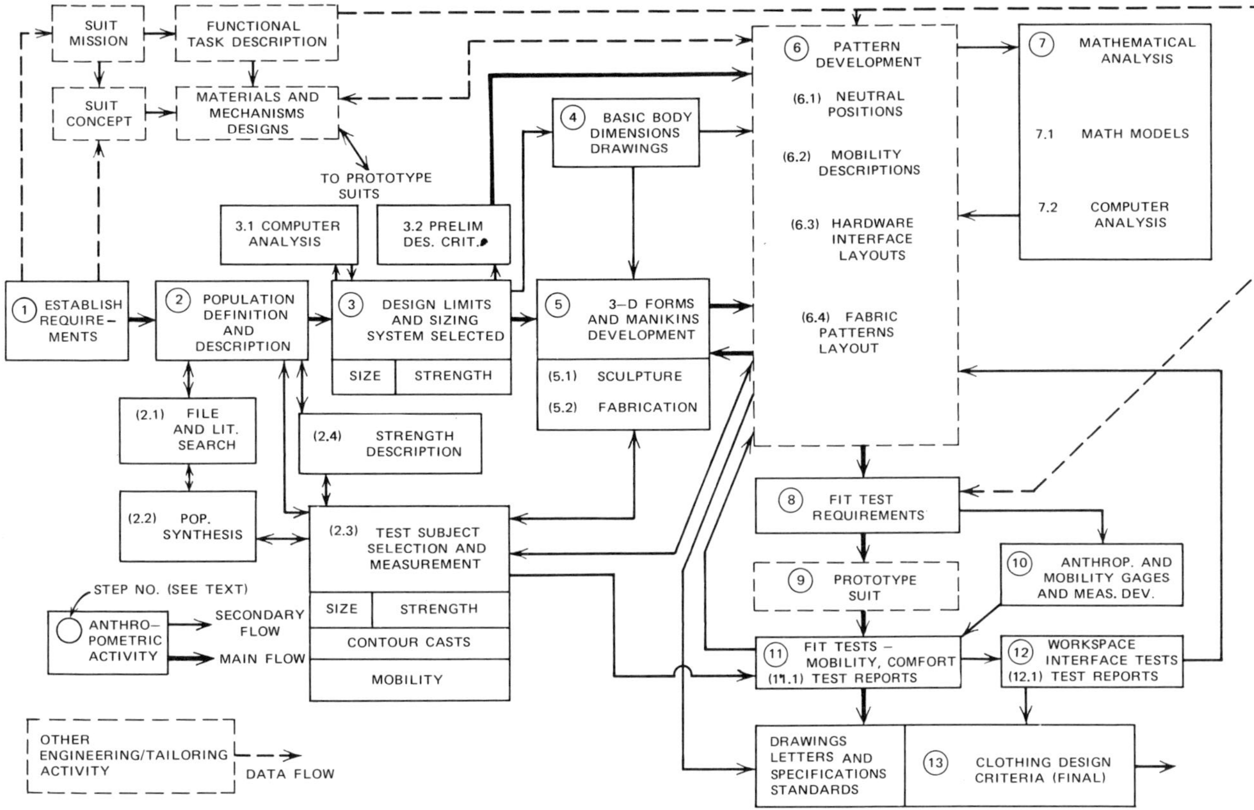

Figure 9-1. Engineering anthropometry clothing design procedures flow chart.

development (Step 6). Making the suit to meet its environmental and mobility constraints requires careful analysis of candidate materials and of mechanization methods for joints and fittings. The selection of mechanisms and materials will be influenced by anthropometric considerations both at the design level and during development of the prototype suit (Steps 9 to 12).

Two types of pressure protective garment are discussed in the following presentation in order to illustrate anthropometric implications of different suit concepts and provide more complete coverage by examples of the various steps in design procedure. These two types are the U.S. Air Force partial pressure suit and the NASA Apollo full pressure space suit. The former receives prime emphasis here, because it must fit the human body so closely in nearly all regions except the face. Both types must completely cover the body, and thus include a helmet, gloves, and boots. Both require connection to outside breathing gas, pressurization gas, and communications.

The major portion (trunk, arms, and legs—called the torso) of the partial pressure suit becomes essentially skin tight when fully activated at high altitudes, and provides mechanical resistance to internal body pressures that would expand the tissues outward. The mechanical pressure is exerted by tension of the cloth which is created by laces wrapped around an inflatable tube (or capstan) running parallel to the sides of the limbs and trunk (Figure 9-2). In contrast, the pressure garment assembly of the Apollo Extravehicular Mobility Unit (EMU) protects by the "full pressure" principle. In this type of suit, gas pressure is applied evenly over the entire body by enclosing man and gas in an impervious, man-shaped "balloon." There must be space between skin and suit to circulate cooling gas. This space is also used for a skintight garment of porous fabric having tubes sewn into it in which cooling liquid is circulated when the suit is worn on the lunar surface. The liquid circulation and cooling, as well as breathing gas (oxygen pressure and circulation and communications are provided by a backpack portable life support system (PLSS) when walking on the moon. As illustrated in Figure 9.3, this suit is significantly more bulky, partly because of its basic pressurization concept and partly due to protective layers providing protection against extremes of temperature, fire hazards, micrometeoroids, and radiation. Waste management is another important function, requiring devices of interest to anthropometric engineering, which are incorporated in the suit.

Sizing of the torso is first considered. Anthropometric aspects of gloves, helmets, and face masks are discussed later as separate topics. Although based on interesting history and unique measurement scales, the design of boots is not discussed, because the general principles described in other applications can be adapted.

Figure 9-2. High altitude partial pressure suit. (Photo courtesy of Messrs. Kent Gillespie and Milton Alexander.)

9.3.2 Step 2. Population Description and Basic Dimensions Presentation

Procedures of population description for clothing design are very similar to those for work space design. Yet, there are important differences in emphasis, such as the interest in circumferences and linear distances along the surfaces of the body, and in description of body contours. Table 9-1 is a list of the body dimensions taken for Apollo suit fitting, and typifies the classes of dimensions of interest in clothing design.

9.3.3 Step 3. Development of Clothing Size Programs and Design Criteria Selection

In clothing size program development, the question of design criteria percentiles is considerably more complex than in work space design because of the added factors of different sizes. Examples following will illustrate the general procedure and related areas of anthropometric complexity. The dis-

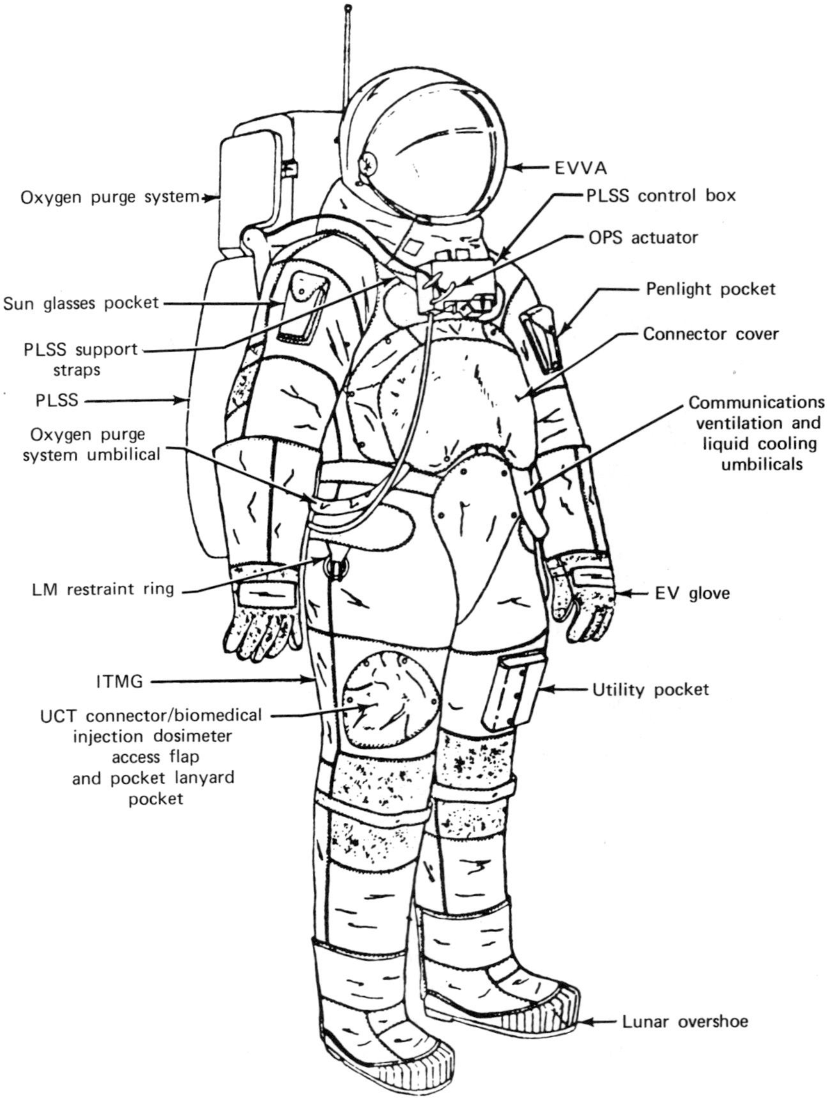

Figure 9-3. Apollo extravehicular mobility unit. The complete assembly includes several layers of fabric clothing, mechanical attachments, helmet, gloves, boots, covers, life support system, and communications apparatus. (Developed by International Latex Corporation, Dover, Delaware for National Aeronautics and Space Administration.)

Table 9-1. Anthropometric Dimensions for Apollo Full-Pressure Suit Design (Courtesy of International Latex Corporation)

Weight	Upper thigh circumference
Height	Mid thigh circumference
Cervical height	Lower thigh circumference
Mid-shoulder height, right	Calf circumference
Mid-shoulder height, left	Lower leg
Shoulder height, right	Ankle bone
Shoulder height, left	Scye circumference, right
Suprasternale height	Scye circumference, left
Nipple height	Axillary arm circumference
Waist height (back)	Biceps flexed circumference
Trochanteric height	Elbow flexed circumference
Knee cap	Wrist circumference
Center knee-floor height	Forearm flexed circumference
Crotch height	Sleeve inseam, right
Shoulder-elbow length	Shoulder-elbow pivot
Inter-scye breadth	Elbow pivot-wrist
Biacromial breadth	Wrist-forefingertip
Shoulder breadth	Vert. trunk circumference, right
Chest breadth	Waist front length
Waist breadth	Anterior neck length
Hip breadth	Posterior neck length
Vert. trunk dia., right	Waist back length
Vert. trunk dia., left	Gluteal arc length
Head circumference	Crotch length
Neck circumference	Span
Shoulder circumference	Span free
Chest at scye	Knee circumference
Chest at nipple	
Waist circumference	
Buttock circumference	
Foot length (both right and left)	
Instep length	
Width	
Instep circumference	

cussion is largely based on a report by Emanuel, Alexander, Churchill, and Truett (1959).

Step 3.1. Selection of Primary Dimension and Size Ranges

In describing clothing sizes, it is convenient and economical to have a small number of basic dimensions that characterize the different sizes. It is recommended that no more than two such key dimensions be used, each divided into a small number of intervals. The number of sizes increases geometrically with every new dimension. The simple case of men's shirt sizes illustrates this point. Suppose one has a shirt sized on the basis of Sleeve Length alone, supplied in five length intervals. The addition of a Neck Circumference size criterion in, say, four circumference intervals is multiplied by the number of Sleeve Lengths to determine the total set, resulting in 20 shirt sizes. Further dimensional description in the form of four different Chest Circumferences would increase the number of shirt sizes to 80. Such a large number would clearly be unwieldy for a retail store or a quartermaster to handle. Also, in most cases two dimensions are sufficient to assure adequate fit.

But which dimensions should be used? Four general qualifications provide guidelines.

1. The dimensions can be easily taken and they are convenient to measure beforehand or at the point of fit of clothing (examples: Height, Weight, Waist Circumference).
2. The dimensions are among the actual design dimensions of the garment, and can be checked by measurement on the garment (example: shirts are sized by Neck Circumference and Sleeve Length).
3. The dimensions have a high correlation with many of the other dimensions that influence the design of the garment (such dimensions must be found by statistical analysis).
4. Dimensions that are commonly measured on the design population would be desirable, because this helps in setting up procurement tariffs (number of articles in each size). Height and Weight are examples of such dimensions applicable to nearly all persons in a civilized, literate society.

Selection of the first, second, and fourth criterion is based on judgments, but only a thorough statistical analysis will determine which dimension(s) candidates best satisfy the requirement of high correlations with other dimensions. High correlations between the basic sizing dimensions and other body dimensions are desirable, because they generally permit small adjustments that minimize unnecessary bulk and weight of the clothing, and reduce costly complexity of design, fabrication, alterations, and maintenance.

Statistical analysis to select dimensions for the partial pressure suit provides an example: The basic data described 4025 flying personnel from the U.S. Air Force (Hertzberg, Daniels, and Churchill, 1954), available on punched cards. A computer analysis was performed to determine which combination of basic dimensions would minimize the variabilities of other dimensions most, particularly those dimensions that are important in the construction of flight clothing. Various pairs of body dimensions, most of which were made up of a length and a circumference, were correlated against other body dimensions. Fifteen pairs of dimensions were examined by determining multiple correlation coefficients with other dimensions applicable to flight clothing. These multiple correlations were then compared in order to see which pair of basic dimensions could be selected to minimize variabilities in general. A portion of the results is summarized in Table 9-2. The table shows the highest correlation coefficient found in all pairs for each dimension, and the pairs that have this value are noted. Each of the alphabetically labeled columns to the right represent a dimension pair. In those columns the *deviation* from the highest correlation is shown. This presentation has the effect of standardizing all the results with respect to a zero baseline. The analysis showed a strong preference for Height and Weight as the basic dimension pair for use in close fitting flight clothing. Specifically, Emanuel and his co-workers found that "for 29, or 58% of the 50 dimensions listed . . . the multiple correlation coefficient with stature and weight is as high or higher than that with any other pair of dimensions. Height and weight have the highest multiple correlation coefficient with all circumferences, dimensions which are very important in clothing design." In all cases in which Height and Weight do not have the highest correlation coefficient, the deviations shown in the table are less than 0.10. It was concluded that this difference would not be of significance from a practical standpoint. The finding, that a combination of Stature and Weight is optimal to minimize variability, is similar to results from other studies (O'Brien, Girshick, and Hunt, 1941); O'Brien and Shelton, 1941; Morant and Gilson, 1945).

The selection of Height and Weight seems to violate the second criterion desirable for selection of dimension pairs; the dimensions do not appear on the garment at all. However, the use of Height and Weight as basic dimensions resulted in an overlap between sizes for all design dimensions. Emanuel et al. stated that "This overlap enables the design range for all dimensions to be reduced without decreasing the percentage of fit of the garment, since upgrading and downgrading of sizes will be more possible than if basic sizing dimensions which are incorporated directly into the suit were used." The authors asserted that even many persons apparently outside the Height-Weight criteria (to be described later) will be fitted, because of indirect control on clothing design dimensions exerted by Height and Weight.

Having selected two primary dimensions on which to base a sizing system, the next task is to divide the combinations of these dimensions into suitable intervals or categories that define the design ranges for each size. This has often been done by a "visual fit" judgment, based on experience and knowledge of the design function, but could be performed using an optimization program. Figure 9-4 illustrates a typical example, the bivariate distribution: Height versus Weight diagram for the eight-size program, in which the eight selected design range areas are depicted with heavy borderlines.

Table 9-2. Comparison of Multiple Correlation Coefficients[a] (Minus Signs Omitted)

	Maximum (Column Number)	Maximum Value	A Stature and Weight	B Stature and Chest Circumference	C Stature and Waist Circumference	D Stature and Buttock Circumference	E Stature and Vertical Trunk Circ.	F Crotch Height and Weight	G Crotch Height and Chest Circumference	H Crotch Height and Waist Circumference	I Crotch Height and Buttock Circumference	J Crotch Height and Vertical Trunk Circ.	K Sleeve Length and Weight	L Sleeve Length and Chest Circumference	M Sleeve Length and Waist Circumference	N Sleeve Length and Buttock Circumference	O Sleeve Length and Vertical Trunk Circ.
Standing Heights																	
Cervicale height	ABCDE	.97	.00	.00	.00	.00	.00	.09	.11	.11	.10	.06	.24	.26	.26	.25	.20
Shoulder height	ABCDE	.95	.00	.00	.00	.00	.00	.07	.09	.09	.08	.03	.23	.26	.26	.25	.19
Suprasternale height	ABCDE	.97	.00	.00	.00	.00	.00	.08	.11	.11	.09	.06	.24	.26	.26	.25	.20
Nipple height	ABCDE	.93	.00	.00	.00	.00	.00	.06	.08	.08	.07	.04	.25	.26	.26	.26	.21
Substernale height	ABCDE	.90	.00	.00	.00	.00	.00	.06	.08	.07	.06	.03	.24	.25	.25	.25	.20
Elbow height	E	.92	.01	.01	.01	.01	.00	.09	.12	.12	.10	.04	.27	.31	.31	.28	.20
Waist height	ABCDE	.90	.00	.00	.00	.00	.00	.04	.05	.05	.04	.03	.23	.23	.23	.23	.21
Penale height	FGHIJ	.93	.07	.07	.07	.07	.05	.00	.00	.00	.00	.00	.26	.25	.25	.26	.26
Crotch height (inseam)	E	.88	.02	.03	.02	.02	.00	—	—	—	—	—	.20	.20	.20	.20	.21
Gluteal furrow height	FGHIJ	.92	.06	.06	.06	.05	.04	.00	.00	.00	.00	.00	.24	.24	.24	.24	.24
Kneecap height	FHIJ	.83	.01	.01	.01	.01	.01	.00	.01	.00	.00	.00	.16	.17	.17	.17	.16
Body Lengths																	
Popliteal height, sitting	FGHIJ	.88	.08	.08	.08	.07	.06	.00	.00	.00	.00	.00	.24	.23	.23	.23	.23
Shoulder-elbow length	ABCDEF	.74	.01	.00	.00	.01	.00	.01	.01	.01	.01	.01	.02	.02	.02	.02	.02
Forearm-hand length	ABCDE	.78	.00	.00	.00	.00	.00	.01	.02	.02	.02	.01	.07	.07	.07	.07	.07
Breadths																	
Biacromial diameter	K	.56	.06	.05	.09	.09	.12	.05	.06	.11	.09	.11	.00	.01	.02	.01	.02
Chest breadth	BGL	.80	.05	.00	.11	.13	.22	.05	.00	.12	.13	.22	.05	.00	.09	.11	.20
Waist breadth	CHM	.82	.04	.11	.00	.09	.26	.04	.11	.00	.09	.26	.05	.11	.00	.09	.26
Hip breadth	DIN	.82	.04	.12	.09	.00	.16	.04	.15	.12	.00	.16	.04	.15	.11	.00	.14
Depths																	
Chest depth	ABGL	.77	.00	.00	.06	.08	.19	.01	.00	.06	.08	.21	.02	.00	.06	.08	.22
Waist depth	CMM	.85	.06	.16	.00	.13	.25	.07	.16	.00	.13	.27	.08	.16	.00	.14	.29
Buttock depth	F	.84	.01	.24	.07	.03	.16	.00	.14	.07	.02	.17	.02	.15	.07	.04	.19

[a] *Interpretation of table:* line 1 indicates that the highest correlation with Cervicale Height is 0.97; this value was obtained from each of the combinations listed in columns A, B, C, D, and E. The value of 0.09 in column F indicates that the correlation of Cervicale Height with Crotch Height and Weight is 0.09 less than the indicated maximum, that is, 0.86. The other entries have similar meanings.

Height (in.)

Weight (lb)	61.4–62.2	62.2–63.0	63.0–63.8	63.8–64.5	64.5–65.3	65.3–66.1	66.1–66.9	66.9–67.7	67.7–68.4	68.4–69.3	69.3–70.1	70.1–70.8	70.8–71.6	71.6–72.4	72.4–73.2	73.2–74.0	74.0–74.8	74.8–75.6	75.6–76.4	76.4–77.1	Totals
227–232										1	1		1	2	1	2	1	1			10
221–226									1		1	2	1	2	3	1	1	1	1		14
215–220									2	2	4	3	2	6	1	2	2	1	1		26
209–214						1			3	2		10	9	6	5	5	3	2	3		49
203–208						1		3	5	4	11	7	7	9	8	5	1	4		1	66
197–203				1			1	3	7	12	14	19	23	10	10	7	6	2		2	117
191–196						2	3	9	8	22	23	22	23	17	15	8	1	4	3		160
185–190					1		6	9	18	38	21	37	20	26	7	6	7	1	2	1	200
179–184				1	1	2	11	14	29	36	35	40	22	29	15	6	6	1	1	1	250
173–178				1	3	4	16	26	38	44	54	48	38	26	16	21	7	2	1		345
167–172	1		2	2	5	14	16	30	45	51	61	56	43	26	13	11	7	2	1		386
161–166			3	4	10	20	25	41	51	85	64	53	42	26	16	12	3		1		456
155–160		2	3	5	10	20	32	45	63	76	71	50	48	25	14	9	3	1	2		479
149–154	2		4	8	17	33	36	54	57	52	61	53	39	14	8	3		1	1		443
143–148		3	2	6	25	28	43	45	51	53	42	34	13	8	7		2		1		363
137–142	2	3	6	13	14	33	49	46	43	32	32	23	12	6	3	2					319
131–136	2	1	1	9	12	24	27	27	30	13	14	11	3	2	1						177
125–130	2	4	3	10	11	22	12	13	16	10	6		1								110
119–124		1	3	5	8	8	4	7	5					1							42
113–118		1	1	3	2	2	1	2	1												13
Totals	9	15	28	68	119	214	282	374	473	533	515	468	347	241	143	100	50	23	18	5	4025

$r = 0.47$

Figure 9-4. Size categories for eight-size program (Emanuel, Alexander, and Truett, 1959).

From such a figure one may determine the number of persons who theoretically will take each size within a given group, data usually referred to as the *tariff.* Table 9-3 is an example of a *fitting table* and suggested tariff in terms of number of persons in a 1000-person sample. From such tariff lists, a quartermaster or storekeeper can select the proportion of each size he will keep in stock, and determine which size to supply to his "clients" for the first fitting.

Step 3.2. Selection of Design Dimensions

Actual design dimensions for clothing adjustment are next determined. Emanuel et al. determined design ranges as the mean plus and minus 1.5 standard deviations, although it is common to use the mean plus and minus 2 standard deviations (yielding a coverage of approximately 95%). They stated that "in cases of inadequate fit for an indicated size, upgrading or downgrading sizes will probably result in a proper fit for another 8%" (thus accommodating about 95% altogether). Experience with protective garments built to Height-Weight standards has confirmed a high percentage fit result. The "mean" referred to above is the midpoint of the design dimension for those persons who fall within each a given size defined by a range of Height and Weight. The "standard deviation" is the standard error of estimate of the design dimension calculated from the trivariate distribution based on the given range of intervals of Height and Weight. An abbreviated table of such standard errors of estimate is illustrated in Table 9-4. From these data and the calculated means for each size

Table 9-3. Example of Fitting Table and Tariff for Clothing Sizes (From Emanuel, Alexander, Churchill, and Truett, 1959)[a]

	Weight (lb)		Height (in.)		Suggested Tariff
Size	From	To	From	To	(per 1000)
Small regular	125	149	63	67.50	127
Small long	125	149	67.50	72	119
Medium regular	150	174	64.50	69	220
Medium long	150	174	69	73.50	243
Large regular	175	199	66	70.50	136
Large long	175	199	70.50	75	105
X-large regular	200	224	67.50	72	31
X-large long	200	224	72	76.50	19
					1000

[a] Proportion of survey sample theoretically included = 94%.

Table 9-4. Standard Errors of Estimate for Combinations of Clothing Dimensions (Emanuel, Alexander, Churchill, and Truett, 1959)

Measurement	Total Sample S.D.	Standard Error of Estimate	4 Size Program	6 Size Program	8 Size Program	9 Size Program	12 Size Program
Axillary arm circ.	1.10	.69		.76	.74	.76	.73
Anterior neck length	.64	.57		.59	.59	.59	.57
Posterior neck length	.61	.59		.59	.59	.59	.59
Shoulder length	.56	.52		.52	.52	.52	.52
Cervicale ht.	2.31	.55		1.23	1.19	1.02	.92
Shoulder ht.	2.28	.70		1.25	1.20	1.06	.96
Suprasternale ht.	2.19	.54		1.14	1.10	.94	.84
Substernale ht.	2.02	.88		1.28	1.24	1.13	1.06
Nipple ht.	2.08	.74	1.24	1.21	1.16	1.04	.96
Elbow ht.	1.77	.73		1.06	1.03	.94	.85
Waist ht.	1.81	.81	1.19	1.17	1.13	1.05	.99
Penale ht.	1.75	.90		1.18	1.17	1.10	1.02
Gluteal furrow ht.	1.62	.82		1.09	1.06	.98	.89
Gluteal arc	.92	.87		.87	.87	.87	.87
Chest breadth	.80	.53		.58	.56	.58	.55
Waist breadth	.94	.58		.65	.64	.65	.62
Hip breadth	.73	.46		.47	.47	.47	.43
Hip breadth (sitting)	.87	.50		.56	.54	.56	.53
Chest depth	.75	.48		.54	.53	.54	.52
Waist depth	.88	.55		.61	.61	.61	.60
Buttock depth	.82	.45		.53	.53	.53	.51
Forearm-hand length	.81	.51		.58	.58	.56	.52
Buttock circ. (sitting)	2.82	1.37		1.70	1.63	1.70	1.58
Shoulder circ.	2.43	1.42		1.61	1.54	1.61	1.49

Note. All values are in inches.

(see example Table 9-5), one can develop tables of *design ranges*. Table 9-6 is a portion of one such table taken from the report by Emanuel et al. The referenced report contains tables for 53 clothing design dimensions and four different size programs. Note that the design ranges are all rounded off to the nearest quarter inch for the convenience of the pattern maker. Such design range tables may be considered as preliminary design criteria (Step 3.2, in Figure 9-1) which have not as yet been validated by fit tests with sample clothing articles on actual subjects. When verified, such tables become part of Step 13, final clothing design criteria.

9.3.4 Step 4. Basic Body Dimensions Drawings

The preparation of drawings of basic body dimensions is recommended for several types of clothing development projects, but is often not as important in

Table 9-5. Calculated Means for Clothing Dimensions Eight-Size Height–Weight Sizing Program

	Weight	Height	Chest Circumference	Waist Circumference
Small regular	125–149	63.00–67.50	36.59	29.45
Small long	125–149	67.50–72.00	36.37	29.12
Medium regular	150–174	64.50–69.00	38.71	31.94
Medium long	150–174	69.00–73.50	38.26	31.14
Large regular	175–199	66.00–70.50	41.06	35.03
Large long	175–199	70.50–75.00	40.51	33.92
X-large regular	200–224	67.50–72.00	43.84	38.75
X-large long	200–224	72.00–76.50	43.01	37.11

	Buttock Circumference	Trunk Vert. Circumference	Waist Back	Waist Front
Small regular	35.38	61.46	16.88	14.41
Small long	35.38	62.72	17.66	14.78
Medium regular	37.64	64.08	17.37	14.97
Medium long	37.40	65.14	18.09	15.34
Large regular	39.95	66.91	17.83	15.69
Large long	39.87	67.57	18.53	15.97
X-large regular	42.30	69.58	18.17	16.43
X-large long	42.18	70.43	18.90	16.83

Note. All dimensions except weight are in inches.

Table 9-6. Example of Clothing Design Ranges for Eight-Size Height–Weight Sizing Program[a]

	Weight	Height	Chest Circumference	Waist Circumference
Small regular	125–149	63.00–67.50	34.25–38.75	26.50–32.25
Small long	125–149	67.50–72.00	34.00–38.50	26.25–32.00
Medium regular	150–174	64.50–69.00	36.50–41.00	29.00–34.75
Medium long	150–174	69.00–73.50	36.00–40.50	28.25–34.00
Large regular	175–199	66.00–70.50	38.75–43.25	32.25–37.75
Large long	175–199	70.50–75.00	38.25–42.75	31.00–36.75
X-large regular	200–224	67.50–72.00	41.50–46.00	36.00–41.50
X-large long	200–224	72.00–76.50	40.75–45.25	34.25–40.00

	Buttock Circumference	Vert. Trunk Circumference	Waist Back	Waist Front
Small regular	33.50–37.25	58.75–64.25	15.50–18.25	13.00–16.00
Small long	33.50–37.25	60.00–65.50	16.25–19.00	13.25–16.25
Medium regular	35.75–39.50	61.50–66.75	16.00–18.75	13.50–16.50
Medium long	35.50–39.25	62.50–67.75	16.75–19.50	13.75–16.75
Large regular	38.00–41.75	64.25–69.50	16.50–19.25	14.25–17.25
Large long	38.00–41.75	64.75–70.25	17.00–20.00	14.50–17.50
X-large regular	40.50–44.25	67.00–72.25	16.75–19.50	15.00–18.00
X-large long	40.25–44.00	67.75–73.25	17.50–20.25	15.25–18.25

[a] From Emanuel, Alexander, Churchill, and Truett (1959). All dimensions except weight are in inches.

many clothing development projects (especially torso patterns) as in work space design. An experienced clothing pattern designer can proceed from properly measured torso dimensions directly to pattern layout.

If one is developing a series of body forms or manikins, the drawings may be used as a basis for designing and fabricating these items. Such drawings should include contours at frequent intervals. Drawings of landmark relationships are very useful in mask and helmet design and development, where many complicated adjustments and spatial relationships of ears, nose, eyes, mouth, chin, cheek, and so forth, must be accommodated with machined or cast rigid parts and mechanical devices.

9.3.5 Step 5. Preparation of Manikins and Body Forms

This task is similar in some respects to the preparation of clearance envelope mockups for work space design. These manikins and forms, described in Chapter VII, represent different parts of the body and may be used as design tools and as fabrication development tools for pattern making.

A sculptor may be employed profitably to prepare the body forms. Using data defining a few key landmark body points, he can "fill in" contours by use of his basic knowledge of human anatomy. This activity is somewhat analogous to the employment of graphic artists in preparing drawings of man from few data.

An excellent report describing development of such body forms for torso suit development has been prepared by McConville, Alexander, and Velsey (1963). The forms were prepared to conform with tables of clothing size body dimensions by a combination of engineering mock-up practice and professional sculpture.

A steel tubular armature, or core, was first designed to the proper scale for each of eight sizes by the sculptor. To facilitate transportation of the manikins, a roman joint (common insertion joint in which one piece slides into the other and is locked in place with a set pin) was incorporated into the arm and leg segments to permit their removal. A heavy wire mesh that would retain its form was fitted over the armature and attached to provide the gross body size. The form was then roughed in with successive layers of plaster of paris. By measuring from known basic points, the sculptor then carefully brought each body dimension to its proper design value and carried the resulting form into the body areas not described by statistical data. The extent of the completed shape of the clothing manikins, and a few of the basic anthropometric dimensions used in their construction are indicated in Figure 9-5. Further details are contained in the original report.

"A tolerance of one-tenth of an inch variation from the design value was considered as an acceptable sculpturing error." However, difficulties appeared that had not been anticipated prior to the actual integration of the statistical

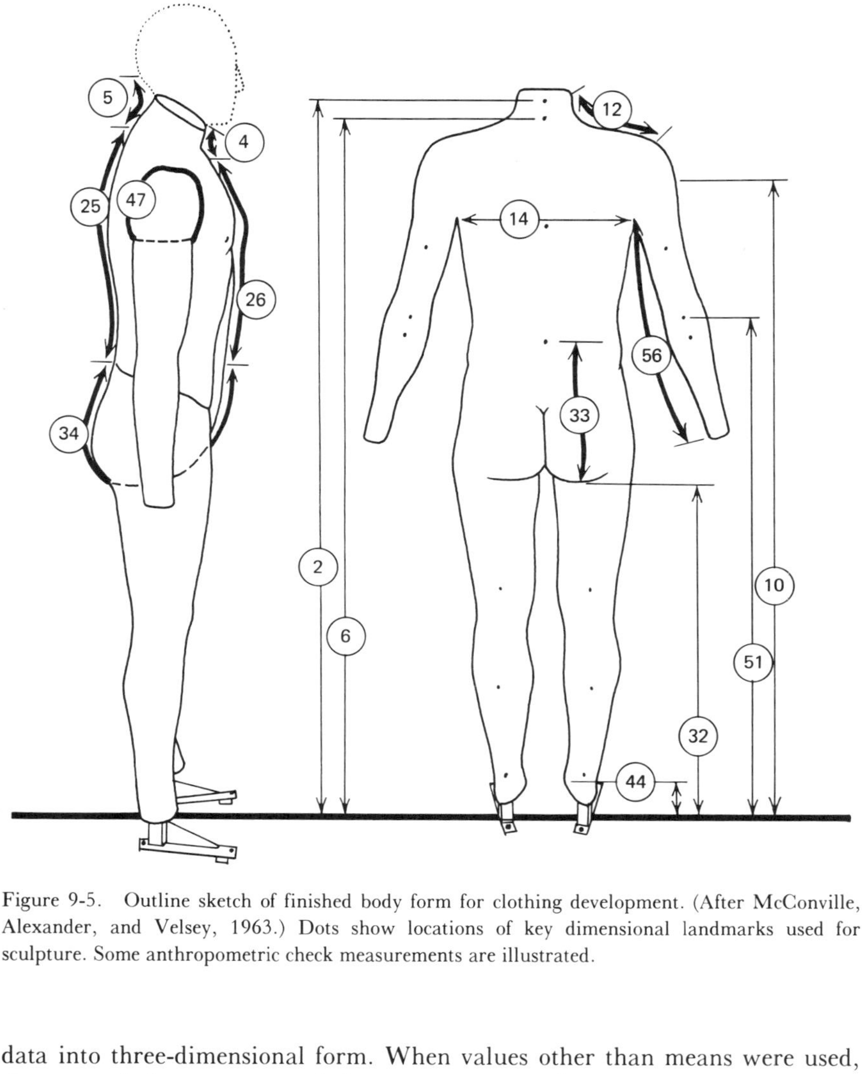

Figure 9-5. Outline sketch of finished body form for clothing development. (After McConville, Alexander, and Velsey, 1963.) Dots show locations of key dimensional landmarks used for sculpture. Some anthropometric check measurements are illustrated.

data into three-dimensional form. When values other than means were used, the sum of the parts exceeded the total value of the dimension. Only if a perfect correlation existed between the segment and the whole would the summation of parts equal the total. In the fabrication of the manikins this problem was encountered in dealing with certain surface lengths of the trunk. For example, the dimensions Waist Front, Waist Back, and Crotch Length approximate the value of the dimension Vertical Trunk Circumference." When the three parts were held to their design values the resulting Vertical Trunk Circumference was excessive. As Vertical Trunk Circumference is a more critical dimension than its parts in sizing programs, it was held to its proper design value and the reduction of variability this enforced upon the values of the component parts was disregarded."

"It was also found desirable to construct the body forms with the arms in somewhat different positions from those specified in the initial program. This would then permit the actual tailoring of the garments on the manikins. The statistical design values were therefore found to be consistently less for the dimensions of Shoulder Breadth and Shoulder Circumference."

9.3.6 Step 6. Pattern Development

The total process of "engineered" clothing pattern development and mechanisms design requires a combination of tailoring art and engineering science to achieve desired mobility, comfort, suit functional capability for environmental protection, and other specified design goals. Much of this approach is not available in documentary form, being as much art as science, and is related to fabrication skills beyond the scope of this text. However, in certain cases, some of the engineering anthropometry tasks associated with work space design may be useful.

Lacing systems, such as used in the Apollo EMU, are frequently placed between the joints of full pressure suits to adjust the length of the limb segments, thus minimizing the number of suit sizes. Early models of the Apollo suit also had, in the front of the torso, a vertical adjustment strap, attached near the groin and near the neck ring, below the helmet. This strap was adjustable by the wearer to permit various trunk section lengths and shapes such as can be accomplished by shortening the front surface of the suit.

Selection of the donning method is a very critical key element in pressure clothing design. Many different systems of arranging zippers and other closure systems have been investigated. An early selection for the Apollo full pressure suit was a zipper running along the back centerline of the suit and under the crotch. Later, this was modified to accommodate hip and trunk bellows, which permit greater trunk/hip mobility (and eliminated the need for the front adjustment strap for trunk positioning).

9.3.7 Step 7. Mathematical Analysis

Mathematical modeling and computer analysis of anthropometric data for the process of *pattern development* in clothing *design* (as opposed to selecting sizes) is relatively less needed than for work space design at the current time, and will not be discussed here. However, in selected cases, such as face mask design, it has been usefully applied. Additional uses are probable as new concepts and application areas develop. Therefore, a separate block of mathematical analysis operations has been included as part of Figure 9-1.

9.3.8 Step 8. Fit and Mobility Test Requirements

As the suit design is being defined, critical fit problems and mobility functions may be identified, which will be the object of study in prototype suit fit and mobility tests (Step 11). Test plans should be defined for the evaluation of these potential problem areas (high-pressure points, chafing, awkward positioning, etc.) and of candidate mobility and operational mechanisms, such as joint systems, helmet locks, donning and doffing activity, and the like. A survey of needed suit mobility, in order to assure safe, efficient operation at the work station in an aircraft or space vehicle, is also highly recommended as an early step in preparing a specification for suit design (see Interface Tests, Step 12).

9.3.9 Step 9. Prototype Suit

The initial integration of the suit fabric and mechanisms usually appears as one or more prototype suits, designed for a specific subject. A variety of candidate features may be incorporated in this suit for evaluation, perhaps a different approach on each arm and leg. Inasmuch as substitute materials and nonfunctional parts are used, this suit is analogous to the work space mock-up.

This is where the mobility mechanisms, pressure points, visibility, and interface problems are first analyzed in three-dimensional reality. Thermal and other protective features may also be evaluated. Appearance may become a critical factor, after basic functional requirements are well accomplished. Again, one subject, for whom the suit has been specifically designed, is usually the "test pilot" of such a creation. Needed engineering and tailoring changes are then recommended for incorporation into a series of differently sized "production articles."

9.3.10 Step 10. Preparation of Anthropometric Measuring Gages and Mobility Measurement Devices

In order to evaluate a suit in terms of its flexibility, or restrictions on mobility of the wearer, special devices are needed, such as the mobility measurement table and various goniometers discussed in Chapter III. Contour measurement devices, also discussed in Chapter III, provide means to record pressurized suit contours and reach envelopes. Such evaluation can take place in the demonstrated movement of the wearer in open rooms or in mock-up evaluations with the devices mounted at the specific work stations.

9.3.11 Step 11. Fit and Mobility Tests

Fit-testing activity, and related mobility testing, may be accomplished at least twice. The first is where the prototype suit, the subject, and the anthropometric gages come together in a process of evaluation to determine if the patterns are correct for the purposes and persons intended. Later, a larger series of clothing sizes may be tested for fit and mobility on a large group of personnel, using a preproduction run of the equipment. Typical goals for the latter type of fit testing emphasize verification of sizing programs. For example, Emanuel, Alexander, Churchill, and Truett (1959) gave determination of the following as their goals in evaluation of three close-fitting garments, designed to Height-Weight standards:

1. "The accuracy of the statistical assumptions and procedures used in deriving these sizing programs;
2. "The adequacy of the techniques used to transform the numerical data into actual acticles of clothing;
3. "The feasibility of fitting a one-piece, snugly-fitting suit on the basis of height and weight alone; and
4. "The practicality of issuing such garments on the basis of the prospective wearer's stated (rather than measured) height and weight."

The methods and results of only one partial pressure suit fit test are summarized herein, as the other tests and results were similar in nature.

Each subject was asked his Height and Weight and was then issued a suit according to the fitting chart without check on the accuracy of the subject's statement. After this suit was donned and adjusted by means by laces, it was evaluated while uninflated for fit in the torso, thigh, legs, and arms. After inflation, the suit was observed for chest-back expansion. The sample consisted of 52 subjects, between 19 and 52 years of age, with Heights ranging from the 5th percentile to above the 99th percentile, and Weights from below the 1st percentile to above the 99th percentile of the reference survey (Hertzberg et al. 1954).

Forty-nine (94%) of the subjects were satisfactorily fitted by suits of the size indicated by the fitting chart, and two more (each on the borderline between two sizes) were fitted by downgrading one size. The remaining unaccommodated subject had dimensions below the planned range of the sizing program.

Mobility of the tested suit was considered to be definitely improved over a previous suit, and comfort was satisfactory. "Many of the men were able to stand erect when the suit was inflated to 10 psi and some were able to join their fingertips overhead while standing."

The latter comment is an example of cursory mobility evaluation, independent of the suit "work space" functions. Standardized and detailed mobility test series, such as those described in Chapter III, were developed as a result of the challenges posed by the Apollo Project. In some early forms they were applied to proposed competitive models of the developing Apollo EMU suit by the NASA (Jones, 1966) and the vehicle contractor, North American Rockwell (Roebuck, 1968; Ryker, 1969). Results of these tests influenced suit specifications and gave impetus to improvement of mobility features in the suit design. Also, mock-up tests yielded desirable capability goals, which were later compared to standardized mobility test scores resulting from tests on actual suits. The mobility profile chart in Figure 9-6, was one of the more effective graphic comparison techniques.

Accurate mobility descriptions are especially useful for clothing systems that contain extensive environmental and/or communications controls and displays, in order to determine locations of such controls and displays on the suit. All the controls must be reachable and all displays visible in this mini-work space. However, these devices should also permit the crewman to do his primary work with a minimum of interference.

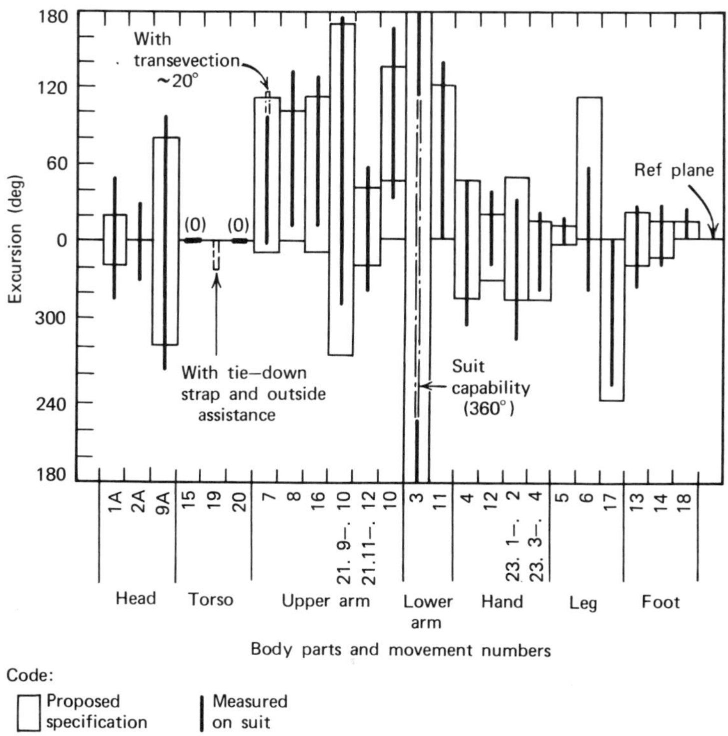

Figure 9-6. Mobility profile chart. Total range of angular movement and absolute position of movement in space with respect to defined reference planes are depicted on this type of profile chart, for the movements coded on the abscissa. Also, comparisons are readily shown between specified magnitudes and measured data, or between measured data on two suits. (Figure from Ryker, 1968.)

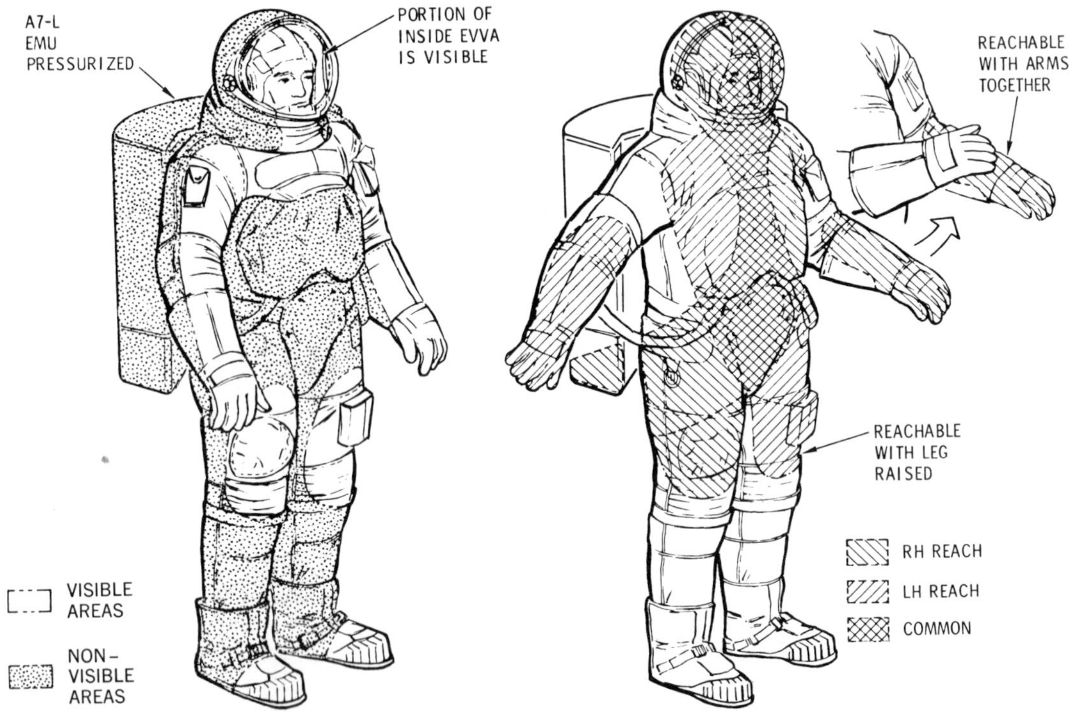

Figure 9-7. Visible and reachable areas on full pressure space suit. This is a preliminary conceptual description, based on observation of suits during mock-up evaluations. Detail refinements would require more extensive and controlled testing. The backpack shape shown is an advanced concept. (Courtesy of Space Division, Rockwell International Corporation.)

A desirable first step in determining optimum locations is to perform a survey of reachable and visible areas on the suit for its operational modes. Figure 9-7 shows a conceptual drawing of how the results of such a survey might look, as mapped onto an existing type of spacesuit. Next, one must analyze the vehicle or other duty station work space interfaces to see where prime duty functions tend to create obstructions or protrusions in the useful space around the suit, which would obviate use of some reachable/visible areas for suit controls and displays. Within such envelopes of constraint, the suit operational controls are located, to the degree possible.

9.3.12 Step 12. Interface Tests

Suit provisions to accommodate special requirements of *work space* include special mobility requirements at joints, particular locations of breathing gas and electrical umbilicals so as to clear restraints and controls, special visibility provisions, scuff protection, breadth and depth dimension limitations, and thermal protection. Work space interface tests to evaluate these aspects are needed frequently in development.

A typical interface problem between pressure suits and vehicle is the location of breathing gas and electrical umbilical hardware as related to seat or couch and restraint system. Figure 9-8 shows a photographic record of a trial to determine if the Apollo couch restraints were compatible with the suit hardware locations. Engineering anthropometrists are in a position to observe such relationships during mock-up testing and are likely to be involved as a consequence of working either with suit design or with vehicle design. Furthermore, their statistical understanding is an aid in extrapolating results from a small number of tests to probable results for a population.

9.4 RIGID, SEGMENTED CLOTHING DESIGN

Another class of torso clothing involves use of large areas of rigid material instead of fabric. Examples include deep water diver's suits, suits for high vacuum work, and some experimental space suits (*Machine Design,* 1967) Much of ancient full body armor and some modern partial body armor for military and police work also fits into this category. A very closely related concept is the "exoskeleton" described by Mizen (1965) and by Johnsen and Corliss (1971). The discussion herein is limited to brief consideration of experimental pressure protective suits (space suits). Readers interested in armor of the modern soldier are referred to articles by Rodzen et al. (1971) and Rolston, Bodine, and Dunleavy (1968). The latter gives a brief, interesting overview of the historical development of armor in the last two centuries.

For several years the National Aeronautics and Space Administration has been developing concepts for a nearly all-metal pressure suit for space ex-

Figure 9-8. Photographic record of test of space suit and restraint harness interface. (Courtesy of Space Division, Rockwell International Corporation.)

ploration work. The potential advantages of such suits include a combination of high strength to resist high internal gas pressures, possibly up to standard earth atmosphere at sea level, and strength to resist micrometeoroid impacts in space and on the moon, or damage by puncture from rocks or other sharp objects in the workspace. Another possible use is to make the suit perform the function of a couch or body support by simple mechanical connections to a framework at selected points on each critical suit segment. Otherwise, the functional requirements are similar to those of full-pressure suits previously discussed.

The peculiar design problems which arise are related to difficulties of adjustment, problems of donning, doffing, and comfort in the suit. In addition, the rigid nature of the materials requires a precise definition of contours of each part from the outset of design, much as the mold lines for an aircraft or automobile, rather than a cloth pattern.

Instead of laces for adjustments of segment length, the concept of multiple parts has been one approach to sizing. Rather than make one whole torso pattern for a size, a series of clothing parts are separately sized, much as one might do for helmets, boots, or gloves. Thus, one may have serveral sizes of thigh section, of lower leg section, of trunk, and of upper arm and lower arm sections. These are then assembled to provide a "best fit" for each individual. In general, all section diameters are set for large sizes, perhaps only one diameter for all lengths of some sections, where variability is small and function permits. However, an upper trunk section probably would not be feasible in a single chest diameter size, due to required arm mobility clearances.

The support of the suit weight on the body will probably require some internal harness as well as padding to protect the subject from injury by non-yielding surfaces. Such problems may be handled by procedures and devices similar to hard helmets, which are discussed later.

At least one problem is minimized by stiff metal suits: that of fabric stretch under pressure. This benefits glove fitting and dexterity of operation because the sleeve length remains constant. Hard suits may have gloves that are mostly fabric in order to retain "feel" feedback and dexterity to some degree.

In addition to the segment sizing/adjustment considerations, the "hard" suit concept tends to place more emphasis on the detail design of joints and their relationships to human joint motions (Fonda-Bernardi, 1965; Radnofsky, 1967; Vykukal, 1968). Although the constant-volume molded bellows may be used, much of the value of "hard suit" construction is thereby lost. There have been several other types proposed and built for test such as the "stovepipe-jointed" system of Vykukal (1968). However, literature on the subject does not generally treat the combination of human motion and suit motion in a manner suitable for inclusion in this text. The emphasis is generally on the mechanical design concepts, with little emphasis on the anthropometric compatibility and sizing problems. Therefore, further discussion of the subject will not be included in this text. The reader is referred to articles and reports that treat the general subject of mobility (Parry, Curry, Hanson, and Towle, 1966; Mizen, 1965; Dempster, 1955; Radnofsky, 1967; Fonda-Bernardi, 1965).

9.5 GLOVE DESIGN APPLICATION

The combination of anthropometric and engineering aspects of glove design is one of the most fascinating and difficult problems in engineered clothing. Not only must the glove provide protection but ideally it should also permit dexterity and transmission of a wide range of pressures (i.e., "feel") for tactile sensation. These requirements tend to work against each other, resulting in a variety of compromises for different environmental conditions, none perfectly satisfactory. The discussion that follows is limited to anthropometric application examples involving development of glove sizing programs, hand forms, and fit tests.

9.5.1 Step 3. Development of Glove-Sizing Programs

Barter and Alexander (1956) have described a special anthropometric survey of hand dimensions and development of a glove-sizing system for a close-fitting partial pressure glove, such as would be used with the partial pressure suit previously described in Section 9.2. Their reasons for concern with close fit had the same basis as that for the torso: application of counterpressure uniformly on the skin of the hand to provide adequate protection against low pressures in the high-altitude environment. Their description of commercial glove-sizing practice is instructive and interesting:

"The prime dimension used by many manufacturers is hand circumference, which more or less corresponds to the anthropometric measurement, Hand Circumference at Metacarpal 2. Commercial sizes are stated in terms of glovers inches which in turn are based on the metric system in some obscure fashion. One glovers inch equals 27.0 millimeters or 1.06 English inches. A size 8 ½ glove then is supposed to fit individuals whose hand circumference is 8 ½ glovers inches or 230 millimeters. Usually commercial glove sizes range from 7 to 10 by glovers half-inch increments. This large number of sizes assures a reasonably good fit for hand circumference. The problem of hand length is solved by a series of even graduations up and down from the arbitrary length decided upon for the size 8 ½ glove. Finger lengths are accommodated by having the fingers of the glove slightly short so that when the hand is inserted into the glove, the tips of the fingers go to the end of the glove. The only problem here is that only one or two of the fingers are accommodated adequately. The manufacturer of leather gloves has the additional factor of natural stretch which helps the glove conform to the hand. Small variations in size are thus taken care of in the course of use."

Barter and Alexander's development of the sizing program illustrates use of some engineering approximations and time-saving synthesis techniques. Because of a short time schedule, they could not perform a statistical analysis to determine the optimum number of sizes. "A twelve size system was chosen arbitrarily, because it was felt that this definitely would be usable, and because it equalled the number of sizes of the partial pressure suit." A second item is the adaptation of a *synthetic bivariate correlation distribution* for two hand dimensions having a correlation coefficient of .60. This was used in place of the actual distribution, for which previous computer calculations indicated a correlation coefficient of .606. The theoretical bivariate distribution covered about 1000 cases, whereas actual new dimensional data for glove design were gathered for only 100 subjects, and would not portray the full range of population characteristics as accurately. On the bivariate distribution, twelve areas (corresponding to the twelve selected glove sizes) were selected by "expert judgment" relating to the proportion to be fitted and the allowable tolerance of fit. Not all of the categories were enclosed by equal ranges, and a small percentage was not included.

The remainder of the analysis follows that for suit torso sizes in general procedures: Regression equations were computed for 31 other dimensions obtained in the 100-sample survey, treating them as independent variables. After obtaining these equations, midpoints of the size ranges of the two basic dimensions were substituted in order to obtain group mean values for the other dimensions. Then one within-size standard deviation was added to each mean value to obtain the design value. This within-size standard deviation is the same for all 12 sizes and may be considered as an average standard deviation. Design values and tariffs are listed in the report by Barter and Alexander for all 12 sizes. They did not discuss pattern making or hand forms for these glove types.

9.5.2 Steps 7 and 11. Fit Testing

Barter and Alexander's (1956) report described an example of a fit-testing procedure for pressure suit gloves. Fifty-one subjects and two sets of gloves fabricated by different manufacturers were involved.

The procedure started with taking of two dimensions, Hand Circumference and Hand Length on the right hand of each subject. These were then compared with a glove sizing chart to determine the proper size for each subject. Gloves were donned and evaluated in both the uninflated and inflated state. The evaluations were based on observations and subject comments, in three main areas: Finger Lengths, Hand Circumference, and Wrist Circumference, with the hand in several positions.

The results indicated good success. Thirty-nine out of 40 subjects were fitted adequately in one manufacturer's gloves and 34 out of 35 were fitted adequately in the second manufacturer's gloves. Downgrading and upgrading schemes are also discussed in the report, which permitted fitting a larger percentage of the population than would be indicated by strict adherence to the sizing criteria.

9.5.3 References to Further Examples

Many other interesting fit, contour, and mobility problems related to glove design are found in the literature: Bradley (1957); Roebuck (1965); Pierce

(1960, 1963); Sheridan (1954); Lyman (1956); Lyman and Groth (1958). The problem of arctic glove design is equally of concern (White, Kobrick, and Zimmerer, 1964) and many other examples of gloves of protective clothing could be named. However, the literature on such glove development is skimpy, at best. Therefore, the subject could well use further detail investigation and application of engineering anthropometry and ergonomic techniques.

9.6 HELMET DESIGN

Space suits for Apollo have a transparent "bubble" helmet attached to the suit torso, in which the crewman's head moves freely. This type requires design concepts closely akin to "work space design." That is, the "bubble" must encompass an *envelope of head movements.* However, close-fitting helmets, which move with the head, are more appropriate to this chapter, dealing with "clothing" concepts, and will be the subject of the following discussion.

The U.S. Air Force has developed several appropriate size programs and, with each, an associated head form series. These and later anthropometric sizing program investigations were described by Zeigen, Alexander, Churchill, Emanuel, and Velsey, (1960) in a report describing a Head Circumference Sizing System for helmet design, which will be the basis for this discussion on helmet sizing.

9.6.1 Sizing Program Concepts

The report of Zeigen et al. (1960) illustrates another application of the philosopy for development of sizes based on selected population anthropometric data. This involves:

1. Selection of key dimension(s).
2. Specification of size intervals or "boxes" for the key dimensions (sizing programs).
3. Selection of percentile ranges for design dimensions related to persons in each specified size interval.
4. Preparation of tariffs and sizing dimensions tables for design.
5. Design and fabrication of forms (head forms in this case) which can be used as models for molds or pattern making.

To form a basis for selection of key dimensions, a statistical analysis of variability of several important head and face dimensions was undertaken. Twenty-one possible choices of key dimensions were analyzed to develop standard errors of estimate for the design dimensions. Minimum values of standard error of estimate were subtracted from all other standard errors in the same column, in order to evaluate conveniently the relative differences.

The resulting differences were tabulated as in Table 9-1. A choice was then made among the combinations and single dimensions that could yield good control and practicality of measurement. It was decided, on statistical evidence, that there was no great advantage in selecting more than a single key dimension, Head Circumference, as the basis of a sizing system. Additional practical reasons were listed as follows:

1. "The probability that equipment personnel, untrained in anthropometric measuring techniques, will make a mistake is increased twofold when both head length and breadth (or any other pair) must be taken for determining a size.
2. "For those helmets in which a close fit is not critical, head circumference may be approximated from standard hat sizes. Furthermore, only an ordinary measuring tape is needed to determine head circumference, while a special instrument must be used to measure head length and breadth. Also in this connection, we know that personnel in the field frequently do not use the fitting instruments provided with an article of personal protective equipment, and the use of the simplest of procedures will enhance the probability of its being applied as directed.
3. "Head length and breadth appear to be really critical only in entirely rigid helmets having no adjustability in the support; in liner, sling, or pad-type helmets, there is always some degree of adjustability, so that if head circumference is controlled, head breath and length will also be readily accommodated as long as sufficient room is provided in the shell. Although head length and breadth may be thought to better represent head shape than head circumference, representative head shapes are still provided by head forms using the key dimension head circumference.
4. "Another important consideration is that of the number of sizes needed. When using head length and breadth it is possible to establish a four- or six-size program, with the latter providing somewhat better coverage than the former. However, it is impossible to eliminate sizes without causing excessive bulk in the remaining helmets. On the other hand, . . . in those instances wherein a larger adjustability can be provided, it is possible to use every other size of a program based on head circumference, and there will be little added bulk since these are graded sizes." (As part of the analyses, theoretical Four- and Six-Size Head Length, Head Breadth programs also were set up.)

Table 9-7 represents a fitting chart and estimated procurement tariff (per 1000) for all Three- and Six-Size Head Circumference programs discussed in this report (mean and liner).

Table 9-7. Fitting Table and Suggested Tariffs for the Three- and Six-Size Head Circumference Programs (From Zeigen et al., 1960)

Program	Size	Interval of Head Circumference (in.)	Suggested Tariff[a] (per 1000)
Six-Size (mean and liner)	1	21.0–21.5	54
	2	21.5–22.0	171
	3	22.0–22.5	310
	4	22.5–23.0	269
	5	23.0–23.5	149
	6	23.5–24.0	47
Three-Size (mean)	1–2	21.0–22.0	225
	3–4	22.0–23.0	579
	5–6	23.0–24.0	196

[a] Proportion of 1950 survey sample theoretically included—97%.

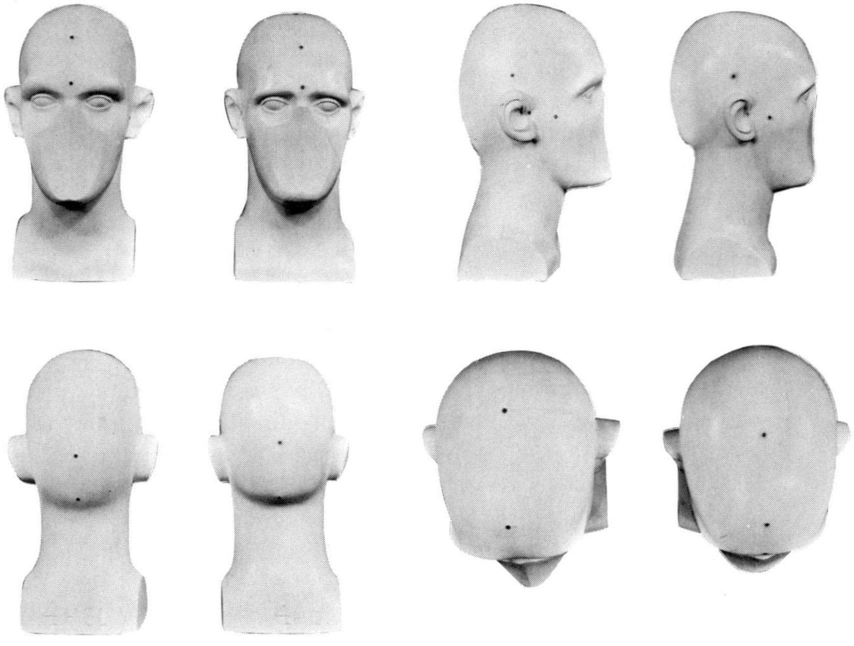

Figure 9-9. Examples of head forms for helmet size development. (Courtesy of Mr. Milton Alexander, USAF Aerospace Medical Research Laboratory.)

9.6.2 Headform Series and Sculpturing Techniques

Headforms have been prepared of plaster of paris in a series of standard sizes to represent significant head measurements in a concrete manner for helmet design. Zeigen et al. (1960) have provided a description of techniques by which such a series may be constructed for helmet shells and helmet liners. Examples of these forms are shown in Figure 9-9.

"Hollow plaster blanks served as the foundations for the desired headforms. As an aid in building up this blank to dimensional values, copper nails were driven into it at various selected points including known landmarks." The procedures were otherwise similar to those for the torso forms (Section 9.3.5). As in those cases, anomalies developed because of the complexity of the design rationale, and compromises had to be made. In order to maintain the values of the maximum frontal diameter, somewhat larger browridges were needed for the linear headform series than for the mean headforms, especially for the largest of the liner headforms.

"After each headform was sculptured, it was measured to insure there was no more than a plus or minus 0.1-in. difference between the statistical and sculptured values. . . . Changes were made as needed." Judgments based on the specific application are needed to resolve such problems, which are typical of headform and other body form constructions (Zeigen et al., 1960). Of course, fit tests finally must be performed to evaluate the effectiveness of these compromises.

X
CONTROLS, DEVICES, AND COMPONENTS DESIGN APPLICATIONS

10.1 INTRODUCTION

There is a class of anthropometric design applications that involve only a small portion of the general space surrounding a person or that involve human mass properties or strength related to a piece or part of clothing or personal equipment that he normally wears. This class consists of applications involving characteristics of objects, devices, and machinery components that are handled by human beings or stepped on, sat in, carried, leaned against, or otherwise manipulated by humans. Subdivisions include objects classifiable as *manipulative* devices such as hand-operated controls: triggers, push buttons, rotary switches, and other hand-operated or grasped devices such as latches, handles, tools, and weapons. A parallel group of devices involve the *feet:* foot-operated controls, foot supports or restraints, certain tools, and ladder rungs. A third group of items involve the dimensions of the *head* to a high degree. These include communications devices such as hand sets, head-mounted microphones, earphones, and various optical devices—binoculars, microscopes, and the like. Another group involves *other special body areas,* characteristics, or *combinations* of various parts of the body: belts, harnesses, holsters, equipment, back or chest packs, consumer appplicances, manipulation/strength enhancement devices, prostheses, and others too numerous to specify. Table 10-1 lists applications in consumer appliance areas not mentioned in preceding chapters.

The detailed specific application examples presented herein constitute only a small sample of the possible range. However, they serve to illustrate the generality of the concepts, anthropometric techniques, and tools described in chapter VII, and the adaptation of procedures described in Chapters VIII and IX.

10.2 HAND-OPERATED CONTROLS

Engineering anthropometry influences the shapes of connectors, latches, knobs, switch resistance or detent systems, the strength of control shaft or handle, or

Table 10-1. Engineering Anthropometry Applications to Consumer Appliances

Class of Device	Anthropometric Application
Clothes irons	Handle grip shape and size, control locations
Vacuum cleaners	Handle grip shape and size, control locations, torque versus size, push buttons
Radios, television, and communications equipment	Knob shapes, torques exertable, handles (for portables), ear to mouth distances, head configurations
Stoves, washing machines, and clothes dryers	Handle size and shape, control knobs and push buttons (also related to work space design principles)
Toasters	Finger grip, push button, and handle shape, sizes and forces
Sewing machines	Knobs sizes and shapes, handles and hand clearances (also related to work space design principles); some have foot pedals for start/stop and speed control
Hearing aids	Ear dimensions and shape factors
Refrigerators and freezers	Handle sizes and shape, control knobs sizes and torques, latches shape, sizes and resistances (some work space design applications)
Cameras and projectors	Knob torques versus sizes, fingertip dimensions, handles and latches, sizes and resistances, locations and orientations of controls for easy reach, location of view finders, and other optics in relation to nose clearance.
Food mixers and blenders	Knob torques versus size, push-button controls, handles and latches (some work space design applications)

of the mechanical stops for limiting motion, and the separation or clearance space around controls, as well as the location of controls relative to the operator (Van Cott, and Kinkade, 1972). Among the commonly encountered examples of hand-operated controls described in human engineering handbooks, the following are selected as examples for this section.

1. Rotary adjustment knobs—continuous motion, cylindrical shape, panel mounted.
2. Rotary selection switches—multiple position detents, bar shape, recessed.
3. Push buttons—in keyboards.

Typically, human engineering handbooks provide dimensional requirements and forces or torques recommended for "optimal" operation of such controls. Many of the control dimensional requirements are related both to body dimensions, particularly the fingers and hand, and to the psychological and physiological characteristics of man as regards his touch sensitivity and ability to perceive and control, to discriminate size, direction, and force, and to perform consistently and accurately under various stress conditions. In this discussion, emphasis will be placed upon the comparison of some very basic anthropometric data with *limiting maximum and minimum functional requirements* of the design.

10.2.1 Hand Grip Types and Terminology

For convenience in later discussions of design aspects of hand-operated controls and tools, primary categories of hand-object prehension grips have been compiled in Figure 10-1. The listing relies to a large degree on published literature (e.g., Ammerman, 1956; Jones, Kobrick, and Gaydos, 1958; Napier, 1956, 1962; Taylor, 1954; Tichauer, 1966), especially on a review by Shah (1973). However, since previous descriptions and terms were not fully satisfactory and have not been generally accepted as standards, the listing in Table 10-1 attempts a new and consistent approach. Here, the primary titles are derived from the anatomy of the hand parts mainly involved, further exemplified and simplified by short secondary names, given in parentheses.

Grip Numbers 1 through 5 are most suitable for finely controlled "precision"* work. Grip Number 6 is a transition to the type used in the transmission of large force or energy, typically represented by Grip Number 7, the "power"* grip. Figure 10-2 illustrates the hook grip which is important for certain types of handholds and drawer pulls, tools, and similar items.

10.2.2 Cylindrical Dial Controls

A classic example of control design is the cylindrically shaped knob, usually recommended for continuous adjustment or used for detented settings at discrete positions. Anthropometric concerns to be considered in this text are minimum and maximum dimensions that the hand can grasp, and maximum torques that may be exerted. Torques can be influenced by several physical

* Napier (1956, 1962) has discussed the differences between "power" and "precision" grip types.

(1) Thumb–fingertip grip (Tip grip):
the thumb tip opposes one fingertip.

(2) Thumb–finger palmar grip (Plier grip):
thumb pad opposes the palmar pad of one finger (or the palmar pads of several fingers) near the tips. This grip evolves easily from the tip grip (1) above.

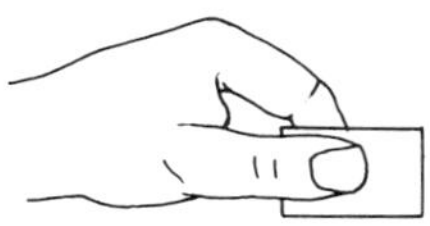

(3) Thumb–forefinger side grip (Lateral grip):
thumb opposes the (radial) side of the forefinger.

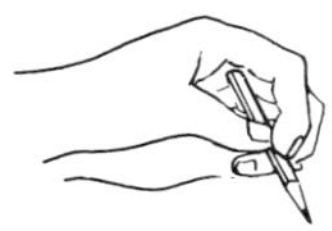

(4) Thumb–two–finger grip (Chuck or writing grip):
thumb and two fingers (often forefinger and index finger) oppose each other at or near the tips.

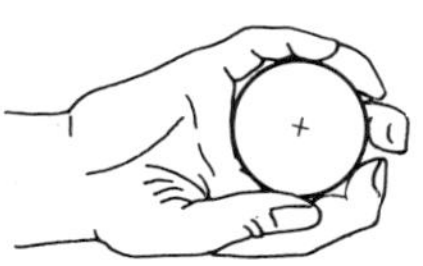

(5) Thumb–fingertip enclosure (Disc grip):
thumb pad and the pads of three or four fingers oppose each other near the tips (object grasped does not touch the palm). This grip evolves easily from grip 4.

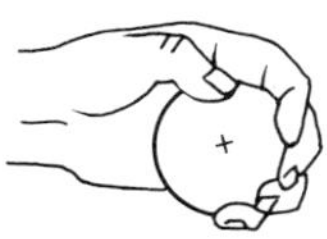

(6) Finger–palm enclosure (Collet enclosure):
a large part, or all, of the inner surface of the hand is in contact with the object while enclosing it. This grip evolves easily from grip 5.

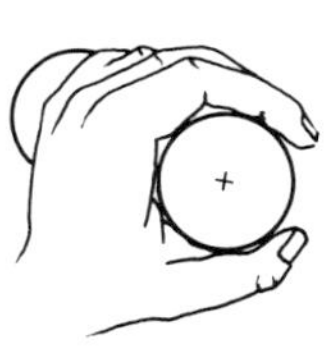

(7) Power grip:
the total inner hand surface is grasping an often cylindrical handle which runs parallel to the knuckles and generally protrudes on one or both sides from the hand.

Figure 10-1. Categories and titles for prehension hand grips.

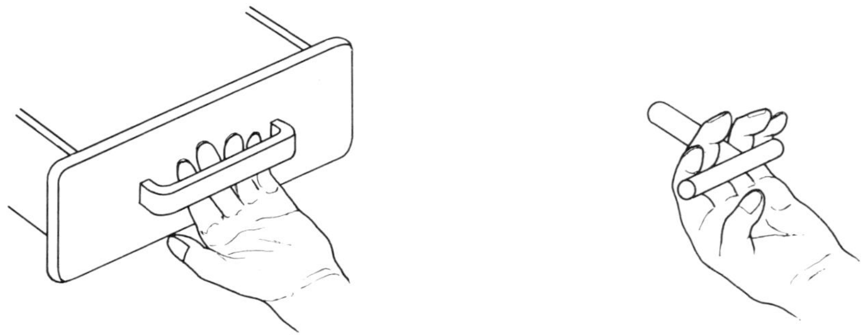

Figure 10-2. Hook grips. This type of finger action is used where thumb counterpressure is not needed.

characteristics and by glove types (Sharp, 1962; Ammerman, 1956; Pierce, 1960, 1963; Hedberg and Lobron, 1954; Roebuck, 1965).

Design considerations related to maximum exertable torques for such knobs are summarized in Table 10-2. An example problem follows which shows typical estimation processes in applications of torque and force data to design requirements development.

Problem Statement:
Determine the upper limit of operating torque and design stress limit for a cylindrical knurled knob ½ in. thick by 2½ in. in diameter which is mounted with lower surface essentially at panel level, axis perpendicular to operator's trunk at approximately chest level. Operator's direction of reach is restricted but not his angular position of starting torque application or method of grasp. Assume bare hand operation only.

Approach to the Solution:
The upper limit of *operating torque* should be set below the lowest measurement of *maximum torque* exertion by the population, so that the weakest person can operate the switch. Review of several sources of data reveals the following:
Data of Sharp (1962) and Roebuck (1965) appear to be applicable as to knob size location and orientation. However, the subject orientation in Sharp's study was rather restricted to a type of "precision grip" on the knob (Figure 10-3*a*) and resulted in magnitudes generally lower than those of Roebuck's study, which permitted a "power grip" technique (Figure 10-3*b*).

1. Operating Torque:
Without further information, Sharp's lower levels of torque are appropriate as design criteria for *operating* torque. These data for knurled knobs indicate a mean of 23.2 in.-lb and standard deviation of 7.1 in.-lb. Selecting a

Table 10-2. Anthropometric Considerations for Design of Cylindrical Knobs

Type of Relationship	Effect of Variations
Torque versus diameter	Mean scores of maximum exertable torque increase monotonically as diameter increases, for all similar hand/glove conditions, texture, and thickness. Effectiveness of torque application increases more rapidly than diameter (nonproportional relationship) (Sharp, 1962; Roebuck, 1965; Ammerman 1956).
Torque versus texture and glove material	Knurling and fluting increase torque transmission by fingers as compared to smooth knobs (Sharp, 1962; Roebuck, 1965). Use of rubber gloves produces similar effect (Roebuck, 1965).
Torque versus glove pressurization (for pressure suits)	Pressurization of space suit glove generally reduces capability for exerting torque as compared to unpressurized condition, except where only fingertips are involved (very small diameters) (Roebuck, 1965; Pierce, 1963).
Torque versus arm/body position	Torque exertion capability is sensitive to body positioning and hand/finger positioning. Roebuck (1965) showed a factor of approximately twice those of Sharp (1962) on similar knobs, for different conditions of grasp and trunk support.
Torque versus axial thickness	Range of effects unknown. Roebuck (1965) showed no significant difference between .5 and .65 in. thickness.
Torque versus distance from panel	Range of effects unknown.

low design value of the first percentile, one may estimate the design limit by the method outlined in Chapter V:

Multiply the standard deviation by the appropriate factor from Table 5-4, then subtract the result from the mean.

$(7.1) \times (2.236) = 15.9$ in.-lb (difference between mean and 1st percentile)

$23.2 - 15.9 \doteq 7.3$ in.-lb (1st percentile)

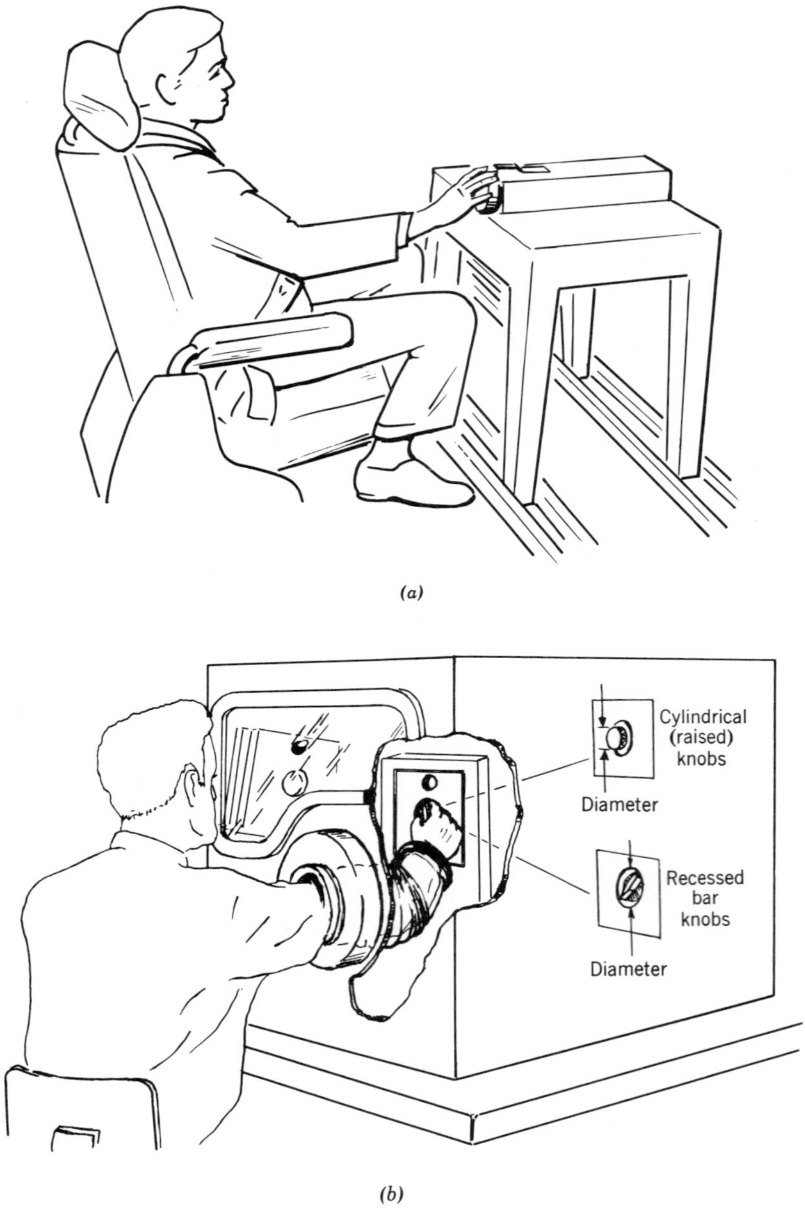

Figure 10-3. Subject position and grip used in two studies of maximum torque on knobs. (*a*) Subject position in Sharp's (1962) study. (*b*) Subject position in study by Roebuck (1965).

Thus the operating torque should be less than 7.3 in-lb for a 99 percentile level of confidence that all operators can turn the knob. (This procedure assumes normally distributed data. However, muscular strength data are often skewed—see Chapters IV and VI.)

2. Design Stress Torque:
The upper limit of torque for *design stress levels* for the switch shaft and motion limit devices (stops) is determined from the maximum exertable torque of a very strong person in the design population. Assume the 95th percentile is used as the criterion. The data of Roebuck (1965) shown in Table 10-3 are more characteristic of data for a maximum stress design, since such forces may be exerted if the proper, effective grip technique is used by the operator. Unfortunately, the data do not go beyond 2.0 in. diameter: However, a number of methods are available to extrapolate to the required diameter. *Such estimation activity is a common requirement in engineering anthropometry.* Hence, for methods are described.

Method 1: Increase in Constant Proportion to Another Study. Since Sharp's data extend into the 2.5 in. range, a ratio of Roebuck's data by Sharp's (1962) data at smaller diameters is a possible approach. Table 10-4 indicates the ratios of Roebuck's data to Sharp's data for both knurled and smooth knobs. The smooth knob (bare hand) data yield higher ratios at 1.0 and 2.0 in. diameters than the knurled knobs, but the pattern is not consistent.

A great many statistical manipulations may be applied to estimate the significance of these differences and the probable errors involved. However, there still remains a need for judgment in the estimate. It appears reasonable that a ratio in the neighborhood of 2.0 leads to a conservative estimate. This would yield a mean torque of 46.5 in-lb. The minimum ratio (1.715) yields 39.8 in-lb, as a potential low figure for the mean.

Estimation of the 95th percentile for these distributions depends on estimating the standard deviations and applying factors from Chapter V to estimate the selected percentile. The estimation of standard deviation is derived from the concept of coefficient of variation $V = S/M$ (see Chapter V), data for which are also shown in Table 10-4.

These tabulated values indicate a significant variation, potentially *as a function of diameter,* which bears further investigation. In Figure 10-4 data from other series are plotted for comparison to the basic conditions. Those selected are the conditions likely to show variational effects related to a "good" grip—for example, unpressurized glove (with high coefficient of friction) on smooth knobs, bare hand on recessed bar knobs, bare hand on knurled cylindrical knobs, and including the above conditions of basic concern. There appears to be a decreasing fluctuation in the coefficient of variation as diameter increases, eventually approaching a relatively steady horizontal trend. Coeffi-

Table 10-3. Mean and Standard Deviation of Maximum Torque[a] by Knob Diameter and Hand Condition

Knob Dia. (in.)	Cond.	Configuration: Recessed Bar .75 thick		Cylindrical Smooth .50 thick		Cylindrical Knurled .50 thick		Cylindrical Knurled .65 thick	
		Mean[b]	S.D.[b]	Mean	S.D.	Mean	S.D.	Mean	S.D.
1/8	B			.255	.067			.749	.103
	U			.531	.165			.786	.105
	P			.635	.221			.964	.364
1/2	B			2.61	.451				
	U			3.71	.769				
	P			3.39	.928				
1	B	6.33	1.40	7.62	2.88	11.9	3.58	11.3	3.08
	U	5.96	1.60	9.50	3.64	10.2	3.08	10.3	3.29
	P	5.96	1.64	8.08	2.27	9.00	1.69	9.54	2.36

1½	B	12.2	3.54	14.6	4.62				
	U	11.9	1.76	17.4	5.15				
	P	11.3	2.80	14.8	3.61				
1¾	B	19.5	3.86						
	U	18.5	3.27						
	P	17.9	3.97						
2	B	24.4	5.71	18.7	5.49	26.5	4.96	27.3	5.38
	U	22.8	3.73	22.9	6.18	26.0	5.34	25.0	5.34
	P	21.1	3.67	21.6	3.94	23.8	4.59	23.2	3.65
2¼	B	29.0	6.76						
	U	27.9	6.74						
	P	25.0	4.19						
2½	B	35.8	7.15	26.5	4.85				
	U	35.1	8.10	28.7	5.72				
	P	30.0	5.09	28.7	6.61				

[a] (From Roebuck, 1965)
[b] All torque values and standard deviations are in inch-pounds.
Key: B = bare hand, U = unpressurized glove, P = pressurized glove—3.5 psig, S.D. = standard deviation.

Table 10-4. Comparison of Knob Torques (Bare Hand Operation) for Two Studies

Cylindrical Knob Texture and Diameter (in.)	Torques						
	Sharp (1962)			Roebuck (1965)			Ratio of Means:
	Mean (in.-lb)	Std. Dev. (in.-lb)	Coef. Var.	Mean (in.-lb)	Std. Dev. (in.-lb)	Coef. Var.	$\left(\frac{\text{Roebuck Data}}{\text{Sharp Data}}\right)$
Knurled							
1.0	7.25	2.22	.306	11.9	3.58	.301	1.175
2.0	13.15	3.06	.233	26.5	4.96	.187	1.925
2.5	23.2	7.09	.306	(to be estimated—see text)			
Smooth							
1.0	3.69	1.33	.361	7.6	2.88	.379	2.03
1.5	6.08	1.59	.369	14.6	4.62	.316	2.40
2.0	9.24	2.29	.249	18.7	5.49	.294	2.03
2.5	14.75	3.95	.268	26.5	4.85	.184	1.78

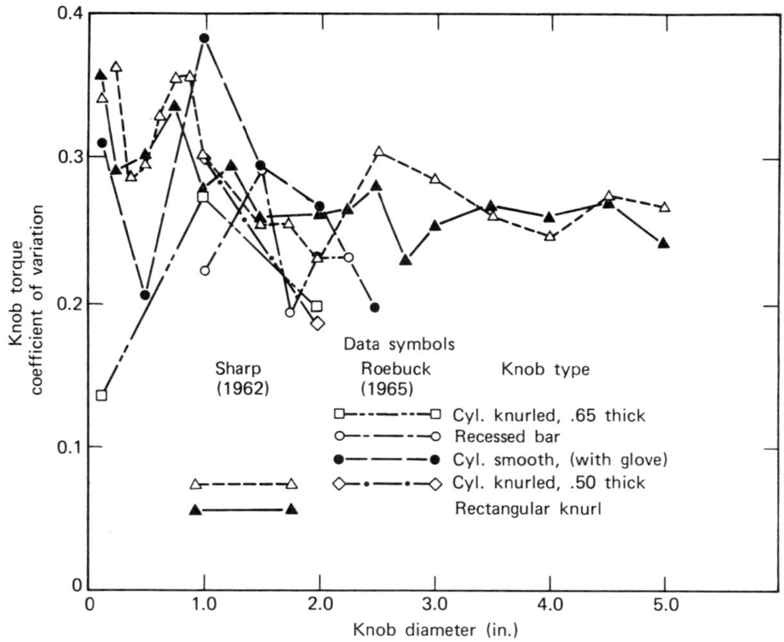

Figure 10-4. Coefficient of variation of torque as a function of knob diameter. Data from several types of small knobs of varying shape, surface texture and operated by subjects under differing glove-hand conditions are compared.

cients of variation for Roebuck's data are generally less than those of Sharp. However, none of the magnitudes go below $V = .187$ in the vicinity of 2.0 to 2.25 in. Visual extrapolation of the trend, following Sharp's data, indicates the coefficient would rise, possibly to .25 (25%), which is a conservative estimate; that is, it will lead to using a higher stress level for design and reduce the probability of breakage. Calculation of the 95th percentiles is shown in Table 10-5 (Method 1).

Method 2: Adjustment of Smooth-Knob Data Using Percentage Increment of Torque for Knurled Knobs. Roebuck's data for smooth knobs extends to 2.5 in. Figure 10-5 shows two types of comparison of incremental torque of knurled knobs: in terms of *percentage* and *absolute* difference for both Sharp's data and Roebuck's data. It may be seen that the trends are similar for both sets of data, although somewhat different in absolute magnitude. The percentage increment drops rapidly as diameter increases to approximately 1.5 in., then appears to begin a slow rise (at about 10% per inch of diameter for Sharp's data). Extrapolating from Roebuck's datum at 2.0 in. (40%) yields ap-

Table 10-5. Calculation of 95th Percentile Torques

Column no.	(1)	(2)	(3)	(4)	
Method Described in Text	Estimate of Mean (M) (in.-lb)	Estimate of Std. Dev. $S = .25\ (M)$	Increment: from Mean to 95th Percentile $\Delta = 1.645\ (S)$	Design Criteria (in.-lb)	Percentile
1. Proportion of Means to	(high) 46.5	11.6	19.1	65.6	95th[a]
another study.	(low) 39.8	10.0	16.4	56.2	95th
2. Percentage increment:	(high) 38.4	9.6	15.8	54.2	95th
Knurled over smooth.	(low) 37.5	9.4	15.5	53.0	95th
3. Extrap. Sample (Maximum)	—	—	—	47[a]	83rd[b]
4. Specification Magnitude		Not applicable		133[a]	unspecified

[a] 95th percentiles calculated as the sum of column (1) and (3).

[b] Maximum of twelve subjects in sample. See text for interpretation.

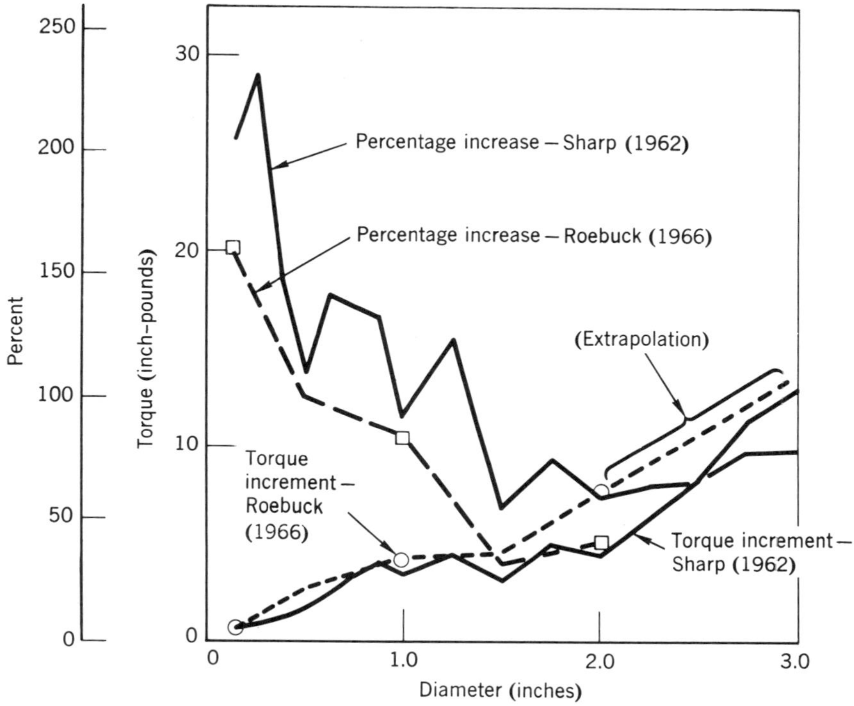

Figure 10-5. Increment of maximum torque due to knurling—as a function of knob diameter. (Roebuck, 1965.) The above data are for bare hand conditions, and compare mean values. Note the similarity in results from two different studies, even though the absolute magnitude of the means for the two studies were significantly different.

proximately 45% increment at 2.5 in. diameter. Since the smooth knob torque at 2.5 in. is 26.5 in-lb, the estimated mean for the knurled knob is $1.45 \times 26.5 = 38.4$ in-lb.

Method 3. Extrapolating directly as shown for the absolute magnitudes, a value of 11 in-lb added to 26.5 yields 37.5 in-lb. The 95th percentile magnitudes also must be calculated for these means based on assumed coefficients of variation as in Table 10-4. Having previously noted that maximum force and torque data are typically assymetrical, there is reason to compare actual maximum data from Roebuck's report. This represents a 100% level of the sample subjects counting from the lowest magnitude upward. However, counting from the top, it represents a rough, small-sample estimate of the 83.5th percentile ($\frac{1}{12}$ of subjects above this value). The linearly extrapolated maximum measurement is approximately 47 in-lb. Thus the estimated "sample maximum" value is slightly less than all the calculated 95th percentile estimates.

Method 4: "By the Book." Another useful checkpoint is that of the aircraft design specification MIL-A-8865 (ASG). These requirements may be called for by the customer in some military vehicles. This specification calls for pilot applied loads for design of 133 in.-lb for a "small wheel or knob . . ." if operated by twisting. Clearly such a magnitude is much higher than expected from the previous discussion of experimental data, and its use could result in an overweight design.

Problem Solution: Typical of many engineering anthropometry problems, the several methods have generated different, relatively close estimates, without a clear choice criterion for selection. Considering other experience of the skewed nature of force data, the highest estimate (65.6 in-lb) is recommended. It is the most conservative, except for the "specification" value.

10.2.3 Recessed Rotary Selector Switch

A second example of the application of engineering anthropometry to the design of small hand controls involves bar-type rotary selector switch knobs that are recessed for pressure suit protection and to help prevent inadvertant actuation. At the beginning of the Apollo program, no anthropometric data were available that could be applied to the design for such knobs. Hence, a study was performed to relate maximum exertable torque to diameter knob size and to the wearing of space suit gloves, for both the recessed bar knobs and cylindrical knobs (Roebuck, 1965). Recessed knob test results are summarized in Table 10-3 along with those for cylindrical knobs. Among the interesting findings was a significant rate of torque increase between 1.5 and 1.75 in. diameter. This phenonomenon appears related to two anthropometric aspects: opposing the thumb by either the tips of the index and middle finger *or* by the length of the second phalanx of the bent index finger provides a grip that seems to fit within the recess (Figure 10-6). Also, the subjects expressed marked preferences for the 1.5 and 1.75 in. diameters, especially for the latter when gloves were worn. Design considerations for such recessed bar knobs are summarized in Table 10-6.

10.2.4 Keyboards for Manual Data Entry

The examples selected here involve the standard typewriter keyboard, which serves as a model for *combinations* of push buttons, called keyboards, such as used on teletypers, desk calculators, consoles, computer keysets, cash registers, and the like. This man-machine interface should be designed to allow high-frequency, error-free operation with the least possible strain on the operator.

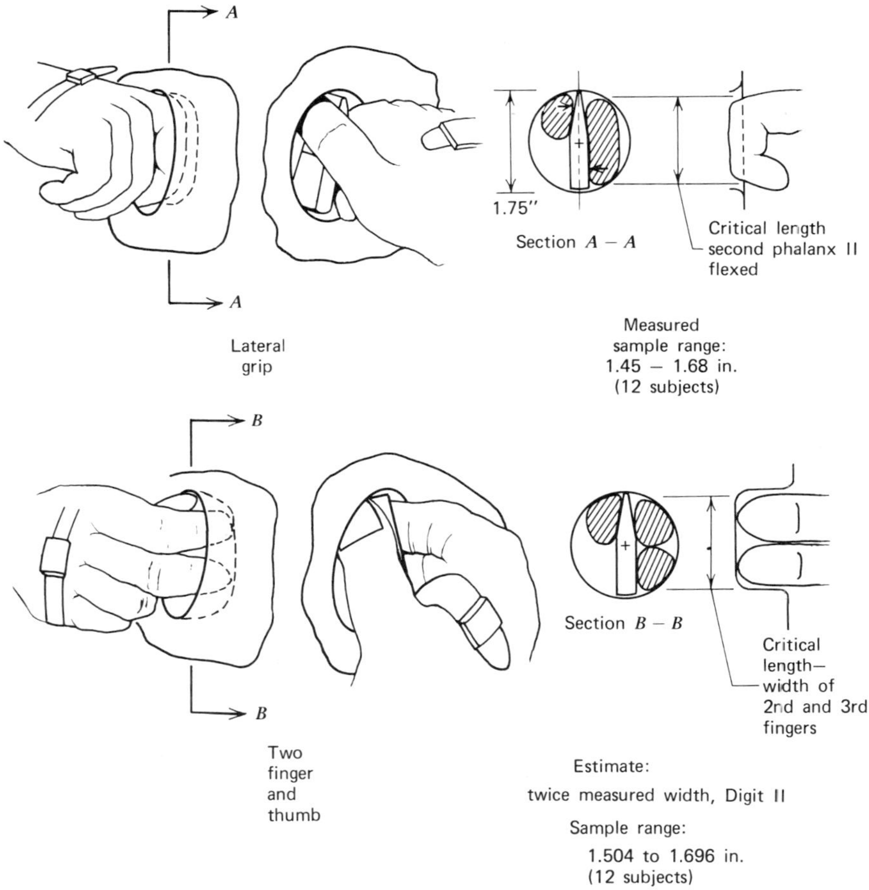

Figure 10-6. Recess of 1.75 in. diameter provides space for two effective grip methods. (Roebuck, 1965.)

The following discussion, based primarily on articles by Kroemer (1964, 1965a, 1965b, 1972c), covers several experiments conducted to find optimum design criteria. These experiments dealt mainly with the lateral tilt of keyboards, or, anthropometrically, with the amount of pronation or supination of the hand of the operator.

Body Positioning in Relation to Keyboards

It has long been known that the typewriter keyboard layout requires the typist to assume postures of the trunk, head, shoulders arms, and hands that are "unnatural, uncomfortable and fatiguing" (Klockenberg, 1926). A brief

Table 10-6. Design Considerations for Recessed Bar Knobs (Based on data from Roebuck, 1965)

Type of Relationship	Effect of Variations
Torque versus diameter of recess	Mean scores of maximum exertable torque increases monotonically as diameter increases. Significantly greater rate of increase from 1.5 to 1.75 in. diameter and between 2.25 and 2.5 in. in diameter
Torque versus texture and glove material	Probably not applicable. No improvement with rubber gloves—either constant or decrement.
Torque versus glove pressurization (for pressure suits)	Pressurization generally reduces torque exertion capability—effect greatest on largest diameters (up to 2.5 in.)
Torque versus axial thickness	Unknown—all knobs tested were 0.75 in. thick, top surface flush with panel.

anthropometric analysis of body position pinpoints the specific problems and suggest potential solutions.

At the standard keyboard, the typist has to hold the palms of the hands about horizontal, that is, rotated inward ("pronated") close to the anatomical limit. This position violates the rule of thumb recommending use of midpoints of motion range for joints. Such static tension, endured over some time, leads to fatigue. To relieve some tension from the pronatory muscles, the operator tends to lift the elbow laterally and forward (the elbows are also lifted if the keyboard is located too high). Thus the operator constantly works against the gravitational pull with the shoulder muscles, which may be overly strained over extended periods of time. Lundervold (1958) recorded increased muscular activity electromyographically in both shoulder/upper arm muscles, but even in forearm muscles when a typist kept the shoulders raised.

From postural principles described thus far, it appears that a keyboard design that permits tilting the hands laterally (about half-way between extreme pronation and supination) should avoid the fatiguing pronation and possibly reduce arm-hand syndromes found among card punchers and typists.

Preferred Posture of Hands and Forearms

In order to more precisely select candidate angles for keyboard designs, Kroemer (1964) investigated preferred angle of tilt of the palms by a simple anthropometric test, using a thin light rod attached across each subject's palm with a rubber band.

Figure 10-7 gives the results in terms of degrees of pronation "α" against vertical at the different upper arm elevations "β." Since the data were not normally distributed, median values are indicated in addition to the usual means. To hold the palm about horizontal was felt comfortable only with the upper arm distinctly raised to the side. With the upper arm hanging, however, most subjects preferred an angular position of the hand in the middle region between extreme pronation and supination. A line extrapolated from Klockenberg's findings shows similar results.

Experiments on Arrangement of Keys and Keyboards

The literature abounds with experiments and suggestions concerning the arrangement of the individual keys in relation to each other (see, e.g., Alden, Daniels, and Kanarick, 1970; Dvorak, 1943; Klockenberg, 1926; Martin, 1949; Remington and Rogers, 1969). However, very few researchers paid attention to the effects of the spatial orientation (lateral declination) of the key-

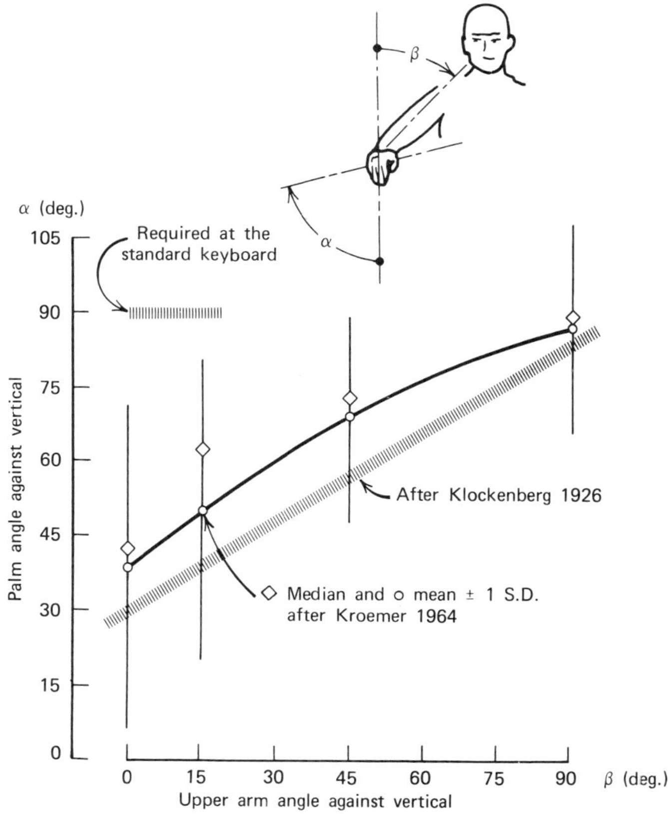

Figure 10-7. Preferred palm position in relation to upper arm posture.) (after Kroemer, 1964.)

Table 10-7. Summary of Four Keyboard Studies

Study Description	Results
Single hand keyboard	
1. "Hand Configured" arrangement 3 curved rows 5 straight columns versus square matrix arrangement 4 keys × 4 keys in straight rows and columns Ref: Webb and Coburn (1959)	At 18° lateral declination, 5 out of 6 subjects preferred "hand configured" keyboard. Mean performance better on hand configured keyboard (647 versus 729 seconds to complete task)
Two-hand keyboard (Typewriter)	
2. Hinged left and right halves at centerline. Sections set at following: 0° horizontal (standard), 22°, 44°, 66°, 88° 3-minute timed sessions each (5 × 5 Latin square experiment design) Ref: Creamer and Trumbo (1960)	Significant differences (statistically) in speed: best at 44°, good at 22° and 66°, worst at 0° and 88°. *But* largest difference between means (44° and 0°) less than 5%. Errors: Greatest at 0°, least at 88°. Fatigue index: independent of declination. Subjects preferred 44° or 66°, found 0° hardest.
3. Standard typewriter keyboard (Fig. 10-8) (Sloped 15° in side view) compared to "K-keyboard" which has left and right halves hinged to truncated 30° triangular horizontal centerpiece. Key arrangement "hand configured" (Fig. 10-9). Sections set at following: 0° (horizontal), 30°, 45°, 60°, 90° Ref: Kroemer (1964)	No statistically significant differences in tapping frequency or number of errors. Only marked preference was the 60° declination as compared to 0° (Each subject had only two settings to test.
4. Standard typewriter keyboard compared to K-keyboard (Fig. 10-9) set at 50° vertex angle, declined at 45° Ref.: Kroemer (1965a, 1965b)	No significant differences in tapping rate (5/sec) or circulatory strain (median heart rate 11 beats/min above resting), but more errors on standard keyboard. (127 versus 77/1000 on K-keyboard). Termination reasons (most frequent): standard keyboard—"aches and pains," K-keyboard—"can't concentrate" but some aches and pains in shoulder region (elbows were lifted).

board on job efficiency or operator strain. Table 10-7 summarizes four studies in which spatial orientation was a key parameter.

The primary purpose of Kroemer's experiments (Numbers 3 and 4 in Table 10-7) was to explore whether or not different postures of the hand-wrist forearm system produce muscular strain that affects the performance of key-

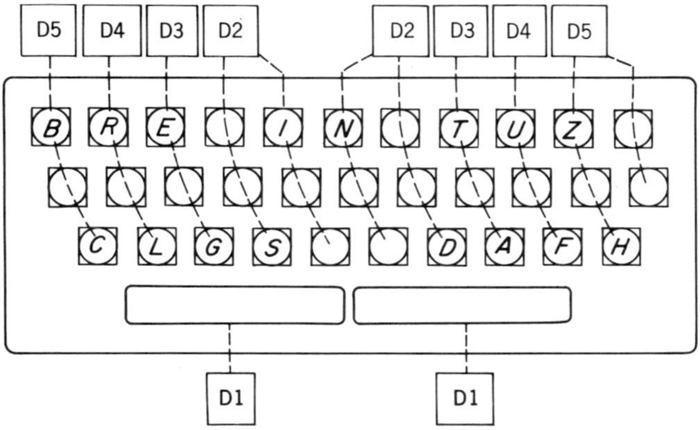

Figure 10-8. Standard keyboard model for typewriter (after Kroemer, 1965a,b). Dashed lines indicate the keys usually allotted to each digit (*D*). Distribution of characters shown was used for research purposes, but is not recommended for general use.

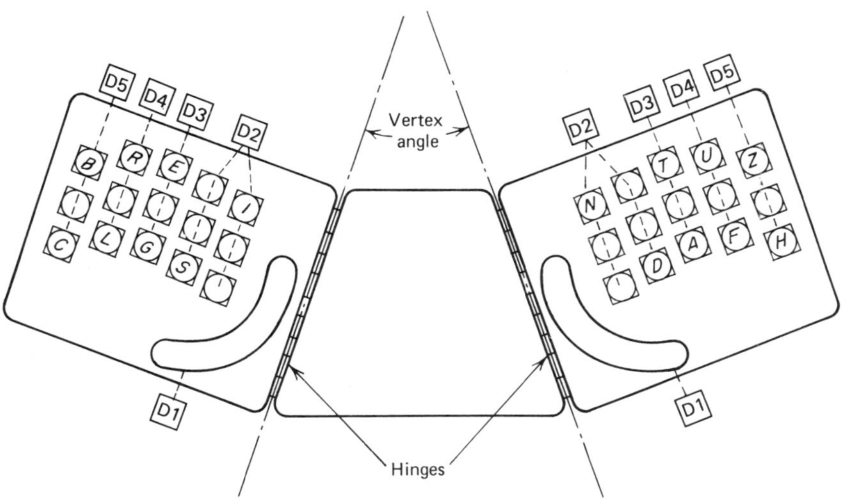

Figure 10-9. K-keyboard model for typewriter (after Kroemer, 1965a,b). Dashed lines indicate the keys usually allotted to each digit (*D*). Distribution of characters shown is not recommended for general use.

board operators. Several of the experimental conditions did necessitate sustained muscular tensions to maintain certain body positions, which were uncomfortable, fatiguing, and straining to the extent of being painful. Complaints about physical discomfort in the arms and wrists after work at the standard keyboard arrangement (Figure 10-8) were mentioned more frequently than with the inclined K-keyboard (Figure 10-9). "Aches and pains" were given as reason for terminating the experiments more frequently after work on the standard keyboard than on the K-keyboard inclined at 45°.

The experiment with the horizontal standard keyboard and the keysets at 45° declination did not show any significant differences in the typing frequency, in the endured typing time, or in the operator's heart rate. However, only about half as many typing *errors* (depressing a key not contained in the "text") were committed at the K-keyboard than at the standard keyboard. This can mainly be attributed to the division of the K-keyboard into two separate keysets with one assigned to each hand.

Summary—General Design Features of Keyboards/Work Stations

Anatomical, physiological, and biomechanical considerations, as well as the discussed experiments suggest that the following design features be thoroughly considered.

1. Separation of the keyboard sections allotted to each hand, and lateral declination of the keyboard sections allotted to each hand.

2. Mechanics of key motion and their effects on the operator (the literature contains almost no information on the forces/impacts exchanged between finger and key, and on their effects concerning the effort, strain, or fatique induced in the operator. Even Hettinger's hypothesis that the frequency is more important than the force, published in 1958, has stirred very little research interest).

3. General work place layout (the numerous system components such as the text to be copied, platen and displays to be scanned, table, stand, console, and chair, foot-operated controls, in addition to the keyboard. These system components interact biomechanically, physiologically, and psychologically with the operator and affect his strain and hence his performance.)

10.3 HANDHOLDS, HANDLES, AND HAND TOOLS

Another class of hand-related devices which have many features similar to hand controls, when considered from an anthropometric/man-machine viewpoint, includes devices that are grasped and manipulated to perform a direct mechanical function (transmit energy) rather than switching (control energy release). For example, a handhold or handle enables persons to assist their own movement, or provide for stability, or facilitate holding or movement of a large package (e.g., suitcase, electronic set) or device, such as a shovel or power drill. See also "Design of Hand Tools," Section 10.3.3.

10.3.1 Functional Requirements

Ostensibly a simple concept, the function of a handle or handhold (separately or on a tool) may vary considerably in usage. Several "mission" considerations (Step 1, Figure 8-1) are listed in Table 10-8, together with pertinent anthropometric dimension and force data which should be available for successful design (Step 2, Figure 8-2).

10.3.2. Design, Development and Evaluation Procedures—Handles

Critical clearance designs justify detailed layout "work space" drawings to evaluate capability of the hand to accomplish its desired grasp. Inspection of the layout drawings may generate requirements for measuring equipment and evaluation procedures. These will usually be simple mock-ups of the work area constraints. Selection of a subject pool and a survey of a large number of subjects may be required. Examples of such studies are described by McFadden and Swearingen (1958), McFadden et al. (1959), Tichauer (1966), Garrett, Alexander, and Bennett (1967), Maul and Solf (1969) and Ramsey (1971). in some cases, casting techniques may be applied, perhaps using a malleable clay to develop contours within the hand or the clearance envelopes outside of it. Handholds, being in intimate contact with the hand, require "clothing" type anthropometric considerations as well as those related to "work space" clearances.

10.3.3 Design of Hand Tools

Hand tools are means of increasing effectiveness and range of limb motions and of boosting power, strength (force and torque) and pressure capacities. Additionally, hand tools can serve to keep the body from close contact with harmful (hot, sharp, noxious) materials. The key man-machine interface is the *handle*. In addition to factors described in Table 10-8, tool handles generally have to "fit the hand" more than those previously described, either resulting in a contour interlocking between hand and tool, or allowing a relative movement. Often, interlocking and force movement must alternate in

Table 10-8. Handhold/Handle Anthropometric Design Considerations and Data Requirements

Design Considerations	Anthropometric Data Types Required
Grip types (see Figures 10-1 and 10-2)	Finger diameters—at various joints and between joints, both breadth and thickness, relaxed and compressed (working positions). External and internal diametral measurements.
Direction(s) of approach of hand	Range of wrist joint movement. Type of grip required.
Forces and torques applied/ resisted (direction and magnitude)	Strength capability versus grip type for design population (including gloves, etc.)
Handle length	Hand breadth, thumb space, glove thickness
Clearance allowed/required around handle	Clearance diameters for gripping actions—knuckles, wrist, heel of hand, glove shape.
Contouring, shape factors	Hand contours in functional positions.
Gloves	Additional clearance for glove material. Mobility/grasp capability reduction Coefficient of friction Reduction of tactile sensations Variations due to suit pressurization/depressurization Metal stiffeners, straps, buckles, etc.

the course of using the tool. Also, tool handles may have finger-operated controls built into them, such as triggers, thumb-operated buttons or thumbwheels, or squeeze levers (pliers, guns, power tools, etc.).

Previously mentioned data tables giving hand dimensions usually do not describe the hand in its working position and give virtually no information on the contours and the surface geometry of the inside of the hand. Hence, molds of the *inside* of the hand in its operational posture can be very useful in determining how a handle can or should be formed to fit snugly into the hand. Unless the custom-form handle is intended for use by one specific individual, the mold has to be smoothed and brought into a more general shape to fit the variety of hands of the user population. Hence, even for tools in general use, simple geometric forms (cylinders, ellipses, cones, etc.) are often the best possible adaptation to the hands of a larger population.

Energy transfer between hand and tool utilizes friction and mechanical interlocking between the surfaces of handle and skin. To avoid slippage, handles are generally made of, or covered with, nonporous material that does not retain fat, water, or other "lubricants." Slippage can also be avoided by shaping the handle so that no continuous layer of "grease" can exist between tool and skin; knurling or grooving or asymmetrical shaping of the handle are often used. Pronounced shape can provide virtual interlocking between hand and handle with no relative motion possible in one or several directions: a T-handle, for example, grasped so that the stem is between the fingers and the bar is at the palm restricts motion between the hand and the tool severely. However, pronounced shaping can lead to excessive pressure at certain points of interaction. Such pressure can be painful and may even damage tissue. Especially susceptible are the interphalangeal points, tendon sheats, and areas close to blood vessels and nerves.

Wearing of mittens or gloves can change the dimensions, tactility, and mobility of the (protected) hand substantially, as noted in Chapters VIII and IX and Section 10.2. Special design allowances must be made for such conditions.

Task requirements, space available, and spatial arrangement of the object to be worked on determine which grip (or grips) (described in Figures 10-1 and 10-2) are used. Each of these "grips" requires different designs of the handle of the tool, and often the handle design for one type of grip is quite inadequate for another way of grasping it.

For conventional tools, the various human factors engineering handbooks (Chapter VII) contain adequate design principles. Even for specific tools to be used either under unusual circumstances, or by selected operators (astronauts, aquanauts, women, etc.) or for tools for special tasks, the previous comments provide some insights into the anthropometric and ergonomic variables that must be considered. Major considerations based on anatomical, anthropometric, biomechanical, and ergonomical research (Damon, 1970; Kroemer 1963, 1966b; Maul and Solf, 1969; Peres, 1961; Ramsey, 1971; Tichauer, 1966) are as follows:

The design and use of the tools must be compatible with the motion inventory and strain capacity of the human body, especially of the forearm/wrist/hand. In general, manipulative work with hand tools is best performed when the wrist is approximately in line with the long axis of the forearm (Fig. 10-10). (This is part of the experience that use of body members in their midranges and functional positions normally results in best performance and least fatigue and strain). Dorsiflection of the wrist in combination

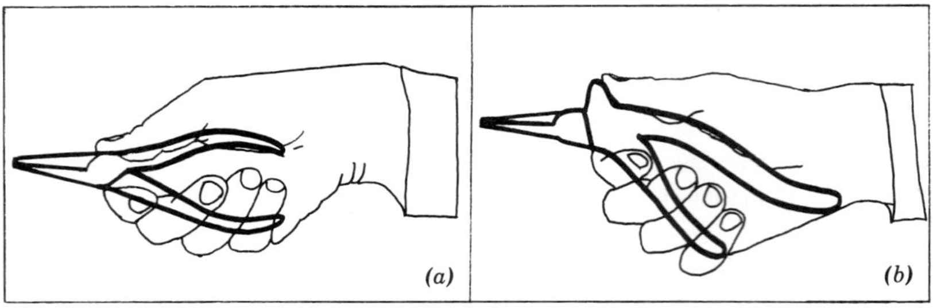

Figure 10-10. Redesign of pliers to reduce wrist stress. (*a*) Conventional hand tool requiring ulnar flexion. (*b*) Redesigned pliers can be manipulated in a less stressful hand and wrist position. (Courtesy Dr. J. D. Ramsey, Texas Tech University.)

with acute pronation is to be avoided particularly as extremely straining. For speed and precision of tool-aided manipulation, the radial side seems to be preferred, while tools are often directed to the ulnar side if slower and stronger movements are required. For exertion of direct strength or force, the direction from the elbow through the forefinger is advantageous. Rotating exertions are executed about an axis of rotation running approximately from the elbow through the ring finger. Continuous or frequent rotations of the wrist should be avoided.

10.4 FOOT-OPERATED CONTROLS

The design of foot-operated controls, involving the large masses and gross motions/positions of the legs is heavily dependent on the same major considerations as general work space design.

10.4.1 Body Positioning in Relation to Foot-Operated Controls

Efficient operation of foot controls generally requires that the operator be seated. As compared to the standing position, sitting is more stable, requires less effort to be maintained, hence is less fatiguing and can be maintained for longer periods of time. Furthermore, the seated position allows simultaneous use of both feet, a requirement for most foot-controlled man-machine systems. The body posture of the pedal operator, and hence his efficiency in operating pedals, depend (1) on the type and size of his seat, (2) on the number, type, size, and mode of operation of the pedal(s), and (3) on the relative spatial arrangement of seat and pedal(s). Other factors such as vehicle dynamics or vibrations in the man-machine environment feedback loop also bear on the operator's efficiency, as discussed in Chapter VIII. The most obvious relationships between seat and pedal are height and (lateral and sagittal) distance: a pedal arranged too far or too close, or displaced too much to the side, will impede proper operation, or render it impossible. However, even when located within easy reach, different arrangements of pedals are likely to be advantageous for, say, rare but forceful operations or continuous fine movements requiring little energy. Adjustability of the seat in height and distance will be required to accommodate operators of different body sizes, especially with different leg lengths. Absence or presence of a backrest and its size and height above the seat pan can be important for the stability of the operator's body position, particularly if he has to apply considerable force to a pedal. Figure 10-11 (from Kroemer, 1970a) identifies most important parameters of body posture and of body support during pedal operation. Thigh angle α, knee angle β, and foot angle γ, determine pedal angle δ. These body position angles α, β, and γ in turn depend on the height of the pedal (H) and its distance (D) from the junction of seat pan and backrest tangents (Seat Reference Point, SRP). Inclination of the seat pan and of the backrest are described by angles ζ and ϵ respectively. Height of the lower edge of the backrest and the size of the backrest are indicated by the letters R and r. Not shown is the lateral dis-

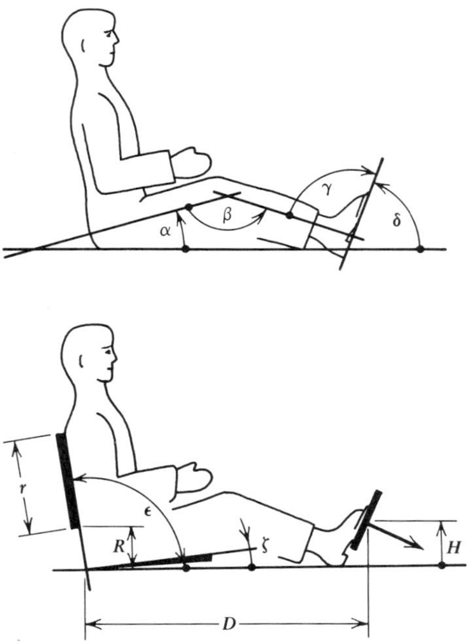

Figure 10-11. Leg angles and body support of the seated operator of pedals. (from Kroemer, 1970a.)

placement (L) of the pedal from the vertical plane dividing the seat into a right and left half. This nomenclature will be used throughout this discussion.

10.4.2 Forces Applicable to Pedals

Design criteria for the largest static forces than can be applied with one leg to a fixed pedal are estimated from knowledge of the seat-pedal relationships, that is, body support and posture, especially knee angle β, described above. Figure 10-12 provides gross guidelines as to relative force than can be exerted as pedal height varies above and below the seat reference point (SRP). The data relate to two percentage values of leg length (reach) from seat back to pedal. These percentage values can also be expressed in terms of knee angle β and thigh angle α as shown in Figure 10-13. In terms of absolute forces, Elbel (1949) has measured almost 520 lb with knee angle β of 110° and ankle angle γ about 120°. Crawford (1954) found maximum pedal forces of nearly 900 lb. Females typically exert about two-thirds of the force exerted by males, but this ratio can be as low as one-half at 95% reach to four-fifths at shorter reach percentages (Rohmert and Jenik, 1971). Martin and Johnson (1952) showed that maximum forces occurred at hip joint height (3 to 5 in. above SRP). This finding agrees with data in Figure 10-12 and with expectations based on mechanical linkage principles. One must also consider the location of the back support, as shown in Figure 10-14. These data from Rees and Graham (1952)

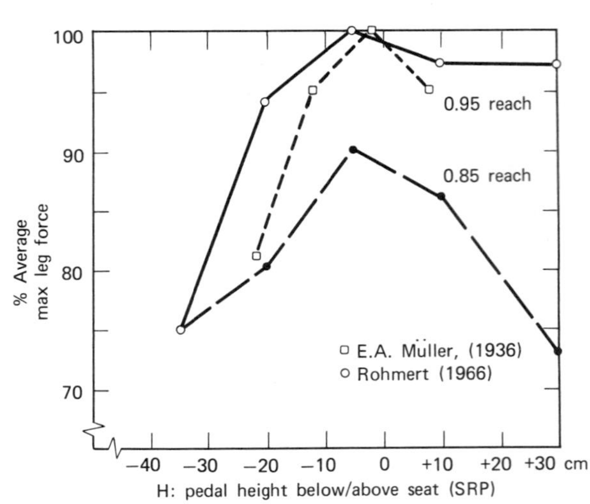

Figure 10-12. Maximal leg force applied to a pedal at different pedal heights. (from Kroemer, 1971b.)

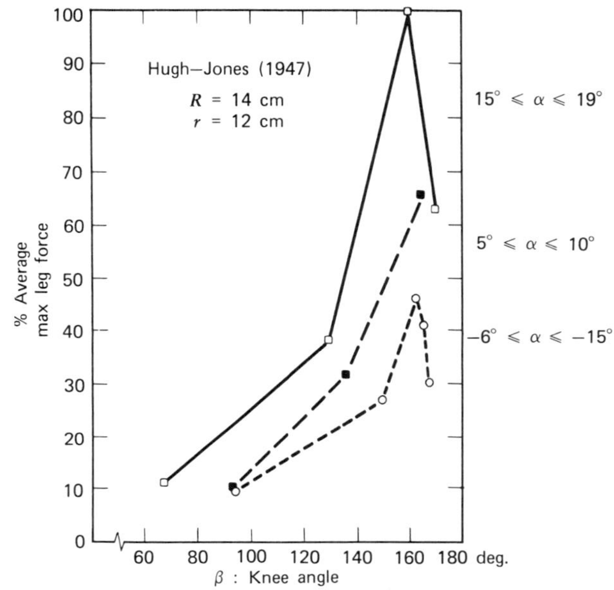

Figure 10-13. Maximal leg force applied to a pedal at different knee angles. (from Kroemer, 1971b.)

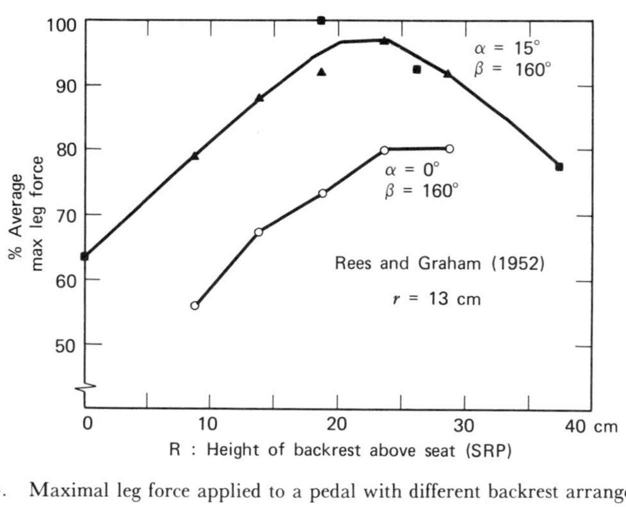

Figure 10-14. Maximal leg force applied to a pedal with different backrest arrangements. (from Kroemer, 1971b.)

are derived from tests of men pushing at the ball of the foot, whereas Hugh-Jones (1947) had his subjects push on pedals pivoted at the instep.

So far, forces were discussed that can be exerted in static thrust of the total leg, that is, accomplished by attempted changes in the knee and hip angles. Figure 10-15, however, presents results of experiments in which the subjects exerted static force in attempted plantar rotation of the foot about the ankle joint (Hertzberg, 1960; Hertzberg and Burke, 1971). Such rotational foot forces were found to depend on the pedal angle δ, that is, on the angle γ between the lower leg and foot. These foot rotation forces are, of course, much lower than the forces exertable in total leg thrust.

10.4.3 Summary of Pedal Design Considerations

Selection and arrangement of the foot-operated controls requires the same type of concern for the operator's anthropometric, biomechanical, and ergonomic characteristics as for hand-operated controls. The findings of the experiments on muscular force capabilities may be summarized as follows:

If very large static forces are to be exerted, the pedal should be at about seat height, in front of the seat, and at such a distance that the leg is almost straight when the foot is placed on the pedal. When large forces are required, the operator must have a backrest to lean against; his thigh should be horizontal or inclined with α up to 30°, the knee angle β between 150° and 165°, and the angle γ between tibia and foot between 80° and 90°.

If only small forces are required, the pedal may be lowered; force then may be exerted either by thrust of the total leg or by rotation of the foot about the ankle. For small forces, or for continuous steering tasks, or for discrete activations, the thigh should be horizontal or slightly elevated with $10° \leq \alpha \leq 15°$;

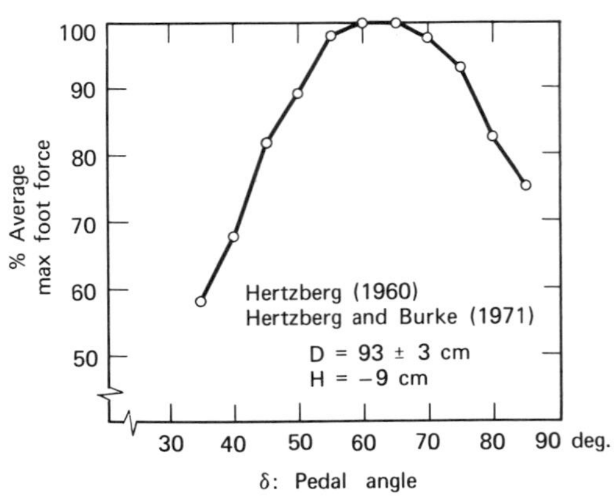

Figure 10-15. Maximal foot force achieved in attempted foot rotation at different pedal angles. (from Kroemer, 1971b.)

the knee angle β could be anywhere between about 90° and 150°, and the foot angle γ between 90° and 120°.

Despite the rather large number of published data, it is often difficult to assess and compare the published data on forces exertable to pedals, mainly for the following reasons. First, the experimental set-up is not always completely described. Second, the instructions to the subjects are often not reported. Third, the score or index the experimenter selected as "maximum" generally was not stated.

Results of experiments on the speed and accuracy of pedal operation do not provide strong guidance for anthropometric criteria development, especially outside the experimentally investigated sets of conditions. Hinging the pedal at the heel, or nearby, and providing for sliding rather than lifting motions and fore-aft motions rather than lateral seem to aid speed of operation (Kroemer, 1969a, 1970a).

BIBLIOGRAPHY

The following abbreviations are used in frequently appearing sources:

Title	*Abbreviation*
Wright-Patterson Air Force Base.	WPAFB
United States Air Force	USAF
United States Army Air Force	USAAF

Decimal number series appearing in brackets [ ] after year of publication designate the section of this book in which the reference to the work appears. Only first- and second-level headings are used; that is, if an item appeared in a subsection of Section 4.3.2, it would be designated as [4.3.2]. For the handbook references listed in Section 7.2.4, only the author and date are listed, together with the table and section number in which they appear.

Abernethey, J. 1793 [2.4.1]. An essay on the nature of the matter perspired and absorbed from the skin. *Surgical and Physiological Essays Part II,* London, 107–165.

Abt, L. E. 1955 [7.7.2]. Anthropometric data in the design of anthropomorphic test dummies. In ed. R. W. Miner, pp. 630–636. Dynamic anthropometry, *Ann. N.Y. Acad. Sci.* **63:**4, pp. 433–636.

Ad Hoc Committee for Standardization of Muscle Strength Testing. 1973 [4.3.1]. A proposed standard procedure for static muscle strength testing. *Proceedings,* 1973 American Industrial Hygiene Conference, Boston, Mass. (May).

Adrian, M. J. 1968 [3.4.2]. An introduction to electrogiometry. *Kinesiology Rev. 1968,* pp. 12–18, Council on Kinesiology, Phys. Ed. Div., Amer. Assoc. for Health, Phys. Ed. and Recreation, Wash., D.C.

Åkerblom, B. 1948 [3.2, 8.5.1, 8.8.3]. *Standing and sitting posture with special reference to the construction of chairs,* Nordiska Bokhandeln, Stockholm.

———. 1954 [8.8.3]. Chairs and sitting. In *Symposium on Human Factors in Equipment Design.* eds. W. F. Floyd and A. T. Welford. London: H. K. Lewis.

Alden, D. G.; Daniels, R. W.; and Kanarick, A. F. 1970 [10.2.4]. *Human factors principles for keyboard design and operation—a summary review.* Report 12180—FR 1 a. St. Paul, Minn.: Honeywell.

Alderman, R. B., and Banfield, T. J. 1969 [4.7.2]. Reliability estimation in the measurement of strength. *Res. Quart.* **40:**3, 338–455.

Alexander, M., and Clauser, C. E. 1965 [8.9.1]. *Anthropometry of common working positions,* AMRL-TR-65-73. WPAFB, Ohio: Aerospace Med. Res. Labs., USAF.

Alexander, M., and Hertzberg, H. T. E. 1957 [9.2]. *A comfort evaluation of a form-fitting high altitude helmet,* WADC TR 56-404. WPAFB, Ohio: Wright Air Dev. Center, USAF.

Altman, J. W.; Marchese, A. C.; and Marchiando, B. W. 1961 [8.9.2, 8.9.4]. *Guide to design of mechanical equipment for maintainability,* ASD TR-61-381. WPAFB, Ohio: USAF (AD-269-322).

Ammerman, F. 1956 [10.2.1, 10.2.2]. Torque requirements in knob design. *Design News* **11:**17, 136–137.

Arkin, H., and Colton, R. R. 1963 [5.2.10]. *Tables for statisticians.* New York: Barnes and Noble.

Asa, M. L. 1942 [8.8.4]. *A study of work place layout.* Master's thesis, Dept. of Ind. Eng., Univ. of Iowa.

Ashe, W. F.; Roberts, L. G.; and Bodenam, P. 1943 [7.5.1]. *Anthropometric measurements,* Project No. 9. Ft. Knox, Ky: Armored Force Med. Res. Lab.

Asmussen, E., and Heeboll-Nielsen, K. 1962 [6.10.1]. Isometric muscle strength in relation to age in men and women. *Ergonomics* **5:**1, 167–169.

Astrand, P. O., and Rodahl, K. 1970 [4.2, 4.7.2, 6.12]. *Textbook of work physiology.* New York: McGraw-Hill.

Ayoub, M. M. 1972 [3.5, 3.5.5]. Human movement recording for biomechanical analysis. *Int. J. Prod. Res.* **10:**1, 35–51.

Ayoub, M. M., and Trombley, D. J. 1967 [10.4.3]. Experimental determination of an optimal foot pedal design. *J. Ind. Eng.* **17:**9, 550–559.

Baker, P. T.; McKendry, J. M.; and Grant, G. 1960a [8.9.2]. *Anthropometry of one handed maintenance actions,* NAVTRADEVCEN 330-1 (Supplement III). Design for Maintainability, Port Washington, N.Y.: U.S. Naval Training Devices Center.

——— 1960b [8.9.2]. Volumetric requirements for hand tool usage. *Human Factors* **2:**3, 156–162.

Band, E. G. U. 1971 [8.4.5]. *Calculation of rocket powered trajectories of a "plane of symmetry" model of a human subject and ejection seat,* AMRL-TR-71-7. WPAFB, Ohio: Aerospace Med. Res. Lab., USAF.

Barnes, R. M. 1949 [3.5.3, 8.8]. *Motion and time study.* New York: John Wiley.

Barnes, R. M.; Hardaway, H.; and Podolsky, O. 1942 [10.4.3]. Which pedal is best? *Factory Management & Maintenance* **100:**98–99.

Barter, J. T., and Alexander, M. 1956 [4.8.2, 9.2, 9.5.1, 9.5.2]. *A sizing system for high altitude gloves,* WADC TR-56-599. WPAFB, Ohio: Wright Air Dev. Center, USAF.

Bashkirew, P. N. 1954 [6.6.1]. Specific gravity of the adult male subject and factors determining its change [in Russian]. Trans. State Univ. of Moscow, 166, Moscow.

Basler, V. E., and Morehouse, L. E. 1948 [3.2, 4.7.2]. *The effects of G on maximum grip strength,* Tech. Rep. ONR. Los Angeles: Dept. Av. Med., USC School of Med. Contract NG Ori 77, Task 1 (AD-110-589).

Baxter, J. H. 1875 [1.2, 1.3]. *Statistics, medical and anthropological, of the Provost-Marshall-General's bureau.* Washington, D. C.: Gov't Ptg. Office.

Behnke, A. R. 1953 [3.2.2]. The relation of lean body weight to metabolism and some consequent systemizations. *Ann. N.Y. Acad. Sci.* **56:**6, 1095–1142.

———. 1954 [3.2]. Body composition. I. *In vivo* estimation of fat and water content from specific gravity (density) determinations. II. *In vivo* estimation of body fat from measurements of gaseous desorption or absorption. In *Methods for evaluation of nutritional adequacy and status,* pp. 294–310, National Research Council, U.S.

Behnke, A. R.; Feen, B. G.; and Welham, W. C. 1942 [3.2, 6.6.1]. The specific gravity of healthy men—body weight-volume as an index of density. *J. Amer. Med. Assoc.* **118:**7, 495–98.

Benedict, F. G. 1916 [2.4.1]. A photographic method for measuring the surface area of the human body. *Amer. J. Physiol.* **41:**275–91.

Berner, J., Jr. 1954 [2.3.2]. Calculation of the body surface area by photogrammetry. *Scand. J. Clin. Lab. Invest.* **6:**4.

Bernstein, N. A. 1931 and 1936. See Clauser, McConville, and Young. 1969 [3.2].

———. 1967 [3.2]. *The co-ordination and regulation of movements.* London: Pergamon Press.

Bertillon, A., and Chervin, A. 1909 [1, 2 historical discussion]. *Anthropologie metrique.* Paris: Imprimerie Nationale.

Best, W. R., and Kuhl, W. J. 1953 [3.2, 3.2.2]. *Estimation of active protoplasmic mass by physical and roentgenological anthropometry.* Report No. 114, Medical Nutrition Lab., 9937 TSU-SGO. Chicago: United States Army.

Bilger, A. J., and Greene, E. H. 1973 [3.4.1]. *"Winters" protective body mechanics. A manual for nurses.* New York: Springer.

Björn, H.; Lundquist, C.; and Hjelmström, P. 1954 [2.3.2]. A photogrammetric method of measuring the volume of facial swellings. *J. D. Res.* **33:**295–308.

Blanton, P. L., and Biggs, N. L. 1968 [3.2, 6.6.2]. Density of fresh and embalmed human compact and cancellous bone. *Amer. J. Phys. Anthropol.* **29:**1, 39–44 (N.S.).

Blesh, T. E.; Meyers, C. R.; and Kiphuth, O. W. 1954 [2.3.2]. *Photometric photography in posture evaluation of Yale University freshmen.* New Haven: Dept. of Phys. Ed., Yale Univ.

Boeing Co. 1970 [7.9.1, 8.4.5]. *Cockpit geometry evaluation*—Phase II, Final Report, Vols. I-V, JANAIR Reports 700201-5, and Phase II A, Final Report, Vols. III and IV, Boeing Reports D162-10127-2A and D162-10128-2A. Seattle: Boeing Co.

Bohnenkamp, H., and Ernst, H. W. 1931 [2.4.2]. *Pfluger's Arch. fid. ges. Physiol.* **228:**40.

Bonney, M. C.; Evershed, D. G.; and Roberts, E. A. 1969 [7.9.1]. Sammie—a computer model of man in his environment. Manuscript of a paper presented at the Ann. Scientific Meeting Ergonomics Res. Soc., Bristol, Eng.

Boyd, E. 1935 [2.3.1, 2.4.1]. *The growth of the surface area of the human body.* Minn.: Univ. of Minn. Press.

Boyd, E.; Scammon, R. E.; and Lawrence, D. 1930 [2.4.1]. The determination of surface area of living children. *Proc. Soc. Exper. Biol. Med.* **27:**445–449.

Bradley, J. V. 1957 [9.5.3]. *Glove characteristics influencing control manipulability,* WADC TR 57-389. WPAFB, Ohio: Wright Air Dev. Center, USAF. Also *Human Factors* (1969) **11:**1, 21–35.

Braune, W., and Fischer, O. 1889 [1.3, 3.2, 3.2.5, 6.6.4, 6.6.6]. *The center of gravity of the human body as related to the German infantryman.* Leipzig (ATI 138, 452. Available from the Defense Documentation Center).

Broadbent, B. H. 1931 [2.3.2]. A new x-ray technique and its application to orthodontia. *Angle Orthodontist* **1:**45.

Broer, M. H., and Galles, N. R. 1958 [6.9.3]. Importance of relationship between body measurements in performance of toe touch test. *Res. Quart.* **29:**257.

Brookes, M. J., and Kaplan, A. 1972 [8.8.2]. The office environment: space planning and affective behavior. *Human Factors* **14:**5, 373–391.

Brown, C. W.; Ghiselli, E. E.; Jerret, R. F.; Minimum, E. W.; and U'Ren, R. M. 1949a [8.4.2]. *Forces which may be applied by the prone pilot to aircraft control devices.* 1. *Three dimensional hand controls.* Memorandum Report MCREXD-694-4J. WPAFB, Ohio: USAF, Eng. Div. (ASTIA No. ATI-52794).

———. 1949b 2. *Two-dimensional hand controls.* AF Technical Report No. 5954. WPAFB, Ohio: Air Materiel Command, USAF (ASTIA No. ATI-72377).

———. 1949c 3. *Foot Controls.* AF TR No. 5955. WPAFB, Ohio: Air Materiel Command, USAF (ASTIA No. ATI-70935).

———. 1950 [8.4.2]. *Comparison of aircraft controls for prone and seated position in three-dimensional pursuit task.* AF Technical Report No. 5956. WPAFB, Ohio: Air Materiel Command, USAF (ASTIA No. ATI-73414).

Brožek, J., and Keys, A. 1951 [3.2]. The evaluation of leanness-fatness in man: norms and interrelationships. *Brit. J. Nut.* **5**:2, 194–206.

Brues, A. M. 1946 [6.2.2]. Regional differences in the physical characteristics of an American population. *Amer. J. Phys. Anthropol.* **4**:463–81 (N.S.).

Bullock, M. I., and Harley, I. A. 1972 [3.5.3, 3.5.5]. The measurement of three-dimensional body movements by the use of photogrammetry. *Ergonomics* **15**:3, 309–22.

Burdi, A.; Huelke, D. F.; Snyder, R. G.; and Lowrey, G. H. 1969 [8.6.3]. Infants and children in the adult world of automotive safety design: pediatric and anatomical considerations for design of vehicle restraints. *J. Biomechanics* **2**:3, 267–80.

Burke, P. H., and Beard, L. F. H. 1967 [2.3.2, 2.5.2]. "Stereophotogrammetry of the face. *Amer. J. Orthodontics* **53**:10, 769–82.

Buxton, D. 1957 [6.9.1]. Extension of the Kraus-Weber test. *Res. Quart.* **28**:210.

Caldwell, L. S. 1961 [4.2]. *The relationship between the maximum force exertable by the hand in a horizontal pull and the endurance of a sub-maximal holding response,* Report 470. Ft. Knox, Ky.: U.S. Army Med. Res. Lab.

———. 1963 [4.2, 6.10.4]. Relative muscle loading and endurance. *J. Eng. Psych.* **2**:155–161.

Carlyle, L. 1960 [1.3, 7.6.1, 8.4.5, 8.4.7]. *Man and space.* Douglas Aircraft Co., Engineering Paper No. 899, January.

Cathcart, E. P. 1927 [6.10.1]. The physique of women employed in industry. *Proc. Roy. Inst. Gr. Brit.* **25**:185–99.

Cathcart, E. P., Hughes, D. E. R., and Chalmers, J. G. 1935 [6.10.1, 6.10.5]. *The physique of man in industry.* Report 71. London: Med. Res. Council.

Chaffee, J. W. 1961a [1.3, 2.3.2]. *Andrometry: a practical application of coordinate anthropometry in human engineering.* (Unpublished) report FZY-012, 18 April, Convair Division of General Dynamics Corporation, Fort Worth, Tex. (Abstracts of material published as Chaffee 1961b below.)

———. 1961b [1.3, 2.3.2]. Anthropometric photogrammetry as applied to escape capsule design. *Human Factors* **3**:1, 36–52.

———. 1961c [3.2, 3.2.3, 6.8.1]. *The effect of acceleration on human centers of gravity.* (Unpublished) report FZY-013. Fort Worth, Texas: Convair Division of General Dynamics Corporation.

———. 1969 [8.3.6, 8.6.8]. *Methods for determining driver reach capability.* SAE Report 690105. New York: Society of Automotive Engineers.

———. 1970 [8.6.7]. *Effect of body restraints on driver reach.* (Equivalent titles in French and German), Paper No. 700359, Intern. Automobile Safety Conf. Comp., P-30. New York: Soc. of Automotive Eng.

Chaffin, D. B. 1969 [4.7.2, 7.9.1]. A computerized biomechanical model—development of and use in studying gross body actions. *J. Biomechanics* **2:**4, 429–41.

Chapanis, A. 1959 [5.2.11]. *Research techniques in human engineering.* Baltimore: The Johns Hopkins Press.

Churchill, E. 1966 [5.2.11, 5.2.12]. Statistical considerations. In *Human Development,* ed. F. T. Faulkner, pp. 40–75. Philadelphia: W. B. Saunders.

Churchill, E., and Truett, B. 1957 [9.6.2]. *Metrical relations among dimensions of the head and face.* WADC TR 56-621. WPAFB, Ohio: Wright Air Dev. Center, USAF (AD-110-629).

Cichowsky, W. G. 1968 [7.6.2, 8.6.10]. A third generation test dummy—Sophisticated Sam. *Proc. General Motors Corp., Automotive Safety Seminar,* GM Safety Research and Developmental Lab., General Motors Proving Ground, Milford, Mich. July 11–12.

Clark, W. A. 1920 [3.4.2]. A system of joint measurements. *J. Ortho. Surg.* **2:**12, 687–700.

Clarke, H. H. 1954 [6.10.4]. Relationship of strength and anthropometric measures to various arm strength criteria *Res. Quart.* **25:**134–43.

Clarke, H. H., and Baley, T. L. 1950 [4.7.2]. Strength curves of fourteen joint movements. *J. Phys. Mental Rehabil.* April–May, 12–19.

Clauser, C. E.: McConville, J. T., and Young, J. W. 1969 [3.2, 3.2.2, 6.4.2, 6.6.2, 6.6.3, 6.6.4, 6.7, 7.6.2, 7.9.1]. *Weight, volume, and center of mass of segments of the human body.* AMRL TR 69–70. WPAFB, Ohio: Aerospace Med. Res. Lab., USAF.

Clauser, C. E.: Tucker, P. E.: McConville, J. T., Churchill, E., Laubach, L. L., and Reardon, J. A. 1972 [2.2.1, 5.2.10, 5.6]. *Anthropometry of Air Force women.* AMRL TR 70–75. WPAFB, Ohio: Aerospace Med. Res. Lab., USAF.

Cleveland, H. G. 1955 [3.2]. *The determination of the center of gravity of segmants of the human body.* Dissertation, Univ. of Calif., Los Angeles.

Cobe, H. M. 1928 [6.9.4]. The range of active motion at the wrist of white adults. *J. Bone and Joint Surgery* **10:**763.

Cochran, L. B. 1953 [4.7.2]. Studies on the ease with which pilots can grasp and pull ejection seat face curtain handles. *J. Aviation Med.* **24:**1, 23–28.

Codman, E. A. 1934 [3.4.1]. *The shoulder.* Boston: Thomas Todd (privately published by the author).

Cotton, F. S. 1932 [3.2]. Studies in centre of gravity changes. *Aust. J. Exp. Biol. Med. Sci.* **10:**16–34, 225–47.

Crawford, W. A. 1954 [10.4.2]. *Pilot foot loads.* FPRC Memo 57. Farnborough, Eng.: RAF Inst. of Aviation Med.

Creamer, L. R., and Trumbo, D. A. 1960 [10.2.4]. Multifinger tapping performance as a function of the direction of tapping movements. *J. Appl. Psych.* **44:**6, 376–80.

Croney, J. 1971 [9.2]. See Section 7.2.4, Table 7.2.

Cumberland, C. H., and Bowey, G. S. 1948 [8.5.1]. *Passenger seats in civil aircraft design considerations.* Air Transport Technical Memorandum No. 11, Ministry of Supply, London.

Damon, A., and McFarland, R. A. 1955 [1.3, 8.6.3]. The physique of bus and truck drivers: with a review of occupational anthropology. *Amer. J. Phys. Anthropol.* **13:**4, 711–42.

Damon, A., and Randall, F. E. 1944 [1.3]. Physical anthropology in the Army Air Forces. *Amer. J. Phys. Anthropol.* **2:**3, 293–316 (N.S.).

Damon, A., Stoudt, H. W.; and McFarland, R. A. 1966 [1.3, 6.10.2, 6.10.4, 6.12.4 8.5, 8.8.4]. See Section 7.2.4, Table 7.2.

Daniels, G. S. 1952 [6.3.3]. *The "average man?"* Technical Note WCRD 53-7. WPAFB, Ohio: Wright Air Dev. Center, USAF (AD-10203).

Darcus, H. D. 1951 [4.5.1, 4.8.2]. The maximum torques developed in pronation and supination of the right hand. *J. Anat. London* **85:**55–67.

Darcus, H. D., and Weddell, A. G. M. 1947 [8.7]. Some anatomical and physiological principles concerned in the design of seats for naval war-weapons. *Brit. Med. Bull.* **5:**1, 31–37.

Davenport, C. B. 1927a [2.1]. Measurement of men. *Amer. J. Phys. Anthropol.* **10:**1, 65–70.

———. 1927b [2.1].* *Guide to physical anthropometry and anthroposcopy.* Eugenics Research Assoc. Handbook Series, Cold Spring Harbor, New York: Waverly Press.

Davenport, C. B., and Love, A. G. 1921 [1.2, 1.3, 7.5.1]. *Army anthropology.* Wash., D. C.: Gov't. Ptg. Office.

Davy, J. 1840 [3.2, 6.6.2]. *Researches, physiological and anatomical.* Philadelphia: Waldie.

Deats, C. V., and Nielsen, G. 1966 [7.8.3]. *Construction of vacuum formed control and display mockup panels.* AMRL-TR-66-175. WPAFB, Ohio: Aerospace Med. Res. Labn., USAF.

Dempsey, C. A. 1953 [3.3]. *Development of a workspace measuring device.* WADC TR 53-53. WPAFB, Ohio: USAF (AD-13206)

Dempster, W. T. 1955a [1.3, 2.5.1, 2.5.2, 3.2, 3.2.5, 3.2.6, 3.2.7, 3.4.1, 3.4.2, 3.4.3, 3.4.4, 3.4.6, 3.5.1, 3.5.3, 6.6.2, 6.6.4, 6.7, 6.9.3, 6.9.5, 7.3.3, 7.6.1, 7.6.2, 7.7, 7.8, 8.4, 8.4.5, 9.4]. *Space requirements of the seated operator: geometrical, kinematic, and mechanical aspects of the body with special reference to the limbs.* WADC TR 55-159. WPAFB, Ohio: Wright Air Dev. Center, USAF (AD-87892) (see also 1955b).

———. 1955b [3.4.1, 3.4.2, 3.5.3, 6.9.5]. The anthropometry of body action. In Dynamic anthropometry, *Ann. N.Y. Acad. Sci., ed. R. W. Miner,* **63:**4, 559–85.

Dempster, W. T., Gabel, W. C. and Felts, W. J. L. 1959 [8.4.8]. The anthropometry of the manual work space for the seated Subject, *Amer. Jour. Phys. Anthrop.* **17:**4, 289–317. Also: (1961) ASD TR 61-89. USAF, WPAFB, Ohio. (AD-258564).

Deschin, J. 1950 [2.3.2]. Photo sculpture. *Popular Photography,* August.

Design News 1971 [7.7.4]. Teleoperator arm demonstrates dexterity. *Design News.* Nov. 22, p. 8.

Devlin, W. A., and Roe, R. 1968 [8.6.6]. The eye ellipse and consideration in the driver's forward field of view. *SAE Report* 680105. New York: Society of Automotive Engineers.

De Vries, H. A. 1966 [4.2]. *Physiology of exercise for physical education and athletics.* Dubuque, Iowa: Wm. C. Brown.

Dixon, W. J., and Massey, F. J. 1969 [5.2.11]. *Introduction to statistical analysis.* 3rd ed. New York: McGraw-Hill.

Dreyfuss, H. 1955 [1.3]. *Designing for people.* New York: Simon and Schuster.

———. 1960a [1.3]. Tailoring the product to fit. *Industrial Design,* June.

———. 1960b; also 1967, 2nd ed. [1.3, 6.2.3]. See Section 7.2.4, Table 7-2.

———. 1966 [1.3, 8.5.1, 8.8]. People come in assorted sizes. *Human Factors* **8:**4, 273–77.

Drillis, R. 1959 [3.2.6, 3.5, 3.5.3]. The use of gliding cyclograms in the biomechanical analysis of movements. *Human Factors* **1:**2, 1–11.

———. 1963 [1.1, 10.3.3]. Folk norms and biomechanics. *Human Factors* **5:**5, 427–441.

Drillis, R., and Contini, R. 1966 [3.2, 3.2.4, 6.4.2, 6.6.1, 6.6.2, 6.6.3, 6.6.4, 6.6.6, 6.7]. *Body*

* Cited in Chaffee (1961a).

segment parameters. Report No. 1166-03 (Office of Vocational Rehabilitation, Dept. of Health, Education and Welfare). New York: N.Y. Univ. School of Eng. and Sci.

DuBois, D. F., and DuBois, E. F. 1915 [2.4.1, 6.5]. The measurement of the surface area of man. 5th paper. *Arch. Intern. Med.* **15:**868.

———. 1916 [6.5]. A formula to estimate the approximate surface area if height and weight be known. *Arch. Intern. Med.* **18:**863–71.

DuBois-Raymond, R. 1900 [3.2]. Über die Grenzen der Unterstützungsfläche baim Stehen. *Arch. Anat. Physiol.* **23:**562–64.

Duggar, B. D. 1962 [3.2, 3.2.3]. The center of gravity of the human body. *Human Factors* **4:**3, 131–48.

Dupertuis, C. W. 1950 [6.6.1]. Anthropometry of extreme somatotypes. *Amer. J. Phys. Anthropol.* **8:**3, 367–83.

Dupertuis, C. W., Pitts, G. C.; Osserman, E. F., Welham, W. C., and Behnke, A. R. 1950 [6.6.1]. *The relation of specific gravity to body build in a group of healthy men.* Western Reserve Univ. and Naval Medicine Res. Inst. Project NM 004 006.03.06.

Dupertuis, C. W., and Tanner, J. M. 1950 [2.3.2]. The pose of the subject for photogrammetric anthropometry, with especial reference to somatotyping. *Amer. J. Phys. Anthropol.* **8:**1, 27–47 (N. S.).

Dvorak, A. 1943 (10.2.4]. There is a better typewriter keyboard. *Natl. Bus. Ed. Quart.* **12:**51–58, 68.

Dzendolet, E., and Rievley, J. F. 1959 [4.5.1, 4.8.2]. *Man's ability to apply certain torques while weightless,* WADC TR 59-94, WPAFB, Ohio: Aero. Med. Lab., USAF.

Eberhart, H., and Inman, V. 1947 [3.5.3]. Fundamental studies of human locomotion and other information related to design of artificial limbs. *Report to National Research Council* **1:**1-6. College of Eng., Univ. of Calif. Berkeley.

Elbel, E. R. 1945 [4.8.1, 6.10.2, 7.5.1]. *Leg strength and leg endurance in relation to height, weight, and other body measurements.* USAAF Sch. Av. Med., Randolph Field, Tex., Project No. 318, Report No. 1.

———. 1949 [10.4.2]. Relationship between leg strength, leg endurance, and other body measurements. *J. Appl. Physiol.* **2:**4, 197–207.

Emanuel, I.; Alexander, M., and Churchill, E. 1959 [9.2]. *Anthropometric sizing and fit-test of the MC-1 oral-nasal oxygen mask.* WADC TR 58-505, WPAFB, Ohio: Wright Air Dev. Center, USAF (AD-213-604).

Emanuel, I.; Alexander, M.; Churchill, E., and Truett, B. 1959 [9.2, 9.3.3, 9.3.4, 9.3.5, 9.3.11]. *A height-weight sizing system for flight clothing.* WADC TR 56-365, Aero Med. lab., WPAFB, Ohio: Wright Air Dev. Center, USAF (AD-130-917).

Englemann, W. F. 1956 [2.3.2]. Photogrammetry applied to making portraits. *Photogrammetric Eng.* **22:**2 (April).

Ensdorff, J. 1964 [10.4.3]. *An optimal design for a foot activated level mechanism.* Master's thesis, Dept. of Ind. Eng., Texas Tech. Univ.

Eshkol, N., and Wachman, A. 1958 [3.4.1]. *Movement notation.* London: Weidenfeld and Nicholson.

Ewing, C. L., and Thomas, D. J. 1972 [8.3.11]. *Human head and neck response to impact acceleration.* Army-Navy Joint Report: USAARL 73-1, NAMRL Monograph 21, U.S. Army Aeromedical Res. Lab., Naval Aerospace Med. Res. Lab.

Fick, R. 1904–1911 [1.3].* *Handbuch der Anatomie und Mechanik der Gelenke.* Part I:

* Cited in Dempster (1955a) and Dempster, Gabel, and Felts (1959).

Anatomie der Gelenke, **2:**1, 512 pp. (1904). Part II: Allgemeine Gelenke und Muskelmechanik, **2:**2, 376 pp. (1910). Part III: Spezielle Gelenk-und Muskelmechanik, **2:**3, 688 pp. (1911). In *Handbuch der Anatomie des Menschen,* ed. K. v. Bardeleben. **2:** Sect. 1, Jena: G. Fischer.

Fischer, O. 1906 [1.3, 6.6.4]. *Theoretical fundamentals for a mechanics of living bodies with special application to man as well as to some processes of motion in machines.* Leipzig (ASTIA No. ATI-153668; Air Technical Intelligence translation from the German).

———. 1907 [1.3]. *Kinematics of organic joints* [in German]. Braunschweig: F. Vieweg and Sohn.

Folley, J. D., Jr., and Altman, J. W. 1956 [8.9.2]. *Guide to design of electronic equipment for maintainability.* WADC TR 56-218. WPAFB, Ohio: Wright Air Dev. Center. USAF (AD-47953).

Fonda-Bernardi, G. 1965 [9.4]. The design of rigid, articulated pressure suits. A paper presented at Internl. Astronaut. Federation, Internl. Astronaut. Congress, 16th, Athens, September 13-18.

Freese, E. I. 1934 [8.8.5]. The geometry of the human figure. *Amer. Architect* **144:**57–60.

Galton, F. et al. 1881 [6.10.1]. Report of the anthropometric committee. *Report of the British Assoc. for the Advancement of Science* 225–72.

———. 1883 [6.10.1]. Final report of the anthropometric committee. *Report of the British Association for the Advancement of Science* 253–306.

Garn, S. M. 1954 [3.2]. Fat patterning and fat intercorrelations in the adult male. *Human Biology* **26:**56–69. (Cited by Brožek, 1955.)

Garrett, J. W. 1968 [4.5.1, 10.2]. *Clearance and performance values for the bare-handed and pressure-gloved operator.* AMRL TR 68-24. WPAFB, Ohio: Aerospace Med. Res. Lab., USAF (AD 681-457).

Garrett, J. W. 1970a [10.2]. *Anthropometry of the hands of male air force flight personnel.* AMRL TR 69-42. WPAFB, Ohio: Aerospace Med. Res. Lab., USAF (AD 709-883).

———. 1970b [10.2]. *Anthropometry of the Air Force female's hand.* AMRL TR 69-26. WPAFB, Ohio: Aerospace Med. Res. Lab., USAF (AD 710-202).

———. 1971a [10-2]. *An introduction to relaxed hand anthropometry.* AMRL TR 67-217. WPAFB, Ohio: Aerospace Med. Res. Lab., USAF.

———. 1971b [10.2]. The adult human hand: some anthropometric and biomechanical considerations. *Human Factors* **13:**2, 117–31.

Garrett, J. W., Alexander, M.; amd Bennett, W. W. 1967 [10.3.2]. *Two-handed retention on various handle configurations.* AMRL TR 67-63. WPAFB, Ohio: Aerospace Med. Res. Lab., USAF (AD 658-441).

Garrett, J. W., Alexander, M., and Matthews, C. W. 1970 [1.3, 8.3.6, 8.4.5]. *Placement of aircraft controls.* AMRL TR 70-33. WPAFB, Ohio: Aerospace Med. Res. Lab., USAF.

Garrett, J. W., and Kennedy, K. W. 1971 [1.2, 2.2.1, 6.3.1]. *A collation of anthropometry.* vol. I. A-H, vol. II, I-Z and index. AMRL TR 68-1. WPAFB, Ohio: Aerospace Med. Res. Lab., USAF. vol. I: 1119 pp. vol. II: 1075 pp. (AD 723-629/30).

Gavan, J. A.: Washburn, S. L.; and Lewis, P. H. 1952 [1.3, 2.3.2]. Photography: an anthropometric tool. *Amer. J. Phys. Anthropol.* **10:**3, 331–53.

Geckeler, E. 1939 [4.4.3]. A pneumatic dynamomoter. *Amer. J. Surgery* **45:**353.

Giedion, S. 1948 [1.3, 3.5, 3.5.3]. *Mechanization takes command.* New York: Oxford Univ. Press.

Gifford, E. C., Provost, J. R., and Lazo, J. 1965 [5.2.9]. *Anthropometry of naval aviators—1964.*

NAEC-ACEL-533. Philadelphia: Aerospace Crew Equip. Lab., U.S. Naval Air Engineering Center.

Gilliland, A. R. 1921 [3.4.1, 3.4.2]. Norms for amplitude of voluntary movement. *J. Amer. Med. Assoc.* **77:**1357.

Glanville, A. D., and Kreezer, G. 1937 [3.4.1, 3.4.2]. The maximum amplitude and velocity of joint movements in normal male human adults. *Human Biology* **9:**2, 197–211.

Goldman, J., and Nadler, G. 1956 [3.5.4]. Electronics for measuring human motions. *Science* **124:**807–10

Gough, M. N., and Beard, A. P. 1936 [10.4.2]. *Limitations of the pilot in applying forces to airplane controls.* Technical Note 550. Washington, D.C.: National Advisory Committee for Aeronautics.

Gould, B. A. 1869 [1.2, 1.3]. *Investigations in the military and anthropological statistics of American soldiers.* Hurd, New York: U.S. Sanitary Commission.

Grandjean, E. 1969a [6.12.4]. *Fitting the task to the man.* London: Taylor and Francis.

Grandjean, E., Ed. 1969b [8.5.1, 8.8.3]. Sitting posture. Proc. Int. Symp. Sitting Posture, Zurich, September 1968. *Ergonomics* **12:**2, 115–367.

Guibert, A., and Taylor, C. L. 1952 [2.4.2]. Radiation area of the human body. *J. Appl. Physiol.* **5:**1, 24–37.

Hamilton, A. 1875 [4.4.3]. A New Dynamometer. *The Psychol. and Medico-Legal J.* **2:**255–256.

Hammer, L. R. 1961 [8.3.13]. *Aeronautical systems division studies in weightlessness: 1959–1960.* WADD TR 60-715. WPAFB, Ohio: Aeronautical Systems Div., Air Force Systems Command, USAF.

Hanavan, E. P., Jr. 1964 [1.3, 6.6.6, 7.9]. *A mathematical model of the human body.* AMRL TR 64-102. WPAFB, Ohio: Aerospace Med. Res. Lab. (AD 608-463).

Hansen, R.; Cornog, D. Y.; and Hertzberg, H. T. E. 1958 [7.5.2]. See Section 7.2.4, Table 7-2.

Harless, E. 1860 [3.2, 3.2.5, 6.6.2, 6.6.4]. The static moments of the component masses of the human body. *Trans. of the Math-Phys. Royal Bavarian Acd. of Sci.* **8:**1, 2, 69–96; 257–94. (Cited by Clauser, McConville, and Young as unpublished English translation, WPAFB, Ohio).

Heath, B. H. and Carter, J. E. L. 1967 [2.6] A modified somatotype method. *Am. J. Physical Anthrop.* **27:**1, 57–74.

Hedberg, R. D., and Lobron, C. M. 1954 [4.5.1, 10.2.2]. *The maximum torque man can apply to a 1-1/8 inch knob.* Human Engineering Report No. 5 (Report No. 4065). Frankford Arsenal Lab., Ordnance Corps, ASTIA No. AD-52903.

Heeboll-Nielsen, K. 1964 [6.10.2]. *Muscular asymmetry in normal young men.* Communication 18. Hellerup, Denmark: Danish Nat. Assoc. for Infant Paralysis.

Hellebrandt, F. A.; Duvall, E. N.; and Moore, M. L. 1949 [3.4.2]. The measurement of joint motion. Part 3: Reliability of goniometry. *Physiotherapy Rev.* **29:**6, 302–07.

Henry, F. M. 1967 [4.7.2]. "Best" versus "average" individual scores. *Res. Quart.* **38:**2, 317–20.

Herren, P. 1961 [2.3.2]. *Statement on new methods in roentgenographic cephalometrics.* Philadelphia: J. B. Lippincott.

Herron, R. E. 1972 [2.3.2]. *Stereophotogrammetry in biology and medicine.* Unnumbered report. Biostereometrics Laboratory, Texas Institute for Rehabilitation and Research. Houston, Tex.: Baylor College of Medicine.

Hertzberg, H. T. E. 1949 [8.6.4]. *Comfort tests of the pulsating seat cushion and lumbar pad.* Report MCREXD-695-82. WPAFB, Ohio: Air Materiel Command (AD 70599).

———. 1955 [4.4.1, 8.5.1]. Some contributions of applied physical anthropology to human engineering. *Ann. N.Y. Acad. Sci.* **63**:4, 616–29.

———. 1960 [10.4.2]. Dynamic anthropometry of working positions. *Human Factors* **2**:3, 147–55. Also published (1960) as ASD TR 61-90. Dayton, Ohio: Aerospace Med. Res. Lab., WPAFB (AD 263-715).

———. 1968 [1.2, 2.2.1]. The conference on standardization of anthropometric techniques and terminology. *Amer. J. Phys. Anthropol.* **28**:1, 1–16 (N.S.).

———. 1969 [7.7.2, 8.4.7]. The anthropology of anthropomorphic dummies. *Proc., 13th Stapp Car Crash Conf.* 201–214. New York: Society of Automotive Engineers.

———. 1972 [8.5.1, 8.8.3]. The human buttocks in sitting: pressures, patterns, and palliatives. *SAE Report* 720005. New York: Society of Automotive Engineers.

Hertzberg, H. T. E., and Burke, F. E. 1971 [10.4.2]. Foot forces exerted at various aircraft brake-pedal angles. *Human Factors* **13**:5, 445–56.

Hertzberg, H. T. E.; Churchill, E.; Dupertuis, C.; White, R.; and Damon, A. 1963 [5.2.9]. Anthropometric survey of Turkey, Greece, and Italy. (AGARDO Graph No. 73). New York: MacMillan (AD 421-428).

Hertzberg, H. T. E., and Colgan, J. W. 1948 [8.4.2]. *A prone position bed for pilots.* Memorandum Report No. MCREXD-695-71D. WPAFB, Ohio: Aero Med. Lab., USAF (ATI-34088).

Hertzberg, H. T. E., and Daniels, G. S. 1950 [3.2, 3.2.3, 3.2.4]. *The center of gravity of a fully loaded F-86 ejection seat in the ejection position.* Memorandum Report No. MCREXD-45341-4-5. WPAFB, Ohio: Air Materiel Command, USAF.

Hertzberg, H. T. E.; Daniels, G. S.; and Churchill, E. 1954 [1.3, 2.2.1, 2.2.4, 2.3.1, 5.2.7, 5.2.9, 5.4, 5.6, 6.2.2, 7.7.1, 8.8.4, 9.3.3, 9.6, 9.7.1]. *Anthropometry of flying personnel—1950,* WADC TR 52-321. WPAFB, Ohio: Wright Air Dev. Center, USAF (AD 47953).

Hertzberg, H. T. E.; Dupertuis, C. W., and Emanuel, I. 1957 [1.3, 2.3.2]. Stereophotogrammetry as an anthropometric tool. *Photogrammetric Eng.,* December, 942–47. Also: WADC TR 58-67. Feb. 1958 (AD 150-964).

Hertzberg, H. T. E.; Emanuel, I.; and Alexander, M. 1956 [8.9.1]. *The anthropometry of working positions.* 1. *A preliminary study.* WADC TR 54-520. WPAFB, Ohio: Wright Air Dev. Center, (AD 110-573).

Hettinger, T. 1958 [10.2.4]. A modification of the skin temperature test to detect the disposition for tendovaginitis [in German]. *Int. Z. Agnew, Physiologie* **17**:271–75.

Hewitt, D. 1928 [6.9.4]. Range of active motion at the wrist of women. *J. Bone and Joint Surg.* **10**:775–87.

Hickey, L. F.; Springer, W. E.; and Cundari, F. L. 1968 [1.3, 7.8.3, 8.4.6]. *A development in cockpit geometry evaluation.* Report D6-53594. Seattle: Boeing. Also presented at the AGARD-NATO Symposium on Problems of the Cockpit Environment, Amsterdam, The Netherlands, Nov. 11–14, 1968. (Astia AD 680-799). Clearing house for Fed. Scientific and Tech. Info., Springfield, Va.

Hofrath, H. 1931 [2.3.2]. Die Bedeutung der Rontgenfera far Diagnostik der Kieferanomolien. *Fortsch. Orthodont.* **1**:232.

Holland, G. J. 1968 [3.4.1, 6.9.1]. The physiology of flexibility: a review of the literature. *Kinesiology Review—1968,* Council on Kinesiology, Phys. Ed. Div. Washington, D.C.: Amer. Assoc. for Health, Phys. Ed., and Recr.

Hooton, E. A. 1945 [1.3, 2.3.1, 7.5.1, 8.5, 8.5.1, 8.5.3]. *A survey in seating.* Gardner, Mass.: Heywood Wakefield.

———. 1949 [1.2]. *Measurements of body build in a sample of the United States Army.* Prepared for Res. and Dev. Br., Mil. Planning Div., Office of the Quartermaster General, Contract No. W44-109-qm-2014. Cambridge: Harvard Univ., Dept. of Anthropol.

Hooton, E. A.; Wulsin, F. R.; Randall, F. E.; Andrews, J. M.; Stagg, F. L.; Seltzer, C. C.; Bill, N.; and Hall, K. G. 1948 [1.2]. *Body build in relation to military function in a sample of the United States Army.* Office of the Quartermaster General, Res. and Dev. Contract W44-109-qm-1078. Cambridge; Harvard Univ., Dept. of Anthropol.

Hoyle, G. 1970 [4.2]. How is the muscle turned on and off? *Scientific American* **222:**4, 85–93.

Hrdlička, A. 1925 [2.3.2]. *The Old Americans.* Baltimore: Williams and Wilkins.

———. 1939 [1.2, 1.3, 2.1, 2.3.1]. *Practical anthropometry.* Philadelphia: Wistar Inst. of Anatomy and Biology.

Hugh-Jones, P. 1947 [6.10.2, 10.4.2]. The effect of limb position in seated subjects on their ability to utilize the maximum contractile force of the limb muscles. *J. Physiol.* **105:**332–344.

Hultkrantz, J. W. 1897 [1.3]. *Das Ellenbogengelenk und Seine Mechanik.* Jena: Fisher.

Hunsicker, P. A. 1955 [4.4, 4.4.1, 4.4.2, 4.4.4, 4.8.1, 6.10.1, 6.10.2, 6.10.4]. *Arm strength at selected degrees of elbow flexion.* WADC TR 54-548. WPAFB, Ohio: USAF.

Hunsicker, P. A., and Donnelly, R. J. 1955 [4.4, 4.4.1, 4.4.2, 4.7.1]. Instruments to measure strength. *Res. Quart.* **26:**4, 408–20.

Hunsicker, P. A., and Greey, G. 1957 [6.10.2]. Studies in human strength *Res. Quart.* **28:**2, 109–22.

Hunt, E. E., and Giles, E. 1956 [2.3.2]. An evaluation of the photometric camera. *Amer. J. Phys. Anthropol.* **14:**3, 429–36 (N.S.).

Hupprich, F., and Sigerseth, P. O. 1950 [6.9.4). Specificity and reliability of measures of flexibility for girls. *Res. Quart.* **21:**25.

Iberall, A. S. 1964 [9.2]. *The use of lines of nonextension to improve mobility in full-pressure suits.* AMRL 64-118. WPAFB, Ohio: Aerospace Med. Res. Lab., USAF (AD 610-519).

Isakawa, T. 1932 [6.10.1]. Power grip measured by dynamometer. *Report of the Inst. of Science and Labor,* No. 12, Japan.

Janousek, J. A. 1970 [8.7]. The use of mockups in the design of a deep submergence rescue vehicle. *Human Factors* **12:**1, 63–68.

Johnsen, E. G. and Corliss, W. R. 1971 [9.4]. *Human factors applications in teleoperator design and operation.* New York: John Wiley & Sons.

Jones, C. E.; Kobrick, T. L.; and Gaydos, H. F. 1958 [10.2.1]. *Anthropometric and biomechanical characteristics of the hand.* Environ. Prot. Res. Div., TR EP-100. Natick, Mass.: Headquarters, Quartermaster Research and Engineering Command, U.S. Army.

Jones, H. E. 1947 [6.10.4]. The relationship of strength to physique. *Amer. J. Phys. Anthropol.* **5:**29–39 (N.S.) (March).

Jones, R. L. 1966 [9.3.11]. *Evaluation and comparison of three space suit assemblies.* NASA Techn. Note NASA TND-3482. Washington, D.C: NASA.

Jones, W. L., and Gifford, E. C. 1964 [8.4.7]. U.S. Navy aircraft weapon systems anthropometry. Unpublished paper. Authors employed at Bureau of Medicine and Surgery, Dept. of the Navy, Washington, D.C. and Aerospace Equipment Laboratory, Naval Air Engineering Center, Philadelphia, respectively.

Kama, W. N. 1965 [8.9.2]. Volumetric workspace study. Part II. Optimum workspace configuration for use of wrenches. AMRL-TDR-63-68 (II). WPAFB, Ohio: Aerospace Med. Res. Lab., USAF.

Kapff and Vierordt. See Vierordt (1906) [3.2, 6.6.2].

Karpovich, P. V. 1960 [3.4.2]. *Electrogoniometer for measuring degree of forearm rotation.* Report to U.S. Army Medical Research and Development Command. Washington, D.C.: Office of Surgeon General.

Karpovich, P. V.; Herden, E. L.; and Asa, M. M. 1960 [3.4.2]. Electrogoniometric study of joints. *U.S. Armed Forces Med. J.* **11:**424.

Karpovich, P. V.; and Wilklow, L. B. 1959 [3.4.2]. A goniometric study of the human foot in standing and walking. *U.S. Armed Forces Med. J.* **10:**885.

Kellog, J. H. 1893 [4.4.1]. A new dynamometer for use in anthropometry. *Modern Medicine and Bacterial World* **2:**260–75.

Kemsley, W. F. F. 1957 [2.2.2, 2.3.1]. *Women's measurements and sizes.* London: Joint Clothing Council, Ltd., Her Majesty's Stationery Office.

Kendall, H. O., and Kendall, F. P. 1949 [6.9.1]. *Muscle testing and function.* Baltimore: Williams and Wilkins.

Kennedy, K. W. 1964 [1.3, 3.3, 8.3.6, 8.4.5]. *Reach capability of the USAF population. Phase 1-The outer boundaries of grasping—reach envelopes for the shirt-sleeved, seated operator.* AMRL-TDR-64-59. WPAFB, Ohio: Aerospace Med. Res. Labs., USAF (AD 608-269).

Kennedy, K. W., and Bates, C. 1965 [8.8.4]. *Development of design standards for ground support consoles.* WPAFB, Ohio: AMRL-TR-65-163. Aerospace Med. Res. Labs., USAF (AD 630-639).

Kennedy, K. W., and Filler, B. E. 1966 [8.9.1]. *Aperture sizes and depths of reach for one and two handed tasks.* TR AMRL-TR-66-27. WPAFB, Ohio: Aerospace Med. Res. Labs., USAF (AD 646-716)

King, B. G. 1948 [3.3]. Measurements of man for making machinery. *Amer. J. Phys. Anthropol.* **6:**3, 341–351 (N.S.).

King, B. G., Morrow, D.; and Vollmer, E. P. 1947 [3.3, 8.3.6]. *Cockpit studies—the boundaries of the maximum area for the operation of manual controls.* Report No. 3, Project X-651 Naval Med. Res. Inst., Bethesda, Md. National Naval Medical Center.

King, B. G.; Patch, C. T.; and Shinkham, P. G. 1960 [6.6.3]. The center of mass of man. ASME Paper Number 60-WA-303. Presented at Winter Annual Meeting, New York, Nov. 27–Dec. 2, American Society of Mechanical Engineers.

Kira, A. 1966 [8.8.5, 8.10]. *The bathroom.* Research Report No. 7, Center for Housing and Environmental Studies. Ithaca: Cornell Univ.

Kirchner, G., and Glines, D. 1957 [6.9.1]. Flexibility of children. *Res. Quart.* **28:**16.

Kirk, S.; Edwards, E.; and Hindle, T. 1964 [8.6.9]. Designing the driver's workspace. *Design* **188:**36–41.

Klockenberg, E. A. 1926 [10.2.4]. *Rationalization of the typewriter and its operation* [in German]. Berlin: Springer.

Krause, H. E.; and Bogner, F. K. 1971 [7.9.1]. *A survey of mathematical man-models as related to the development of COMBIMAN.* UDRI-Report 71-30. Dayton, Ohio: Univ. of Dayton.

Krause and Vierodt. See Vierordt, 1906 [3.2].

Kroemer, K. H. E. 1963 [10.3.3.]. *Controls on punch presses and other machine tools* [in

German]. Research Report No. 1269 of the State of Northrhine-Westfalia. Koeln-Opladen: Westdeutscher Verlag.

———. 1964 [10.2.4]. On the effects of the spatial orientation of keyboards on the efficiency of typing [in German]. *Int. Z. angew Physiologie* **20:**5, 240–51.

———. 1965a [10.2.4]. Comparison of a standard typewriter keyboard with a K-keyboard [in German]. *Int. Z. angew. Physiologie* **20:**6, 453–64.

———. 1965b [10.2.4]. Improvements of the keyboard of the typewriter [in German]. *Arbeitswissenschaft* **4:**1, 11–16.

———. 1966a [1.3, 8.6.9]. Insufficient consideration of the findings of work physiology in the design of automobiles as a cause of automobile accidents [in German]. *ATZ-Automobil-techn. Z.* **68:**11, 380–85.

———. 1966b [10.3.3]. *On the ergonomic effects of the location of rotary controls* [in German]. Research Report No. 1687 of the State Northrhine-Westfalia. Koeln-Opladen: Westdeutscher Verlag.

———. 1967a [1.3]. *What you should know of switches, cranks and pedals. Selection, arrangement, and use of controls* [in German]. Berlin: Beuth.

———. 1969a [10.4.3]. *Foot operation of controls: speed and accuracy of foot motions between targets.* Conference Record No. 69 C 58-MMS. New York: Inst. of Electrical and Electronic Engineers.

———. 1969b [4.4.4, 4.7.2, 6.10.6, 8.9.1]. *Push forces exerted in sixty-five common working positions.* AMRL TR 68-143. WPAFB, Ohio: Aerospace Med. Res. Labs., USAF (AD 695-040).

———. 1970a [10.4, 10.4.1, 10.4.3]. *Foot operation of controls: speed of activation and exertion of force to pedals; perception, speed and accuracy of leg and foot motions.* AMRL TR 69-57. Aerospace Med. Res. Labs., USAF, WPAFB, Ohio.

———. 1970b [4.2, 4.3.1]. Human strength: terminology, measurement and interpretation of data. *Human Factors* **12:**3, 297–313.

———. 1971a [8.8, 8.8.3]. *Seating in plant and office.* AMRL TR 71-52. WPAFB, Ohio: Aerospace Med. Res. Labs., USAF. Also published in *J. Am. Indust. Hygiene Assoc.* **32:**10, 633–52.

———. 1971b [10.4, 10.4.2]. *Pedal operation by the seated operator.* AMRL TR 71-102. WPAFB, Ohio: Aerospace Med. Res. Labs., USAF. Also as SAE Preprint 72004. New York: Society of Automotive Engineers, 1972.

———. 1971c [10.4]. Foot operation of controls. *Ergonomics* **14:**3, 333–61.

———. 1972a [4.7.2]. *The effect of G_z-vectors on muscular force exerted to controls.* AMRL TR 72-192. WPAFB, Ohio: Aerospace Med. Res. Labs., USAF.

———. 1972b [7.9, 7.9.1]. *COMBIMAN-Computerized biomechanical man-model.* AMRL TR 72-16. WPAFB, Ohio: Aerospace Med. Res. Lab., USAF. Also, pages 73–88 in *Proc. IFU Colloquium* "Space Technology-A Model for Safety Techniques and Accident Prevention?" Cologne, Germany, April, 1972. Cologne: Verlag TUV Rheinland, 1973.

———. 1972c [10.2.4]. Human engineering the keyboard. *Human Factors* **14:**1, 51–63.

———. 1972d [4.7.2, 6.10.7]. *Designing for muscular strength of various populations.* AMRL TR 72-46. WPAFB, Ohio: USAF. Also published in *Proc. Symposium on National and Cultural Variables in Human Factors Engineering.* Oosterbeek, The Netherlands, June 1972.

———. 1973 [4.7.2]. Effects of high G on pilot muscle strength available for aircraft control operation. *Proc. 44th Ann. Meeting of the Aerospace. Med. Assoc.,* Las Vegas, Nev., 255–256.

Kroemer, K. H. E., and Gienapp, E. M. 1970 [4.4.4]. Hand-Held Device to Measure Finger (Thumb) Strength. *J. Appl. Physiol.* **29:**4, 526–27.

Kroemer, K. H. E., and Howard, J. M. 1970a [4.3.1, 4.72]. *Problems in Assessing Muscle Strength.* AMRL TR 68-144. WPAFB, Ohio: Aerospace Med. Res. Lab., USAF (AD 708-741).

Kroemer, K. H. E., and Howard, J. M. 1970b [4.7.2]. Toward standardization of muscle strength testing. *J. Medicine and Science in Sports* **2:**4, 224–30.

Kroemer, K. H. E., and Robinette, J. C. 1968 [8.8.3]. *Ergonomics in the design of office furniture.* AMRL TR 68-80. WPAFB, Ohio: Aerospace Med. Res. Lab., USAF.

Kroemer, K. H. E., and Robinson, D. E. 1971 [4.4.4, 4.7.2, 4.8.1, 6.10.4, 6.10.6, 8.9.1]. *Horizontal static forces exerted by men standing in common working positions on surfaces of various tractions.* AMRL Tr 70-114. WPAFB, Ohio: Aerospace Med. Res. Lab., USAF.

Kubokawa, C. C. 1968 [7.8.3]. *Instant modular 3D mockup for configuring control and display equipment.* NASA Paper N68-34665.

Kyropoulos, P., and Roe, P. W. 1968 [8.6.2]. The application of anthropometry to automotive design. *Proc. General Motors Corp. Automotive Safety Seminar,* Safety Res. and Dev. Lab., G. M. Proving Ground, Milford, Mich., July 11–12.

Lacmann, O. 1950 [2.3.2]. *Die Photogrammetrie in Ihrer Anwendung auf Nicht-Topographischen Gebieten.* Leipzig: S. Hirzel Verlag.

Lange, W. 1971 [8.6.10]. *Mechanical and physiological response of the human cervical column to severe impacts relative to the torso.* In AMRL TR 71-29, pp. 141-67. WPAFB, Ohio: Aerospace Med. Res. Lab., USAF.

Laubach, L. L. 1969 [6.9.2]. Body composition in relation to muscle strength and range of joint motion. *J. of Sports Medicine and Physical Fitness* **9:**5, 89–97.

———. 1972 [6.12.3]. *A selected literature review pertaining to the relationships between static and dynamic muscular strength.* Interim Report, Contract F33615-72-C-1006 with the Aerospace Med. Res. Lab., WPAFB, Yellow Springs, Ohio: Webb Associates, Inc.

Laubach, L. L.; Kroemer, K. H. E.; and Thordsen, M. L. 1972 [4.2, 4.7.2, 6.10.4, 6.10.7]. Relationships among isometric forces measured in aircraft control locations. *Aerospace Medicine* **43:**7, 738–42.

Laubach, L. L., and McConville, J. T. 1966 [6.10.4]. Relationships between flexibility, anthropometry and the somatotype of college men. *Res. Quart.* **37:**2, 241–51.

———. 1969 [6.9.2, 6.10.4]. The relationship of strength to body size and typology. *Medicine and Science in Sports* **1:**4, 189–94.

Lauru, L. 1957 [10.4.3]. Physiological study of motions. *Advanced management* **22:**3, 17–24.

Lay, W. E., and Fisher, L. C. 1940 [1.3, 7.7.1, 8.5.1]. Riding comfort and cushions. *Soc. of Automotive Engineers J.* (Transactions) **47:**5, 482–96.

Lear, Inc. 1960 [8.1]. *Whole panel control-display study. Vol. 1, Methodology for control-display systems development.* Lear Engineering Report GR-1364 (I) Lear, Inc., Grand Rapids Advance Eng. Div., Contract AF 33(616)-5901 for Fl. Control Lab. WPAFB, Ohio: USAF.

LeGros, L. A., and Weston, H. C. 1926 [1.3]. *On the design of machinery in relation to the operator.* Industrial Fatigue Research Board Report 36, p. 9.

Lehmann, G., ed. 1961 [4.2, 6.12]. Arbeitsphysiologie. Vol. 1 of *Handbuch der gesamten Arbeitsmedizin,* ed. A. Baader. Berlin: Urban and Schwarzenberg.

Leider, M., and Buncke, C. M. 1954 [3.2, 6.6.2]. Physical dimensions of the skin. *Arch. Dermat. and Syph.* **69:**563–69.

Leighton, J. R. 1942 [3.4.2]. A simple objective and reliable measure of flexibility. *Res. Quart.* **13:**205–16.

———. 1955 [3.4.1, 3.4.2]. An instrument and technique for measurement of range of joint motion. *Arch. Phys. Med. Rehabil.* **36:**571–78.

———. 1956 [3.4.1, 6.9.1]. Flexibility characteristics of males ten to eighteen years of age. *Arch. Phys. Med. Rehabil.* **37:**494–499.

———. 1957 [3.4.1, 3.4.2]. Flexibility characteristics of four specialized skill groups of college athletes. *Arch. Phys. Med. Rehabil.* **38:**24–28.

———. 1960 [3.4.1, 3.4.2, 6.9.4]. On the significance of flexibility for physical education. *J. Health, Phys. Educ., Recr.* **31:**27.

———. 1964 [3.4.1, 3.4.2, 6.9.4]. A study of the effect of progressive weight training on flexibility. *J. Assoc. Phys. Ment. Rehabil.* **18:**101–05.

Letulle and Pompillion 1906 [2.4.1]. Methode de Recherche Applicable a L'étude de la Nutrition. *Rev. Soc. Scient. d'Hyg. Aliment* **3:**645–708.

Lieber, L. 1960 [6.2.3]. We're getting too big for our britches!" *This Week,* Nov. 6, 18–20, Los Angeles Times supplement.

Linford, A. G., and Rarick, G. L. 1968 [4.7.2, 6.10.6]. The effect of knee angle on the measurement of leg strength of college males. *Res. Quart.* **39:**3, 582–86.

Lippert, S. 1949 [1.3, 8.5, 8.5.1]. *Notes on method of photographic contour map for head.* Douglas Aircraft Co.

———. 1950 [1.3, 8.4, 8.5]. Designing for comfort in aircraft seats. *Aeronautical Engr. Rev.* **9:**9.

———. 1957 [1.3, 8.5]. *An engineering approach to the human factors problems of jet transport aircraft.* A presentation to the Airlines Medical Directors Association. Denver. May 5.

———. 1958. [1.3, 8.5.3]. *The engineering approach to the human factors problems of jet aircraft.* Remarks prepared for presentation at the Panel on the Jet Age and Chest Medicine, 24th Annual Meeting of the Amer. College of Chest Physicians, San Francisco, June 19.

———. 1965 [1.3, 7.3.3]. *Estimated body dimensions of the adult male Jewish population of Israel.* Technion Aeronautical Engr. Report TAE No. 40, Technion-Israel Inst. of Technology, Dept. of Aeronautical Engr., Haifa, Israel.

Lissauer, W. 1903 [2.4.1]. Ueber Ober flächen messungen und Säuglingen und ihre Bedeutung für den Nahrungsbedarf. *Jahrbuch für Kinderheilkunde* **58:**392–411.

Lombard, C. F.; Canfield, A. A.; Wilson, R. C.; Warren, N. D.; and Drury, D. R. 1951 [4.7.2]. *The influence of positive (head to foot) centrifugal force upon a subject's (pilot) ability to exert maximum pull on an aircraft control stick.* TR ONR, Jan. 1948, Dept. of Av. Med., USC Sch. Med., L. A., Calif., Contract N6Ori77, Task 1 and 2.

Lombard, C. F., and Drury, D. R. 1947 [4.7.2]. *The influence of positive (head to foot) radial acceleration upon the ability of a subject (pilot) to manipulate a control stick.* TR ONR, July 1947, Dept. of Av. Med., USC Sch. of Med., L. A., Calif., Contract N6Ori77, Task. 1.

Lonie, M. 1948 [9.2.]. Anthropometry and apparel. *Amer. J. Phys. Anthropol.* **6:**3, 353–61.

Lundervold, A. 1958 [10.2.4]. Electromyographic investigations during typewriting. *Ergonomics* **1:**3, 226–33.

Lyman, J. 1956 [9.5.3]. *Final report on studies of some variables relating hand-covering design to manual performance in extreme environments.* Dept. of Eng. Report No. 56-7, Univ. of Calif., Los Angeles.

Lyman, J., and Groth, H. 1958 [9.5.3]. Prehension force as a measure of psychomotor skill for bare and gloved hands. *J. Applied Psych.* **42:**18–21.

MacConaill, M. A. 1966 [3.4.1]. The ergonomic aspects of articular mechanics. In *Studies on the Anatomy and Function of Bone and Joints,* ed. F. G. Evans, pp. 69–80. New York: Springer-Verlag.

Machine Design (1967) [9.4]. Clothes that clank. *Machine Design,* August 17, 28–32.

———. 1970 [8.6.11]. Adjustable fixture previews car design. *Machine Design* **42:**7 March 19, 29.

Malina, R. M.; Hamill, P. V. V.; and Lemeshow, S. 1973 [6.2.4]. *Selected body measurements of children 6-11 years, United States.* Vital and Health Statistics, Series 11, No. 123, Public Health Service, HEW. Washington, D.C.: U.S. Govt. Ptg. Office.

Martin, E. 1949 [10.2.4]. *The typewriter and its history* [in German]. Aachen: Basten.

Martin, R. 1928* [1.2, 6.2.2]. *Lehrbuch der Anthropologie.* 2nd ed. 3 vols. Jena: Fischer Verlag. *Also: 1914, 1st ed.; same title and publisher. [1.2, 6.2.2].

Martin, W. B., and Johnson, E. E. 1952 [10.4.2]. *An optimum range of seat positions as determined by exertion of pressure upon a foot pedal.* Report No. 86. Fort Knox, Ky.: U.S. Army Medical Res. Lab.

Martin, W. E. 1953 [6.2.4]. *Basic body measurements of school age children.* Washington D.C.: U.S. Dept. of Health, Education, and Welfare, Office of Education.

Martin, W. E. et al. 1954 [6.2.4]. *The functional body measurements of school age children.* Chicago: National School Service Institute.

Martinez, J. L. 1968 [8.6.10]. Headrest and seat back design proposals. SAE Paper No. 680775, *Proc. of Twelfth Stapp Car Crash Conf.,* Oct. 22–23, pp. 164–71.

Mathews, D. K. 1959 [6.9.3]. Hip flexibility of elementary school boys as related to body segments. *Res. Quart.* **30:**297–302.

Mathews, D. K., and Kruse, R. 1957 [6.9.3]. Effects of isometric and isotonic exercises on elbow flexor muscle groups. *Res. Quart.* **28:**26.

Mathews, D. K. et al. 1957 [6.9.3]. Hip flexibility of college women as related to length of body segment. *Res. Quart.* **28:**352–56.

Maul, H., and Solf, J. 1969 [10.3.2, 10.3.3]. *Selecting the right handle* [in German]. Special Issue, REFA-Nachrichten. Berlin: Beuth.

Mayo, A. M. 1953 [8.1]. Designing the cockpit to the man. *Amer. Aviation* **17:**3, 23–26 and **17:**4, 48–53.

McConville, J. T.; Alexander, M.; and Velsey, S. 1963 [9.3.5]. *Anthropometric data in three-dimensional form: development and fabrication of USAF height-weight manikins.* AMRL TDR 63-55. WPAFB, Ohio: 6570th Aerospace Med. Res. Lab., USAF (AD 410-451).

McFadden, E. B., and Swearingen, J. J. 1958 [10.3.2]. Forces that may be exerted by man in the operation of aircraft door handles. *Human Factors* **1:**1, 16–22.

McFadden, E. B., Swearingen, J. J.; and Wheelwright, C. D. 1959 [10.3.2]. The magnitude and direction of forces that man can exert in operating aircraft emergency exists. *Human Factors* **1:**4, 16.

McFadden, E. B., and Young, J. W. 1971 [6.2.4]. *Evaluation of an improved flotation device for infants and small children.* Report No. FAA-AM-71-37. Oklahoma City: Federal Aviation Admin., Office of Aviation Medicine, Civil Aeromedical Institute.

McFarland, R. A.; Damon, A.; Stoudt, H. W.; Moseley, A. L.; Dunlap, J. W.; and Hall, W. A. 1953 [8.6.3]. *Human body size and capabilities in the design and operations of vehicular equipment.* Boston: Harvard School of Public Health.

McFarland, R. A.; Damon, A.; and Stoudt, H. W. 1955 [8.6.9]. *The application of human body size data to vehicular design.* Special Publication No. 142. New York: Society of Automotive Engineers, [See also McFarland et al. 1953]

McFarland, R. A.; Domey, R. G.; Duggar, B. C.; Crowley, T. J., and Stoudt, H. W. 1968 [8.6.3, 8.6.4]. *An evaluation of the ability of amputees to operate highway equipment.* Report RD-592. Boston: Harvard School of Public Health.

McHenry, R. R. 1971 [8.6.10]. *Multidegree, nonlinear mathematical models of the human body and restraint systems.* AMRL TR 71-29-7. WPAFB, Ohio: Aerospace Med. Res. Lab., USAF.

McHenry, R. R., and Naab, K. N. 1966 [1.3, 8.6.10]. *Computer simulation of the automobile crash victim in a frontal collision—a validation study.* CAL Report No. YB-2126-V-1R. Buffalo: Cornell Aeronautical Lab.

McKendry, J. M.; Grant, G.; Corso, J. F.; and Brubaker, R. 1960 [8.9.1, 8.9.2]. Supplement IV, Maintainability handbook for electronic equipment design to NAV TRAVDEVCEN 330-1. Design for Maintainability, Technical Report NAVTRADEVCEN 330-1-4, U.S. Navy.

McNemar, Q. 1962 [5.2.10]. *Psychological statistics* New York: John Wiley.

Meeh, C. 1879 [2.4.1]. Surface measurements of the human body [in German]. *Ztsch. f. Biol.* **15:**425–58.

———. 1895* [3.2, 3.2.5]. Volummessungen des menschlichen Körpers und seiner einzelnen Theile in den verschiedenen Altersstufen. *Zts. f. Biol.* **13:**125–47. *Date cited by Dempster (1955), but listed as 1894 by Clauser, McConville, and Young (1969).

Meister, D., and Farr, D. E. 1966a [8.1.]. *Designers guide for effective development of aerospace ground equipment control panels.* AMRL TR 66-29. WPAFB, Ohio: Aerospace Med. Res. Labs., USAF.

———. 1966b [8.1]. *A methodology of control panel design.* AMRL TR 66-28. WPAFB, Ohio: Aerospace Med. Res. Labs., USAF.

———. 1967 [7.4.4]. The utilization of human factors information by designers. *Human Factors* **9:**1, 71–87.

Meldrum, J. F. 1966 [8.6.6]. Automobile driver eye position. *SAE Transactions* **74,** Paper 650464.

Michel, C. H., and Perret, M. 1907 [2.4.1]. La Ration Alimentaire de l'Enfant Depuis sa Naissance Jusqua l'age de Duex Ans. *L'Obstetrique* **12:**145–56, *Bulletin de Science Pharmacologique* **14:**287–95.

Miles, M. 1963 [7.7.3]. Mechanized dummies to test space suits. *Los Angeles Times,* Nov. 13, p. 24.

Miller, W. K., and Katz, S. 1968 [7.6.2]. A technique for measuring local impact pressures. *Proc. Automotive Safety Seminar,* General Motors Corp., G. M. Proving Ground, Milford, Mich., July 11–12.

Miskin, E. A. 1956 [2.3.2]. The application of photogrammetric techniques to medical problems. *The Photogrammetric Record* **II:**8, 92, October.

———. 1960 [2.3.2]. Simple photogrammetric methods in medicine. *Med. & Biol. Illus.* **10:**230.

Mizen, N. J. 1965 [7.6.3, 9.4]. *Preliminary design for the shoulders and arms of a powered exoskeletal structure.* Final Technical Report, Contract No. Nonr-3830(00). Buffalo: Cornell Aeronautical Lab.

Molbech, S. 1963 [4.2]. *Average percentage force at repeated maximal isometric muscle contractions at different frequencies.* Communication 16. Hellerup, Denmark: Danish Nat. Assoc. for Infant. Paralysis.

Monod, H. 1956 [4.2]. *Contribution a l'étude du travail statique.* Medical dissertation, Univ. de Paris.

Montagu, M. F. A. 1960 [2.1]. *A handbook of anthropometry.* Springfield, Ill.: Charles C. Thomas.

Montoye, H. J., and Faulkner, J. A. 1964 [4.4.1]. Determination of the optimum setting of an adjustable grip dynamometer. *Res. Quart.* **35:**1, 29–36.

Moore, M. L. 1949a [3.4.2]. The measurement of joint motion: Part 1-Introductory review of the literature. *Physiotheraphy Rev.* **29:**195–205.

———. 1949b [3.4.2]. The measurement of joint motion: Part 2-The technique of goniometry. *Physiotherapy Rev.* **29:**254–64.

Morant, G. M. 1945 [2.3.1]. Anthropometric Investigations for Air Force Purposes, Great Britain, FPRC 609.

———.1947 [7.5.1]. *Dimensional requirements for seats in R.A.F. aircraft.* Flying Personnel Research Committee (Great Britain), Report 682.

———. 1954 [7.8]. Body size and work space. In *Symposium on human factors in equipment design,* eds. Floyd and Welford. London: H. K. Lewis.

———. 1955 [8.1]. Body measurements in relation to work space. In *Anthropometry and human engineering.* Advisory Group for Aeronautical Research and Development (AGARD), North Atlantic Treaty Org. London: Butterworths Scientific Publications.

Morant, G. M., and Gilson, J. C. 1945 [2.3.1, 7.5.1, 9.3.3]. *A report of body and clothing measurements of Royal Air Force personnel.* Flying Personnel Research Committee Report 633(a), Farnsborough, Eng.: R.A.F. Institute of Aviation Medicine.

Morehouse, L. E., and Wells, J. G. 1948 [4.7.2]. *An electromyographic study of the effects of various positive G forces upon the pilot's ability to perform standardized pulls on an aircraft control stick.* Technical Rep. ONR, June 1948. Los Angeles: Dept Av. Med., USC Sch. Med.

Morgan, C. T.; Cook, J. S.; Chapanis, A.; and Lund, M. W., eds. 1963 [6.12.4, 8.1.1, 8.4.5, 8.8.4, 8.9.2]. See Section 7.2.4, Table 7-2.

Moroney, W. F. 1971 [6.4.3]. *Selected bivariate anthropometric distributions describing a sample of naval aviators—1964.* NAMRL-1130. Pensacola: Naval Aerospace Med. Res. Lab.

———. 1972 [6.4.3]. The use of bivariate distributions in achieving anthropometric compatibility in equipment design—Part I: The requirement. *Proc. of the 16th Ann. Meeting of the Human Factors Soc.,* Oct. 17–19, 1972, Los Angeles.

Moroney, W. F., and Smith, M. J. 1972a [6.4.3]. *Empirical reduction in potential user population as the result of imposed multivariate anthropometric limits.* NAMRL-1164. Pensacola: Naval Aerospace Med. Res. Lab.

———. 1972b [6.4.3]. *Intercorrelations and selected descriptive statistics for 96 anthropometric measures on 1549 naval aviation personnel.* NAMRL-1165. Pensacola: Naval Aerospace Med. Res. Lab.

Mosso, A. 1884 [3.2, 3.2.3]. Application de la balance a l'etude de la circulation du sang chez l'homme. *Arch. Ital. Biol.* **5:**130–43.

Müller, E. A. 1936 [10.4.2]. The best arrangement of foot controls operated in the seated position [in German]. *Arbeitsphysiologie* **9:**2, 125–37. Also: Optimum arrangement of pedals to be operated from sitting position. Air Technical Intelligence Translation 182580, F-TS-8336/VV. WPAFB, Ohio: Air Technical Intelligence Center (ATI-138641).

———. 1957 [4.7.2]. The regulation of muscular strength. *J. of the Assoc. for Phys. and Mental Rehab.* **11:**2, 41–47.

———.1970 [4.7.2]. Influence of training and inactivity on muscle strength. *Arch. Phys. Med. and Rehability* **51:**449–62.

Munro, E. H. 1952 [7.4.2, 9.2]. *Preparation of anthropometric nomographs.* Environmental Protection Division, Report No. 184. Natick, Mass.: Quartermaster Research and Development Command.

Muybridge, E. 1955 [1.3]. *The human figure in motion.* New York: Dover Publication.

Napier, J. R. 1956 [10.2.1]. The prehensile movements of the hand. *J. of Bone and Joint Surg.* **38B:**4, 902–13.

Napier, J. R. 1962 [10.2.1]. The evolution of the hand. *Scientific American,* December.

Newman, L. 1949 [4.4.2]. A new device for measuring muscle strength. *Archives of Phys. Med.* **30:**234–37.

Newman, R. W. 1952 [3.2, 3.2.2]. *Measurement of body fat in stress situations.* Report No. 193. Natick, Mass.: Environmental Protection Division, Quartermaster Res. and Dev. Command.

———. 1953 [9.2.]. *Model and size data for the design of men's clothing.* Environmental Protection Division, Report No. 217. Lawrence, Mass.: Natick, Quartermaster Res. and Dev. Lab. (AD-21553).

———. 1963 [6.2.3]. The body sizes of tomorrow's young men. Chapter 8 In *Human Factors in Technology,* eds. E. Bennett, J. Degan, and J. Spiegel, chapter 8. New York: McGraw-Hill.

Newman, R. W., and Munro, E. 1955 [6.2.2]. The relation of climate and body size in U.S. males. *Amer. J. Phys. Anthropol.* **13:**1, 1–18 (N.S.).

Newman, R. W., and White, R. M. 1951 [9.2]. *Reference anthropometry of Army men.* Report No. 180, Environment Protection Section, Res. and Dev. Branch, Mil. Protection Div., Off. of Quartermaster General, Dept. of the Army.

Nichols, D. E., and Amrine, H. T. 1959 [10.4.3]. A physiological appraisal of selected principles of motion economy. *J. Ind. Eng.* **10:**5, 373–78.

O'Brien, F.; Girshick, M. S.; and Hunt, E. P. 1941 [9.2, 9.3.3]. *Body measurements of American boys and girls for garment and pattern construction.* Miscellaneous Publication No. 366. Washington, D.C.: U.S. Dept. of Agriculture.

O'Brien, R., and Shelton, W. C. 1941 [7.5.1, 9.2, 9.3.3]. *Women's measurements for garments and pattern construction.* Miscellaneous Publication No. 454. Washington, D.C.: U.S. Dept. of Agriculture in cooperation with the Work Projects-Administration, Textiles and Clothing Div., Bureau of Home Economics.

Oresme, N. [1.3]. *Tractatus de unifornitate et difformitate intensium.* MS, Bibliotheque Nationale, Paris. Printed in several editions toward the end of the fifteenth century.

Oshima, M.; Fujimoto, T.; Oguro, T.; Tobimatsu, N.; Mori, T.; Tanaka, I.; Watanabe, T.; and Alexander, M. 1965 [9.4]. *Anthropometry of Japanese pilots.* AMRL TR 65-74. WPAFB, Ohio: Aerospace Med. Res. Lab., USAF (AD 462-062).

Oxford, H. W. 1969 [6.2.4, 8.8.3]. Anthropometric data for educational chairs. *Ergonomics* **12:**2, 140–61.

Panel on Psychology and Physiology 1949 [8.7]. *A survey report on human factors in undersea warfare.* Committee on Undersea Warfare. Washington, D.C.: National Research Council.

Pangle, R., and Garrett, L. 1966 [4.4.1]. Origin of the spring scale dynamometer. *Res. Quart.* **37:**1, 155–56.

Parker, J. F., and West, V. R., eds. 1973 [6.8.2]. *Bioastronautics data book.* 2nd ed. National Aeronautics and Space Admin. Washington, D.C.: U.S. Govt. Ptg. Office.

Parry, D. G.; Curry, L. R.; Hanson, D. B.; and Towle, G. B. 1966 [7.6.3, 9.4]. *A study of techniques and equipment for the evaluation of extravehicular protective garments.* AMRL TR 66-4. WPAFB, Ohio: Aerospace Med. Res. Labs., USAF.

Pascale, L. R. M.; Grossman, M. I.; and Sloane, H. S. 1955 [3.2]. *Correlation between thickness of skinfolds and body density in 88 soldiers.* Army Medical Nutr. Lab. Rep. No. 162, Denver.

Passerello, C. E., and Huston, R. L. 1971 [7.9.1]. Human attitude control. *J. Biomechanics* **4:**4, 95–102.

Payne, P. R., and Band, E. G. U. 1971 [7.6.2]. *Development of a dynamic analog anthropomorphic dummy for aircraft escape system testing.* AMRL TR 71-10. WPAFB, Ohio: Aerospace Med. Res. Lab., USAF.

Pearson, J. R.; McGinley, D. R.; and Butzel, L. M. 1963 [3.2.6, 3.5.3]. Dynamic analysis of the upper extremity: planar motions. *Human Factors* **5:**1, 59–70.

Perbix, J. 1954 [6.9.2]. Relationship between somatotype and motor fitness in women. *Res. Quart.* **25:**841.

Peres, N. J. C. 1961 [10.3.3]. Process Work without strain. *J. Australian Factory,* Special Feature Article, July 1.

Phillips, M. et al. 1955 [6.9.1]. Analysis of results from the Kraus-Weber test of minimum muscular fitness in children. *Res. Quart.* **26:**314.

Pierce, B. F. 1960 [9.5.3, 10.2.2]. Manual force capabilities of a pilot in a full-pressure suit: techniques of measurement and data presentation. *Eng. Ind. Psychol.* **1960:**2, 27–33.

———. 1963 [9.5.3, 10.2.2]. Effects of wearing a full-pressure suit on manual dexterity and tool manipulation. *Human Factors* **5:**5, 479–84.

Pigg, L. D., and Kama, W. N. 1961 [8.3.13]. *The effect of transient weightlessness on visual acuity.* WADD TR 61-184. WPAFB, Ohio: Behavioral Sciences Lab., Aerospace Med. Lab., Wright Air Dev. Div., Air Res. and Devel. Command. USAF.

Product Engineering Staff 1967 [3.2.4]. New data should help fit people better to machines. *Product Engineering,* Sept. 11, 173–175.

Product Engineering Staff 1968 [6.2.3]. Planes must keep on growing to keep up with passengers. *Product Engineering.* Mar. 25, 123.

Quetelet, A. 1835 [1.2, 6.10.5]. *Sur l'homme et le developpement de ses facultes* (Paris) A treatise on man and the development of his faculties. Translation published in 1842. Edinburg: W. and R. Chambers.

Raber, B. F., and Hutchinson, F. W. 1947 [2.4.2]. *Panel Heating and Cooling Analysis.* New York: John Wiley.

Radnofsky, M. I. 1967 [9.4]. Space Suits. *Intern. Science and Technology,* Feb., p. 32.

Ramsey, C. G., and Sleeper, H. R. 1941 [8.8.5]. *Architectural Graphic Standards.* 3rd ed. New York: John Wiley.

Ramsey, J. D. 1971 [10.3.2, 10.3.3]. *Ergonomic guidelines for design and use of hand tools.* Synopsis, Ergonomics Refresher Course. Toronto: American Industrial Hygiene Assoc.

Randall, F. E. 1947 [1.2]. *Survey of body size of Army personnel, male and female: Phase 4—Body dimensions of army females—methodology and general considerations.* Environmental Protection Division, Report No. 123, Project No. E-59-46. Natick, Mass.: Quartermaster Res. and Dev. Command.

———. 1948a [1.2, 1.3, 9.2]. *Applications of anthropometry to the determination of size in clothing.* Environmental Protection Div., Report No. 133. Natick, Mass.: Quartermaster Res. and Dev. Command.

———. 1948b [1.2, 1.3]. Anthropometry in the Quartermaster Corps. *Amer. J. Phys. Anthropol.* **6**:3, 373–80 (N.S.).

———. 1949 [1.2]. Anthropometric nomograph of Army white men. *Human Biology* **21**:4, 218–32.

Randall, F. E., and Baer, M. J. 1951 [1.2]. *Survey of body size of Army personnel, male and female—methodology.* Environmental Protection Section, Report No. 122 Revised. Lawrence, Mass.: Quartermaster Climatic Res. Lab., Res. and Dev. Div., Office of the QM General.

Randall, F. E.; Damon, A.; Benton, R. S.; and Patt, D. I. 1946 [1.3, 5.3, 7.5.1, 8.5, 8.5.1]. *Human body size in military aircraft and personal equipment.* Army Air Force TR 5501. Dayton: Air Materiel Command, Wright Field.

———. 1949a [9.2]. *Anthropometric nomograph of Army women.* Environmental Protection Div., Report No. 148. Natick, Mass.: QM Res. and Dev. Center.

———. 1949b [9.2]. *Reference anthropometry of Army women.* Environmental Protection Division, Report No. 149. Natick, Mass.: QM Res. and Dev. Center.

Rebiffé, R.; Zayana, O.; and Tarrière, C. 1969 [7.6.2, 8.3.6]. Determination des zones optimales pour l'emplacement des commandes manuelles dans l'espace de travail. *Ergonomics* **12**:6, 913–24.

Rees, J. E., and Graham, N. E. 1952 [10.4.2]. The effect of backrest position on the push which can be exerted on a isometric foot-pedal. *J. of Anat.* **96**:3, 310–19.

Remington, R. J., and Rogers, M. 1969 [10.2.4]. *Keyboard literature survey. Phase I: bibliography.* TR 29.0042. Research Triangle Park, N.C.: IBM Systems Develop. Div.

Reynolds, E., and Lovett, R. W. 1909 [3.2, 3.2.3]. A method of determining the position of the center of gravity in its relation to certain bony landmarks in the erect position. *Amer. J. Physiol.* **24**:289–93.

Ricci, B. 1970 [4.7.2]. For a moratorium on "physical fitness testing." *JOHPER* **4**:3, 28–29.

Rockwell International 1962 [8.3.3]. Apollo design criteria specification. (Unpublished document). SID 62-65, Rev. 15 May 1962, Space and Information Systems Division, North American Aviation, Downey, Calif. (present title of company is listed above as author).

Rodzen, R.; Mayerhofer, K.; George, D.; O'Shea, R.; Watmough, T.; and Scribano, F. C. 1971 [9.4]. *Development of aircrew body armor.* IITRI Project Report J6190. Chicago: IIT Research Institute.

Roe, R. W., and Hammond, D. C. 1972 [8.6.6]. Driver head and eye position. *SAE Report* 720200. New York: Society of Automotive Engineers.

Roebuck, J. A., Jr. 1952 [1.3]. Anthropometric data: human body dimensions and weights. Douglas Aircraft Co. Report No. SM-14617. Douglas Aircraft Co., Santa Monica, Calif.*

———. 1954 [8.4.3]. Pilot's eye and control wheel position. Model 1859, Douglas Aircraft Co., Report No. SM-18668. Douglas Aircraft Co., Santa Monica, Calif.*

———. 1957 [1.3, 5.2.10, 5.3, 5.5.1, 5.5.2, 6.3.1, 7.3.3, 7.5.1, 7.7.1, 8.5, 8.5.2, 11.3]. Anthropometry in aircraft engineering design. *J. Aviation Med.* **28**:1, 41–56.

———. 1965 [4.5.1, 4.8.2, 9.5.3, 10.2.2, 10.2.3, 10.2.4]. Knob torque strength requirements for space suit glove operation. Master's thesis, Univ. of Calif., Los Angeles.

* Unpublished—proprietary data. May be available to readers upon special request to McDonnell Douglas Co., Long Beach, Calif.

———. 1968 [1.3, 3.4.1, 3.4.2, 3.4.3, 3.4.4, 3.4.6, 9.3.11]. A system of notation and measurement for space suit mobility evaluation. *Human Factors* **10:**1, 79–94.

Roebuck, J. A., Jr.; Kroemer, K. H. E.; and Thomson, W. G. 1973 [6.2.3, 8.3.11]. Frontiers in Workspace Applications of Anthropometry. pp. 319–329 In K. D. Cross and J. J. McGrath, Eds., *Crew System Design*-Proceedings of an interagency conference at Los Angeles, Calif., September 12-14, 1972. Santa Barbara, Calif.: Anacapa Sciences, Inc.

Roebuck, J. A., Jr., and Levedahl, B. H. 1961 [6.9.1, 8.5]. Aircraft ground emergency exit design considerations. *Human Factors* **3:**3, 174–209.

Rogers, R. A., and Silver, J. N. 1968 [8.6.7]. Elements of an effective child restraint system. In *Proc. of 12th Stapp Car Crash Conf.,* Oct. 22–23, 1968, Detroit, pp. 172–187. New York: Society of Automotive Engineers.

Rohmert, W. 1960 [4.2]. Determination of recovery periods for static work of man [in German]. *Int. Z angew. Physiologie* **18:**175–90.

———. 1966 [10.4.2]. *Maximal forces of men within the reach envelope of the arms and legs* [in German]. Research Report No. 1616 of the state of Northrhine-Westfalia, Westdeutscher Verlag Koeln-Opladen.

Rohmert, W., and Jenik, P. 1971 [6.10.6, 10.4.2]. Isometric muscular strength in women. in *Frontiers of Fitness,* ed. R. J. Shephard, Chapter 4, pp. 79–97. Springfield, Ill.: C. C. Thomas.

Rosen, N. G. 1922 [3.4.2]. A simplified method of measuring amplitude of motion in joints. *J. Bone and Joint Surg.* **20:**3, 570–79.

Rolston, R. F.; Bodine, E.; and Dunleavy, J. 1968 [9.4]. Breakthrough in armor. *Space/Aeronautics,* July, 55–63.

Roussy, B. See Boyd, E. (1935) for extensive list of Roussy's works. [2.4.1].

Ryker, N. J. 1968 [9.3.11]. Man/equipment tasks systems for Apollo. Paper presented at Gilbreth Centennial, combined meeting of American Management Assoc. and ASME, December, New York.

SAE 1967 [8.6.6]. Passenger car driver's eye range. *SAE Recommended Standard* J 941a. New York: Society of Automotive Engineers.

SAE 1970 [8.6.1]. Devices for use in defining and measuring vehicle seating accommodation. *SAE Standard* J 826a. New York: Society of Automotive Engineers.

Sahley, L. W. 1957 [1.3]. *Dimensions of the human figure—male and female.* Cleveland: Cleveland Designers and Consultants.

Sandover, J. 1971 [7.9]. *A study of human analogues, part I. A survey of the literature.* Report PD-170-01. Loughborough, Eng.: Dept. of Ergonomics and Cybernetics, Loughborough Univ. of Technology.

Santschi, W. R.; DuBois, J.; and Omoto, C. 1963 [3.2, 3.2.4, 6.6.3]. *Moments of inertia and centers of gravity of the living human body.* AMRL TDR 63-36. WPAFB, Ohio: Aerospace Med. Res. Lab., USAF (AD 410-451).

Saralegui, A. M. 1954 [2.3.2]. What is photosculpture?" *Photogrammetric Eng.* **XX:**1, March.

Sargent, D. A. 1897a [4]. Strength tests and the strong man of Harvard. *Amer. Phys. Ed. Rev.* **2:**108–19 (June).

———. 1897b [4]. Intercollegiate strength tests. *Amer. Phys. Ed. Rev.* **2:**216–20 (Dec.).

Savara, B. S. 1965 [2.3.2]. Applications of photography for quantitative study of tooth and face morphology. *Amer. J. Phys. Anthropol.* **23:**427–34.

Schaffer, G. K. 1959 [6.9.1]. Variables affecting Kraus-Weber failures among junior high girls. *Res. Quart.* **30:**75.

Scherrer, J. 1967 [6.12]. *Physiologie de travail (ergonomie).* 2 Vols. Paris: Masson et Cie.

Schneider, M. 1966 [10.4.3]. Letter to K. H. E. Kroemer, April 4.

Schochrin, W. A. 1935 [6.10.1]. Die Muskelkraft der Beuger und Strecker des Unterschenkels. *Arbeitsphysiologie* **8:**251–60.

Schroeder, F. de N. 1951 [8.8.5]. *Anatomy for interior designers.* 2nd ed., New York: Whitney Publications.

Schwartz, S. A., and Visconti, V. 1965 [3.4.1]. Proposed spacesuit mobility notation standards. Grumman Aircraft Engineering Co., Eng. Rep. No. LED-480-13A (unpublished).

Seaford, H. W. 1959 [1.3, 2.3.2]. Comments on the PhotoMetric system. *Amer. J. Phys. Anthropol.* **17:**1, 83–85 (N.S.).

Sendroy, J., Jr., and Cecchini, C. P. 1954 [6.5]. *The determination of human body surface area from height and weight.* Research Report Project NM 004 006.05.01. Bethesda, Md.: Naval Med. Res. Inst., National Naval Med. Center.

Sendroy, J., Jr., and Collison, H. A. 1960 [6.5]. Nomogram for determination of human body surface area from height and weight. *J. Appl. Physiol.* **15:**958–59. Also: NMRI Report No. 2, MR. 005.12-3001.01, Bethesda, Md.: Naval Medical Res. Inst.

Severy, D. M.; Brink, H. M.; and Baird, J. D. 1968 [8.6.7]. Vehicle design for passenger protection from high speed rear-end collisions. Paper No. 680774. *Proc. of 12th Stapp Car Crash Conf.* New York: Society of Automotive Engineers.

Shah, M. J. 1973 [10.2.1]. *Biomechanics of hand control interactions.* Final Report, Contract No. F 33615-71-Q-1113, P00009, with the Aerospace Med. Res. Lab. Dayton: WPAFB: University of Dayton Res. Inst.

Shapiro, H. L., and Hulse, F. S. 1939 [7.5.1]. *Migration and environment.* New YorK: Oxford Univ. Press.

Sharp, E. D. 1962 [10.2.2]. *Maximum torque exertable on knobs of various sizes and rim surfaces,* Medical Res. Lab., Report MRL-TDR 62-17. WPAFB, Ohio: Aerospace Med. Res. Lab., USAF.

Sheldon, W. H.; Dupertuis, C. W. and McDermott, E. 1954 [2.6]. *Atlas of Men.* New York: Harper and Brothers.

Sheldon, W. H.; Stevens, S. S.; and Baker, W. B. 1940 [2.3.2, 2.6]. *The varieties of human physique.* New York: Harper and Bros.

Sheridan, T. B. 1954 [9.5.3]. *An experimental study of physical criteria for handcovering designs.* Master's thesis; Univ. of Calif., Los Angeles.

Siber, Hegner and Co., Inc. 1956 [2.3.1]. GPM Anthropological Instruments, April 1956, Switzerland.

Siegel, A. W.; Nahum, A. M.; and Appleby, M. R. 1968 [8.6.3, 8.6.7]. *Injuries to children in automobile collisions.* SAE Report No. 680771. New York: Society of Automotive Engineers.

Simon, P.* 1926 [2.3.2]. *Fundamental principles of a systemic diagnosis of dental anomolies,* Trans. B. E. Lischer. Boston: The Stratford Co. *Cited by Burke and Beard, 1967.

Sinelnikoff, E., and Grigorowitsch, M. 1931 [3.4.1, 3.4.2]. Die Beweglichkeit der Gelenke als sekundäres Geschlechtliches und Konstitution elles Merkmal. *Zts. f. Konstitutions lehre* **15:**6, 679–93.

Slowik, J. 1965 [7.7.3]. *Power driven articulated dummy.* Final Report, Contract NAS 9-1370. Chicago: IIT Research Institute.

Smedley, F. 1900 [4.4.1]. Report on child study investigation. *Forty Sixth Annual Report of the Chicago Board of Education for the Year Ending June 30, 1900,* p. 47–116.

Smith, M. J. 1972 [6.4.3]. The use of bivariate distributions in achieving anthropometric compatibility in equipment design—Part II: The development. *Proc. of the 16th Ann. Meeting of the Human Factors Soc.,* Oct. 17–19, Los Angeles, p. 19.

Snook, S. H.; Irvine, C. H.; and Bass, S. F. 1970 [6.12]. Maximum weights and work loads acceptable to male industrial workers. *Amer. Ind. Hygiene Assoc. J.* **31**:4, 579–86.

Snyder, R. G. 1970a [8.6.3, 8.6.7]. *Human impact tolerance.* SAE Reprint 700398. New York: Society of Automotive Engineers.

———. 1970b [8.6.7]. Occupant restraint systems of automotive, aircraft and manned space vehicles: an evaluation of the state of the art and future concepts. In *Impact Injury and Crash Protection,* ed. E. S. Gurdjian et al., Chapter 22, pp. 496–561. Springfield, Ill.: C. C. Thomas.

Snyder, R. G.; Chaffin, D. B.; and Schutz, R. K. 1972 [1.3, 6.4.2, 8.4.6]. *Link system of the human torso.* AMRL TR 71-88. WPAFB, Ohio: Aerospace Med. Res. Lab., USAF.

Synder, R. G.; Crosby, W. M.; Snow, C. C.; Young, I. W.; and Hanson, P. 1966 [8.6.7]. *Impact injury to the pregnant female and fetus in lap belt restraint.* SAE Report 66081. New York: Society of Automotive Engineers.

Snyder, R. G.; Spencer, M.; Owings, C.; and Van Eck, P. 1972 [6.2.4]. *Source data of infant and child measurements. Interim data, 1972.* Report, University of Michigan for Children's Hazard Division, Food and Drug Administration, Ann Arbor.

Soberman, R.; Brodie, B. B.; Levy, B. B.; Axelrod, J.; and Steele, J. M. 1949 [3.2.]. The use of antipyrine in the measurement of total body water in man. *J. Biol. Chem.* **179**:31 (May). (Cited by Behnke, 1953.)

Society of Automotive Engineers 1968 [8.6.10]. *Proc. of 12th Stapp Car Crash Conf. New York:* Society of Automotive Engineers.

Spiegel, M. R. 1961 [5.4.]. *Schaum's outline series: theory and practice of statistics.* New York: Schaum Publ.

Springer, W. E., and Bommarito, C. L. 1960 [3.4.1]. *Mobility of men in full pressure suits.* Document DZ-7418. Seattle: Boeing.

Squires, P. C. 1959 [8.8.4]. Proposed shape of the normal work area. *Eng. and Ind. Psychol.* **1**:1, 12–17.

Sroka, F., and Hill, R. 1967 [8.7.2]. *Console design for Star III research vehicle.* General Dynamics Res. Report P-417-67-078, Electric Boat Div., Gen. Dynamics.

Staples, M. L. 1966 [9.2]. *A bibliographical survey and critical review of the role of anthropometry in the sizing of clothing and personal equipment.* EP Report 10, Directorate of Biosciences Records, Defense Research Board (2nd ptg).

Stevens, P. H.; Chase, D. O.; and Brownlie, A. W. 1966. Industrial design of a narrow aisle sitdown lift truck. *Human Factors* **8**:4, 317.

Stevenson, P. H. 1928 [6.5]. Calculation of the body-surface area of Chinese. *Chinese J. of Physiol.,* Report Series **1**:13–24.

Stoudt, H. W.; Crowley, T. J.; McFarland, R. A.; Ryan, A.; Gruber, B.; and Ray, C. 1970 [8.6.3]. *Static and dynamic measurements of motor vehicle drivers.* Report HS-800 261. Washington, D.C.: U.S. Dept. of Transportation.

Stoudt, H. W.; Damon, A.; McFarland, R. A.; and Roberts, J. 1965 [5.2.9, 6.2.4, 8.6.3]. *Weight, height and selected body dimensions of adults, U.S. 1960–1962,* Report No. 8, Series 11, National Center for Health Statistics, Public Health Service Publication No. 1000. Washington, D.C.: U.S. Dept. of Health, Educ. and Welfare.

Strasser, H. 1917 [1.3]. Lehrbuch der Muskel—und Gelenkmechanik. 4 vols. 1913–1917. Berlin: J. Springer.

Strasser, H., and Gassmann, A. 1893 [1.3]. Hülfsmittel und Normen zur Bestimmung und Veranschaulichung der Stellungen, Bewegungen und Kraftwirkungen am Kugelgelenk, inbesondere am Hüft-und Schulter gelenke des Menschen. *Anat. Hefte* **2:**6/7, 389–434.

Stuart, H. C. 1961 [6.2.4]. *Stuart growth charts.* Enclosure, with personal communication to author, from Mead Johnson Lab., Mead Johnson and Co., Evansville, Ind. Also: Dept. of Maternal and Child Health, Harvard School of Public Health, Boston, Mass. Also: Children's Medical Center, Boston, Mass.

Stuart, H. C.; Hill, P.; and Shaw, C. 1940 [3.2]. *Growth of bone, muscle and overlying tissues as revealed by studies of roentgenograms of the leg area.* Monogr. Soc. Res. Child Develop. No. 26. Evanston, Ill.: Child Develop. Publ.

Swearingen, J. J. 1949 [3.3, 8.5.2]. *Determination of the most comfortable knee angle for pilots.* Report No. 1, Biotechnology Project No. 3-48. Oklahoma City: Civil Aeronautics Med. Res. Lab.

———. 1953 [3.2, 3.2.3, 3.2.4, 6.6.3]. *Determination of centers of gravity of man.* Oklahoma City: Civil Aeronautics Med. Res. Lab., Project No. 53-203.

Swearingen, J. J.; Badgley, J. M.; Braden, G. E.; and Wallace, T. F. 1969 [3.2, 3.2.3]. *Determination of centers of gravity of infants.* Report No. AM 69-22, Office of Aviation Medicine. Oklahoma City: Federal Aviation Admin., Dept. of Transportation.

Swearingen, J. J.; Hasbrook, A. H.; Snyder, R. G.; and McFadden, E. B. 1962 [3.5.2, 8.3.11, 8.5]. *Kinematic behavior of the human body during deceleration.* Report No. 62-13. Oklahoma City: Civil Aeromedical Res. Inst.

Swenson, L. S.; Grimwood, J. M.; and Alexander, C. C. 1966 [8.3.2]. *This new ocean—a history of Project Mercury.* NASA SP-4201, National Aeronautics and Space Administration, Washington, D.C. Washington, D.C.: U.S. Govt. Ptg. Office.

Sytcheff, A. I. 1902 [2.4.1]. *Measurement of the volume and surface of the body of children according to age.* Dissertation, St. Petersburg, 1902, Translated for the Nutrition Lab. of the Carnegie Institution of Washington by H. B. Dine in 1914.

Tanner, J. M. 1962 [2.3.2]. *Growth at adolescence.* 2nd ed. Oxford: Blackwell Scientific Publications.

Tanner, J. M., and Weiner, J. S. 1948 [1.3, 2.3.2]. *The reliability of the photogrammetric method of anthropometry with a description of a miniature camera technique.* Gt. Brit. Roy. Nav. Pers. Res. Comm. Report No. RNP 48/497. Also: 1949 *Amer. J. Phys. Anthropol.* **7:**2, 145–186 (N.S.).

Taylor, C. L. 1954 [10.2.1]. The biomechanics of the normal and of the amputated upper extremity. In *Human Limbs and Their Substitutes,* eds. P. E. Klopsteg and P. D. Wilson, Chapter 7, pp. 169–221. New York: McGraw-Hill.

Taylor, C. L., and Blaschke, A. C. 1951 [3.5.3]. A method for kinematic analysis of motions of the shoulder, arm and hand complex. *Ann. N.Y. Acad. Sci.* **51:**1251—65.

Teeple, J. B.; Bond, H. J.; and Sleight, R. B. 1956 [8.1]. How to design a cockpit: from the man out. *Aviation Age* **25:**1.

Thalmann-Degan, P. 1944 [2.3.2]. Stereo photogrammetry, a diagnostic tool in mandibular orthopedics [in German]. Doctoral dissertation, Univ. of Zurich, Switzerland.

Thomson, W. G. 1969 [5.2.9, 8.4]. *Anthropometric research for aircraft crew station geometry evaluations.* GDC-ERR-1380 (Life Sciences), General Dynamics, Convair Div., San Diego, Calif. (Approval for distribution only from Engineering Offices Services.)

Thompson, J. E. 1968 [8.6.10]. Occupant response versus vehicle crush: a total system approach. 680780, *Proc. of 12th Stapp Car Crash Conf.,* pp. 220–239. New York: Society of Automotive Engineers.

Thordsen, M. L.; Kroemer, K. H. E.; and Laubach, L. L. 1972 [4.2, 4.7.2]. *Human force exertions in aircraft control locations.* AMRL TR 71-119. WPAFB, Ohio: Aerospace Med. Res. Lab., USAF.

Tichauer, E. R. 1966 [10.2.1, 10.3.2, 10.3.3]. Some aspects of stress of forearm and hand in industry.*J. Occupational Medicine* **8:**2, 63–71.

Tipton, C. M., and Karpovich, P. V. 1964 [3.4.2]. Clinical electrogoniometry. *J. Assoc. Phys. Ment. Rehabil.* **18:**90.

Tornvall, G. 1963 [6.10.4]. Assessment of physical capabilities, with special reference to the evaluation of maximal voluntary isometric muscle strength and maximal working capacity. *Acta Physiologica Scandinavica* **53,** Suppl. 201.

Trombley, D. J. 1966 [10.4.3]. Experimental determination of an optimal foot pedal design. Master's thesis, Texas Tech. Univ.

Trotter, M., and Gleser, G. 1951a [6.2.4]. Effect of aging on stature. *Amer. J. Phys. Anthropol.* **9:**3, 311–24 (N.S.).

———. 1951b [6.2.3]. Trends in stature of American whites and Negroes born between 1840 and 1924. *Amer. J. Phys. Anthropol.* **9:**4, 427–40 (N.S.).

Trumbo, D. A., and Schneider, M. 1963 [10.4.3]. Operation time as a function of foot pedal design. *J. Eng. Psychol.* **2:**4, 139–43.

Ufland, J. M. 1953 [6.10.1]. Einfluss des Lebensalters, Geschlects, der Konstitution und des Berufs au der Kraft Verschiedener Muskelgruppen. *Arbeitsphysiologie* **6:**653–63 (May).

U.S. Air Force 1968a [8.4.5]. Cockpit-basic dimensions, fixed wing. Subnote 1 (1) in *AFSC Design Handbook,* 2-2, 1—May ed.

———. 1968b [8.3.11, 8.4.5]. Full restraint extremity strike envelope. Subnote 2 (2) in *AFSC Design Handbook,* 1-6.

———. 1969, 1972 [7.4.1]. Anthropometry and biomechanics—design note 2 B 11. In *AFSC Design Handbook, 1-3.* 1st ed. 1969; 2nd ed. Jan., 1972. WPAFB, Ohio: Aeronautical Systems Div.

U.S.D.C. 1954 [9.2.]. *Recommended commercial standards on body measurements for the sizing of women's patterns and apparel.* Report 5200A, Commodity Standards Division, Office of Technical Services. Washington, D.C.: U.S. Dept. Commerce.

U.S. Navy 1962 [8.9.4]. *Human factors standards for the fleet ballistic missile weapon system. vol. 2—Design of equipment.* NAV WEPS OD 18413A, vol. II, Special Projects Office. Washington, D.C.: U.S. Navy.

U.S. Selective Service System 1943 [1.2]. *Causes of rejection and incidence of defects* (T. I. Edwards, Med. Stat. Bull. No. 2, Washington, D.C.

Van Cott, H. P., and Kinkade, R. G., eds., 1972 [10.2]. See Sect. 7.2.4, Table 7–2.

Van Patten, R. E., and Rubinstein, M. 1970 [4.4.2]. *Development of a hydraulic grip dynamometer.* AMRL TR 70-71. WPAFB, Ohio: Aerospace Med. Res. Lab.

Variot and Saint Albin 1903 [2.4.1]. La mensuration delâitre cutanée des jeunees enfants par l'enveloppement avec des feulles détain. *Bull. Soc. de Pediat de Paris* **1903:**V, 307.

Vicinus, J. H. 1962 [10.2]. *X-ray anthropometry of the hand.* AMRL TR 62-111. WPAFB, Ohio: Aerospace Med. Res. Labs., USAF (AD 291-412).

Vierordt, H. 1906 [3.2, 6.6.2]. *Anatomical, physiological and physical data and tables* [in German]. Jena: G. Fischer.

Von Gierke, H. E. 1971 [7.9]. *Biodynamic models and their applications.* AMRL TR 71-51. WPAFB, Ohio: Aerospace Med. Res. Lab., USAF. Also in: *J. Acoustical Soc. of Amer.* **50:**6, 1397–1413.

Vykukal, H. C. 1968 [9.4]. Advanced developments in hard space suit technology. *J. Eng. for Ind.,* Nov., pp. 577–83.

Walmsley, J. R., and Roberts, J. E. 1963 [3.2]. Body composition of USAF flying personnel. *Aerospace Medicine,* May, pp. 403–05.

Washburn, C. T. 1932 [8.8.5]. Stadium seating, *Architectural Record* **71:**270–72.

WCS Institute 1969 [7.4.4].*Regulatory and advisory documents applicable to human factors, personnel, and training requirements.* 3rd ed. Report No. MF1 69-1. San Diego: Man Factors, Inc.,

Wear, C. A. 1963 [6.9.3]. The relationship of flexibility to length of body segments. *Res. Quart.* **34:**234.

Webb Associates. 1962. See Sect. 7.2.4, Table 2.

Webb, S., and Coburn, R. 1959 [10.2.4]. *Development and testing of a hand-configured keyset.* TM-357, San Diego: U.S. Navy Electronics Lab.

Weber, E., and Weber, W. 1836 [3.2]. *Mechanik der menschlichen Gehwerkzeuge.* Gottingen.

Weinbach, A. P. 1938 [2.5.2, 3.2, 3.2.7]. Contour maps, center of gravity, moment of inertia, and surface area of the human body. *Human Biology* **10:**356–71.

Weis, E. B.; Jr., Leysath, W. Q.; and Horning, K. R. 1967 [3.5.3]. *Development of a pulsed x-ray television fluoroscope for biodynamic research.* AMRL TR 66-189. WPAFB, Ohio: Aerospace Med. Res. Lab.

Weis, E. B., Jr., and Mohr, G. C. 1967 [3.5.3]. Cineradiographic analysis of human visceral responses to short duration impact. *Aerospace Medicine* **38:**10, 1041–44.

Weis, E. B., Jr., and Primiano, F. P., Jr. 1966 [3.2.3]. Motion of the human center of mass and its relationship to mechanical impedence. *Human Factors* **8:**5, 399–406.

White, R. M. 1961 [5.2.7, 5.2.8, 5.2.9, 9.7.1]. *Anthropometry of army aviators.* Technical Report EP-150. Natick, Mass.: Quartermaster Res. and Engr. Center.

White, R. M.; Kobrick, J. L.; and Zimmerer, T. R. 1964 [9.5.3]. *Anthropometry of the arctic-equipped soldier.* Technical Report EPT-2. Natick, Mass.: U.S. Army Natick Lab.,

White, R. M., and Winston, G. 1951 [9.2]. *A nine size system for functional clothing.* Special Report No. 50. Lawrence, Mass.: Environmental Protection Section, Quartermaster Res. Lab.,

Wiechec, F., and Krusen, F. 1939 [3.4.2]. A new method of joint measurement and a review of the literature. *Amer. J. Surg.* **43:**3, 659–68.

Wilkie, D. R. 1960 [6.12]. Man as a source of mechanical power. *Ergonomics* **3:**1, 1–8.

Williams, M., and Stutzman, L. 1959 [4.7.2, 6.10.6]. Strength variation through the range of joint motion. *Phys. Therapy Rev.* **39:**3, 145–52.

Wilmart, L. 1896 [2.4.1]. Arpeutage de la peau humaine. *La Clinique, Brussels* **10:**113–16.

Wilson, C. L. 1961a [6.8.2]. *Reaction of human tissues to high vacuum exposure.* Presented at the 32nd Annual Meeting of the Aerospace Medical Assoc., 24-27 April 1961, Chicago.

———. 1961b [6.8.2]. *Production of gas in human tissues at low pressures.* 61-105, August 1961, School of Aerospace Medicine, USAF Aerospace Med. Center (ATC).

Wilson, G. D., and Stasch, W. H. 1945 [3.4.2]. Photographic record of joint motion. *Arch. Phys. Med.* **26:**361–62.

Winters, M. C. 1951 [3.4.1]. *Protective body mechanics in daily life and nursing.* Philadelphia: W. B. Saunders.

Woodson, W. E. 1954 [7]. See Section 7.2.4, Table 7-2.

Woodson, W. E., and Conover, D. W. 1970 [8.7.1, 8.8.4]. (also published 1964, 1st Ed.). *Human engineering guide for equipment designers.* 2nd ed., 3rd printing. Berkeley/Los Angeles: Univ. of Calif. Press.

Worner, H. 1923 [2.4.1]. The surface of the human body [in German]. *Z. ges. Experiment. Medizin* **33:**510–26.

Wright, I. B. 1963 [3.3]. Application of a system of functional anthropometry in pressure suit design. *J. Brit. Interplanet. Soc.* **19:**2, 31–41.

Young, J. W. 1967 [8.3.11]. A functional comparison of basic restraint systems. FAA Report AM 67–13. Oklahoma City: Federal Aviation Adminstration, Office of Aviation Medicine, Aero-Medical Institute.

Zeigen, R. S.; Alexander, M.; Churchill, E.; Emanuel, I.; and Velsey, S. 1960 [9.2, 9.6, 9.6.1, 9.6.2, 9.6.3]. *A head circumference sizing system for helmet design.* WADD TR 60-631. WPAFB, Ohio: Wright Air Dev. Div., (AD 251-939).

Zeller, M. 1939 [2.3.2]. Photogrammetric techniques and their applications [in German]. Section in "Vermessung-Grundlage-Karte" Festschrift zur schweitzerischen Landesausstellung.

———. 1952 [2.3.2]. Textbook of stereo-photogrammetry. Trans. E. A. Miskin. London: H. K. Lewis.

APPENDIX A: GLOSSARY

The terms in this glossary are divided into three parts:

Part 1 General anthropometric and anatomical terms and colloquial engineering expressions.
Part 2 Terms for description of movement used by the classical anatomical systems.
Part 3 Terms for description of movement recently developed for engineering anthropometry usage.

The same word might appear in different parts because of multiple usage.

PART 1—GENERAL TERMINOLOGY

Abduction	Movement laterally, away from body centerline. See Figure 3.13, page 78.
Acromial	Pertaining to acromion.
Acromion	The highest point on the lateral edge of the shoulder bone.
Adduction	Opposite of abduction.
Anterior	The front part of the body, or pertaining to the front part of the body.
Axillary	Referring to the armpit region.
Ball and socket joints	Those joints that permit movement in all planes and rotation as well, as in the case of the shoulder and hip.
Biceps	The large muscle at the front of the upper arm.
Bite board	A piece of wood, plastic, and the like of suitable size and shape for clamping between the teeth, attached in a fixed relation to an object from which head measurements are to be made.
Brow ridge	The bony elevation covered by the eyebrows.
Canthus	A corner or angle formed by the meeting of the eyelids.
Cervicale	The largest bony bump on the spinal column in the region of the base of the neck.
Deltoid muscle	The large muscle on the outer side of the upper arm in the shoulder region.
Distal end	End of a limb away from trunk.

Drivers, design	The most significant concepts, constraints or criteria which define and shape a design. The term is derived from the concept of a "forcing function" in dynamic analysis, sometimes called a "driver".
Ectomorphic	A type of body build characterized by relatively little fat or muscle, often smaller bones and a somewhat thin chest. See text discussion on somatotyping for further references.
Endomorphic	A type of body build characterized by relatively large amounts of soft, fatty tissue, larger abdominal protrusions of the stomach area, and often relatively less muscular tissue. See text discussion on somatotyping for further references.
External	Away from the central long axis of the body; the outer portion of a body segment.
Fiducial markers	Pieces of tape, pins, and the like used to locate particular points on a body for measuring. (See also "landmarks.")
Forehead rod	A rod extending from a fixed wall or object to the forehead to help position the head while measurements are made.
Frankfort plane	The standard plane of orientation of the head, determined by locating the lower edges of the eye sockets and a single tragion in the same horizontal plane. This can be closely approximated when the subject looks directly forward.
G, g	Capital G is used to express inertial resultant to whole body acceleration in multiples of the magnitude of the acceleration of gravity. Lower case g represents the exact numerical acceleration of earth gravity (980.665 cm/sec^2 or 32.1739 ft/sec^2). (Gell, *Aerospace Med.* 32:1110, 1961)
Glabella	The most forward point in the midline of the forehead between the brow ridges.
Gluteal furrow	The furrow formed by the overhang of the buttock on the back of the upper leg.
Helix	The rolled outer part of the ear.
Hinge joints	Those joints that permit wide range of movement in only one direction, such as the elbow and knee joints.
Humerus	The bone of the upper arm.
Internal	Near the central long axis of the body; the inner portion of a body segment.
Knuckle	The joint formed by the meeting of a finger bone (phalanax) with a palm bone (metacarpal).
Kyphosis	Curvature of the spinal column, such that the central part is more dorsally displaced than the ends.
Landmarks	Readily distinguishable and describable features of the human body suitable for use as measuring points. Exam-

	ples: nipples, navel, gluteal furrow, eye, lip, seventh cervical vertebra, malleolus, acromion, and other bony prominences. Such features should be commonly found in all body types, ages, and conformations in the population to be surveyed.
Lateral	Lying to the right or left side of the midsagittal plane of the body; opposed to medial. See Part 2.
Lordosis	Curvature of the spinal column, such that the central part is more forward than the ends.
Malleolar	Referring to the malleolus.
Malleolus	A rounded bony projection in the ankle region. There is one on both the lateral and medial sides of the leg.
Mandible	The lower jaw.
Medial	Lying near the midsagittal plane of the body; opposed to lateral.
Mesomorphic	A type of body build characterized by relatively predominent muscular tissue and heavy bones, often a "barrel" chest. See text discussion on somatotyping for further references.
Metacarpal bone	A bone of the palm of the hand.
Metacarpale	The point of juncture on the back of the hand of the palm bone (metacarpal) with the first bone of the finger (phalanx).
Metatarsal	A bone of the instep of the foot.
Midplane	Same as midsagittal plane.
Midsagittal plane	The plane which divides the body into symmetrical right and left sections.
Nasal root	The area of greatest indentation where the nose meets the forehead.
Natural waist line	The level of greatest lateral indentation in the abdomen region. If no natural waist line is visible the level at which the belt is worn is used instead.
Occipital region	The back of the head.
Olecranon	The bony tip of the elbow.
Orbital	(1) Relating to the eye ball. (2) Relating to space flight around a planet-in "free fall" or weightlessness.
Orbitale	In the area of the eyeball.
Parting agent	A chemical, or material applied to a part or portion of the body before casting to prevent sticking of casting material.
Patella	The kneecap.
Phalangeal	Referring to a phalanx or to the phalanges.
Phalanx	(Plural, phalanges) a bone of the fingers or toes.

Popliteal area	The area of the back of the leg directly behind the knee.
Posterior	The back of the body or referring to the back of the body.
Proximal end	The end of a limb nearest the trunk; opposed to distal.
Radial	Referring to the radius.
Radius	One of the two forearm bones. This bone runs from the lateral side of the elbow region to the wrist on the same side as the thumb.
Scye	The sleeve hole.
Sits erect	Subject sits on a flat horizontal surface, his weight distributed equally, with his back held in and his shoulders held back. This position requires holding the torso straight, but not rigid.
Somatotype	A classification of body build, involving the type of tissues which seem to predominate, general shape characterizations and secondary indications of skin type, hair, etc. Many schemes have been devised, but most commonly referred to in this text is that of Sheldon, Stevens and Baker (1940), having three main groups: Mesomorphic, Endomorphic and Ectomorphic which are defined in this glossary. See text discussion on somatotyping for further references.
Stands erect	Subject stands on a flat surface, his weight distributed equally, with his back held in and his shoulders held back and his legs fully straightened. This position requires holding the body straight but not rigid.
Sternum	The breastbone.
Stylion	The point at the center of the notch just distal to the styloid process of the radius.
Subnasale	The point where the base of the nasal septum meets the philtrum.
Substernale	The point located at the middle of the lower edge of the breastbone.
Suprasternale	The lowest point of the notch in the upper edge of the breastbone.
Temporal crest	A narrow, bony ridge running along the side of the head, curving up from the upper lateral margin of the eye socket, above and past the ear, and downward, ending behind the ear. This serves as the area of attachment for the temporal muscles.
Temporal muscles	The muscles of the temple region.
Tragion	The point located at the notch just above the tragus of the ear. This point corresponds approximately to the upper edge of the ear hole.

Tragus	The small cartilaginous flat in front of the ear hole.
Trapezius muscle	The large muscle at the back of the neck and shoulder.
Ulna	One of the two forearm bones; this bone runs from the tip of elbow to the wrist on the same side as the little finger.
Ulnar	Referring to the ulna.
Virtual image	The apparent location of a scene as seen through optical devices. See a text on optics.
Visco-elastic properties	Denoting characteristics of materials which are both viscous and elastic in nature, tend to have resistance to movement related both to velocity of movement and to amount of deflection and tend to return to an original state when force is removed.

PART 2—CLASSIC MOVEMENT TERMINOLOGY

Terms listed and explained below supplement those in Figure 3-13 and are commonly found in medical texts and related texts on kinesiology, physical therapy, prosthetics, and so forth. Part 3 of this appendix suggests new movement terminology based on a different concept of human movement (see text, Sections 3.4.1, 3.4.2)

Surfaces of the trunk or limbs

Dorsum	Back surface.
Ventral	Belly surface.
Lateral surfaces	Side surfaces.

Directional terms

Cranial, cephalic	Toward the head.
Caudal	Toward the tail.
Superior	Up or upward in anatomical position toward the head.
Anatomical position	Erect, with heels together and feet pointing somewhat outward, the arms by the sides and the palms facing forward.
Inferior	Downward, toward the feet—caudal.
Anterior	The part habitually carried forward in progression = ventral.
Posterior	Dorsal.
Medial	Toward the midline.
Lateral	Toward a side.

(Above two best used only when referring to a limb as a whole.)

Distal	Away from the base of the limb or away from the trunk.
Proximal	Toward the attachment of the limb to the trunk.

Descriptions of terms within a limb, mediolateral sense:

Radial	Toward the thumbside, the radial bone side of the arm on hand.
Ulnar	Toward the little finger side, the ulna bone side of the arm or hand.
Tibial	Toward the great toe side, the tibia bone side.
Fibular	Toward the little toe side, the fibula bone side.

Planes of the body

Sagittal plane	One passing through the midline of the body so as to divide it into right and left halves.

Parasagittal plane	One parallel to the sagittal plane, but to one side of it.

(The prefix "para" may be used for any plane considered to have a parallel relationship to a defined principal plane in space)

Coronal or frontal plane	One dividing the body into an anterior and a posterior (ventral and dorsal portion), thus running roughly parallel with the front of the body and with a suture of the skull called the coronal suture.
Horizontal or transverse plane	One dividing the body or limbs into upper and lower parts in relation to gravity and the anatomical position.

Terms denoting type and direction of movement

(Other than those illustrated and described on page 78 of text—Figure 3-13)

Circumduction	Circular movement of a joint, as in swinging the arm around in a roughly parasagittal plane.
Elevation	Upward movement of a limb or body segment.
Eversion	Movement of the foot away from the sagittal plane. Concurrent rotation occurs around two axes to face the plantar surface outward.
Inversion	Movement of the foot toward the sagittal plane. Concurrent rotation occurs around two axes to face the plantar surface inward.
Pronation	Rotation of the hand about the long axis of the forearm such as to face the palm downward when the forearm is held horizontally forward.
Supination	Opposite of pronation—turning the palm upward.

PART 3—ENGINEERING ANTHROPOMETRY MOVEMENT TERMINOLOGY

Terms denoting type of movement*

1.	Vection (vek'shun)	Pivoting or revolving a link director (the principal director unless otherwise noted), or its projection on a principal plane, about an axis perpendicular to itself.
2.	Rotation	A rotatory movement of a link about its major axis, or principal director. Described as an angular direction-change (vection) of the rotary director.

* The major terms for dual links are formed by combining the three terms denoting type of movement with the following prefix elements indicating direction:

(1) -E-	A positive upward- or outward-tending movement (from the standard position), or any motion resulting in an increasing angular coordinate of the right limb.
(2) -IN-	Opposite to -E-, an inward or downward movement.
(3, 4, 5)	The first syllable of each of the names for the principal planes (front, sag, trans).

3.	Torsion	Twisting of a link about its major axis, described as an angular direction-change (vection) of the rotary director assuming the tail of the principal director is fixed.

Terms denoting direction of movement—single links*

1.	Posivection (pos'i-vek-shun)	Vection in any plane producing an increasing angular reading in that plane. The plane in which action is measured must be specified by a preceding term; that is, frontal, sagittal, transversal.
2.	Negivection	Opposite of posivection.
3.	Positive rotation	As seen from the tail of the principal director, rotation resulting in clockwise vection of the rotary director.
4.	Negative rotation	Opposite to positive rotation.
5.	Positive torsion	As seen from the tail of the principal director, torsion resulting in clockwise vection of the rotary director.
6.	Negative torsion	Opposite to positive torsion.

Terms denoting direction of movement—dual links†

1.	Frontevection (frunt'e-vek-shun)	As seen from the front, clockwise vection of the right limb together with counterclockwise vection of the left limb about axes perpendicular to the frontal plane.
2.	Frontinvection (frunt'in-vek-shun)	Opposite to frontevection.
3.	Sagevection (saj'e-vek-shun)	As seen from the right, counterclockwise vection of the limbs about an axis perpendicular to the sagittal plane.
4.	Saginvection (saj'in-vek-shun)	Opposite to sagevection.
5.	Transevection (trans'e-vek-shun)	As seen from above, clockwise vection of the right limb together with counterclockwise vection of the left limb about axes perpendicular to the transverse plane.
6.	Transinvection (trans'in-vek-shun)	Opposite to transevection.
7.	Fronterotation (frunt'e-roh-tay-shun)	Frontevection of the rotary directors of the limbs. *Positive fronterotation* implies that the principal director is pointing in the positive X direction, or forward. *Negative fronterotation* implies that the principal director is pointing aft, or in the minus X direction.

* Additional necessary distinctions for attitude of the limbs when performing rotational and torsional movements are defined by the terms *positive* and *negative,* which also serve to indicate direction for single links.

† See footnote p. 423.

8.	Frontinrotation (frunt'in-roh-tay-shun)	Opposite to fronterotation. Frontinvection of the rotary directors of the limbs. As in above, *positive* implies that the principal director points forward; *negative* implies that the principal director points aft.
9.	Sagerotation (saj'e-roh-tay-shun)	Sagevection of the rotary directors of dual links. *Positive* implies that the principal director of the right limb is pointing to the right, or in the positive *Y* direction, and opposite for the left limb. *Negative* implies that the right limb is pointing left and the left limb is pointing right.
10.	Saginrotation (saj'in-roh-tay-shun)	Saginvection of the rotary directors of dual links. The terms *positive* and *negative* apply as in sagerotation above.
11.	Transerotation (trans'e-roh-tay-shun)	Transevection of the rotary directors of the limbs. *Positive* implies that the principal director of the links points downward, in the direction of the plus Z axis, *negative* implies the opposite.
12.	Transinrotation (trans'in-roh-tay-shun)	Transinvection of the rotary directors of limbs. The terms *positive* and *negative* apply as in transerotation above.
13.	Frontetorsion (frunt'e-tor-shun)	Frontevection of the rotary directors of the limbs with the tail end of the principal directors held fixed. The terms *positive* and *negative* apply as for fronterotation.
14.	Frontintorsion (frunt'in-tor-shun)	Opposite of frontetorsion.
15.	Sagetorsion (saj'e-tor-shun)	Sagevection of the rotary directors of the limbs with the tail end of the principal directors held fixed. The terms *positive* and *negative* apply as for sagerotation.
16.	Sagintorsion (saj'in-tor-shun)	Opposite of sagetorsion.
17.	Transetorsion (trans'e-tor-shun)	Transevection of the rotary directors of the limbs with the tail end of the principal directors held fixed. The terms *positive* and *negative* apply as for transerotation.
18.	Transintorsion (trans'in-tor-shun)	Opposite to transetorsion.

APPENDIX B: CORRELATION COEFFICIENT TABLES*

These data were developed from a random sample of 1000 persons selected from over 4000 measured in a study conducted in 1950 (Hertzberg, Daniels and Churchill, 1954). Although best arranged as a complete 96 × 96 matrix, the original data have been divided here into parts to facilitate publication. The dimensions are identified with a number and a title in the left column of each page. Across the top of each page at the head of each column of three-digit numbers (correlation coefficients) is a series of numbers corresponding to those associated with the titles in the left column. Thus, to find the correlation coefficient between Sitting height (No. 19) and Stature (No. 2), one may look at the set of three digits at the intersection of row 19 and column 2, finding 743. The decimal is understood to precede the three-digit set ($r = .743$). Similarly, at the intersection of row 2 and column 19 the same numbers (743) occur.

* Prepared from data compiled by U.S. Air Force, Anthropology Branch, Aerospace Medical Research Laboratories, Wright Air Development Center, Wright-Patterson Air Force Base, Ohio. Courtesy of Mr. H. T. E. Hertzberg.

Table C-1. Body Dimension Correlation Coefficients for U.S. Air Force Flying Personnel—1950 96 × 96 Matrix

	1	2	3	4	5	6	7	8	9	10	11	12	13	14	15	16	17	18	19	20	21	22	23	24	25
WEIGHT																									
1 Weight		493	484	487	481	506	525	530	471	448	531	397	300	501	309	398	477	440	418	410	429	100	213	738	553
BODY LENGTHS																									
2 Stature	493		975	976	982	965	954	962	940	901	901	893	844	841	862	867	794	826	743	695	633	279	187	237	883
3 Nasal root height	484	975		987	975	957	950	956	937	894	896	889	839	837	853	863	793	829	725	711	434	278	192	227	878
4 Eye height	487	976	987		977	956	952	957	938	894	897	892	843	837	858	867	794	834	724	707	630	278	187	225	879
5 Tragion height	481	982	975	977		963	952	960	940	899	898	890	840	838	861	865	791	826	731	691	631	270	185	223	879
6 Cervicale height	506	965	957	956	963		956	953	937	896	897	894	849	832	870	882	790	836	686	644	618	253	172	240	887
7 Shoulder height	525	954	950	952	952	956		948	947	897	942	894	836	879	857	874	844	832	682	653	684	266	247	262	879
8 Suprasternale height	530	962	956	957	960	953	948		942	921	899	885	848	837	851	868	796	835	693	662	618	255	177	267	888
9 Nipple height	471	940	937	938	940	937	947	942		906	906	887	837	852	853	875	809	832	656	627	615	252	193	243	874
10 Substernale height	448	901	894	894	899	896	897	921	906		847	840	788	789	817	842	758	797	620	586	567	224	156	199	832
11 Elbow height	531	901	896	897	898	897	942	899	906	847		841	762	918	785	810	888	783	672	643	688	286	348	284	823
12 Waist height	397	893	889	892	890	894	894	885	887	840	841		848	785	864	867	734	824	571	535	524	444	97	186	861
13 Penale height	300	844	839	843	840	849	836	848	837	788	762	848		681	919	879	614	833	436	422	391	121	−079	127	864
14 Wrist height	501	841	837	837	838	832	879	837	852	789	918	785	681		685	719	940	697	662	639	681	313	404	318	737
15 Crotch height	309	862	853	858	861	870	857	851	853	817	785	864	919	685		912	637	842	464	429	409	133	−036	75	874
16 Gluteal furrow height	398	867	863	867	865	882	874	868	875	842	810	867	879	719	912		676	864	458	434	418	111	−027	152	899
17 Knuckle height	477	794	793	794	791	790	844	796	809	758	888	734	614	940	637	676		664	632	610	665	295	428	273	679
18 Kneecap height	440	826	829	834	826	836	832	835	832	797	783	824	833	697	842	864	664		436	427	389	99	−031	222	886
19 Sitting height	418	743	725	724	731	686	682	693	656	620	672	571	436	662	464	458	632	436		887	822	523	584	216	512
20 Eye height sitting	410	695	711	707	691	644	653	662	627	586	643	535	422	639	429	434	610	427	887		807	500	569	239	488
21 Shoulder height sitting	429	633	634	630	631	618	684	618	615	567	688	524	391	681	409	418	665	389	822	807		527	737	237	454
22 Waist height sitting	100	279	278	278	270	253	266	255	252	224	286	444	121	313	133	111	295	99	523	500	527		485	66	134
23 Elbow rest height sitting	213	187	192	187	185	172	247	177	193	156	348	97	−079	404	−036	−027	428	−031	584	569	737	485		110	−005
24 Thigh clearance height sitting	738	237	227	224	223	240	262	267	243	199	284	186	127	318	75	152	273	222	216	239	237	66	110		316
25 Knee height sitting	553	883	878	879	879	887	879	888	874	832	823	861	864	737	874	899	679	886	512	488	454	134	−005	316	
26 Popliteal height sitting	331	821	817	819	817	820	817	819	821	771	749	821	871	674	862	862	610	834	453	430	401	131	−031	154	889
27 Buttock-knee length	601	820	812	813	807	836	826	825	815	774	772	777	769	704	789	824	664	774	451	422	417	67	−010	363	822
28 Buttock-leg length	495	829	818	820	822	836	830	826	821	786	775	798	785	703	802	833	670	797	459	424	417	107	−013	274	848
29 Shoulder-elbow length	382	736	733	738	739	750	742	731	709	683	596	702	722	490	739	723	434	680	451	427	438	123	−112	172	727
30 Forearm-hand length	427	793	788	788	788	790	783	786	767	740	705	747	763	569	770	764	504	760	500	472	446	126	13	185	811
31 Span	437	819	815	814	818	814	794	809	779	744	682	772	782	551	792	777	487	762	528	494	447	161	−052	188	818
32 Arm reach from wall	429	695	686	691	690	703	680	695	671	646	598	674	661	497	666	676	452	678	413	397	344	115	−077	228	719
33 Maximum reach from wall	410	682	674	679	677	690	669	677	648	604	594	663	664	487	670	662	420	632	451	435	408	185	20	208	689
34 Functional reach	376	622	611	618	624	633	605	621	596	574	519	603	609	431	600	616	390	610	363	338	295	83	−103	196	647

Table C-1 (continued)

	1	2	3	4	5	6	7	8	9	10	11	12	13	14	15	16	17	18	19	20	21	22	23	24	25
BODY BREADTHS																									
35 Elbow-elbow breadth	805	168	168	169	162	189	229	210	163	140	256	110	43	261	40	135	261	200	132	152	188	−044	138	636	269
36 Hip breadth sitting	836	352	342	347	339	363	384	384	329	313	404	292	186	380	192	263	364	295	332	327	354	139	205	630	408
37 Knee-knee breadth sitting	713	316	304	309	303	319	318	336	276	267	346	244	166	329	164	211	311	256	299	313	304	127	178	595	373
38 Biacromial diameter	440	447	441	438	445	444	381	438	393	387	331	384	339	283	363	370	246	407	325	305	180	87	−076	253	441
39 Shoulder breadth	787	343	339	340	338	353	357	366	314	302	336	261	183	312	199	265	292	319	291	293	275	52	91	554	399
40 Chest breadth	734	276	278	276	267	288	316	303	261	235	320	209	161	297	164	231	285	278	211	213	254	−014	115	499	352
41 Waist breadth	793	218	214	219	211	252	262	263	216	197	252	160	116	244	119	222	229	271	124	149	165	−093	41	613	335
42 Hip breadth	781	475	470	472	465	486	488	494	441	411	489	408	320	453	327	371	428	404	395	385	384	144	161	564	512
43 Chest depth	757	202	205	208	202	230	252	261	233	202	263	159	100	246	88	194	228	225	155	184	214		105	583	298
44 Waist depth	755	170	163	172	164	200	216	225	182	180	223	115	35	213	43	152	203	206	104	134	153	−066	84	600	258
45 Buttock depth	820	211	194	201	197	235	253	254	211	187	277	151	36	282	43	158	272	199	216	210	251	57	195	695	286
CIRCUMFERENCES																									
46 Neck circumference	676	232	233	227	222	246	254	263	212	209	254	156	78	252	85	165	246	225	236	248	247	46	152	514	282
47 Shoulder circumference	791	285	282	287	279	301	311	328	276	273	305	221	150	287	144	233	273	293	218	233	227	16	86	586	376
48 Chest circumference	843	300	299	300	294	317	347	350	296	266	350	237	180	324	172	266	302	304	243	247	284	15	132	629	396
49 Waist circumference	826	207	203	208	198	240	260	258	205	194	268	138	83	248	88	192	245	251	122	149	184	−098	88	647	321
50 Buttock circumference	913	370	358	365	361	385	403	406	346	331	422	290	180	406	191	270	391	322	324	317	341	85	192	729	432
51 Thigh circumference	826	240	234	238	231	258	279	277	230	217	309	171	93	294	92	162	279	219	221	235	258	32	168	721	313
52 Lower thigh circumference	740	241	236	241	235	252	255	272	227	232	285	173	107	282	116	166	268	224	225	232	232	48	146	644	321
53 Calf circumference	738	231	222	222	222	229	245	254	202	211	256	150	89	243	93	146	226	201	233	230	224	58	135	605	317
54 Ankle circumference	626	253	249	252	250	250	263	276	227	229	285	169	125	259	136	175	255	245	226	207	227	29	126	464	332
55 Scye circumference	601	291	289	293	290	286	317	318	284	270	311	240	166	310	170	234	295	271	243	256	272	79	121	450	329
56 Axillary arm circumference	760	136	131	134	126	147	176	186	139	112	204	77	1	210	−003	81	204	137	155	191	201	38	161	631	208
57 Biceps circumference flexed	785	138	136	139	131	153	181	184	139	123	203	70	8	209	1	87	198	146	141	162	178	−015	139	653	228
58 Elbow circumference flexed	635	326	324	327	313	326	336	349	300	281	334	258	227	299	229	269	287	326	237	245	242	29	72	500	404
59 Lower arm circumference flexed	763	253	251	252	248	258	280	291	240	221	295	183	111	296	113	180	283	238	256	256	263	68	168	606	325
60 Wrist circumference	589	275	274	275	270	278	283	294	247	237	275	208	148	251	148	183	247	228	264	255	261	95	140	442	322
61 Sleeve inseam	202	616	616	614	618	618	595	611	597	590	501	601	634	392	643	623	337	576	366	358	302	118	−078	48	612
62 Sleeve length	488	716	711	712	716	716	699	715	681	654	598	681	664	494	676	676	440	664	481	453	417	151	−033	246	720
63 Anterior neck length	−180	289	301	302	294	244	228	192	199	190	201	218	232	178	230	191	159	137	280	269	177	126	51	−204	143
64 Posterior neck length	11	173	150	157	172	61	100	127	112	114	92	75	87	106	91	64	105	55	239	216	100	50	70	−015	67
65 Shoulder length	162	388	380	375	390	382	296	369	329	329	250	331	350	175	345	322	146	335	299	251	121	70	−100	26	354
66 Waist back	322	576	561	560	578	612	557	559	525	514	522	357	418	483	416	441	464	424	524	480	467	−059	201	172	464
67 Waist front	552	416	410	410	414	413	423	470	428	418	439	208	247	434	252	329	417	326	406	415	386	−104	248	395	373
68 Gluteal arc	302	274	275	269	269	248	276	280	247	220	291	353	139	306	136	104	283	140	372	353	355	549	290	231	181

69	Crotch length	628	277	273	271	269	282	308	295	258	245	338	342	65	347	62	118	340	166	381	363	394	511	339	512	233
70	Vertical trunk circumference	808	569	562	561	564	570	604	588	538	510	624	443	292	622	290	353	608	397	613	592	630	269	435	601	486
71	Interscye	464	214	217	213	214	217	242	218	187	167	279	165	70	300	80	121	302	168	239	266	272	104	237	364	190
72	Interscye maximum	553	314	311	308	306	309	324	328	280	291	315	230	173	310	166	222	292	279	267	286	265	45	133	431	315
73	Buttock circumference sitting	870	312	305	309	305	334	352	356	300	291	369	258	146	353	148	239	332	272	273	269	301	89	171	699	380
74	Knee circumference sitting	787	475	469	470	464	484	491	506	451	446	508	407	341	468	342	400	454	437	352	343	360	86	154	597	544
THE FOOT																										
75	Foot length	440	696	691	694	692	687	676	684	658	620	628	645	625	556	631	629	512	642	492	460	419	180	77	220	704
76	Instep length	412	660	658	657	660	649	647	650	623	606	605	605	590	533	589	592	498	606	469	434	408	155	75	199	657
77	Foot breadth	483	427	429	426	414	415	422	428	392	388	411	350	313	376	318	315	347	385	366	346	336	117	128	311	447
78	Heel breadth	530	319	318	316	305	328	323	340	280	271	311	273	232	251	242	254	234	283	297	263	281	111	132	341	388
79	Bimalleolar breadth	438	465	460	461	462	450	431	460	405	380	420	408	354	385	366	343	358	387	409	395	357	223	144	277	466
80	Medial malleolus height	349	414	410	410	419	406	398	397	381	353	383	349	317	379	337	349	342	379	335	320	300	125	114	223	447
81	Lateral malleolus height	273	395	394	391	400	403	399	383	391	355	378	389	362	383	379	404	342	405	242	226	214	75	27	172	459
82	Ball of foot circumference	532	414	413	414	403	408	410	421	372	367	395	346	318	367	308	322	336	353	343	329	325	131	125	363	455
THE HAND																										
83	Hand length	377	654	662	655	651	646	643	645	628	586	591	612	597	497	602	595	448	617	464	451	400	158	77	159	657
84	Palm length	339	566	565	562	564	557	552	555	538	497	505	531	520	423	519	513	381	533	392	398	348	134	54	153	577
85	Hand breadth at thumb	385	402	404	402	398	383	393	396	371	342	368	344	311	310	312	319	275	342	334	327	309	122	88	210	402
86	Hand breadth at metacarpale	425	390	392	387	383	384	385	386	357	332	365	322	291	310	304	282	280	333	344	333	318	138	117	255	390
87	Thickness metacarpal III	406	269	271	272	277	280	292	294	263	263	296	247	192	274	184	215	246	261	240	232	255	116	104	284	296
88	First phalanx III length	400	611	612	609	606	605	599	614	574	560	547	566	569	469	553	557	418	580	444	428	385	167	59	173	640
89	Finger diameter III	459	321	324	321	305	314	313	333	277	263	306	241	216	268	211	215	239	255	337	314	316	133	163	299	339
90	Grip diameter inside	142	453	459	454	448	441	429	439	434	408	373	433	439	305	442	416	266	416	307	285	240	107	11	−011	447
91	Grip diameter outside	273	459	466	462	453	445	440	445	432	401	394	419	417	313	411	399	276	398	359	332	300	124	45	100	454
92	Fist circumference	473	376	384	384	373	364	363	386	342	329	348	310	255	311	269	278	283	327	347	344	317	134	126	265	395
THE HEAD AND FACE																										
93	Head length	255	253	233	227	232	228	227	226	215	213	220	186	159	198	174	205	192	176	238	178	178	83	110	136	237
94	Head breadth	326	95	87	93	67	98	105	106	78	76	105	64	53	83	50	63	66	101	94	89	121	28	53	256	143
116	Head height	257	210	178	177	164	180	182	190	152	141	185	165	138	174	144	156	177	151	248	179	164	109	85	203	203
122	Head circumference	471	277	270	263	249	265	281	277	248	249	282	213	181	254	178	225	240	227	266	220	254	79	128	337	310

Table C-1 (*continued*)

	26	27	28	29	30	31	32	33	34	35	36	37	38	39	40	41	42	43	44	45	46	47	48	49	50
WEIGHT																									
1 Weight	331	601	495	382	427	437	429	410	376	805	836	713	440	787	734	793	781	757	755	820	676	791	843	826	913
BODY LENGTHS																									
2 Stature	821	820	829	736	793	819	695	682	622	168	352	316	447	343	276	218	475	202	170	211	232	285	300	207	370
3 Nasal root height	817	812	818	733	788	815	686	674	611	168	342	304	441	339	278	214	470	205	163	194	233	282	299	203	358
4 Eye height	819	813	820	738	788	814	691	679	618	169	347	309	438	340	276	219	472	208	172	201	227	287	300	208	365
5 Tragion height	817	807	822	739	788	818	690	677	624	162	339	303	445	338	267	211	465	202	164	197	222	279	294	198	361
6 Cervicale height	820	836	836	750	790	814	703	690	633	189	363	319	444	353	288	252	486	230	200	235	246	301	317	240	385
7 Shoulder height	817	826	830	742	783	794	680	669	605	229	384	318	381	357	316	262	488	252	216	253	254	311	347	260	403
8 Suprasternale height	819	825	826	731	786	809	695	677	621	210	384	336	438	366	303	263	494	261	225	254	263	328	350	258	406
9 Nipple height	821	815	821	709	767	779	671	648	596	163	329	276	393	314	261	216	441	233	182	211	212	276	296	205	346
10 Substernale height	771	774	786	683	740	744	646	604	574	140	313	267	387	302	235	197	411	202	180	187	209	273	266	194	331
11 Elbow height	749	772	775	596	705	682	598	594	519	256	404	346	331	336	320	252	489	263	223	277	254	305	350	268	422
12 Waist height	821	777	798	702	747	772	674	663	603	110	292	244	384	261	209	160	408	159	115	151	156	221	237	138	290
13 Penale height	871	769	785	722	763	782	661	664	609	43	186	166	339	183	161	116	320	100	35	36	78	150	180	83	180
14 Wrist height	674	704	703	490	569	551	497	487	431	261	380	329	283	312	297	244	453	246	213	282	252	287	324	248	406
15 Crotch height	862	789	802	739	770	792	666	670	600	40	192	164	363	199	164	119	327	88	43	43	85	144	172	88	191
16 Gluteal furrow height	862	824	833	723	764	777	676	662	616	135	263	211	370	265	231	222	371	194	152	158	165	233	266	192	270
17 Knuckle height	610	664	670	434	504	487	452	420	390	261	364	311	246	292	285	229	428	228	203	272	246	273	302	245	391
18 Kneecap height	834	774	797	680	760	762	678	632	610	200	295	256	407	319	278	271	404	225	206	199	225	293	304	251	322
19 Sitting height	453	451	459	451	500	528	413	451	363	132	332	299	325	291	211	124	395	155	104	216	236	218	243	122	324
20 Eye height sitting	430	422	424	427	472	494	397	435	338	152	327	313	305	293	213	149	385	184	134	210	248	233	247	149	317
21 Shoulder height sitting	401	417	417	438	446	447	344	408	295	188	354	304	180	275	254	165	384	214	153	251	247	227	284	184	341
22 Waist height sitting	131	67	107	123	126	161	115	185	83	−044	139	127	87	52	−014	−093	144		−066	57	46	16	15	−098	85
23 Elbow rest height sitting	−031	−010	−013	−112	13	−052	−077	20	−103	138	205	178	−076	91	115	41	161	105	84	195	152	86	132	88	192
24 Thigh clearance height sitting	154	363	274	172	185	188	228	208	196	636	630	595	253	554	499	613	564	583	600	695	514	586	629	647	729
25 Knee height sitting	889	822	848	727	811	818	719	689	647	269	408	373	441	399	352	335	512	298	258	286	282	376	396	321	432
26 Popliteal height sitting		714	757	692	755	773	637	649	573	89	210	167	355	235	203	161	323	123	81	90	126	194	222	137	210
27 Buttock-knee length	714		803	682	695	715	650	603	592	356	458	369	421	435	421	420	579	384	374	393	293	393	451	411	505
28 Buttock-leg length	757	803		683	717	720	671	604	615	226	351	287	388	328	303	295	459	289	274	235	249	318	342	308	391
29 Shoulder-elbow length	692	682	683		736	804	662	641	618	103	273	219	404	315	242	218	390	174	152	132	186	236	249	187	273
30 Forearm-hand length	755	695	717	736		869	737	701	668	154	303	277	460	362	286	220	430	212	166	164	247	302	292	202	305
31 Span	773	715	720	804	869		761	741	697	160	306	265	555	414	330	232	432	192	143	142	242	342	319	196	306
32 Arm reach from wall	637	650	671	662	737	761		695	903	180	305	246	437	348	279	273	406	246	208	207	278	326	308	231	331
33 Maximum reach from wall	649	603	604	641	701	741	695		657	172	297	233	414	329	298	249	383	253	185	201	215	287	338	221	301
34 Functional reach	573	592	615	618	668	697	903	657		158	277	210	423	323	255	239	373	212	172	160	265	297	266	196	292

BODY BREADTHS

35	Elbow-elbow breadth	89	356	226	103	154	160	180	172	158		706	580	270	740	748	761	642	673	694	721	598	732	784	778	753
36	Hip breadth sitting	210	458	351	273	303	306	305	297	277	706		654	308	642	616	695	808	648	657	742	527	655	708	731	877
37	Knee-knee breadth sitting	167	369	287	219	277	265	246	233	210	580	654		281	542	475	552	608	511	522	605	465	538	567	565	690
38	Biacromial diameter	355	421	388	404	460	555	437	414	423	270	308	281		693	450	323	400	224	228	229	389	534	379	287	367
39	Shoulder breadth	235	435	328	315	362	414	348	329	323	740	642	542	693		780	679	647	583	575	630	626	831	750	668	707
40	Chest breadth	203	421	303	242	286	330	279	298	255	748	616	475	450	780		680	609	579	544	607	538	745	779	657	653
41	Waist breadth	161	420	295	218	220	232	273	249	239	761	695	552	323	679	680		643	671	764	741	586	682	747	852	754
42	Hip breadth	323	579	459	390	430	432	406	383	373	642	808	608	400	647	609	643		579	562	609	488	618	639	647	812
43	Chest depth	123	384	289	174	212	192	246	253	212	673	648	511	224	583	579	671	579		648	690	566	648	777	710	693
44	Waist depth	81	374	274	152	166	143	208	185	172	694	657	522	228	575	544	764	562	648		766	523	595	678	842	732
45	Buttock depth	90	393	235	132	164	142	207	201	160	721	742	605	229	630	607	741	609	690	766		556	631	710	784	820

CIRCUMFERENCES

46	Neck circumference	126	293	249	186	247	242	278	215	265	598	527	465	389	626	538	586	488	566	523	556		640	623	580	602
47	Shoulder circumference	194	393	318	236	302	342	326	287	297	732	655	538	534	831	745	682	618	648	595	631	640		777	691	748
48	Chest circumference	222	451	342	249	292	319	308	338	266	784	708	567	379	750	779	747	639	777	678	710	623	777		759	755
49	Waist circumference	137	411	308	187	202	196	231	221	196	778	731	565	287	668	657	852	647	710	842	784	580	691	759		810
50	Buttock circumference	210	505	391	273	305	306	331	301	292	753	877	690	367	707	653	754	812	693	732	820	602	748	755	810	
51	Thigh circumference	113	396	275	169	193	203	214	213	180	714	773	645	286	648	606	683	655	649	672	767	539	682	717	726	846
52	Lower thigh circumference	116	344	264	174	197	201	229	200	221	620	652	634	276	576	503	584	590	553	555	626	517	638	574	609	748
53	Calf circumference	125	318	222	165	209	216	189	169	170	623	638	634	342	611	515	537	562	538	532	603	498	616	592	588	709
54	Ankle circumference	156	301	253	190	261	233	209	187	189	507	548	545	279	501	435	444	518	441	418	458	424	531	482	467	611
55	Scye circumference	185	332	320	251	265	268	269	230	267	526	462	403	287	542	461	475	459	507	455	489	495	580	525	504	543
56	Axillary arm circumference	35	280	176	72	115	113	161	144	142	731	675	547	260	669	596	676	582	659	659	709	579	678	709	722	721
57	Biceps circumference flexed	33	298	198	90	150	128	175	158	162	744	667	568	264	679	612	681	584	686	650	703	624	712	721	715	744
58	Elbow circumference flexed	255	381	352	280	364	339	337	292	299	539	511	491	339	547	483	486	509	479	447	482	521	572	536	519	585
59	Lower arm circumference flexed	157	349	252	201	248	235	243	198	218	706	630	575	313	647	580	607	582	612	588	632	608	664	668	640	699
60	Wrist circumference	149	306	247	243	333	293	288	237	274	505	477	508	332	539	461	446	474	450	410	452	474	530	477	461	531
61	Sleeve inseam	621	526	529	614	641	673	563	536	515	−024	119	99	328	154	88	49	231	63	27	−007	61	83	131	12	79
62	Sleeve length	660	672	634	719	731	785	652	625	587	255	366	300	546	485	391	316	477	272	218	232	312	392	416	283	354
63	Anterior neck length	182	91	156	180	161	196	124	165	120	−252	−198	−106	41	−145	−179	−253	−081	−316	−259	−260	−192	−232	−254	−286	−203
64	Posterior neck length	78	59	72	55	70	72	27	12	28	−061	14	9		−004	−018	−050	12	−035	−073	−049	−024	−041	−009	−070	6
65	Shoulder length	347	298	323	312	374	444	316	274	285	7	72	102	519	282	152	58	196	−001	−023	−023	49	204	108	22	98
66	Waist back	405	443	454	413	475	467	414	381	391	135	204	217	273	215	156	177	296	171	132	133	198	170	197	156	244
67	Waist front	266	421	325	280	308	318	265	324	230	404	436	351	241	394	413	446	437	438	476	467	352	399	478	473	475
68	Gluteal arc	123	184	143	129	151	176	151	207	108	174	310	239	157	210	191	128	290	158	171	282	176	155	232	152	291
69	Crotch length	88	278	219	133	145	164	182	174	148	502	593	474	227	475	419	449	507	455	483	602	414	502	485	482	641
70	Vertical trunk circumference	318	525	452	378	414	417	389	376	337	608	691	575	371	620	561	558	657	564	567	669	534	606	628	607	757
71	Interscye	89	267	185	100	132	141	161	163	141	481	354	305	262	470	452	410	371	364	367	388	337	460	461	408	431
72	Interscye maximum	186	354	281	234	292	315	340	294	329	474	435	365	436	582	505	479	432	407	402	433	504	594	530	466	507
73	Buttock circumference sitting	159	454	343	246	267	263	300	265	268	725	843	654	314	661	637	743	747	682	745	794	578	683	734	799	885
74	Knee circumference sitting	317	558	481	361	421	406	406	358	364	580	688	699	336	566	537	594	660	571	560	623	507	575	622	618	736

Table C-1 (continued)

	26	27	28	29	30	31	32	33	34	35	36	37	38	39	40	41	42	43	44	45	46	47	48	49	50
THE FOOT																									
75 Foot length	626	597	623	562	725	682	579	575	547	188	330	321	399	320	243	230	449	219	189	197	245	281	294	214	356
76 Instep length	582	568	617	534	665	624	543	468	498	186	309	307	340	284	205	213	418	206	174	172	216	257	274	217	341
77 Foot breadth	332	383	356	368	425	414	369	348	332	325	379	408	343	414	341	315	419	277	256	293	352	377	363	303	422
78 Heel breadth	256	329	298	288	345	346	289	325	262	404	430	414	259	412	388	387	424	349	383	370	330	386	438	399	472
79 Bimalleolar breadth	356	396	355	376	444	443	352	437	337	272	336	468	358	356	284	245	426	256	207	249	273	282	316	226	369
80 Medial malleolus height	366	339	330	334	376	382	306	257	287	222	295	389	279	311	223	184	367	173	152	194	208	252	213	172	318
81 Lateral malleolus height	419	343	354	318	378	377	282	300	256	170	215	214	231	243	207	170	265	157	112	160	155	204	187	151	230
82 Ball of foot circumference	342	394	348	361	416	416	344	345	313	375	424	465	323	444	387	341	454	332	293	358	391	391	442	328	439
THE HAND																									
83 Hand length	594	533	559	565	795	721	619	559	553	148	263	286	392	315	240	186	374	178	133	149	239	262	243	155	274
84 Palm length	502	468	489	497	676	621	539	464	499	162	235	262	343	295	220	197	329	178	130	136	225	253	222	152	251
85 Hand breadth at thumb	327	336	330	352	483	471	348	312	311	251	262	307	326	369	298	225	328	238	158	187	325	332	311	198	292
86 Hand breadth at metacarpale	306	341	330	355	470	453	374	322	319	300	294	334	331	405	328	259	339	262	216	231	391	363	336	246	324
87 Thickness metacarpal III	206	260	235	250	298	271	243	198	218	329	307	346	240	362	283	255	324	261	254	267	315	334	318	265	343
88 First phalanx III length	575	496	527	542	747	711	591	571	516	189	282	289	385	316	248	198	372	231	155	159	274	279	287	180	287
89 Finger diameter III	252	282	241	272	383	333	255	296	225	359	354	380	279	413	343	275	375	311	271	298	377	372	366	310	383
90 Grip diameter inside	425	331	385	409	555	523	436	436	390	−058	69	54	265	123	85	28	167	27	−016	−001	40	75	77	1	70
91 Grip diameter outside	409	367	411	405	537	498	423	419	383	67	173	177	283	225	165	113	257	125	84	93	166	171	202	105	180
92 Fist circumference	300	316	312	322	409	398	314	331	280	349	333	363	344	434	385	301	354	311	273	283	396	396	389	208	382
THE HEAD AND FACE																									
93 Head length	195	196	194	183	247	232	181	199	163	165	181	191	206	239	217	159	181	96	114	165	202	199	191	122	187
94 Head breadth	90	114	87	105	119	144	116	128	78	291	270	225	176	296	270	285	225	230	223	228	311	276	297	260	260
116 Head height	151	134	150	117	101	148	143	176	118	139	198	184	86	150	130	194	116	78	149	196	182	183	223	172	241
122 Head circumference	226	276	246	231	260	285	243	255	216	366	365	323	279	416	388	364	339	308	273	331	424	373	404	327	376

Table C-1 (continued)

	51	52	53	54	55	56	57	58	59	60	61	62	63	64	65	66	67	68	69	70	71	72	73	74	75
WEIGHT																									
1 Weight	826	740	738	626	601	760	785	635	763	589	202	488	−180	11	162	322	552	302	628	808	464	553	870	787	440
BODY LENGTHS																									
2 Stature	240	241	231	253	291	136	138	326	253	275	616	716	289	173	388	576	416	274	277	569	214	314	312	475	696
3 Nasal root height	234	236	222	249	289	131	136	324	251	274	616	711	301	150	380	561	410	275	273	562	217	311	305	469	691
4 Eye height	238	241	222	252	293	134	139	327	252	275	614	712	302	157	375	560	410	269	271	561	213	308	309	470	694
5 Tragion height	231	235	222	250	290	126	131	313	248	270	618	716	294	172	390	578	414	269	269	564	214	306	305	464	692
6 Cervicale height	258	252	229	250	286	147	153	326	258	278	618	716	244	61	382	612	413	248	282	570	217	309	334	484	687
7 Shoulder height	279	255	232	263	317	176	181	336	280	283	595	699	228	100	296	557	423	276	308	604	242	324	352	491	676
8 Suprasternale height	277	272	254	276	318	186	184	349	291	294	611	715	192	127	369	559	470	280	295	588	218	328	356	506	684
9 Nipple height	230	227	202	227	284	139	139	300	240	247	597	681	199	112	329	525	428	247	258	538	187	280	300	451	658
10 Substernale height	217	232	211	229	270	112	123	281	221	237	590	654	190	114	329	514	418	220	245	510	167	291	291	446	620
11 Elbow height	309	285	256	285	311	204	203	334	295	275	501	598	201	92	250	522	439	291	338	624	279	315	369	508	628
12 Waist height	171	173	150	169	240	77	70	258	183	208	601	681	218	75	331	357	208	353	342	443	165	230	258	407	645
13 Penale height	93	107	89	125	166	1	8	227	111	148	634	664	232	87	350	418	247	139	65	292	70	173	146	341	625
14 Wrist height	294	282	243	259	310	210	209	299	296	251	392	494	178	106	175	483	434	306	347	622	300	310	353	468	556
15 Crotch height	92	116	93	136	170	−003		229	113	148	643	676	230	91	345	416	252	136	62	290	80	166	148	342	631
16 Gluteal furrow height	162	166	146	175	234	81	87	269	180	183	623	676	191	64	322	441	329	104	118	353	121	222	239	400	629
17 Knuckle height	279	268	226	255	295	204	198	287	283	247	337	440	159	105	146	464	417	283	340	608	302	292	332	454	512
18 Kneecap height	219	224	201	245	271	137	146	326	238	228	576	664	137	55	335	424	326	140	166	397	168	279	272	437	642
19 Sitting height	221	225	233	226	243	155	141	237	256	264	366	481	280	239	299	524	406	372	381	613	239	267	273	352	492
20 Eye height sitting	235	232	230	207	256	191	162	245	256	255	358	453	269	216	251	480	415	353	363	592	266	286	269	343	460
21 Shoulder height sitting	258	232	224	227	272	201	178	242	263	261	302	417	177	100	121	467	386	355	394	630	272	265	301	360	419
22 Waist height sitting	32	48	58	29	79	38	−015	29	68	95	118	151	126	50	70	−059	−104	549	511	269	104	45	89	86	180
23 Elbow rest height sitting	168	146	135	126	121	161	139	72	168	140	−078	−033	51	70	−100	201	248	290	339	435	237	133	171	154	77
24 Thigh clearance height sitting	721	644	605	464	450	631	653	500	606	442	48	246	−204	−015	26	172	395	231	512	601	364	431	699	597	220
25 Knee height sitting	313	321	317	332	329	208	228	404	325	322	612	720	143	67	354	464	373	181	233	486	190	315	380	544	704
26 Popliteal height sitting	113	116	125	156	185	35	33	255	157	149	621	660	182	78	347	405	266	123	88	318	89	186	159	317	626
27 Buttock-knee length	396	344	318	301	332	280	298	381	349	306	526	672	91	59	298	443	421	184	278	525	267	354	454	558	597
28 Buttock-leg length	275	264	222	253	320	176	198	352	252	247	529	634	156	72	323	454	325	143	219	452	185	281	343	481	623
29 Shoulder-elbow length	169	174	165	190	251	72	90	280	201	243	614	719	180	55	312	413	280	129	133	378	100	234	246	361	562
30 Forearm-hand length	193	197	209	261	265	115	150	364	248	333	641	731	161	70	374	475	308	151	145	414	132	292	267	421	725
31 Span	203	201	216	233	268	113	128	339	235	293	673	785	196	72	444	467	318	176	164	417	141	315	263	406	682
32 Arm reach from wall	214	229	189	209	269	161	175	337	243	288	563	652	124	27	316	414	265	151	182	389	161	340	300	406	579
33 Maximum reach from wall	213	200	169	187	230	144	158	292	198	237	536	625	165	12	274	381	324	207	174	376	163	294	265	358	575
34 Functional reach	180	221	170	189	267	142	162	299	218	274	515	587	120	28	285	391	230	108	148	337	141	329	268	364	547

Table C-1 (*continued*)

	51	52	53	54	55	56	57	58	59	60	61	62	63	64	65	66	67	68	69	70	71	72	73	74	75
BODY BREADTHS																									
35 Elbow-elbow breadth	714	620	623	507	526	731	744	539	706	505	−024	255	−252	−061	7	135	404	174	502	608	481	474	725	580	188
36 Hip breadth sitting	773	652	638	548	462	675	667	511	630	477	119	366	−198	14	72	204	436	310	593	691	354	435	843	688	330
37 Knee-knee breadth sitting	645	634	634	545	403	547	568	491	575	508	99	300	−106	9	102	217	351	239	474	575	305	365	654	699	321
38 Biacromial diameter	286	276	342	279	287	260	264	339	313	332	328	546	41		519	273	241	157	227	371	262	436	314	336	399
39 Shoulder breadth	648	576	611	501	542	669	679	547	647	539	154	485	−145	−004	282	215	394	210	475	620	470	582	661	566	320
40 Chest breadth	606	503	515	435	461	596	612	483	580	461	88	391	−179	−018	152	156	413	191	419	561	452	505	637	537	243
41 Waist breadth	683	584	537	444	475	676	681	486	607	446	49	316	−253	−050	58	177	446	128	449	558	410	479	743	594	230
42 Hip breadth	655	590	562	518	459	582	584	509	582	474	231	477	−081	12	196	296	437	290	507	657	371	432	747	660	449
43 Chest depth	649	553	538	441	507	659	686	479	612	450	63	272	−316	−035	−001	171	438	158	455	564	364	407	682	571	219
44 Waist depth	672	555	532	418	455	659	650	447	588	410	27	218	−259	−073	−023	132	476	171	483	567	367	402	745	560	189
45 Buttock depth	767	626	603	458	489	709	703	482	632	452	−007	232	−260	−049	−023	133	467	282	602	669	388	433	794	623	197
CIRCUMFERENCES																									
46 Neck circumference	539	517	498	424	495	579	624	521	608	474	61	312	−192	−024	49	198	352	176	414	534	337	504	578	507	245
47 Shoulder circumference	682	638	616	531	580	678	712	572	664	530	83	392	−232	−041	204	170	399	155	502	606	460	594	683	575	281
48 Chest circumference	717	574	592	482	525	709	721	536	668	477	131	416	−254	−009	108	197	478	232	485	628	461	530	734	622	294
49 Waist circumference	726	609	588	467	504	722	715	519	640	461	12	283	−286	−070	22	156	473	152	482	607	408	466	799	618	214
50 Buttock circumference	846	748	709	611	543	721	744	−585	699	531	79	354	−203	6	98	244	475	291	641	757	431	507	885	736	356
51 Thigh circumference		731	698	565	482	696	717	527	657	466	33	253	−238	7	30	167	420	260	588	656	389	453	794	677	228
52 Lower thigh circumference	731		702	630	503	599	661	535	638	495	−003	191	−196	13	74	163	369	180	516	572	307	392	673	646	262
53 Calf circumference	698	702		700	447	599	649	536	666	518	52	269	−215	9	123	161	349	198	477	566	292	390	649	654	312
54 Ankle circumference	565	630	700		421	465	526	480	566	518	52	232	−159	48	116	171	291	157	392	485	259	329	536	581	366
55 Scye circumference	482	503	447	421		519	576	515	575	477	55	272	−115	9	50	153	341	135	388	477	299	387	497	432	269
56 Axillary arm circumference	696	599	599	465	519		792	555	676	480	−016	239	−268	−038	21	106	413	215	496	581	377	462	712	562	175
57 Biceps circumference flexed	717	661	649	526	576	792		618	767	533	−036	211	−278	−024	8	101	398	188	484	573	361	464	718	575	181
58 Elbow circumference flexed	527	535	536	480	515	555	618		728	565	113	353	−128	22	112	198	340	149	359	494	275	398	527	520	345
59 Lower arm circumference flexed	657	638	666	566	575	676	767	728		627	41	304	−211	12	69	166	409	193	470	591	380	448	662	578	290
60 Wrist circumference	466	495	518	518	477	480	533	565	627		90	297	−091	17	105	190	304	142	371	488	263	382	487	481	321
61 Sleeve inseam	33	−003	52	52	55	−016	−036	113	41	90		617	188	68	336	359	199	175	19	219	16	142	87	203	473
62 Sleeve length	253	191	269	232	272	239	211	353	304	297	617		101	73	440	417	317	216	209	442	212	353	340	427	578
63 Anterior neck length	−238	−196	−215	−159	−115	−268	−278	−128	−211	−091	188	101		−013	110	213	−084	34	−120	−036	−081	−025	−236	−119	169
64 Posterior neck length	7	13	9	48	9	−038	−024	22	12	17	68	73	−013		91	−029	81	78	25	36	34	59	−042	23	77
65 Shoulder length	30	74	123	116	50	21	8	112	69	105	336	440	110	91		290	50	49	41	155	40	143	78	148	292
66 Waist back	167	163	161	171	153	106	101	198	166	190	359	417	213	−029	290		389	−043	24	452	186	239	209	293	403
67 Waist front	420	369	349	291	341	413	398	340	409	304	199	317	−084	81	50	389		80	173	541	225	316	461	431	291
68 Gluteal arc	260	180	198	157	135	215	188	149	193	142	175	216	34	78	49	−043	80		550	380	170	158	301	256	197
69 Crotch length	588	516	477	392	388	496	484	359	470	371	19	209	−120	25	41	24	173	550		686	346	336	631	499	222
70 Vertical trunk circumference	656	572	566	485	477	581	573	494	591	488	219	442	−036	36	155	452	541	380	686		434	483	715	646	427

71	Interscye	389	307	292	259	299	377	361	275	380	263	16	212	−081	34	40	186	225	170	346	434		575	373	324	118
72	Interscye maximum	453	392	390	329	387	462	464	398	448	382	142	353	−025	59	143	239	316	158	336	483	575		476	479	246
73	Buttock circumference sitting	794	673	649	536	497	712	718	527	662	487	87	340	−236	−042	78	209	461	301	631	715	373	476		715	287
74	Knee circumference sitting	677	646	654	581	432	562	575	520	578	481	203	427	−119	23	148	293	431	256	499	646	324	479	715		455
	THE FOOT																									
75	Foot length	228	262	312	366	269	175	181	345	290	321	473	578	169	77	292	403	291	197	222	427	118	246	287	455	
76	Instep length	216	259	300	355	275	162	182	340	284	299	436	530	154	105	305	387	239	168	201	406	128	239	268	437	893
77	Foot breadth	346	374	437	440	302	305	338	391	393	415	238	367	9	70	169	282	277	189	287	455	227	344	367	492	485
78	Heel breadth	424	418	442	451	311	376	397	373	426	401	166	339	−059	8	118	192	296	186	332	446	204	248	439	485	420
79	Bimalleolar breadth	275	343	417	459	299	242	249	380	390	464	275	421	109	47	162	274	296	243	259	408	189	283	316	446	571
80	Medial malleolus height	228	254	291	333	240	205	187	276	255	342	253	335	95	34	184	294	214	130	171	329	138	181	255	329	333
81	Lateral malleolus height	166	163	171	180	200	150	133	205	183	219	261	294	63	21	109	229	205	86	133	259	115	134	195	231	275
82	Ball of foot circumference	389	345	479	479	298	394	375	406	431	426	289	417	15	37	165	272	295	244	286	468	250	360	407	545	494
	THE HAND																									
83	Hand length	171	193	212	278	226	119	156	334	259	332	468	568	175	63	321	416	261	155	163	383	94	254	240	387	722
84	Palm length	172	186	199	283	228	125	161	280	248	296	411	512	154	25	274	374	217	148	138	344	91	237	216	367	627
85	Hand breadth at thumb	254	288	293	339	298	228	291	384	382	413	263	414	91	93	186	264	205	131	213	339	178	320	244	339	427
86	Hand breadth at metacarpale	283	334	341	368	335	274	332	443	449	489	244	401	58	67	186	258	231	147	238	372	213	341	265	386	414
87	Thickness metacarpal III	297	320	332	328	300	285	332	408	425	401	147	286	−015	15	72	188	199	119	270	358	207	267	318	337	248
88	First phalanx III length	191	217	244	295	287	138	194	388	316	365	450	539	110	68	282	357	264	180	187	383	129	246	247	379	671
89	Finger diameter III	328	341	366	362	341	327	379	440	480	527	174	307	−027	64	146	225	276	185	294	413	201	281	340	402	375
90	Grip diameter inside	4	26	45	96	58	−037	−024	137	51	79	362	394	157	35	252	266	134	120	33	156	27	103	44	191	502
91	Grip diameter outside	134	147	153	220	153	89	117	276	209	237	362	397	163	93	248	266	158	147	126	258	65	163	156	268	501
92	Fist circumference	329	337	400	392	379	323	363	450	470	471	219	386	−011	78	197	236	267	176	286	413	212	318	321	397	419
	THE HEAD AND FACE																									
93	Head length	150	125	161	170	144	147	160	168	163	200	170	213	−022	−003	132	165	160	53	114	231	128	162	175	207	201
94	Head breadth	242	262	234	219	183	246	277	231	269	192	26	159	−123	−049	60	51	145	75	187	229	136	162	272	240	110
116	Head height	208	218	171	158	106	202	187	147	171	117	76	138	−002	81	58	81	111	109	181	211	175	158	215	212	138
122	Head circumference	330	312	333	300	265	322	345	298	339	288	159	298	−092	4	120	192	261	124	284	392	240	340	384	413	236

Table C-1 (*continued*)

	76	77	78	79	80	81	82	83	84	85	86	87	88	89	90	91	92	93	94	116	122
WEIGHT																					
1 Weight	412	483	530	438	349	273	532	377	339	385	425	406	400	459	142	273	473	255	326	257	471
BODY LENGTHS																					
2 Stature	660	427	319	465	414	395	414	654	566	402	390	269	611	321	453	459	376	253	95	210	277
3 Nasal root height	658	429	318	460	410	394	413	662	565	404	392	271	612	324	459	466	384	233	87	178	270
4 Eye height	657	426	316	461	410	391	414	655	562	402	387	272	609	321	454	462	384	227	93	177	263
5 Tragion height	660	414	305	462	419	400	403	651	564	398	383	277	606	305	448	453	373	232	67	164	249
6 Cervicale height	649	415	328	450	406	403	408	646	557	383	384	280	605	314	441	445	364	228	98	180	265
7 Shoulder height	647	422	323	431	398	399	410	643	552	393	385	292	599	313	429	440	363	227	105	182	281
8 Suprasternale height	650	428	340	460	397	383	421	645	555	396	386	294	614	333	439	445	386	226	106	190	277
9 Nipple height	623	392	280	405	381	391	372	628	538	371	357	263	574	277	434	432	342	215	78	152	248
10 Substernale height	606	388	271	380	353	355	367	586	497	342	332	263	560	263	408	401	329	213	76	141	249
11 Elbow height	605	411	311	420	383	378	395	591	505	368	365	296	547	306	373	394	348	220	105	185	282
12 Waist height	605	350	273	408	349	389	346	612	531	344	322	247	566	241	433	419	310	186	64	165	213
13 Penale height	590	313	232	354	317	362	318	597	520	311	291	192	569	216	439	417	255	159	53	138	181
14 Wrist height	533	376	251	385	379	383	367	497	423	310	310	274	469	268	305	313	311	198	83	174	254
15 Crotch height	589	318	242	366	337	379	308	602	519	312	304	184	553	211	442	411	269	174	50	144	178
16 Gluteal furrow height	592	315	254	343	349	404	322	595	513	319	282	215	557	215	416	399	278	205	63	156	225
17 Knuckle height	498	347	234	358	342	342	336	448	381	275	280	246	418	239	266	276	283	192	66	177	240
18 Kneecap height	606	385	283	387	379	405	353	617	533	342	333	261	580	255	416	398	327	176	101	151	227
19 Sitting height	469	366	297	409	335	242	343	464	392	334	344	240	444	337	307	359	347	238	94	248	266
20 Eye height sitting	434	346	263	395	320	226	329	451	398	327	333	232	428	314	285	332	344	178	89	179	220
21 Shoulder height sitting	408	336	281	357	300	214	325	400	348	309	318	255	385	316	240	300	317	178	121	164	254
22 Waist height sitting	155	117	111	223	125	75	131	158	134	122	138	116	167	133	107	124	134	83	28	109	79
23 Elbow rest height sitting	75	128	132	144	114	27	125	77	54	88	117	104	59	163	11	45	126	110	53	85	128
24 Thigh clearance height sitting	199	311	341	277	223	172	363	159	153	210	255	284	173	299	−011	100	265	136	256	203	337
25 Knee height sitting	657	447	388	466	447	459	455	657	577	402	390	296	640	339	447	454	395	237	143	203	310
26 Popliteal height sitting	582	332	256	356	366	419	342	594	502	327	306	206	575	252	425	409	300	195	90	151	226
27 Buttock-knee length	568	383	329	396	339	343	394	533	468	336	341	260	496	282	331	367	316	196	114	134	276
28 Buttock-leg length	617	356	298	355	330	354	348	559	489	330	330	235	527	241	385	411	312	194	87	150	246
29 Shoulder-elbow length	534	368	288	376	334	318	361	565	497	352	355	250	542	272	409	405	322	183	105	117	231
30 Forearm-hand length	665	425	345	444	376	378	416	795	676	483	470	298	747	383	555	537	409	247	119	101	260
31 Span	624	414	346	443	382	377	416	721	621	471	453	271	711	333	523	498	398	232	144	148	280
32 Arm reach from wall	543	369	289	352	306	282	344	619	539	348	374	243	591	255	436	423	314	181	116	143	243
33 Maximum reach from wall	468	348	325	437	257	300	345	559	464	312	322	198	571	296	436	419	331	199	128	176	255
34 Functional reach	498	332	262	337	287	256	313	553	499	311	319	218	516	225	390	383	280	163	78	118	216

BODY BREADTHS

35	Elbow-elbow breadth	186	325	404	272	222	170	375	148	162	251	300	329	189	359	−058	67	349	165	291	139	366
36	Hip breadth sitting	309	379	430	336	295	215	424	263	235	262	294	307	282	354	69	173	333	181	270	198	365
37	Knee-knee breadth sitting	307	408	414	468	389	214	465	286	262	307	334	346	289	380	54	177	363	191	225	184	323
38	Biacromial diameter	340	343	259	358	279	231	323	392	343	326	331	240	385	279	265	283	344	206	176	86	279
39	Shoulder breadth	284	414	412	356	311	243	444	315	295	369	405	362	316	413	132	225	434	239	296	150	416
40	Chest breadth	205	341	388	284	223	207	387	240	220	298	328	283	248	343	85	165	385	217	270	130	388
41	Waist breadth	213	315	387	245	184	170	341	186	197	225	259	255	198	275	28	113	301	159	285	194	364
42	Hip breadth	418	419	424	426	367	265	454	374	329	328	339	324	372	375	167	257	354	181	225	116	339
43	Chest depth	206	277	349	256	173	157	332	178	178	238	262	261	231	311	27	125	311	96	230	78	308
44	Waist depth	174	256	383	207	152	112	293	133	130	158	216	254	155	271	−016	84	273	114	223	149	273
45	Buttock depth	172	293	370	249	194	160	358	149	136	187	231	267	159	298	−001	93	283	165	228	196	331

CIRCUMFERENCES

46	Neck circumference	216	352	330	273	208	155	391	239	225	325	391	315	274	377	40	166	396	202	311	182	424
47	Shoulder circumference	257	377	386	282	252	204	391	262	253	332	363	334	279	372	75	171	396	199	276	183	373
48	Chest circumference	274	363	438	316	213	187	442	243	222	311	336	318	287	366	77	202	389	191	297	223	404
49	Waist circumference	217	303	399	226	172	151	328	155	152	198	246	265	180	310	1	105	308	122	260	172	327
50	Buttock circumference	341	422	472	369	318	230	439	274	251	292	324	343	287	363	70	180	382	187	260	241	376
51	Thigh circumference	216	346	424	275	228	166	389	171	172	254	283	297	191	328	4	134	329	150	242	208	330
52	Lower thigh circumference	259	374	418	343	254	163	345	193	186	288	334	320	217	341	26	147	337	125	262	218	312
53	Calf circumference	300	437	442	417	291	171	479	212	199	293	341	332	244	366	45	153	400	161	234	171	333
54	Ankle circumference	355	440	451	459	333	180	479	278	283	339	368	328	295	362	96	220	392	170	219	158	300
55	Scye circumference	275	302	311	299	240	200	298	226	228	298	335	300	287	341	58	153	379	144	183	106	265
56	Axillary arm circumference	162	305	376	242	205	150	394	119	125	228	274	285	138	327	−037	89	323	147	246	202	322
57	Biceps circumference flexed	182	338	397	249	187	133	375	156	161	291	332	332	194	379	−024	117	363	160	277	187	345
58	Elbow circumference flexed	340	391	373	380	276	205	406	334	280	384	443	408	388	440	137	276	450	168	231	147	298
59	Lower arm circumference flexed	284	393	426	390	255	183	431	259	248	382	449	425	316	480	51	209	470	163	269	171	339
60	Wrist circumference	299	415	401	464	342	219	426	332	296	413	489	401	365	527	79	237	471	200	192	117	288
61	Sleeve inseam	436	238	166	275	253	261	289	468	411	263	244	147	450	174	362	362	219	170	26	76	159
62	Sleeve length	530	367	339	421	335	294	417	568	512	414	401	286	539	307	394	397	386	213	159	138	298
63	Anterior neck length	154	9	−059	109	95	63	15	175	154	91	58	−015	110	−027	157	163	−011	−022	−123	−002	−992
64	Posterior neck length	105	70	8	47	34	21	37	63	25	93	67	15	68	64	35	93	78	−003	−049	81	4
65	Shoulder length	305	169	118	162	184	109	165	321	274	186	186	72	282	146	252	248	197	132	60	58	120
66	Waist back	387	282	192	274	294	229	272	416	374	264	258	188	357	225	266	266	236	165	51	81	192
67	Waist front	239	277	296	296	214	205	295	261	217	205	231	199	264	276	134	158	267	160	145	111	261
68	Gluteal arc	168	189	186	243	130	86	244	155	148	131	147	119	180	185	120	147	176	53	75	109	124
69	Crotch length	201	287	332	259	171	133	286	163	138	213	238	270	187	294	33	126	286	114	187	181	284
70	Vertical trunk circumference	406	455	446	408	329	259	468	383	344	339	372	358	383	413	156	258	413	231	229	211	392
71	Interscye	128	227	204	189	138	115	250	94	91	178	213	207	129	201	27	65	212	128	136	175	240
72	Interscye maximum	239	344	248	283	181	134	360	254	237	320	341	267	246	281	103	163	318	162	162	158	340
73	Buttock circumference sitting	268	367	439	316	255	195	407	240	216	244	265	318	247	340	44	156	321	175	272	215	384
74	Knee circumference sitting	437	492	485	446	329	231	545	387	367	339	386	337	379	402	191	268	397	207	240	212	413

Table C-1 (*continued*)

	76	77	78	79	80	81	82	83	84	85	86	87	88	89	90	91	92	93	94	116	122
THE FOOT																					
75 Foot length	893	485	420	571	333	275	494	722	627	427	414	248	671	375	502	501	419	201	110	138	236
76 Instep length		438	362	487	275	188	436	646	575	395	389	248	596	322	445	472	365	177	95	105	198
77 Foot breadth	438		510	488	342	227	711	432	368	461	532	341	446	487	240	367	524	206	206	159	341
78 Heel breadth	362	510		443	259	161	487	377	356	378	409	320	374	477	204	365	453	287	208	226	371
79 Bimalleolar breadth	487	488	443		401	212	510	454	417	404	437	324	476	444	249	331	456	185	156	101	229
80 Medial malleolus height	275	342	259	401		651	396	373	342	263	266	270	364	323	194	220	275	187	74	85	199
81 Lateral malleolus height	188	227	161	212	651		270	330	300	163	135	157	327	215	154	154	194	121	51	77	166
82 Ball of foot circumference	436	711	487	510	396	270		399	349	423	494	337	417	464	222	359	487	184	206	157	341
THE HAND																					
83 Hand length	646	432	377	454	373	330	399		849	520	486	256	766	403	626	593	438	238	89	102	250
84 Palm length	575	368	356	417	342	300	349	849		459	393	179	608	329	491	496	370	186	88	108	200
85 Hand breadth at thumb	395	461	378	404	263	163	423	520	459		713	391	503	475	319	431	548	260	127	142	291
86 Hand breadth at metacarplae	389	532	409	437	266	135	494	486	393	713		413	509	572	247	377	603	226	203	125	310
87 Thickness metacarpal III	248	341	320	324	270	157	337	256	179	391	413		387	447	67	250	437	188	119	133	236
88 First phalanx III length	596	446	374	476	364	327	417	766	608	503	509	387		480	528	536	499	220	113	106	256
89 Finger diameter III	322	487	477	444	323	215	464	403	329	475	572	447	480		143	329	575	209	195	130	294
90 Grip diameter inside	445	240	204	249	194	154	222	626	491	319	247	67	528	143		639	239	124	24	41	142
91 Grip diameter outside	472	367	365	331	220	154	359	593	496	431	377	250	536	329	639		392	150	66	84	194
92 Fist circumference	365	524	453	456	275	194	487	438	370	548	603	437	499	575	239	392		239	181	164	321
THE HEAD AND FACE																					
93 Head length	177	206	287	185	187	121	184	238	186	260	226	188	220	209	124	150	239		67	184	646
94 Head breadth	95	206	208	156	74	51	206	89	88	127	203	119	113	195	24	66	181	67		228	496
116 Head height	105	159	226	101	85	77	157	102	108	142	125	133	106	130	41	84	164	184	228		263
122 Head circumference	198	341	371	229	199	166	341	250	200	291	310	236	256	294	142	194	321	646	496	263	

INDEX*

* Authors listed in Bibliography, and indexed by section number where they appear in text